SOUTHEAST ASIA

This comprehensive and absorbing book traces the cultural history of both Mainland and Island Southeast Asia from 3000 BC to around AD 1300, across an extensive region that extends from Burma in the west to the eastern regions of Indonesia. It commences with Neolithic and Bronze–Iron Age prehistoric cultures and continues through to the major Hindu and Buddhist civilizations and burgeoning international contacts of the early Christian Era. Southeast Asia incorporated the region of origin for the Austronesian population dispersal across Indonesia and the Pacific, commencing about 5,000 years ago, and was an arena for the development of many archaeologically rich Neolithic and metal-using communities, especially in Thailand and Vietnam. It served as the backdrop for several unique and strikingly monumental Indic civilizations; such as the Khmer civilization centred around Angkor and the Cham kingdoms of coastal Vietnam. This book will be invaluable to anyone interested in the full history of the region.

Ian Glover is Emeritus Reader in Southeast Asia Archaeology at the Institute of Archaeology, University College London. He has undertaken excavations in East Timor, Sulawesi, western Thailand and central Vietnam on periods ranging from Late Pleistocene cave deposits, Iron Age cemeteries and the emerging Cham Civilization of Central Vietnam. His academic interests include early technologies of bronze, iron and glass and the effects of inter-regional trade on cultural evolution.

Peter Bellwood is Professor of Archaeology at the Australian National University in Canberra. He has carried out field research since 1967 in Southeast Asia (Brunei, Malaysia, Indonesia, Philippines) and numerous Polynesian islands. He has a special interest in archaeological and linguistic aspects of Austronesian prehistory in both Southeast Asia and Oceania, and in the prehistories of early farming populations in all parts of the world.

SOUTHEAST ASIA

From prehistory to history

Edited by Ian Glover and Peter Bellwood

RoutledgeCurzon
Taylor & Francis Group
LONDON AND NEW YORK

First published in 2004
by RoutledgeCurzon
2 Park Square, Milton Park, Abingdon, Oxfordshire OX14 4RN

Simultaneously published in the USA and Canada
by RoutledgeCurzon
270 Madison Ave, New York NY 10016

RoutledgeCurzon is an imprint of the Taylor & Francis Group

Transferred to digital printing 2006

Typeset in Bembo by LaserScript Ltd, Mitcham, Surrey

British Library Cataloguing in Publication Data
A catalogue record for this book is available from the British Library

Library of Congress Cataloging in Publication Data
A catalog record for this book has been requested

ISBN 0–415–29777–X
ISBN 0–145–39117–2

Printed and bound by Antony Rowe Ltd, Eastbourne

CONTENTS

List of plates vii
List of illustrations viii
List of tables xiv
List of contributors xv
Foreword xviii
ANDREW SHERRATT

Introduction **1**
IAN GLOVER AND PETER BELLWOOD

1 **Southeast Asia: foundations for an archaeological history** **4**
PETER BELLWOOD AND IAN GLOVER

2 **The origins and dispersals of agricultural communities in Southeast Asia** **21**
PETER BELLWOOD

3 **Mainland Southeast Asia from the Neolithic to the Iron age** **41**
CHARLES HIGHAM

4 **The archaeology of early contact with India and the Mediterranean World, from the fourth century BC to the fourth century AD** **68**
BÉRÉNICE BELLINA AND IAN GLOVER

5 **Pre-Angkorian and Angkorian Cambodia** **89**
MIRIAM T. STARK

6 **The archaeology of the early Buddhist kingdoms of Thailand** **120**
PHASOOK INDRAWOOTH

7 **The archaeology of Burma (Myanmar) from the Neolithic to Pagan** 149
PAMELA GUTMAN AND BOB HUDSON

8 **Northern Vietnam from the Neolithic to the Han period** 177
NGUYEN KHAC SU, PHAM MINH HUYEN AND TONG TRUNG TIN

9 **The coastal states of Champa** 209
WILLIAM A. SOUTHWORTH

10 **The classical cultures of Indonesia** 234
JOHN N. MIKSIC

11 **The archaeology of the Philippine Archipelago** 257
ELISABETH A. BACUS

12 **The archaeology of early maritime polities of Southeast Asia** 282
PIERRE-YVES MANGUIN

13 **Indigenous traditions and exogenous influences in the early history of Peninsular Malaysia** 314
DAVID BULBECK

14 **Retrospect and prospect** 337
IAN GLOVER AND PETER BELLWOOD

Index 346

PLATES

Between pages 202 and 203

1 Noen U-Loke burial of a man wearing four bronze belts, bronze ear ornaments and many bangles, finger and toe rings, Thailand. (Burial 69)
2 Alkaline etched beads of agate and carnelian *in situ*, Context 73, Ban Don Ta Phet, Thailand
3 Carnelian lion pendant from Context 73, Ban Don Ta Phet, Thailand
4 Angkor Wat, Cambodia
5 Carnelian 'tigers' from Halin and Binnaka, Myanmar
6 Seated Buddha from Vesali, stylistically linked with Pyu and Dvaravati types. Kept at Lat-kauk-zay monastery, Mrauk-U, Myanmar
7 The Shwezigon pagoda at Nyaung-u, Myanmar
8 Ear-shaped wooden cups from Lach Tuong and Nghi Ve, Vietnam
9 Ovoid jars excavated at Go Cam, Vietnam, 2001
10 The Vo Canh inscription, perhaps the earliest in Southeast Asia, in the National Museum of History, Vietnam
11 Islamic turquoise-glazed pottery from Bai Lang site, Culao Cham, Quang Nam province, Vietnam
12 The principal shrine of Po Nagar at Nha Trang, Khanh Hoa Province, Vietnam
13 The great Buddhist monument at Borobudur, Central Java, Indonesia
14 'Ship-of-the Dead' burial jar from Manunggul Cave, chamber A, Palawan Island, Philippines
15 Excavation across the central canal, Oc Eo, Vietnam, 2002

ILLUSTRATIONS

1.1	The major language families and subgroups with a selection of the major ethnolinguistic populations of modern Southeast Asia mentioned in the text	5
1.2	Traditional and present day Southeast Asians: (a) Temiar people of interior Kelantan, Malaysia (b) Burmese monks at Prome (c) Bunak bards, dressed in ceremonial attire to recite the Bei Gua, or 'Itinerary of the Ancestors' before the altar of war, East Timor (d) People on the Xieng Khouang Plateau, northern Laos	6
1.3	Pleistocene movements and colonizations across land and sea in Southeast Asia	8
1.4	Rainfall and monsoon wind patterns in Southeast Asia	10
1.5	The Tingkayu biface industry from Sabah, tentatively dated to the late Pleistocene	17
1.6	Maros Points from the Toalian industry from South Sulawesi	17
2.1	Putative homelands of the major language families of China and Southeast Asia	22
2.2	Overall distribution of the Austronesian language family	26
2.3	Approximate dates from archaeological and linguistic data for initial Austronesian colonizations across Southeast Asia and the Pacific	27
2.4	The higher-level structure of the Austronesian language family	28
2.5	Sites with Neolithic red-slipped pottery in Island Southeast Asia	32
2.6	A selection of dentate- and circle-stamped pottery, from southern China to Melanesia	33
2.7	Indian pottery from the Sembiran site, north Bali	37
3.1	Location of the Southeast Asian sites mentioned in the text	43
3.2	The reconstructed coastline in the vicinity of Nong Nor 4,500 years ago	44
3.3	Pottery vessel from mortuary phase 7 at Khok Phanom Di	45
3.4	Mortuary vessel from Khok Phanom Di	45
3.5	Location of key sites in China and Burma mentioned in the text	47
3.6	Stone adzes recovered from Phung Nguyen	48
3.7	Pottery from Phung Nguyen, Vietnam	49
3.8	The Bronze Age cemetery of Nong Nor	54
3.9	Bronze dagger from the Dong Son cemetery of Lang Vac	58
3.10	Aerial view of the prehistoric site of Noen U-Loke	61

3.11 Plan of the Noen U-Loke cemetery, showing the five mortuary phases 62
3.12 Agate jewellery found in the later graves of Noen U-Loke 62
3.13 Noen U-Loke burial of a woman wearing gold, agate, silver and bronze jewellery 63
4.1 A copper coin of Western Roman Emperor Victorinus (AD 268–70) found at U-Thong, Thailand 71
4.2 Ivory comb from Chansen Phase II, Western Thailand 71
4.3 Sa Huynh style two-headed animal ear pendant of nephrite from Vietnam 75
4.4 Translucent glass beads from Ban Don Ta Phet 76
4.5 High-tin bronze bowl with central cone and concentric rings from Ban Don Ta Phet 77
4.6 Black granite bowl with central cone from the reliquary chamber of a stupa near Taxila, Pakistan 77
4.7 Rouletted ware bowls from Kobak Kendal and Cibutak, Java 79
4.8 Megalithic stone circle at Batu Kantan, West Java, Indonesia 79
4.9 Kundika from Kausambi, Uttar Pradesh, India 80
4.10 Stamped pottery from Beikthano, Burma (Myanmar) 81
4.11 Sherds stamped with radiating petal motifs from Beikthano, Burma (Myanmar) 82
5.1 Archaeological sites in Cambodia, mentioned in the text 90
5.2 Excavation in progress at Laang Spean in 1969 92
5.3 Pedestal vessel with impressed decoration found during excavation at Laang Spean 93
5.4 Plan of the Krek earthwork 93
5.5 Drawings of Krek pottery 94
5.6 Sambor Prei Kuk 95
5.7 Bronze bell from Samrong Sen and bone spear or harpoon shafts 95
5.8 Angkor Borei digital elevation map 98
5.9 Stratigraphic profile at Angkor Borei 99
5.10 Pre Rup 102
5.11 Khmer brown glazed footed jar 103
5.12 Khmer green glazed jar and cover 103
5.13 Bakong step-temple 106
5.14 Face towers in the Bayon temple 110
6.1 Some of the main prehistoric sites in Southeast Asia 121
6.2 Important sites of the Iron Age and the Post-Iron Age in South Asia 123
6.3 Sea routes and ancient ports in South and Southeast Asia 124
6.4 Late Roman bronze lamp from Pong Tuk, Kanchanaburi Province 125
6.5 Indian bronze coin from Klong Thom, Krabi Province 125
6.6 Important archaeological sites in Southeast Asia during the Dvaravati Period 126
6.7 The main Dvaravati sites in Central and Northeast Thailand 127
6.8 Stone slab showing seated Buddha under a Naga, from Nagarjunakonda, Southeastern India 128
6.9 Stone *Dharmacakra* and pillar, U-Thong 128

6.10 Plan of ancient Nakhon Pathom 129
6.11 Terracotta relief of a foreigner from Ku Bua, Ratchaburi Province 130
6.12 Wat Klong, Ku Bua, Ratchaburi Province 130
6.13 Terracotta seal from Chansen 131
6.14 Silver coins from U-Thong 133
6.15 Stone mould from Chansen 133
6.16 Saddle quern and roller from Dong Khon, Chainat Province 134
6.17 Terracotta images of women, Ku Bua 134
6.18 Stucco figures of musicians from Ku Bua 134
6.19 Stone *Dharmacakra*, inscribed with a Buddhist text, Lopburi 137
6.20 Stone image of a seated Buddha on Vanaspati from Nakhon Pathom 139
6.21 Headless terracotta images of men with monkeys from U-Thong 140
7.1 The main river systems of Burma, showing walled settlements, Pyu sites and Iron Age archaeological finds 150
7.2 Neolithic and Bronze Age archaeological finds in upper Burma 153
7.3 Stone bracelets of the Neolithic or early metal age from Halin 154
7.4 Bronze implements from Halin 155
7.5 Pyu coin from Halin 156
7.6 Bronze coffin decoration, Samon Valley 156
7.7 Archaeological research at Halin, 1905–2001 159
7.8 The Bawbawgyi pagoda at Sriksetra (Thayekittaya) 161
7.9 A walled elite site at Dhanyawadi surrounded by an irregular, curving outer city wall 162
7.10 Archaeological and epigraphically recorded sites of the Pagan period 164
7.11 Pagan at the end of the thirteenth century AD 167
7.12 The building cycle at Pagan 168
8.1 The locations of some important archaeological sites in Vietnam 178
8.2 Unifacially flaked Hoabinhian pebble tools from Xom Trai Cave 179
8.3 Hoabinhian flaked axes from Xom Trai Cave 179
8.4 "Bacsonian marks" on river pebbles from Hang Doi Cave 180
8.5 Artefacts of the Da But Culture 181
8.6 Artefacts of the Quynh Van Culture 182
8.7 Artefacts of the Ha Long Culture 184
8.8 Grooved sandstone grinding stones of the Ha Long Culture from Dong Mo site 185
8.9 Artefacts of the Bau Tro Culture 186
8.10 Artefacts of the Bien Ho Culture 187
8.11 Artefacts of the Phung Nguyen Culture 191
8.12 Double stone mould for casting bronze arrowheads from Dong Dau 192
8.13 Artefacts of the Hoa Loc Culture 194
8.14 Dong Son burial material from Cau Can, Ha Tay Province 196
8.15 Plan of the Dong Son site, Thanh Hoa Province 197
8.16 Excavations at Dong Son in 1960 198
8.17 Dong Son Culture bronzes from a grave at Hop Minh, Yen Bai Province 198
8.18 Dong Son bronze pediform axe from Ha Dong 199
8.19 Bronze pediform axe and casting mould from Lang Ca 199

8.20 Bronze toothed implement – possibly a brush used in textile manufacture 199
8.21 Bronze drum, Heger I type, Dong Son Culture 200
8.22 Bronze dagger with entwined tigers and elephant from Lang Ca site 200
8.23 Eastern Han Period brick tomb, Mao Khe, Quang Ninh Province 203
9.1 Sites of the Champa culture in modern Vietnam 210
9.2 Jean-Yves Claeys with Henri Parmentier and his daughter at Tra Kieu in 1927 211
9.3 Sa Huynh burial jars at Tam My, Quang Nam Province 212
9.4 Two-headed animal earrings from Giong Ca Vo (Ho Chi Minh City) 213
9.5 Han seal impressions from Go Cam, Quang Nam Province 213
9.6 Roofing tiles of Chinese design excavated at Go Cam in 2000 214
9.7 Remains of a large timber structure from the first or second century AD, excavated at Go Cam, 2001 215
9.8 Face tiles from the 1993 excavations at Buu Chau Hill, Tra Kieu 215
9.9 The main forms of pottery excavated at Tra Kieu 217
9.10 Plan of a columned hall at Hoan Chau, Tra Kieu, excavated between 1997 and 2000 218
9.11 Kendis and bowls *in situ* at the Go Du De location, Tra Kieu, 1996 219
9.12 Stone sculpture of a male figure from Phu Ninh 222
9.13 Stone relief carving of a seated male figure from Tra Kieu, 1927 223
9.14 Sculptured pediment from My Son E1 225
9.15 Detail of the flautist on the My Son E1 pedestal 225
9.16 North shrine at Hoa Lai, Ninh Thuan Province 227
9.17 Bronze statue of Tara or a female Avalokiteshvara from Dong Duong 229
9.18 Gajasimha ('Elephant-lion') from Thap Mam 230
10.1 Western Indonesia locating places mentioned in the text 235
10.2 The Kutei inscription dated to *c.* AD 400 – perhaps the earliest in Indonesia 236
10.3 The inscription from Telaga Batu recording an "oath drinking" ceremony 238
10.4 The eighth-century Candi Canggal at Gunung Wukir, Central Java 241
10.5 The Arjuna group of temples on the Dieng Plateau, Central Java 241
10.6 The architectural complex at Ratu Boko, Central Java 243
10.7 Carved relief at Candi Loro Jonggrang 244
10.8 Carved relief image of a dancer at Candi Loro Jonggrang 244
10.9 Spout of a gold ritual vessel with *makara* face 245
10.10 Carved relief image of a woman paddling pottery and men carrying clay, second level at Borobudur, Central Java 246
10.11 Gold coins from Central Java, ninth century 246
10.12 Carved stone relief from East Java showing an agricultural landscape 247
10.13 Candi Singasari, East Java 249
10.14 Large fourteenth-century stone image of a Bhairawa found in the Rambahan area of Sumatra 249
10.15 Stone carving of Bima as a blacksmith working a piston bellows, Candi Sukuh, East Java 253
11.1 Location of archaeological sites in the Philippines mentioned in the text 258

11.2	Flake tools, basalt chopper and a quartz hammer-stone from Tabon Cave, Palawan	260
11.3	House plans from Dimolit, northern Luzon	262
11.4	Double-headed jade earring/pendant and jade *lingling-o* from Tabon Cave, Palawan	263
11.5	Bronze axes, adzes and earthenware casting moulds from the Tabon Caves, Palawan	264
11.6	Anthropomorphic earthenware burial jars from Ayub Cave	265
11.7	Earthenware vessel with female figures from Burial II, Magsuhot site	266
11.8	Stoneware jars from Vietnam	268
11.9	Copper-plate inscription from Laguna de Bay, Luzon	269
11.10	Gold ornament with Garuda image from Palawan	272
11.11	Iron daggers and carved pieces of bone and antler from Cebu City	274
11.12	Distribution of glazed tradeware ceramics within the Dumaguete polity	276
11.13	Burials of a fifteenth- or sixteenth-century mass grave at Tanjay	278
12.1	Maritime Southeast Asia, locating the main known polities and major archaeological sites mentioned in the text	284
12.2	Indian coin (possibly Satavahana) with a ship design found at Khuan Luk Pad, Krabi, Peninsular Thailand	286
12.3	Gold ornaments from the site of Air Sugihan (South Sumatra)	287
12.4	Batu Gajah (Elephant stone) from the Pasemah megalithic region, South Sumatra	288
12.5	Gold seal of Indian or Hellenistic influence, from Pekalongan, north coast of Central Java	289
12.6	Glass and stone beads from Oc Eo	290
12.7	Wooden pole pattern from Phase I (first to third century AD) at Go Oc Eo (2001)	291
12.8	Wooden pole from Phase I (first to third century AD) at Go Oc Eo (2001)	292
12.9	Terracotta tile from Phase I (first to third century AD) at Go Oc Eo (2001)	292
12.10	Large burial jar with lid and small adjoining jarlet from Linh Son, Oc Eo, Vietnam (1998)	293
12.11	Fifth-century mitred Vishnu from Chaiya, Peninsular Thailand	295
12.12	Brick structure at Go Cây Thi (1999), dating from Oc Eo Phase II	298
12.13	Stratigraphical section, Go Cây Thi (1999), showing brick structure and settlement chronology (Oc Eo Phases I and II)	299
12.14	Glass effigy of an Iranian-looking man, Oc Eo	299
12.15	Vaishnava inscription of Purnavarman, king of Tarumanagara, at Ci Aruteun, West Java	302
12.16	Vishnu statue from late sixth- to early seventh-century temple at Kota Kapur, Bangka, South Sumatra	305
12.17	Late seventh-century Old Malay 'oath drinking' inscription from Sebokingking, Palembang, South Sumatra	306
12.18	A Malay-world sailing vessel depicted on the eighth-century reliefs at Borobudur, Central Java	307

13.1	West Malaysia and surrounding historical sites	316
13.2	Major Malaysian sites compared to Orang Asli groups	320
13.3	Iron tools from Perak slab graves	321
13.4	Iron Age finds in West Malaysia compared to Aslian languages	321
13.5	The Tantric shrine of Candi Bukit Batu Pahat, Bujang Valley, Kedah	324
13.6	A Buddhist votive tablet from the cave of Gua Chawas	326
13.7	A model for changes in group ranges and networks of interconnection in West Malaysia over the last five thousand years	328

TABLES

5.1	Temporal framework (used in Chapter 5)	91
5.2	Royal succession in the Khmer Empire	104
13.1	Fordisc 2.0 analysis of Malay Peninsula craniometric affinities in terms of closest relationship of each specimen to the recent populations measured by Howells	317
13.2	Average stature and ranges over time and by location in West Malaysia	318

CONTRIBUTORS

Elisabeth A. Bacus is Lecturer in Southeast Asian Archaeology at the Institute of Archaeology, University College London. Her current research focuses on investigating the transformation to early states in Bali, Indonesia, and on analyses of Northeast Thailand mortuary remains to elucidate gender relations in the Bronze Age. In addition, she is currently completing a monograph on her archaeological research in southeastern Negros Island, Philippines, entitled, *The Dumaguete Polity: Archaeological Investigations of Politics, Economy and Identity*. Dr Bacus is also editor, with L. Lucero, of *Complex Polities in the Ancient Tropical World* 1999.

Bérénice Bellina studied Archaeology and Art History of South and Southeast Asia at Sorbonne Nouvelle University (Paris III) and has participated in excavations in France, the UK, Laos, Thailand and India. After completing her doctoral dissertation in 2001, entitled *Témoinages archéologiques d'échanges entre l'Inde et l'Asie du Sud-Est: morphologie, morphométrie et techniques de fabrication des perles en agate et en cornaline*, she was awarded a French Ministry of Foreign Affairs Fellowship at the Research Laboratory for Archaeology and the History of Art, University of Oxford. She is Chargée de Recherche au CNRS, FRE 2350 – Université Paris III, Sorbonne Nouvelle. Dr Bellina's research interests are cultural exchange processes in Asia and especially between South and Southeast Asia, focusing on the analysis of technological transfers; and material sciences.

Peter Bellwood is Professor of Archaeology at the Australian National University in Canberra. He has carried out field research since 1967 in Southeast Asia (Brunei, Malaysia, Indonesia, Philippines) and numerous Polynesian islands. He has a special interest in archaeological and linguistic aspects of Austronesian prehistory in both Southeast Asia and Oceania, and in the prehistories of early farming populations in all parts of the world. He is the author of *Man's Conquest of the Pacific* (1978), *The Polynesians* (rev. ed. 1987), *Prehistory of the Indo-Malaysian Archipelago* (rev. ed. 1997), *The First Farmers* (in press for 2005), and has *edited Recent Advances in Indo-Pacific Prehistory* (with V. N. Misra, 1985), *The Austronesians* (with J. Fox and D. Tryon 1995) and *Examining the Farming/Language Dispersal Hypothesis* (with C. Renfrew 2003).

Francis David Bulbeck is Australian Research Fellow in the School of Archaeology and Anthropology, The Australian National University, Canberra. His main research interests focus on human adaptation and cultural change, particularly in Southeast Asia, but with growing attention to the southwest Pacific, including Australia, and South

Asia. These interests incorporate perspectives from biological anthropology, archaeology, ethnography, and history. He is the author (with Ian Caldwell) of *Land of Iron: The Historical Archaeology of Luwu and the Cenrana Valley* (2000), and editor (with Noel Barnard) of *Ancient Chinese and Southeast Asian Bronze Age Cultures* (2 volumes, 1996–7).

Ian Glover is Emeritus Reader in Southeast Asian Archaeology at the Institute of Archaeology, University College London. He has undertaken excavations in East Timor, Sulawesi, western Thailand and central Vietnam on periods ranging from Late Pleistocene cave deposits, Iron Age cemeteries and the emerging Cham Civilization of Central Vietnam. His academic interests include early technologies of bronze, iron and glass and the effects of inter-regional trade on cultural evolution.

Pamela Gutman is an Honorary Associate of the Department of Art History and Theory in the University of Sydney, Australia. She writes on the early art of Southeast Asia, with special reference to Burma. Her most recent book is *Burma's Lost Kingdoms: Splendours of Arakan* (2001).

Charles Higham has been active in archaeological research in Southeast Asia since 1969. Having retired as Professor of Anthropology at Otago University, Dunedin, New Zealand, he was awarded the James Cook Research Fellowship, funded by the New Zealand Government. He has published a series of final excavation reports on the sites of Ban Na Di, Nong Nor and Khok Phanom Di in Thailand, and is the author of many journal articles and four major syntheses of Southeast Asian prehistory. These are *The Archaeology of Mainland Southeast Asia – from 10 000 BC to the Fall of Angkor* (1989); *The Bronze Age of Southeast Asia* (1996); *Prehistoric Thailand – from Early Settlement to Sukhothai* (1999); and *Early Cultures of Mainland Southeast Asia* (2002). He is a Fellow of the British Academy and visiting scholar at St. Catharine's College, Cambridge.

Bob Hudson is due to complete a Ph.D. thesis entitled *Upper Burma from the Neolithic to Bagan* in 2004, in the Department of Prehistoric and Historic Archaeology, University of Sydney, Australia. His research interests include the use of GIS applications in the study of early urbanism in Southeast Asia, with a strong focus on Burma/Myanmar.

Pham Minh Huyen is Assistant Professor and has been working at the Institute of Archaeology of Vietnam since 19610. Her interests are in the Metal Age of Vietnam and ancient bronze drums. She has published extensively, in both Vietnamese and English, on the Dong Son Culture, on Dong Son drums, and on prehistory in North Vietnam.

Phasook Indrawoorth is Professor of Archaeology at Silpakorn University, Bangkok, Thailand. She obtained her BA Degree in Archaeology from MS University of Baroda, Gujerat, India. Her main research interest is in the field of historical archaeology in Thailand, from the late Prehistoric Period (*c.*300 BC) to the early Historic Period. Her main publications in Thai include *Report on the Excavation at Tambon Phra Praton, Amphoe Muang, Changwat Nakhon Pathom* (1984); *The Ancient Civilization in Lumphun Province* (1993); *Report on the Excavation at Muang Fa Daed Song Yang, Kamalasai District, Kalasin Province* (2001); and *Buddha Images of Mahayana Buddhism* (2001). She has also published *Dvaravati: a critical study based on archaeological evidence* (1999) (in Thai and English) and *Index of the Pottery of the Dvaravati Period* (1985).

Pierre-Yves Manguin is a member of the École Française d'Extrême-Orient. His research focuses on the history and archaeology of the coastal states and maritime trade networks of Southeast Asia. He is the author of *Les Portugais sur les côtes de Viet-nam et du Champa.* (1972); *Nguyên Anh, Macau et le Portuga: aspects politiques et commerciux d'une relation privilégiée* (1984); *O'Ribeiro das cousas do Achem' de D. João Ribeiro Gaio (with Jorge M. dos Santos Alves),* (1997) and many journal and conference articles in English, French, Indonesian and Portuguese. He undertakes archaeological work in Indonesia and Vietnam.

John N. Miksic is Associate Professor in the Southeast Asian Studies Programme, National University of Singapore. He is also a Visiting Fellow in the Asia Research Institute, National University of Singapore, and a board member, Center for Khmer Studies, Siem Reap, Cambodia. His research interests include the historical archaeology of Southeast Asia between the fifth and fifteenth centuries; Chinese and Southeast Asian ceramics; Chinese glass; Southeast Asian gold jewellery; urbanization; maritime trade; and cultural resource management, including tourism. He is the author of numerous journal articles and his main publications include *Archaeology on the Forbidden Hill of Singapore* (1985), and *Old Javanese Gold* (1990). He is editor of *Earthenwares of Southeast Asia* (2003).

Nguyen Khac Su is Assistant Professor and has been head of the Stone Age Section at the Institute of Archaeology, Vietnam, since 1971. He has published (in Vietnamese) on the Son Vi and Hoa Binh cultures and on the prehistory of the mountain provinces of North Vietnam.

William A. Southworth completed his Ph.D. thesis entitled *The Origins of Champa: A preliminary review* at the School of Oriental and African Studies, London, in 2001 and has published a number of articles on Champa. He was a Research Fellow at the Center for Khmer Studies in Siem Reap, Cambodia, 1999–2001, and is now an independent researcher on early Southeast Asian art and archaeology at the University of Bonn. His main interest lies in the relationship between the material evidence from archaeological excavation and historical texts.

Miriam Stark is an Associate Professor, University of Hawai'i at Manoa, Honolulu. Her research specialities are in Cambodian archaeology and Philippine ethnoarchaeology. She is editor of the journal *Asian Perspectives* and has published extensively on ancient economic systems, emergent complexity in the Mekong Delta, ceramic ethnoarchaeology, and technology and culture. Her papers include Angkor Borei and the Archaeology of Cambodia's Mekong Delta, in *Art & Archaeology of Fu Nan: Pre-Khmer Kingdom of the Lower Mekong Valley*, J. Khoo (ed.), Bangkok 2005. Since 1996, she has directed the Lower Mekong Archaeological Project. This research program examines state formation in southern Cambodia during the first millennium AD.

Tong Trung Tin is Assistant Professor and has been Vice-Director of the Institute of Archaeology of Vietnam, where he has worked since 1977. His research interests are in the historical archaeology of Vietnam, sculpture, art and architecture. He has published, in Vietnamese, on Vietnamese sculpture and art in the Ly and Tran dynasties, on the architecture of Buddhist temples, and on *stupa* in the Ly dynasty.

FOREWORD

Andrew Sherratt

As Jared Diamond has observed, the Old World has its axis from east to west, and the New World from north to south. The mountain spine of the Americas extends all the way down the Pacific coast from Alaska to Patagonia – a cumulative crumpling caused by the slow westward movement of those continents over geological time. The Old World, on the other hand, is crumpled in the middle, along a line which extends from western Europe to New Guinea. More complex in its origin, this chain of mountains resulted from multiple continental collisions: the northward movement of Africa and India, creating mountain pile-ups from the Pyrenees and the Alps to the Himalayas; and the slow, inexorable movement of the tectonic plate underlying the Pacific Ocean, as it dives beneath the eastern borders of Asia, leaving the arcs of volcanic islands which festoon Eurasia's eastern edge. In between the solid mass of India, and the volcano-fringed Philippine Sea, the continental shelf of Southeast Asia forms an archipelago – an island world astride the Equator, many of whose languages belong to the family called Austronesian, "Southern Islands". Like the Mediterranean Sea, at the opposite end of the Old World axis, it has been a cradle of seafaring skills and a crossroads between surrounding cultures and civilizations. It is high time for a biographical portrait of this region, showing how its personality emerged over the formative period which encompasses both later prehistoric and early historic times, and making full use of the flood of new information provided by archaeology. This book is it: the first integrated account of the emergence of Southeast Asia on the stage of world history.

The natural borders of Southeast Asia are unusually clear. A glance at a map of earthquake activity shows a line which runs from the eastern end of the Himalayas, through Burma and the Andaman Islands, to follow the mountain spine of Indonesia (and its parallel deep-sea trench) as far as the Moluccas; thereafter it swings back northwards, up past the Philippines (with an even deeper trench on the Pacific side) to Taiwan, whence it continues parallel to the Asian Mainland up to Japan and so to Kamchatka and the Aleutian Islands. The area so enclosed is, geologically speaking, the eastern borderland of Eurasia: and Southeast Asia is its southernmost extension, with its chains of islands continuing the ridges and fissures of the continental mass. These have naturally acted, therefore, as stepping-stones into the unknown, leading down from either India or China to the tropical resources on either side of the equator, or the new (to humans) world of Australasia with its distinctive animals and plants. The early arrival of human populations in Australia, on the other side of a substantial sea-crossing, suggests that Southeast Asia was humankind's first training-ground in making the most of marine environments – and perhaps that the Americas were first reached by comparable groups moving north and east along the island arcs to travel clockwise around the Pacific. As one of the first areas outside Africa to be occupied by human populations, therefore, Southern and Southeast Asia had a crucial role in world prehistory; and since the mega-explosion of the Toba magma-chamber in northern Sumatra some 70,000 years ago (a massive event much larger than any volcanic eruption in historical times) may have killed off a substantial proportion of contemporary humankind, through the "nuclear winter" it initiated, it may well have had a significant effect on the entire human species. Southeast Asia's second claim to fame is as the largest area of the Earth's surface to be inundated by rising sea-levels at the end of the last glaciation some ten thousand years ago, as the ice melted and water was transferred from land to sea, flooding the shallow continental shelves. This created the island world as it appears today, a southern Cyclades with its hub as Borneo and an elongated outer circle of islands, together separating the Indian from the Pacific Oceans like a semi-permeable membrane. These two roles, therefore – as a series of steps from north to south, and as a mediator between east and west – have alternated throughout its career on a continuously increasing scale.

The period after the retreat of the ice saw the beginnings of farming in several areas of the world. The first great expansion of farming populations in the Old World had its origins in the Levant, where wheat and barley were first cultivated; but although its effects reached as far as northwest India (where these crops formed the basis for the Indus Valley civilization), this expansion had no impact on Southeast Asia. It was the second great centre of crop-domestication, the rice-growing area of central China, which was to provide a carbohydrate staple for the monsoon lands. Unlike the explosive demographic effects which accompanied the first use of wheat and barley, however, rice-growing seems to have spread relatively slowly, perhaps as new methods of cultivating it in a wider range of environments were pioneered. Thus it was not until the third millennium BC that large areas of continental Southeast Asia were introduced to farming, even later that it became widespread in the islands; and down to very recent times there was an intimate mosaic of different ways of life in the archipelago. This makes it possible to make use of ethnological, linguistic and anthropological evidence alongside the archaeological reconstruction of Southeast Asian prehistory, in a way which makes it particularly vivid and exciting – though also the subject of lively debates – in a rapidly improving understanding of what was happening in this area in early times. One hotly disputed topic has been the beginnings of bronze metallurgy, in which the whole area came to have notable expertise, especially in the casting of elaborate hollow items such as drums. These techniques again provide a link with China, and perhaps beyond to the bronze-working tradition of Siberia and northern central Asia. The outlines of a pattern of interconnections and influences are only now becoming clear. By the closing centuries of the first millennium BC, a chain of sophisticated bronze-working cultures existed between the southern border of Han China and the Gulf of Thailand, whose products were distributed as far south as New Guinea. Just as in Europe an "amber route" connected urban consumers at one end of a supply-chain with populations at the other end of a continent, able to provide them with a precious and desirable product, so it has been suggested that a "feather route", supplying bird-of-paradise feathers across the whole extent of island Southeast Asia, carried these exotic items as far as China – bringing prosperity to trading-centres along the route. Such long-distance luxuries, along with more local items of trade, passed through areas of continental Southeast Asia now practising rice cultivation in irrigated fields, living in fortified settlements, and making tools and ornaments out of bronze.

From some time around 700 BC, an important focus of urban development had once again emerged in India; this time in the rice-growing Ganges valley rather than the Indus, and with a maritime outlet to the east of the peninsula, on the Bay of Bengal. Links to the west first came by way of Afghanistan from Persia and its rising empire, later conquered by Alexander the Great. The Ganges corridor thus connected the Persian-Hellenistic world with the rising world to the east of India, via ports such as Tamluk near the Ganges mouth. Northern Burma (Myanmar) provided a nodal connection, both indirectly with China itself (via the hard, mountainous route through Yünnan) and with the riches of peninsular and island Southeast Asia. This provided the entry-point to a network of connections with centres of population in the alluvial valleys of the Irrawaddy, the Salween and the Mekong (in southern Burma, Thailand and Cambodia respectively), where the distinctive lowland methods of floodwater farming, leading to ever more elaborate systems of water-control, were able to sustain increasing densities of population. The volume of Indian trafficking grew substantially in the final centuries BC, as trade with the West was carried in sailing-boats using the seasonally complementary monsoon winds to travel between the west coast of India and up the Persian Gulf or the Red Sea to supply consumers in the Roman Empire. Southern India and Sri Lanka acquired a new centrality within these sailing-routes, which now began to extend across the Bay of Bengal to tap into the web of connections established in Southeast Asia, and to acquire the first Chinese products, by sea. Like the Silk Road, which was developing at the same time to link Rome, Persia and China across the scattered oases in the deserts north of the Himalayas, traffic was indirect and passed through many hands: but the attraction of items such as silk and pearls was enough to pull them across continents. Southeast Asia was the maritime hub of these connections, perhaps (with its delta farmers and seagoing traditions) integrating land and water more intimately than anywhere else on Earth. It should be no surprise, therefore (although it is an astonishing observation) that languages of the Austronesian family came in the next millennium to be spoken over an area from Madagascar to Easter Island – a third of the entire circumference of the world. This in itself is a reflection of the scale of voyaging, far beyond the regular trade routes between urban centres, which carried explorers of the oceans off into the unknown.

As the scale of global connections grew rapidly during the first millennium AD, the strategic position of Southeast Asia, at the interface between the China Sea and the Indian Ocean, became increasingly evident; and as the civilizations of both India and China grew in scale and reach, traffic both within and beyond Southeast Asia grew commensurately. The term "Indochina" (nowadays often resented as a colonial hangover), nonetheless serves to convey something of these dual influences from larger and longer-established urban traditions – even if this term leaves no room for the local root-stock, creative blending of influences, and unique achievements which characterize this area as much as its proximity to sometimes more powerful neighbours. The cultures both of the mainland and the islands retained their distinctiveness, even when amplified by population movements from the north and new cultural and linguistic affiliations, and even – perhaps especially – when they adopted religious ideas and practices from their neighbours.

The story of this crucial and cosmopolitan region is still being put together, from the details won from the study of monuments and manuscripts, and the excavation of settlements, ports, towns and temples. It is less well known, and less appreciated in the world as a whole, than it deserves to be – in part, because writing an account of it requires a range of knowledge and collaborative research which is breathtaking in its scope, combining the skills of the scientist and the humanist familiar with a dozen different disciplines. This book will introduce many readers for the first time to the coherence of our present knowledge of these developments. It shows how artificial are the boundaries which we often impose on our understanding, by separating "history" from "prehistory", or dividing the history of humankind into neat (often national) boxes. The interlinked islands and peninsulas of Southeast Asia, with their boundless external horizons, provide a metaphor for the whole intellectual enterprise of compiling a common history of humankind.

INTRODUCTION

Ian Glover and Peter Bellwood

Southeast Asia is attracting increasing interest among archaeologists and those interested generally in the documentation of human cultural achievements in the remote past. During Neolithic times the Southeast Asian islands served as the source region for one of the greatest population dispersals on record, that of the Austronesians, spreading ultimately to as far afield as Madagascar and Polynesia. Similarly, the Southeast Asian Mainland was the arena for the development of a series of rich Neolithic and Bronze Age communities. Out of the latter evolved widespread and densely populated Iron Age cultures, followed quickly by several unique and strikingly monumental "Indic" civilizations after 1500 years ago, when this part of the world yielded products sought after in India, China and the Mediterranean. Many of the eastern regions of Southeast Asia, especially in Indonesia and the Philippines, witnessed the coexistence of colourful tribal cultures alongside these developing civilizations with their distant trading links. All of these cultural foundations live on today, in society, language and ethnic affiliation, despite the changes wrought by the more recent arrivals of Islamic and western influences. This book addresses these foundations.

The rationale for this book developed out the earlier series *Peoples of Southeast Asia and the Pacific*, which both of us had been editing for the publisher Blackwell between 1993 and 1997. The aim of this series was to examine the cultural history of the peoples of specific islands and ethnolinguistic groups, up to their incorporation into modern nation states, as well as past archaeological complexes.[1] These books were to draw, as relevant, on whatever good data was available from archaeology, ethnography, art history, comparative linguistics, historical sources, and the political science of modern nation building. We were both trained in the disciplines of anthropology and prehistoric archaeology but felt that the archaeological record of Southeast Asia was too often reported out of its broader cultural context. Technical studies of ceramics, metals, dating, plant remains, monumental structures and sculpture abounded in a rather specialized literature, but not much attempt was made to present archaeological research to educated non-specialists and help inform the ever increasing number of western visitors and tourists to the region. Of course, some exceptions had appeared from time to time: Peter Bellwood's *Man's Conquest of the Pacific* (1979); Charles Higham and Rachanie Thosarat's *Prehistoric Thailand – from Early Settlement to Sukhothai* (1998); Higham's own *Early Cultures of Mainland Southeast Asia* (2002); *Ancient Trade and Cultural Contacts in Southeast Asia*, edited by Amara Srisuchat (1996); and *Southeast Asia: a Past Regained* (Conlan 1995). But the time seemed ripe for a fairly general but authoritative review of the whole field.

In 1996 John Davey, Blackwell's commissioning editor, left for another position and the publishers decided not to continue the series after just six of the planned series had appeared. The new editor suggested in its place a book of 'readings'; a compilation of articles of lasting importance from a range of archaeological and anthropological journals as a university textbook. Both of us favoured instead a book of newly commissioned articles by specialists to cover broad time ranges, focused on the main modern nations of Southeast Asia. While modern national boundaries are often of little relevance for an understanding of prehistory or ancient history, the modern world nevertheless "recognizes" Southeast Asia as divided into nation states, and it is the modern world to which this book is addressed.

The authors were asked to concentrate on the period running from the emergence of settled food-producing Neolithic cultures (mainly third and second millennia BC) down to the establishment of Islamic trading principalities in parts of the region starting around the fourteenth century AD. Earlier periods of hunter-gatherer archaeology are outlined where necessary for background purposes, but do not form a major part of this book, which is essentially focused on the themes of early farming societies and early states. Beyond these recommendations, we left the authors to write on what they knew best and what they considered most significant for the cultural history of the countries and places with which they were most concerned. In particular, we wanted the authors to bridge the gaps which so often exist between prehistoric and historic archaeology in Southeast Asia, a gap which resembles that between prehistoric and Classical archaeology that has existed for so long in the western part of the Old World.

Originally, we had hoped to have a significant proportion of the book written by archaeologists from the countries of Southeast Asia. But for various reasons – poor communications, problems with language, illness and accidents – we found harder than we had imagined. That said, we are delighted to be able to include major chapters on Thailand by Professor Phasook Indrawooth of Silpakorn University, Bangkok, and on Vietnam by Drs Nguyen Khac Su, Pham Minh Huyen and Professor Tong Trung Tin, all of the Institute of Archaeology, National Institute of Social Sciences, Hanoi.

After this Introduction and a preliminary chapter by Bellwood and Glover which introduces the region, its people and their geographic setting and, very briefly, the Pleistocene peopling of Southeast Asia, there are twelve substantive chapters; by Bellwood on the origins and dispersal of agricultural communities of insular Southeast Asia; by Charles Higham on the Neolithic cultures of the continental region and their cultural trajectory into an Iron Age in the last centuries BCE; by Bérénice Bellina and Ian Glover on early contact with India and the Mediterranean world; by Miriam Stark on early Cambodia and the emergence of the great Angkorian civilization; by Phasook Indrawooth on early Buddhist and Hindu civilization in the region of modern Thailand; by Pamela Gutman and Bob Hudson on Burma/Myanmar; by Nguyen Khac Su, Pham Minh Huyen and Tong Trung Tin on the rich and complex early cultures in the region of present-day northern Vietnam; by William Southworth on the Champa kingdoms of central Vietnam; by John Miksic on the Classical cultures of Indonesia; by Elisabeth Bacus on the island world of the Philippines; by Pierre-Yves Manguin on the early maritime states of western Indonesia, Malaysia and southern Vietnam; and by David Bulbeck on indigenous and extraneous influences which have affected cultural developments in Peninsular Malaysia. These are followed by a final chapter by Bellwood and Glover which attempts to identify the long-term achievements of Southeast Asian societies on a world scale. Essential themes include the roles of indigenous creativity versus external influence, the value of Southeast Asia as a crossroads of cultural interaction, and why a knowledge of the history and archaeology of the region is of especial importance today as the region goes through a period of transition from a long stage of economic and political domination by European and American power to one where the "Middle Kingdom", China, appears to be reasserting its ancient ascendancy.

Note

1 The books published in this series are *The Peoples of Borneo* (V. T. King 1993); *The Khmers* (I. Mabbett and D. Chandler 1995); *The Bugis* (C. Pelras 1996); *The Peoples of Bali* (A. Hobart, U. Ramseyer and A. Leeman, 1996); *The Lapita Peoples* (P. V. Kirch 1997); and *The Island Melanesians* (M. Spriggs 1997).

Bibliography

Bellwood, P. (1979) *Man's Conquest of the Pacific*, Auckland: Collins.
Conlan, R. (ed.) (1995) *Southeast Asia: a Past Regained* in the series "Lost Civilizations", Alexandra: Time-Life Books.
Higham, C. F. W. (2002) *Early Cultures of Mainland Southeast Asia*, Bangkok: River Books and Thames & Hudson.
Higham, C. F. W. and Thosarat, R. (1998) *Prehistoric Thailand: From Early Settlement to Sukhothai*, Bangkok: River Books.
Srisuchat, A. (ed.) (1996) *Ancient Trade and Cultural Contacts in Southeast Asia*, Bangkok: Office of the National Cultural Commission.

1

SOUTHEAST ASIA

Foundations for an archaeological history

Peter Bellwood and Ian Glover

The modern nations of Southeast Asia contain a total population of over 450 million people, spread through a large number of different ethnic and linguistic groups (Figures 1.1 and 1.2). Some of these peoples, particularly in coastal and riverine wet rice-growing areas, are extremely numerous today and have had a history marked in recent centuries by the attainment of high levels of political and socio-cultural complexity. Such people include the Thais, Khmers, Vietnamese, Burmans, Malays, Javanese and Balinese, to name some of the largest in terms of population. Others are extremely small, such as the bands of hunters who still survive in a marginal way in the ever-diminishing rainforests. Examples of these groups include the Agta of Luzon, the Semang of the Malay Peninsula, the Punan of Borneo and the Mani of Southern Thailand. Between the numerically-dominant lowlanders and the hunters, we have many other groups of farming populations, frequently located in rugged upland or remote areas, whose remarkable traditions, lifestyles and patterns of diversity contribute to one of the richest ethnographic records in the world. This last group is too numerous for a short and succinct list, since literally hundreds of ethnolinguistic groups exist in the hinterlands of Mainland Southeast Asia and in the multitudinous islands which stretch from Sumatra to Luzon and New Guinea.

All of the native peoples of Southeast Asia have ancestries, in terms of culture, language and genotype, firmly grounded in the Southeast Asian region. This becomes very clear when we examine languages and physical appearance. At no time in the recorded history of Southeast Asia, extending back for at last 2,000 years, can we see any major replacements of native languages or populations by immigrants from outside the region. Undoubtedly, contacts with India and China through the past 2,000 years have transformed much of the cultural history of Southeast Asia and brought many settlers. So, too, have contacts with Islamic powers after AD 1200 and with European powers after AD 1500. But in no case were populations from any of these regions able to settle in significant numbers. The Southeast Asians themselves do not speak descendant forms of Sanskrit, Chinese or Arabic as their vernaculars and have never done so; neither are they biologically derived from South, East or West Asia. As Alfred Crosby[1] has so evocatively described, regions such as Southeast Asia were far too densely settled and too tropical in environment to attract successful European settlement. Likewise, the Indian, Chinese and Arab trading states and empires, despite their undoubted contributions to Southeast Asian culture history, never dispatched large numbers of settlers into the region.

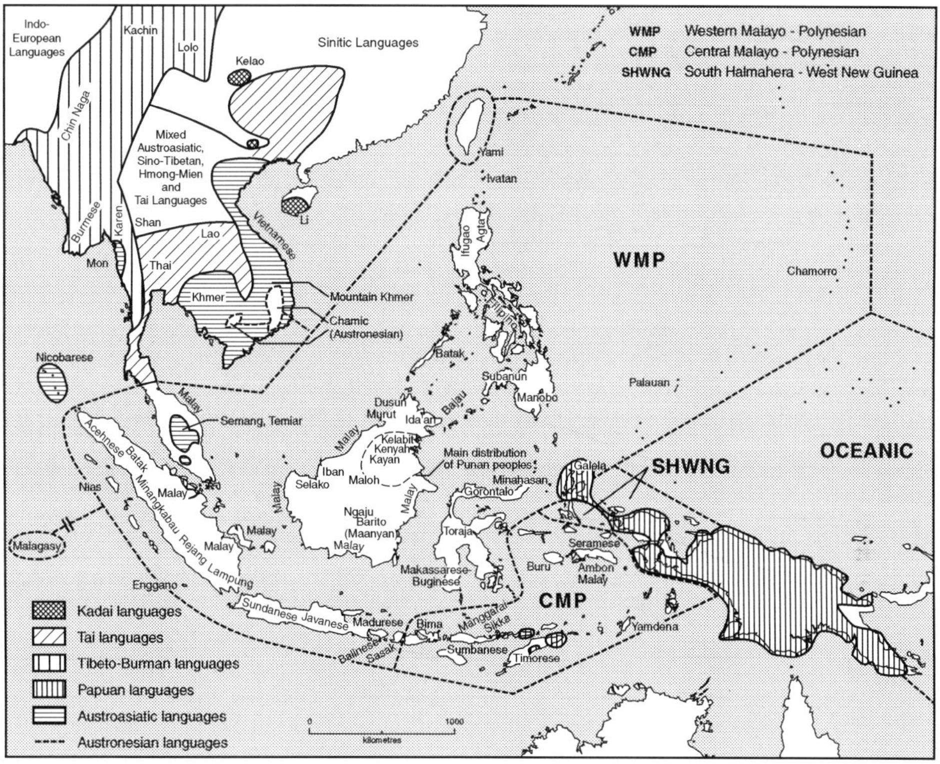

Figure 1.1 The major language families and subgroups with a selection of the major ethnolinguistic populations of modern Southeast Asia mentioned in the text.

As far as we know, Southeast Asia did not witness any truly independent developments of early agriculture, urban civilization or literacy, but it did witness the oldest recorded sea crossings by humans, the genesis of the greatest ethnolinguistic dispersal in human history (that of the Austronesians), and the evolution of some major historical civilizations. Southeast Asian populations during the Neolithic and Early Metal periods also contributed much to human achievements in agriculture, art, metallurgy, boat construction and ocean navigation. Southeast Asia, indeed, must have served as the proximal source during the past 60,000 years for all the populations of Australasia and the Pacific Islands, from the Aboriginal Tasmanians to the Hawaiians and Easter Islanders.

So this book is about the history of the native peoples of Southeast Asia, as visible mainly in the data of archaeology, but with excursions when necessary into the fields of documentary history, art and architecture, language and human biology. We examine the flowering of indigenous traditions across the millennia, often stimulated by external contacts, and often in turn stimulating developments in other regions. In order to put the following chapters in perspective, the remainder of this chapter will be devoted to three themes: the environments, the people, and the deeper foundation levels of prehistory before the beginnings of systematic cereal agriculture and animal domestication.

(a) Temiar people of interior Kelantan, Malaysia. (Photograph by P. Bellwood.)

(b) Burmese monks at Prome. (Photograph by I. C. Glover.)

(c) Bunak bards, dressed in ceremonial attire to recite the Bei Gua, or 'Itinerary of the Ancestors' before the altar of war, East Timor. (Photograph by C. Friedberg.)

(d) People on the Xieng Khouang Plateau, northern Laos. (From François Garnier 1873.)

Figure 1.2 Traditional and present day Southeast Asians.

Southeast Asian environments

Southeast Asia comprises a remarkable array of peoples and cultures located across two geographical divisions. These are *Mainland Southeast Asia* (Burma, Laos, Thailand, Cambodia, Vietnam, Peninsular Malaysia) and *Island Southeast Asia* (Taiwan, Philippines, East Malaysia, Indonesia, Brunei). These divisions have not always had the same geographical shapes or environmental characteristics as today. During the Pleistocene Epoch of geological time (*c.*1.8 million to 10,000 years ago), the earth's climate was drastically cooled by a series of ice ages. At the peaks (or maxima) of such cold phases, land temperatures dropped on average by 5 or 6 degrees Celsius, sea levels fell to over 100 metres below their present levels, and rainfall and vegetation appear to have been greatly reduced, even in the tropics. The last glacial maximum occurred about 20,000 years ago, the previous one about 130,000 years ago, and between these glacial maxima the climates of the world oscillated very frequently, generally being less warm and wet than those of today. We are now in the peak of an interglacial which has lasted for the past 10,000 years, a veritable paradise of climate and environment during which time all human complex cultures, with farming and cities, have evolved. Without the existence of this current interglacial, life as we know it would not exist, hence, in part, our current fears over which way the climate will turn in the future.

When sea levels fell during the long periods of cold climate during the Pleistocene, Mainland Southeast Asia was extended by land bridges to the Sunda Shelf islands of Sumatra, Java, Borneo and Bali, forming a huge southeasterly dry land extension to the Asian continent. This massive ancient land mass is termed "Sundaland" by biogeographers (Figure 1.3). Taiwan was also joined to the Chinese Mainland. However, the islands of the Philippines and eastern Indonesia (Sulawesi, Moluccas, Lesser Sundas) were never land-bridged either to Asia or to Greater Australia (Australia plus New Guinea and Tasmania), although the distances between them were sometimes much reduced. These eastern Indonesian islands belong to the biogeographical province of "Wallacea", through which human migration beyond the Sunda Shelf has always involved sea crossings, generally between about 10 and 90 kilometres and thus too wide to allow migration by swimming alone. Boats or rafts of some kind must have been used, even for the first crossings to Australia between 40,000 and 60,000 years ago.

As biogeographers have long observed since the days of Alfred Russel Wallace, a contemporary of Charles Darwin, Sundaland continentality equates with richness in terms of native faunas and floras, whereas Wallacean insularity equates with endemicity and pauperization. The Asian Mainland, together with the Sunda Shelf islands to as far east as Bali and Borneo, has varied placental mammal faunas, including some very large species such as elephants, rhinos, cattle, deer, pigs and tigers. Greater Australia has a marsupial fauna, with animals such as wallabies, bandicoots and cuscuses (possums) occurring in New Guinea and adjacent islands. Colonists in Wallacea found fewer animal resources, although a number of endemic mammal species existed in the Philippines and Sulawesi, in the latter island even including two endemic genera of cuscuses whose ancestors rafted on continental crust aeons ago from Greater Australia. The Lesser Sundas and Moluccas, however, had precious few mammalian faunal resources in the Late Pleistocene until people learnt the values of animal translocation although stegodonts (elephant-like creatures, now extinct) had reached Sulawesi and the Lesser Sundas before modern humans entered the region about 50,000 years ago. The first evidence for purposeful

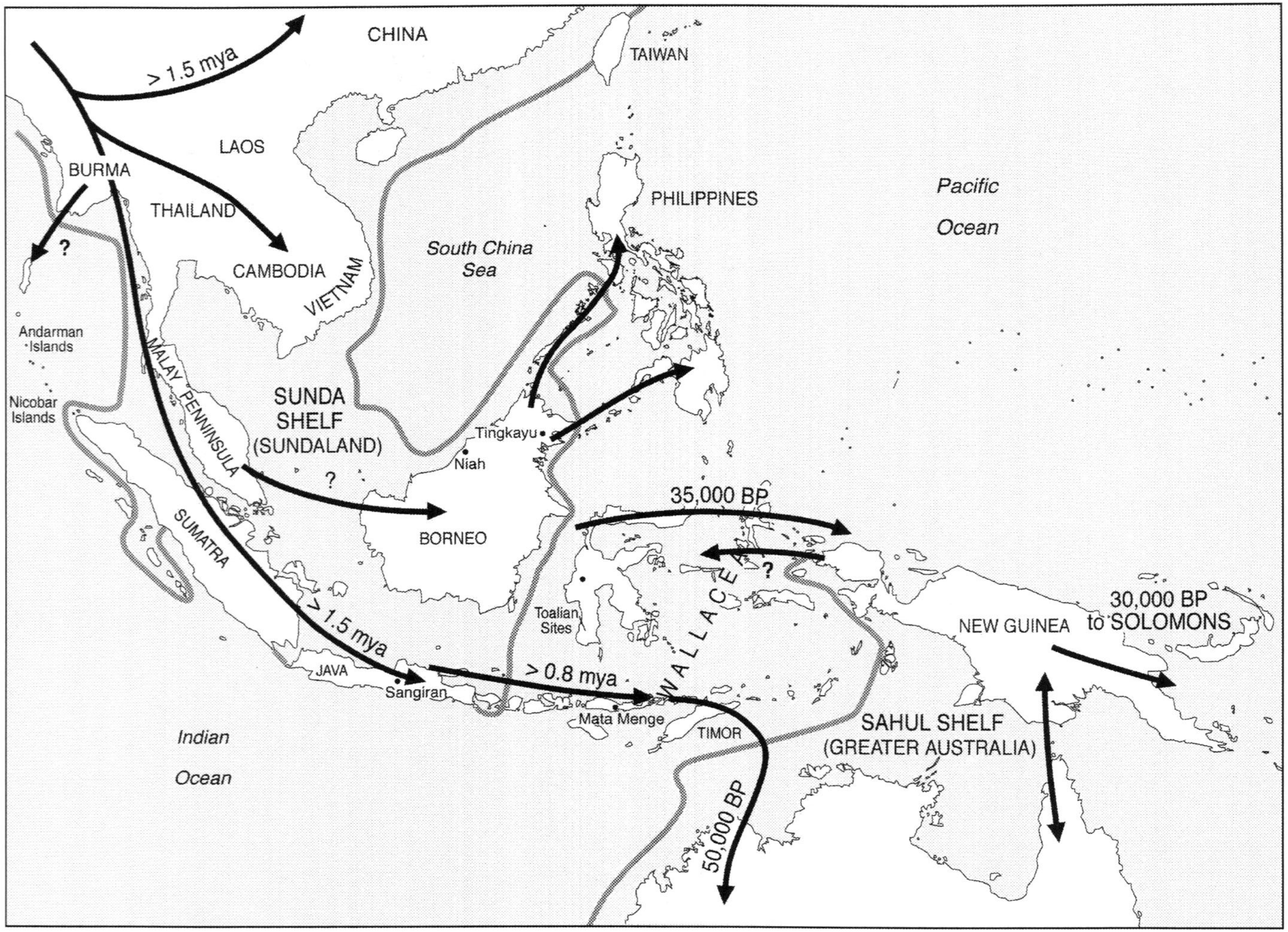

Figure 1.3 Pleistocene movements and colonizations across land and sea in Southeast Asia.

animal translocation falls between the late Pleistocene and middle Holocene, when marsupials were taken from New Guinea to the northern Moluccas Islands, Timor and the Bismarck Archipelago.

The modern environments of Southeast Asia are essentially tropical (Figure 1.4). There is increasing dry season length as one moves polewards beyond 5 degrees north and south of the equator, along which rain falls during much of the year. Equatorial populations living below these latitudes today tend to be small, and in eastern Indonesia often dependent for subsistence on tubers and tree crops such as yams, taro, various palm starches and bananas. The major cereals of the Southeast Asian and Chinese Neolithic cultures, especially rice and foxtail millet, are not well suited to hot and ever-wet equatorial climates and evolved beyond the equatorial zone in tropical to temperate monsoon regions with long dry seasons. Today, and in the historical past, the greatest population densities have occurred in these monsoon regions, especially in alluvial lowlands in southern China and Mainland Southeast Asia north of the Malay Peninsula, and in alluvial/volcanic landscapes in Luzon, Java and Bali.

As human prehistory in Southeast Asia progressed, so human relationships with landscapes and environments changed. Hunters, farmers, and urban dwellers tend to use different parts of the landscape, with increasing population density becoming focused through time in ever-smaller areas of high productive potential. Ten thousand years ago, human populations were mobile and dispersed, with periodic concentrations in rich coastal regions. By 1,000–1,500 years ago, wet-field rice landscapes and urban/temple complexes occupied the richest and most accessible lowlands, village farmers occupied the less central valleys and slopes, and hunter-gatherers occupied the remotest interiors and coasts. By 1,000 years ago also, the ethnic patterns which still join and divide the peoples of Southeast Asia were already well and truly in place.

The peoples of Southeast Asia

Since several chapters in this book extend well into the historical period, with decipherable inscriptions and written records, it is necessary briefly to describe the main ethnolinguistic divisions within the recent and modern populations of Southeast Asia. This may best be done with reference to language, since there can be no doubt that language, on the large scale of the language family, is intimately correlated with the cultural and geographical origins of different peoples. The language families of Southeast Asia will be discussed in more detail in the following two chapters, when we come to examine their suggested origins and early dispersal patterns.

At this point, however, the main language families, together with brief statements on their possible origins and histories, may be introduced. Approximate modern distributions are shown in Figure 1.1. Excluding minority languages which have spread in recent centuries, particularly from Europe and China, we have five major families:

1. Tibeto-Burman languages within the Sino-Tibetan family. These languages occupy the western mainland of Southeast Asia and northern South Asia, and today their speakers include major populations such as the Burmese and Karen. Exactly when they first entered Southeast Asia is unclear, but their homeland lies further north in western or central China, possibly Sichuan.

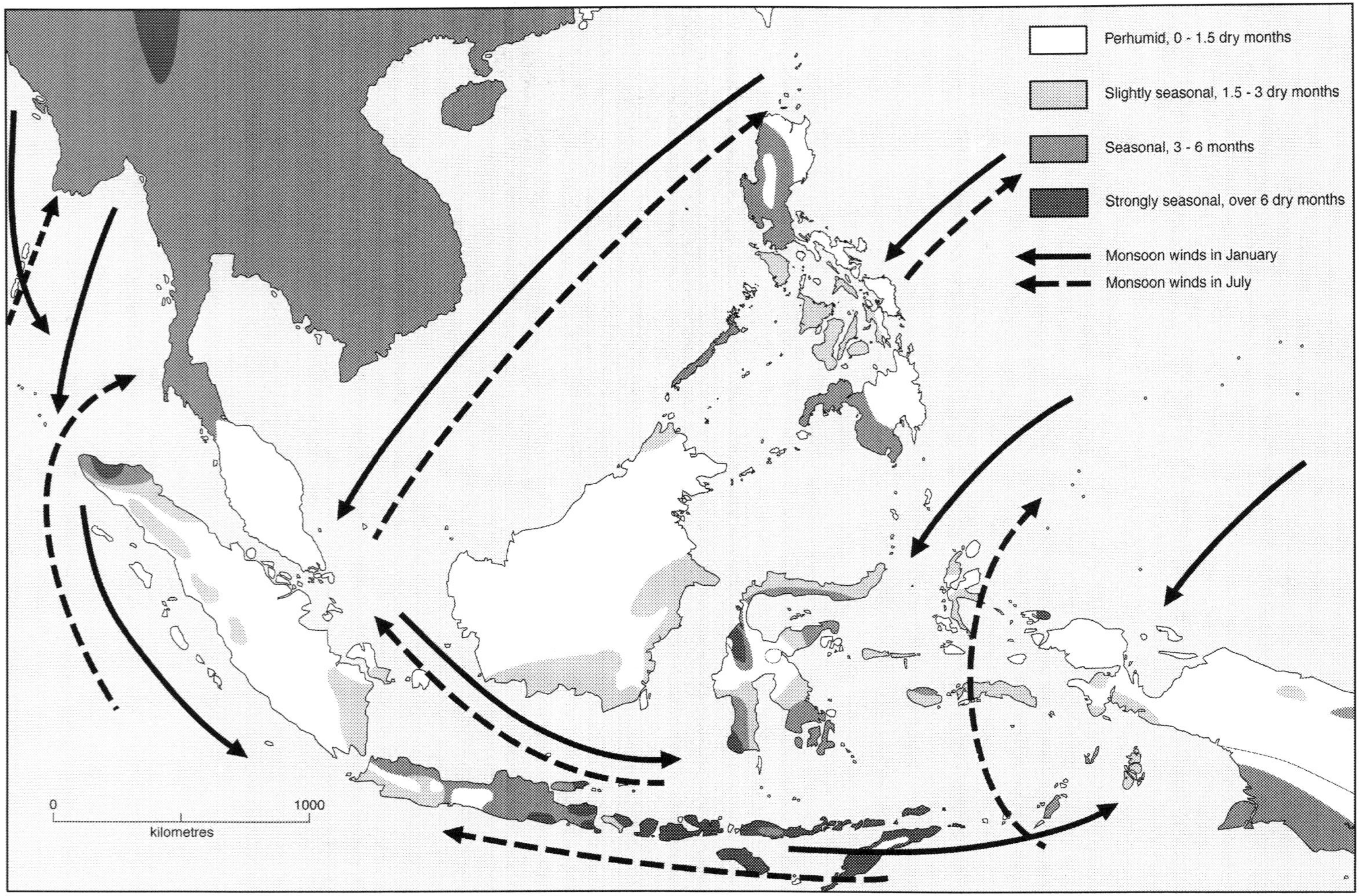

Figure 1.4 Rainfall and monsoon wind patterns in Southeast Asia (from Bellwood 1992).

2 Austroasiatic languages. These include major languages such as Khmer and Vietnamese, and many small isolated linguistic pockets scattered through Mainland Southeast Asia, Peninsular Malaysia (the Aslian languages), the Nicobars and northeastern India (Munda). There is one opinion that the Austroasiatic languages derive from the earliest agricultural colonization of Mainland Southeast Asia, a process possibly commencing out of southern China about 3000 BC (see Higham, chapter 3), because early Austroasiatic populations grew rice.[2] But it is also possible that Austroasiatic languages were widely dispersed on the mainland of Southeast Asia before the Neolithic and that rice farming was taken up by some of these groups in appropriate habitats from earlier rice cultivators in the north, who may have belonged to the Hmong-Mien language family.[3]

3 Tai (Daic) languages, including Kadai. These also have an origin in southern China and have spread into Thailand and Laos mainly within the past millennium. Thus, it is unlikely that they featured greatly in the prehistory of Southeast Asia proper, although their speakers may have been involved in the creation of the Bronze-Iron Age civilization of Dian in Yunnan.

4 Hmong-Mien languages. These originated probably in the middle Yangzi region of China and have spread south in recent centuries as a result of Chinese pressure on the homeland region of their speakers. Many Hmong and Mien (also called Meo, Miao and Yao) live at high altitudes and form the so-called "hill tribes" of many regions of northern Mainland Southeast Asia.

5 Austronesian languages. These are spoken by the major seafaring population which spread from southern China and Taiwan, commencing about 3000 BC, to settle all of Island Southeast Asia and most of the Pacific Islands. Austronesians also colonized the Malay Peninsula, southern Vietnam and Madagascar. In AD 1500 they formed the most widespread ethnolinguistic population in world history.

These major ethnolinguistic populations will be referred to again as the chapters in this book unfold, since it is possible from time to time to make useful comparisons between the linguistic and archaeological records, even for reconstructed linguistic stages which occurred prior to the beginnings of writing.

The archaeological foundations

So far, our knowledge of the prehistory and archaeology of Southeast Asia is a little uneven, not only in geographical coverage – many countries such as Burma, Laos and Cambodia are only just commencing archaeological research on pre-Classical periods – but also in content. For instance, we have an excellent burial and subsistence economy record for the Neolithic and Bronze-Iron Ages on the mainland of Southeast Asia, but almost no data on the internal housing plans of individual settlements. Much of the Holocene information on hunter-gatherers and farmers from Malaysia and Indonesia is derived from caves and rock-shelters, so we know little here of open site (camp or village) distributions, but we have good data on lithics and pottery sequences. Some of the lacunae reflect the nature of the tropical environment: preservation is never good in the equatorial zone and leaching is also a major problem in the monsoonal tropics. However, the monsoon regions of Thailand, Cambodia and Vietnam encouraged more stable lowland settlements that offer excellent site visibility in the form of settlement mounds belonging to the agricultural period, an advantage denied in the more equatorial regions of Malaysia, Indonesia and the Philippines.

Moving now to the broadest scale of prehistoric reconstruction, archaeology and allied disciplines tell us that the main roots of the pre-Colombian patterns of worldwide cultural and biological diversity can be traced, subsequent to the biological evolution of humanity itself, to a number of human migratory achievements. One was the colonization of the Old World beyond the African homeland. This probably spanned at least two distinct stages, the first involving an out-of Africa movement by early *Homo* populations, with a later one involving further movements, perhaps out of Africa again, by anatomically modern populations of *Homo sapiens*, our direct ancestors. The early *Homo* populations settled in Southeast Asia and extended northwards and eastwards to China and Java by perhaps 1.5 million years ago. The most recent and extensive bursts of colonization, involving the anatomically modern humans, extended across the sea gaps of eastern Indonesia to reach Australia, New Guinea and possibly the Philippines around 35,000 to 50,000 years ago (Figure 1.2). The Americas were reached more recently, perhaps about 14,000 years ago.

The second major series of human expansions resulted from the establishment and growth of the earliest agricultural economies. These arose independently, at various times between 12,000 and about 5,000 years ago, in regions such as the Middle East, central China, the New Guinea Highlands, and some tropical regions of Africa and the Americas. Here we witness, in the archaeological record, the oldest systematic ways of producing rather than collecting or hunting food – in other words, agriculture and animal husbandry. These developments allowed a spurt of human population growth in the agricultural latitudes of the earth unprecedented in the previous two million years of human evolution. The ethnolinguistic map of Southeast Asia today, with its major language families (Figure 1.1), is almost entirely a creation of this recent period of remarkable social and economic development.

The first humans in Southeast Asia

Because this book focuses on the antecedents of living peoples and societies in Southeast Asia, it is not necessary to focus in detail on *Homo erectus*. But they do deserve recognition as the human pioneer species. Discovered in greatest fossil numbers in the eroded anticline of Sangiran in central Java, this early human species has become known popularly to the world by the rather patriarchal term "Java Man" (yes, some were women too, and even children!), or *Pithecanthropus*, the latter term bestowed by the original discoverer, Eugene Dubois, following his epochal discoveries at Trinil in 1891.

Today, research on *Homo erectus* in East Asia is proceeding apace. Large populations are now known in fossil form from sites in many parts of China and Java. This species evolved in Java for upwards of 1.5 million years, probably in semi-isolation and probably reaching extinction as recently as 50,000 years ago. Did modern humans apply the *coup-de-grâce*, as many suggest for the Neanderthals? We may never know, and it must be acknowledged here that opinions on the extinction issue are varied and often heated. There are many issues of chronology, species definition and genetic affinity which will need to be addressed before we can come close to any final conclusion.

Extinct or not, *Homo erectus* was clearly human. Bipedal like us, but somewhat smaller-brained, they made stone tools in China and possibly in Java, and also may have made narrow sea crossings (see next section). They were perhaps hunters – at least, their fossils often occur with the bones of the large Early and Middle Pleistocene mammals of Java, species such as elephants, stegodonts, rhinos, hippos, water buffalo, deer, pig and tiger. Most of these animals favoured fairly open forest or grassland, and the rainforests of Java with their orang-utans (no longer extant in Java) and gibbons emerged later, during the final interglacial about 130,000 years ago. A hunter's life in 800 000 BC, if indeed they hunted, was perhaps a good one. The problem is that most fossils are found in water-laid deposits, rather than in primary circumstances, therefore "proving" an activity such as hunting, as opposed to scavenging, is not an easy matter. Apart from some very simple stone tools, we know nothing of the cultural capacities of these early humans. Did they create art, imagine the future, bury their dead, decorate their bodies? We do not know.

So let us move on a million years or so, to the first activities of the direct ancestors of modern populations. The strong evidence for an anatomically modern human presence in Australia by 50,000 years ago makes it fairly certain that such populations were also present at that time in Southeast Asia. A skull from Niah Cave in Sarawak dated perhaps to 40,000 years ago, and younger skull fragments from Tabon Cave in the Philippines, attest the Late Pleistocene presence in Island Southeast Asia of anatomically modern humans of a phenotype resembling ancient Australians and Melanesians. These populations travelled far across both land and sea.

The first crossings of the sea

The ability to build a raft or canoe, however primitive, in order to cross a body of water is one which has characterized most coastal human societies in history. Growing evidence for the existence of such ability in the prehistoric record of humanity makes us wonder: how long ago did people begin to launch themselves at sea, not just to cross a narrow channel to an offshore island but to reach places close to and even over the horizon? Were such crossings done deliberately? Data on the first ocean crossings of humanity may be ambiguous about dates and degrees of intentionality, but current archaeological investigation is opening some remarkable new perspectives.

In most areas of the world, the ability to cross oceans seems to have developed within the time span of anatomically modern humans like ourselves. The only exception to this generalization, publicized very recently and still under debate, is a claim that *Homo erectus* was able to cross one or more sea gaps up to 19 km wide about 800,000 years ago in order to travel from Bali across the Wallace Line to the eastern Indonesian island of Flores. This is a remarkable claim, so far unprecedented and obviously rather isolated, given that no other ocean crossing can be positively attested until about 40,000 to 60,000 years ago, when humans probably reached Australia. But, if true, the Flores discovery indicates just how much we have yet to learn about the capabilities of hominins very remote in time, even though the sea crossings concerned in this instance were not out of sight of land.

Let us focus now on the remarkable new information about the capacity of early modern humans to cross sea between 50,000 and 30,000 years ago, information recovered from archaeological sites of Late Pleistocene age in the islands of Southeast Asia and western Oceania (Figure 1.3). Although most major islands in the Philippines and eastern Indonesia were high enough to be visible to their neighbours, the crossing from Roti or

Timor to the Sahul shelf of northwestern Australia, perhaps via now-drowned intervening islands, would have involved one crossing of at least 90 km even at times of lowest sea level. This could have required sailing completely out of sight of land for a short period, and we know this crossing was done at least 45,000 years ago. Such relatively narrow sea gaps, mostly under 90 km wide, which were negotiable for Pleistocene seafarers, continued east of New Guinea to as far as the southern Solomons, beyond which lay much wider expanses of sea, crossed on present evidence only by Austronesians with sailing and outrigger canoe technology after 3,500 years ago.

In recent years, archaeologists and natural scientists working in Wallacea and Australasia have produced astounding evidence for the early human colonization of this whole region, from Sulawesi, the Talaud Islands, the Moluccas, New Guinea, the Bismarck and Solomon Islands, and, most importantly perhaps, from Australia itself.

In terms of the date of the first modern human crossing of the Wallace Line, leaving aside issues over *Homo erectus*, Australia has so far the oldest evidence. Optical luminescence dates (a trapped-electron-based technique) for quartz particles in sandy sediments from two sites in the Northern Territory suggest a human presence, with associated stone flake tools, grindstones and ground pieces of red ochre, by as much as 50,000 years ago. New dates from Lake Mungo in western New South Wales are of a similar antiquity. So far, available radiocarbon dates suggest that the islands of Sulawesi, Talaud, the Moluccas, Bismarcks and Solomons were first settled between 28,000 and 35,000 years ago. These date distributions raise the possibility that Australia was reached from the Lesser Sundas perhaps 20,000 years before many of the islands in eastern Indonesia, but at present this can be no more than a possibility, subject to future testing by different dating methods. Dates for initial human occupation in the Philippines, a process that almost certainly occurred from Borneo rather than from Taiwan, fall generally within the past 30,000 years and a former presence here of *Homo erectus* seems very unlikely.

Let us now look at what is known of the lives of these first humans to cross the seas of Wallacea and Melanesia. The precise types of watercraft used by these first colonists will remain forever unknown, but the large rafts made of lashed-together bamboo poles which still ply some Southeast Asian rivers for transport purposes might give some clues. Lithic technology certainly included simple flake and pebble tools, together with the use of red and yellow ochre for pigment and heated stones for cooking. Shellfish and inshore fish provided protein, as did the rather limited mammal species of these island regions. A constantly-expanding archaeological record tells us that the descendants of these early Wallacean migrants adapted rapidly to the very different inland environments of Australia and New Guinea, where mammal faunas were far more plentiful. The prehistory of Greater Australia, including New Guinea, is of course a topic for another venue, but the original island and coastal maritime lifestyle of the first settlers did continue in the small equatorial islands of the Moluccas and Bismarck Archipelagoes, located to west and east of New Guinea respectively. The record of this lifestyle over the past 35,000 years shows some very interesting developments.

In the archaeological records of these two archipelagos there appear to be two successive periods of activity. The first, from before 35,000 down to about 20,000 years ago, reveals a fairly simple lifestyle of strandline exploitation with inshore fishing, shellfishing and crab collection, combined with only very limited evidence that communities were in frequent inter-island contact. For instance, in this early period we see few signs of any trade in tool stones such as obsidian or chert, or any deliberate translocation of animals or plants between islands. This may reflect deficiencies of the record, but taken at face value the picture indicates that, once a new island was reached, people settled in, retaining mostly a localized form of mobility.

Gradually, more regular inter-island contacts for trade purposes seem to have developed. A black volcanic glass called obsidian, collected from at least two sources in central New Britain, was taken by about 20,000 years ago, in small amounts, to sites up to 350 km away in New Ireland. Even more surprisingly, people began to carry marsupials, evidently from the New Guinea Mainland, to those islands both west and east of New Guinea where they did not occur in the native fauna. Cuscuses (*Phalanger orientalis*) were taken to New Ireland by 15,000 years ago, bandicoots (*Echymipera* sp.) to the Admiralties by 12,000 years ago, and wallabies (*Thylogale brunii*) to New Ireland by possibly 7,500 years ago. In the northern Moluccas, a species of wallaby (*Dorcopsis muelleri*) was translocated to Gebe Island, immediately west of New Guinea, at about 9,000 years ago, apparently from a source on Misool Island. A related species of wallaby occurred on Halmahera, perhaps also translocated from New Guinea, although this remains uncertain. Sadly, these wallabies were extirpated for reasons unknown in the northern Moluccas by 800 years ago.

Although these animal movements were probably uncoordinated – currently they appear to have been drawn out over a period of perhaps 10,000 years – they do indicate that conscious attempts to increase food supplies on relatively impoverished islands were taking place. This record of animal translocation is at present unique in world prehistory.[4] New tool forms also appeared after about 10,000 years ago in several islands. The most significant are adzes made from large reef shells such as *Tridacna* and *Hippopus*, ground with hollowed cutting edges, found in excavations in Gebe and the Admiralty Islands. These shell adzes could have been used in dug-out canoe construction, a development which might have led to the seeming florescence in human contacts around this time. Edge-ground stone axes also made an appearance as early as 25,000 to 30,000 years ago in northern Australia, Japan and the New Guinea Highlands, where they might have been used for forest clearance activities by hunter-gatherers. Other examples, less certainly dated, are known from Vietnam, Peninsular Malaysia and Borneo.

Did the earliest Palaeolithic colonists of Australia, New Guinea and the islands as far east as the Solomons, in some cases no doubt the contemporaries of late Neanderthals in Europe and western Asia, cross the sea with intent? This, naturally, is a question of some contention which will perhaps never be answerable with great conviction. But as the colonization of these islands progressed, so the cultural practices required to make colonization successful were developed. These practices included translocation of food animals and plants and an increasing sophistication of watercraft technology, perhaps even involving use of the sail before Austronesian times. However, it is interesting that at European contact the inhabitants of Australia, except for those in northern Australia close to the zone of outrigger canoe distribution in Indonesia and New Guinea, did not use sails or manufacture large canoes. Thus, it is likely that advanced boat-building concepts such as the uses of outriggers, sails and dug-out log hulls only evolved in quiet equatorial waters towards the end of the Pleistocene, long after Australia and New Guinea were initially settled. The first settlers probably used paddles rather than sails.

The Sunda Islands and the Southeast Asian Mainland

The above evidence for maritime activities and sea crossings is of course best known to us from the island world of Wallacea and Melanesia rather than from the continental regions, including the massive islands of Sumatra, Borneo and Java, which lie immediately to its west. On the Southeast Asian Mainland, cave occupation by populations assumed to be anatomically modern dates back to at least 40,000 years ago, particularly in Thailand and Vietnam, although skeletal material older than 20,000 years has not yet been found. By the end of the Pleistocene, at about 10,000 years ago, a series of lithic assemblages termed "Hoabinhian" became very widespread in southern China and through the whole of Mainland Southeast Asia to as far as northern Sumatra. These are characterized by unifacial or bifacial axe-like tools made on river pebbles and seem to reflect a hunting and gathering economy, perhaps with some degree of plant management. Most interestingly, the Hoabinhians seem to have been adept inhabitants of the interior rainforests of the Malay Peninsula, an environment which surely involved a substantial investment in plant exploitation. Clear signs of animal or plant domestication are, however, entirely absent.

In the islands of western Indonesia the contemporary populations are represented by the "Deep Skull" at Niah and by a series of flake-based, rather than pebble-based, lithic industries. Such industries have been found widely in caves in Sumatra, Java and northern Borneo, and the tools concerned are essentially very similar to those manufactured by the contemporary sea-crossing populations located to the east, in Wallacea. An unusual industry of chert bifaces of possible Late Pleistocene age from Tingkayu in Sabah (Figure 1.5) does little to modify the general picture of lithic simplicity and uniformity, an impression which has suggested to many that bamboo[5] rather than stone was the real provider of working edges in this part of the world. Of art we have little, especially when compared to the rich cave tapestries of northern Australia, but fairly schematic examples of human and animal figurative art, created from ochre or charcoal by late hunting populations, do occur in caves and rockshelters scattered across the region. None can be securely dated. Negative "hand stencils", an art form so well known in Australia and in the Palaeolithic cave art of Europe, are reported from Sulawesi, the southeastern Moluccas and West Papua, and the Mangkalihat Peninsula of eastern Kalimantan (Borneo), suggesting perhaps a greater antiquity than hitherto expected for some of the cave art of the region.[6]

During the middle Holocene, commencing about 7,000 years ago, the southwestern arm of the island of Sulawesi witnessed a most unusual efflorescence of lithic technology, typified by backed blades and "microliths" and a series of remarkable serrated-edged and hollow-based projectile points termed "Maros Points". This industry, termed the Toalian (Figure 1.6), appears to have existed in a rather splendid isolation, with contemporary parallels found only to the south in Australia. Perhaps there were links, although the absence of such technology in the intervening Lesser Sunda Islands, including Timor, makes one wonder.

By 4,500 years ago, many of the hunter-gatherer societies of Southeast Asia, particularly those located in northerly regions, must have begun to suspect that something new was in the wind. Farming societies had already been in existence for 4,000 years by this time in the middle Yangzi region of China. As farmers and their subsistence economy slowly spread south, reaching the Pearl Delta and Taiwan by 5,000

Figure 1.5 The Tingkayu biface industry from Sabah, tentatively dated to the late Pleistocene. (Photograph by P. Bellwood.)

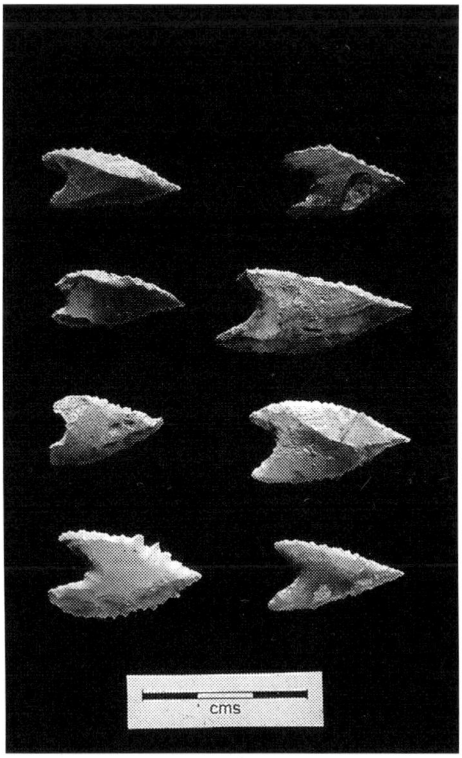

Figure 1.6 Maros Points from the Toalian industry from South Sulawesi. (Photograph by I. C. Glover.)

years ago, so a halo of interaction would have formed between them and the surrounding hunters. In many cases, the hunters probably managed to continue their mobile lifestyles through a kind of exchange-based mutualism with the farmers. Others converted to the new, more sedentary lifestyles, with their considerable baggages of new technology and food production, mostly becoming absorbed into the foundation dispersals of the major ethnolinguistic groups who occupy Southeast Asia today. In particular, in the strictly Southeast Asian geographical sense, these dispersals involved the ancestral speakers of the Austronesian and Austroasiatic languages, and possibly the speakers of ancestral Tibeto-Burman languages to the west. These populations, and their prehistories since Neolithic times, occupy the next two chapters.

Acknowledgement

We wish to thank Jenny Sheehan for drawing Figures 1.1, 1.3 and 1.4.

Notes

1 Crosby 1986.
2 For rice terminology amongst early speakers of Austroasiatic languages, and the general history of this family, see Luce, G. H. 1985; Mahdi, W. in Blench and Spriggs 1998; Peiros 1998.
3 The authors have different opinions on this, with Bellwood favouring an agricultural/ Neolithic dispersal of early Austroasiatic speakers, together with Higham in Chapter 3, whereas Glover prefers a pre-Neolithic dispersal.
4 On translocation, see Spriggs, M. (1997) *The Island Melanesians*, Oxford, Blackwell; and Flannery, T. *et al.* (1998) Mammals from Holocene archaeological sites on Gebe and Morotai Islands, northern Moluccas, Indonesia, *Australian Mammalogy* 20/3: 391–400.
5 There is an argument that the large bamboos which could have provided cutting tools on the mainland were taken by people from the Asian Mainland into Sahul and Wallacea in mid-Holocene times. This could offer a partial explanation for the dichotomy between pebble/core tools + bamboo on the mainland of Southeast Asia, and sharp-edged flake tools in the islands to the east. However, Dr Soeyatmi Dransfield of the Royal Botanic Gardens, Kew notes that, "There are several large bamboos in Indonesia, *Dendrocalamus giganteus*, was introduced from Burma probably in the early nineteenth century while other large bamboos, such as *Dendrocalamus asper, Gigantochloa robusta*, and *Gigantochloa pseudoarundinacea*, have been in Java or Sumatra for a long time, either planted or naturalized, and their origins are not known. So far they have never been recorded to occur in Mainland Asia".
6 For Kalimantan hand stencils, see J. M. Chazine *et al.* at http://www.kalimanthrope.com.

Select Bibliography

Peoples of Southeast Asia: anthropology and history

Albrecht, G. and Moser, J. (1999) "Recent Mani settlements in Satun Province, South Thailand". *Journal of the Siam Society* 86 (1&2): 161–99.
Bellwood, P., Fox, J. J. and Tryon, D. (eds) (1995) *The Austronesians: Comparative and Historical Perspectives*, Canberra: Dept. Anthropology, Research School of Pacific and Asian Studies, Australian National University.
Chazine, J. M. *et al.* at http://www.kalimanthrope.com.
Crosby, A. (1986) *Ecological Imperialism*, Cambridge: Cambridge University Press.
Garnier, F. (1873) *Voyage d'Exploration en Indochine*, Paris: Hachette.
Geertz, H. (1963) "Indonesian cultures and communities", in R. McVey (ed.) *Indonesia*, New Haven: Yale University Press, pp. 24–96.
Hobart, A., Ramseyer, U. and Leemann, A. (1996) *The Peoples of Bali*, Oxford: Blackwell.
King, Victor T. (1993) *The Peoples of Borneo*, Oxford: Blackwell.
Lebar, F. M. (ed.) (1972–5) *Ethnic Groups of Insular Southeast Asia*, vols 1 and 2, New Haven: HRAF Press.
Lebar, F. M., Hickey, G. C. and Musgrave, J. K. (1964) *Ethnic Groups of Mainland Southeast Asia*, New Haven: HRAF Press.
Lee, R and Daly, R. (eds) (1999) *The Cambridge Encyclopaedia of Hunters and Gatherers*, Cambridge: Cambridge University Press.
Luce, G. H. (1985) *Phases of Pre-Pagan Burma*, 2 vols, Oxford: Oxford University Press.
Mabbett, I. and Chandler, D. (1995) *The Khmers*, Oxford: Blackwell.
Mahdi, W. (1998) Linguistic data on transmission of Southeast Asian cultigens to India and Sri Lanka, in R. Blench and M. Spriggs (eds), *Archaeology and Language* II, pp. 390–415. London: Routledge.
Pelras, C. (1996) *The Bugis*, Oxford: Blackwell.
Spriggs, M. (1997) *The Island Melanesians*, Oxford: Blackwell.

Environments and pleistocene archaeology

Bellwood, P. (1997) *Prehistory of the Indo-Malaysian Archipelago*, 2nd edition, Honolulu: University of Hawai'i Press.
Bellwood, P. *et al.* (1998) "35,000 years of prehistory in the northern Moluccas", in G-J. Bartstra *et al.*, *Bird's Head Approaches, Modern Quaternary Research in Southeast Asia* 15: 233–75. Rotterdam: Balkema.
Bergh, G. van den (1999) *The Late Neogene Elephantoid-bearing Faunas of Indonesia and their Palaeogeographic Implications*, Leiden: Nationaal Natuurhistorisch Museum.
Bergh, G. van den, de Vos, J., Sondaar, P. and Aziz, F. (1996). "Pleistocene zoogeographic evolution of Java (Indonesia) and glacio-eustatic sea level fluctuations: a background for the presence of Homo", *Bulletin of the Indo-Pacific Prehistory Association* 14: 7–21.
Bergh, G. van den, Mubroto, B., Aziz, F., Sondaar, P. and de Vos, J. (1996) "Did *Homo erectus* reach the island of Flores?", *Bulletin of the Indo-Pacific Prehistory Association* 14: 27–36.
Flannery, T., Bellwood, P., White, J. P., Ennis, T., Irwin, G., Schubert, K. and Balasubramanian, S. (1998) "Mammals from Holocene archaeological sites on Gebe and Morotai Islands, northern Moluccas, Indonesia", *Australian Mammalogy* 20/3: 391–400.
Keates, S. and Bartstra, G-J. (2001) "Observations on Cabengian and Pacitanian artefacts from Island Southeast Asia", *Quartär* 51/52: 9–32.
Morwood, M., O'Sullivan, P. B., Aziz, F. and Raza, A. (1998) "Fission-track ages of stone tools and fossils on the east Indonesian island of Flores", *Nature* 392: 1773–6.
Simanjuntak, T., Prasetyo, B. and Handini, R. (eds) (2001) *Sangiran: Man, Culture and Environment in Pleistocene Times*, Jakarta: National Research Centre of Archaeology.
Wallace, A. R. (1962) *The Malay Archipelago* (originally published 1869), New York: Dover.
Watanabe, N. and Kadar, D. (eds) (1985) *Quaternary Geology of the Hominid Fossil Bearing Formations in Java*, Bandung: Geological Research and Development Centre.

Linguistic history in Southeast Asia

Blench, R. and Spriggs, M. (eds) (1998) *Archaeology and Language*, vol. 2 (this volume contains several papers on Southeast Asian language history), London, Routledge.
Blust, R. A. (1995) "The prehistory of the Austronesian-speaking peoples: a view from language", *Journal of World Prehistory* 9: 453–510.
Pawley, A. K. (2003) "The Austronesian dispersal: languages, technologies and people", in P. Bellwood and C. Renfrew (eds) *Examining the Farming/Language Dispersal Hypothesis*, pp. 251–74, Cambridge: McDonald Institute for Archaeological Research.
Peiros, I. (1998) *Comparative Linguistics in Southeast Asia*, Canberra: Pacific Linguistics Series C-142.
Wurm, S. A. and Hattori, S. (eds) (1983) *Language Atlas of the Pacific Area*, Part II. Canberra: Australian Academy of the Humanities.

Holocene archaeology, pre-neolithic

Anderson, D. (1990) *Lang Rongrien Rockshelter*, Philadelphia: University of Pennsylvania Museum.
Bellwood, P. (1992) "Southeast Asia before history", in N. Tarling (ed.) *The Cambridge History of Southeast Asia*, vol. I, pp. 55–136, Cambridge: Cambridge University Press.
Bellwood, P. (1993) "Cultural and biological differentiation in Peninsular Malaysia: the last 10,000 years", *AP* 32: 37–60.
Bellwood, P. (1997) *Prehistory of the Indo-Malaysian Archipelago*, 2nd edn, Honolulu: University of Hawai'i Press.
Bellwood, P. (1998) "Human dispersals and colonizations in prehistory – the Southeast Asian data and their implications", in K. Omoto and P. Tobias (eds) *The Origins and Past of Modern Humans*, pp. 188–205. Singapore: World Scientific.
Glover, I. C. (1981) "Leang Burung 2: an Upper Palaeolithic rock shelter in South Sulawesi, Indonesia", *Modern Quaternary Research in Southeast Asia* 6: 1–38.

Glover, I. C. and Presland, G. (1985) "Microliths in Indonesian flaked stone industries", in V. N. Misra and P. Bellwood (eds) *Recent Advances in Indo-Pacific Prehistory*, pp. 185–95. New Delhi, Oxford and IBH.

Higham, C. F. W. (2002) *Early Cultures of Mainland Southeast Asia*, Bangkok: River Books.

Peregrine, P. and Ember, M. (eds) (2001) *Encyclopaedia of Prehistory*, vol. 3: East Asia and Oceania (numerous chapters by different authors), New York: Kluwer.

Pookajorn, S. (1996) "Human activities and environmental changes", in L. G. Strauss *et al.* (eds) *Humans at the End of the Ice Age*, p. 208. New York: Plenum.

Reynolds, T. (1993) "Problems in the Stone Age of South-east Asia", *Proceedings of the Prehistoric Society* 59: 1–16.

Veth, P., Spriggs, M., Jatmiko, A., and O'Connor, S. (1998) "Bridging Sunda and Sahul: the archaeological significance of the Aru Islands, southern Moluccas", in G.-J. Bartstra (ed.) *Bird's Head Approaches, Modern Quaternary Research in Southeast Asia* 15: 157–78. Rotterdam: Balkema.

2

THE ORIGINS AND DISPERSALS OF AGRICULTURAL COMMUNITIES IN SOUTHEAST ASIA

Peter Bellwood

After 5,000 years ago, the world of the hunter-gatherer economy across Southeast Asia and on the western edge of the Pacific was confronted rather suddenly by another economic system: that of the first agricultural populations. New populations and languages, with close links with contemporary populations in central and southern China, began to spread across the region to form the foundation of the pattern of ethnolinguistic groups which exists today, beneath the veneer of twenty-first-century global civilization (see Figure 1.1).

This is not to state that there were ever mass migrations of early farmers who marched their way across the landscape, eradicating all former hunter-gatherer presences. The reality was far more complex, and must be modelled demographically in terms of what we know of differing farmer and hunter population profiles under differing environmental circumstances. More importantly, we need to understand the historical processes concerned in terms of the distinct and independent data sets from archaeology, linguistics, genetics and palaeoanthropology.[1] It is not sufficient simply to accumulate all the data into a vague concept of "migration", and then to visualize something akin to the observations of Julius Caesar on the migrations of the Helvetii into Gaul in 58 BC, complete with their families, pack animals, wagons and seed corn. Of course, some ancient populations perhaps did migrate in this way. But we must also think hard about how archaeological and economic items (e.g. stamped pottery, rice, domestic pigs), proto-languages, and specific "marker" genes might have originated and moved through space, sometimes in fairly independent ways.

Archaeologists, linguists and geneticists are currently very interested in the question of how agriculture spread after its initial appearances in various parts of the world. Was it through the demographic increase and range expansion of farmers, via a process termed "demic diffusion" by geneticists? Or was it through hunter-gatherer adoption of agriculture? The problem is, rather often, that the relevant archaeological, linguistic and genetic data does not always point with perfect precision to one or other of these polar options. This doubtless means that the reality was somewhere in-between.

The archaeological assemblages we associate with early agriculture – the crops, domesticated animals, pottery, ornaments of stone and shell, ground stone tools, spindle whorls (for spinning fibre) and village-sized settlements – all spread far and wide within various cultural complexes during the early Neolithic of Southeast Asia, essentially spanning the whole area between 3000 and 1500 BC (and being generally earlier in the north than in the south). The foundation movements of the major agriculturalist language families of Southeast Asia (Figure 2.1), especially Austroasiatic and Austronesian, also spread far and wide, carried in the main by populations of native speakers of the proto-languages concerned, although localized instances of language shift doubtless occurred as well.

However, genetic data in Southeast Asia does not point clearly to total replacement of pre-agricultural peoples, and this is true in terms of nuclear DNA markers as well as mitochondrial DNA and Y chromosome haplotypes (the last two being inherited without recombination through females and males respectively).[2] In fact, genes sometimes give away processes of population admixture far more clearly than do languages. Indeed, if we think about modern situations carefully, it is apparent that even recent colonial episodes of truly mass migration into the Americas and Australasia have

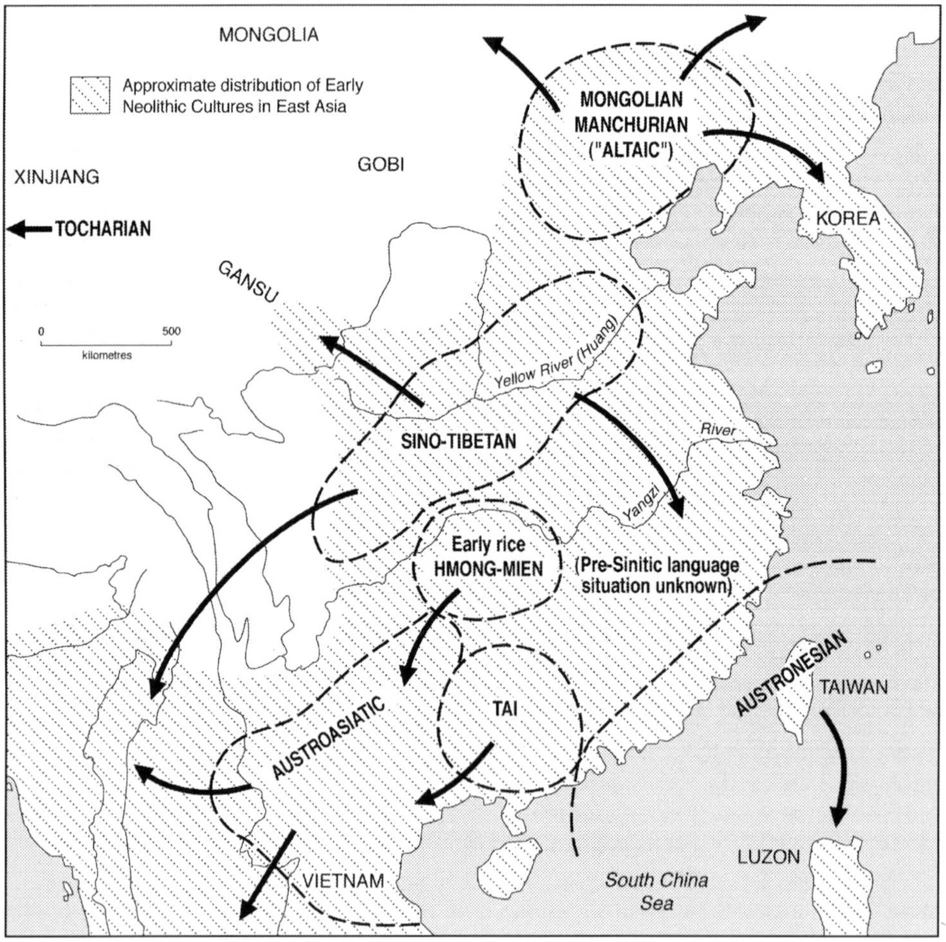

Figure 2.1 Putative homelands of the major language families of China and Southeast Asia.

not completely removed all traces of previous peoples. Native peoples of course live on, very vigorously indeed in many regions of the recently-colonized world.

So, with this introduction, we can perhaps begin to consider the Neolithic prehistory of Southeast Asia in terms of real ancestral populations, their movements, and their interactions.

The first farmers

Why did transitions to agriculture occur, all within the past 12,000 years or less, sufficient to shake the human world irreversibly from its two-million-year Palaeolithic state of relative hunter-gatherer demographic equilibrium? The "bottom-line" answer, if we wish to search for ultimate causes, probably lies in the post-glacial climatic amelioration after 15,000 years ago. This led, as a result of warmer and wetter climates, to a massive increase in the productivity of the earth's tropical and subtropical surface, at least from a human viewpoint.

The three most significant of the indigenous transitions to agriculture in the world, in terms of population growth and impact on later history, occurred in the Middle East, China, and the tropical Americas. These regions are all in fairly low latitudes with strongly seasonal rainfall distributions, where combinations of domesticable animals and plants, especially annual large-grained cereals and other seed crops, proliferated in the warmer post-glacial conditions. In the Middle East and China, we know that some populations turned to harvesting these resources, particularly wheat and barley in the former region, and rice, foxtail millet and broomcorn millet in the latter. In good times, such plentiful cereal foods would have encouraged a degree of sedentism and population growth. But the warmth was not continuous and ever-increasing; unstable climatic fluctuations are known to have occurred, leading to periodic quite severe cold reversals. Perhaps, as a result of stresses in food supply because of these climatic fluctuations, some groups in the Levant and China began to select for domesticated features in their animals and plants. Such selection, whether conscious or unconscious, increased productivity via a number of changes promoting better yields and easier processing. The results would have benefitted pure subsistence as well as those competitive aspects of affluence, such as feasting and wealth accumulation, which have always tended to characterize increasingly large and sedentary populations. Thus, both social and environmental factors could have reinforced each other within this very important developmental trajectory.

The first such development of agriculture with morphologically domesticated cereals occurred in the Middle East about 10,500 years ago, followed closely by China by about 9,000 years ago. The Americas followed much later, with their first major domesticated food crops, especially maize, being dated to about 5,000 years ago. The absolute reasons for the many indigenous transitions to agriculture are still not totally understood by archaeologists and each region has to be examined on its own merits, but one fact remains transparently obvious. These transitions were fundamental for the present demographic situation of humanity – they unleashed a cycle of population growth without which none of the ancient or modern civilizations, nor the problems of overpopulation and poverty in the modern world, would exist.

Early agriculturalists in China, Southeast Asia and New Guinea

The islands of Southeast Asia and the Pacific witnessed a two-part development and dispersal of agricultural populations. In the Highlands of New Guinea, agricultural systems based on the drainage of swamps and the shifting cultivation of tubers on surrounding slopes had developed indigenously by at least 6,000 years ago. But the absences of cereals and domesticated animals in this island meant that populations were generally small. Pigs were not introduced to New Guinea until about 3,000 years ago, and the American sweet potato, a major highland food source today, perhaps not until after AD 1550 (although it might have been a little earlier, particularly if it could have been transmitted from prehistoric Polynesia where it was present from about 1,000 years ago). The relatively low demographic profile of prehistoric New Guinea societies meant that no agricultural colonization of Australia, the last completely hunter-gatherer continent to survive until European contact, ever occurred. This remarkable fact did not reflect any inherent deficiency in the Australian environment. Rather, it reflected the absence of any sizeable agricultural population in the malarial southern lowlands of New Guinea, combined with the geographical circumstance whereby the migrations of Austronesian agriculturalists into Oceania occurred along the northern side of New Guinea, not the less hospitable southern side.

After 5,000 years ago, both the mainland and the islands of Southeast Asia eventually became incorporated into a phase of increasing agricultural activity, characterized by the spread of a basically Neolithic set of artefacts of types generally absent in Australia and the New Guinea Highlands (apart from ground stone axes). To understand these trends we need to examine the beginnings of agriculture in China, the second but by far the most significant of the two regions of early agriculture in the Indo-Pacific region.

By 8,500 years ago, the archaeological record reveals the first village-agricultural societies in the Yellow and Yangzi river basins of China. These people grew foxtail and broomcorn millet in the north and rice in the south, and kept domesticated pigs, dogs and poultry. They made pottery, used polished stone tools, lived in substantial villages of timber houses, and knew such important technological innovations as kiln-firing for pottery (in the Yellow River valley), weaving, jade working and skilled carpentry. By 5,500 years ago the agricultural way of life had spread through the coastal provinces of China and southwards through interior valleys to the Pearl Delta and Taiwan.

It would be a cardinal mistake to regard all these people as "Chinese", in the sense of speaking ancestral Sinitic languages and being genetically ancestral only to modern Chinese ethnic groups. "China" at 6,000 years ago was an ethnic mosaic, presumably with early Sino-Tibetan-speaking societies in the north, and societies in the south ancestral to the present Tai, Austroasiatic and Austronesian peoples (Figure 2.1). At 5,500 years ago it is most unlikely that the major modern language families would have been delineated as they are now. Instead, a time-travelling linguist would have noted a network of languages and dialects of tribal size spread over the whole region, from only some of which are descended modern language subgroups and families such as Sinitic, Austroasiatic and Tai. These modern subgroups and families have arisen because, in certain places and under certain demographic conditions, some early societies underwent processes of expansion. The oldest of them spread with agricultural colonists into a world peopled by fairly sparse groups of hunters and gatherers.

This leads us to an important observation about the totality of language distribution in Southeast Asia. Figure 1.1 indicates that Austronesian languages have spread like a blanket over Island Southeast Asia, with no surviving remnants of earlier linguistic landscapes west of the Moluccas. This situation only changes as one approaches West Papua (Irian Jaya), with Papuan languages having a relatively restricted presence in parts of Halmahera and the eastern Lesser Sundas. As will be demonstrated below, the Austronesian dispersal was mainly a Neolithic phenomenon, and since then only within-family linguistic rearrangements have occurred, for instance the expansions of Malay and Javanese.

However, the Southeast Asian Mainland is a veritable mosaic of many language families, often rather chaotically interdigitated, particularly in the mountain regions between the major rivers in the northern zone. The Austroasiatic family evidently spread first, to judge from its fragmented distribution, and the more recent spreads of languages of early civilizations, such as Mon, Khmer and Vietnamese, still render the Austroasiatic family one of major significance. The spreads of the Tai (especially Thai and Lao) and Hmong-Mien languages, together with Burmese, have taken place into Southeast Asia very much more recently, indeed mainly within the past millennium or so according to historical accounts. The mainland has thus had a much more complex ethnolinguistic history than the islands, possibly because of the greater number of large-scale societies here, from Iron Age times (*c.*500 BC) onwards, that have periodically reconfigured the political and ethnic landscape through colonization, assimilation, and on occasion downright conquest. In this sense, while the foundation dispersals of some of the major language families undoubtedly occurred in the Neolithic, much linguistic rearrangement on the mainland has occurred since, especially in the regions of Indic kingdom formation.

In the remainder of this chapter, I wish to focus on the Austronesians and their colonization of Island Southeast Asia and Oceania, since the question of the contemporary Austroasiatic dispersal through the mainland of Southeast Asia is dealt with by Charles Higham in the following chapter. These two language families appear to have been the first to spread with agricultural populations through Southeast Asia, although it is also possible that the Tibeto-Burman languages could have commenced their spread into the Himalayan and Burma regions with early farmers – we simply do not have much information on this family and its possible archaeological record at present. Austronesian prehistory gives us one of our best-studied examples of a successful, and hugely long-distance, spread of Neolithic agriculturalists well over half way around the circumference of the world.

The Austronesian dispersal

The expansion of the Austronesian-speaking peoples undoubtedly involved a real colonization process by ethnolinguistically-coherent groups who spoke early Austronesian languages. As the most widespread ethnolinguistic population on earth prior to the European colonizations of the last few centuries, the Austronesians settled more than half of the earth's circumference in tropical latitudes, only escaping into cooler climates to reach New Zealand and Easter Island. Today they number well over 350 million people and speak more than 1,000 different, although related, languages. Their dispersal, a process which took place in various stages between 5,000 and 1,000 years ago, took them ultimately from a homeland in the region of southern China and Taiwan to places as far away as Madagascar, Hawai'i and Easter Island (Figures 2.2 and 2.3).

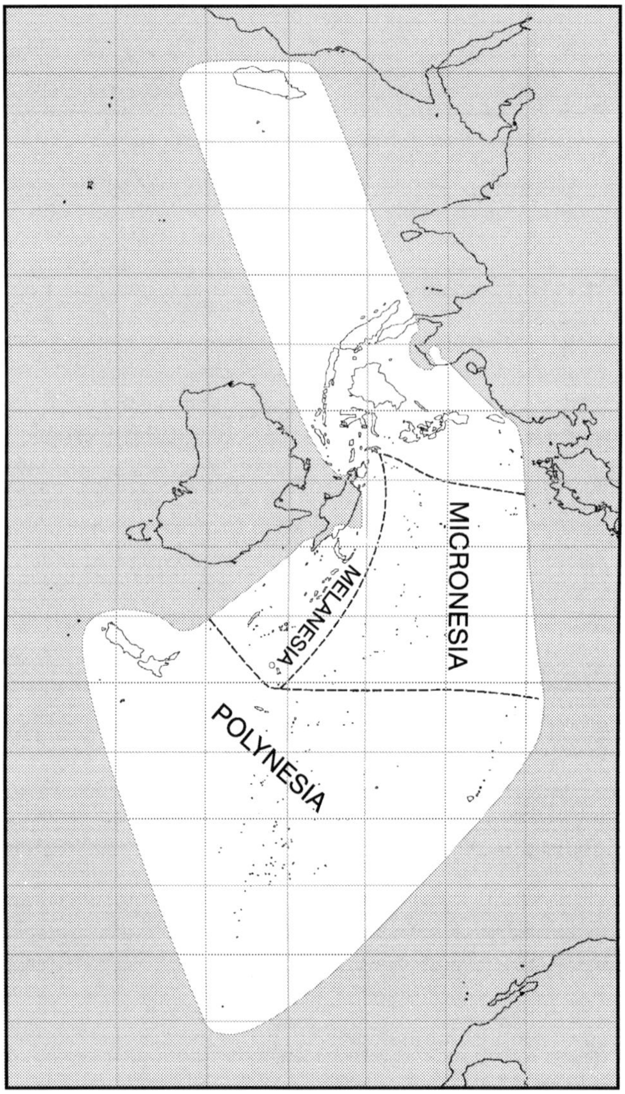

Figure 2.2 Overall distribution of the Austronesian language family.

Research on the prehistory of the Austronesians has now become a multidisciplinary industry involving the work of many scholars; not just linguists and archaeologists, but also social anthropologists, geneticists, palaeoanthropologists, palynologists and environmental scientists of many kinds.[3] From the outset, it is essential to remember that the Austronesians are defined as such because *they all speak Austronesian languages.* This circumstance alone is a guarantee of a high degree of shared ancestry and history, but it is easy to observe that Austronesians today are not a unified population in terms of biological affinity – the speakers of Austronesian languages share a wide range of Asian and Melanesian phenotypes. Neither are the Austronesians a single "type" in terms of

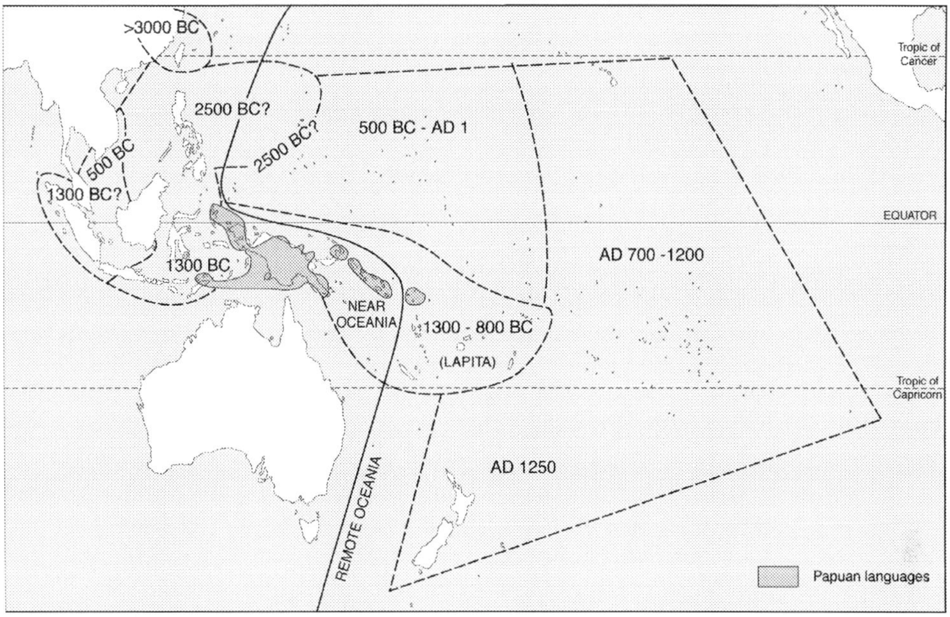

Figure 2.3 Approximate dates from archaeological and linguistic data for initial Austronesian colonizations across Southeast Asia and the Pacific.

society or culture. Essentially, we must be aware that Austronesian languages, cultures and biological gene pools have not evolved locked together as a single entity through prehistoric times, but have blended together or drifted apart from time to time according to historical circumstances.

The languages of the Austronesian family, and the cultures to which they belong, share to varying degrees an ultimate common ancestry located on the Asian Mainland at least 6,000 years ago. This can be seen not only through the languages, but also (admittedly to a hazier extent) through comparative archaeological, anthropological and art-historical observations. Since 5,500 years ago the Austronesians have undertaken an immense amount of colonization, leading to cultural divergence and adaptation to new, strange and often highly challenging environments. Their colonizations also brought them into varying degrees of contact with the pre-Austronesian populations of Island Southeast Asia and Melanesia – people whose ancestors had settled in these islands more than 35,000 years ago and who, for example, in parts of New Guinea, had already developed systems of agriculture independently of the Austronesians. In the case of Indonesia and the Philippines it appears that the pre-Austronesian populations were hunter-gatherers, and in these areas the dominance of Austronesian languages and cultures at the present time is much stronger than is the case in New Guinea. In this chapter there is not space to examine these issues of interaction in depth, but assimilation of, and interaction with, pre-existing peoples have clearly been of significance in regions as far east as the Solomons, beyond which no pre-Austronesian populations ever managed to penetrate. The extent of Pleistocene, pre-Austronesian, colonization in Island Southeast and the western Pacific is shown in Figure 1.3.

The foundation of our knowledge of Austronesian prehistory must clearly come in the first instance from linguistic rather than biological or archaeological evidence. The Austronesian languages form a coherent phylogenetic grouping, with only very rare examples which resist classification, characterized by a great deal of shared and inherited core vocabulary and many other aspects of grammar and phonology. In order to study the prehistories of unwritten languages, linguists favour a process of comparison involving the identification and geographical plotting of cognate items in living or recently recorded languages (cognates are features shared by languages as a result of shared common origin rather than borrowing). They are then able to identify genetic subgroups of languages by plotting the distributions of uniquely shared and innovated cognate features. These language subgroups can be ordered hierarchically, as in the case of the most widely accepted classification of the high-order Austronesian subgroups, that by Robert Blust, shown in Figure 2.4.

The historical implication of Figure 2.4 favours a southern coastal Chinese origin for the pre-Austronesian roots of the family, at which stage the pre-Austronesian languages concerned were perhaps related in some way (by borrowing or genetic affinity) to the contemporary roots of the Tai, Austroasiatic and possibly also Sino-Tibetan language families. Thus, the deep roots of Austronesian expansion were sown several millennia before the Austronesians themselves began to differentiate as an ethnolinguistically-distinct people via their migrations to and beyond Taiwan. Austronesians, technically speaking, have only existed in an ethnolinguistic sense *since* the period of Proto-Austronesian, located in Taiwan about 5,500 years ago. Earlier populations are, by definition, Pre-Austronesian.

According to the linguistic evidence, the pre-Austronesian phase was followed by a colonization of Taiwan (the linguistic homeland of Proto-Austronesian), and then a dispersal southwards through the Philippines into northern Indonesia. From here, in the general region of northern Borneo, Sulawesi and the Moluccas, later population dispersals

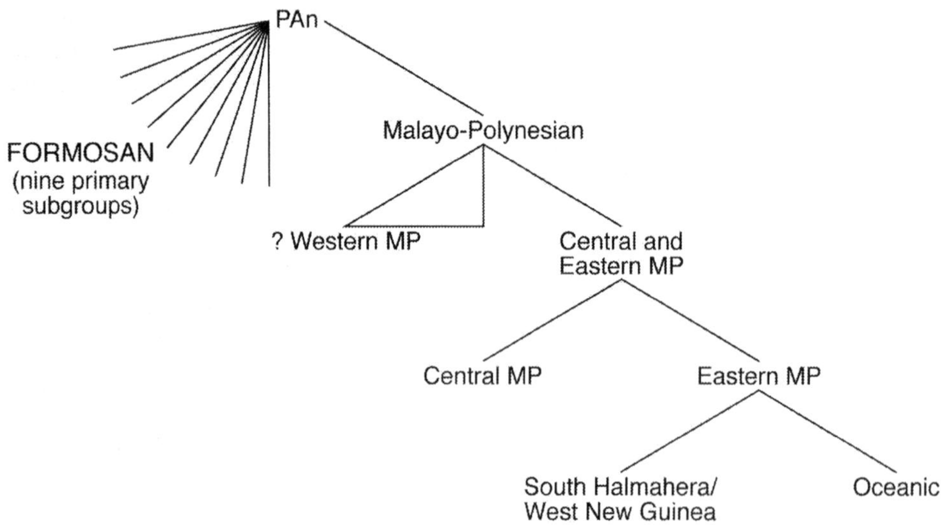

Figure 2.4 The higher-level structure of the Austronesian language family (after Robert Blust).

proceeded westwards to the Malay Peninsula, southern Vietnam and Madagascar, and eastwards into Oceania. These colonizations followed the development, presumably in the Philippines and Indonesia, of sufficient maritime technology to cross oceans easily and regularly. However, despite the glamour of ethnographically-recorded Oceanic voyaging traditions, maritime skills alone were not the sole cause of Austronesian expansion, at least not in the earlier stages (although the status given to navigators was an increasingly important reason for later voyages of discovery in Remote Oceania). Systematic agriculture and animal husbandry were probably of far greater overall significance in the earliest days of expansion, since they would have been indispensable for the rapid growth of a healthy population and indispensable later on for colonizing Oceanic islands with limited terrestrial resources.

One of the earliest mainstays of the Austronesian economy in Southeast Asia was rice, although this crop was never taken as far as Oceania and many tropical crops such as coconuts, taro, yams and sago were added to the economic plant roster as Austronesians expanded southwards into equatorial regions. Concerning the early Austronesian economy in more detail, it is crucial to note that the reconstructed Proto-Austronesian vocabulary[4] indicates a people growing rice and millet, with domestic pigs and dogs (and perhaps chickens too), canoes, knowledge of tattooing, and use of the bow and arrow. By very soon after the Proto-Austronesian phase, in the Proto-Malayo-Polynesian phase of Figure 2.4 (perhaps located *c.*4,500–4,000 years ago in the northern Philippines), they were building substantial timber houses and using pottery, sails and outriggers on canoes, looms (probably backstrap type) for weaving, and chewing betel. They had also added the tropical tuber and fruit crops listed above to their diet. Indeed, most of these Proto-Malayo-Polynesian additions (except for the tropical crops) probably existed in the climatically more temperate Proto-Austronesian phase in Taiwan as well, but clear linguistic proof of this in the form of pan-Austronesian cognates has not always survived since many Formosan Aboriginal languages have now been replaced by Sinitic languages (Taiwanese and Mandarin).

In terms of archaeology, the signatures of agricultural societies with sedentary villages, domesticated pigs and dogs, pottery, polished stone tools and the remains of rice are clearly marked in the coastal southern Chinese record, extending southwards from Zhejiang through Fujian to Guangxi, Guizhou and Guangdong Provinces, and Taiwan, and perhaps into northern Vietnam and Thailand too, by about 5,000 years ago. Some of these early Mainland Southeast Asian Neolithic assemblages cannot yet be associated directly with evidence for agriculture, especially in Vietnam and Thailand and some coastal regions of southern China, leading Charles Higham in the following chapter to associate them with foraging. However, we have firm dates for rice in Taiwan by at least 5,000 years ago (see below), and the Taiwan situation indicates clearly that poor conditions for preservation might have led to cereal invisibility in earlier excavations. While it would be imprudent to state that all Neolithic cultures in the region were *dependent* on rice cultivation, and while some were undoubtedly still harvesting available wild resources, the fact remains that we have no long-lived or significant complex of Neolithic cultures in China or Southeast Asia for which some degree of agricultural subsistence can be confidently ruled out. Future improvements in the recognition of carbonized tubers such as yams and taro, as well as the recognition of rice in the form of charred grains, as chaff in pottery or in phytolith form, should increase greatly our knowledge of early farming economies in the future.

Whatever the precise economies present in southern China before 5,000 years ago, it is again important to stress that such early East Asian Neolithic cultures cannot be equated with Austronesians *per se*. However, it is interesting to note that many artefact types typical of later Island Southeast Asian and Oceanic archaeological cultures are very widespread on the Asian Mainland as well. These include red-slipped and/or painted, stamped and cord-marked styles of pottery, knee-shaped wooden adze handles, untanged or stepped and polished stone adzes, art styles emphasizing the uses of spirals and circles, and bones of potentially-domesticated pigs, dogs and chickens (the wild ancestors of domesticated dogs are not native to Island Southeast Asia, and neither are wild pigs native to islands east of Sulawesi). An excellent assemblage of this early and potentially-ancestral type comes from the *c*.7,000 year-old site of Hemudu, in the lowland coastal region of Zhejiang Province, where it is associated with prolific evidence for rice cultivation.

In Taiwan, archaeological cultures identified by such features made an appearance at some uncertain time between 4000 and 3000 BC. The carriers of a Neolithic economy to Taiwan and the P'eng-hu (Pescadores) Islands made cord-marked and incised pottery and used polished stone adzes, slate spear points and stone barkcloth beaters. Archaeological evidence for rice cultivation is present in Taiwan by 3000 BC in the form of carbonized grains in the Nan-kuan-li site near Tainan,[5] and similar evidence for rice is already attested before 2000 BC far to the south in the cave of Gua Sireh, located in the equatorial latitude of Sarawak, Borneo. At Nan-kuan-li the rice was harvested using reaping knives of shell.

By about 3000 to 2500 BC, the Austronesian population which had colonized Taiwan, presumably replacing or incorporating earlier populations of hunters and gatherers, was ready to move further. One of the next steps according to the dated archaeological record, with the linguistic record in strong support (see above), seems to have been a southwards and eastwards move which incorporated, around 2500–1500 BC, the Batanes Islands and the rest of the Philippines, eastern Indonesia and northern Borneo. By 1500 BC people had reached the Mariana Islands of western Micronesia across an absolutely astonishing 2,500 km of open sea to the east of Luzon. Soon afterwards, parts of island Melanesia were reached (especially the Bismarcks, Solomons, New Caledonia, Vanuatu, Fiji), and then, by about 1000 to 800 BC, the islands of western Polynesia (Tonga, Samoa, Wallis and Futuna). This southwards and eastwards move was undoubtedly one of the most astonishing bouts of colonization ever to occur in early human history, and as we learn more about the archaeologically less-known regions of western Austronesia it may turn out to have been even more extensive than we now realize (dates for initial Austronesian colonization in western regions such as Borneo, Sumatra and Java are still uncertain, but are also perhaps likely to fall between 2000 and 1000 BC). In a period of under 1,000 years, Austronesian ancestors spread from Taiwan, through Island Southeast Asia into Melanesia and central Oceania, over about 7,000 km of land and sea. In order to do this they had to develop systematic strategies for the exploration and colonization of faraway islands, strategies well described by Irwin and Anderson.[6]

In the islands of Southeast Asia, the early Austronesians moved rapidly around coastlines already settled, as in Taiwan, by sparse groups of hunters and gatherers. In New Guinea, however, the indigenous peoples (as noted above) seem to have already developed techniques of taro, sugar cane and fruit (banana, pandanus) agriculture, at least in the highlands, and possibly intensive harvesting of yams, sago and other tree products in many lowland regions. For various reasons little understood, but perhaps reflecting both the prior existence of large populations and environmental factors (malaria?), New Guinea together with much of the Solomons seem to have been relatively avoided by the *earliest* Austronesian colonizers, although our knowledge of prehistory in many of these regions is still subject to constant revision. Later on, Austronesian descendants filled in some of the available gaps, except in the New Guinea Highlands, where Austronesian settlement never penetrated.

One point to remember is that this amazing phase of coastal dispersal from Taiwan to as far as Samoa took place at least 1,500 years *before* the better-known phase of Eastern Polynesian colonization and long-distance voyaging during the first millennium AD (see Figure 2.3). In Island Southeast Asia, the archaeological traces of this expansion of the second and early first millennia BC are visible in a number of sites, mainly caves and rockshelters, with red-slipped pottery, shell tools and polished stone adzes, found through the Batanes Islands and the northern Philippines, Sabah (northern Borneo), the Talaud Islands, northern Sulawesi, eastern Java and the northern Moluccas (Figures 2.5 and 2.6). A site called Andarayan in northern Luzon has yielded rice husks embedded in potsherds dated to 1500 BC, and, as noted above, rice had already reached Sarawak before 2000 BC, although here in association with a type of paddle-impressed pottery quite different from the eastern red-slipped ware. At the site of Bukit Tengkorak in Sabah, the Neolithic red-slipped pottery, here dated from about 1300 BC onwards, was found with two rather surprising occurrences of a lithic nature; an industry of agate microblade drills used for drilling shell artefacts, and obsidian imported from sources in New Britain in Melanesia, located over 3,500 km to the east and probably representing one of the longest-distance transfers of a Neolithic commodity in world prehistory. New research in the Batanes Islands and the Cagayan Valley in the northern Philippines has produced many sites with stamped red-slipped pottery and stone artefacts related to contemporary sites in Taiwan, and in the case of the Pamittan site in the Cagayan Valley (northeastern Luzon) the dates for red-slipped pottery range back to about 2000 BC.[7]

Palynological results from lakes in the highlands of Taiwan, Java and Sumatra also indicate clearance for agriculture from 2000 BC onwards, although the exact dates for these activities are not very secure. As noted, dates for Austronesian colonization in the large islands of Borneo, Sumatra and Java, and also the Malay Peninsula, remain uncertain owing to the sparseness of the archaeological record, but dates in the second or first millennia BC seem very likely. One of the problems in these large islands with their powerful erosion regimes is that the oldest coastal Neolithic sites are likely to be buried under huge depths of alluvium, and so extremely hard to find and excavate. The Malay Peninsula, which still today has many interior regions populated by Austroasiatic-speaking (Aslian) populations, was probably only first settled, in coastal areas, by Austronesians less than 2,500 years ago. These Austronesians would have found agriculturalists, ancestors of some of the modern Aslians, already in occupation since at least 2000 BC.

Madagascar was probably only reached in the mid-first millennium AD, evidently by colonists from southern Borneo, perhaps with Malay- or Javanese-speaking leaders according to recent linguistic analyses.[8] In the other direction, the furthest reaches of eastern Micronesia (Carolines, Marshalls, Kiribati) and eastern Polynesia (Societies, Marquesas, Hawai'i, Easter Island) were reached at various times between 500 BC and AD 1000, and perhaps only by AD 1200 in the case of New Zealand.

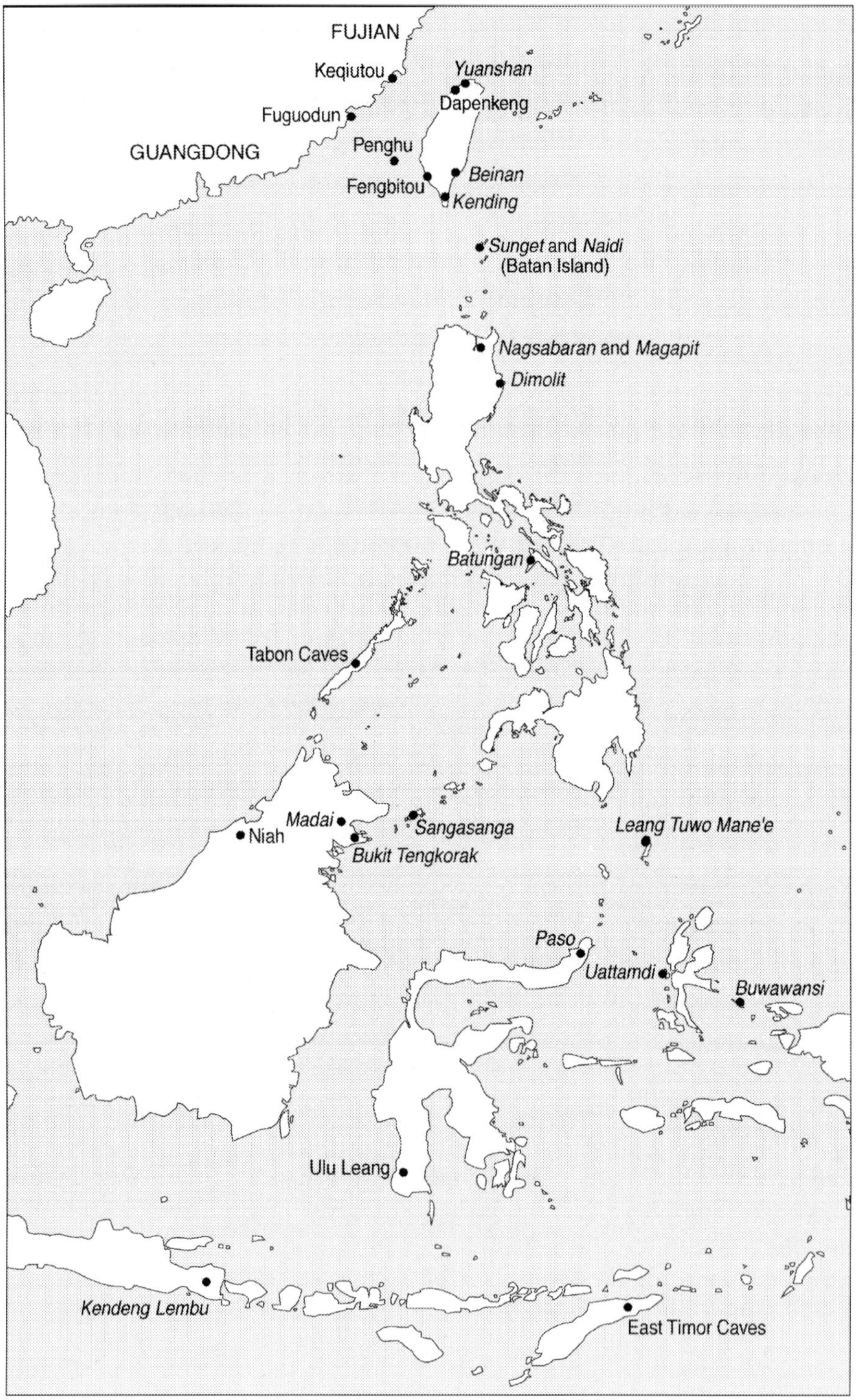

Figure 2.5 Sites (in italics) with Neolithic red-slipped pottery in Island Southeast Asia.

Figure 2.6 A selection of dentate- and circle-stamped pottery, from southern China to Melanesia. All sherds except a) are red-slipped and have lime or white clay decorative infil. **a)** Xiantouling, Guangdong coast, China (c. 3000 BC). Courtesy Yang Yaolin. **b)** Magapit, Cagayan Valley, Luzon (1500–1000 BC). Courtesy Yoji Aoyagi. **c)** Yuanshan, Taipei, Taiwan (1000 BC). Courtesy National Taiwan University. **d)** Nagsabaran, Cagayan Valley (1500–1000 BC). Courtesy Tsang Cheng-hwa. **e)** and **h)** Batungan Cave, Masbate, central Philippines (800 BC). Courtesy Social Science Research Institute, University of Hawai'i. f) Kamgot, Anir Islands, Bismarck Archipelago (Lapita – 1300 BC). Courtesy Glenn Summerhayes. **g)** Lapita (Site 13), New Caledonia (1000 BC). Courtesy Christophe Sand. **i)** and **j)** Achugao, Saipan, Mariana Islands (1500 BC). Courtesy Brian Butler. **k)** Bukit Tengkorak, Sabah, 1300 BC.

Why did the initial Austronesian dispersal occur?

At this stage it is necessary, before continuing the record after 1000 BC, to move back to the linguistic and archaeological evidence in Southeast Asia to consider just what promoted all this movement and activity into lightly settled, or, in the case of Oceania beyond the Solomons, totally uninhabited regions. Why did the Austronesians, like many peoples in history, not simply stay at home? In fact, the Austronesians were not particularly unusual in being colonists since the development of agriculture allowed population expansions to occur in many regions of the world. The main claim to fame of the Austronesians is that their migrations ultimately crossed such vast ocean spaces. They were able to develop their maritime skills for the simple reason that their homeland zone was located in a strategic location, close to the Asian end of the greatest series of island chains in the world. Chance dealt a good geographical hand to the Austronesians, a chance which they did not ignore.

Of course, there are many more specific reasons why individual Austronesian colonies were founded. One important social reason is that the process of colonization itself can increase the status of an individual and his/her descendants. Micronesian and Polynesian legends (e.g. the famous Maori "Fleet" traditions) are full of the exploits of founder-figures, after whom kin groups were named and whose direct descendants still form aristocratic lineages today. Such a "founder-focused ideology"[9] would always be sufficient to foment a desire to discover new territory. In addition, some small islands in Oceania might also have become overpopulated quite quickly, especially if we think of birth-rates similar to those typical of recent European colonists into fertile, relatively disease-free and only lightly populated land masses such as the more heavily colonized parts of Australia and North America (averaging seven children per family in European Australia in the 1840s and 1850s). The Bounty Mutineers and their Austronesian (Tahitian) wives in Pitcairn recorded similarly spectacular growth rates. Yet overpopulation was clearly not the real reason for Austronesian expansion, certainly not in the huge islands of Indonesia and the Philippines, and high rates of population growth might have been the results rather than the causes of such large-scale population dispersals.

The main *underlying* reason for the Austronesian diaspora, the *sine qua non* (albeit not necessarily the main immediate reason for all individual population movements), was surely the possession of an efficient agricultural economy combined with reliable access to meat sources, especially in the form of domesticated animals and fish. A successful agricultural economy is a way of life transportable to any new and suitable environment. Hunters and gatherers cannot colonize and permanently settle small isolated islands on a continuing basis with guaranteed success; often there is simply insufficient food to support a viable population. The Neolithic inhabitants of southern coastal China, between 5000 and 3000 BC, by developing both systematic food production and also successful methods of maritime travel, were able to put their tremendous potential for demographic growth to work in new and welcoming environments. Once colonization began, the only process to stop it, apart from geographical or technological barriers, would have been other populations equally empowered with demographic and cultural muscle.

The early Austronesians of course met such populations: the Austroasiatic speakers of Peninsular Malaysia, Vietnam, perhaps parts of Borneo, and the Papuan speakers of New Guinea. Such prior populations, when strongly entrenched like the Papuans, delayed the process of colonization and in the case of interior New Guinea made it non-existent prior to the period of modern Indonesian transmigration. Austronesians have only settled minor pockets of coastline around New Guinea, seemingly only within the past 2,000 years according to both archaeological and linguistic evidence. Indeed, the impressive dominance of the Melanesian phenotype in the western Pacific indicates strongly that some of the Austronesian languages of Melanesia spread via processes of language shift rather than colonization. In other words, some coastal and island populations, descended genetically from the initial colonists of Melanesia, also migrants from Southeast Asia, but over 35,000 years ago, abandoned their native languages to adopt the incoming languages of the Austronesians, in many cases at relatively early dates in the trajectory of Austronesian dispersal.

Yet it must be remembered that this kind of language shift, while common in some regions, was probably rare in the totality of Austronesian history. It is not possible to explain the vast extent and relative homogeneity of the Austronesian family of languages by a process of language shift alone. Unmoving indigenous populations did not simply adopt some form of early Austronesian language and abandon their own vernaculars all the way from Sumatra to the Solomons; there are no known social mechanisms at a tribal social level which could account for such a phenomenon. For instance, none of the historical empires – Roman, Inca, Mongol nor any others – were capable of such a feat over such a large area. English and Spanish only spread through such vast regions because of deliberate and sustained policies of colonization by European powers. Also, there are no *widespread* indications in Austronesian language history (e.g. strong traces of substrata or interference through shift) that such a massive process of language shift ever occurred. The dispersal of the Austronesian languages must be, at a guess, for at least 80 per cent of the geographical distribution of the family, the result of colonization by Austronesian-speaking founder communities. This is one of the greatest, perhaps *the greatest*, human dispersal on record since our common ancestors left Africa.

There remains one unanswered question. Why did the Austronesian dispersal commence *when* it did? As noted, we cannot trace back the early Austronesians directly to the earliest farmers in central China, so some kind of "sealed" origin within an early rice-cultivating Hemudu-type Neolithic at 5000 BC would not be a very viable hypothesis. The main Austronesian migrations commenced quite late in terms of the chronology of Neolithic China, at about 3500 BC or later, with the main phase following 2000 BC. Agriculture had already been in existence in central China for 3,500 years by this time. The factors which allowed the Austronesian dispersal to occur – the agricultural and maritime skills, the demographic profile required to encourage expansion, the social desires to initiate colonization – did not develop overnight and probably increased in impact as the expansion process unfolded. It also seems likely that "domino effects" in some form might have contributed, with rising agricultural population densities in China stimulating, even pushing, populations in more peripheral areas into movement. Robert Suggs once suggested that the Polynesian migrations could have been stimulated by the rise of Shang power in Bronze Age China after 1800 BC.[10] We know now that Suggs' dates were too recent to explain Austronesian dispersal as a whole, but the general idea makes good sense. Humans then, as now, were inexorably bound up in networks of mutual relationship – a major rearrangement of population in one region could have had effects far beyond the immediate social horizon.

The prehistory of the Austronesians since the "big bang" of colonization from the Philippines to Polynesia in the second millennium BC has obviously been complex and detailed, the more so because, as with the aftermaths of all great population dispersals, the archaeological and cultural records simply become more regionalized everywhere with time and so more difficult to read in terms of long-distance correlations. People clearly stopped moving very far once the initial phase of colonization in each area was over, as one might expect. Settling in became the norm, albeit with some continuing degree of trade and intermarriage, often over long distances (witness the extensive trade networks of the New Guinea region last century, albeit in situations of remarkable cultural and linguistic heterogeneity). For instance, Island Melanesia at 1000 BC was extensively occupied by culturally-homogeneous bearers of the Lapita culture, who probably spoke only one of a few closely related Austronesian (Proto-Oceanic) dialects and made very similar types of decorated pottery (Figure 2.6) and shell ornaments across an island region almost 5,000 km from west to east. But by AD 1000 the Melanesian islands were dotted with literally hundreds of "settled-in" local cultures and languages, despite the existence of trade and interaction. We see the same pattern in the later prehistory of eastern Indonesia, Polynesia, or wherever we look in the Austronesian world beyond the influences of the relatively homogenizing Indianized and Islamic civilizations. Initial population dispersals are therefore much easier to describe than their ultimate regionalized products, and the intensely diversified ethnographic record of Austronesia, today with more than 1,000 languages and cultures, gives a graphic picture of just how much diversification has occurred.

Some highlights of later Austronesian archaeology

The Austronesian colonization process must have passed through all significant coastal regions of Island Southeast Asia during the second millennium BC, perhaps earlier in the Philippines and, of course, Taiwan. After this time, despite the tendency to develop cultural diversity, the region has seen a number of periodic but widespread stylistic horizons. The most significant of these is generally dated to between 300 BC and AD 700, when metallurgy, widespread styles of decorated pottery and the beginnings of trade contact with India and China spread through huge parts of the Indo-Malaysian Archipelago and adjacent regions of the mainland. The ancestors of the Malays and Chams (southern Vietnam) probably owed their arrivals on the Asian Mainland to the activities of this phase, and by its end the first Austronesian migrants had reached Madagascar. Late in the first millennium AD we witness the beginnings of another very widespread stylistic horizon, this time based on the import of glazed ceramics from Chinese kilns to all parts of Southeast Asia.

The circumstances surrounding the arrival of Indian contacts, iron metallurgy, glass beads and other exotic trade items in Southeast Asia are touched upon in several of the following chapters. In Island Southeast Asia, bronze and iron metallurgy appear to have arrived together, perhaps soon after 300 BC. By the first century AD, the presence of plentiful sherds of Indian Rouletted Ware and moulded pottery at Sembiran in Bali, together with a sherd graffito in Brahmi or Kharoshthi script, inform us that contact with India was well underway (Figure 2.7). Just who travelled where, of course, is hard to know, but it is possible at this stage that most movement was by Austronesians, who after all were soon to colonize Madagascar and perhaps to carry Southeast Asian crops such as bananas and taro to eastern Africa, from where they were incorporated into West African agricultural systems. Yet the graffito also hints at an Indian presence, as also do the oldest

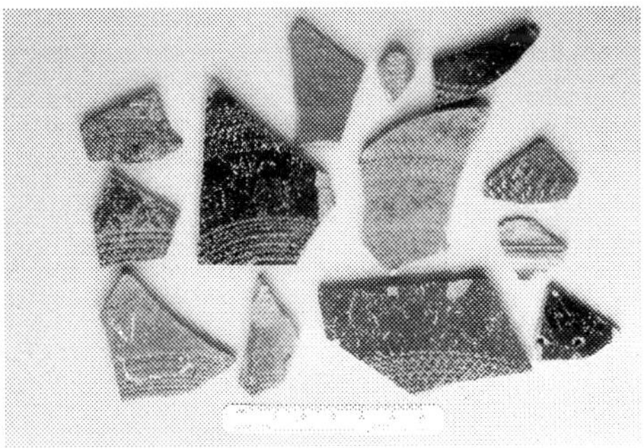

Figure 2.7 Indian pottery from the Sembiran site, north Bali: Above left: Rouletted Ware; Above right: mold-made pottery of Wheeler's Arikamedu type 10, stamped with a bird design; Left: a black slipped sherd with a graffito in Brahmi or Kharoshthi script. AD 100–200.

inscriptions in Southeast Asia, all in Sanskrit and some dating as early as AD 400. As noted in the introduction to this volume, Indians never colonized Southeast Asia, but the impressive Indic temples constructed after the seventh century could hardly have come into existence without *considerable* Indian knowledge and bodily presence.

From the indigenous perspective, the period of initial contact with India was a period of considerable efflorescence of style and material culture. Not only did bronze and iron come into common use, but massive bronze drums of Dong Son style, mainly originating in northern Vietnam, spread rapidly down the length of Indonesia, particularly along the islands of the Sunda Chain and ultimately to as far east as the Bird's Head of New Guinea. Sulawesi and the Philippines have so far produced almost none of these drums, and they are rather rare in southern Vietnam. But all of this makes sense when we realize that southern Vietnam during the Iron Age was the home of the Chamic-speaking Austronesian populations, close linguistic relatives of the Malays and, like the Malays, believed to be of immediate origin in Borneo. The Dong Son drums themselves, manufactured most vigorously in northern Vietnam and Yunnan, were probably made under the aegis of Tai- or Viet-speaking kingdoms whose trade and alliance links with the rest of Mainland Southeast Asia appear to have followed interior riverine rather than coastal routes. Thus, Dong Son drums are common in Thailand, Laos and West Malaysia. They probably spread easily into Sumatra, Java and the Lesser Sunda Islands since these regions form virtually a continuous chain of land.

Contemporary with the spread of these drums went the spread of beads of coloured glass or stone, ultimately of Indian inspiration (where carnelian and agate beads were made before 4,500 years ago – witness their presence in the Royal Graves of Ur in

Mesopotamia), but sometimes of local manufacture. Local traditions of bronzeworking sprang up on the Southeast Asian Mainland and Java/Bali, characterized by large bells and "flasks" with spiral surface decoration, a variety of bronze weapons (spearheads and daggers), and kettledrums in the special Pejeng style manufactured in Eastern Java and Bali, these being rather different from the more standardized "Heger 1" types made in Vietnam and Yunnan. Many of these objects in western Indonesia come from uncertain archaeological contexts, but some of the drums were used as bone containers for burial in sites in Java.

In recent years, knowledge of Bronze-Iron Age developments in Indonesia has grown most quickly in the Borneo-Sulawesi-Philippines region. Here, as noted many years ago by Solheim, much of the pottery of the period between 500 BC and AD 1000 is intricately decorated by incision and stamping. It has been termed the "Sa Huynh-Kalanay Style" by Solheim, after two sites in southern Vietnam and the central Philippines respectively. Sa Huynh-Kalanay regional similarities subsume the Philippines, southern Vietnam and Sulawesi, with extensions into eastern Borneo and the Moluccas. They reflect style diffusion and trade rather than migration, and thus cannot be considered a similar phenomenon to the spread of red-slipped and incised/stamped pottery with Austronesian colonization 1,500 years before. But they do indicate the significance of inter-island relationships 2,000 years ago, pulsating in time with much vaster linkages as Rome, India and Han China first stimulated the global economy on the largest scale, up to that time, in human history.

Acknowledgements

I wish to thank Jenny Sheehan of the Cartography Unit at ANU for drawing Figures 2.1–2.5. Lyn Schmidt and Dominique O'Dea of Archaeology and Natural History at ANU drew Figure 2.6.

Notes

1 See Bellwood 2001a; Bellwood and Renfrew 2003 on these issues.
2 See Hurles 2003 for a good discussion of the genetic history of Austronesian dispersal.
3 Surveys of the results of some of these disciplines are presented in Bellwood *et al.* 1995.
4 Vocabulary reconstructions for Proto-Austronesian are discussed by Blust 1995.
5 Tsang Cheng-hwa, personal communication.
6 See Irwin 1992; Anderson 2000.
7 See Tanaka and Orogo 2000 for Pamittan.
8 This book does not cover the societies and history of Madagascar, even though the major populations there are Austronesian. For some recent linguistic and archaeological observations see Adelaar 1995; Dewar and Wright 1993.
9 For a discussion of this in the Austronesian context, see Bellwood 1996b.
10 Suggs 1960: 225–6.

Select Bibliography

Early agriculture – general

Bellwood, P. (1996a) "The origins and spread of agriculture in the Indo-Pacific region", in D. Harris (ed.) *The Origins and Spread of Agriculture and Pastoralism in Eurasia*, pp. 465–98. London: UCL Press.

Bellwood, P. (2001a) "Early agriculturalist population diasporas? Farming, languages and genes", *Annual Review of Anthropology* 30: 181–207.
Bellwood, P. and Renfrew, C. (eds) (2003) *Examining the Farming/Language Dispersal Hypothesis*. Cambridge: McDonald Institute for Archaeological Research.
Denham, T. P., Harberle, S. G., Lentfer, C., Fullager, R., Field, J., Therin, M., Porch, N. and Winsborough, B. (2003) "Origins of agriculture at Kuk Swamp in the highlands of New Guinea", *Science* 301: 189–93.
Golson, J. and Gardner D. (1990) "Agriculture and sociopolitical organisation in New Guinea Highlands prehistory", *Annual Review of Anthropology* 19: 395–417.
Lu, Tracey Lie-dan (1998) *The Transition from Foraging to Farming and the Origin of Agriculture in China*, Oxford: BAR International Series 774.
Malone, C. (ed.) (1998) "Special Section: Rice Domestication", *Antiquity* 72: 857–907.
Price, T. D. and Gebauer, A. B. (eds) (1995) *Last Hunters First Farmers*, Santa Fe: School of American Research.
Smith, B. (1995) *The Emergence of Agriculture*, New York: Scientific American.

Austronesian and other areas of linguistic history

Adelaar, A. (1995) "Borneo as a cross-roads for comparative Austronesian linguistics", in P. Bellwood, Fox J. J. and Tryon D. (eds) (1995) *The Austronesians: Historical and Comparative Perspectives*, pp. 75–95, Canberra: Department of Anthropology, Research School of Pacific and Asian Studies, Australian National University.
Bellwood, P., Fox, J. J. and Tryon, D. (eds) (1995) "The Austronesians: Comparative and Historical Perspectives". Canberra: Department of Anthropology, Research School of Pacific and Asian Studies, Australian National University.
Blust, R. A. (1984–5). "The Austronesian homeland: a linguistic perspective", *Asian Perspectives* 26: 45–67.
Blust, R. A. (1995) "The prehistory of the Austronesian-speaking peoples: a view from language", *Journal of World Prehistory* 9: 453–510.
Blust, R. A. (1996). "Austronesian culture history: the windows of language", in W. H. Goodenough (ed.) *Prehistoric Settlement of the Pacific*, pp. 28–35. Philadelphia: American Philosophical Society.
Collins, J. (1998) *Malay, World Language*, Kuala Lumpur: Dewan Bahasa dan Pustaka.
Driem, G. van (1999) "A new theory on the origin of Chinese", *Bulletin of the Indo-Pacific Prehistory Association* 18: 43–58.
Dutton, T. (1995) "Language contact and change in Melanesia", in P. Bellwood, J. J. Fox and D. Tryon (eds) (1995) *The Austronesians: Historical and Comparative Perspectives*, pp. 192–213, Canberra: Department of Anthropology, Research School of Pacific and Asian Studies, Australian National University.
Hurles, M. (2003) "Can the hypothesis of language/agriculture co-dispersal be *tested* with Archaeogenetics?", in P. Bellwood and C. Renfrew (eds) *Examining the Farming/Language Dispersal Hypothesis*, pp. 299–31, Cambridge: McDonald Institute for Archaeological Research.
Pawley, A. K. (2003) "The Austronesian dispersal: languages, technologies and people", in P. Bellwood and C. Renfrew (eds) *Examining the Farming/Language Dispersal Hypothesis*, pp. 251–74, Cambridge: McDonald Institute for Archaeological Research.
Pawley, A. and Ross, M. (1993) "Austronesian historical linguistics and culture history", *Annual Review of Anthropology* 22: 425–59.

Neolithic archaeology – Mainland Southeast Asia

Bellwood, P. (1993) "Cultural and biological differentiation in Peninsular Malaysia: the last 10,000 years", *Asian Perspectives* 32: 37–60.
Higham, C. F. W. (2002) *Early Cultures of Mainland Southeast Asia*, Bangkok: River Books.
Higham, C. and Thosarat, R. (1998) *Prehistoric Thailand: from early settlement to Sukhothai*, London: Thames & Hudson.

Neolithic archaeology – Island Southeast Asia and Oceania

Anderson, A. (2000) "Slow boats from China: Issues in the prehistory of Indo-Pacific seafaring", in S. O'Connor and P. Veth (eds) *East of Wallace's Line*, pp. 13–50, Rotterdam: Balkema.
Bellwood, P. (1996b) "Hierarchy, founder ideology and Austronesian expansion", in J. Fox and C. Sather (eds) *Origins, Ancestry and Alliance*, pp. 118–40, Canberra: Department of Anthropology, Research School of Pacific and Asian Studies, Australian National University.
Bellwood, P. (1997) *Prehistory of the Indo-Malaysian Archipelago*, 2nd edn, Honolulu: University of Hawai'i Press.
Bellwood, P. (2001b) "Southeast Asia Neolithic and Early Bronze", in P. Peregrine and M. Ember (eds) *Encyclopaedia of Prehistory, vol. 3: East Asia and Oceania*, pp. 287–306.
Bellwood, P. (in press) "Formosan prehistory and Austronesian dispersal", in D. Blundell (ed.) *Austronesian Taiwan*, Taipei: SMC.
Chang, K. C. and Goodenough, W. H. (1996) "Archaeology of Southeast China and its bearing on the Austronesian homeland", in W. H. Goodenough (ed.) *Prehistoric Settlement of the Pacific*, pp. 36–56, Philadelphia: American Philosophical Society.
Ipoi Datan and Bellwood, P. (1991) "Recent research at Gua Sireh and Lubang Angin", *Bulletin of the Indo-Pacific Prehistory Association* 10: 386–405.
Irwin, G. J. (1992) *The Prehistoric Exploration and Colonization of the Pacific*, Cambridge: Cambridge University Press.
Kirch, P. V. (1997) *The Lapita Peoples*, Oxford: Blackwell.
Kirch, P. V. (2000) *On the Road of the Winds*, Berkeley: University of California Press.
Solheim, W. G. II. (1967) "Two pottery traditions of late prehistoric times in Southeast Asia", in F. S. Drake (ed.) *Symposium on Historical, Archaeological and Linguistic Studies on Southern China, Southeast Asia, and the Hong Kong Region*, pp. 15–22, Hong Kong: Hong Kong University Press.
Spriggs, M. (1997) *The Island Melanesians*, Oxford: Blackwell.
Suggs, R. (1960) *The Island Civilizations of Polynesia*, New York: New American Library.
Tanaka, K. and Orogo, A. B. (2000) "The archaeological excavation at the Pamittan site", *Journal of Environmental Studies* 8: 113–41, Japan: Keiai University.
Tsang, C-h. (1995) "New archaeological data from both sides of the Taiwan Straits", in P. J-k. Li, C-h. Tsang, Y-k. Huang, D-a. Ho and C-y. Tseng (eds) *Austronesian Studies Relating to Taiwan*, pp. 185–226, Taipei: Institute of History and Philology, Academia Sinica.

Post-Neolithic archaeology

Bernet Kempers, A. J. (1988) *The Kettledrums of Southeast Asia*, Rotterdam: Balkema.
Dewar, R. E. and Wright, H. T. (1993) "The culture history of Madagascar", *Journal of World Prehistory* 7: 417–66.
Glover, I and Syme, B. (1993) "The Bronze Age in Southeast Asia: its recognition, dating and recent research", *Man and Environment* 18/2: 41–74.
Higham, C. (1996) *The Bronze Age in Southeast Asia*, Cambridge: Cambridge University Press.

3

MAINLAND SOUTHEAST ASIA FROM THE NEOLITHIC TO THE IRON AGE

Charles Higham

The period covered by this chapter witnessed a series of major cultural changes on the mainland of Southeast Asia which were ultimately to set the stage for the development of the first civilizations. There are four major phases. The first involved hunters and gatherers, some of whom lived relatively mobile lives in the forested interior, while others occupied the rich coasts. A major change occurred during the third millennium BC when rice farmers, who raised domestic cattle and pigs, infiltrated and occupied the inland river valleys. Their origin is not known with certainty, but present evidence drawn from both archaeology and linguistics points to an ultimate homeland in the middle reaches of the Yangzi valley. Between 1500 and 1000 BC, these agricultural communities became familiar with the properties of copper and tin, and began mining, smelting and casting copper and bronze artefacts. Again, the origins of this Bronze Age are not firmly established, but the accumulating evidence points to stimulus from China. The fourth phase involved the adoption of iron working, the earliest forged iron implements being dated to about 500 BC. Until recently, the vital millennium from 500 BC until AD 500 was little known, but a series of excavations are now beginning to illuminate this as a period of deep-seated cultural change.

This period of prehistory in Thailand and Vietnam may thus be divided into an early period of hunting and gathering, followed by successive Neolithic, Bronze and Iron Ages, the latter being succeeded in the early centuries AD by the initial emergence of the historical states and civilizations. The principal features of each will be considered by reference to major representative sites, discussing how these harmonize with the generality of accumulating evidence.

Tropical hunters and gatherers of Central Thailand

Prehistoric hunters and gatherers in tropical latitudes are usually accorded a poor press in comparison with their more affluent temperate cousins. There is a widespread assumption that they were constantly on the move seeking food, were not endowed with more than the most parsimonious material culture and led simple, rather wretched lives. This was not the case generally, and certainly not in Southeast Asia, where evidence for hunting and gathering groups in the interior uplands has accumulated in the forefronts of caves.[1] Such protected environments provide evidence for intermittent occupation, to take advantage of the local resources of plants and animals, from at least 35,000 years ago. This does not mean that these same groups were not also taking advantage of river and stream valleys, but the many changes to these more open and less protected habitats means that the archaeological evidence within them has not survived so well.

The coasts of Southeast Asia, and in particular river estuaries, offer one of the world's richest habitats in terms of natural bounty. On a world scene, hunter-gatherers living in such marine habitats can secure their territory through permanent occupation and become very rich in social, technological and economic terms. A very early pottery tradition known, for example, comes from the Jomon cultures of postglacial Japan, essentially hunter-gatherer in subsistence, albeit possibly with some incipient forms of cultivation and plant management. The ethnographic Calusa of Florida, and the Kwakiutl, Nootka and Haida of British Columbia and Washington State, all essentially hunters and gatherers, sustained royal elites, commoners and slaves.

The culture of early hunting and gathering coastal groups in Thailand and Vietnam (Figure 3.1) has recently been illuminated by two excavations in the Gulf of Siam and by an increasing number of investigations at sites located on the raised beaches of Vietnam. Nong Nor in Central Thailand was excavated over three seasons in 1990–2.[2] It lies about 25 km behind the present shore of the Gulf of Siam, but during its first occupation phase it was located on the edge of an extensive marine embayment, no more than half an hour by canoe from the outlet to the open sea (Figure 3.2). The embayment supported many other, similar sites. Nong Nor comprises what looks like a thick shell midden, in which the small cockle *Meretrix lusoria* predominates.

Careful excavation and analysis of the finds from Nong Nor have revealed how the occupants spent their time. They went out to the open sea to hunt the eagle ray, bull and tiger sharks. They hunted dolphins and a wide range of fish from the inlet and the offshore coral reef. Only one grave was found, that of a relatively old woman, buried in a crouched position under a group of pottery vessels. A round white pebble was found with her body. Close inspection revealed that it had been used to rub and polish the surfaces of pottery vessels before they were fired. Many pots were made and fired at the site, and the surfaces of the finer wares were decorated by polishing and incised designs. Very few land mammals were hunted. Indeed, nearly all the small sample of mammal bones recovered had been converted into useful tools. There was no evidence for domestic animals, no remains of the domestic dog, and a complete absence of rice. It is likely that this site was only occupied for a season. It only has a thin layer of occupation. Perhaps the inhabitants stayed for the dry season and moved to a more permanent base for the rest of the year. According to the radiocarbon dates, Nong Nor was visited in this way in about 2300 BC.

Just such a permanent base site has been found 14 kilometres to the north of Nong Nor at Khok Phanom Di, a large site occupied between 2000 and 1500 BC, during which time its cultural deposits accumulated to a depth of over 9 m.[3] The pottery vessels and bone tools from the lowest layers at Khok Phanom Di mirror those from Nong Nor (Figures 3.3–4). The economy was also similar. We find thick deposits of shellfish that prefer to live in muddy, estuarine conditions. There was also much fishing, and crabs were collected in considerable numbers from the nearby mangrove forests. The hunter-gatherers of Khok Phanom Di commanded a river estuary. The thick layers of ash, the caches of the clay anvils for shaping clay into pots, and the burnishing stones used to decorate the finished vessels reveal a vigorous ceramic industry. The polished adzes were

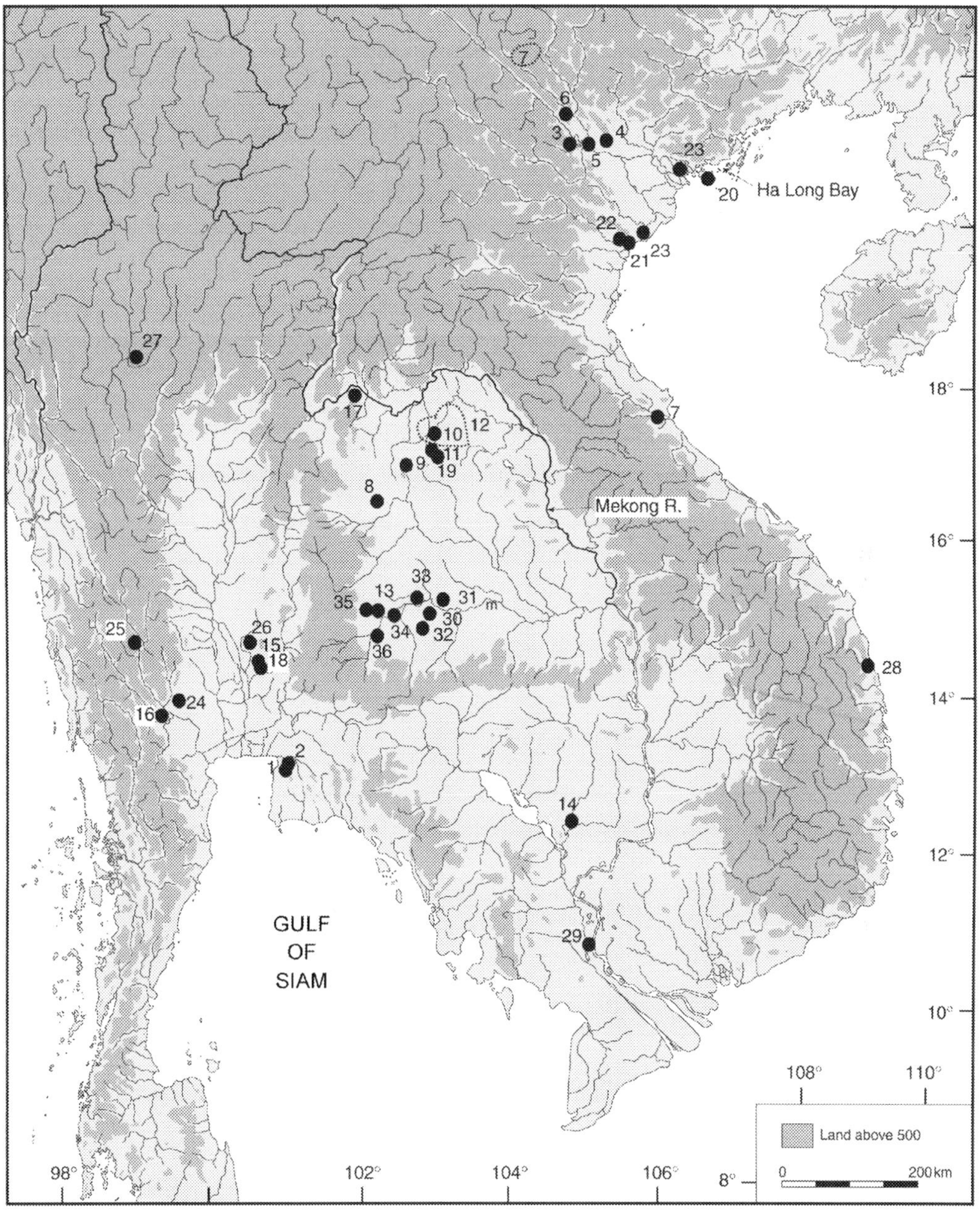

Figure 3.1 Location of the Southeast Asian sites mentioned in the text. **1.** Nong Nor, **2.** Khok Phanom Di, **3.** Phung Nguyen, Go Bong, **4.** Co Loa, Dong Dau, **5.** Lung Hoa, Thanh Den, Go Mun, Viet Tri, Lang Vac, **6.** Xom Ren, **7.** Ha Giang, **8.** Non Nok Tha, **9.** Ban Phak Top, **10.** Ban Chiang, **11.** Non Kao Noi, **12.** Upper Songkhram Valley, **13.** Ban Lum Khao, **14.** Samrong Sen, **15.** Non Pa Wai, **16.** Ban Kao, **17.** Phu Lon, **18.** Nil Kham Haeng, **19.** Ban Na Di, **20.** Cai Beo, **21.** Da But, **22.** Dong Son, **23.** Hoa Loc, **23.** Viet Tri, **24.** Ban Don Ta Phet, **25.** Ongbah, **26.** Noen Ma Kok, **27.** Ban Wang Hi, **28.** Sa Huynh, **29.** Angkor Borei, **30.** Ban Don Phlong, **31.** Non Yang, **32.** Ban Takhong, **33.** Ban Krabuang Nok, **34.** Phimai, **35.** Noen U-Loke, Ban Lum Khao, **36.** Phanom Wan.

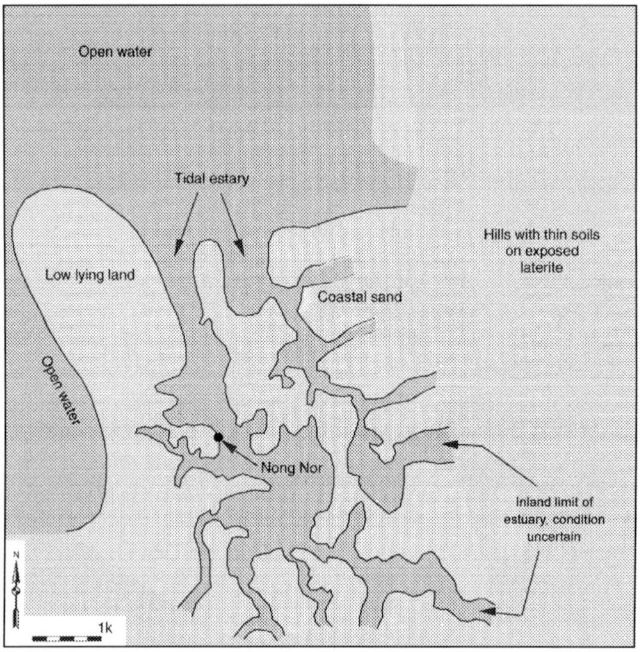

Figure 3.2 The reconstructed coastline in the vicinity of Nong Nor 4,500 years ago. It reveals that the site was located on the edge of a marine inlet. Such information is made possible by the fieldwork of geomorphologists.

made of stone quarried in the interior and were given heavy use. We can imagine their importance in clearing the mangrove forest, and in making houses and boats. There is also some tantalizing evidence for rice cultivation in the form of rice temper in a few imported pottery sherds. The low-lying marine or brackish water habitat of Khok Phanom Di would have ruled out local rice farming. Perhaps the inhabitants were exchanging goods with inland rice farmers.

Well over 100 different species of shellfish were identified at Khok Phanom Di, as well as microscopic forams and ostracods, and different varieties of salt or freshwater fish and crabs, so we can follow the history of this community as it adapted not only to environmental, but also social changes. In the case of the latter the inhabitants had to cope with the challenges posed by intrusive agricultural groups in the hinterland.

Paradoxically, cemeteries provide the best evidence for assessing the nature of this extinct society. The dead at Khok Phanom Di were interred in clusters, each including the skeletons of men, women, children and infants. The mortuary rites remained basically unaltered through 20 or so generations of occupation. The corpse was wrapped with a range of grave goods in an asbestos or beaten bark shroud and laid on a wooden bier in a grave orientated so that the head pointed to the rising sun. Red ochre was powdered over the body, sometimes in a considerable quantity. Grave goods included complete, very beautiful pottery vessels, shell and fish bone beads and bangles, as well as tools probably used by the individual in life, such as stone adzes, fish hooks, clay potters' anvils and burnishing stones.

Figure 3.3 Pottery vessel from mortuary phase 7 at Khok Phanom Di. It includes motifs of human-like figures paralleled in such inland sites as Khok Charoen. The vessel diameter is 20 cm.

Figure 3.4 Mortuary vessel from Khok Phanom Di. They were made with considerable expertise and finished by burnishing. This example is 14 cm in diameter.

Time, however, also wrought changes, visible in the record of seven successive mortuary phases. The first saw scattered burials with very few grave goods. This contrasts with the second and third phases, in which the dead were buried in discrete clusters accompanied by pottery vessels, shell beads and fish bone jewellery. There was a very high proportion of infants, their early death probably reflecting an inherited blood disorder known as thalassemia. This condition conferred some resistance to malaria, but could also induce anaemia when inheritance was homozygous for the recessive alleles concerned. Despite the malarial environment, the men during these two phases had strongly developed upper body musculature and their tooth wear differed from that seen in women.[4] It would seem likely that these men spent time away from Khok Phanom Di, perhaps in coastal or inland travel. Their subsistence was strongly based upon hunting, gathering and fishing.

Several changes were noted midway through the third mortuary phase. The sea level fell. Shellfish, fish and crabs now show a sharp bias towards freshwater species. At the same time, granite hoes were found for the first time, along with shell knives that, according to the wear pattern on the blades, were used for cutting cereal stems. The first bones of the domestic dog also appeared. Taken in conjunction, these variables are compatible with the local cultivation of rice. This finding is further supported by the recovery of partially-digested stomach contents and human faeces from burials of this phase. The former included rice chaff and freshwater fish remains, the latter the remains of mouse hair and a beetle known to inhabit rice stores. The rice consumed may have been stored in conditions which harboured such vermin and beetles.

Men and women of mortuary phases 3B and 4 were distinguished on the basis of grave goods, the former being interred with large turtle shell ornaments. Women, on the other hand, were accompanied in death by the clay anvils used for shaping pottery vessels. At the same time, we find that men were less powerfully built and did not live so long. While the situation is not completely clear, these changes might reflect a change which saw rice cultivation becoming more important at the expense of fishing and collecting. The men and women also seem to have shared a similar diet, for their patterns of tooth wear were no longer distinct.

This episode did not endure, for during the ensuing fifth mortuary phase there was a reversion to marine conditions. Hoes and sickles were no longer found. Phase 5, however, saw unprecedented mortuary wealth. One woman was interred in an unusually long and deep grave. Cylinders of unfired clay had covered her body, with each probably representing sufficient to manufacture an individual vessel. She was buried with over 100,000 shell disc beads, a shell bangle, and shell ear ornaments (or perhaps parts of a headdress). A ceramic anvil and two burnishing stones lay beside her right ankle. To judge from her strong wrist musculature, she was almost certainly a potter. The grave beside her contained an infant with a virtually identical set of grave goods, even including a miniature clay anvil. These very rich burials portray a society in which pottery makers were able to gain considerable personal wealth and prestige. By exchanging the vessels they made, it seems likely that they were able to secure exotic shell ornaments in extraordinary quantities.

This expanding involvement in trade seems to have continued into the penultimate mortuary phase (phase 6), in which again we find richly-endowed female burials in association with clay anvils and shell jewellery. One group of three such graves was found within a rectangular clay and timber mortuary building, while a second but contemporary group was contained within a wooden structure, albeit with far less mortuary wealth. The impression given by these late burials is that of a rich hunter-gatherer community which engaged in an exchange network that incorporated inland rice farmers.

Khok Phanom Di was probably abandoned in the mid-second millennium BC. No coastal settlement in Southeast Asia has revealed a comparable sequence, or similarly intimate insight into associated environmental and cultural changes. We do know, however, that the coasts of Vietnam and southern China were thickly studded with settlements most easily recognized by their deep shellfish deposits. These sites are often termed coastal Neolithic by local scholars. Yet it seems much more likely that they reflect a widespread adaptation by hunter-gatherers to the rich resources of the shore and estuaries of Southeast Asia. Few, if any, are documented beyond the period when Khok Phanom Di was abandoned, for by then the centre of gravity had moved to the inland river valleys and the foundation of villages based on the cultivation of rice, and the raising of domestic stock.

The Neolithic societies of Mainland Southeast Asia

Rice grows wild in Thailand and Vietnam, but all attempts to trace a local Southeast Asian transition from hunting and gathering to farming societies have been fruitless. Given the bounty of the coastal environment and the relatively thin population of hunters and gatherers in the forested interior, there seems to have been no stimulus to change. Present evidence rather suggests that the transition to rice cultivation and stock raising took place under conditions of an oscillating climate in the middle reaches of the Yangzi Valley, between about 8000 and 6000 BC.[5] The permanent village communities documented at such early village sites as Pengtoushan in Hunan Province represent the initial stages in an expansionary process which saw rice cultivators spread to the west, east and south (Figure 3.5). The arrival of the first such rice farmers in southern China, Vietnam and Thailand appears to have taken place during the third millennium BC. Shixia and related sites in the upper Beijiang Valley of Guangdong reveal a surely-intrusive settlement phase, represented by a novel mortuary ritual and a range of artefacts paralleled in the Liangzhu culture of the lower Yangzi region to the north. Inhumation

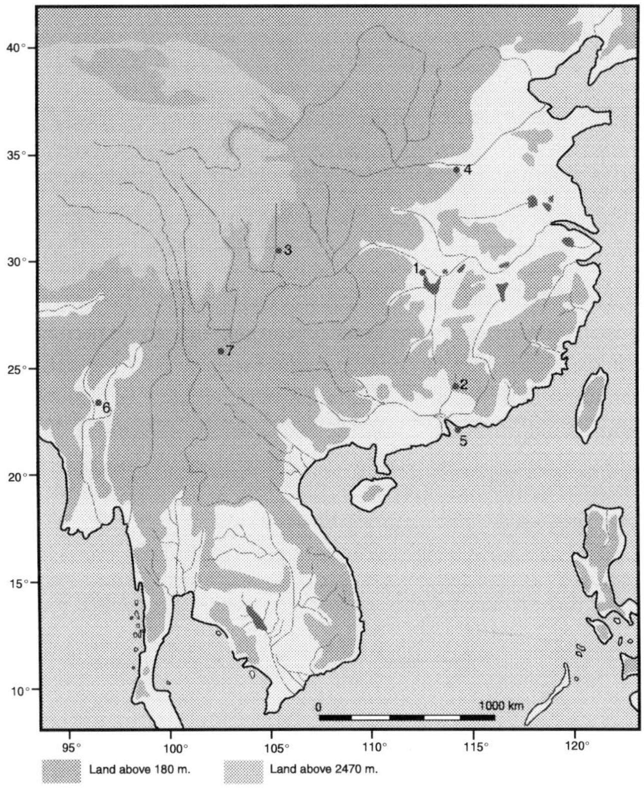

Figure 3.5 Location of key sites in China and Burma mentioned in the text. 1. Pengtoushan, 2. Shixia, 3. Sanxingdui, 4. Erlitou, 5. Sham Wan, Kwo Lo Wan, 6. Nyaunggan. 7. Baiyangcun.

graves were orientated with the head directed to the east, and incorporated ceramic vessels and jade ornaments among the mortuary offerings.

The pattern of intrusive agriculturalists settling inland valleys in southern China, while the coast continued to be occupied by affluent foraging groups, is repeated in the Red River area and the contiguous coast of Vietnam. The earliest agricultural settlements take their name from Phung Nguyen, a site which has been extensively investigated. There are relatively few radiocarbon dates for this sequence, but the Phung Nguyen phase probably extends from the late third to the mid-second millennium BC. Recent research at Co Loa has revealed initial settlement from about 2000 BC.[6] Most settlements are found above the confluence of the Red and Black rivers. They cover between 1 and 3 hectares and are found on slightly elevated terrain near small stream confluences. The principal excavated site is at Phung Nguyen itself,[7] which covers 3 hectares, of which 0.4 hectare has been excavated. The stratigraphy, as in most Phung Nguyen sites, is shallow, barely exceeding 1 metre in depth. Excavations commenced in 1959 and were followed by two further campaigns.

All this activity provided a large sample of most interesting material culture. No trace of bronze was recovered, but there was a substantial sample of ceramic, bone and stone artefacts. Spindle whorls attest to a weaving industry and bone harpoons suggest some form of hunting. The stone adzes take a variety of forms (Figure 3.6). Only four of the shouldered variety were found, compared with 777 examples of a quadrangular form, some of which were sharpened so consistently that they are broader than they are long. When one adds stone adze fragments for which the shape is indeterminate, a total of 1,138 adzes or adze fragments were recovered. There are also 59 small stone chisels, some with cutting edges only 10 millimetres wide. Almost 200 whetstones were found. They bore grooves that result from sharpening the stone adzes and chisels. Stone projectile points were rarer. Three reach the dimensions of a spear point, the remainder are more likely to be tanged arrowheads.

The inhabitants of Phung Nguyen also fashioned stone rings, mostly in nephrite. The total sample of 540 specimens has been subdivided into eight types based on the shape of the cross-section. Most are rectangular, but some are much more complex, having a range of ribs and flanges. While some are large enough to rank as adult bracelets, others have small diameters and were either designed for children or perhaps for display as earrings. Stone beads were also made, most being tubular and measuring up to 1.3 centimetres in length. There was also a vigorous tradition of working clay. There are pellet-bow pellets and clay net weights, but most attention was accorded to the manufacture of clay vessels.

It is on the basis of changing decorative styles on pottery that the Vietnamese archaeologists have designated phases to this culture (Figure 3.7). The earliest, called after the site of Go Bong, is characterized by incised parallel bands infilled with rows of impressions done with a pointed implement. The favoured motif is in the shape of an "S" meander. The second sub-phase incorporates a range of designs based, according to Ha Van Tan,[8] on "geometric asymmetry". Incised bands infilled with dentate impressions alternate with bands left blank, to form a series of most attractive design fields. This form of decoration has clear parallels with the Yunnan Neolithic sites of Baiyangcun and Dadunzi.

The late Phung Nguyen style of pottery is found at the site of Trang Kenh, near Haiphong. Nguyen Kim Dung's excavations there have revealed a sophisticated workshop for the manufacture of nephrite bracelets and beads, involving working with chisels, drill points, saws and grinding stones.[9] The radiocarbon dates suggest that the

Figure 3.6 Stone adzes recovered from Phung Nguyen.

workshop dates to about 1650–1500 BC, but the introduction of craft skills in working nephrite and jadeite ornaments represents a key link with the later Chinese Neolithic. The bangles from Phung Nguyen are the product of highly-skilled lapidaries. The value attached to stone jewellery and weaponry is also in evidence at Lung Hoa, a second late Phung Nguyen site characterized by deep graves, some cut over 5 metres into the ground and equipped, as in the Lingnan Fubin culture of southern China, with ledges.[10] Two graves include stone bracelets, beads and earrings, as well as ceramic vessels, as mortuary offerings. One *ge* halberd is particularly interesting because it matches those found in southern China and northwards into the Bronze Age early urban states in Sichuan (Sanxingdui) and the Huanghe basin (Erlitou). The *yazhang* jade blade is also a central feature of the latter two Chinese assemblages, and specimens have been recovered from Phung Nguyen and Xom Ren. Even at this late stage in the expansion and establishment

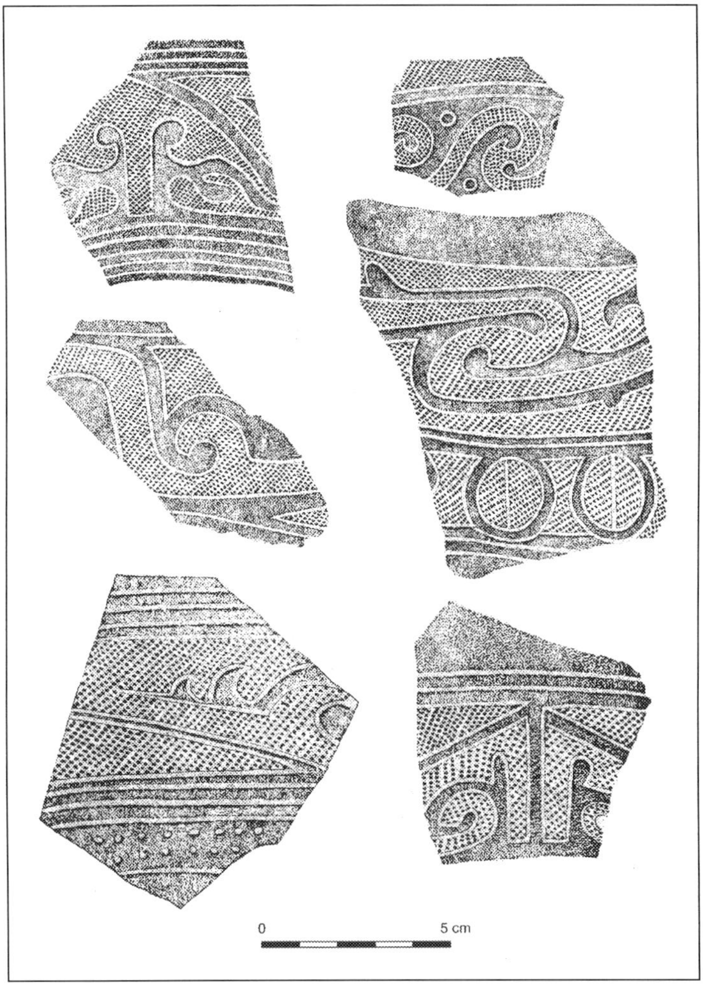

Figure 3.7 Pottery from Phung Nguyen, Vietnam decorated in a wide variety of motifs and in a style found widely in Neolithic sites in Southeast Asia.

of Neolithic communities in Southeast Asia, contact was maintained with the increasingly complex societies of the Yangzi and Huanghe rivers.[11]

Archaeological fieldwork in the uplands north of the Red River has resulted in an appreciation that Neolithic sites were not confined to the relatively open terrain above Viet Tri. The Lo River, for example, attracted intrusive settlements characterized by a range of stone adze forms, stone bangles and a ceramic industry. These sites, known collectively as the Ha Giang culture, might well have been sources for the high quality stone found in such profusion at the many Phung Nguyen settlements.[12] Further south, recent excavations at the coastal late Neolithic site of Con Nen have yielded tubular stone beads, stone bangles and adze heads, decorated potsherds and tubular ceramic feet for pottery vessels. The settlement of Central Vietnam during the late Neolithic period is a major area of future research.

The singular style of decorated pottery in these Phung Nguyen sites is matched further up the Red River valley in the southern Chinese province of Yunnan. A deep sequence at Baiyangcun incorporated the foundations of at least 11 houses, in addition to an inhumation cemetery dated to the second half of the third millennium BC. A second but rather later site at Dadunzi also revealed house foundations and a cemetery in which infants were interred in large ceramic jars.[13] These two sites are within striking distance of the Mekong River, and as we follow this great thoroughfare south, so we encounter many more prehistoric settlements linked by a common economy of rice farming and stock raising, in conjunction with incised and burnished ceramics.

In Thailand, the earliest settlement phase at Non Nok Tha in the northeast belongs to this horizon; here again we find inhumation graves associated with incised ceramics as mortuary offerings.[14] Ban Phak Top has furnished spectacular examples of the black burnished and incised wares, but sadly this site has been completely destroyed by looting. A handful of graves at the nearby site of Ban Chiang belong to the same tradition and have been dated between 2500–2000 BC, while at Non Kao Noi, in the same area of the upper Songkhram Valley, further undated graves have been uncovered. The site of Ban Lum Khao in the upper Mun Valley, excavated in 1995–6, has revealed a series of pits and associated occupation material dated to about 1500 BC. Again, the black incised pottery belongs to the same intrusive tradition, while the faunal remains from the pits illuminate the environment which these settlers sought. The majority of the remains come from fish, some of remarkable size when compared with their modern counterparts. The Ban Lum Khao village was located in a low-lying riverine habitat which attracted deer and water buffalo, both of which were hunted. Indeed, the large, wild water buffalo appear to have been rapidly eliminated, for they only appear in the early phase of occupation.

Ban Non Wat lies about 15 kilometres to the west of Ban Lum Khao, and three seasons of excavations there beginning in 2002 have uncovered Neolithic occupation and a cemetery dating between 2000–1300 BC. Adult burials were found with fine incised and painted pottery vessels, and bivalve shells thought to represent fertility. One man was found in a seated position within a large, lidded ceramic vessel. A woman had been interred with three pig skeletons, decorated pots, and cowry shells placed as ear ornaments. A ring of five lidded infant jar burials were found disposed round her head. One infant jar burial contained a rice grain, while many shellfish in the occupation layers indicate the exploitation of a watery environment.

As we proceed still further south, the same pottery style and forms with incised and burnished decoration are found at the site of Samrong Sen in Cambodia, where prehistoric archaeology in Southeast Asia had its beginnings over a century ago. They occur also at Non Pa Wai just north of Lopburi, again in a familiar inhumation cemetery.[15] Such settlements must have entered the exchange orbit of affluent coastal settlements like Khok Phanom Di, bringing with them knowledge of rice cultivation, domestic stock and the dog.

To the southwest, in the valleys of central and western Thailand, Neolithic settlement has long been known following Sørensen's pioneering excavations at Ban Kao in Kanchanaburi Province.[16] The earlier of the two major occupation phases included a series of inhumation graves, wherein the dead were accompanied by a wide range of pottery vessel forms. There is little evidence here for the incised and burnished style, the hallmark of the ceramic industry being a bowl raised on pointed tripod feet. Similar forms have been found to the south into the coastal plains of Malaysia, at such sites as Jenderam Hilir in Selangor.[17] Radiocarbon dates from Ban Kao indicate initial settlement in the late third millennium BC, and two determinations from Jenderam Hilir straddle 2000 BC.

The similar dates of the early Neolithic sites from Guangdong to Peninsular Malaysia probably indicate related expansionary movements southwards, following the courses of the major rivers. Linguists have identified inherited similarities in many of the languages spoken over much of Mainland Southeast Asia, from eastern India to southern China and southwards to Malaysia and the Nicobar Islands,[18] sufficient to classify them within the Austroasiatic family (which excludes the Tai languages). There are three major subdivisions within Austroasiatic; Mundaic in India, Mon-Khmer (which includes Vietnamese and the Aslian languages of Malaysia), and Nicobarese. Cognates for rice and aspects of its cultivation are known over much of this area, suggesting that this crop was grown by the earliest Austroasiatic speakers. The deep differences between the Munda branch on the one hand and Mon-Khmer on the other indicate a considerable time depth for Proto-Austroasiatic, measured in millennia rather than centuries. This has encouraged both linguists and archaeologists to seek a pattern whereby the Austroasiatic languages had a common origin in the Yangzi Valley, their present distribution reflecting the diaspora of agricultural societies which began over 8,000 years ago. This expansionary model gathers force with the appreciation that Austroasiatic and Austronesian languages probably have a common ancestry in the Austric phylum. Whereas the former expanded from the Yangzi Valley by continental riverine routes, the latter followed an Island Southeast Asian and ultimately Oceanic route. This model has the advantage of being testable through the study of ancient DNA in bone, not only from the human beings deemed to have participated but also from their dogs, for the latter have no ancestor in Southeast Asia or the Pacific and must have originated ultimately in a region such as China, where the wolf is native.

The Bronze Age of Mainland Southeast Asia

The origins of the Mainland Southeast Asian Bronze Age have a history of controversy initiated by claims dating from the 1960s and 1970s for remarkably early dates for two sites in Thailand, Non Nok Tha and Ban Chiang.[19] These claims can now be set aside. New accelerator radiocarbon dating techniques allow fragments of rice chaff, used to temper the clay used to manufacture mortuary vessels, to be dated. This permits the precise dating of items from assured contexts in a prehistoric site. The results for Non

Nok Tha reveal that the Bronze Age cemetery was in use within the period 1500–1000 BC. Bronze Age burials at Ban Chiang belong to the same period.

Freeing the issue from chronological controversy now allows for a much more interesting assessment of the Mainland Southeast Asian Bronze Age. The emerging pattern indicates that, from Hong Kong and coastal Guangdong to the Chindwin Valley in Burma, a distinctive tradition of bronze casting developed during the second half of the second millennium BC.[20] This was rooted in local Neolithic communities and poses the issue not only of origins, but of the implications of metallurgical skill.

Understanding origins involves an appreciation of bronze casting traditions beyond Southeast Asia, because either the local bronze working had a local and independent origin, or the knowledge of smelting and casting was introduced from an established exotic source. Now that we can set aside claims for a Southeast Asian bronze industry as early as the fourth millennium BC, which would have ruled out any form of introduced knowledge, it is possible to consider possible outside sources. The closest and most likely such source lies in the bronze-casting tradition of China. We have already noted that the Neolithic communities of southern China and Vietnam obtained exotic northern jades by exchange. There is also evidence that these groups were familiar with bronzes which originated within the Shang and Zhou tradition of casting. The site of Xing'an, for example, has furnished a late Shang period bronze *you* vessel.[21] A bronze halberd of similar age has been found at Xinjie in Guangxi Province.[22] The maintenance of exchange relations between Lingnan (southern China) and the Yangzi Valley during the second millennium BC could well account for not only the transmission of jades and finished bronzes, but the vital knowledge of the properties of copper and tin ore.

One can, however, proceed a stage further. The origins of the Chinese Bronze Age itself have long been enigmatic, not least because of the recovery of the earliest bronze artefacts in the remote northwestern province of Gansu. Now, however, it is possible to trace the expansion across the Eurasian Steppes of bronze industries from west to east, thus making the Chinese tradition itself derivative from a western source.[23] Within this broad pattern of the diffusion of knowledge in its many regional bronze-working expressions, the Mainland Southeast Asian province is distinct on several counts.

The mouth of the Pearl River and the general area of Hong Kong has been known as a centre of bronze casting for the past 60 years. Schofield, for example, recovered six bivalve sandstone moulds for casting socketed bronze axes at Shek Pik, on Lantau Island, in 1937. Excavations at Sham Wan in 1971 recovered bronze fishhooks and arrowheads made of a 10 per cent tin alloy. Meacham has added further to our understanding of the Hong Kong bronze industry through the recovery of bivalve sandstone casting moulds used as grave goods in a cemetery at Kwo Lo Wan.[24] These sites belong within the period 1300–1000 BC. Both the finished bronzes and the techniques of manufacture are precisely matched to the west and south in Thailand, Vietnam and Cambodia.

Our understanding of this Bronze Age tradition has been greatly enhanced by recent research in Thailand, both at the copper mines themselves and in the villages which acquired and cast the ingots. Two mining complexes have been examined. The first lies on the southern bank of the Mekong River at Phu Lon in northern Thailand, and the other is found in the Khao Wong Prachan Valley in central Thailand.[25] The rich veins of copper, recognized on the surface by characteristic green staining, were followed into the hillsides and the mined ore was crushed and concentrated before being placed into clay reaction vessels. These were then probably covered with ceramic chimneys pierced to admit tuyères, in order to raise the furnace heat sufficiently for successful smelting. At Non Pa Wai in the Khao Wong Prachan Valley, smelting operations covered an area of 5 hectares to a depth of 3 metres. Most of the resulting copper was poured into moulds to produce circular ingots, surely destined for exchange. Some, however, was also locally cast in bivalve moulds. One of the graves, of a young man, contained the mould for casting an axe. None of the copper artefacts found at Non Pa Wai contained any tin.

This intensive mining activity has been dated to the second half of the second millennium BC, but it continued into the first millennium, as seen at the very deep deposits of casting debris recovered at the neighbouring site of Nil Kham Haeng. Here, the thin horizontal lenses are thought to result from metal-working debris being redeposited by monsoon rains. Indeed, Andrew Weiss has proposed that the smelting activity was itself a dry season activity undertaken by the occupants of the many settlements which concentrate in the vicinity of the rich copper deposits.

Most Bronze Age settlements are found in the small stream valleys which feed the major rivers of Mainland Southeast Asia. They were linked by far-reaching exchange networks which saw marine shell reaching settlements over 1,000 km from the coast, and copper and tin entering villages far removed from the ore sources. One of the advantages of relatively extensive excavations in Bronze Age sites in Thailand has been the recovery of both cemeteries and the industrial areas in which bronzes were cast. For example, a clay-lined furnace has been recovered at Ban Na Di in Udorn Province of the Khorat Plateau.[26] It was surrounded by crucible fragments, copper staining and a sandstone mould for casting a socketed axe. The ceramic crucibles still contained the remains of bronze resulting from a 10 per cent admixture of tin with the copper. This produced a tougher alloy than copper alone, and finished bronzes include axes as well as a range of arrowheads, socketed spears, fishhooks, bangles and anklets. A similar casting area was found at nearby Ban Chiang, while at the Bronze Age cemetery of Non Nok Tha, several male graves contained either socketed axes or axe moulds in sandstone.

Judicious interpretation of the mortuary remains from these Bronze Age cemeteries has provided some insight into social organization. This begins with the premise that a person's status may be indicated by the quantity and quality of accompanying mortuary offerings. At Ban Na Di, we find that men, women, infants and children were interred in groups, although the restricted area of the excavation ruled out the complete exposure of any single cluster or row. Grave goods included ceramic vessels, some of which contained food in the form of fish or pig bones, the complete limbs of cattle and pigs, exotic shell and stone beads and bangles, clay figurines of cattle, deer, elephants and people, and bronze jewellery in the form of bangles, anklets and possibly earrings. It was found that one of the two groups of interments included most of the exotic offerings, all the figurines and most of the bronzes. Since both groups were interred over the same period of time, it is possible that one commanded rather higher wealth and status than the other, but not to a dominant degree.

Testing this hypothesis would necessitate a much more extensive excavation. At Nong Nor, in the valley of the Bang Pakong River in central Thailand, a much larger area of a Bronze Age cemetery has indeed been exposed.[27] This overlay the hunter-gatherer settlement discussed above and over 160 Bronze Age graves were uncovered (Figure 3.8). Unfortunately, a high proportion had suffered disturbance. Nevertheless, it is possible to recognize a basic mortuary tradition similar to that in northeastern Thailand. The dead were interred in rows and groups which incorporated men, women, infants and children,

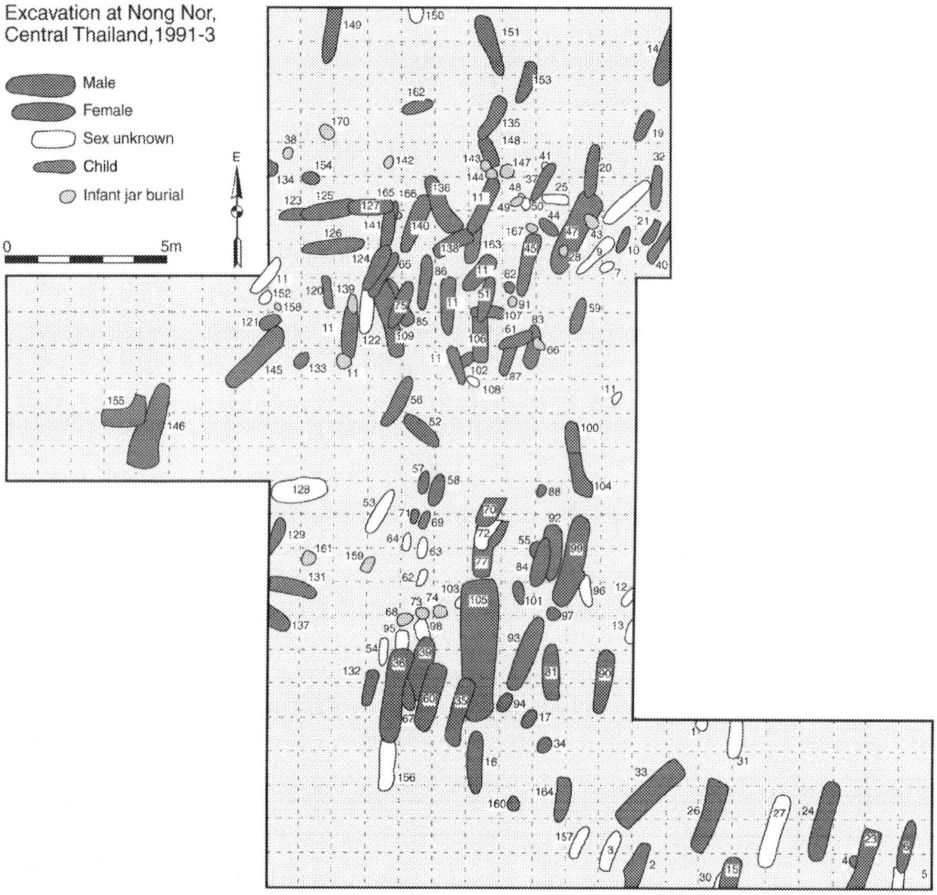

Figure 3.8 The Bronze Age cemetery of Nong Nor reveals two major groups, and a preference to inter the dead in rows.

the infants often being interred in large lidded jars. Grave goods included pottery vessels, ornaments of exotic talc, carnelian, serpentine and marble, bronze and tin bangles, and animal bones. Whereas the people of Ban Na Di selected the left forelimbs of cattle or pigs, the occupants of Nong Nor preferred a dog's skull for interment with the dead. One man was found associated with the horns of a large bull. This cemetery formed over a period of several centuries, so identifying contemporaneous social variables is by no means straightforward. However, one group of five burials included a male interred in a particularly large grave. He was accompanied by a unique large bronze bangle and some fine pottery vessels. Moreover, the women buried in his immediate vicinity were unusually wealthy in terms of their multiple bangles from distant sources. As at Ban Na Di, there is a hint of social inequality, but again not to a marked degree.

The excavations of Non Nok Tha were also extensive and, while some individuals were relatively well endowed with offerings, there is no evidence for a particular group defined by sex, age or preferred location being singled out for special attention. Indeed, no grave from the Bronze Age approaches burial 15 from the hunter-gatherer community of Khok Phanom Di in terms of mortuary wealth. At Non Nok Tha, the basic Bronze Age pattern recurs: the dead were set out in rows, with ceramic vessels, bronzes, and animal bones, which in this site included the complete skeletons of dogs and the limb bones of pigs and cattle.

At Ban Lum Khao in Nakhon Ratchasima Province we again find a similar pattern. The dead were laid out in rows. The pottery vessels at this site included many particularly attractive red forms with trumpet-shaped rims, and animal bones included the extremities of pigs and, on occasion, complete bivalve shellfish and the skeletons of fish. Some were buried with stone adze heads, but none of the 111 graves uncovered included a single bronze artefact. This rarity of bronze at Ban Lum Khao, despite clear evidence for local casting, follows a wide pattern. Bronzes were always rare in Thai Bronze Age cemeteries. The recovery of tin ornaments at Nong Nor also reveals that copper-based alloys were but one aspect of the employment of metals in display and ritual during this period.

The Neolithic layers at Ban Non Wat, in the upper Mun Valley, lay beneath a Bronze Age cemetery. Previous exposures of Bronze Age settlements in Thailand have been relatively small. At Ban Non Wat, however, the opening of nearly 400 square metres over three seasons has uncovered some burials of surprising and unparalleled wealth. While most of the dead were found with a handful of pottery vessels and some shell and marble ornaments, a few were interred in very large graves with a rich array of offerings. One such grave measured 5 by 3.5 metres. Nearly 80 pottery vessels, some of considerable size, were disposed in rows round the two burials. Both skeletons had been partially removed from the grave soon after death, and then carefully replaced. Grave goods included socketed bronze axes, fine marble bangles, and thousands of shell beads. A second such outstandingly rich burial matched the number and size of pottery vessels. One skeleton was found intact, the other had been removed and then replaced. The latter was associated with a fine socketed bronze axe, the arms of the former were covered in large trochus shell and marble bangles. Two bronze axes and a socketed bronze knife were found in a third rich grave, along with 30 finely decorated pottery vessels. The bronzes at this site were restricted to these special burials. Although excavations are continuing, it is evident that this site requires a complete reappraisal of the social organization of the Bronze Age. Specifically, there is strong evidence for a socially elite group at this particular site by at least 1000 BC.

There is no doubt that more extensive excavations in Vietnam and Cambodia would greatly expand our knowledge of this distinctive Bronze Age tradition. At present, the sequence is best known in Bac Bo, the area centred on the Red River Valley where Dong Dau is the most important site, not least because of the unusually deep stratigraphic record.[28] It is located to the east of most Phung Nguyen sites, within sight of the Red River. It was recognized in 1961, and excavations undertaken in 1965 and 1967–8 uncovered 550 square metres to a depth of between 5 and 6 m. A fourth season in 1981 added further to our understanding of the material culture of this phase.[29] The mound itself covers about 3 ha. Its basal cultural material has been ascribed to the final Phung Nguyen subphase, and while the pottery of the Dong Dau site reveals Phung Nguyen origins, at least in style and mode of decoration, we also find compelling evidence for a local and vigorous bronze industry. Ngo Si Hong has published half a bivalve mould for casting a socketed bronze axe, while Trinh Sinh[30] has stressed that many of the Phung

Nguyen phase stone artefacts were copied in bronze. There are also intriguing parallels with material from the Northeastern Thai sites, not only in the small furnaces for casting bronze items, but in the ceramic cattle figurines.

The bivalve moulds recovered by Ha Van Tan from a small (50 square metres) excavation in a Dong Dau context at Thanh Den are virtually identical with those from the Khorat plateau. The 30 or so fragments of stone and clay moulds were designed for casting axes and fish hooks. The site has a cultural stratigraphy of only one metre, and the three radiocarbon dates match very closely the dates obtained for the Bronze Age in Northeast Thailand. Bronze was also employed to make socketed spearheads, arrowheads and chisels. The Dong Dau phase axes began to take on the initial pediform shape so diagnostic of later decorated examples from the Dong Son Iron Age. Thanh Den has also yielded nephrite bangles and rings which recall Phung Nguyen prototypes, some of which appear to have been manufactured at the site.[31]

Towards the end of the second millennium BC, the Dong Dau phase developed into the Go Mun phase. Go Mun is located only 3 km northeast of Phung Nguyen, and indeed the 30 or so known Go Mun sites are located within the same general area as those of the Phung Nguyen and Dong Dau phases. There have been four campaigns of excavations at Go Mun, commencing in 1961 and finishing a decade later. In all, 1,500 square metres were excavated, the cultural stratigraphy being only 1 metre deep. As at Phung Nguyen, stone adzes were in the main quadrangular in section, and only one shouldered. Similar stone chisels to those from Phung Nguyen were also encountered. The inventory of bronze artefacts reveals that many forms in stone were copied in metal. There are also bivalve moulds for casting axes and arrowheads. Thirteen axes have been found, and seven chisels. The spearheads, arrowheads and bracelets were likewise rendered in bronze. Fishhooks were the most abundant bronze artefact, followed by narrow projectile points. One sickle was recovered, and the figure of a seated individual which was presumably cast by means of the lost wax technique. The Dong Dau pottery bears curvilinear and rectangular patterns which look like developed Phung Nguyen motifs, and it is in these that Ha Van Tan[32] sees models for the decoration later found on the well-known Dong Son drums. It is apparent from the excavation carried out at Go Mun and related sites that bronze working was increasing in intensity and range of artefacts.

There was also a coastal aspect to settlement in the Bac Bo area. Vietnamese archaeologists see the early Neolithic site of Cai Beo and the Da But grouping of sites as ancestral to various so-called middle and late Neolithic cultures which occupied the coastal tract north and south of the Red River delta. Thus, the Ha Long culture of the islands in the northern sector of the Gulf of Bac Bo is seen as derivative from a Cai Beo context. They base this opinion on the similarities in the rectangular and shouldered adzes recovered. Sites of this group also yield polished stone bracelets, beads and pendants not dissimilar to Phung Nguyen examples.

Moving south of the delta, we encounter sites of another coastal group, called after the site of Hoa Loc. This group is known for a most unusual form of decorated pottery with a quadrangular shaped rim. They also used clay seals with deeply excised patterns resembling those found much later in Iron Age contexts in Northeast Thailand. Stone adzes and grinding stones are common and large stone hoes occur. The faunal associations from Hoa Loc are dominated by marine species, but Vu The Long has also noted the remains of domesticated dog, pig and probably cattle. Le Van Thieu[33] has indicated that some of the pigs' teeth display a bimodal size distribution, probably reflecting the presence of both wild and domesticated animals. Hoa Loc itself is located on a raised sand bar now about 4 kilometres behind the shoreline. It is evident that as the sea level fell back from its post-Pleistocene high, so coastal settlement followed it. A few pieces of bronze were found at Hoa Loc when it was excavated in 1976. The site seems to equate, in terms of its metallurgy, with the latest Phung Nguyen subphase in the inland area.

The geographic extent of the Southeast Asian Bronze Age tradition is not yet defined. Although many sites are known from the mouth of the Mekong to Yunnan, and from Lingnan (southern China) to central Thailand, its western limits have only recently been extended with the discovery of the Nyaunggan cemetery in Burma.[34] The Chindwin Valley is rich in copper ore, and Nyaunggan lies on the flank of an old volcano overlooking its broad flood plain. Excavations there have revealed an extensive cemetery in which the dead were buried with many pottery vessels, stone ornaments and bronze spearheads which recall Mainland Southeast Asian forms. Once again, animal bones accompanied the dead. This must be one of many such sites in the Chindwin and presumably the Irrawaddy Valley, and a new chapter in defining the Bronze Age of Southeast Asia is now unfolding.

The Bronze Age thus developed within those late Neolithic communities exposed through exchange to knowledge and ideas originating in the early states of China. The economy continued to be based on rice cultivation, domestic livestock and hunting, fishing and collecting, and there is some limited evidence for social distinctions based on inherited wealth and status. Copper and tin ores are relatively abundant, but have a restricted distribution far away from the majority of agricultural settlements. Hence, metal ingots were distributed by long-established exchange routes firmly related to passage by river. Marble, marine shell, serpentine, talc, carnelian, fine ceramics and doubtless many perishable items exchanged hands, all employed to exhibit status and to be immolated with the dead.

The Iron Age of mainland Southeast Asia

The Bronze Age began within the period 1500–1000 BC and came to a close when iron entered the technological repertoire by approximately 500 BC. Iron ore is more widespread than copper or tin in Southeast Asia, and it is also available in the river valleys that attracted Neolithic and Bronze Age agricultural settlement. Relative abundance, coupled with the superior qualities of iron once effectively worked, are qualities with profound cultural implications.

The Iron Age of Southeast Asia can be divided into two distinct provinces. The first involved societies that lay in the path of the predatory imperial ambitions of the Han Dynasty of China. The second comprised those groups further south which were only indirectly affected by Han expansion. By the first century BC, the Han had annexed much of southern China and were actively incorporating the tribes of Yunnan and Vietnam into their imperial schemes. The result was a marked surge in militarism, the rise of powerful local chiefdoms and the investment of much energy into war. When not directly confronting the Chinese, these chiefdoms engaged in strife with their neighbours (Figure 3.9).

This phenomenon is nowhere better illustrated than in the Dian chiefdom of Yunnan. Here, we find royal cemeteries dating to the first century BC in which men and women of the elite lineage were interred with extraordinary mortuary wealth. Their large lacquered wooden coffins were filled with outstanding bronzes, including drums containing thousands of exotic cowry shells. These drums commonly bore bronze figures set in compositions on their tympana participating in scenes of war and ritual. Thus we can admire the chief, resplendent in golden armour on his horse, surrounded by his followers engaged in vicious hand-to-hand conflict. One is loading a crossbow, a weapon taken directly from the Chinese armoury. Ritual scenes fulfilling the agricultural round can also be recognized, often directed by high-status women. Indeed, the royal cemeteries include the graves of women interred with superb bronze weaving implements. Again represented as gilded figures, these female leaders are seen receiving gifts, or ringed by a group of weavers. Pride of place among these scenes, however, must be accorded a meeting between the paramount and his subsidiary chiefs. Seated in a roofed pavilion surrounded by ceremonial drums, the leader was the focus for the preparation of a feast involving the slaughter of cattle and pigs and the execution of war captives. Unfortunately, this luminous chiefdom, which on its own accord stands out as one of the best documented from the prehistoric world, was extinguished by incorporation as a province of Han Dynasty China.[35]

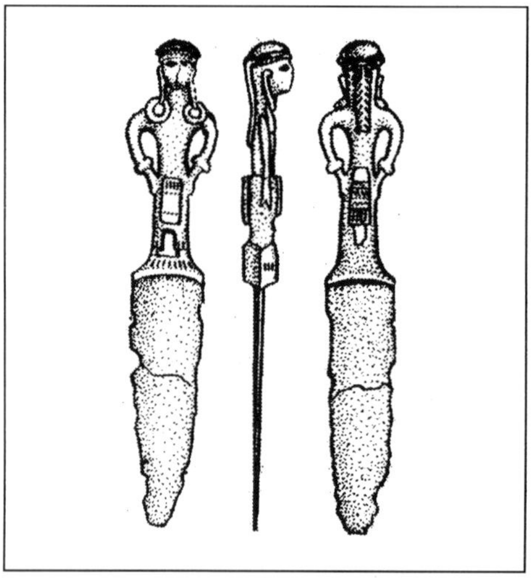

Figure 3.9 Bronze dagger from the Dong Son cemetery of Lang Vac incorporating a hilt showing a man wearing fine ornaments and a headband.

A similar florescence, followed by military defeat, afflicted the Dong Son culture of the Red, Ma and Ca valleys of northern Vietnam. First recognized on the basis of excavations at the cemetery and settlement of Dong Son, this group is renowned for its giant ceremonial bronze drums. The drums were lavishly decorated with ritual and battle scenes. We are treated to vivid pictures of war canoes bristling with plumed warriors brandishing spears and firing bows and arrows from fighting platforms. There are processions, musical ensembles, rice threshing, even a scene of four Dong Son drums set on a platform being beaten from above. The casting of such drums, together with the variety of large bronze vessels, must have required specialist workers under the control of elite leaders.

The huge settlement of Co Loa, which dominates the Red River plain north of Hanoi, likewise reflects control over a substantial labour force. Excavations within this site have uncovered a large ceremonial bronze drum, many socketed bronze implements which might have been used as ploughshares or hoes, and a cache of bronze arrowheads.[36] Several Dong Son cemeteries have also been examined. In the Red River valley, the dead were often placed in coffins fashioned from hollowed tree trunks. Their contents include weaponry with the wooden hafts of bronze spears and axes, imported Chinese coins, wooden bowls and the remains of woven clothing. The richest boat coffin from Viet Khe includes many bronzes, some of which were clearly of Chinese origin.[37]

While there was a proliferation of bronzes in the Dong Son cemeteries, iron objects were relatively rare.

The Chinese referred to the Truong Son Cordillera of northern Mainland Southeast Asia as the "Fortress of the Sky", and their energy for colonial expansion ebbed beyond its northern and eastern foothills. Beyond lay the rich lowlands of the Mekong and Chao Phraya river systems, and a long coastline offering opportunities for regional and international trade. Such trade could have been the spark which ignited the major social changes which took place during the Iron Age of the Southeast Asian Mainland, especially with the trading opportunities offered by the establishment of the Roman and Chinese empires. However, the ready and local availability of iron, and the potential for competitive emulation already apparent in the Bronze Age, should not be overlooked as contributors to increasing social complexity.

All these variables are manifested in the wealth of the mortuary offerings recovered during the excavation of the site of Ban Don Ta Phet in central Thailand.[38] This site commands the eastern approaches to the Three Pagodas Pass, a trade route linking the Chao Phraya plains with the Gulf of Martaban and ultimately, India. It represents a departure from earlier mortuary traditions in that it appears to have been a designated cemetery with no associated occupation or industrial remains, confined within a ditched enclosure. The available radiocarbon dates suggest an early fourth-century BC date for commencement, by which time exchange contact with India brought in glass, carnelian and agate ornaments, including a carnelian figurine of a rampant lion. Unfortunately the acidic soils have militated against the survival of human bone, so we have no means of identifying the age and sex of the burial assemblages. Yet the wealth of the grave goods far exceeds any encountered during the Bronze Age. There are iron spears, harpoons, axes, billhooks, bronze ornaments, and a type of bronze bowl of probable Indian origin, fashioned from an alloy containing over 20 per cent of tin. This provides a golden finish, but also makes the metal so brittle that it is easily prone to fracture. These bowls, turned on a lathe to produce a very thin wall, were decorated with languid images of elegant women, animals, plants and structures quite at variance with the austere ceremonies and battles seen on the contemporary Dong Son drums.

This bronze tradition, which must have called upon specialist craftspeople, also fed exchange networks. High tin bronzes have been found in Khorat Plateau sites such as Ban Na Di. A double-headed animal ornament of nephrite was also found at Ban Don Ta Phet, the parallels for which lie mainly to the east along the coast of Vietnam and into the Philippines.[39]

Ban Don Ta Phet is the best documented site in Central Thailand which exhibits Iron Age burial complexity. The great limestone cavern of Ongbah was also used as a cemetery, the dead there being interred in hardwood boat coffins.[40] We know few details, for the site was looted before the Danish archaeologist Per Sørensen could conduct proper excavations, but the wealth of the offerings gleaned from local villager reports might have been based on the output from the local lead mines. Lead is an essential component of Iron Age bronzes, for it eases castability. At Noen Ma Kok, Mankong has reported a range of artefacts which matches that from Ban Don Ta Phet.[41] Further north, at Ban Wang Hi, Pautreau has recovered a sample of Iron Age graves in which the dead were accompanied by iron weaponry and exotic ornaments.[42]

Similar trends to wealth and social complexity have long been recognized in large urnfield cemeteries on the long coast of Vietnam. These sites have been named collectively after the village of Sa Huynh, near which Vinet discovered jar burials as long ago as 1909. The mortuary remains include small pottery vessels, iron tools, glass and carnelian beads, and sites extend from the Hai Van Pass to the vicinity of Saigon, a distance of over 700 kilometres.[43] The cremation rite, in which the incinerated bones were placed in lidded vessels, again means that we know nothing of the age or sex of individual interments. This mortuary ritual contrasts with the widespread and enduring tradition of inhumation. It is highly likely that the Sa Huynh people were directly ancestral to the Cham civilization which dominated this long coastline for a thousand years from the first few centuries AD. The Chamic languages are Austronesian, with closest relationships with Malay and other languages in Island Southeast Asia. At present, it seems likely that the Sa Huynh culture represents a first millennium BC move into southern Vietnam by groups speaking an Austronesian language.

Until recently our knowledge of the Iron Age in the Mekong Valley, a vital area that was later to witness the rise of the state of Angkor, was little known. The period between AD 1 and 500 in particular was barely documented through excavation. This situation is now being addressed. Excavations at the great urban centre of Angkor Borei, just above the delta, have revealed an Iron Age cemetery at the base of the sequence (see Miriam Stark's chapter in this volume). A separate field programme in the upper valley of the Mun River in eastern Thailand has involved the opening of two large Iron Age settlements with startling results.

The broad floodplain of the Mun River suffers one of the longest dry seasons in Mainland Southeast Asia, yet aerial photographs taken half-a-century ago reveal a dense distribution of settlement mounds which seem to have been ringed by broad moats and raised banks. Small test excavations in several sites before 1996 had revealed evidence for Iron Age occupation, with deep sequences and intriguing evidence for clay structures. At Ban Don Phlong, Nitta[44] uncovered a series of 17 iron-smelting furnaces overlying an Iron Age cemetery in which the dead were interred within clay-lined coffins which date to the last centuries BC. One man had been interred wearing a necklace of agate and glass beads, while bronze bangles and rings were relatively abundant, especially when compared with the numbers in Bronze Age assemblages. At Non Yang, Nitta's excavations revealed a series of timber and clay structures, the wall of one room surviving to a height of 30 cm. A ditch associated with a curving row of post holes also ran across the excavated area. Excavations at Ban Takhong and Ban Krabuang Nok comprised deep occupation layers, evidence for iron smelting and burials within lidded jars.[45] All these excavations encouraged a programme of fieldwork designed to uncover an extensive area, linked with the examination of the moats and evidence for environmental change.

Such a programme began in 1995, in a defined study area west of the later Angkorian centre of Phimai. There is a dense concentration of Iron Age settlements in this region, on occasion so close that they are almost within hailing distance. Noen U-Loke was chosen for the closest attention, largely because an earlier excavation by Wichakana had revealed a deep, stratified sequence containing inhumation burials (Figure 3.10). An area 15 by 14 metres has been opened to a depth of 5 metres, while long cuts up to 6 metres deep have been placed through the surrounding moats to define their form and function.

Noen U-Loke was first occupied during the late Bronze Age and was finally abandoned about AD 400–500. Most fortunately, the soil conditions favour the survival of bone and 126 burials have been recovered, divided into five successive phases (Figure 3.11).

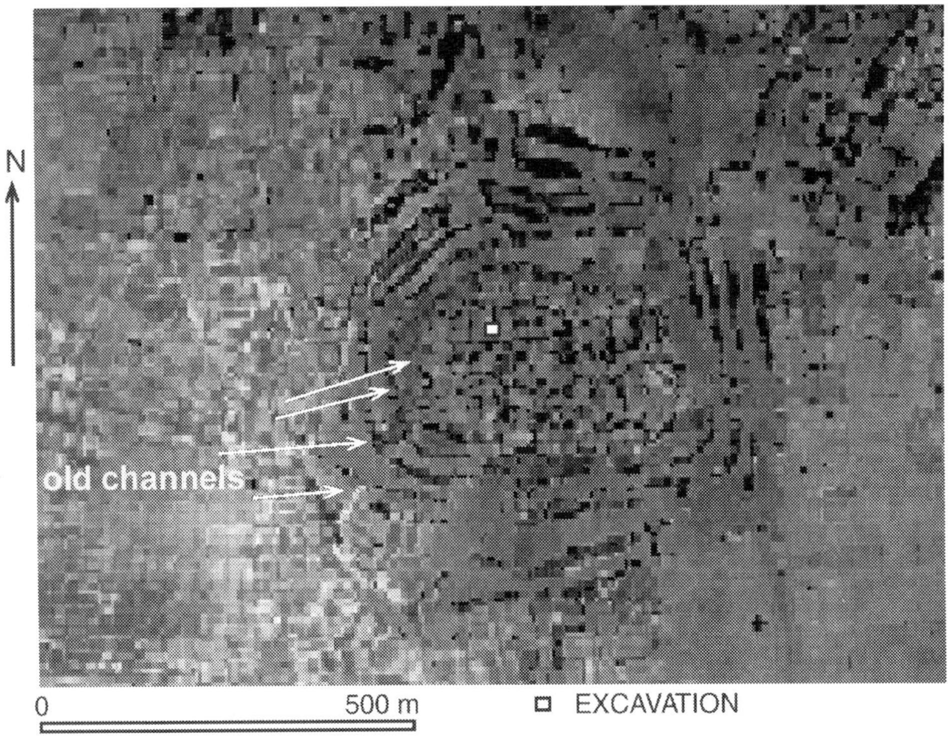

Figure 3.10 Aerial view of the prehistoric site of Noen U-Loke, showing the area excavated and the old channels.

There is also a wealth of evidence for the technological and economic activities at the site. Thus, for the first time, it has proved possible to trace the fortunes of an Iron Age community over a period of a thousand years.

The most compelling evidence comes from the remains of the people and their mortuary rituals. The deepest layers record the transition from the Bronze into the Iron Age, when the site was still relatively small and surrounded by a braided network of streams and swamps. One of the earliest graves contained a woman, interred with iron grave goods in the form of bangles and neck rings. The use of iron for ornaments was short-lived, for a slightly later grave of a man included bronze bangles and neck rings, but also an iron socketed spearhead and a socketed hoe. He was accompanied by a tiger canine necklace, two bronze spearheads, pottery vessels containing fish skeletons, shell discs for insertion in the ear lobes, and several other shell discs. The second and third mortuary phases saw clusters of graves, each containing the remains of men, women, children and infants. These people wore bronze ornaments including rings, bangles and anklets with bells, as well as the earliest glass and agate jewellery in the sequence and the entire skeletons of young pigs. Carnelian was confined to the third phase graves, which also revealed an interesting innovation in the form of a burial in a grave filled with white, silificied rice. The carnelian and agate ornaments (Figure 3.12) have been subjected to detailed examination and are thought to have come from Thai quarry sites. These phases date to the last centuries BC.

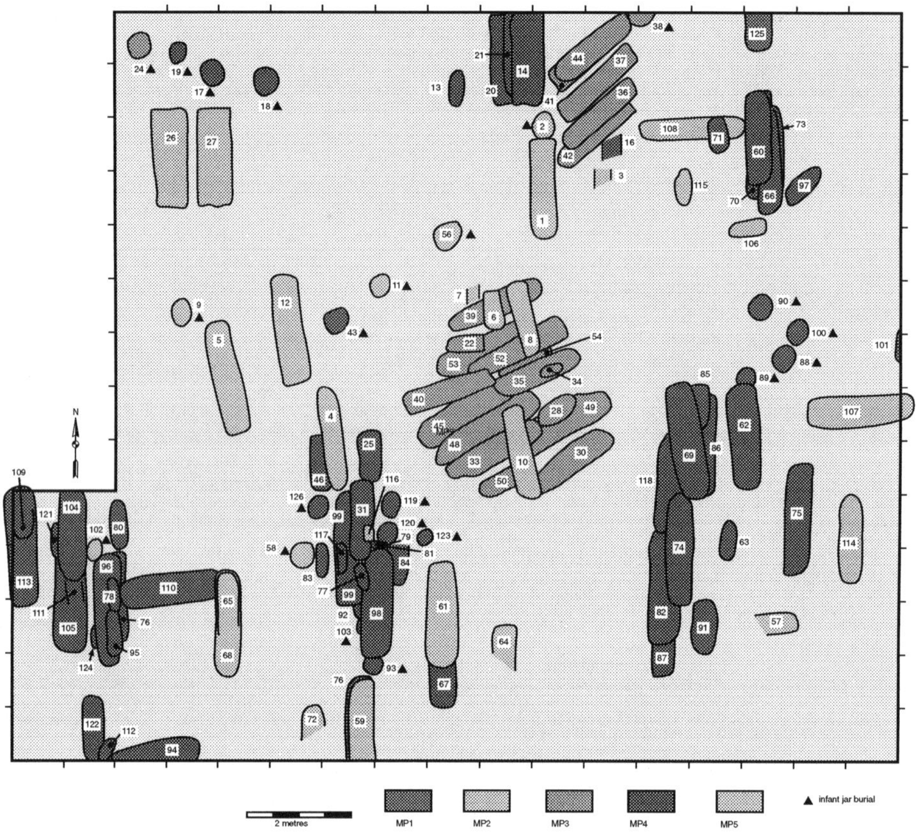

Figure 3.11 Plan of the Noen U-Loke cemetery, showing the five mortuary phases.

There were major changes with the fourth phase. Again, we find rice-filled graves, but the range and quantity of grave goods in each of the grave clusters greatly increased, and clay-lined and lidded coffins were now favoured. At least one outstandingly rich individual was present in each cluster. One contained the remains of a male with arguably more bronze than the accumulated total of all Bronze Age graves previously known in Thailand. He wore 150 bronze bangles, equally distributed on each arm, bronze toe and finger rings, and three bronze belts. His ear coils were made of silver covered in gold foil and an iron knife lay beside his left hand. Further grave goods included several splendid pottery vessels and glass beads by the neck and ankles. Burial 69 in a second cluster, also a male, wore four bronze belts, heavy bronze

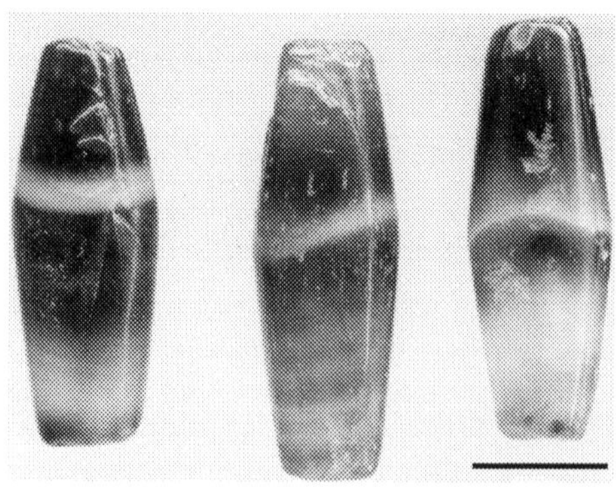

Figure 3.12 Agate jewellery found in the later graves of Noen U-Loke. (Scale 1 cm.) (Charles Higham.)

ear discs and many bangles and rings (Plate 1). Again, he was accompanied by an iron knife. The woman in a third cluster had an iron knife and wore a necklace of gold and agate beads, silver bangles and bronze rings, anklets and bangles (Figure 3.13). Large, thin-walled pottery vessels were placed beyond her head. These rich graves have been dated to between AD 100 and 300, a period when exchange up and down the Mekong and its tributaries grew in response to the rapid developments in maritime trade. In microcosm, we can see at Noen U-Loke the swift rise of leaders, whose wealth turned not only on more intensive agriculture, but also on the production of salt on an industrial scale and participation in burgeoning trade.

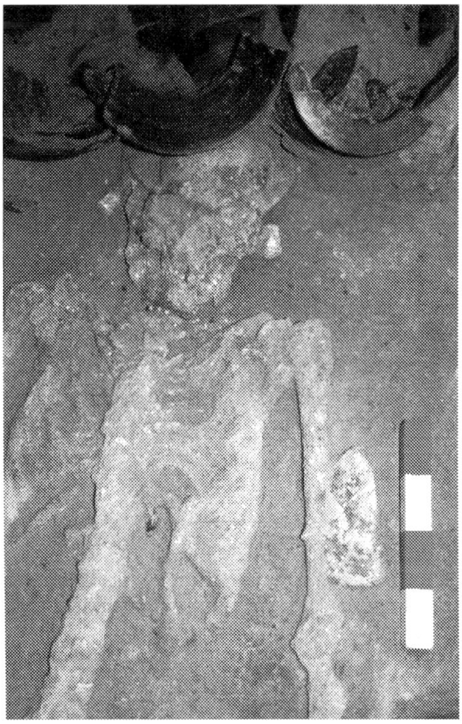

Figure 3.13 Noen U-Loke burial of a woman wearing gold, agate, silver and bronze jewellery. (Burial 113.) (Charles Higham.)

The fifth and final mortuary phase at Noen U-Loke saw the end of the rice-filled graves and tight clustering of burials, and a reduction in the wealth of grave goods. However, we can also recognize other important changes. One man was found interred with an arrowhead through his spine. This was also a period when iron weaponry proliferated in the occupation layers. Iron sickles were now placed as grave goods. There appears to have been a growth in militarism and agricultural intensity with the growing population and foundation of new settlements in the valley. This final phase before the site was abandoned brings us to the verge of early states in the region, manifested in the construction of brick temples dedicated to the ancestors, local gods and gods from the Hindu pantheon.

For years, the nature of the moats around many of these Iron Age settlements in Mainland Southeast Asia has been enigmatic. By cutting deep sections through them at Noen U-Loke and other sites in the study area, William Boyd and his colleagues have identified their structure and date.[46] He has found that the banks round the site confined water brought into the moats by natural stream channels. AMS radiocarbon dates from the banks and the channels themselves date these huge water-control structures to the late Iron Age, between about AD 100 and 500.

We still lack evidence for the purpose of the moats, which might well have been multiple. Defence of the settlements is one possibility, for this was the period when the number of iron arrowheads increased markedly. As populations grew, so there would also have been a need for a predictable domestic water supply in the dry season, while extensive moats would also have provided a source of food. However, changing river patterns, quickened by deforestation and increased siltation, may well have caused the river channels to move away from some Iron Age sites, thereby encouraging abandonment. Noen U-Loke now lies, unoccupied, some distance from the village of Ban Nong Na and its river. In this regard, the local smelting of iron, casting of bronze and production of salt had profound environmental consequences, for all led to increasing deforestation.

The upper Mun Valley contains two major temple sites dating to the period of Angkor (from AD 800). Excavations at both have revealed earlier Iron Age occupation. At Phanom Wan, an Iron Age cemetery flanks the central sanctuary and contains a grave similar to those from Noen U-Loke lying on the same orientation as the sanctuary above. A layer with Iron Age pottery underlies the central temple at Phimai.[47] These sequences strongly support local origins for the regional expressions in Thailand of the civilization of Angkor. In central Thailand, sites like Ban Don Ta Phet anticipate the genesis of the state of Dvaravati, while the Sa Huynh culture was to develop into the civilization of Champa. Thus can we appreciate how the first civilizations of Southeast Asia had their origins deep in the prehistoric past.

Notes

1 Anderson 1990, Albrecht *et al.* n.d.
2 Higham and Thosarat 1998; Boyd 1998; Mason 1998; O'Reilly 1998.
3 Higham and Bannanurag 1990, Higham and Thosarat 1994, Pisnupong 1993; Mason 1991.
4 Tayles 1999.
5 Higham and Lu 1998, Pei 1998.
6 Lai Van Toi 1999.
7 Hoang Xuan Chinh and Nguyen Ngoc Bich 1978.
8 Ha Van Tan 1980.
9 Nguyen Kim Dung 1990, 1998.
10 Hoang Xuan Chinh 1968.
11 Ha Van Tan 1993.
12 Bui Vinh 1995.
13 YPM 1977, 1981.
14 Bayard 1971, 1972a, 1972b.
15 Rispoli 1997.
16 Sørensen and Hatting 1967.
17 Leong Sau Heng 1991.
18 Diffloth 1994.
19 Solheim 1968, Gorman and Charoenwongsa 1976.
20 Meacham 1993, Moore and Pauk 2001.
21 Liang Jingjin 1978.
22 GXBWG 1984.
23 An Zhimin 1998.
24 Meacham 1975, 1994.
25 Natapintu 1988, Pigott *et al.* 1997, Pigott and Weisgerber 1998.
26 Higham and Kijngam 1984.
27 Higham and Thosarat 1998.
28 Ha Van Phung 1979.
29 Ngo Si Hong 1987.
30 Trinh Sinh (1977).
31 Nguyen Kim Dung 1998.
32 Ha Van Tan (1980).
33 Le Van Thieu (1979).
34 Moore and U Pauk 2001.
35 Pirazzoli-t'Serstevens 1974.
36 Nguyen Giang Hai and Nguyen Van Hung 1983.
37 VMH 1965.
38 Glover 1980, 1983; Rajpitak and Seeley 1979.

39 Reinecke 1996.
40 Sørensen 1979.
41 Mankong 1989.
42 Pautreau *et al.* 1997, Pautreau and Mornais 1998.
43 Reinecke 1996, 1998.
44 Nitta 1991.
45 Indrawooth *et al.* 1990.
46 McGrath and Boyd 2001.
47 Talbot and Janthed 2001.

Select Bibliography

General

Blust, R. (1996) "Beyond the Austronesian homeland: the Austric hypothesis and its implications for archaeology", in W. H. Goodenough (ed.), *Prehistoric Settlement of the Pacific*, 117–40. Philadelphia: American Philosophical Society.

Diffloth, G. (1994) "The lexical evidence for Austric, so far", *Oceanic Linguistics* 33: 309–22.

Higham, C. F. W. (1996) *The Bronze Age of Southeast Asia*, Cambridge University Press.

Higham, C. F. W. and Lu, T. (1998) "The origins and dispersal of rice cultivation", *Antiquity* 72: 867–77.

Higham, C. F. W. (2002) *Early Cultures of Mainland Southeast Asia*, Bangkok: River Books.

Pei, A. (1998) "Notes on new advancements and revelations in the agricultural archaeology of early rice domestication in the Dongting Lake region", *Antiquity* 72: 878–85.

Archaeology – Thailand, Burma, Malaysia

Albrecht, G., Berke, H., Burger, D., Moser, J., Muller-Beck, H., Pookajorn, S., Rahle, W. and Urban, N.D. B. (1993) "Sakai Cave, Trang Province, Southern Thailand", report on the Field Work.

Anderson, D. D. (1990) *Lang Rongrien Rockshelter: a Pleistocene-Early Holocene Archaeological Site from Krabi, Southwestern Thailand*, Philadelphia: University Museum Monograph 71.

Bayard, D. T. (1971) "Non Nok Tha: the 1968 excavation, procedure, stratigraphy and a summary of the evidence", New Zealand: Otago University Studies in Prehistoric Anthropology No. 4.

Bayard, D. T. (1972a) "Excavations at Non Nok Tha, Northeastern Thailand 1968: an interim report", *Asian Perspectives* 13: 109–43.

Bayard, D. T. (1972b) "Early Thai bronze: analysis and new dates", *Science* 176: 1411–2.

Boyd, W. E. (1998) "The palaeoenvironment of the archaeological site at Nong Nor", in C. F. W. Higham and R. Thosarat (eds) *The Excavation of Nong Nor, a Prehistoric Site in Central Thailand*, 27–86, New Zealand: Otago University Studies in Prehistoric Anthropology No. 18.

Glover, I. C. (1980) "Ban Don Ta Phet and its relevence to problems in the pre- and protohistory of Thailand", *Bulletin of the Indo-Pacific Prehistory Association* 2: 16–30.

Glover, I. C. (1983) "Excavations at Ban Don Ta Phet, Kanchanaburi Province, Thailand, 1980–1", *South-East Asian Studies Newsletter* 10: 1–4.

Gorman, C. F. and Charoenwongsa, P. (1976) "Ban Chiang: a mosaic of impressions from the first two years", *Expedition* 8(4): 14–26.

Higham C. F. W. and Bannanurag, R. (1990) *The Excavation of Khok Phanom Di, Volume I: The Excavation, Chronology and Human Burials*, London: Society of Antiquaries.

Higham, C. F. W. and Kijngam, A. (eds) (1984) *Prehistoric Investigations in Northeast Thailand*, Oxford: British Archaeological Reports (International Series) 231 (1–3).

Higham, C. F. W. and Thosarat, R. (1994) *Khok Phanom Di. Prehistoric Adaptation to the World's Richest Habitat*, Dallas-Fort Worth: Harcourt Brace Jovanovich.

Higham, C. F. W. and Thosarat, R. (eds) (1998) *The Excavation of Nong Nor, a Prehistoric Site in Central Thailand*, New Zealand: Otago University Studies in Prehistoric Anthropology No. 18.

Indrawooth, P., Krabuansang, S. and Narkwake, P. (1990) "Archaeological study of Ban Krabuang Nok", *SPAFA Digest*, XI: 12–20.

Leong Sau Heng (1991) "Jenderam Hilir and the mid-Holocene prehistory of the west coast plain of Peninsular Malaysia", *Bulletin of the Indo-Pacific Prehistory Association* 10: 150–60.

Mankong, S. (1989) *Noen Ma Kok* (in Thai), Bangkok: Fine Arts Department.

Mason, G. M. (1991) "The molluscan remains", in C. F. W. Higham and R. Bannanurag (eds) *The Excavation of Khok Phanom Di, Volume II: The Biological Remains (Part I)*, pp. 259–319, Research Reports of the Society of Antiquaries of London No. XLVIII.

Mason, G. M. (1998) "The shellfish, fish and crab remains", in C. F. W. Higham and R. Thosarat (eds), *The Excavation of Nong Nor*, pp. 173–211, Oxford: Oxbow.

McGrath, R. and Boyd, W. E. (2001) "The chronology of Iron Age 'moats' of northeast Thailand", *Antiquity* 75: 349–60.

Moore, E. and Pauk Pauk, U. (2001) "A preliminary note on a Bronze Age cemetery near Mandalay, Myanmar (Burma)", *Asian Perspectives* 40(1); 35–47.

Natapintu, S. (1988) "Current research on ancient copper-base metallurgy in Thailand", in P. Charoenwongsa and B. Bronson (eds) *Prehistoric Studies: the Stone Age and Metal Ages in Thailand*, pp. 107–24. Bangkok: Thai Antiquity Working Group.

Nitta, E. (1991) "Archaeological study on the ancient iron-smelting and salt-making industries in the northeast of Thailand: Preliminary report on the excavations of Non Yang and Ban Don Phlong", *Journal of Southeast Asian Archaeology* 11: 1–46.

O'Reilly, D. J. W. (1998) "Comparative analysis between Nong Nor phase I and Khok Phanom Di", in C. F. W. Higham and R. Thosarat (eds) *The Excavation of Nong Nor*, pp. 161–72, Oxford: Oxbow Books.

Pautreau, J.-P. and Mornais, P. (1998) "Le cimetière protohistorique de Ban Wang Hi", *Archeologia* 351: 46–54.

Pautreau, J.-P., Matringhem, A. and Mornais, P. (1997) "Excavation at Ban Wang Hi, Lamphun Province, Thailand", *Journal of the Siam Society* 85: 161–72.

Pigott, V. C. (1998) "Prehistoric copper mining in the context of emerging community craft specialization in northeast Thailand", in A. B. Knapp, V. C. Pigott and E. W. Herbert (eds) *Social Approaches to and Industrial Past. The Archaeology and Anthropology of Mining*, pp. 205–25, London: Routledge.

Pigott, V. C. and Weisgerber, G. (1998) "Mining archaeology in geological context: The prehistoric copper mining complex at Phu Lon, Nong Khai Province, northeast Thailand", in T. Rehren, A. Hauptmann and J. D. Muhly (eds) *Metallurgica Antiqua: In Honor of Hans-Bert Bachmann and Robert Maddin*, pp. 135–62, Bochum: Deutsches Bergbau-Museum.

Pigott, V. C., Weiss, A. D. and Natapintu. S. (1997) "The archaeology of copper production: excavations in the Khao Wong Prachan Valley, Central Thailand", in R. Ciarla and F. Rispoli (eds) *South-East Asian Archaeology 1992*, pp. 119–57, Rome: Istituto Italiano per L'Africa e L'Oriente.

Pisnupong, P. (1993) "The industrial stone technology", in C. F. W. Higham and R. Thosarat (eds) *The Excavation of Khok Phanom Di, Volume III: The Material Culture (Part I)*, London: Society of Antiquaries.

Rajpitak, W. and Seeley, N. J. (1979) "The bronze bowls from Ban Don Ta Phet: an enigma of prehistoric metallurgy", *World Archaeology* 11(1): 26–31.

Rispoli, F (1997) "Late 3rd–2nd millennium BC. pottery traditions in Central Thailand: some preliminary observations in a wider perspective", in R. Ciarla and F. Rispoli (eds) *South-East Asian Archaeology 1992*, pp. 59–97, Rome: Istituto Italiano per L'Africa e L'Oriente.

Solheim, W. G. II (1968) "Early bronze in Northeastern Thailand", *Current Anthropology* 9: 59–62.

Sørensen, P. (1979) "The Ongbah cave and its fifth drum", R. B. Smith and W. Watson (eds) *Early South East Asia*, pp. 78–97, Oxford: Oxford University Press.

Sørensen, P. and Hatting, T. (1967) *Archaeological Investigations in Thailand, Vol. II, Ban Kao, Part 1: The Archaeological Materials from the Burials*, Copenhagen: Munksgaard.

Talbot, S. and Janthed, C. (2001). "Northeast Thailand before Angkor: evidence from an archaeological excavation at the Prasat Hin Phimai", *Asian Perspectives* 40(2): 179–94.

Tayles, N. G. (1999) *The Excavation of Khok Phanom Di: A Prehistoric Site in Central Thailand, Vol. V, The People*, London: Research Reports of the Society of Antiquaries of London, No. LXI.

Archaeology – China, Vietnam, Central Asia

An Zhimin (1998) "Cultural complexes of the Bronze Age in the Tarim Basin and surrounding areas", in V. H. Mair (ed.) *The Bronze Age and Early Iron Age Peoples of Eastern Central Asia*, pp. 45–62, Philadelphia: Institute for the Study of Man.
Bui Vinh (1995) "Initial steps on determining areas of distributions and characteristics of stone artefacts of the Ha Giang culture" (in Vietnamese), *Khao Co Hoc* 3: 33–45.
GXBWG (Museum of the Guangxi Zhuang Autonomous Region) (1984) "Pre-Qin bronze artefacts recovered from Guangxi in recent years" (in Chinese), *Kaogu* 798–806.
Ha Van Phung (1979) "In search of relations between Go Mun and Dong Son cultures" (in Vietnamese), *Khao Co Hoc* 29: 43–61.
Ha Van Tan (1980) "Nouvelles récherches préhistoriques et protohistoriques au Viet Nam", *Bulletin de l'École Française d'Extrême Orient* 68: 113–54.
Ha Van Tan (1993) "*Yazhang* plaques in the Phung Nguyen culture sites" (in Vietnamese), *Khao Co Hoc* 86: 16–27.
Hoang Xuan Chinh (1968) *Bao Cao Khai Quat Dot Di Chi Lung Hoa*, Hanoi: Nha Xuat Ban Khoa Hoc Xa Hoi.
Hoang Xuan Chinh and Nguyen Ngoc Bich (1978) *The Excavation of the Archaeological Site of Phung Nguyen* (in Vietnamese), Hanoi: Nha Xuat Ban Khoa Hoc Xa Hoi.
Lai Van Toi (1999) "The initial inhabitants of Co Loa" (in Vietnamese), *Khao Co Hoc* 3: 39–54.
Le Van Thieu (1979) "The wild pig and the domestic swine from the site of Hoa Loc (Thanh Hoa)" (in Vietnamese), *Khao Co Hoc* 2: 37–42.
Liang Jingjin (1978) "Bronze artefacts recovered in Guanxi" (in Chinese), *Wenwu* 10: 93–6.
Meacham, W. (1975) "Schofield and Shek Pik in retrospect", in W. Meacham (ed.) *An Archaeological Site at Shek Pik*, pp. v–ix. Journal Monograph I, Hong Kong: Hong Kong Archaeological Society.
Meacham, W. (1993) "New C14 dates and advances in establishing a precise chronology for Hong Kong's prehistory", *Journal of the Hong Kong Archaeological Society* XIII: 115–7.
Meacham, W. (1994) "On the dating of painted pottery in Hong Kong", unpublished paper read at the conference on Painted Pottery, Chinese University of Hong Kong, February.
Ngo Si Hong (1987) "Back to Dong Dau and fresh knowledge of it" (in Vietnamese), *Khao Co Hoc* 1: 22–35
Nguyen Giang Hai and Nguyen Van Hung (1983) "Bronze items just unearthed at Co Loa (Hanoi)" (in Vietnamese), *Khao Co Hoc* 47: 21–32.
Nguyen Kim Dung (1990) "The lithic workshop at Trang Kenh" (in Vietnamese), *Khao Co Hoc* 3: 64–82.
Nguyen Kim Dung (1998) "Nephrite and jadeite manufacturing tradition in prehistoric Vietnam" (in Vietnamese), *Khao Co Hoc* 4: 15–22.
Pirazzoli-t'Serstevens, M. (1974) *La Civilization du Royaume de Dian à l'Époque Han*, Paris: Ecole Française d'Extrême-Orient.
Reinecke, A. (1996) "Ohrringe mit tierkopfenden in Sudostasien", *Beitrage zur Allgemeinen und Vergleichenden Archaeologie* 16: 5–51.
Reinecke, A. (1998) *Einführung in die Archäeologie Vietnams*, Cologne: Linden Soft.
Trinh Sinh, (1977) "From the stone ring to the bronze rings" (in Vietnamese), *Khao Co Hoc* 2/3: 51–6.
VMH (Vietnam Museum of History) (1965) *Ngoi Mo Co Viet Khe*, Xuet Ban, Hanoi.
YPM (Yunnan Provincial Museum) (1977) "The Neolithic site of Ta-Tun-Tzu in Yuan-Mo County, Yunnan Province" (in Chinese), *Kaogu Xuebao* 43–72.
YPM (Yunnan Provincial Museum) (1981) "The Baiyangcun site in Binchuan County, Yunnan Province" (in Chinese), *Kaogu Xuebao* 349–68.

4

THE ARCHAEOLOGY OF EARLY CONTACT WITH INDIA AND THE MEDITERRANEAN WORLD, FROM THE FOURTH CENTURY BC TO THE FOURTH CENTURY AD

Bérénice Bellina and Ian Glover

Introduction

From early in the first millennium AD, elite groups in many parts of Southeast Asia, except in the remote and forested interior of the mainland or in the eastern islands of Indonesia and the Philippines, adopted Hindu and Buddhist cults, political ideologies and ritual language as shown by the many religious monuments, images and inscriptions. There are some ambiguous external historical sources, Chinese and Indian, such as the accounts of the mysterious kingdom of Funan in the Mekong River Delta of present-day Cambodia and Vietnam, translated from Chinese sources and compiled by the French scholar Paul Pelliot, and the *Arthasastra* of Kautilya, which record the process of "Indianization". The textual data are presented and analysed in numerous books and articles[1] and this historical information is not considered in this chapter, which deals almost exclusively with the surviving material evidence from archaeology.

According to the periods in which they wrote, and the scholars' background, various explanations have been proposed for this process. Early in the twentieth century, the European colonization of Asia led many scholars to think that the transfer of Indian culture was due to large-scale migration of Indians to Southeast Asia. This scenario was carried to an extreme by supporters of the "Greater India" movement, such that the renowned scholar R. C. Majumdar could assert that "the Hindu colonists brought with them the whole framework of their culture and civilization and this was transplanted in its entirety among the people who had yet not emerged from their primitive barbarism".[2] In contrast to this colonialist approach, O. W. Wolters has written of the selective "localization" of Indian cultural elements and emphasized the innovative and dynamic character of Southeast Asian societies.[3] In a rather similar vein, Kulke speaks of "convergence" between small principalities on both sides of the Bay of Bengal, linked by a complex network of exchange relations and being partners in a mutual process of civilization.[4] Nowadays, all regional specialists agree that acculturation in this region, whether one wants to call it "Indianization", "localization" or "convergence", was clearly linked to expanding trade networks and more especially to the maritime routes. In order to understand this process, it is necessary to study the formation and evolution of these networks across an area from the eastern coasts of the Indian subcontinent to the different regions of Southeast Asia.

Exchange networks in South Asia and Southeast Asia*

During the period under study, India witnessed the emergence of several mature states: the Mauryas, Kushanas and the Guptas in North India, and the Satavahanas in the Deccan. South India also contained some powerful chiefdoms such as the Cheras, Cholas and the Pandyas, some of which emerged as urbanized kingdoms such as that of the Pallavas, who ruled modern-day Tamil Nadu during the third/fourth to the ninth centuries AD. Despite the political plurality, what mattered for trade was the codification of crafts under guilds, which acted as banks and places for investment and the monetarization of parts of the economy, as shown by the wide range of coins issued by cities in different areas. Trade based on profit is well described in the *Arthasastra*, and an elaborate bureaucracy developed, especially in the Mauryan state. There was a considerable development of both overland and maritime trade routes, although with many regional variations in the organization of trade. The period also saw the rise of specialized trading communities (*vanijas* and *setthis*) in the middle Ganga Valley, dealing in salt, textiles, metals and pottery.

The newly spreading cults of Buddhism and Jainism accepted the accumulation and reinvestment of wealth; a concept quite alien to the culture of the earlier Vedic period in which reciprocal exchange of the "prestige goods" type had been the normal method of distributing exotic and luxury items. Long-distance trade between the agricultural hinterland of the middle Ganga Valley, ports such as Gange and Tamralipti in the Delta, and those at the mouth of the Narmada Valley on the west coast such as Broach (Barygaza in the *Periplus*), developed rapidly at this time. The gemfields and gold-rich deposits of South India were quickly integrated into these trading systems.[5]

With a lack of written records, we cannot analyse in the same detail as India the structure of exchange within Southeast Asia for the thousand years from the fifth century BC onwards. Good archaeological documentation is still scarce and we depend overmuch on models based on analogies from more recent historical and ethnographic situations. For instance, Bronson, Wheatley, Wolters, Miksic and Wisseman Christie have all proposed evolutionary or structural models for Southeast Asian exchange systems.[6] Although useful, these are generalized and abstract and, for the most part, lack firm support from empirical data from the past.

However, we know that late prehistoric settlements of the second and early first millennia BC in Mainland Southeast Asia regularly occur in small stream valleys which feed the major river systems. These, perhaps quite isolated, villages were linked by far-reaching exchange networks which saw marine shell ornaments being taken over 1,000 km from the coast, and copper and tin ingots and artefacts entering communities far removed from the ore sources. Marble, marine shell, serpentine and other rare stone material, ceramics and doubtless many perishable items exchanged hands along the river systems. As Higham in chapter 3 makes clear, the middle of the first millennium BC in

*See Chapter 6, Figure 6.3.

Southeast Asia was a period of profound economic, social and political change. The Iron Age in Southeast Asia was marked by increases in wealth and social complexity leading to powerful territorial polities. Large or valuable objects, such as Dong Son bronze drums and nephrite ornaments from Vietnam, arrived by sea to enter long-established exchange routes along the rivers. Thus, it is evident that intra and inter-regional exchange routes were well developed before they were linked to the more developed South Asian trading systems.

Wisseman Christie has argued for the emergence of three clusters of producer-trading states in Peninsular Malaysia during late centuries BC.[7] But throughout most of Southeast Asia at this time, the highest level of political organization was what might be called chiefly society, or at best some nascent states in which and barter and gift-giving were likely to have been the principal modes of exchange, since there is no evidence for coinage. In central Vietnam, the Sa-Huynh Culture probably represented a culturally-related series of chiefdoms which were closely involved in overseas trade, as shown by the Sa-Huynh, or Sa-Huynh influenced, artefacts and urn burials widely distributed in the Philippines, northern Indonesia and parts of Thailand.

The role of Indo-Roman trade in the articulation of South and Southeast Asian exchange networks

Although our knowledge of intra-regional trading networks is uneven, archaeology provides evidence enough to demonstrate that they were already dynamic and expanding before they became interlinked. These networks were greatly stimulated by their integration into Indian trade to the west. Indo-Roman commerce had generated a rising demand for exotic and prestigious items of consumption and adornment in the urban civilizations of the Mediterranean Basin – that "splendid and trifling" trade in spices, perfumes, precious stones and pearls, silks and muslin, tortoiseshell, ivory and rhinoceros horn, dyes and ungents, ghee, lac and so on scorned by the high-minded historian, Edmund Gibbon, for undermining Roman republican virtues. Unfortunately most of the traded items mentioned in the classical texts were perishable and archaeologists can rely only on those surviving the tropical conditions.

As an example of the demand for exotic products in the west, one need only look at the spice trade and particularly at the trade in cloves, the unopened flower buds of the tree *Eugenia aromatica*, whose home was in the northern Moluccan islands of eastern Indonesia. Cloves were already known in China in the third century BC, and were described by Pliny in Rome in the first century AD. At the production end, the trade in cloves, nutmeg and mace transformed Moluccan society from scattered kin-based communities of hunter-gatherers and shifting cultivators to stratified coastal trading states and petty empires. As one author has pointed out,

> It was the spice trade which was partially responsible for the Indianization of Southeast Asia and which later facilitated the spread of Islam. So this western demand for an aromatic flower bud of rather little value to the native peoples of the Moluccas transformed, in the long run, the economic and political face of Asia.[8]

Later in this chapter we emphasize some of the most frequent and enduring materials found in late prehistoric archaeological contexts in India and Southeast Asia which provide evidence for this contact and exchange; especially pottery and bronze vessels and ornaments of semiprecious stone and glass, coins and seals. However, it must also be remembered that ideas and technologies also travelled; glass-making was one, as some of its products survive to bear witness. We also believe that the techniques of iron-smelting and forging were taken from India to Southeast Asia in the mid-first millennium BC, although no iron products of certain Indian manufacture have so far been identified from Southeast Asian sites. The tradition of making large stone slab tombs and other "megalithic" structures in western Indonesia and the Malay Peninsula may also reflect these early links, although those of Neolithic Beinan in southeastern Taiwan probably have an entirely local origin.

Coins, seals and other rarely found objects

Roman coins of gold, silver and copper have been found in very large quantities in India, particularly in the south, but only a few seem to have been carried further east and the contexts of these finds are always unclear. They include the well-known second century AD medallions of Marcus Aurelius and Antoninus Pius found at Oc Eo, a third-century copper coin of Victorinus from U-Thong in Thailand (Figure 4.1), and another Roman coin, too worn to be properly identified, found at Khuan Lukpad in Peninsular Thailand (see Figure 6.5). Of clear Indian origin is an ivory comb from Chansen Phase II decorated with a pair of horses, a *hamsa* and a "vase of abundance" (Figure 4.2). Carnelian intaglios and seals, two at least of well-known second-century AD Roman types, were found at Khuan Lukpad. Many other seals and sealings, some "classicizing" and others with Brahmi or Kharoshthi inscriptions, or images of boats, have been found

Figure 4.1 A copper coin of Western Roman Emperor Victorinus (AD 268–70) found at U-Thong, Thailand. (Photograph by I. C. Glover.)

Figure 4.2 Ivory comb from Chansen Phase II, Western Thailand, decorated with a pair of horses, a *hamsa* and a "vase of abundance". The find was dated to the third century AD. (Drawing courtesy of the publishers of *Asian Perspectives*.)

there as well as at a number of other Southeast Asian sites. This material is quite well known and has recently been described in a number of books and articles by Himanshu Ray; it is more thoroughly discussed and illustrated in chapter 6 by Phasook Indrawooth. Unfortunately, very little of this material may be attributed to a specific context and the date of its arrival in Southeast Asia may only be guessed at. What we can be reasonably sure of is that all these western items came to the region from, or via, India; thus they provide support for the development of early contacts across the Bay of Bengal.

Stages in the development of Indian – Southeast Asian exchange links

A study of the different traded materials allows us to confirm the existence of two distinct phases. The first seems to start about the fourth century BC and to end around the second century AD. The scattered evidence of this phase (Phase I) enabled the Dutch historian Van Leur to refer to regular but less intense and archaeologically less-visible contacts that preceded Indianization.[9] During Phase II (second–fourth century AD), intra and inter-regional exchange intensified. From about the mid-fifth century AD, fully Indianized kingdoms appear in Burma, Thailand, Cambodia, coastal Vietnam and western Indonesia, and this theme is taken up in subsequent chapters of the book.

Phase I (fourth century BC to second century AD)

Trade between the classical world and India

Indo-Roman commercial undertakings seem to have been highly organized and are quite well documented in classical writing dating from the second century AD, even though there is much uncertainty about the details. Revisions are regularly proposed for dating the growth of this trade from the evidence provided by archaeology. We argue that virtually all new data on this trade is likely to come from archaeology, which has barely started to research the problem, rather than from literary and historical sources, which seem to be finite and mostly known.

In India, there is abundant physical evidence of trade in the form of Mediterranean amphorae and Italic Arretine ware on the South Indian coast, of Roman gold-coin hoards throughout South India, and of numerous classical intaglios and seals throughout southern India and Sri Lanka. There is also Mediterranean lead in the Satavahana coinage of Central and Eastern Deccan. In the Mediterranean, although Asian imports have largely died (slaves and elephants) or decayed beyond recognition (silks and cotton, wood and lacquer), there exists a remarkable reminder of this trade in the form of the exquisite Indian ivory figurine buried under the ash of Pompeii.[10]

But what is lacking in identifiable artefacts is more than made up by the wealth of textual data. For instance, there are detailed contemporary descriptions of the structure of the trade in the *Periplus*, in Strabo's and Ptolemy's *Geographies* and Pliny's *Natural History*.[11] There is sufficient detail that historians such as Rashke and archaeologists such as Wheeler have been able to develop a comprehensive and, on the whole, convincing structure for trade between India and the Roman world, as it existed at the beginning of the Christian era.[12] These exchange systems were more developed than those described for Southeast Asia and approximate to the "Middleman", and "Port of Trade" modes. In many cases, particularly at the western ends of the trade routes, these were entrepreneurial ventures undertaken for commercial profit, facilitated by the use of coinage and underwritten by accumulated capital.

The trade between India and Southeast Asia

In Southeast Asia, very few items may securely be assigned to the western world. Those reaching the region, such as a few coins and intaglios, came through South Asia. The bulk of the archaeological evidence consists of Indian or Indian-made objects, some of which show western influence. In Phase I they are found in non-Indianized contexts. The first evidence of regular exchange consists in glass and stone beads and ornaments, and ceramic and bronze vessels. It seems to us that vessels of this phase are very similar to Indian types, whether imported or locally made. They testify already frequent exchange. Three types of vessels seem to characterize this period; bronze containers with a central knob or cone, pottery rouletted wares, and stamped wares.

SEMIPRECIOUS STONE BEADS AND PENDANTS

During Phase I, the semiprecious stones agate and carnelian, and to a lesser extent rock crystal and nephrite, were used for most of the beads and pendants widely found in Southeast Asia, replacing the softer materials such as serpentine, limestone, marble and shell used to make ornaments beforehand. These new types of ornament have chiefly been discovered unevenly distributed in burials, indicating that they were probably the valued possessions of an emerging elite who used them in life, as in death, as indicators of status. The rich finds of agate and carnelian beads at sites such as Ban Don Ta Phet (Plate 2), Khao Sam Kaeo and Noen U-Loke in Thailand, at Giong Ca Vo and other Sa Huynh sites in Vietnam, at Gilimanuk in Bali and Leang Buidane in the Talaud Islands, Indonesia, show the wide acceptance of these new materials.[13]

In addition to the simple beads of agate and carnelian there are some very unusual lion pendants from Ban Don Ta Phet (Plate 3), Ban U Taphao and Khao Sam Kaeo. (They occur also in Han Period tombs in South China), all of which have close Indian correlates. Alkaline-etched agate and carnelian beads must also be brought into the picture. This very specialized craft tradition originated 4,500 years ago in the Harappan period and such beads were widely manufactured in India from about 600 BC. The presence in the late centuries BC of spectacular decorated stone beads in Burma, Thailand, Vietnam, Yunnan, Indonesia and in the Philippines may best be understood through the operation of exchange networks.

For a long time it has been assumed that all the agate and carnelian found in Southeast Asia in this early period (as with glass ornaments – see below) originated in India. This is because South Asian workshops developed the highly skilled techniques to make fine beads out of these hard stones. The richest sources of microcrystalline quartz rocks known in antiquity are also in the volcanic rocks of the Deccan Plateau. Furthermore, no beads made of these materials have yet been found in Southeast Asian contexts prior to the Iron Age.

Until the early centuries AD, the assumption of Indian origin probably remains true. But from this period onwards we find evidence of local manufacture at Khuan Lukpad and Kuala Selinsing, both on the western coast of the Thai-Malay Peninsula, and to a lesser extent at Oc Eo in southern Vietnam. Whether the raw materials came from South

Asia or if Southeast Asians had found and started to exploit local sources, as some recent trace element studies seem to suggest, is not yet known.[14]

Agate and carnelian are difficult to work and require skilled techniques including the knowledge of how to heat the stone to make it easier to knap and to induce changes in colour by heating and staining. This led Peter Francis to suggest, and Bérénice Bellina to demonstrate, that some Indian craftsmen probably settled in Southeast Asia.[15] When local workshops first developed, and how much Indian influence was involved in the specialized craft of bead-making, are among important topics currently being investigated.[16]

GLASS IN SOUTH AND SOUTHEAST ASIA

Glass, mainly in the form of beads, appears commonly in archaeological sites in South and Southeast Asia in the first millennium BC and more or less accompanies the regular adoption of iron. The first finds of true glass from the Indian subcontinent occur in the Iron Age painted grey-ware culture of northern India from about 1000 BC. From this time onwards glass beads were regularly made in many parts of the subcontinent, although few sites are closely dated and most beads are casual finds lacking specific contexts.[17] Francis identified four regional traditions of early-glass making in India, of which by far the most important for the exchange with Southeast Asia was on the Tamil Nadu coast. Here, Arikamedu and Karakaidu, south of Madras, were the best-known production sites, where the beads were drawn into long hollow tubes and then cut into sections to be annealed. Francis refers to these as "Indo-Pacific Monochrome Drawn Glass Beads", or more simply "Indo-Pacific Beads", and they were manufactured in Southern India from at least the fourth century BC. They were widely traded for over 1,500 years to Africa, Japan and Korea, as well as to Southeast Asia. Production was dominated by small opaque monochrome red beads often known as *mutisalah* ("false pearls") in Indonesia, where they are particularly common.

Based on a study of manufacturing debris from archaeological sites, Francis concluded that beads of this tradition were also made at various times from the first century BC onwards at Mantai and Anuradhapura in Sri Lanka, Khuan Lukpad and Satingpra in southern Thailand, Kuala Selinsing in Malaya, Muara Jambi in Sumatra, and Oc-eo in Vietnam.[18] Two features tend to distinguish early South Asian from West Asian and European glasses, these being a high alumina (Al2O3 >3.5–4 per cent) and low lime content (CaO <4.5–5 per cent). From compositional analyses it is clear that Indian glass-makers at the turn of the Christian era used a number of distinct batch compositions to produce a range of clear, translucent coloured and opaque glass beads.

EARLY GLASS IN SOUTHEAST ASIA

A number of researchers have recently reviewed the evidence for early (i.e. prehistoric) glass in Southeast Asia and discussed the relationships with India.[19] The first glass is found in the middle of the first millennium BC at Iron Age sites in Peninsular and Central Thailand. Its spread closely matches that of iron. Indo-Pacific beads are the most common type, and among them opaque brown-red and orange-red *mutisalah* are most frequently found. In Thailand, they have been found in sites such as Ban Chiang, Ban Na Di, Non Muang, Ban Tha Kae, Ban Don Ta Phet, Prasat Muang Singh, Khao Sam Kaeo and Kok Ra Ka. They have also been found at Kuala Selinsing in Peninsular Malaysia and at Sembiran in Bali. Oc Eo in Vietnam has yielded the largest number of glass beads of any site in Southeast Asia and there was some local manufacture there, although some importation is also likely.

Ban Don Ta Phet (Kanchanaburi, Thailand) is important because it has yielded the best dated and widest range of glass beads with secure contexts of any site in Southeast Asia. A few bangles and distinctive ear ornaments were also found, and one typical Sa Huynh style two-headed animal ear pendant of nephrite from Vietnam (Figure 4.3). The site is an Iron Age secondary burial location dated to the early part of the fourth century BC (360–390 BC), with many semiprecious stone and glass beads, bronze vessels and ornaments, iron tools and weapons. Glover mentions that a number of the translucent glass beads at Don Ta Phet have cubic, bi-pyramidal, square prismatic or hexagonal prismatic shapes (Figure 4.4) and imitate the forms of natural mineral crystals, especially the famous beryl crystals of South India. Such crystal-shaped glass beads have been recorded only rarely in Southeast Asia.[20]

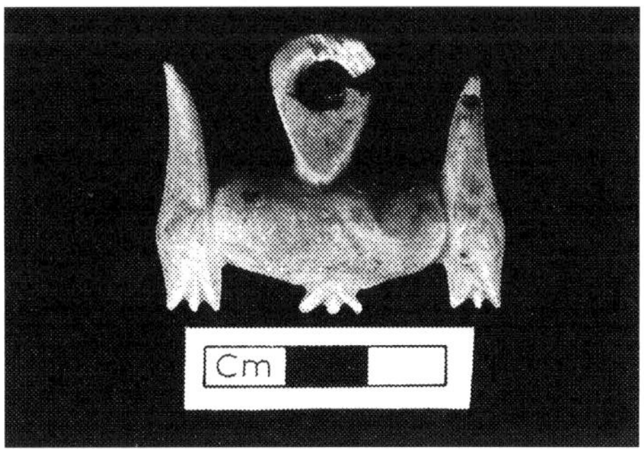

Figure 4.3 Sa Huynh style two-headed animal ear pendant of nephrite from Vietnam. Excavated at Ban Don Ta Phet, 1985. (Photograph by I. C. Glover.)

Early Southeast Asian glass beads may be grouped into two broad compositional types: mixed-alkali glass, and potash glass. The mixed alkali glass beads are all opaque red *mutisalah* beads with a high copper content, probably of Indian manufacture. The potash glasses include all colours and degrees of opacity and it is now generally thought that some were made locally in Southeast Asia, even at this early date, since they include forms never found in India. Khuan Lukpad, Tha Muang (U-Thong) and Oc Eo were glass bead manufacturing sites during the early centuries AD, but they have been much disturbed by bead diggers. There is as yet no unequivocal evidence to date the manufacture of raw glass back to the prehistoric period in Southeast Asia, although raw glass cullet may have been imported earlier than this and worked into beads and other ornaments.

BRONZE VESSELS WITH A CENTRAL CONE

This appears to be the most ancient container type indicating links between India and Southeast Asia, occurring at a few sites in central and western Thailand such as Ban Don Ta Phet, a cave at Khao Kwark in Ratchaburi Province (where a Dong Son Drum was also recovered) and from looted sites around Lopburi. At Ban Don Ta Phet about 30 high-tin bronze containers were excavated, many incomplete and very fragmentary. They have relatively flat bases and some have a number of concentric circles surrounding a central cone (Figure 4.5). The vessel walls are very thin – sometime less than 1 millimetre – and usually, but not always, have rather low sides, slightly curved to the exterior.[21] Metal vessels, probably bronze, also with a central cone, were found in the 1930s by the Swedish archaeologist Olov Janse in brick-built tombs of Chinese Han style at Dong Son, Thanh Hoa Province, dated to about the first century AD. Other, rather similar high-tin bronze bowls, but without the conical boss, have been found during tin-dredging operations in West Malaysia.

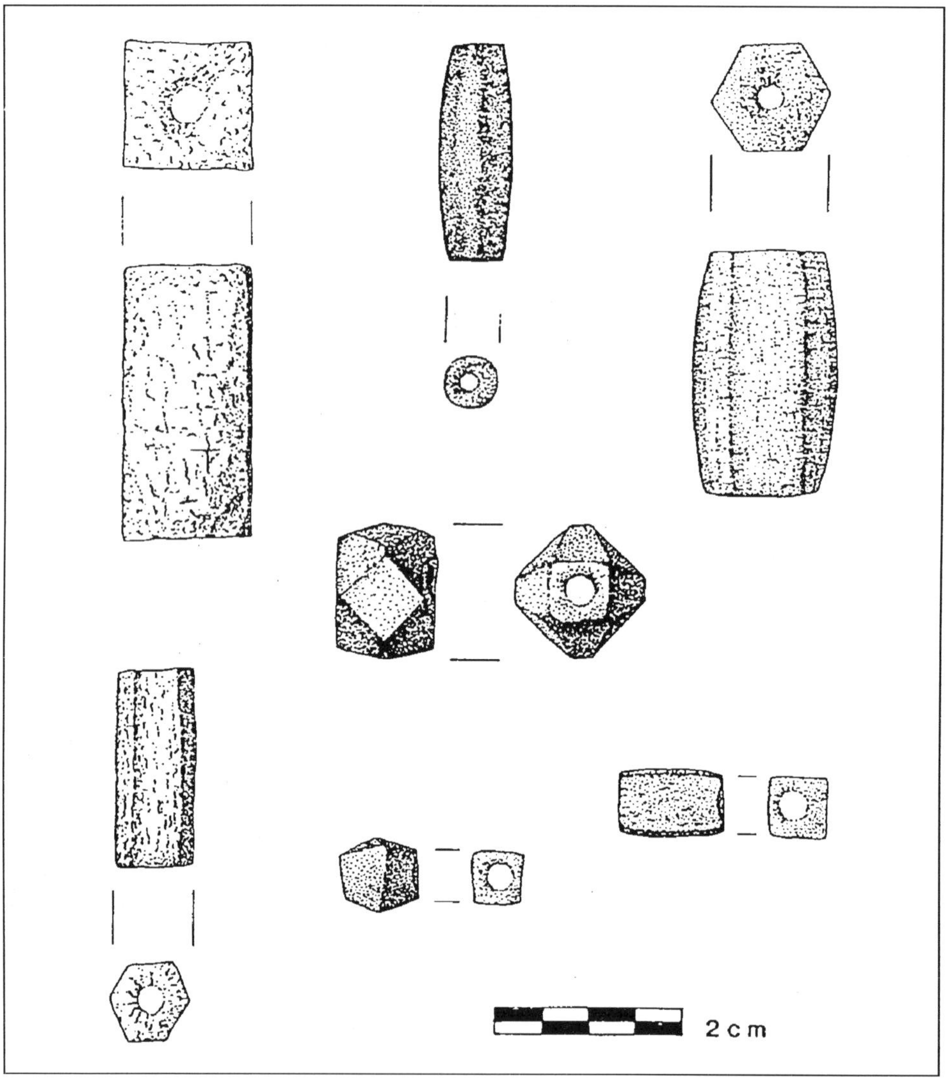

Figure 4.4 Translucent glass beads from Ban Don Ta Phet with cubic, bi-pyramidal, square prismatic or hexagonal prismatic shapes imitating the forms of natural mineral crystals, especially the famous beryl crystals of South India. (Drawing by A. Farrer.)

Examples of this type of container made from pottery, stone, bronze and silver have been found widely distributed in many different cultural settings in the Indian subcontinent. In pottery they occur in levels of the last centuries BC at Taxila in Pakistan, Varanasi in Uttar Pradesh, Nevasa in Maharashtra, Sisulpalgarh in Orissa, in Bengal and Bangladesh, in Andhra Pradesh, and at Arikamedu in Tamil Nadu. At Mahastangarh, in Bangladesh, vessels of this type in Northern Black Polished Ware are dated to the third–second centuries BC. One complete specimen made from black granite was recovered in the nineteenth century from the reliquary chamber of a ruined early Buddhist *stupa* near Taxila (Figure 4.6).

A great variety of silver, copper and bronze knobbed-base bowls were also found at both the Bhir and Sirkap mounds in Taxila. In southern India, bronze bowls of this type occur in megalithic graves in the Nilgiri Hills of Tamil Nadu. Casal excavated one at Souttoukeny dated to about the second century BC. Janse referred to a comment by Bruce Foote to the effect that such vessels "greatly resemble Graeco-Roman art works". In summary, these distinctive bowls, though far from common in Southeast Asia, can be said to be widespread in the subcontinent. It seems highly probable that the form has its origins in the West, even though the Asian examples exhibit shapes and decorative variations not known there. Janse compared the Vietnamese examples with the Megarian type of bronze bowl found in Macedonia, and when Marshall described the knobbed base vessels from Taxila he suggested that they may have been stylized versions of a Greek ceramic type known as the *phiales* bowl, common in the Mediterranean world in the third and second centuries BC.

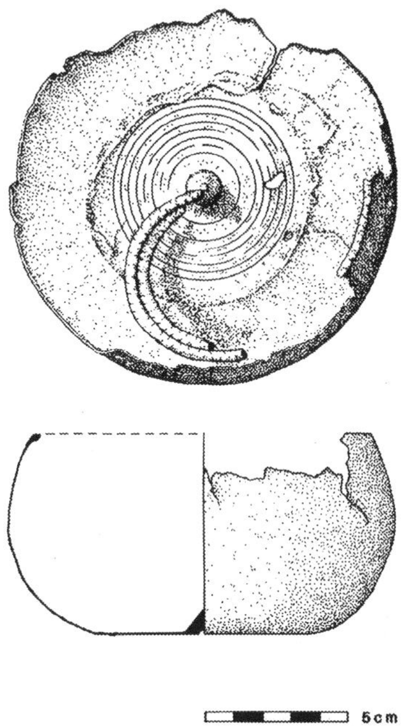

Figure 4.5 High-tin bronze bowl with central cone and concentric rings from Ban Don Ta Phet. (Drawing by Anne Farrer.)

Figure 4.6 Black granite bowl with central cone from the reliquary chamber of a stupa near Taxila, Pakistan. (Photograph courtesy of The British Museum.)

If the ultimate origin of this vessel form was among the western classical civilizations, they quickly spread into South Asia and soon after that into Southeast Asia. Arrival in India by the maritime route is unlikely owing to their absence on the western coast and it is more likely that they came by a land route. Gardin, who studied the pottery from Aï Khanum, commented that Hellenistic pottery forms, including Megarian bowls, very quickly reached Central Asia;[22] and it is possible to follow and date their spread via the Near East, Afghanistan and Pakistan, along the Ganga Valley, and then down the east coast of India into Tamil Nadu. Once they reached South Asia, the knobbed base bowl with a central cone underwent modifications in form and probably in function. Specification of the route(s) for the transmission of this vessel type to Southeast Asia remains for the future.

ROULETTED WARE

This wheel-made pottery constitutes a very significant item in the evidence for exchange between South and Southeast Asia. It has been well known in India since the excavations of Wheeler at Arikamedu in the 1940s. The most common form is a flat-based shallow dish, about 6 centimetres deep and up to 32 centimetres in diameter. The bevelled rim curves slightly inwards. The surface is highly polished, brown to red-grey in colour, and the interior body mainly grey. Decoration comprises one to three interior bands of impressed rouletted designs.[23] The flat vessel shape derives from the forms of protohistoric Black and Red Ware pottery (BRW) found in the earliest levels at Arikamedu which, together with Northern Black Polished Ware (NBPW), spread from the Ganga Valley into southern India during the Mauryan period.

Rouletted ware is found in many sites in the subcontinent, from the south to the northeast. Among these are Anuradhapura, Kantarodai and Mantai in Sri Lanka; Arikamedu, Karaikadu and Kodumanul in Tamil Nadu; Amaravati and Brahmagiri in Andhra Pradesh; Sisulpalgarh in Orissa; Tamluk and Chandraketugarh in Bengal; and Mahasthangarh in Bangla Desh. This distribution shows a pattern of trade along the east coast.

A tight chronology for rouletted ware remains a matter of debate. Wheeler dated it to the first and second centuries AD. Begley placed its appearance in the second century BC and suggests that it could have lasted until the first century AD. In Sri Lanka, Deraniyagala suggested an even earlier origin based on radiocarbon dates for the oldest levels of Period IV at Anuradhapura, between 500 and 250 BC. However, such early dates need confirmation before they can be accepted. It is generally agreed that rouletted ware was locally made in only a few centres, probably in Tamil Nadu,[24] since the fabric is very homogenous. These centres are still to be identified and we find it difficult to accept Gogte's arguments that it all came from Bengal where very little, and that not typical rouletted ware, has been found.[25]

In Southeast Asia, rouletted ware has been excavated, sometimes in dated contexts, in Bali, Java and Vietnam. Walker and Santoso were the first to identify three rouletted ware bowls from sites of the Buni Complex on the north coast of Java.[26] Two of these are of the classic Indian type (Figure 4.7) while the third is better compared to an Indian ceramic type called "russet coated painted Andhra ware", contemporary with rouletted ware. Sembiran, a coastal site on the north coast of Bali, is especially rich in rouletted ware sherds, Arikamedu Type 10 stamped ware (see Figure 2.7) and Indo-Pacific beads. This site was excavated by Ardika and Bellwood and dates from the last centuries BC to the early centuries of the Christian Era.[27] The vessels are wheel-made with a fine fabric and decorated with two or three bands of rouletting. Some sherds were examined by neutron activation analysis and compared with samples from Arikamedu, Karaikadu and Anuradhapura. The results showed a great similarity between the rouletted ware from all these sites, confirming the concept of a single source.[28] Finally, one sherd of dark grey rouletted ware was found in Phase 1 at Tra Kieu in Central Vietnam, dated to the first century BC and the first half of the first century AD. Mineralogical analysis by Prior confirmed that the fabric was indistinguishable from that of sherds from Wheeler's excavations at Arikamedu.[29]

Thus, the presence of Indian-made rouletted ware in Southeast Asia puts the matter of contact between these regions beyond question. Although the chronology for these imports needs greater precision, it seems likely that the appearance of rouletted ware in Southeast Asia was just a little later than the knobbed bronze vessels.

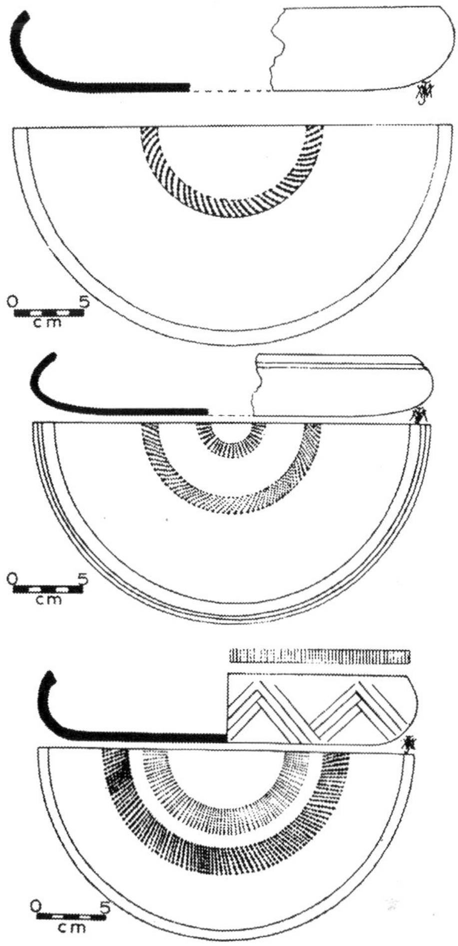

Figure 4.7 Rouletted ware bowls from Kobak Kendal and Cibutak, Java. (Courtesy of the National Museum, Jakarta.)

MEGALITHS IN SOUTHEAST ASIA

Megalithic graves are generally thought to be collective tombs for clans or other kin groups (Figure 4.8). Such tombs, and sometimes alignments and other structures, are relatively common in south-central Sumatra, the Malay Peninsula, parts of Java and some of the eastern Indonesian islands. They are very rare in most of Mainland Southeast Asia. Links with the well-known Iron Age megalithic graves of southern India have long been proposed. In the 1930s, van der Hoop carefully surveyed and excavated in Java and Sumatra a range of stone images, dolmens, menhirs, circles, terraces and slab graves. He showed that they were, for the most part, constructed by indigenous iron-using peoples. However, he also recognized external contact in the form of the glass and stone beads to which he attributed an Indian origin, and in the carvings of Vietnamese Dong Son drums on the stone reliefs at Batu Gajah and Airpurah on the Pasemah Plateau in southern Sumatra.

Because of the lack of well-dated megalithic structures, the exact timing for the arrival of these external cultural traits and materials is still unresolved, but it seems probable that they belong to the early Metal Age of the late centuries BC to early centuries AD, when prestige items such as Dong Son bronze drums and semiprecious stone and glass beads were coming through the developing exchange networks.[30] At this time it seems that links between Sumatra and southeastern India, the centre of the Indian Iron Age megalithic tradition, were particularly close. The Sumatran megalithic graves regularly contain agate, carnelian, crystal and glass beads of exactly

Figure 4.8 Megalithic stone circle at Batu Kantan, West Java, Indonesia. (Photograph courtesy of N. Y. Kim.)

the same varieties as those found in India, so it seems reasonable to see the fashion for building such tombs as introduced at this time.

Phase II (second to fourth centuries AD)

During the second phase, inter and intra-regional exchange intensified and is marked by a lesser diversity but greater quantity of items available for study. Most of the archaeological evidence now consists of Southeast Asian-made ceramics inspired by Indian models. These include the *kundika* and *kendi* pottery types, and stamped and moulded ceramics, which clearly show the adoption of Indian forms and decorative techniques. From this time, objects in contexts referred to as "Indianized" may be found. Glass and stone beads still came from India along the oceanic trade routes. But local manufacturing in an Indian tradition is now beyond doubt and it is difficult to separate imported from locally-made products on the data so far available.

The Kundika

This is a form of pitcher with a long neck and a spout swelling at the base (Figure 4.9). The *kundika* (sometimes referred to as a "sprinkler") is an Indian ceramic form extensively adopted in Southeast Asia from the last centuries BC, but only for a brief period. It is a specialized form of the more common spouted vessel commonly known in Southeast Asia as the *kendi*.[31] The *kundika* becomes rare in South Asia after the sixth–seventh centuries and was primarily associated with Hindu rituals. However, it has also been found in Buddhist sites dating from the beginning of the historical period and was frequently made in the distinctive Red Polished Ware. Easily identifiable *kundika* vessels occur in Pyu sites in Burma, such as Beikthano, in the Mon site of Winka south of Thaton on the Tenasserim coast, in Dvaravati sites in Central Thailand (Chansen and Ban Khu Muang), at Oc Eo in South Vietnam, at Tra Kieu in Central Vietnam and in Central Java.

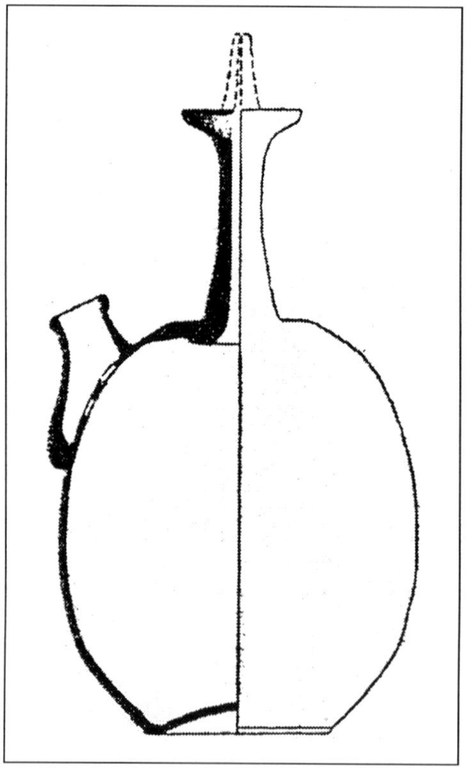

Figure 4.9 Kundika from Kausambi, Uttar Pradesh, India. (Drawing by B. Bellina from Sharma 1969: 178.)

Stamped and moulded ceramics

Southeast Asian pottery with stamped or moulded designs (Figure 4.10) also derives from Indian prototypes which remain to be studied in detail. In South Asia, such forms occur for the first time during the

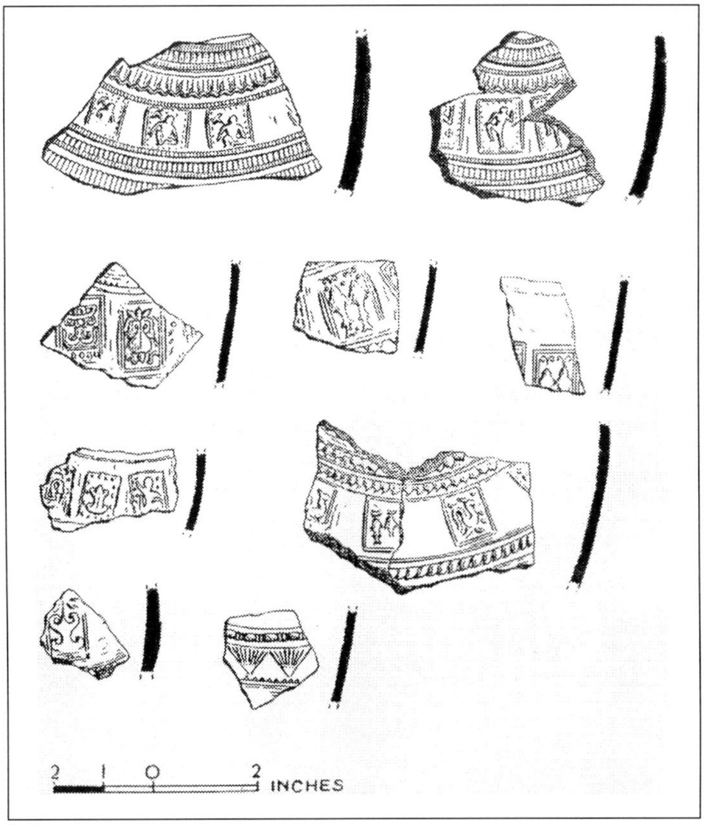

Figure 4.10 Stamped pottery from Beikthano, Burma (Myanmar). (Drawn by B. Bellina from Aung Thaw 1968, fig. 71.)

last centuries BC and last until the sixth–seventh centuries. They are found in major early historic sites such as Mathura, Ujjain, Chichli and Paithan. Most often, this ceramic is red and the stamped or moulded decoration, located on the shoulder, consists of symbolic motifs like the *srivatsa* (vase of abundance), the wheel, the *svastika*, the *hamsa* (goose), plant motifs like rosettes and leaves, or geometrical motifs. At Mathura, for example, this type of ceramic appears in the Kushana levels and continues into the Gupta levels of the fourth–fifth centuries. A moulded pitcher found in the Gupta levels displays on its shoulder three decorated bands ranged in tiers. A bowl found in Ujjain phase III, first century BC to sixth/seventh centuries AD, displays a series of *astamangala*.

The Burmese stamped ceramics show strong similarities to those discovered in India and are commonly found in early Buddhist sites such as Beikthano, Halin and Sri Ksetra. Other local adaptations of this stamped or moulded ceramic type are found in Thailand, in Dvaravati sites such as Chansen Phase V (see chapter 6). As in Pyu sites, the decoration comprises a series of rectangular frames, each separated by a vertical dotted band, enclosing an animal such as an elephant or a cow, a floral motif, or a scene with a horse and rider or a dancer. Sherds with a band of rosettes from Phra Praton in Central Thailand strongly resemble examples excavated in Kondapur, Andhra Pradesh. Although occasional vessels may have been imported from India, we believe that the Southeast Asian stamped ceramics are a local product, one that reflects the adoption and adaptation of Indian techniques and style.[32]

Moulded ware ornamented with radiating flower petals

This type of pottery has been found in the Pyu site of Beikthano (Figure 4.11) and also seems to be a local product derived from an Indian model. The Beikthano sherds are decorated with bands of lotus or acanthus flowers radiating towards the edge of the vessel. Such radiating lotus flower decoration is common in South Asia, as for instance on the Kundla vase, and is also seen on some of the earlier bronze bowls found at Ban Don Ta Phet and Khao Jamook in Thailand. A stone vessel with such a design comes from Taxila, but the most significant comparison is between the pottery from Beikthano and Ter in Maharashtra.

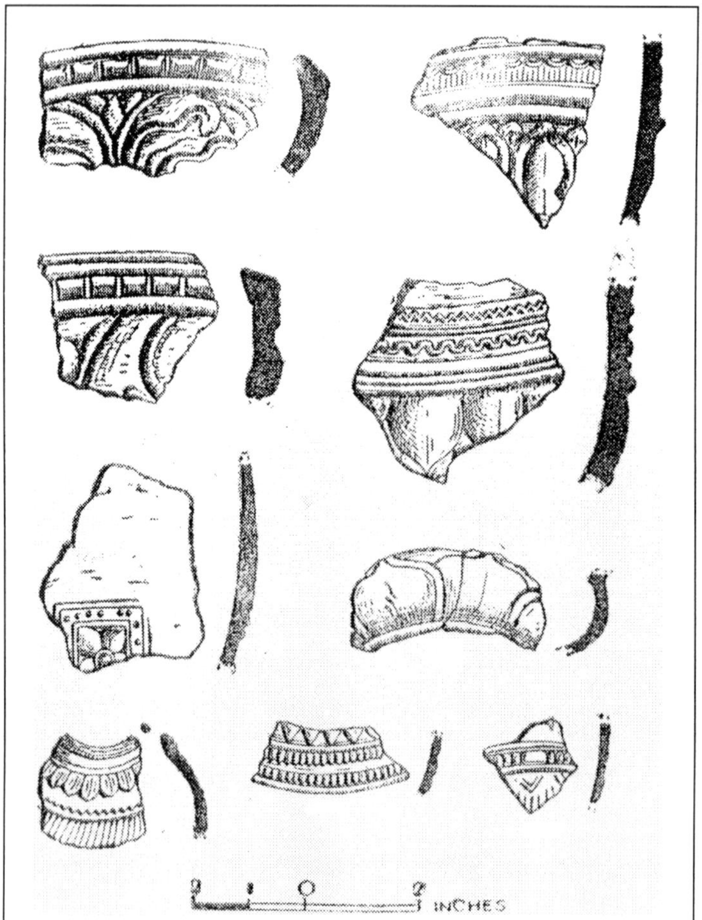

Figure 4.11 Sherds stamped with radiating petal motifs from Beikthano, Burma (Myanmar). (Drawing by Aung Thaw 1968, fig. 72.)

Mould-decorated pottery has a long history in South Asia and has been found primarily in the western Deccan, with only one fragment coming from Kanchipuram in Tamil Nadu. Characteristic vessels of this type, made with two vertical moulds, come from Nevasa, Ter, Kondapur and Kolhapur. Begley has suggested an origin for this ware in an earlier Hellenistic tradition. However, in considering its origins we must also take into account the evidence from Aï Khanum in Afghanistan. Here, fragments of moulds for producing imitation megarian bowls have been dated to the last quarter of the third century BC and these could well be prototypes for the South Asian Moulded Ware.

Conclusions

The discovery of Indian-made, or Indian-influenced, objects in archaeological sites in Southeast Asia in the late centuries BC enables examination of the formation and evolution of regional and inter-regional trading networks. During Phase I, this material occurs in non-Indianized sites. During Phase II, the stamped and moulded ceramics and seals provide valuable data which complement those gained from art history and epigraphy. Art historical research for this later phase shows that the Indian influences into Southeast Asia were multiple and did not originate in any one area. The material evidence from archaeological sites for Phase I also suggests that almost every coastal region of South Asia was involved in these trading networks, although most emanated from the east coast and Bengal. During the last centuries BC the local networks of regional exchange were linked together such that, with the exception perhaps of Indonesia, which seems to have had closer contacts with southern India and Sri Lanka, it has not been possible to identify any direct and exclusive link between any region of the Indian subcontinent and any region in Southeast Asia.

A generation ago, on the basis of the few items then known to be derived from India or the Roman world, Wheeler was perhaps correct to argue that there were only sporadic exchange visits between communities situated on both sides of the Bay of Bengal. Enough evidence is now at hand to refute this interpretation and to show that, by the late centuries BC, Southeast Asia was already part of a world trading system linking the civilizations of the Mediterranean Basin and Han China. Thus, the process of Indianization had long roots reaching back into prehistory.

Notes

1 Coedès 1968; Kangle 1963; Kulke 1990; Mabbett 1977; Pelliot 1903; Wheatley 1983.
2 Majumdar 1952.
3 Wolters 1999.
4 Kulke 1990.
5 Ray 1991, 1994.
6 Bronson 1977; Wheatley 1983; Wolters 1967; Miksic 1984; Wisseman Christie 1990.
7 Wisseman Christie 1995.
8 Ellen 1977: 25.
9 Van Leur 1955.
10 During Caspers 1981.
11 Casson 1989.
12 Wheeler 1954; Raschke 1978.
13 Glover 1990; Francis 2002.
14 Theunissen *et al.* 2000; Bellina 2001.

15 Francis 1991.
16 Bellina 2001.
17 Glover and Henderson 1995.
18 Francis 2002: Part 2.
19 Basa 1991; Glover and Henderson 1995.
20 Glover, (1990a) dated the burials at Ban Don Ta Phet to the early fourth century BC using AMS dates on rice fragment inclusions in the pottery. However, Bellina, on the basis of stylistic comparisons with materials found in India, prefers to date this material to the third or second century BC. More evidence is needed to put the early dating beyond doubt.
21 Janse 1962.
22 Gardin 1985.
23 Begley (1986) argues that, contrary the common opinion, the decoration was not made with a roulette but with a pointed tool held against the body which "chattered" on the interior surface while the vessel was turned. Nevertheless, as it is in common use, we still use the term "rouletted ware".
24 Both Wheeler (1954) and Casal (1956) believed that rouletted ware was directly imported from the Mediterranean, but it seems that only a few recent excavators in India accept this.
25 Gogte 1997.
26 Walker and Santoso 1980.
27 Ardika and Bellwood 1991.
28 Ardika and Bellwood *et al.* 1993.
29 Prior 1998: 106.
30 Megalithic structures of course continued to be built into modern times in many parts of Indonesia. Here we are concerned only with the earliest forms.
31 Adhyatman 1987.
32 Bellina 1999.

Select Bibliography

The bibliography presents a reasonably comprehensive introduction to the main publications on the subject matter discussed organized by theme, and roughly in the order they are discussed in the chapter. Most of the books listed and some of the articles touch on more than one theme but they are included here under the most relevant heading. The books and articles themselves contain many additional bibliographic references for readers who want to go further into the beginnings of economic exchange and cultural contacts between India, the classical world of the Mediterranean and the various countries making up modern Southeast Asia.

Indianization/localization

Bellina, B. (2001) "Témoinages archéologiques d'échanges entre l'Inde et l'Asie du Sud-Est: morphologie, morphométrie et techniques de fabrication des perles en agate et en cornaline (VIe siècle avant notre ère – VIe siècle de notre ère)", thèse de doctorat, Université Sorbonne Nouvelle, Paris III.

Coedès, G. (1968) *The Indianized States of Southeast Asia*, W. F. Vella (ed.), S. B. Cowing (trans.), Canberra: Australian National University Press.

Dagens, B. (1994) "Le temple indien en Asie du Sud-Est: archéologie d'une forme", in F. Bizot (ed.) *Recherches nouvelles sur le Cambodge*, Paris: École Française d'Extrême-Orient, pp. 259–72.

Kangle, R. P. (1963) *The Kautilya Arthasastra*, Bombay: University of Bombay Press.

Kulke, H (1990) "Indian colonies, Indianization, or cultural convergence? Reflections on the changing image of India's role in South-East Asia", in H. Schulte Nordtholt (ed.) *Onderzoez in Zuidoost-Azië: Agenda's voor de Jaren Negentig*, pp. 8–32, Leiden: Rijksuniversiteit te Leiden, Vakgroep Talen en Culturen van Zuidoost-Azië en Oceanië.

Mabbett, I. W. (1977) "The 'Indianization' of Southeast Asia: reflections on historical sources", *Journal of Southeast Asian Studies* 8 (1 & 2): 1–14, 143–61.
Majumdar, R. C. (1952) *Greater India*, Delhi: Motilal Banararsidas.
Malleret, L. (1960–62) *L'Archéologie du Delta du Mekong*, Tomes II–III, Paris: Publications de l'École Française d'Extrême-Orient 43.
Pelliot, P. (1903) "Le Founan", *Bulletin de l'École Française d'Extrême-Orient* 2: 248–333.
Wheatley, P. (1983) "Nagara and Commandery: Origins of Southeast Asian Urban Traditions", research papers 207–8, Department of Geography.
Wolters, O. W. (1999) "History, Culture and Religion in Southeast Asian Perspectives", *Studies on Southeast Asia No.26*, Singapore: Institute of Southeast Asian Studies.

South Asian exchange

Dutta, A. (1998) "Ancient ports of coastal Bengal and its overseas trade with Southeast Asia: an archaeological overview", in M. J. Klokke and T. de Bruijn (eds) *Southeast Asian Archaeology 1996*, Hull: Centre of South-East Asian Studies, University of Hull, pp. 87–98.
Ray, H. P. (1989) "Early maritime contacts between South and Southeast Asia", *Journal of Southeast Asian Studies* XX (1): 42–54.
Ray, H. P. (1991a) "In search of Suvanabhumi: early sailing networks in the Bay of Bengal", in P. Bellwood (ed.) *Indo-Pacific Prehistory 1990*, Vol. 1, pp. 557–65, Canberra and Jakarta: Indo-Pacific Prehistory Association.
Ray, H. P. (1991b) "Seafaring in the Bay of Bengal in the early centuries AD", *Studies in History* 6 (1): 1–14.
Ray, H. P. (1994) *The Winds of Change – Buddhism and the Maritime Links of Early South Asia*, Delhi: Oxford University Press.

Southeast Asian exchange

Bellina, B. (1997) "Les témoignages archéologiques d'échanges entre le sous-continent indien et l'Asie du Sud-Est (VIe siècle avant notre ère – VIe siècle de notre ère)", unpublished dissertation for the DEA, Université Sorbonne-Nouvelle, Paris III.
Bellina, B. (1998) "La formation des réseaux d'échanges reliant l'Asie du Sud et l'Asie du Sud-Est à travers le matériel archéologique (VIe siècle av. J.-C. – VIe siècle ap. J.-C.). Le cas de la Thaïlande et de la Péninsule Malaise", *Journal of the Siam Society* 86 (1 & 2): 89–105.
Bronson, B. (1977) "Exchange at the upstream and downstream ends: notes towards a functional model of the coastal state in Southeast Asia", in K. Hutterer (ed.) *Economic Exchange and Social Interaction in Southeast Asia: perspectives from Prehistory, History and Ethnography*, Michigan Papers on South and Southeast Asia 13: 39–52.
Cribb, J. (1981) "The date of the symbolic coins of Burma and Thailand – a re-examination of the evidence", *Seaby Coin and Medal Bulletin* 75: 224–6.
Glover, I. C. (1990a) "Early Trade between India and Southeast Asia – a link in the development of a World Trading System", Occasional Paper No. 16, University of Hull: Centre for South-East Asian Studies (2nd revised edition).
Higham, C. F. W. (1996) *The Bronze Age of Southeast Asia*, Cambridge. Cambridge University Press.
Leur, J. C. van (1955) *Indonesian Trade and Society: Essays in Asian Social and Economic History*, The Hague: W. van Hoeve.
Miksic, J. (1984) "A comparison between some long distance trading institutions of the Malacca Straits area and the Western Pacific", *Southeast Asian Archaeology at the XVth Pacific Science Congress*, University of Otago Monographs in Prehistoric Anthropology, 16: 235–53.
Wisseman Christie, J. (1990) "Trade and State Formation in the Malay Peninsula and Sumatra, 300 BC–AD 700", in J. Kathirithamby-Wells and J. Villiers (eds) *The Southeast Asian Port and Polity: rise and demise*, Singapore: Singapore University Press, pp. 39–60.
Wisseman Christie, J. (1995) "State formation in Early Maritime Southeast Asia: a consideration of the theories and the data", *Bijdragen tot de Taal-, Land- en Volkenkunde* 151(2): 235–88.

Wolters, O. W. (1967) *Early Indonesian Commerce: a study of the origins of Srivijaya*, Ithaca: Cornell University Press.

Indian trade with the classical world

Begley, V. (1983) "Arikamedu reconsidered", *American Journal of Archaeology* 87: 461–81.
Begley, V. and R. D. De Puma (eds) (1991) *Rome and India – the Ancient Sea Trade*, Madison: University of Wisconsin Press.
Brown, R. L. and A. M. MacDonnel (1989) "The Pong Tuk Lamp: a reconsideration", *Journal of the Siam Society* 77(2): 9–20.
Casson, L. (ed.) (1989) *The Periplus Maris Erythraei*, Princeton: Princeton University Press.
During Caspers, E. C. L. (1981) "The Indian ivory figurine from Pompeii – a reconsideration of its functional use", pp. 341–53, in H. Hartel (ed.) *South Asian Archaeology 1979*, Berlin: Dietrich Reimer Verlag.
Ellen, R. F. (1977) "The trade in spices", *Journal of the Indonesia Circle* 12: 21–5.
Gardin, J. C., (1985) "Les relations entre la Méditerannée et la Bactriane dans l'Antiquité, d'après des données céramologiques inédites", in, *De l'Indus aux Balkans; recueil à la mémoire de J. Deshayes*, (contributions rassemblées et éditées par J.-L. Huot, M. Yon et Y. Calvet) Paris, Éditions Recherches sur les civilisations, pp. 447–60.
Miller, J. I. (1969) *The Spice Trade of the Roman Empire, 29 BC–AD 641*, Oxford: Oxford University Press.
Raschke, M. G. (1978) "New Studies in Roman Commerce with the East", in *Aufstieg und Niedergang der Romischen Welt* II.9, pp. 604–1378, Berlin and New York: de Gruyter.
Turner, P. (1989) "Roman Coins in India", Occasional Paper No.12, London: Institute of Archaeology.
Warmington, E. H. (1928) *The Commerce between the Roman Empire and India*, Cambridge: Cambridge University Press.
Wheatley, P. (1983) *Nagara and Commandery: Origins of the Southeast Asian Urban Traditions.* Department of Geography Research Papers 207–8, Chicago: University of Chicago.
Wheeler, R. E. M., Ghosh, A. and Deva, Krishna (1946) "Arikamedu: an Indo-Roman trading station on the east coast of India", *Ancient India* 2: 17–124.
Wheeler, R. E. M. (1954) *Rome Beyond the Imperial Frontiers*, Harmondsworth: Penguin.

Semiprecious stone beads

Bellina, B. (2001) "Témoinages archéologiques d'échanges entre l'Inde et l'Asie du Sud-Est: morphologie, morphométrie et techniques de fabrication des perles en agate et en cornaline (VIe siècle avant notre ère – VIe siècle de notre ère)", thèse de doctorat, Université Sorbonne Nouvelle, Paris III.
Francis, P. (1982) "When India was bead maker to the World", *Ornament* 6(2): 33–4 and 56–7.
Francis, P. (2002) *Asia's Maritime Bead Trade – 300 BC to the Present*, Honolulu: University of Hawai'i Press.
Glover, I. C. (1990b) "Ban Don Ta Phet: the 1984–85 excavation", in I. C. and E. A. Glover (eds) *South Asian Archaeology 1986*, Oxford: BAR S-561, pp. 139–84.
Possehl, G. (1981) "Cambay beadmaking", *Expedition* 23(4): 39–47.
Theunisson, R., Grave, P. and Bailey, G. (2000) "Doubts on diffusion: challenging the assumed Indian origin of Iron Age agate and carnelian beads in Southeast Asia", *World Archaeology* 32: 184–105.
Veraprasert, M. (1992) "Khlong Thom: an ancient bead and manufacturing location and an ancient entrepôt", in I. C. Glover, P. Suchitta and J. Villiers (eds) *Early Metallurgy, Trade and Urban Centres in Thailand and Southeast Asia*, Bangkok: White Lotus, pp. 149–61.

Glass in South and Southeast Asia

Basa, K. K. (1991) "The Westerly Trade of Southeast Asia From *c.*400 BC to *c.* AD 500 with Special Reference to Glass Beads", PhD Thesis, University of London.

Francis, P. (1991) "Beadmaking at Arikamedu and beyond", *World Archaeology* 23(1): 28–43.
Glover, I. C and Henderson, J. (1995) "Early glass in South and Southeast Asia and China", in R. Scott and J. Guy (eds) *China and Southeast Asia – Art, Commerce and Interaction*, London: Percival David Foundation of Chinese Art, pp. 141–69.
Salisbury, A. and Glover, I. C. (1997) "New analyses of early glass from Thailand and Vietnam", *Bead Study Trust Newsletter* 30: 7–14.
Shuhaimi, Nik Hassan (1991) "Recent research at Kuala Selinsing, Perak", in P. Bellwood (ed.) *Indo Pacific Prehistory 1990*, Vol. 2, Canberra and Jakarta: the Indo-Pacific Prehistory Association, pp. 141–52.

Bronze vessels

Batchelor, B. C. (1978) "Post 'Hoabinhian' coastal settlement indicated by finds in stanniferous Langat River Alluvium near Dengkil, Selangor, Peninsular Malaya", *Federation Museums Journal* (n.s.) 2: 1–55.
Bennett, A. N. and Glover, I. C. (1992) "Decorated high-tin bronzes from Thailand's prehistory", in I. Glover (ed.) *Southeast Asian Archaeology 1990*, Hull University: Centre for Southeast Asian Studies, pp. 187–208.
Breeks, J. W. 1873 *An Account of the Primitive Tribes and Monuments of the Nilgiris*, London: William H. Allan.
Gardin, J. C. (1985) "Les relations entre la Méditerannée et la Bactriane dans l'Antiquité, d'après des donées céramologiques inédites", in *De l'Indus aux Balkans; recueil à la mémoire de J. Deshayes*, Paris: Éditions Recherches sur les civilisations, pp. 447–60.
Janse, O. R. T., (1962) "Quelques réflexions à propos d'un bol de type mégaréen trouvé au Vietnam", *Artibus Asiae* XXV(4): 280–92.
Marshall, J. (1951) *Taxila: an illustrated account of the archaeological excavations*, Cambridge: Cambridge University Press.
Rajpitak, W. and Seeley, N. (1979) "The bronze bowls from Ban Don Ta Phet: an enigma of prehistoric metallurgy", *World Archaeology* 11(1): 26–31.

Rouletted ware

Ardika, I. W. and Bellwood, P. (1991) "Sembiran: the beginnings of Indian contact with Bali", *Antiquity* 65(247): 221–32.
Ardika, I. W., Bellwood, P., Eggleton, R. A. and Ellis, D. J. (1993) "A single source for South Asian export-quality Rouletted Ware?", *Man and Environment* 18(1): 101–9.
Begley, V. (1986) "Rouletting and chattering: decoration on ancient and present day pottery in India", *Expedition* 28(1): 47–54.
Begley, V. (1991) "Ceramic evidence for Pre-Periplus trade on the Indian coasts", in V. Begley and R. D. De Puma (eds) *Rome and India – the Ancient Sea Trade*, Madison: University of Wisconsin Press, pp. 157–196.
Begley, V. (1996) *The Ancient Port of Arikamedu: new Excavations and Researches, 1989–92*, Paris: Pondichery.
Casal, J.-M. and Germaine, G. (1956) *Site urbaine et sites funéraires des environs de Pondichéry*, Paris: Presses Universitaires de France.
Deraniyagala, S. (1992) "The proto- and early-historic radiometric chronology of Sri Lanka", in, *The Prehistory of Sri Lanka: an ecological perspective (addendum 2)*, Colombo: Archaeological Survey Department of Sri Lanka, pp. 707–38.
Gogte, V. D. (1997) "The Chandraketugarh-Tamluk region of Bengal: source of the Early Historic Rouletted Ware from India and Southeast Asia", *Man and Environment* 22(1): 69–85.
Prior, R. (1998) "The ceramics from early historic sites in Vietnam", in P.-Y. Manguin (ed.) *Southeast Asian Archaeology 1994*, Hull: Centre for South-East Asian Studies, pp. 94–110.
Walker, M. and Santoso, S. (1980) "Romano-Indian rouletted pottery in Indonesia", *Asian Perspectives* 20(2): 228–35.

Megaliths

Glover, I. C., Bronson, B. B. and Bayard, D. T. (1979) "Comment on 'Megaliths' in South East Asia", in R. B. Smith and W. Watson (eds) *Early South-East Asia: essays in Archaeology, History and Historical Geography*, Oxford: Oxford University Press, pp. 253–4.
Heine-Geldern, R. (1928) "Die Megalithen sudostasiens und ihre Bedeutung für die Megalithenfrage in Europa und Polynesia", *Anthropos* 23: 276–315.
Heine-Geldern, R. (1959) "Das Megalithproblem", *Beiträge Österreichs zur Erforschung der Vergangenheit und Kulturgeschichte der Menscheit*, Symposium 1958, pp. 162–82.
Hoop, A. N. J. Th. van der (1932) *Megalithic Remains in South Sumatra*, Zutphen: Thieme.
Kim, Myung-jin (1988) *Megaliths in East Asia with Particular Reference to Indonesia*, Seoul: privately printed.
Perry, W. J. (1918) *The Megalithic Culture of Indonesia*, Manchester: Manchester University Press.
Smith, G. Elliot (1916) *The Influence of Ancient Egyptian Civilization in the East and in America*, Manchester: African Islamic Mission Publications.
Soejono, R. P. (1982) "On the megaliths in Indonesia", in B-m. Kim (ed.) *Megalithic Cultures in Asia*, Monograph 2, Seoul: Hanyang University Press, pp. 73–98.

Kundika *and* Kendi

Adhyatman, S. (1987) *Kendi. Wadah air minum tradisional* (The Kendi: the traditional drinking water container), Jakarta: Himpunan Keramik Indonesia.
Coomaraswamy, A. K. and F. S. Kershaw (1928–9) "A Chinese Buddhist water vessel and its Indian prototype", *Artibus Asiae* 3: 122–41.
Sharma, G. R. (1969) *Excavations at Kausambi 1949–50*, Delhi: Memoir of the Archaeological Survey of India 74.

Stamped and moulded ceramics

Aung Myint (1970) "The excavation at Halin", *Journal of the Burma Research Society* 2: 55–64.
Aung Myint (1977) "The capital of Suvannabhumi unearthed?", *Shiroku* 10: 41–53.
Aung Thaw (1968) *Report on the Excavations at Beikthano*, Rangoon: Ministry of Culture.
Bellina, B. (1999) "La vaisselle dans les échanges entre le sous-continent indien et l'Asie du Sud-Est", *Bulletin de l'École Française d'Extrême-Orient* 86: 161–84.
Bronson, B. (1979) "The later prehistory and early history of Central Thailand", in R. B. Smith and W. Watson (eds) *Early South-East Asia – Essays in Archaeology, History and Historical Geography*, Oxford: Oxford University Press, pp. 313–36.
Bronson, B. and Dales, G. F. (1972) "Excavations at Chansen, Thailand, 1968 and 1969: a preliminary report", *Asian Perspectives* 15(1): 15–46.
Élaigne-Pardon, S. (1996) *Étude des céramiques fines de Mahastangarh (Bengale) aux époques maurya et shunga dans les perspectives techniques et culturelles*, Lyon: Université de Lyon.
Härtel, H. (1989) "Pottery of Mathura", in D. M. Srinivasan (ed.) *Mathura. The Cultural Heritage*, New Delhi: Manohar/American Institute of Indian Studies, pp. 181–92.
Härtel, H. (1993) "Excavations at Sonkh. 2500 years of a town in the Mathura District", *Monographien zur indischen Archäologie, Kunst und Philologie, Band 9*, Berlin: Dietrich Reimer Verlag.
Indrawooth, P. (1985) *Index Pottery of Dvaravati Period*, Bangkok: Silpakorn University.
Indrawooth, P. (1999) *Dvaravati. A Critical Study based on Archaeological Evidence*, Bangkok: Silpakorn University.
Stargardt, J. (1990) *The Ancient Pyu of Burma, Vol. 1: Early Pyu Cities in a Man-madeLandscape*, Cambridge and Singapore: PACSEA/ISEAS.
Wheeler, R. E. M., Gosh, A. and Krishna Deva (1946) "Arikamedu: an Indo-Roman trading station on the East coast of India", *Ancient India, Bulletin of the Archaeological Survey of India* 2: 17–125.

5

PRE-ANGKORIAN AND ANGKORIAN CAMBODIA

Miriam T. Stark

Introduction

Cambodia's past has left the world a rich archaeological heritage. The country is best known for the many temples that marked the apex of the Khmer Empire, leaving a lasting monumental legacy in stone. To Southeast Asian archaeologists, however, Cambodia is also known as the locus of some of the earliest archaeological work in the region undertaken during the late nineteenth century. Unfortunately, this rich cultural heritage was severely damaged during the Indochinese wars and subsequent revolutions and field research virtually ceased between the mid-1960s and 1990s. Less than a decade after the end of its civil war, archaeological research in Cambodia resumed in the mid-1990s.

This chapter reviews key cultural developments in pre-Angkorian and Angkorian Cambodia, and seeks to find the roots of the great Khmer empire that dominated much of Mainland Southeast Asia from the ninth–fourteenth centuries AD. Figure 5.1 locates prehistoric, pre-Angkorian, and Angkorian archaeological sites. The temporal framework used in this summary tacks between a fine-grained approach and the more generalized sequence presented in Table 5.1. The time period described covers two-and-a-half millennia, to the fifteenth century AD.

The scope of this review of Cambodian archaeology is largely restricted to the country's present-day boundaries. However, some attention is paid to the archaeology of two areas that were ethnically Khmer in the recent past: these are the Mekong Delta of southern Vietnam, and the Khorat Plateau of northeastern Thailand. In the former area, starting in the seventeenth century, Vietnamese settlers and later French administrators wrested control of the delta from Cambodia, but a sizable population of ethnic Khmer who call themselves "Khmer Krom" still live there.

The boundary of northwestern Cambodia has also long been contested and the provinces (Buri Ram, Surin, Si Sa Ket, and Nakhon Ratchasima) of northeastern Thailand (*Isan*) that border Cambodia retain sizable ethnic Khmer populations today. It is not surprising, then, that these same provinces bear the archaeological signature of the Khmer civilization, from the late prehistoric period to the expansionist impulses of some Khmer rulers of the Angkor period.

Interest in Cambodian prehistory began in 1876, when Roque (or Roques) discovered the archaeological site of Samrong Sen, along the Chinit river in central Cambodia.[1] The discoveries there and in other localities attracted some attention from

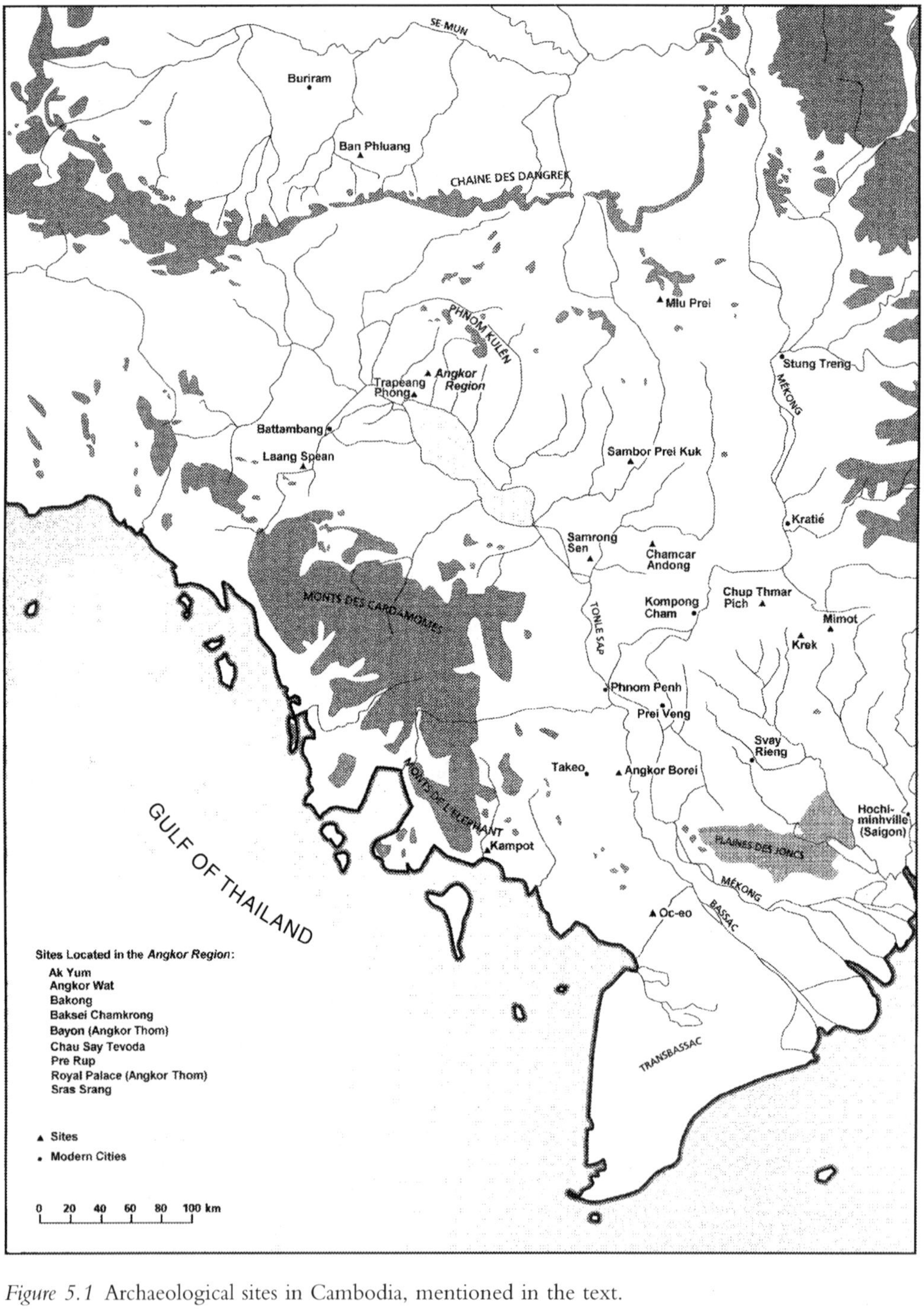

Figure 5.1 Archaeological sites in Cambodia, mentioned in the text.

Table 5.1 Temporal framework used in this chapter

Southeast Asian time periods	*Dates* (BC/AD)	*Cultural developments*
Late Hoabinhian and Early Neolithic	*c*.5200–2500 BC	Late Paleolithic, terminal and post-Pleistocene life based on a mobile hunting and gathering with some more sedentary settlement along the coasts
Neolithic and Bronze Age	*c*.2500–500 BC	Introduction of agriculture and more settled village life, basically with a stone technology with bronze working developing from *c*.1500 BC
Early Historic period	*c*.500 BC–AD 500	Arrival and local development of iron tools and weapons, development of international maritime trade especially with South Asia. Increasing evidence for warfare and tools and the development of early states
Pre-Angkor Period	c. AD 500–802	Appearance of writing using modified Indian scripts and first Sanskrit, then later old Khmer language. Expansion of early states and inter-regional conflict
Angkor, or Historic Period	AD 802–1431	Consolidation and expansion Khmer empire into much of present-day Thailand, Laos and southern Vietnam before fragmentation and withdrawal during conflict with emerging Thai kingdoms.

European prehistorians. Later, the French turned their attention to studying and restoring the great temples of Angkor, north of Tonle Sap – the Great Lake. During the colonial period the French rulers wanted to associate themselves with Cambodia's former greatness through studies of its architecture, art, and ancient language. The emphasis of most archaeological research at this time was given to the Angkor period from the ninth to the fifteenth centuries and very substantial achievements were made there under the leadership of the scholars of the École Française d'Extrême-Orient (EFEO).

Prehistoric Cambodia

This section draws primarily on well-dated archaeological sites; these have been dated using available radiocarbon dates, or absolute dates from Khmer or Sanskrit inscriptions which used a standardized Indic calendar.[2] For a number of reasons, Cambodia's neighbors, Vietnam and Thailand, have a much better documented archaeological record.

The Paleolithic to Hoabinhian, c.5200–3000 BC

Little reliable evidence currently exists for a Pleistocene occupation of Cambodia, despite various efforts to find it. The French geologist Edmond Saurin described quartz and quartzite pebble tools from the Mekong River terraces in the area between Stung Treng and Kratie provinces in eastern Cambodia that might date to the Pleistocene. He argued that they resemble Pleistocene assemblages in Vietnam and may have been associated with a Pleistocene fauna. However, such material cannot easily be dated and Mourer has dismissed these estimates on paleontological and chronometric grounds. Jean-Pierre

Carbonnel also assigned a Paleolithic age to finds from Phnom Loang in Kampot Province, based on their association with Lower Pleistocene fauna.[3]

Our current knowledge of Cambodia's history thus begins in the Holocene epoch (nearly 8,000 years ago) with a hunting and gathering way of life. This period is generally glossed as the "Hoabinhian" throughout Southeast Asia and is associated with a broad-spectrum diet and occupation of riverine areas and forest edges. Cambodia's only documented Hoabinhian site, Laang Spean, lies in a limestone hill in the Sangker river valley in Battambang province (Figure 5.2). French archaeologists Roland and Cecile Mourer excavated portions of this karst cave from 1966–68 with students from the Faculty of Archaeology of the Royal University of Fine Arts in Phnom Penh.[4] Their excavations produced a series of reliable radiocarbon dates that began in the sixth millennium BC, and a collection of flaked stone tools that characterize the Hoabinhian period at sites throughout much of Mainland Southeast Asia. Faunal remains recovered at the site suggest a broad diet of small animals (bats, rodents, birds and frogs), river resources (molluscs and turtles), and a variety of forest animals including deer and small bovids.

The Hoabinhian to Neolithic transition

The cave of Laang Spean also contained an upper "Neolithic" component that is associated with the earliest dated earthenware ceramics in Cambodia (Figure 5.3). Archaeologists agree on little about the Neolithic period across Mainland Southeast Asia beyond its general, but not exclusive association with earthenware pottery, polished stone adzes and plant domestication.[5] While our knowledge of the Southeast Asian Neolithic has increased substantially in the last 50 years, the Cambodian archaeological record for this phase remains limited.

Figure 5.2 Excavation in progress at Laang Spean in 1969. (Photograph courtesy of R. Mourer.)

The province of Kampong Cham contains a series of circular earthwork sites that Bernard-Philippe Groslier and Louis Malleret assigned to the Neolithic period. Fieldwork at these "doughnut-like embankments", such as Krek and Mimot (Figure 5.4), has consistently produced flaked and polished stone tools, stone bracelets and pottery (Figure 5.5) that we tend to associate stylistically with the Neolithic and Bronze Age. Groslier undertook excavations at a site in Mimot District and produced a ceramic collection now held at the National Museum in Phnom Penh. A few years later, Carbonnel also documented circular structures and tumuli in the region and obtained chronometric samples from Chamcar-Andong (1150 ± 100 BP, cal. AD 760–925: Gif-447) and Chup-Thmar Pich (2130 ± 100 BP, cal. 440–375 BC: Gif-1448). Vietnamese archaeologists surveyed the twelve sites Malleret had noted in southern Vietnam and added four more to the list in Binh Phuoc province, which is adjacent to Kampong Cham.[6]

Figure 5.3 Pedestal vessel with impressed decoration found during excavation at Laang Spean. (Photograph courtesy of R. Mourer.)

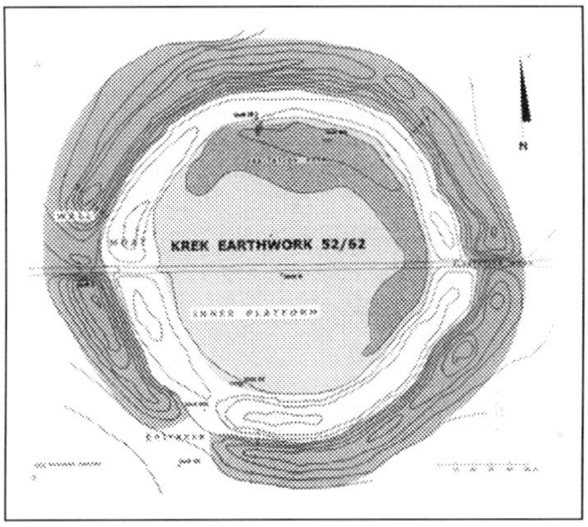

Figure 5.4 Plan of the Krek earthwork. (Courtesy of G. Albreht and M. Haidle.)

Recent excavations by international archaeological teams, working in collaboration with Cambodia's Ministry of Culture and Fine Arts, have provided a more detailed view of the distribution, morphology and material culture of these sites.[7] By May 2000, members of the Memot Research Center team had identified a total of 23 circular earthworks within Cambodia and researchers estimate that there are at least 50 such sites in Cambodia and Vietnam. That these circular earthwork sites display marked similarities to each other is indisputable, but their age and function are currently under debate. The earthworks may have been constructed for defense against other human populations or wild animals, to pen domestic cattle at night, or possibly for other reasons. It remains unclear whether these sites date exclusively to the Neolithic period, or whether they represent a settlement type began in the third millennium and continued into the mid-first millennium BC.

Several historic sites may overlie prehistoric occupation layers in several parts of Cambodia. In northwestern Cambodia, for example, Groslier reported that stone adzes were recovered during excavations and architectural restoration of eighth–fourteenth-century monuments around Angkor. These sites include Ak Yum, Baksei Chamkrong,

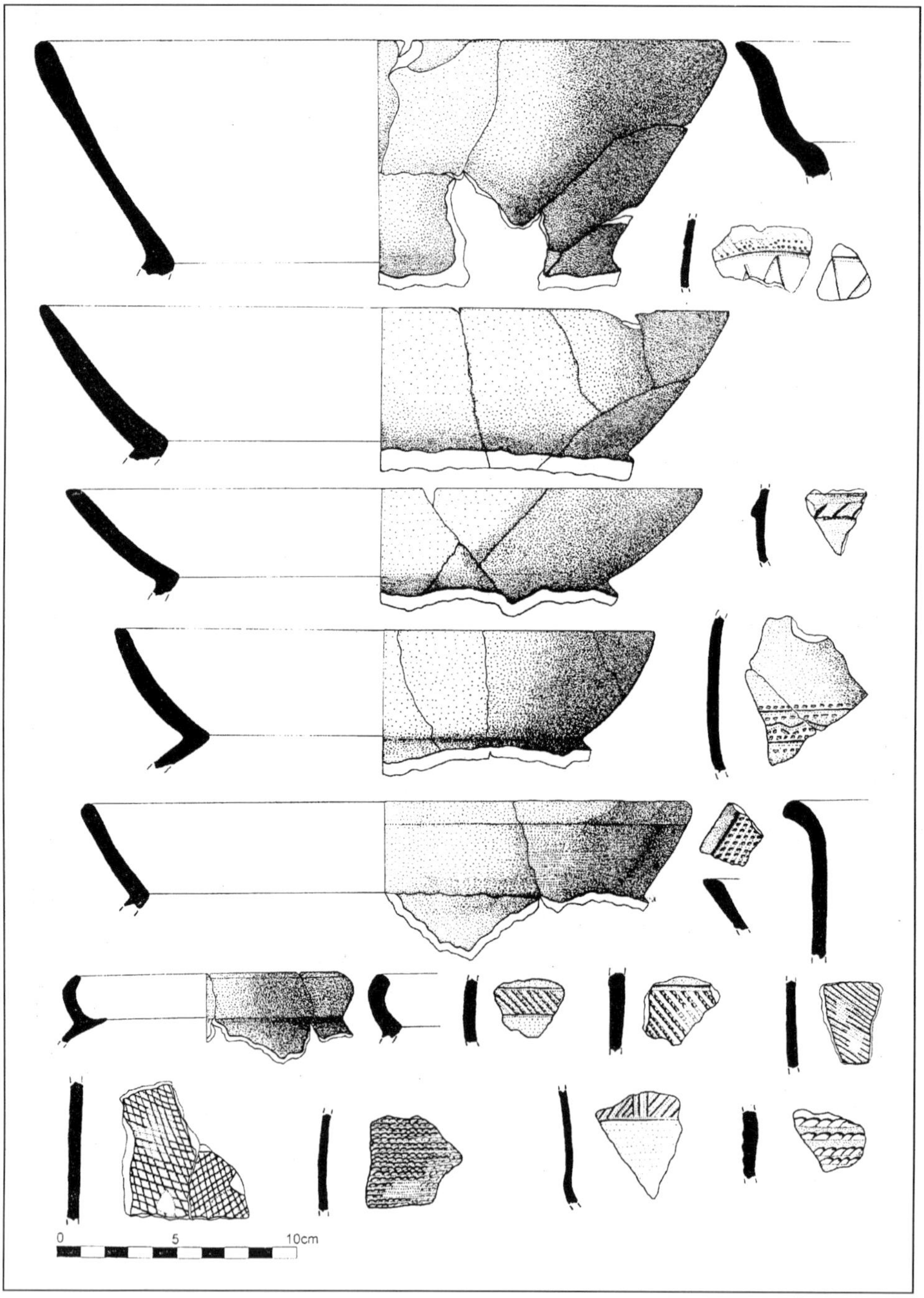

Figure 5.5 Drawings of Krek pottery. (Courtesy of G. Albrecht and M. Haidle.)

Chau Say Tevoda and Trapeang Phong.[8] Even the sixth–eighth-century site of Sambor Prei Kuk (Kompong Thom Province) may sit atop a Neolithic foundation[9] (Figure 5.6), although no one has yet conducted excavations that might provide empirical support for this claim.

Figure 5.6 Sambor Prei Kuk. (Photograph by P. Bion Griffin.)

The Neolithic-Bronze Age (c.1500–500 BC)

The Neolithic-Bronze Age transition is also poorly known in Cambodian archaeology. Few such sites are known and none have been excavated since the Pacific War. Samrong Sen,[10] perhaps the best-known site, lies in Kompong Chhnang Province. Similarities between the finds made there (Figure 5.7) and those from Bronze Age sites in Thailand and Vietnam have led some archaeologists to assign Samrong Sen to the Bronze Age, but the age of the occupation is far from resolved. During the nineteenth century, the Somrong Sen prehistoric shell midden attracted notice from early colonial administrators and European prehistorians for its wealth of artifacts that included ceramics, stone tools and small amounts of bronze. Collecting expeditions

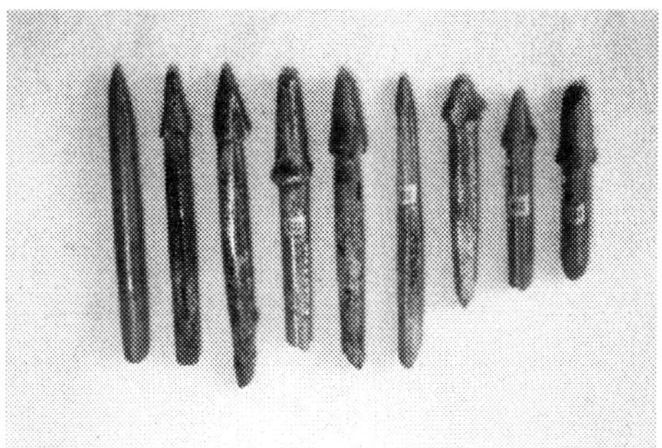

Figure 5.7 Left: Bronze bell from Samrong Sen, decorated with spiral motifs, 19.7 cm in height. Above: Bone spear or harpoon shafts. Both in the Museum of Natural History, Lyon. (Photographs courtesy of R. Mourer.)

and excavations at the site occurred throughout the late nineteenth century but lacked the scientific rigor and expertise necessary to understand the site's occupational sequence. Henri Mansuy recovered a collection of stone adzes, bronze objects and human remains that suggested a Bronze Age occupation. The Swedish archaeologist Olov Janse subsequently tested the site and purchased from villagers bronze artifacts that included bracelets, socketed spearheads, axes and a bell. The lack of scientific dating techniques available at the time of Mansuy's research, however, limited the utility of these findings.

Paul Lévy[11] subsequently examined open-air sites around Mlu Prei (Preah Vihear Province) that also contributed to our meager knowledge of the Cambodian Bronze Age. Lévy's more systematic excavations recovered not only bronze implements, including fragments of a socketed axe and a bronze sickle, but also moulds used to cast bronzes. These included portions of a sandstone bivalve mould and of a ceramic crucible for bronze casting with metal dross still adhering to its surface. The site of O Yak also contained human burials adorned with bronze bracelets, but this site had been previously disturbed.

Other prehistoric sites

Two other regions of Cambodia have produced what may be prehistoric archaeological sites: Rattanakiri in the northeast and Banteay Mean Chay in the north. The province of Rattanakiri is famous for its gem-mining industry, and local miners often encounter prehistoric artifacts during their mining activities. Archaeological reconnaissance at sites in the central part of Rattanakiri Province during 1995 recovered evidence of shouldered stone axes and earthenware ceramics, suggestive of either Neolithic or Bronze Age occupation.[12]

In May 2000, authorities were alerted to looting at a prehistoric mortuary site known locally as Phum Snay, located north of Siem Reap in the Preah Net Preah district of Banteay Mean Chey Province. Among the archaeological materials revealed were human burials, numerous pottery sherds (primarily earthenware, with some celadon), various bronze fragments, nearly intact but oxidized, as well as iron tools, and beads of glass, quartz and carnelian. This site has provisionally been dated to the Iron Age, with a possible extension into the Early Historic period.[13]

Systematic archaeological investigations at Phum Snay were undertaken in February 2001 under the direction of Dougald O'Reilly for the Royal University of Fine Arts (with assistance from Charles Higham). Excavation of a 5 meter by 15 meter unit reached a depth of 1.5 meters, uncovering nine intact human burials and a limited number of tools. The site may cover an area as large as 50 hectares.[14]

The protohistoric period in Cambodia

In Mainland Southeast Asia, the transition from the prehistoric period to the historic period, sometimes called the protohistoric period, falls approximately between 200 BC and AD 500. During this period, Southeast Asians first settled in large nucleated communities, organizing themselves into small warring polities whose political structure has been described by Wolters[15] as of *mandala* type in terms of their alliance-based spheres of influence focused on a ruler. They also became engaged in international maritime trade.[16] The organizational changes at this time were marked by greater social stratification and, ultimately, emergent states. Earlier historians like Coedès suggested that such changes must have been brought about by Indian settlement, and the "Indianization" hypothesis colored most interpretations of the region until the last few decades. Archaeological research on the late prehistoric period, which chronicles a gradual, indigenous trend toward sociopolitical complexity, has compelled most historians to revise their frameworks and assign more agency to indigenous Southeast Asians in the process of early state formation.[17]

It is likely that this process occurred separately in northwestern and southeastern Cambodia.[18] Archaeological excavations at sites in northeast Thailand, which was at various times Khmer-dominated, has begun to document these organizational shifts. Moore's research[19] using the UNESCO ZEMP data base has identified more than 60 probably prehistoric habitation mounds, whose forms and distribution parallel prehistoric earthworks in northeast Thailand.

While our knowledge of this period remains limited in the Tonle Sap region, documentary sources suggest that the lower Mekong and its delta served as a central node for international and regional exchange networks in the early centuries of the Christian Era, housing major population centers that formed organized polities. In Cambodia, the archaeological record of this transition has been illuminated by current research at the site of Angkor Borei (Takeo Province) by the Lower Mekong Archaeological Project (LOMAP).

The transition to history in the Lower Mekong Basin

By the end of the prehistoric period, complex societies arose in the Mekong Delta of southern Cambodia that participated in international maritime trade and vied for power with each other. These delta-based polities established many of the rules which the Khmer empire used to dominate its neighbours in later centuries. The period of the first to eighth centuries AD witnessed the emergence of the earliest states in Cambodia, with an indigenous writing system, monumental architecture, and shifting power centers that moved ever northward through central to northwestern Cambodia. In AD 802, Jayavarman II established his kingdom in the Tonle Sap region. In so doing, he launched a six-century Khmer empire that, at its peak, dominated much of what is now Mainland Southeast Asia. Architecture, inscriptions and art tell a tale of Cambodia's ancient elites, while the humble remains of the common people – from their tableware to their bones – inform about changes in the local population of Cambodia through time.

Information sources used in this summary include archaeological and documentary data. Documentary data include descriptions from visiting Chinese dignitaries and inscriptions in Khmer and Sanskrit.[20] Each source has its strengths and weaknesses. Moving between these sources, however, provides a workable framework for understanding changes in Cambodian history and emergence of its great empire.

The early historic period, or pre-Angkorian Cambodia and "Funan"

Historians and archaeologists have long looked to the Mekong Delta to study the transition to history that began at some point in the early centuries of the Christian Era.[21] Chinese documentary evidence described walled and moated cities that probably were located in this region, which today includes several provinces in southern Cambodia and

Vietnam (Figure 5.1). The largest collection of pre-Angkorian Khmer and Sanskrit inscriptions derive from this region. Many images of the earliest Khmer art also derive from the delta, and French reconnaissance in the area identified a series of archaeological sites that appeared to belong to the Angkorian period.[22]

In the third century AD, the Kingdom of Wu, the southernmost state in post-Han China, sent a number of emissaries into Mainland Southeast Asia to establish trading partners. The great French historian Paul Pelliot translated the accounts of these mission which referred to a "Kingdom of Funan", a polity that flourished between the second and sixth centuries AD.[23] Archaeological research in both Vietnam and Cambodia has begun to provide a substantive basis to these historical sources.

One of the most prominent sites in Cambodia's Mekong Delta is Angkor Borei, Takeo Province. Today, Angkor Borei is a small town within a large walled settlement that covers an area of 300 hectares (Figure 5.8) and contains more than one dozen collapsed brick monuments, most associated with artificial ponds of various sizes. A 4-meter high wall capped with brick masonry still encircles much of the site. Angkor Borei lies immediately north of the hill of Phnom Da, which has produced some of the finest examples of early Khmer art. Geographer Pierre Paris used aerial photographs to argue

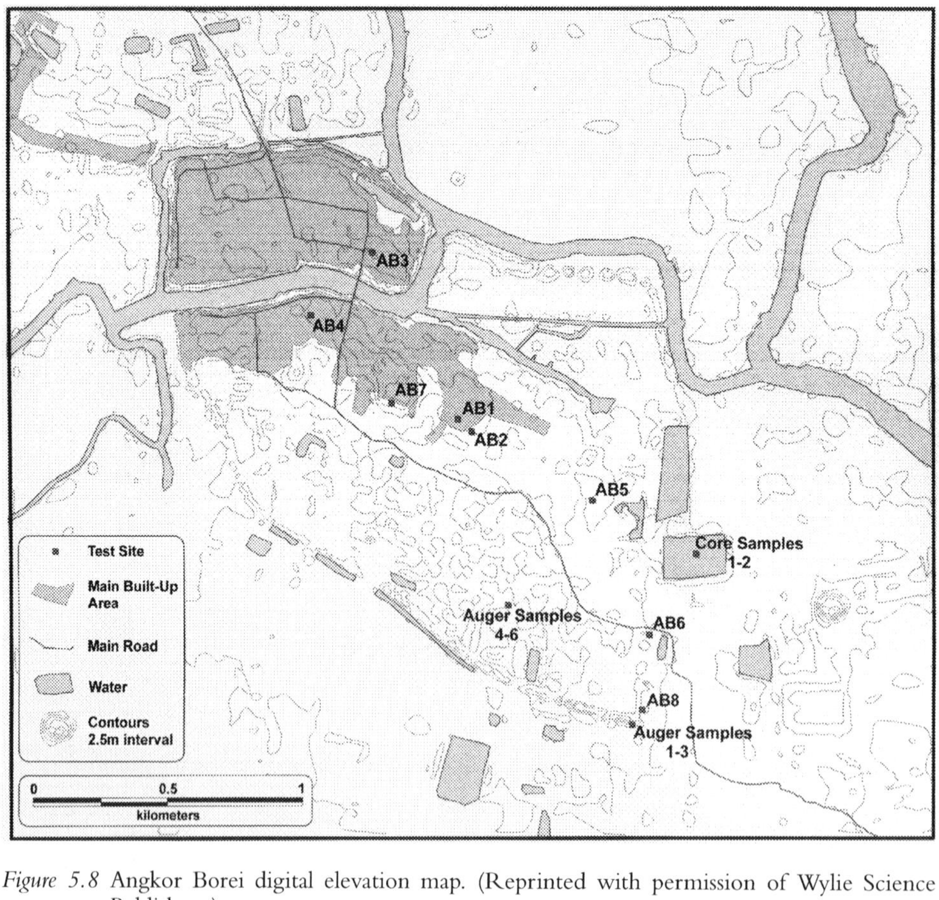

Figure 5.8 Angkor Borei digital elevation map. (Reprinted with permission of Wylie Science Publishers.)

that canals linked Angkor Borei to the Vietnamese site of Oc Eo. These features of Angkor Borei persuaded some scholars that the site was an inland capital of Funan linked to trading ports like Oc Eo, occupied primarily during the second to sixth centuries AD.[24]

Recent excavations at Angkor Borei by the Lower Mekong Archaeological Project have begun to outline its occupational history and to disentangle the collection of brick structures, *baray* (reservoirs) and artifacts that accrued during more than two millennia of occupation. This research at Angkor Borei provides the largest collection of radiocarbon dates yet published for a pre-Angkorian site in Cambodia. These extend the site's occupational sequence back to the fifth or fourth century BC, and ongoing research suggests that Angkor Borei may have been occupied continuously up to the present. Excavations in 1999 and 2000 revealed portions of an ancient cemetery in the center of the site (Figure 5.9) whose dates range from *c.*200 BC–AD 200 and provide a rare mortuary sample from this transitional period.

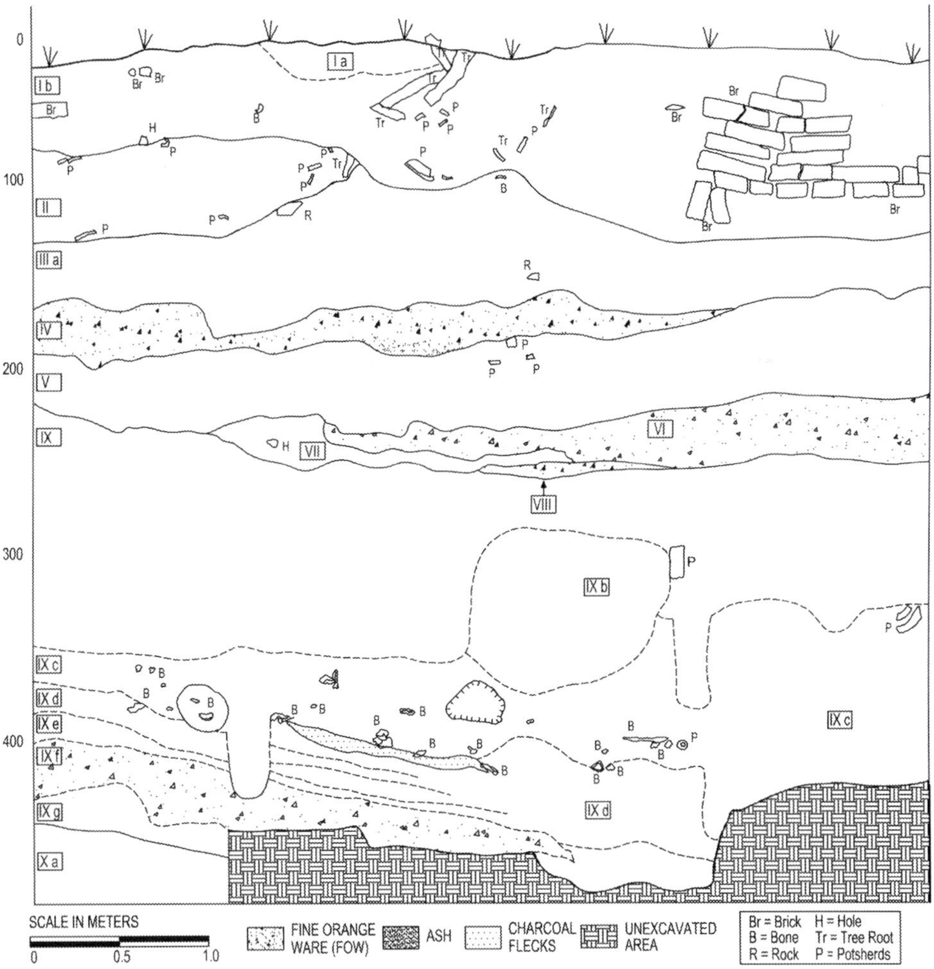

Figure 5.9 Stratigraphic profile at Angkor Borei. (Miriam T. Stark.)

So little archaeological research has been done on this time period in Cambodia that we are only beginning to see the outline of the region's settlement pattern during the early first millennium AD. The site of Ba Phnom in Prey Veng province may have been founded during this time, and still others await identification in southern Cambodia. Vietnamese excavations at more than 70 "Oc Eo culture" sites in their portion of the Mekong Delta reinforce the idea that the delta was a central hub during this time. Analysis of seventh–eighth-century inscriptions suggests that the region contained multiple rather than a single political structure.[25]

The Pre-Angkorian Period and "Chenla"

Historians refer to the sixth–eighth centuries AD as the "Pre-Angkorian Period", signaled by a shift of the power base out of the delta and a movement further up the Mekong River. By the seventh–eighth centuries AD an important center emerged in what is now central Cambodia, whence it came to dominate Cambodia's political landscape for at least two centuries. One reason behind this shift perhaps lay in a change in the regional trade networks accompanying the rise of Srivijaya in southern Sumatra. The Mekong Delta may have lost its significance in international maritime trade networks by this time. The rise of powerful and enterprising leaders of inland agricultural communities, detailed recently in Michael Vickery's study of Khmer inscriptions,[26] may also have played a role.

Evidence for this power shift derives from documentary and archaeological data. Chinese accounts describe the "Kingdom of Chenla" that wrested power from Funan and indigenous inscriptions describe a series of individuals who conquered their enemies by military might. Our knowledge of "Chenla" derives largely from Khmer and Sanskrit inscriptions[27] and largely undocumented finds of sculpture, rather than field archaeology. These are too numerous and the issues too complex to describe here. Earlier scholars like Briggs believed the capital of Chenla lay north at Wat Phu in southern Laos, near the confluence of the Mekong and Mun Rivers. More recent scholars suggest that the capitals of Chenla lay in what is now east-central Cambodia, in the province of Kompong Thom. Foremost among these pre-Angkorian settlements is Sambor Prei Kuk in Kompong Thom Province, known in the inscriptions as Isanapura.

The walled complex of Sambor Prei Kuk encloses an area of at least 400 hectares, and contains three separate precincts, each of which is surrounded by a wall. Standing brick architecture, in varying degrees of preservation (Figure 5.6), dots the landscape of this large site. Outside the external city wall is a reservoir, and the water control system at Sambor Prei Kuk has sparked interest regarding the relationship between water management and elite control.[28] Analysis of inscriptions identifies three possible Chenla rulers: Bhavavarman in the late eighth century; his successor Citrasena, who called himself Mahendravarman; and Isanavarman, who ruled during the early seventh century AD and extended his control to the Thai coast.

Although settlement at Sambor Prei Kuk continued into the Angkorian period – as did sites in the delta like Angkor Borei – its political prominence had diminished by the late eighth century AD, when Jayavarman II established a new capital that he called Isanapura. Today, we know that site as Banteay Prei Nokor, in Kompong Thom Province. Aerial reconnaissance there in the mid-1930s[29] revealed a large, square-moated and walled settlement. Outside the enclosed area were five reservoirs aligned on the same axis, one measuring 200 by 250 meters in size. Two roads radiate outward from Banteay Prei Nokor: one to the north, traceable for 20–25 kilometers, and one to the northwest, to the Mekong River. It is thought that Jayavarman II moved from this capital to the northwest within a few decades, to found his next capital at Hariharalaya north of Tonle Sap, near present-day Siem Reap. However, although several other pre-Angkorian sites have now been identified through their inscriptions and art styles, little systematic archaeological research has been undertaken to resolve their chronology and relative importance.

Northwestern Cambodia's developmental trajectory from the late prehistoric period appears to have had more in common with northeast Thailand than with central and southern Cambodia, and it is likely that the region witnessed a substantial pre-Angkorian period of settlement. At least one ruler emerged in the Tonle Sap region during the pre-Angkorian period: Jayavarman I, who established himself at Ak Yum (just west of Phnom Bakheng, Siem Reap Province) during the seventh–eighth centuries. It is also possible that the Angkorian period monuments have covered and perhaps, in some cases, obliterated earlier settlements.

The historic, or Angkor period – the Khmer Empire

Most accounts of the pre-Angkorian period describe a decentralized collection of polities that vied with each other for power from the sixth–eighth centuries AD. In the ninth century a powerful Khmer state emerged in an area in the lower Mekong River Basin that included the Tonle Sap. Perennial rivers and annual flooding, in addition to access to the lake, facilitated rice agriculture and fishing. The Tonle Sap is one of the most productive freshwater fisheries in the world. In addition, substantial areas in this region remain free from wet-season flooding and are ideal for settlement. More than 50 major monuments and dozens of smaller buildings are found on the Tonle Sap plain. Scholars often use the term "Angkor" to describe the complex of archaeological sites found between the Tonle Sap and the Kulen hills to the northeast.

Cambodia is perhaps most famous for the great ceremonial center of Angkor Wat (Plate 4), built in the twelfth century in an area which served as the imperial capital from the tenth century. At its peak in the twelfth–thirteenth centuries the Khmer Empire was far larger than the present-day kingdom of Cambodia and included large areas of Vietnam, Laos and Thailand. The expansionistic impulse drove the Khmer rulers eastward and into conflict with the Cham principalities of the central coast of Vietnam, and westwards almost to the borders of Burma to gain control over people and for access to maritime commerce via the Malay Peninsula. The archaeological record of this history consists largely of monumental constructions (Figure 5.10) in laterite, sandstone and brick that mark the ancient boundaries and provincial capitals of the Khmer Empire. This summary focuses on sociopolitical and economic trends during the Angkorian period, and how these trends are reflected in the material record.

Information on ancient Khmer history comes from four primary sources:

1 archaeological remains;
2 Khmer and Sanskrit inscriptions;
3 bas-relief iconography and statuaries; and
4 Chinese historical accounts.

Figure 5.10 Pre Rup: Mid-10th century temple built by Rajendravarman. (Photography courtesy of P. Bion Griffin.)

Historians and archaeologists have used the foregoing sources to reconstruct the royal succession, the temple-based economy, and state ideology of the Khmer Empire.

Most archaeological research during the French colonial period focused on the restoration and study of the great monuments, while art historical work was dominated by studies of style and chronology. Even today, field research currently underway in the Angkor area usually takes place within larger restoration projects for specific monuments. However, Moore's use of remote sensing to locate moated sites in the Siem Reap region and Groslier's excavations at the Royal Palace and at the cemetery of Sras Srang are two examples of research-oriented field projects in the region.[30] In addition, researchers of the École Française d'Extrême-Orient since 1992 have produced an archaeological map that sheds light on urban and rural patterning during the Khmer empire.[31] Archaeological survey and excavation in northeast Thailand has also contributed to our knowledge of regional settlement variability and economy throughout the Angkorian period.[32] In recent decades, art historians and archaeologists have also turned to the study of Khmer ceramics and their production localities (Figures 5.11 and 5.12).[33]

Translations of Khmer and Sanskrit inscriptions on stelae in temples or other sacred areas yield information on economy and society, as well as on royal lineages and religious affairs.[34] The Sanskrit inscriptions are concerned directly with the gods while Khmer inscriptions largely deal with the administration of the temple properties. References to commoners in these inscriptions are limited, but the inscriptions hold some information on the Khmer non-elite and the environment in which they lived. Additionally, Chou Ta-Kuan, a Chinese emissary who visited Angkor during 1295–6, wrote on his return to China a fascinating report which we know as "Notes on the Customs of Cambodia", following its

Figure 5.11 Khmer brown glazed footed jar with a form derived from metal vessels. Late twelfth to thirteenth century. Height 39 cm. (Photograph courtesy of Dawn Rooney.)

Figure 5.12 Khmer green glazed jar and cover, ninth or tenth century. Height 18 cm. (Photograph courtesy of Dawn Rooney.)

translation by the French sinologist Pelliot.[35] Drawing on these sources, Khmer scholars have tended to emphasize historical rather than purely archaeological perspectives.

The following sections provide a chronological framework and general background to the sociopolitical organization of the Angkorian period, and concentrate on two subjects to which archaeological and geographic research have made major contributions. The first concerns archaeological evidence for economic organization. The second examines the debate over the role that water control played in the Khmer Empire from the ninth to the fifteenth centuries AD.

Chronology and political history

Khmer inscriptions tell us that the imperial kingdom was founded *c.* AD 802 by Jayavarman II through pacification and unification of the Cambodian countryside. This established the foundations for the supra-regional power that would dominate an enormous area for several hundred years, only to decline during the first part of the fifteenth century. Newly published translations of inscriptions are compelling historians to alter their chronological framework, but an outline of royal succession as it now seems more or less accepted is provided in Table 5.2.

Some of the longer reigns were notable for their construction of monumental temples and palaces or the construction of waterworks, while others were marked by internal and

Table 5.2 Royal succession in the Khmer Empire.

Time Period	*Ruler*	*Selected Developments*
*c.*770–*c.*834	Jayavarman II	Founded kingdom by building Harihāralaya; established cult of the royal *linga*
*c.*834–*c.*870	Jayavarman III	Son of Jayavarman II
*c.*877–889	Indravarman I	Built two portions of Roluos group (Preah Koh, Lolei and Bakong) and *baray* called *Indratataka*
*c.*889/890–*c.*910/912	Yaśovarman I	Built Phnom Bakheng as new capital (called Yaśodharapura), the Eastern Baray (*Yasodharatataka*); introduced Nagari alphabet of North India
*c.*910/912–*c.*923	Harsavarman I	Built Baksei Chamkrong
*c.*923–*c.*928	Isanavarman II	– no major constructions –
928–*c.*941	Jayavarman IV	Moved royal residence away from Angkor to Koh Ker; begins Phimeanakas and Ta Keo.
*c.*941–944	Harsavarman II	– no major constructions –
944–*c.*968	Rājendravarman II	Restored capital at Yasodharapura and built temples of East Mebon and Pre Rup; raided Champa, Dvaravati, and Sukothai areas
*c.*968–*c.*1000	Jayavarman V	Consolidated Rajendravaman's conquests; constructed and dedicated Banteay Srei (Fortress of Women) in AD 968; built Ta Keo
1002–1002	Udayādityavarman I	Disappeared after one year as king
1003–1010	Jayavīravarman	Civil war rages: battle for sovereignty between Jayavīravarman and Sūryavarman. (Not usually in king lists.)
1002–1050	Sūryavarman I	Sūryavarman became king after civil war; built Phimeanakas and Western Baray; expands territory to southwest toward Gulf of Thailand and established Khmer center at Louvo (Lopburi).
1050–*c.*1066	Udayadityavarman II	Built Baphuon, West Mebon
1066/1077–1080	Harsavarman III	– no major constructions –
1080–*c.*1107	Jayavarman VI	Beginning of Mahīdhara dynasty; built Phimai.
1107–1112	Dharanīndravarman I	– no major constructions –
1113–*c.*1150	Suryavarman II	Established relations with China and fought the Chams and the Dai Viet; constructed Angkor Thom and portions of Angkor Wat, Beng Mealea and Chausay Tevoda
*c.*1150–*c.*1165	Yasovarman II	– no major constructions –
*c.*1165–1177	Tribhuvanadityavarman	Cham invasion (and Khmer defeat) ended his reign in 1177
1181–*c.*1218	Jayavarman VII	Expanded Khmer empire on the east to the South China sea, on the northeast far into Champa, and west to the borders of Pagan; built roads, bridges, hospitals and resthouses across kingdom; strengthened centralized bureaucracy; built more than 10 major monuments, including Angkor Thom and most of its contents (e.g. Bayon, Preah Khan, Ta Prohm) and Banteay Kdei and Sras Srang

Time Period	*Ruler*	*Selected Developments*
1218–1243	Indravarman II	– no major constructions –
1243–1295	Jayavarman VIII (abdicated)	May have sponsored the last known royally endowed temple
*c.*1295–1308	Indravarman III	Theravāda Buddhism became state religion; Chinese emissary Chou Ta-Kuan spends year at Angkor Wat
1300–1307*	Srindravarman (abdicated)	– no major constructions –
1308–1327*	Indrajayavarman	– no major constructions –
1330–1353*	Paramathakemaraja	– no major constructions –
1371–?*	Hou-eul-na	– no major constructions –
1404*	Samtac Pra Phaya	– no major constructions –
1405*	Samtac Pra Phaya, Phing-ya	– no major constructions –
1405–1409*	Nippean-bat	– no major constructions –
1409–1416*	Lampong or Lampang Paramaja	– no major constructions –
1416–1425*	Sorijovong, Sorijong, or Lambang	– no major constructions –
1425–1429*	Barom Racha, or Gamkhat Ramadhapati	– no major constructions –
1429–1431*	Thommo-Soccorach, or Dharmasoka	– no major constructions –
1432–?*	Ponha Yat, or Gam Yat	– no major constructions –

Note: This chronology follows the chronology presented in Mabbett and Chandler (1995: 261–68). Those marked with "*" designate contested rulers, offered by contradictory Cambodian and Thai court chronicles; these were taken from chronology in Jessup and Zephir (1997).

international warfare. Military conquest characterized Khmer rulers throughout the first three centuries of their rule. The empire of the ninth–twelfth centuries appears to have derived from a simple quest for power supported by the preceding Hindu cult. In the late twelfth century, the Khmer ruler Jayavarman VII patronized Buddhism (arguably less expansionist in ideology than Saivism) with its outward focus on commercial enterprise rather than military expansion.

Jayavarman II established his rule at Hariharalaya in the early ninth century and his successors ruled at this capital for much the remainder of the century. Indravarman I dedicated a tower of shrines (Preah Koh) to his immediate ancestors, and built the step-temple called Bakong (Figure 5.13). Yasovarman I gained the throne after battles with his brother which may have destroyed much of the royal city and built his capital city of Yasodharapura with its Eastern baray. This walled city, measuring 4 kilometres on each side, housed Phnom Bakheng as the capital.

Several decades of political fragmentation characterized the period after Yasovarman, and it took Rajendravarman to reunify the polity and restore Yashodhapura as his capital. This king's building program included several major shrines: Pre Rup (Figure 5.10), the East Mebon (built on an artificial island in the center of the Eastern Baray) and also perhaps Banteay Srei, a construction attributed to both Rajendravarman and Jayavarman

Figure 5.13 Bakong step-temple built in the ninth century by Indravarman I. (Photography courtesy of P. Bion Griffin.)

V. Rajendravarman's conquests, from the borders of Burma to Champa, brought wealth and power to his empire. In so doing, he also centralized power at Angkor and sent out groups of officials to administrate newly conquered territories.

Following Rajendravarman's reign there was a struggle for power that culminated in the ascendance of Suryavarman I, about AD 1011. Although the extent of his empire fell short of his predecessors, Suryavarman I ordered the construction of the Western Baray, which measured 8 kilometres in length and 2.1 kilometres in width. Recent estimates suggest that it held 156,240,000 cubic meters of water each year.[36] Suryavarman I also encouraged the growth of a commercial economy, along major river networks and overland routes, that connected the Khmers to Vietnam, China and to international maritime trade through the South China Sea.

The Khmer empire reached its apogee during the eleventh century. Following a series of other rulers (see Table 5.2) came Suryavarman II (AD 1113–*c.*1150), who oversaw the construction of Angkor's most famous monument, Angkor Wat, thought to be a funerary temple to his deified ancestors. The walls of this great religious monument's galleries, considered to be one of the largest religious shrines of the ancient world, are adorned with bas-relief scenes that chronicle the history and glory of the Khmer Empire. Suryavarman II also waged war against the Chams of Vietnam and sent embassies to China. Yasovarman, one of the rulers who followed Suryavarman II, was overthrown after a short reign and his successor, Tribhuvanaditya, was defeated by the Chams, weakening the Khmer empire.

Political and economic organization from the ninth to the late twelfth century

Religion and society were intimately linked throughout the Angkorian period. The ninth to the twelfth centuries were dominated by the rulers' Shaivite cults in the most common reconstructions of this period. At the top of the cosmic order were the gods and their human emissary, the king, who, by virtue of his position, was associated with divine power. The prosperity of the kingdom was bound up with the welfare of the royal *lingam*, a phallic-shaped stone that was the physical manifestation of the Hindu god Siva and also of the royal lineage.[37] Khmer rulers erected temples to house the *lingam* at the center of the current capital.

The king and his court resided in his palace in the imperial *nagara* (later corrupted to *nokor* and to Angkor under the French). The ceremonial center was an economic and social institution with a centralized administration and abundant temple complexes, under direct control of the king. It was also the physical embodiment of the heavens.[38] Aided by their Brahman priests, the Khmer kings embodied the concept of royal divinity and dedicated numerous temples to their divine ancestors.

Most historical studies of the Angkorian period have emphasized divine kingship and the structuring role of Indic ideologies rather than examining the economic infrastructure of the empire. Yet some research suggests that the Khmer state was based on an agrarian infrastructure which future archaeological research has great potential to illuminate.[39]

Socioeconomic structure

A fundamental class distinction divided Khmers into elites versus commoners, with gradations in each group.[40] Elites included royalty, bureaucrats, and wealthy landowners – some of whose names are inscribed and acts of beneficence recorded in the stone stelae erected in religious monuments. These elites, referred to as "mandarins" (or *mai-chieh*) in Chou Ta-Kuan's thirteenth-century memoirs, were found in more than 90 provinces throughout the countryside. The secular, landed elite-controlled temples throughout the empire managed irrigation systems and channeled the distribution of agricultural surpluses.

The commoner population consisted of free people, including small landholders, and slaves, most of whom lived in villages associated with particular temple complexes. Others may have lived within the walls of the Khmer ceremonial centers. Commoners plied non-agricultural professions that included artisans, traders, religious personnel, and administrative officials.[41] Documentary accounts and bas-reliefs from the Bayon suggest that male commoners were likely to be farmers, hunters, metal workers, and craftsmen. Female commoners engaged in agriculture, market trade, diplomacy, warfare, and the performing arts. Slaves comprised a large proportion of the commoner population and worked for temples, wealthy families and small farmers.

The Khmer Economy

The Khmer Empire depended on an infrastructure of wet-rice agriculture, fishing, trade tribute, taxation and corvée labor. Since most archaeological work in the Angkor region has concentrated on historic preservation and restoration rather than on research, little is yet known about the pattern of land use beyond the temple complexes. What seems clear, however, is that agricultural surpluses, gleaned from efficient rice farming, underwrote the Angkor economy. Chou Ta-Kuan reported that farmers could harvest up to four crops a year, but this is unlikely to be from the same fields but rather from cultivation of successive fields behind the receding flood from the Tonle Sap. Remote sensing techniques have identified ancient field systems throughout portions of the Angkor region today, and Van

Liere estimated that more than 50 million bunded fields were cultivated between the ninth and fifteenth centuries, using a combination of floating rice and flood recession techniques.[42]

Integral to this economy were the water control systems that facilitated settlement and farming throughout the Angkor region. The Khmers were consummate hydraulic engineers: they cut canals, dredged and straightened rivers, built dikes into the floodplain to deflect and hold back floodwaters, dug moats around their temples and some residential areas, and built countless small reservoirs to tap the high water-table found in the region. The precise role of water control systems in the historical trajectory of the Khmer Empire and of its agrarian systems, however, remains unclear. Several prominent Khmer kings also engaged in large-scale public works projects to build enormous *baray*, so large that they are visible from space by satellite.[43] The Indratataka (or Lolei *baray*), built between *c.* AD 877–890, was 3 kilometres long while the Yasodharatataka, or East Baray, constructed during the reign of Yasovarman, was 7 kilometres long.

The role of these giant reservoirs for subsistence continues to be a source of debate, and the issue is sometimes glossed as the "hydraulic paradigm".[44] For a long time it was held that the agrarian economy of Angkor rested on irrigation.[45] This has been challenged through the analysis of aerial and satellite imagery. Work by van Liere and Acker suggests that the total irrigable land available was far smaller than Groslier calculated. And they argued that the ancient Khmers relied on the traditional rain-fed techniques of floating-rice and recession agriculture that are still in use in the region today, rather than on irrigation. Khmer-built dams may have functioned as flood retardation devices rather than for irrigation and the ponded water was primarily intended for the temples.

No evidence has yet been found for a centralized system of water control and it is possible that water control for farming was organized at the local level administered by the temples. Documentary evidence suggests that the temple functioned as a center for administration and for the collection of tributes and gifts for redistribution, and this pattern may have begun during the pre-Angkorian period. Careful records were maintained of gifts to the temple, both in terms of human labor – commonly through gifts of slaves – and goods. Business transactions that occurred at the temple were also recorded, and the temple served as a type of "bank" for the harvests and seed stores of commoners.

Regional economic and political organization

Regional and possibly international trade had become important by the eleventh–twelfth centuries, yet we still know little about intra- and inter-regional trade networks at this time. Across the Khmer Empire, a series of local systems were controlled by a provincial elite, appointed by the rulers. Government officials comprised at least some portion of this provincial elite, and the wealth they collected from the countryside was channeled to the center to support temple construction and the range of attached specialists who worked for the ruler. These elites formed a caste-like group, occasionally referred to as a *varna*[46], and who were obligated to provide duties, rather than simply tribute, to their king. Markets were focal points for local systems, and temples were located near these markets served to link the Khmer center to its periphery through a series of mutual dependencies.

Research on both production localities and on the goods that artisans produced at these places sheds some light on aspects of the economy. Art historians have produced extremely useful studies on the chronology and function of Khmer glazed ceramics.[47] Brown's chronology for Khmer glazed wares (Figures 5.11 and 5.12) helps archaeologists to date a series of kiln sites that have been discovered recently both in northeastern Thailand and in the Angkor region. These kiln sites contain firing installations and a variety of ceramic wares, including jars, bowls, and roof tiles. Brown[48] suggests that these glazed wares emulated metal and Chinese containers used by the ruling elite in the Khmer capital, and were also a provincial substitute for these imported vessels. Khmer glazed wares were not intended for export and few are found beyond the boundaries of the former empire. Glazed ceramics did, however, circulate within Khmer territory, and ceramic studies indicate that artisans in the central area (Angkor and Phnom Kulen) manufactured green glazed wares primarily from the late ninth to mid-eleventh centuries, and introduced two-color glazed wares by the mid-eleventh century. Provincial potters in Buriram Province of Thailand also made green and a variety of brown glaze wares that are known as "*lie-de-vin*".[49]

Archaeological settlement survey and research on Khmer kiln sites in northeast Thailand suggests the development of regional and markets that may have preceded the founding of the Khmer state in this region. Such data, coupled with the known transportation system with its bridges and 7 meter-wide laterite roads,[50] supplement historical evidence for the economic structure of the Khmer empire. Analysis of documentary data suggests that the seventh–eighth century pre-Angkorian economy was monetized and relied on a value system with widely recognized exchange media and measures of value.[51] No convincing evidence of currency has been found, however, in either the material culture inventory (e.g. coinage) or in documentary evidence of the Angkorian period. The Khmer economy, between the ninth and twelfth centuries, relied on tribute, taxation, and corvée labor which enabled each new ruler to construct public works (usually large reservoirs) and build temples to honor his ancestors. This surplus also supported attached specialists who worked for the ruler and his entourage.

The fact that the state was based on a network of dependence in addition to economic tribute, as in many other ancient states in Southeast Asia, may be one reason why the Khmer kings pursued military expansion to finance the activities of the court. The limiting resource in the expanding Khmer empire was labor: for hydraulic works, for monumental construction and for war. Rain-fed agriculture created the surplus that could release labor for state-financed projects such as monumental construction and water engineering. While the practical function of these great water works is a matter of dispute, the Khmer state's ability to harness labor to create such works is not.

Political and economic organization in the thirteenth century

Jayavarman VII (AD 1181–1218) gave the Khmer Empire its last burst of glory. He conquered the Chams, extended Khmer dominion from Thailand into Laos, south throughout much of the Mekong Basin and west to the borders of Burma with the uncompleted city Prasat Muang Singh near Kanchanaburi on the Kwae Noi River. For Jayavarman VII, imperial expansion meant monumental construction: great stone temples and their *baray*, resthouses, hospitals, and raised roadways and stone bridges to link the provinces to the capital. Portions of the road between Angkor and Phimai, which stretched at least 225 kilometres, are visible by remote sensing today; other roads radiated west, east and southeast. Jayavarman VII also made his mark in the capital with the 3 square kilometres' walled city of Angkor Thom and its dominating Buddhist shrine, the Bayon, and two temple monasteries dedicated to his parents: Ta Prohm (to his mother) and Preah Khan (to his father). He celebrated both Hindu and Buddhist ideologies, and the four-faced towers that epitomize the Bayon are said to reflect the Buddhist incarnation of the *Boddhisattva* known as *Avalokitesvara* (Figure 5.14).

The nature of the Khmer state – and of state ideology – changed at some point in the thirteenth century, when Theravada Buddhism replaced the earlier syncretic form of Hinduism. One major reason for these changes may lie in the increased interaction between Khmers and Mon-speaking residents of Thailand's central plain,[52] where Theravada Buddhism, introduced from Sri Lanka, was widely practised during this time. Theravada Buddhism encouraged a more egalitarian structure replacing the divine cult of kings (*devaraja*) with a national religion by the end of the thirteenth century. Chou

Figure 5.14 Face towers in the Bayon temple. (Miriam T. Stark.)

Ta-Kuan's description of the court emphasizes the accessibility of the king, who held audiences at least twice a day for "functionaries and ordinary people".[53] At approximately the same time, the Khmer economy moved away from militarism and towards international commerce. Cambodia, like other regions in Mainland Southeast Asia, entered the China-based maritime trade network by the early 15th century. As happened in Thailand and Burma, Cambodia's center of power shifted southward to Udong and ultimately to the intersection of the "*quatres bras*" that we now call Phnom Penh.

The end of the reign of Jayavarman VII signaled the beginning of the Khmer empire's two-century decline. Subsequent kings continued their lives of pomp and grandeur, which Chou Ta-Kuan recorded during his visit at the end of the thirteenth century. The Khmer kings also continued to send embassies to China during this time. Yet after Jayavarman's reign, the monumental construction projects that celebrated the Khmer rulers ceased, and Khmer political control weakened with the rise of Thai states such as Sukhothai. When Thai neighbors overwhelmed Angkor in the fifteenth century AD, the era of Angkor's greatness had ended.

Several other reasons have been offered, in addition to macroeconomic reasons, to explain the decline and collapse of the Khmer Empire; among these, ecological factors related to water control technology remain popular. Use of remote sensing data from the Angkor region illuminates environmental changes that are likely to have affected the economy and society. Groslier's "hydraulic city" model, for example, linked Angkor's decline directly to siltation in the massive *baray* that ostensibly fed a complex of irrigation canals. As noted previously, whether these *baray* played an important role in providing food for the 1.9 million Angkor inhabitants that Groslier estimated remains a matter of some debate. What seems clear is that ecological factors played some role, and Heng Thung's geological analysis suggests that the region experienced significant geological uplift that caused downcutting and erosion in the rivers that fed the giant reservoirs.[54]

Economic overshoot through the massive building campaigns of the twelfth and thirteenth centuries under Jayavarman VII has also been suggested as a cause for Angkor's demise.[55] This argument, while attractive, cannot yet explain the relationship between Angkor's collapse during a period in which the first classical states[56] developed in Vietnam (Champa), Thailand (Sukhothai) and Burma (Pagan). Ecological factors like the reduction in control over the water regime may have been "more a symptom than a cause" of Angkor's decline. Social and ideological factors played a key role in the process, including the structural instability in relations between kings and officials, the growing self-sufficiency of the periphery – particular with its growing incorporation into a commercial economy – and the influence of Buddhist values on a Hindu-Saivite community.

Conclusions

The preceding journey through seven millennia of Cambodian history, from its earliest foraging origins to its period of Angkor's glory, has emphasized the high points as these are illuminated from the archaeological record. Cambodia's recent history of war and political instability have limited our knowledge of Cambodia's prehistoric past, which remains shadowy at best. Decades of concentrated research are necessary to fill the gaps in our knowledge of when and where populations became dependent on food production, and of how changes in production strategies precipitated the adoption of metal working in the region. What was the role of the Great Lake (Tonle Sap) in the process of agricultural intensification? Did foragers first experiment with domesticating plants at the lake's margins, or do we see the beginning of agricultural experimentation elsewhere, like in the Mekong Delta? Might studying the metallurgical tradition of prehistoric Cambodia – a country deficient in copper and tin – hold clues for understanding the sources of technological change that are so evident in both Thailand and Vietnam, and that take such different forms? Cambodia's location and its unique geography make it an important locus of research on these topics, and findings from such research will doubtless force revisions in our understanding of the archaeology of Mainland Southeast Asia.

The foregoing summary has sought to illustrate how the balance of knowledge regarding the Cambodian archaeological record has overwhelmingly emphasized the great monuments of the Angkorian period. Key questions concerning urban settlement and growth, provincial organization *vis-à-vis* the political center, and the operation of regional economic networks remain to be explored. Future archaeological research holds great potential to enlarge our understanding of Cambodian archaeology and thus to expand our knowledge of the archaeology of Mainland Southeast Asia.

Acknowledgments

Some research for this study, undertaken in 1994–5, was supported by the Conservation Analytical Laboratory through a Smithsonian Institution post-doctoral fellowship. My sincere thanks go to Jo Lynn Gunness, for her assistance in producing some of this article's illustrations. Figure 5.8 was generated by the Department of Geography and Topographic Sciences, University of Glasgow. Figure 5.4 was drafted by Chhor Sivleng, Mao Someaphyvath, and Vin Laychour, and Figure 5.5 was drafted by Heng Sophady. Dawn Rooney kindly provided Figures 5.11 and 5.12 for use in this article. Thanks also to faculty members of the Royal University of Fine Arts (Phnom Penh) and Ministry of Culture, who sponsor all extant archaeological research in Cambodia. I am also grateful to the institutions and organizations who have provided administrative or financial support for my ongoing research at Angkor Borei (Takeo Province, Cambodia): her Royal Highness Princess Norodom Bopha Devi and the Cambodian Ministry of Culture and Fine Arts, the Royal University of Fine Arts, the University of Hawaii, and the East–West Center for funding the Cambodia project both in Cambodia and at the University of Hawaii. Comments from, and conversations with, Yasushi Kojo, Michael Vickery, Charles Higham, Christophe Pottier, Ashley Thompson, Dawn Rooney, and James Bayman strengthened this manuscript considerably. I am also grateful to Ian Glover for his careful editorial and graphics assistance on this chapter. Mistakes or misrepresentations in this paper are, however, my own responsibility.

Note on sources for the history and archaeology of Cambodia:
Scholarly research on Cambodia started in the late nineteenth century and the overwhelming bulk of published material is in French with lesser amounts in English, German and Japanese. For this essay, primarily French and English sources have been used and only writings in western languages are cited below.

Research on the inscriptions and art history of Cambodia was quite intensive between about 1900 and 1940 before being interrupted by the Second World War. Research resumed after the war; archaeological research and architectural conservation then continued until the early 1970s when insurgency, revolution and war brought a halt to all fieldwork. From the early 1990s Indian, French and many foreign scholars have taken up active research in Cambodian archaeology; a few scholars currently work on the earlier prehistory of the country.

Notes

1 Mourer 1986: 72–5, 1994: 143–6; Worman 1949: 321–2.
2 Dates using surface finds, freshwater or marine shell, or bone collagen, were excluded from the sample because of methodological problems with dating these materials.
3 See Saurin 1963, 1966; Mourer 1994: 165–8; Carbonnel 1970.
4 Mourer 1977, 1986, 1988, Mourer and Mourer 1970, 1973.
5 White 1995.
6 On these sites see Groslier 1966: 193; Malleret 1959; Kojo and Pheng 1997: 181; Carbonnel 1979.
7 Albrecht *et al.* 2000; Dega 1999; Kojo and Pheng 1997, 1998; Thung 2002.
8 Groslier 1979: 165; Mourer 1977: 52.
9 Mourer 1977: 52, 1994: 172.
10 On Samrong Sen, see Cartailhac 1890; Janse 1951; Mansuy 1902, 1923: 2–8; Mourer 1986: 94–7; Worman 1949.
11 Lévy 1943.
12 Kojo 1998.
13 Pottier 2000.
14 O'Reilly and Pheng 2001.
15 Wolters 1999.
16 Glover 1998; Ray 1989.
17 Coedès 1968; Kulke 1990.
18 Higham 1989: 245–54, 279–87.
19 Moore 1992, 1998.
20 Several historians, most notably Georges Coedès (1937, 1942, 1951, 1952, 1953, 1954, 1964, 1966), have devoted their scholarly careers to translating inscriptions. Interpretations of this corpus of documentary data, by Coedès (1968), Claude Jacques (e.g. 1979, 1986, 1990, 1995) and Michael Vickery (1986, 1994, 1998), provide an indispensable data source for studying pre-Angkorian and Angkorian Cambodia (see also Ishizawa 1995; Jacob 1978, 1979; Mabbett 1969, 1977, 1983; Wheatley 1983). See also Stark 1998.
21 Pelliot 1903; Wheatley 1983.
22 Aymonier 1900; Malleret 1959–1962; Parmentier 1927.
23 Pelliot 1903.
24 On Angkor Borei, see Stark *et al.* 1999; Stark and Bong 2001; Paris 1931, 1941; Bishop *et al.* 2003.
25 Jacques 1990; Vickery 1998; see Stark 2001 for dating of Angkor Borei cemetery.
26 Vickery 1998.
27 Vickery 1994.
28 Groslier 1979; van Liere 1980.
29 Goloubew 1936.
30 Moore 1992, 1998; Courbin 1998.
31 Pottier 1998, 1999.

32 Welch 1989.
33 Brown 1988; Rooney 1981, 1984.
34 Coedès 1968; Jacques 1986, 1990; Jacob 1978, 1979; Mabbett 1969, 1977, 1983; Ricklefs 1967: 418.
35 Pelliot 1951.
36 Acker 1998.
37 Aeusrivognse 1976; Mabbett 1969.
38 Wheatley 1983; Mabbett 1969: 211; Mannikka 1996.
39 Wheatley 1975. Research recently started by Pottier (EFEO) and Fletcher and Barbetti (University of Sydney) promises to shed new light on domestic settlement and the Angkor agricultural economy.
40 Jacques 1986: 331.
41 Jacob 1979: 407–8.
42 Acker 1998; van Liere 1980.
43 Parry 1996.
44 Acker 1998; Groslier 1979; Moore 1989; Pottier 1998; Stott 1992; van Liere 1980.
45 Groslier 1956, 1966b, 1979.
46 Mabbett 1977.
47 Brown 1988; Rooney 1981, 1984; Aoyagi *et al.* 2000.
48 Brown 1988: 47.
49 Brown 1988.
50 Parry 1996: 29–30.
51 Wicks 1992: 186–93.
52 Briggs 1951: 242, 259.
53 Chou Ta-Kuan 1987: 40.
54 Thung 2002.
55 Giteau 1976.
56 Southeast Asian historians customarily refer to the thirteenth–fifteenth century polities as "the Classical States", and the term is used in that sense here.

Select Bibliography

General books and articles

Aymonier, E. (1900) *Le Cambodge. Le Royaume Actuel*, Paris: Ernest Leroux.

Boisselier, J. (1966) *Asie du Sud-Est. Tome I, Le Cambodge*, Tome I. Paris: Picard et C[ie].

Briggs, L. P. (1951) *The Ancient Khmer Empire*, Philadelphia: Transactions of the American Philosophical Society, New Series vol. 41(1), Part I.

Chou Ta-Kuan (1987) *The Customs of Cambodia* (translated from the French by Paul Pelliot), Bangkok: Siam Society.

Coe, M. (2003) *Angkor and the Khmer Civilization*, London: Thames & Hudson.

Coedès, G. (1968) *The Indianized States of Southeast Asia* (translated by S. B. Cowing), Honolulu: University of Hawai'i Press.

Freeman, M. and Jacques, C. (1999) *Ancient Angkor*, Bangkok: Asia Books.

Groslier, B-P. (1956) *Angkor, hommes et pierres*, Arthaud, Paris (revised 1966; English edition published as *Angkor, Art and Civilization*, New York: F. A. Praeger.

Groslier, B-P. (1966b) *Indochine*, Archaeologia Mundi. Geneva, Paris, and Munich: Nagel (English edition, *Indochina*, London: F. Muller Ltd.

Groslier, B-P. (1979) "La cité hydraulique angkorienne: exploitation ou surexploitation du sol?" *Bulletin de l'École Française d'Extrême-Orient* 66: 181–202.

Ishizawa, Y. (1995) "Chinese chronicles of 1st–5th century AD Funan, Southern Cambodia", in R. Scott and J. Guy (eds) *South East Asia & China: Art, Interaction & Commerce, Colloquies on Art and Archaeology in Asia* 17: 11–31, London: Percival David Foundation of Chinese Art, School of Oriental and African Studies.

Jacques, C. (1990) *Angkor*, Paris: Bordas.

Jacques, C. (1995) "China and ancient Khmer history". in R. Scot and J. Guy (eds) *South East Asia & China: Art, Interaction & Commerce, Colloquies on Art and Archaeology in Asia* 17: 32–40, London: Percival David Foundation of Chinese Art, School of Oriental and African Studies.

Janse, O. R. T. (1951) *Archaeological Research in Indo-China. Volume I*, Boston: Harvard-Menching Monograph Series 2, Harvard University Press.

Kulke, H. (1990) "Indian Colonies, Indianization or Cultural Convergence? Reflections on the changing image of India's role in South-East Asia", in H. Schulte Norholt (ed.) *Onderzoek In Zuidoost-Asië*, pp. 8–32, Leiden: Vakgroep Talen en Culturen van Zuidoost-Asië en Oceanië, Rijksuniversiteit te Leiden.

Mabbett, I. and Chandler, D. (1995) *The Khmers*, Oxford: Blackwell.

Pelliot, P. (1903) "Le Fou-nan", *Bulletin de l'École Française de l'Extrême Orient*, 3: 248–303.

Pelliot, P. (1951) *Mémoires sur les Coutumes du Cambodge de Tcheou Ta-Kouan*, (version nouvelle, suivie d'un commentaire inachevé), Paris: Libraire d'Amérique et d'Orient, Adrien-Maisonneuve.

Ray, H. P. (1989) "Early maritime contacts between South and Southeast Asia", *Journal of Southeast Asian Studies* 10(1): 42–54.

Stark, M. T. (1998) "The transition to history in the Mekong Delta: a view from Cambodia", *International Journal of Historic Archaeology* 2(3): 175–204.

Wheatley, P. (1975) "Satyanrta in Suvarnadvipa: from reciprocity to redistribution in ancient Southeast Asia", pp. 227–83, in J. A. Sabloff and C. C. Lamberg-Karlovsky, (eds). *Ancient Civilization and Trade*, Albuquerque: University of New Mexico Press.

Wheatley, P. (1983) "Nagara and Commandery: Origins of the Southeast Asian Urban Traditions", research papers Nos 207–8, Chicago: Department of Geography, University of Chicago.

Wolters, O. W. (1999) *History, Culture, and Region in Southeast Asian Perspectives* (revised edn) Southeast Asia Program, New York: Cornell University, Ithaca (in cooperation with the Institute for Southeast Asian Studies, Singapore).

Archaeology

Albrecht, G., Haidle, M. N., Sivleng, C., Hong, H. L., Sophady, H., Than, H., Someaphyvath, M., Kada, S., Sopahl, S., Chanthourn, T. and Laychour, V. (2000) "Circular earthwork Krek 52/62, recent research on the prehistory of Cambodia", *Asian Perspectives* 39(1–2): 20–46.

Bruguier, B. (1998) "L'organisation spatial des sanctuaires Khmers: plan axé ou concentrique?", in P.-Y. Manguin (ed.) *Southeast Asian Archaeology 1994*, pp. 173–8. Hull: Centre for Southeast Asian Studies, University of Hull.

Carbonnel, J.-P. (1979) "Recent data on the Cambodian Neolithic; the problem of cultural continuity in southern Indochina", in R. B. Smith and W. Watson (eds) *Early South-East Asia: Essays in Archaeology, History and Historical Geography*, pp. 223–226. Oxford: Oxford University Press.

Cartailhac, É. (1890) "Les bronzes préhistoriques du Cambodge et les recherches de M. Ludovic Jammes", *L'Anthropologie* 6: 641–50.

Courbin, P. (1988) *La Fouille du Sras-Srang*, Collection de Textes et Documents Sur L'Indochine, XVII. Paris: École Française d'Extrême-Orient.

Dega, M. F. (1999) "Circular settlements within Eastern Cambodia", *Bulletin of the Indo-Pacific Prehistory Association* 18: 181–90.

Dega, M. F. (2002) *Prehistoric Circular Earthworks*, Oxford: Archaeopress.

Glover, I. C. (1998) "The role of India in the later prehistory of Southeast Asia", *Journal of Southeast Asian Archaeology* 18: 21–49.

Goloubew, V. (1936) "Reconnaissances aériennes au Cambodge I. Survol de Bantay Prei Nokor dans la Province de Kompon Cam", *Bulletin de l'École Française d'Extrême-Orient* 36: 465–9.

Groslier, B-P. (1966a) "Découvertes archéologiques récentes au Cambodge", *Kambuja* 16: 76–81. Phnom Penh.

Higham, C. F. W. (2002) *The Early Cultures of Mainland Southeast Asia*, Bangkok: River Books.

Higham, C. F. W. (2002) *The Civilization of Angkor*, Berkeley: University of California Press.

Kojo, Y. and Pheng, S. (1997) "A newly discovered circular earthwork in Southeastern Cambodia", *Anthropological Science* 105(3): 181–7.

Kojo, Y. and Pheng, S. (1998) "A preliminary investigation of a circular earthwork at Krek, southeastern Cambodia", *Anthropological Science* 106(3): 229–44.

Lévy, P. (1943) *Recherches Préhistoriques dans la Region de Mlu Prei*, Hanoi: Imprimerie d'Extrême-Orient.

Ly, Vanna (2001) "Recent archaeological research in the floodplain of the Tonle Sap River: the Shell Midden site of Samrong Sen and its pottery characteristics", *Journal of Southeast Asian Archaeology* 21: 47–81.

Malleret, L. (1959) "Ouvrages circulaires en terre dans l'Indochine meridionale", *Bulletin de l'École Française d'Extrême-Orient* 59(2): 409–34.

Malleret, L. (1959–62) *L'Archéologie du Delta du Mékong, Parts 1–3*, Paris: Publication de l'École Française d'Extrême-Orient.

Mansuy, H. (1902) *Stations Préhistoriques de Somrong-Seng de Long Prao (Cambodge)*, Hanoi: F. H. Schneider.

Mansuy, H. (1923) "Contribution à l'étude de la préhistoire de l'Indochine, III. Résultats de nouvelles recherches effectuées dans le gisement préhistorique de Somrong Sen (Cambodge). Suivi d'un résumé de l'état de nos connaissances sur la préhistoire et sur l'ethnologie des races anciennes dans l'Extrême-Orient mêridional", Hanoi: Mémoires du Service Géologique de l'Indochine, 10.

Moore, E. H. (1998) "The prehistoric habitation of Angkor", in Pierre-Yves Manguin (ed.) *Southeast Asian Archaeology 1994, Volume 1*, pp. 27–36, Hull: Centre for Southeast Asian Studies, University of Hull.

Mourer, R. (1977) "Laang Spean and the prehistory of Cambodia", *Modern Quaternary Research in Southeast Asia* 3: 29–56.

Mourer, R. (1986) "La Poterie au Cambodge: histoire et developpement. Essai d'ethnotechnologie", PhD thesis, Paris: École des Hautes Études en Sciences Sociales.

Mourer, R. (1994) "Contribution a l'étude de la préhistoire du Cambodge", in F. Bizot (ed.) *Récherches Nouvelles sur le Cambodge*, pp. 143–87, Paris: L'École Française d'Extrême Orient.

Mourer, R. and Mourer, C. (1970) "The prehistoric industry of Laang Spean, Province of Battambang, Cambodia", *Archaeology and Physical Anthropology in Oceania* 5(2): 128–46.

Mourer, R. and Mourer, C. (1973) "Prehistoric research in Cambodia during the last ten years", *Asian Perspectives* 14: 35–42.

Murowchick, R. E. (1988) "The development of early bronze metallurgy in Vietnam and Kampuchea: a re-examination of recent work", in R. Maddin (ed.) *The Beginning of the Use of Metals and Alloys*, pp. 175–81, Boston: Massachusetts Institute of Technology.

O'Reilly, D. and Peng Sytha (2001) "Recent excavations in Northwest Cambodia", *Antiquity* 75: 265–66.

Pottier, C. (1998) "Elaboration d'une carte archéologique de la region d'Angkor: l'organisation du territoire Angkorien", in Pierre-Yves Manguin (ed.) *Southeast Asian Archaeology 1994*, pp. 179–94. Hull: Centre for Southeast Asian Studies, University of Hull.

Pottier, C. (1999) "Carte archéologique de la région d'Angkor: Zone Sud", PhD thesis, 3 vols. Université Paris III-Sorbonne Nouvelle (UFR Orient et Monde Arabe).

Pottier, C. (2000) "Rapport sur la visite d'une nécropolie de l'âge du fer", report submitted to the Ministry of Culture and Fine Arts, Cambodia: École Française d'Extrême-Orient, Centre de Siemreap-Angkor.

Qiao Liang and Li Yu-Qun (2000) "Report on archaeological research at Chao Say Tevoda Temple, Angkor", *Udaya* 1: 255–94.

Saurin, E. (1963) "Premiers élements sur la présence de galets aménagés et de vieux paléolithiques au Cambodge", *Comptes-Rendus Sommaires de la Société Géologique de France* 259–60.

Saurin, E. (1966) "Le Paléolithique du Cambodge Oriental", *Asian Perspectives* IX: 96–110.

Saurin, E. (1969) "Les recherches préhistoriques au Cambodge, Laos, et Vietnam (1877–1966)", *Asian Perspectives* 12: 27–41.

Stark, M. T. (2001) "Some preliminary results of the 1999–2000 archaeological field excavations at Angkor Borei, Takeo Province", *Udaya* 2: 19–36.

Stark, M. T. and Sovath, B. (2001) "Recent research on the emergence of early historic states in Cambodia's Lower Mekong Delta", *Bulletin of the Indo-Pacific Prehistory Association* 19: 85–98.

Stark, M. T., Bion Griffin, P., Phoeurn, C., Ledgerwood, J., Dega, M., Mortland, C., Dowling, N., Bayman, J., Sovath, B., Van, T., Chamroeun, C. and Latinis, K. (1999) "Results of the 1995–1996 field investigations at Angkor Borei, Cambodia", *Asian Perspectives*, 38(1): 7–36.

Vickery, M. (1994) "Where and what was Chenla?", in F. Bizot (ed.) *Récherches Nouvelles sur le Cambodge*, pp. 197–212, Paris: L'École Française d'Extrême-Orient.

Welch, D. J. (1989) "Late prehistoric and early historic exchange patterns in the Phimai region, Thailand", *Journal of Southeast Asian Studies* 10(1): 11–26.

White, J. (1995) "Incorporating heterarchy into theory on socio-political development: the case from Southeast Asia", pp. 101–23, in R. M. Ehrenreich, C. L. Crumley and J. E. Levy (eds), *Heterarchy and the Analysis of Complex Societies*, Washington: Archaeological Papers of the American Anthropological Association, No. 6.

Worman, E. C. (1949) "Samrong Sen and the reconstruction of prehistory in Indochina", *Southwestern Journal of Anthropology* 5(4): 318–29.

Art history

Boisselier, J (1989) *Trends in Khmer Art* (trans. and ed. N. Eilenberg), New York: Cornell University, Southeast Asia Program, Ithaca.

Giteau, M. (1965) *Khmer Sculpture and the Angkor Civilization*, London: Thames and Hudson.

Giteau, M. (1976) *The Civilization of Angkor*, New York: Rizzoli.

Jessup, H. I. and Zephir, T. (eds) (1997) *Sculpture of Angkor and Ancient Cambodia*, Washington: National Gallery of Art.

Parmentier, M. H. (1927) *L'Art Khmer Primitif*, Paris: Publications de l'École Française de l'Extrême-Orient.

Rooney, D. F. (2000) *Angkor: An Introduction to the Temples*, Hong Kong: Odyssey.

Ceramics

Aoyagi, Y., Sasaki, T., Marui, M. and Miyata, E. (1998). "Investigation of Tani Kiln Site Group, Angkor". *Reconnaissance Culturelle de Cambodge* 15.

Aoyagi, Y., Sasaki, T., Tanaka, K., Nogami, T., Marui, M. and Sumida, T. (2000) "Excavation of a Khmer Ceramic Kiln Site: Report of the Investigation of Kiln B1, Tani Kiln Complex", *Udaya* 1: 235–53.

Brown, R. (1988) *The Ceramics of South-East Asia: Their Dating and Identification*, (2nd edn), Oxford and New York: Oxford University Press.

Dumarçay, J. (1973) *Charpentes et Tuiles Khmères*, Paris: École Française d'Extrême-Orient.

Franiatte, M. (2000) "Nouvelle Analyses de la céramique khmère du Palais Royal d'Angkor Thom: Etude préliminaire", *Udaya* 1: 91–124.

Groslier, B-P. (1981) "Introduction to the ceramic wares of Angkor", in D. Stock (ed.) *Khmer Ceramics, 9th–14th Century*, pp. 9–40. Singapore: Southeast Asian Ceramic Society.

Guy, J. (1996–1997) "A reassessment of Khmer ceramics", *Transactions of the Oriental Ceramic Society* 61: 39–63.

Rooney, D. F. (1981) "Uses of Khmer ceramics", in D. Stock (ed.) *Khmer Ceramics, 9th–14th Century*, pp. 51–55, Singapore: Southeast Asian Ceramic Society.

Rooney, D. F. (1984) *Khmer Ceramics*, Oxford: Oxford University Press.

Stark, M. T. (2000) "Pre-Angkor earthenware: ceramics from Cambodia's Mekong Delta", *Udaya* 1: 69–90.

Stock, D. (ed.) (1982) *Khmer Ceramics, 9th–14th Century*, Singapore: Southeast Asian Ceramic Society.

Epigraphy

Coedès, G. (1937–66) *Inscriptions du Cambodge*, vols. 1–8, École Française d'Extrême Orient, Collection de textes et documents sur l'Indochine III, Hanoi: Imprimerie d'Extrême Orient.

Jacques, C. (1979) "Funan, Zhenla: The reality concealed by these Chinese views of Indochina", pp. 371–9, in R. Smith and W. Watson (eds) *Early South East Asia: Essays in Archaeology, History, and Historical Geography*, pp. 371–9, Oxford: Oxford University Press.

Jacob, J. M. (1978) "The ecology of Angkor: evidence from the Khmer inscriptions", in P. A. Stott (ed.) *Nature and Man in South East Asia*, pp. 109–27, London: School of Oriental and African Studies, University of London.

Jacob, J. M. (1979) "Pre-Angkor Cambodia: evidence from the inscriptions in Khmer concerning the common people and the environment", in R. B. Smith and W. Watson (eds) *Early South East Asia: Essays in Archaeology, History, and Historical Geography*, pp. 406–26. Oxford: Oxford University Press.

Geology, ecology, hydrology, water management and land use

Acker, R. (1998) "New geographical tests of the hydraulic thesis at Angkor", *South East Asia Research* 6(1): 5–47.

Bishop, P., Sanderson, D. C. W. and Stark M. T. (2003) "OSL and radiocarbon dating of a pre-Angkorian canal in the Mekong Delta, southern Cambodia", *Journal of Archaeological Science* 31 (3) 319–36.

Carbonnel, J.-P. (1970) "Le Quaternaire cambodgien. Structure et straigraphie", Doctorat d'Etat, University of Paris.

Groslier, B-P. (1979) "La cité hydraulique angkorienne: exploitation ou surexploitation du sol?", *Bulletin de l'École Française d'Êxtrème Orient* 66: 161–202.

Jacob, J. M. (1978) "The ecology of Angkor: evidence from the Khmer inscriptions", in P. A. Stott (ed.) *Nature and Man in South East Asia*, pp. 109–27, London: School of Oriental and African Studies, University of London.

Moore, E. H. (1989) "Water management in Cambodia: evidence from aerial photography", *Geographical Journal* 155(2): 204–14.

Moore, E. H. (1992) "Water enclosed sites: links between Ban Takhong, Northeast Thailand and Cambodia", in J. Rigg (ed.) *The Gift of Water: Water Management, Cosmology and the State in South East Asia*, pp. 26–46, London: School of Oriental and African Studies.

Paris, P. (1931) "Anciens canaux reconnus sur photographies aeriennes dans les provinces de Ta-Keo et de Chau-doc", Paris: *Bulletin de l'École française d'Extrême-Orient* 31: 221–4.

Paris, P. (1941a) "Anciens canaux reconnus sur photographies aeriennes dans les provinces de Ta-Keo, Chau-doc, Long Xuyen", Paris: *Bulletin de l'École française d'Extrême-Orient* 41: 365–70.

Paris, P. (1941b) "Autres canaux à l'est du Mékong par examen d'autres photographies aeriennes provinces de Ta-Keo, Chau-doc et de Long Xuyen", Paris: *Bulletin de l'École Française d'Extrême-Orient* 41: 371–2.

Parry, J. T. (1996) "A new perspective on Angkor – the spatial organization of an historical landscape viewed from Landsat", *Geocarto International* 11(2): 15–32.

Stott, P. (1992) "Angkor: shifting the hydraulic paradigm", in J. Rigg (ed.) *The Gift of Water: Water Management, Cosmology and the State in South East Asia*, pp. 47–58, London: School of Oriental and African Studies.

Thung, Heng (2002) "Angkor revisited: lessons to learn?" *SPAFA Journal* 12(2): 5–17.

Van Liere, W. J. (1980) "Traditional water management in the Lower Mekong Basin", *World Archaeology* 11(3): 265–80.

Politics and economics

Jacques, C. (1986) "Sources on economic activities in Khmer and Cham Lands", in D. G. Marr and A. C. Milner (eds) *Southeast Asia in the 9th to 14th Centuries*, pp. 327–34, Singapore: Institute of Southeast Asian Studies and Research School of Pacific Studies, Australian National University.

Vickery, M. (1986) "Some remarks on early state formation in Cambodia", in D. G. Marr and A. C. Milner (eds) *Southeast Asia in the 9th to 14th Centuries*, pp. 95–115, Singapore: Institute of Southeast Asian Studies.

Vickery, M. (1998) *Society, Economics and Politics in pre-Angkor Cambodia: The 7th and 8th Centuries*, Tokyo: The Centre for East Asian Cultural Studies for Unesco, The Toyo Bunko.

Wicks, R. L. (1992) "Money and society in ancient Cambodia and Champa", in *Money, Markets and Trade in Early Southeast Asia*, pp. 183–218. Ithaca: Southeast Asia Program, Cornell University.

Religion and iconography

Aeusrivognse, Nidhi (1976) "The *Devaraja* Cult and Khmer Kingship at Angkor", in K. R. Hall and J. K. Whitmore (eds) *Explorations in Early Southeast Asian History*, pp. 107–148, Ann Arbor: University of Michigan.

Mabbett, I. W. (1969) *Devaraja. Journal of Southeast Asian History* 10(2): 202–23.

Mabbett, I. W. (1977) "*Varnas* in Angkor and the Indian Caste System", *Journal of Asian Studies* 36(3): 429–42.

Mannikka, E. (1996) *Angkor Wat: Time, Space, and Kingship*, Honolulu: University of Hawaii Press.

Social organization

Kirsch, A. T. (1976) "Kinship, genealogical claims, and societal integration in Ancient Khmer society: an interpretation", in C. D. Cowan and O. W. Wolters (eds) *Southeast Asian History and Historiography*, pp. 190–202, Ithaca: Cornell University Press.

Mabbett, I. W. (1983) "Some remarks on the present state of knowledge about slavery in Angkor", in A. Reid (ed.) *Slavery, Bondage and Dependency in Southeast Asia*, pp. 44–63, New York: St. Martin's Press.

Ricklefs, M. C. (1967) "Land and law in the epigraphy of tenth century Cambodia", *Journal of Asian Studies* 26(3): 411–20.

6

THE ARCHAEOLOGY OF THE EARLY BUDDHIST KINGDOMS OF THAILAND

Phasook Indrawooth

Literary and archaeological evidence has confirmed that Central Thailand was the homeland of an early kingdom, or kingdoms, referred to in inscriptions as "Dvaravati". In the seventh century, Chinese historians and pilgrims to India spoke of the existence of a kingdom that they called *To-lo-po-ti*, situated to the west of Isanapura (Cambodia) and to the east of Sri Ksetra (Burma).[1] The Chinese name for this civilization was interpreted as representing the Sanskrit word Dvaravati, meaning "which has gates". But it was not until 1964 that this interpretation was confirmed by two inscribed silver coins found at Nakhon Pathom.[2]

Our knowledge of this civilization was expanded when Paul Pelliot suggested that the people of Dvaravati were Mons. Coedès[3] attributed the "Hindu non-Cambodian" images around the Gulf of Siam described by Lajonquière to the Mons of Dvaravati. He also identified some of the contemporary inscriptions found in the area as being in the Mon language, In 1959, Pierre Dupont convinced most scholars that Dvaravati was indeed a great Mon kingdom[4] whose culture extended widely and came to embrace virtually the whole area of modern Thailand. Not long after that came the supposition that Dvaravati formed part of a Mon confederacy centered at Thaton in Lower Burma. However, this supposition had no support beyond vague legendary and linguistic evidence. Scholars have long been troubled by the absence of early Buddhist remains in the Mon country of Lower Burma, as compared with their abundance in Central Thailand. For a good understanding of the formation of Dvaravati kingdom, one must study the chronological development of the cultural history of Central Thailand.

Central Thailand before the Dvaravati period

In Chapter 3, Higham treats the main aspects of prehistoric Thailand and here we merely mention that archaeological research carried out by foreign and Thai archaeologists shows that the western part of Central Thailand had long been inhabited by prehistoric peoples (Figure 6.1). Evidence of their occupation may be found in caves, and in riverside camps along the Khwae Noi and Khwae Yai Valleys in Kanchanaburi Province. The earliest recognized groups, often referred to as Hoabinhian,[5] were mobile hunters and gatherers and their remains have been excavated at Sai Yok, Phra and Heap caves among other locations. From the late third millennium BC onwards, more permanent settlements such

Figure 6.1 Some of the main prehistoric sites in Southeast Asia.

as Ban Kao and Ban Na Khun Saenae occur along river terraces in the Meklong-Tha Chin Valleys. These Neolithic communities practiced rice cultivation, animal husbandry, and made pottery and used polished stone axes that replaced the flaked tools of the Hoabinhian tradition. From about 1500 BC bronze tools came into common use, particularly in central and northeastern Thailand, but are less commonly found in western and southern regions where iron was introduced, perhaps from India, about 600–500 BC.

Many Iron Age sites in Thailand, such as Rim Khwae Noi, Ban Don Ta Phet and Khok Plub in the Meklong – Tha Chin Valleys, reveal evidence of exchange with India during the Maurya-Sunga Period (*c*.350–50 BC). Of these, Ban Don Ta Phet is one of the most important Iron Age sites yet excavated in Thailand. According to the available radiocarbon dates, the occupation at Ban Don Ta Phet dates from the early fourth century BC and includes good evidence for exchange with sites in South Asia such as Taxila (a subsidiary capital of the Mauryas in northern Pakistan), where very similar bronze bowls and lion amulets have been found.[6] These links are described in detail in chapter 4.

The development of trade within the Indian subcontinent

Trade between Taxila and other centers such as Bharukaccha, Tamralipti, Vidisa and Ujjain was facilitated by the Royal Highways constructed under the Mauryans. Asokan inscriptions[7] show that under more energetic governments, roads were well developed in order to maintain law and order and to provide facilities for long distant trade (Figure 6.2). The Mauryan Royal Highway ran through the entire length of the country, from the capital Pataliputra in Bihar, passing modern Delhi, and crossing the five rivers of the Panjab to the north-western city of Taxila. From Taxila there was a trunk road through the Khyber Pass to the Upper Kabul valley which led across the Hindu Kush to Bactria, an important centre for the transit trade between India, China, Central Asia and the Mediterranean world. From Tamralipti in Bengal, ships not only sailed to Sri Lanka, but also to Southeast Asia and Indonesia (Figure 6.3). Other authors have given full accounts of the development of trade between India and Southeast Asia.[8]

During the Proto-historic Period, contemporaneous with the Indo-Roman Period in India (*c*.50 BC–AD 300), trade relations between India and Central Thailand became more extensive. In India, there was also an active trade between India and the Roman Empire from about the middle of the first century AD, via ports along the Andhra coastline.[9]

Trade goods from Indian ports to Southeast Asia include glass beads, stone beads made from varieties of semi-precious stones, ivory combs, ivory or bone dice, as well as Mediterranean-made objects such as bronze Roman lamps, intaglio seals, local imitations of Roman Arretine ware and Indo-Roman Rouletted pottery bowls. Especial mention should be made of the following:

- A bronze Roman lamp comes from Pong Tuk, Kanchanaburi Province (Figure 6.4). Picard thought this came from Hellenistic Alexandria during the third century BC, whereas Brown and Macdonnel have argued that it is of late Roman–Byzantine manufacture from Greece.[10]
- A Roman coin, issued by the Western Roman Emperor Victorinus (AD 268–70), comes from U Thong in Suphanburi Province[11] (see Figure 4.1).
- An ivory comb, clearly of Indian manufacture, incised on one side with a design depicting an ornate goose or *hamsa* and on the other side with a pair of horses

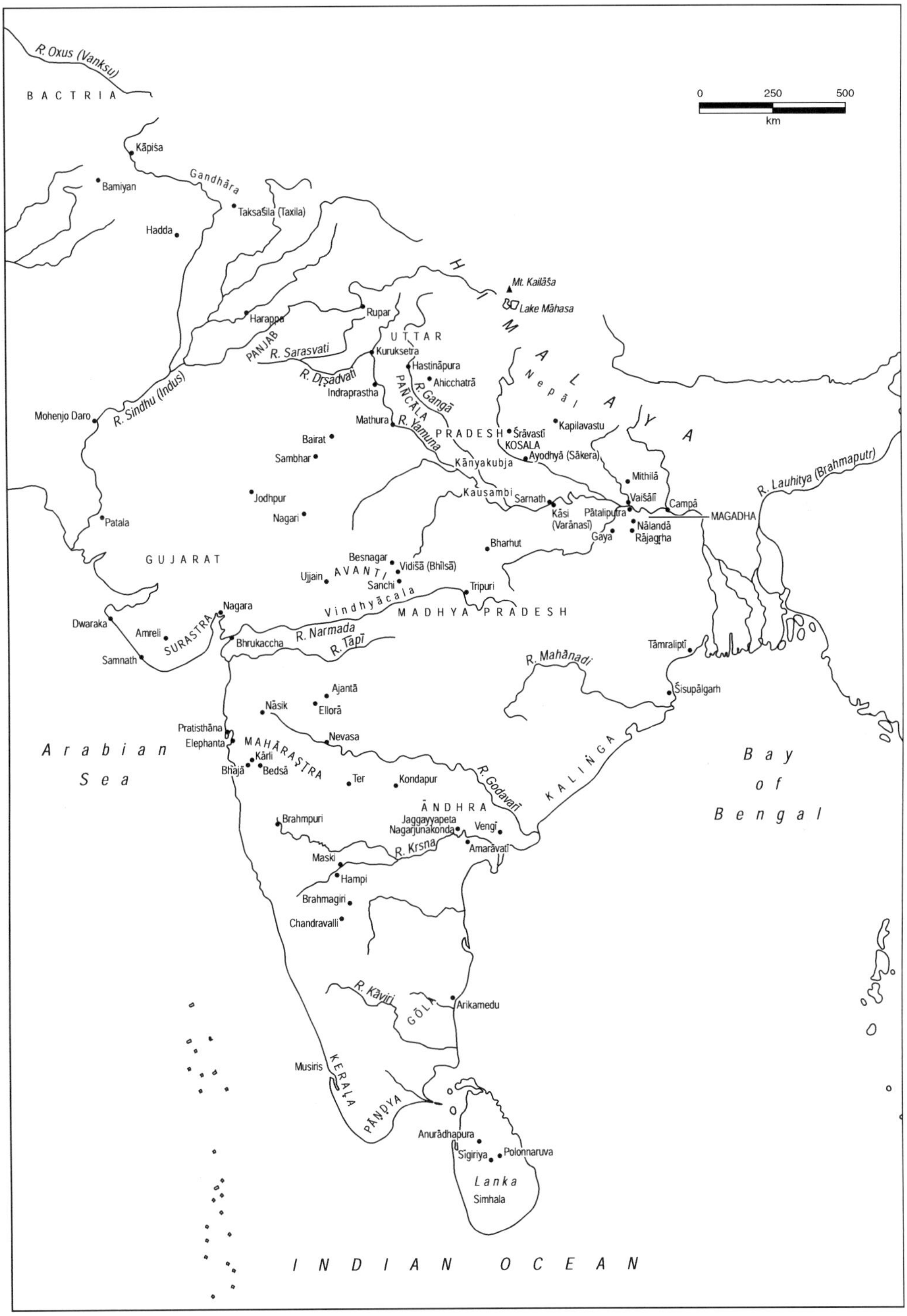

Figure 6.2 Important sites of the Iron Age and the Post-Iron Age in South Asia.

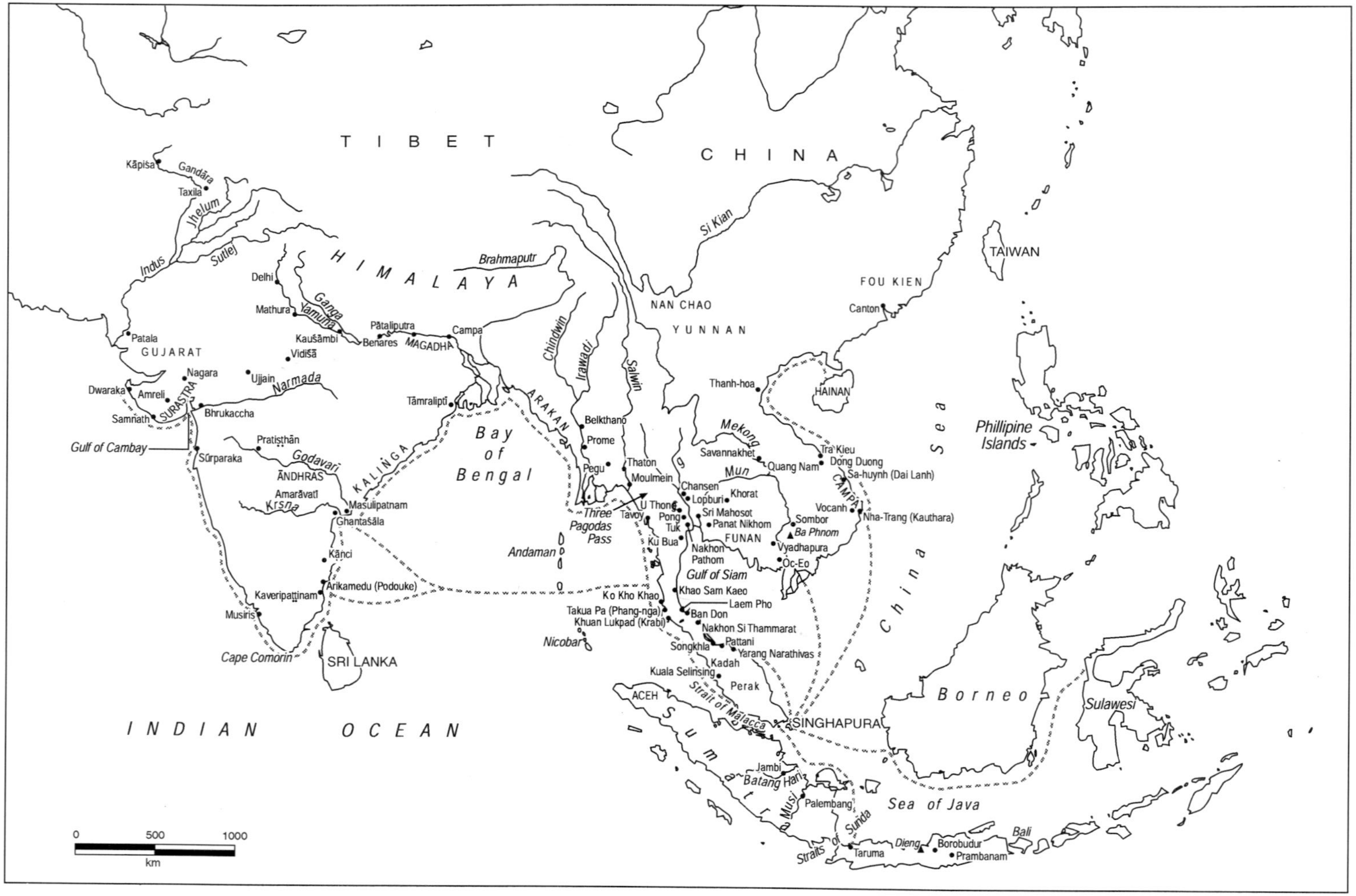

Figure 6.3 Sea routes and ancient ports in South and Southeast Asia.

beneath a row of auspicious emblems (rising sun, *purnaghata, srivatsa, sankha, camara*), comes from Chansen in Ta Khli District, Nakhon Sawan Province (see Figure 4.2).[12] In India, similar combs made from ivory and bone and dating between the fourth century BC and the first century AD have been reported from Taxila (Marshall 1975), Ujjain and Baroda.

- A rectangular ivory or bone dice with the sides numbered 1–4 was unearthed from Nern Makok, Khok Samrong District, Lopburi. This dice was most probably another product from India where, apart from gambling, a game of dice occurred in the consecration ceremony *Rajasuya*, in which the king threw a dice to show how food should be divided.[13]
- A number of Indian coins have been reported from trading centers like Ban Tha Khae in Lopburi Province and Khuan Luk Pad in Krabi Province. At the first site a silver or lead coin was discovered depicting an elephant, probably of Satavahana origin (*c.*500 BC–AD 225). At Khuan Luk Pad, a copper coin was found bearing a humped bull on the obverse and a double-masted ship on the reverse (Figure 6.5), popular symbols of the Pallavas of Tamil Nadu (AD 500–900).[14]

Figure 6.4 Late Roman bronze lamp from Pong Tuk, Kanchanaburi Province. (Phasook Indrawooth.)

Figure 6.5 Indian bronze coin from Klong Thom, Krabi Province. (Phasook Indrawooth.)

By early centuries AD, local rulers probably recognized the political value of Indian concepts of kingship as a means to legitimize their rule and in order to enhance their status. Thus they summoned priests and literati to their courts. Buddhist monks also were zealous in spreading their doctrine, while learned Brahmins introduced Hindu concepts and rites, as well as the sciences, arts and techniques of India.

Dvaravati, The early Buddhist kingdoms in Central and Northeast Thailand

The seventh century AD saw a large number of moated sites in occupation located along the margins of the Central Plain of Thailand (Figures 6.6). According to Vanasin and Supajanya, sea level was higher at that time and so these settlements were accessible by boat. Most sites were also located near rivers that supplied water to the moats (Figure 6.7).

Figure 6.6 Important archaeological sites in Southeast Asia during the Dvaravati Period.

Large religious buildings were constructed within the moats, and major moated sites have been found in the Meklong–Ta Chin valleys, in the Lopburi–Pasak valleys and in the Bang Pakong Valley. Some sites, such as Dong Khon, Muang Bon, U Ta Pao and Thap Chumphon, are located near the Chao Phraya River. Sites in these regions include a number of important Dvaravati towns, such as U-Thong, Nakhon Pathom and Ku Bua.

U-Thong is situated in Suphanburi Province, some 30 miles east of the Meklong River, and in early times was more accessible from the coast than is now the case. The moats here enclose an area of 1,690 by 840 meters and traces of a stone wall on the top of a clay rampart for defensive purposes can still be seen. That U-Thong had participated in trading networks since prehistoric times is shown by nephrite ornaments found there; a two-headed animal ear pendant and a penannular earring with three sharp protuberances, both characteristic products of the Sa Huynh Culture (*c.*600 BC–AD 200) of Central Vietnam. These are surface finds but another animal-headed pendant was also found in a

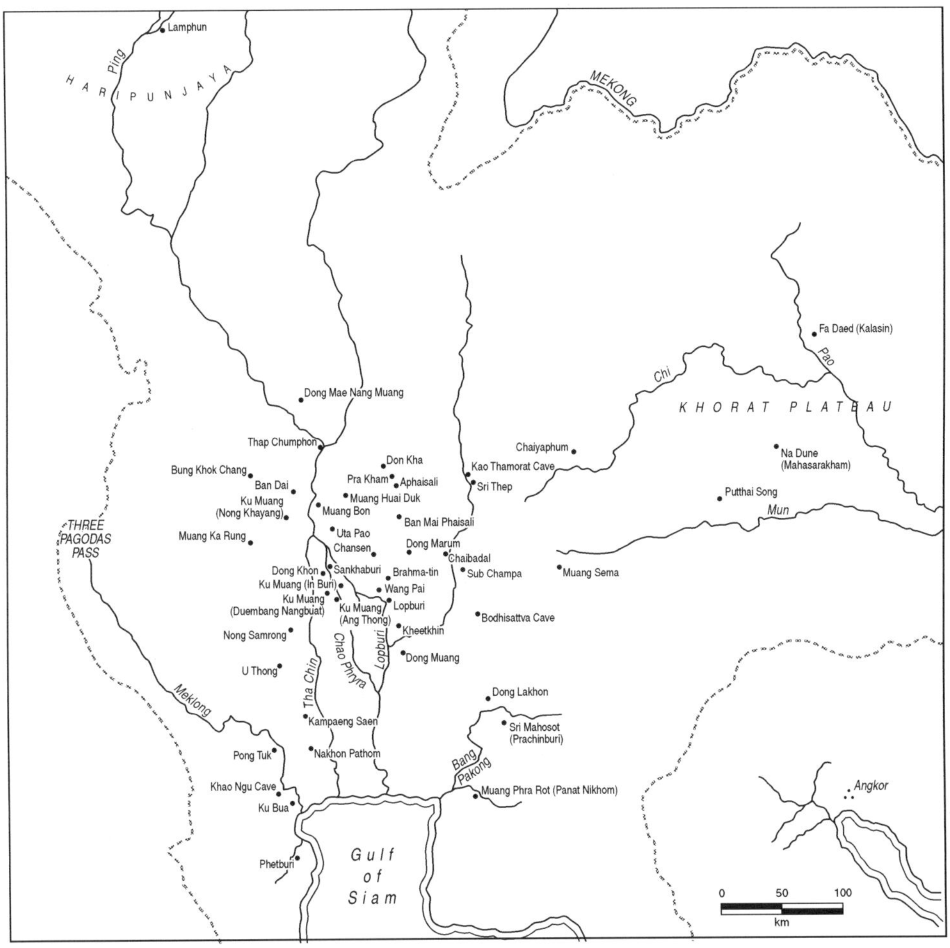

Figure 6.7 The main Dvaravati sites in Central and Northeast Thailand.

burial dated to the fourth century BC at Ban Don Ta Phet, 25 kilometers south of U-Thong.[15]

Many of these pieces can also be paralleled at Oc Eo, the "port" of Funan (see chapter 12). Among other items in the U-Thong Museum, or in private collections, are large quantities of glass and stone beads, tin and lead earrings, medallions, seals and amulets and the stone moulds for making them, as well as gold ornaments including an earring in the form of a *kinnari* (bird-woman). Some of these might have been imported from India.

Figure 6.8 Stone slab showing seated Buddha under a Naga, from Nagarjunakonda, South-eastern India. (Phasook Indrawooth.)

Figure 6.9 Stone *Dharmacakra* and pillar, U-Thong. (Phasook Indrawooth.)

Besides being an important port of the Dvaravati Kingdom, U-thong was also an important early Buddhist center (Figure 6.9). We have, among other finds preserved in the museum at U-Thong, portions of beautiful stucco and terracotta architectural decoration in a pure Amaravati style, such as a terracotta relief with Buddhist disciples carrying their bowls and the lower part of a stucco image of the Buddha sheltered by the *Naga*. These finds imply the former existence at U-Thong of Buddhist constructions of the third or fourth centuries AD. The most important of these is the stone *Dharmacakra*, the well-known symbol of Buddhism, on a pillar unearthed near stupa No. 11 (Figure 6.9).

Nakhon Pathom, situated near the west bank of the Ta Chin river, is nearer to the Gulf of Thailand than is U-Thong. This was a large city covering an area of 3,700 by 2,000 meters (Figure 6.10), with a central mound being all that remains of the ancient brick monument of Chula Paton. Excavations here by the late Pierre Dupont[16] provide the most important contribution to our knowledge of Dvaravati architecture. Chula Paton is one of the most characteristic types of Dvaravati monument, modified several times. In its first state, it consisted of a central square platform ornamented on each face by five standing Buddhas of stucco, placed in niches. This stood on a base, of the same plan, but a little wider, with facings ornamented with mouldings and, on the projecting angles, *makaras* in relief. The whole was supported on a rectangular terrace ornamented with panels bearing alternatively a *Garuda* and an elephant. Four axial flights of steps, with the bottom step semi-circular, gave access to the terrace. These were flanked by lions carved on the facing and had balustrades issuing from the mouths of monsters.

In the second stage, the decoration of the base was simplified. In the third stage, new Buddha images were substituted for the old ones in the niches, and changes were made simplifying the much enlarged terrace.

The most important small finds from Nakhon Pathom are two inscribed silver coins found in a small earthen jar beneath a ruined sanctuary at Nern Hin, west of Pra Praton

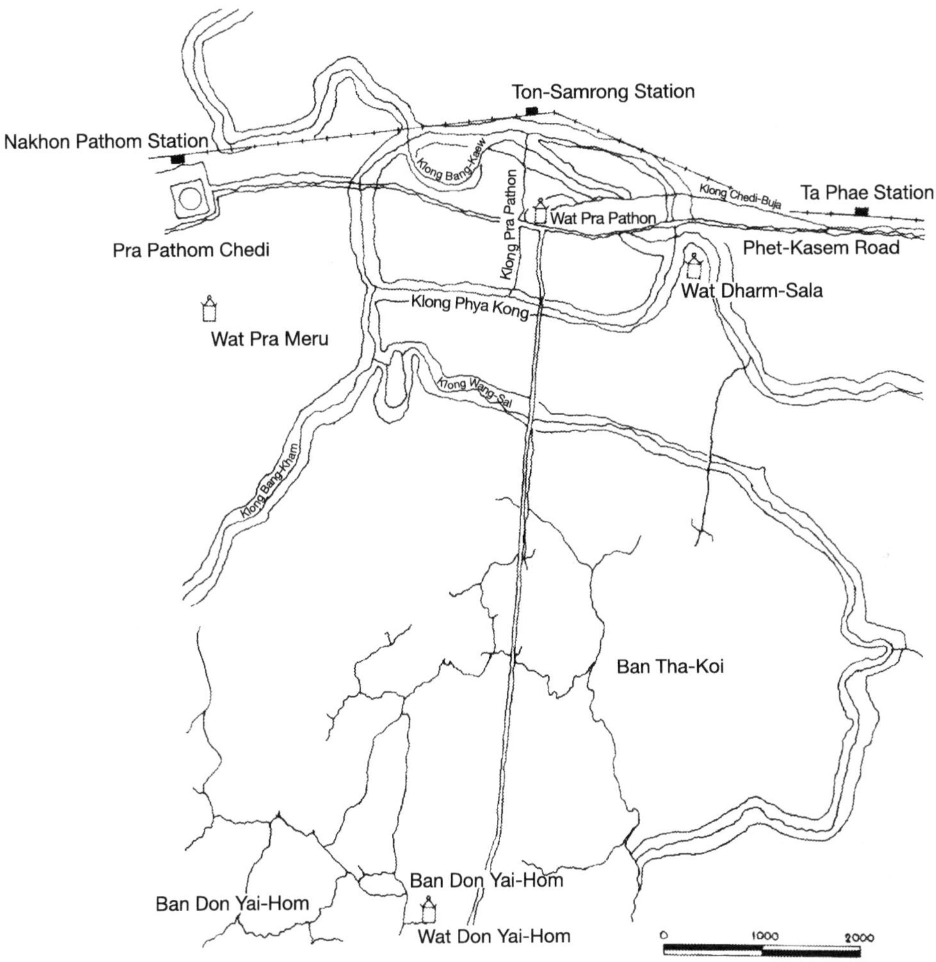

Figure 6.10 Plan of ancient Nakhon Pathom.

Chedi.[17] On the reverse of each coin are engraved the Sanskrit words *sridvaravati svarapunya*, meaning "meritorious deed of the King of Dvaravati". On the obverse of one coin is a *purnaghata* (vase of plenty), from which two creepers are sprouting. On the other is a cow with its calf, symbols of fertility and prosperity. Coedès, who read the inscriptions, stated that they are in South Indian characters of the seventh century and recognized their importance as confirming the Sanskrit name of the kingdom referred to in Chinese sources as *To-lo-po-ti*.[18]

Apart from being regarded as a capital of the Dvaravati kingdom, ancient Nakhon Pathom had an important role as one of the trading centers of Dvaravati. A large number of terracotta seals and sealings and some amulets used by merchants have been found. Other important finds include over 30 pieces of stone *Dharmacakra* (Wheels of the Law), one with two figures of crouching deer to symbolize the First Sermon in the Deer Park at Sarnath, as well as images of the Buddha made of stone and bronze. Thus, the Buddhist monuments at Nakhon Pathom, including Pra Pathon Chedi, emphasize its importance as a Buddhist center during Dvaravati times. In addition, the Pali texts engraved on some stone *Dharmacakra*, mostly with *Patieeasamappada-sutta*, provide evidence of familiarity with the Pali canon.

Subsequent excavations in the occupation area at Nakhon Pathom have also expanded our knowledge of this site. Many artefacts resemble those common in earlier prehistoric objects, such as bronze ornaments, iron spears and spindle whorls. However, such forms clearly continued in use into early historical times, since the settlement appears to have been founded in the eighth and ninth centuries and was probably abandoned when the river changed its course, not long after the tenth century AD.[19]

Figure 6.11 Terracotta relief of a foreigner from Ku Bua, Ratchaburi Province. (Phasook Indrawooth.)

Ku Bua was a relatively small early town, measuring 800 meters north to south and 200 meters east to west, in Ratchaburi Province west of the mouth of the Meklong River.[20] Its coastal location would have facilitated participation in early trading networks. A bronze kettle drum, a product of the Dong Son Culture (*c.*500 BC–AD 100) of northern Vietnam and southern China, has been reported from the site. Regular trade links with China started in the Tang Period (AD 618–906) and continued through the Song Period (AD 960–1279), as shown by the large number of Chinese ceramics recovered from the Meklong River. Besides Indian and Chinese, other foreign traders also visited Ku Bua. Terracottas depicted with distinctive high peaked hats (Figure 6.11) might have been Scythians from the communities known in India as the Saka-Kshatrapas, who ruled the western part of the subcontinent between AD 100 and 400 and sent their traders to Southeast Asia.

Figure 6.12 Wat Klong, Ku Bua, Ratchaburi Province. (Phasook Indrawooth.)

Excavations conducted by Rattanakun in 1961 revealed a series of Buddhist structures inside and outside the moats. Among them, Wat Klong, a large rectangular structure standing almost at the center of the enclosure (Figure 6.12), is considered to be the most important. Despite differences in planning and having its lower foundation courses made of laterite, it has much in common with Chula Pathon at Nakhon Pathom, especially in its brick mouldings. The central structure above, with its pilasters and niches, so far as it has survived, also resembles that at Pra Praton.

The Lopburi–Pasak valleys include a number of important Dvaravati towns, of which Chansen, Sab Champa, Lopburi and Sri Thep can be described. Chansen is located on the west side of the Pasak River in Nakhon Sawan Province. It was evidently a roughly circular town about 780 meters in diameter. Excavations in the occupation area in the late 1960s identified six phases of occupation. The earliest phase is late prehistoric, and in the second there is evidence of trade contact with India, as confirmed by pottery forms and the discovery of the ivory comb (see Figure 4.2), an important trade product of India during that period. Chansen is comparatively rich in seals and sealings, both with and without inscriptions (Figure 6.13).[21]

Figure 6.13 Terracotta seal from Chansen. (Phasook Indrawooth.)

Sab Champa is another moated site, about 834 by 700 meters, on the eastern side of the Pasak river in Lopburi Province. Excavations in 1971 by Maleipan revealed evidence of prehistoric settlement followed by a Dvaravati phase. A large number of terracotta medallions depicting Gaja-Laksmi and Kubera, resembling those from Nakhon Pathom, have usually been identified as amulets for merchants, indicating that this site was also a Dvaravati trading center. Pali inscriptions on an octagonal pillar used to support a *Dharmacakra* confirm the use of Pali texts at Sab Champa during this time.[22]

Lopburi lies on the eastern side of the Lopburi river, mostly under the modern city, and so the plan of the ancient town cannot be determined. As the seat of a Khmer viceroyalty (*c.* AD 1000–1300), later developed as the second capital of King Narai in the seventeenth century, Lopburi has yielded only rare evidence from the Dvaravati period. However, there are sufficient archaeological finds to establish that it was a Dvaravati city of considerable importance. Apart from the discovery of a coin bearing the inscription *Lava pura*, which confirms the original name of the town, Lopburi is comparatively rich in inscriptions in Pali, Sanskrit and Mon, the latter usually mentioning offerings of slaves and carts to a monastery. Some inscribed fragments of a *Dharmacakra* found in Wat Mahathat clearly confirm knowledge of the Pali scriptures in Lopburi during Dvaravati times. Finally, in 1983, when the Fine Arts Department excavated a Khmer monument at Wat Nakhon Kosa, they recognized the remains of a Dvaravati stupa below it with a large number of stucco and terracotta architectural decorations in purely Dvaravati style.[23]

Sri Thep is situated about 2 kilometres east of the Pasak River in Petchabun Province. Here one can clearly observe how the town grew from an oval village about 1,500 meters in diameter into a huge city. East of the original site is an extension covering 4.7 square kilometers. Archaeological research by the Fine Arts Department during 1988–91 revealed evidence of occupation here from the Iron Age to the thirteenth century. The discovery of Hindu images of Vishnu, Krishna and Surya confirms the presence of an Indianized settlement at Sri Thep during the Gupta and post-Gupta periods (*c.* AD 500–800), as does a Sanskrit inscription mentioning a hermit's daughter. Sri Thep was one of the major Dvaravati towns, comparable to Nakhon Pathom and Ku Bua, in which the main religious structure, today known as Khao Klang Nai, was constructed in the center of the city. Rectangular in plan, it measures about 40 by 20 meters, the long axis running north–south. The stucco ornamentation includes a row of crouching dwarves (*Yakshas*) and figures with lion's or cow's heads, which recall similar representations at Monument 18 (Wat Klong) at Ku Bua and the ninth–tenth-century terracotta plaques at Mainamati in northern Bangladesh. A stone *Dharmacakra* was also found within the moat, as well as Buddha images and votive tablets. After the mid tenth century Sri Thep was occupied by the Khmers, whose ruined temples are much in evidence at the site.[24]

The Bang Pakong Valley southeast of modern Bangkok also includes a number of important Dvaravati towns, such as Muang Phra Rot and Muang Sri Mahosot. Evidence of trade contact with India during the Maurya–Sunga Periods was revealed at Ban Khok Raka (Chonburi Province), where a number of glass and stone beads, typical products of India during the late Iron Age, have been reported.

Muang Phra Rot is in Chonburi Province near the mouth of the Bang Pakong River, about 20 km from the Gulf of Thailand. Its predecessor in pre-Dvaravati times might have been Khok Raka, situated nearby. This moated town covers 1500 by 750 meters. Excavations by Sulaksananont[25] revealed evidence of Dvaravati occupation from the seventh to the eleventh centuries, with imported Tang and Song Chinese ceramics and early Islamic turquoise-blue glazed earthenware jars from lower Mesopotamia or Iran.

Muang Sri Mahosot is located in Prachinburi Province. The site measures about *c.*1,550 by 700 meters and has provided sufficient archaeological evidence to establish that it was the chief trading center in the Bang Pakong Valley. Trade contact with India during the Indo-Roman Period is indicated by polychrome striped glass beads as well as beads of agate and carnelian. Artistic remains confirm a close relationship with the Krishna-Godavari valleys of eastern India during the early historic period. Reliefs on the laterite walls of the Sra Keo tank depict animals (lions, elephants and *makara*) in a style often compared to that of Amaravati. The Buddha footprints near Sra Morakot[26] are undoubtedly the products of Dvaravati artists, inspired by Krishna-Godavari Buddhist art.

The town of Muang Sri Mahosot was occupied by the Khmers after their conquest of Dvaravati, as shown by the remains of Khmer monuments and a bronze mirror frame with an inscription in Khmer, dated AD 1193, giving what seems to be the Khmer name of the town – *Sri Vatsapura*.[27]

Material culture

The archaeological remains of Central Thailand during the Dvaravati period provide clear perspectives on themes in Dvaravati material culture, such as town plans, buildings, implements, domestic utensils, ornaments and ceramics.

Town plans

Although irregular moated sites occurred in the dry northeast of Thailand during the local Iron Age, the series of large moated towns along the margins of the Central Plains of Thailand during the Dvaravati period undoubtedly reflect a high degree of Indianization. In the Ganga Plains of northern India, almost all the principal Iron Age sites were located on river banks upon which the inhabitants erected clay embankments to prevent flood waters from entering the habitation area. During the Indian Iron Age (*c*.700–350 BC), earth embankments and moats as flood protective devices occur at sites such as Kausambi, Varanasi and Pataliputra. During the early historic period these were developed into substantial defensive ramparts. Pataliputra and Kausambi are examples where the clay embankments of the early phase, with certain modifications, were converted to defensive purposes.

In some Dvaravati towns there is an expansion of the irregular, more or less circular or oval plans of the earlier Iron Age occupations by constructing new ramparts and moats, as at Muang Bon in Nakhon Sawan Province, or by grafting on a secondary enclosure, as at Sri Thep and Muang Fa Daed in Kalasin Province. At U-Thong, a stone wall, now destroyed, was built on top of the clay rampart.[28]

Buildings

During the Dvaravati period, houses were generally built of wood while fired brick and laterite were used for religious structures. The larger Buddhist monuments, mostly of brick, were constructed within the moats, while smaller ones were built outside the enclosures.

Objects of trade and communication

The occurrence of a large number of uninscribed silver coins throughout the Dvaravati kingdom(s), in contemporary Pyu cities in Myanmar (Beikthano, Sriksetra and Halin), and in Mon-speaking Pegu and the ancient Funan port of Oc Eo, indicates that coinage was used for commercial exchange. Most coins bear Indian symbols of kingship and prosperity, such as the rising sun, *sankha* (conch shell) and *srivatsa* (the abode of Sri, goddess of fertility) (Figure 6.14).[29]

Figure 6.14 Silver coins from U-Thong. (Phasook Indrawooth.)

Large numbers of seals of clay and other materials belonging to kings, royal officials and private individuals, as well as administrative, mercantile and religious organizations, have been discovered in the main Dvaravati cities such as Nakhon Pathom and Chansen (Figures 6.13 and 6.15) in Nakhon Sawan Province. The writing on the seals is usually in positive relief. Some seals have also been found with legends in negative relief, probably used for sealing documents.

Figure 6.15 Stone mould from Chansen. (Phasook Indrawooth.)

Implements and domestic utensils

A wide range of implements and domestic utensils occur in the occupation areas of sites such as Nakhon Pathom. These include polished stone axes, iron tools, terracotta spindle whorls, and stone saddle querns and rollers (Figure 6.16) derived from Indian prototypes. The latter were probably used for grinding spices such as garlic and pepper, and other foodstuffs. Other commonly-found objects include the clay pellets assumed to have been used with a pellet bow for hunting small animals, and numerous terracotta disks that might have been gaming pieces or tokens for commodity exchanges (they occur in a regular series of weights and sizes). Personal toilet items, such as square or rectangular terracotta skin rubbers, occur in the domestic areas of most Dvaravati cities, such as Sri Mahosot in Prachinburi Province. Such skin-rubbers were used in place of soap in the Ganga Valley.

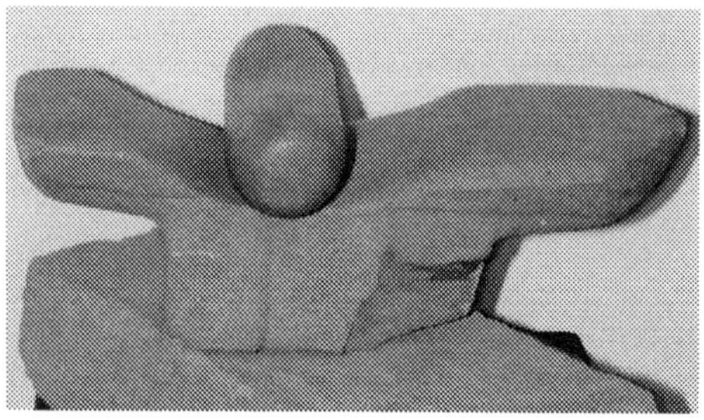

Figure 6.16 Saddle quern and roller from Dong Khon, Chainat Province. (Phasook Indrawooth.)

Ornaments

A wide range of personal ornaments have been reported, such as large flat tin and lead earrings, bronze bells, bronze rings, and beads of glass, carnelian, agate and gold. The stucco images from Ku Bua, Ratchaburi Province, show women – perhaps a princess with her attendant – with elaborate hairstyles, large flat ear-ornaments and elegant clothing (Figure 6.17).

Figure 6.17 Terracotta images of women, Ku Bua. (Phasook Indrawooth.)

Musical instruments and dancing poses

Many of the stucco and terracotta architectural decorations from Ku Bua illuminate Indian dancing poses and a variety of Indian musical instruments such as harps, cymbals and flutes (Figure 6.18).

Figure 6.18 Stucco figures of musicians from Ku Bua. (Phasook Indrawooth.)

Ceramics

Dvaravati ceramics are unglazed, mainly wheel-thrown, and fired in an open hearth rather than in a closed kiln. Analytical studies on Dvaravati pottery indicate that raw materials were locally acquired. Dvaravati pottery basically continued forms of the prehistoric period, such as the dish-on-stand, but strongly carinated vessels with ridges perhaps followed Indian ceramic styles.

Jars with spouts (*kendi*), sprinklers (*kundika*) (see chapter 4) and small cups used as lamps also show close similarity in shape and design to Indian prototypes dating from the early Christian era up to the post-Gupta period (AD 500–800). Western influences may also be seen in the terracotta Roman-style lamps, thought to be local imitations of bronze Roman lamps such as that found at Pong Tuk (Figure 6.4).

Decorative techniques and designs used by the Dvaravati potters include incised lines and wave designs, and impression using cord and mat wrapped paddles, fingers, and snail and shell edges. A technique of decorating pots in relief used carved stamps following a technique introduced by Indian potters of the Gupta (*c.* AD 300–500) and the post-Gupta periods (*c.* AD 500–800). Such stamped designs include human figures in different poses, animals and flowers. The fashion for stamp-decorated pottery during the Gupta period perhaps reflected imitation of Italian Arretine ware, some of which reached India along the maritime trade routes, as well as Hellenistic stamped pottery, which reached northern India from Afghanistan and central Asia.[30]

Social relations

Many of the stucco and terracotta architectural decorations from Ku Bua illuminate social relations during Dvaravati times. The image of a princess with her attendant mentioned above (Figure 6.17) indicates the sophistication of court life. Other scenes show servants bearing objects, musicians, dancers, and even a group of prisoners being kicked by their guard.

Languages

Based on inscriptions, literate Dvaravati people were familiar with three languages: Sanskrit, Pali and Old Mon. The first two were Indian official, scholarly and religious languages, probably not used in everyday speech. The presence of Old Mon in Central Thailand seems surprising today, since Mon is generally known as a language of lower Burma. However many Old Mon inscriptions of the sixth to the ninth centuries AD have come to light in Central Thailand and the connection of these with the Dvaravati kingdom(s) cannot be refuted. From northeast Thailand, a number of Old Mon inscriptions have been ascribed to the tenth century.[31]

The presence of the Old Mon has led scholars to conclude that the Dvaravati people were Mons, or at least that Mons formed the ruling elite. However, scholars have been troubled by the absence of early Buddhist remains in the Mon areas in lower Burma as compared with their abundance in Central Thailand. At Thaton (ancient *Sudhammavati*), in the present-day Mon heartland of Lower Burma, Old Mon inscriptions appear only after the eleventh century. The languages of the Thaton inscriptions and of subsequent ones at Pagan, and throughout Burma during the reign of King Kyanzittha (twelfth century), are also Old Mon. Therefore, there is a gap of about 400 years between these two Old Mon-speaking communities.[32]

We can conclude with a fair degree of certainty that the Dvaravati kingdom(s) did not form part of the Mon Confederacy centered at Thaton in lower Burma, but they developed out of the earlier Austroasiatic-speaking chiefdoms of prehistoric Central Thailand. Languages of the Austroasiatic stock are distributed for the most part through the mainland of Southeast Asia and include the Munda languages of northeastern India and the Mon-Khmer languages, which in turn include a host of minority languages such as Stieng, Bahar, Wa and Palaung.

Concepts of state and kingship

Dvaravati coinage suggests that some of the Indian concepts of state and kingship were accepted by Dvaravati rulers. Inscribed silver coins from sites such as Nakhon Pathom, U-Thong, Ku Bua, Ku Muang, Brahma-tin, Dong Khon and U Ta-Pao indicate the reality of Dvaravati kingship. On the obverse sides of these coins are engraved Indian symbols of fertility and prosperity, such as *purnaghata* (vase of plenty) or an animal – cow or deer – with its offspring. On the reverse sides occur the words *sridvaravatisvarapunya*, meaning "meritorious deeds of the King of Dvaravati". A large number of uninscribed silver coins (Figure 6.14) bear Indian symbols of kingship and prosperity such as the rising sun or *sankha* (conch shell) and *srivatsa* (indicating the abode of Sri, goddess of fertility). These have been found throughout the Dvaravati region and in contemporary cities influenced by Indian civilization, from Burma to the lower Mekong Valley.[33]

These coins were issued by Dvaravati kings, as confirmed by the discovery of stone moulds bearing the *sankha* symbol from U-Thong and Chansen (Figure 6.15), and a clay mould bearing the sun symbol from U-Thong. Rulers aspired to expand the economy and to enhance their position at the head of it. The description in Tung-tien (a Chinese encyclopaedia) of the Dvaravati kingdom, compiled by Tu Yu in the late eighth century AD, recorded that if a man cast silver coins without permission, his arm was to be cut off.[34]

Although some Dvaravati kings patronized Buddhist temples and no doubt followed the Buddha's teaching, it is believed that they were exalted far above ordinary mortals through the magical power of the *Rajasuya*, or Royal Consecration, which imbued the king with divine powers. Objects with ritual purposes carved on stone tablets depicting a series of royal insignia include *camara* (flywhisks), *sankha* (conch shells), *vajra* (thunderbolts), *valvijani* (fans), *ankusa* (elephant goads) and *chhatra* (umbrellas). Such tablets are reported from Nakhon Pathom and from Dong Khon, Chainat Province.[35] It is presumed that the ivory or bone dice from Nern Makok, Lopburi Province, is another kind of ritual object. According to the Vedic text, *Satapatha Brahmana*, these objects might have been used in a series of rituals performed during the *Rajasuya* ceremony, the main features of which were as follows:

1 Offering to the household deities;
2 The sprinkling ceremony (*abhisecaniya*);
3 The king's symbolic walk towards the four quarters, as an indication of his universal rule;
4 Treading upon the tiger's skin in order to gain its strength;
5 Enthronement;

6 A mimic cow raid, symbolizing the king as the war leader of pastoral peoples;
7 Narration by a priest of the *Sunhsepa* legend of *Aitareya Brahmana*, which reflects the structure of class society;
8 A game of dice – the eighth item of the *Rajasuya* in which the king takes part in order to symbolize the division of food.

The stone tablets have small central circular depressions and might have served as receptacles for holding a pot of water for use in the sprinkling ceremony (*abhisecaniya*), the second item mentioned above.

According to Buddhist tradition, Dvaravati kings could also be regarded "Universal Emperors" (*Chakravartin*), as recorded in the *Chakravathisihanada Sutta*. This states:

> Just as Buddha appears from time to time in the cosmic cycle, heralded by auspicious omens and endowed with favorable signs, to lead all living beings along the road to enlightenment, so does a Universal Emperor appear, to conquer all *Jambudvipa* and rule prosperously and righteously.[36]

The concept of *Cakravartin* indicates that the *cakra* or wheel (symbol of sovereignty) of the state chariot rolls everywhere without obstruction. It is believed that the Mauryas developed the concept of *Cakravartin*, which was incorporated into Buddhist tradition. One relief from the second century BC stupa of Jaggayyapeta in Andhra Pradesh depicts a *Cakravartin* scene with the Emperor in the center, on his right the wheel symbolizing the Universal Empire, and on his left the chief Queen, the Chief Minister and Crown Prince, and at his feet the imperial elephant and horse.[37] This concept was blended with later Vedic imperialistic ideas, which were then taken over by mainstream Hinduism. In the Mahabharata, many legendary kings such as Yudhisthira and Rama are said to have been *digvijayins*, conquerors of the four quarters.

Stone *Dharmacakra* that symbolize the Universal Empire (Figures 6.9 and 6.19) and Buddha images, together with Buddhist monuments of typical Dvaravati style, have been discovered at the main Dvaravati sites in Central Thailand and in other regions to which Dvaravati culture spread. These include the northern region of Haripunjaya; the northeastern sites of Muang Sema, Fa Daed and Na Dune; and the southern sites of Chaiya and Yarang.[38] These examples all indicate that the Dvaravati kings followed Buddhist practice as recorded in the *Chakkavathisihanada Sutta*,

Figure 6.19 Stone *Dharmacakra*, inscribed with a Buddhist text, Lopburi. (Phasook Indrawooth.)

and as practiced by Asoka. The Dvaravati kings tried to follow Asoka in establishing *Dharma* or the "Law of Piety" (*dharma-vijaya*) in foreign regions, in order that they could be regarded as *digvijayins* – conquerors of the four quarters.

Religious beliefs

While Buddhism was the dominant religion of the Dvaravati elite, we should not lose sight of the Hindu elements in Dvaravati religion, especially at U-Thong, where a stone *Mukhalinga* in the Pre-Angkorian style of the seventh–eighth centuries was unearthed to the south of the city. The existence of *Saivism* at U Thong is indicated by a mid-seventh-century copper-plate inscription which mentions gifts of a jeweled litter, a parasol and musical instruments to the *Amratakesvara* (a form of linga) by *Sri Harsvarman*, grandson of King Sri Isanavarman. Not only *Saivism*, but traces of *Vaisnavism* are also evident in two steles with rough figures of Visnu in high relief, probably in Pallava style, kept in the U-Thong *San Chao* or spirit shrine. They seem to belong to the same group as the Pallava-derived mitred Visnus found at Muang Sri Mahosot in Prachinburi Province.[39]

Nevertheless, the earliest evidence of religious belief at U Thong is still Buddhist. A number of stucco or terracotta architectural decorations in Amaravati style indicate that Buddhist monuments already existed at U-Thong in the third or fourth centuries.[40] Most scholars agree that Buddhist beliefs were introduced here from Nagarjunakonda in the Krishna-Godavari region of South India, when it was under Ikshvaku rule between AD 200 and 350.

Inscriptions and Buddhist remains from excavations at Nagarjunakonda show that it was the home of different Buddhist sects during the Ikshvaku period. Religious orders such as *Mahaviharavasins, Mahi-sasaka, Bahusrutiya, Apara-mahavinaseliya* and *Chaityakas*, which split from the Hinayana sect, and *Mahasanghikas, Vibhajavadins* and *Lokottaravadins* – which were more inclined to Mahayana concepts – co-existed there in harmony.

Many stupa slabs at Nagarjunakonda depict symbols such as *Dharmacakra, Purnaghata* (Vase of Plenty), and the *Bodhi* tree. Similarly, anthropomorphic forms of the Buddha, often protected by *Naga Muchalinda*, occur in the reliefs. However, since only the sculptural representation of both forms survive, their chronological sequence cannot be determined. The Hinayanists preferred symbols whereas the Mahayanists preferred to depict the Buddha in human form. Even though many sects began without using Buddha images, most finally incorporated the idea.

The different Buddhist sects which flourished at Nagarjunakonda were introduced to U-Thong by the fourth century, if not earlier. They established Buddhist symbols, such as the stone *Dharmacakra* on a pillar found near *stupa* No. 11 at U-Thong. They worshipped Buddha images and we have many bronze and stone images from the main Dvaravati sites. They also believed in *stupa* worship since a large number of small *stupas* were constructed inside and outside the moats of sites such as U-Thong and Ku Bua and Muang Bon. Most of these *stupas* were similar in plan, having a square brick base with a stairway on each face. Devout Buddhists preferred to construct *Mahachaityas* in the centers of important cities, such as Chula Paton at Nakhon Pathom, Wat Klong at Ku Bua (Figure 6.12), and Kao Klang Nai at Sri Thep.[41]

We also learn from epigraphical records that Dvaravati Buddhism was influenced not only from the Krishna-Godavari region, but also from Buddhist centers in other parts of India. For instance, the religious beliefs held by the *Hinayana Sammitiya* sect of Indian

Buddhism, centered at Valabhi in Gujarat and under the patronage of the Saka-Kshatrapas (*c.* AD 200–400) and Maitrakas (*c.* AD 400–800), seem to have had much influence on Dvaravati Buddhism.

The Dvaravati people not only created a large number of *stupas*, *Mahastupas* and Buddha images, but they also produced a large number of religious objects. Archaeologists have discovered votive stupas, terracotta tablets, terracotta begging bowls inscribed in Pali with the Buddhist creed *Ye Dhamma*, and stone *Dharmacakra* (Figure 6.19) inscribed in Pali with the *Patieeasamappada-sutta*. This was the essence of the Buddha's teaching, considered to be of paramount importance at Valabhi during the sixth and seventh centuries. The Chinese pilgrim I-tsing did not fail to notice this widely prevalent practice. According to his record, when people made images and *chaityas* of gold, silver, copper, iron, earth, lacquer, bricks and stone, they put in them two kinds of *Sariras* relics. First came the relics of the Great Teacher, and second the *Gatha* of the Chain of Causation (*Patieeasamappada-sutta*). The merits derived from enshrining these two kinds of *sarira* were supposedly enormous. The fact that the *Gatha* (sacred stanzas from the Buddhist texts) was called *sarira* shows that it had assumed the sanctity of a relic of Buddha himself.[42]

The sculptural art of Dvaravati also came under the influence of Buddhism from northern, eastern and Deccan centres. From Sarnath in the north, a wheel flanked by two deer symbolizing the First Sermon in the Deer Park became the accepted emblem of the seals of almost all the *mahaviharas* of India. This motif was also considered to be of paramount importance by the Dvaravati people. Stone *Dharmacakra* and deer images have been reported from most of the main Dvaravati sites.

The art of Dvaravati was also influenced by Mahayana Buddhism, emanating from the Deccan under the patronage of the Gupta and Vakataka rulers (*c.* AD 300–600). The art of the Deccan caves at Ajanta, Karla and Kanheri was also imitated, in particular the colossal images of Buddha seated in *pralambapada-asana* position, reliefs of preaching Buddha and of the Great Miracle of Sravasti.[43]

A number of colossal images of Buddha are recorded from Dvaravati sites, including the quartzite statues of Wat Pra Men, Nakhon Pathom and the relief carving of the Buddha in Khao Ngu cave, Ratchaburi Province. Terracotta votive tablets depicting the Buddha giving a discourse on the True Doctrine (The Lotus Sutra and the Great Miracle of Sravasti), as described in the *Divyavadana*, were also made by Dvaravati artists.[44]

Figure 6.20 Stone image of a seated Buddha on Vanaspati from Nakhon Pathom. (Phasook Indrawooth.)

A number of stone bas-reliefs are known from sites such as Nakhon Pathom, Sri Thep and Sab Champa.[45] Each depicts the curious bird vehicle on which the Buddha and his two attendants are standing. The vehicle (*vahana*) is labelled as *Vanaspati*, this being a combination of the characteristics of the *hamsa, garuda* and bull vehicles of Brahma, Vishnu and Siva, three gods of Hindu Trinity. I argue that this is a peculiarly Dvaravati concept, although influenced by the Vajrayana school of Mahayana Tantra which flourished in northeastern India under the patronage of the Pala kings (*c.* AD 800–1200).

Lastly, we should mention the amulets that were prevalent during Dvaravati times. The round terracotta medallions found at the main Dvaravati sites depict *Gaja-Laksmi* on one side and *Kubera* on the other, or simply depict *Kubera* or *Gaja-Laksmi* on one face. These were used to ward off misfortune and to bestow wealth from trade. Human-shaped amulets were quite popular. A number of headless human figurines both male and female, particularly a headless man with monkeys (Figure 6.21), have been reported from the main Dvaravati sites. However, it seems that lion amulets were most popular. The lion not only symbolizes power, but it signifies also the Buddha's status as *Sakya Simha* the lion of the Sakyas.

Figure 6.21 Headless terracotta images of men with monkeys from U-Thong. (Phasook Indrawooth.)

The expansion of Dvaravati culture

The northeastern region

The Dvaravati culture was not restricted to the Central Plains but extended also to the Khorat Plateau of northeastern Thailand. A large number of moated sites have been investigated by the Fine Arts Department, such as Muang Sema in Nakhon Ratchasima Province, Muang Fa Daed in Kalasin Province and Muang Nadune in Mahasarakham Province. Of these, Muang Fa Daed is the most remarkable. Located a few kilometres from the Lam Pao tributary of the Chi River, the site is surrounded by a series of moats representing successive stages of enlargement.[46] The town plan grew from an original oval village site called Non Muang Kao. A first extension seems to have ended with an intrusive rampart turning in on the eastern side. South of this is the second extension, with a straight rampart and corners. Including the moat and rampart it measures 1,800 meters long by 1,000 meters wide.

The *sema* stones from Muang Fa Daed have attracted most attention. Many of them are 1.5 meters high, some finely carved with Buddhist scenes. In an important short article, Prince Subhadradis suggested that the *sema* stones of Muang Fa Daed reflected the Dvaravati style which flourished in the Chao Phraya Valley between the seventh and eleventh centuries AD.[47]

The excavations by the Fine Arts Department in 1968 revealed 14 monuments of typical Dvaravati style. Buddha and Bodhisattva images of stucco and bronze are among the finds, together with seven types of votive tablets in Dvaravati style. Excavations in the occupation area revealed inhumation burials indicating that the site was occupied from the Iron Age onwards. Some of the graves contained Iron Age red on buff pottery, while later burials, stratified over the Iron Age material, incorporated iron artefacts with bronze, carnelian and agate jewellery. A group of jar burials typifies the special funeral rites of the inhabitants in the Mun and Chi valleys during the Protohistoric period. Confirmation of occupation contemporary with the Dvaravati Period in Central Thailand is shown by carinated pottery bowls and *kendi*, the *sema* stones and the Buddhist votive tablets.[48]

The northern region

Lamphun Province in northern Thailand is the site of the capital of the ancient kingdom of Haripunjaya which, according to the fifteenth century *Camadevivamsa* – a chronicle of considerable historical value – was founded in the eighth century by Queen Camadevi from Lopburi. The dynasty reigning at Lamphun in the twelfth century is known from several Mon inscriptions found there. Dupont regarded Wat Kukut at Lumphun, and other similar *chedis* there and at Chieng Mai, as examples of late Dvaravati architecture of the twelfth–thirteenth centuries. This view has been generally accepted.

Excavations in front of the Lamphun City Hall and at Wat Prathat, Haripunjaya, revealed clear evidence for Dvaravati settlement in the lowest layers. The ceramic assemblage has strong parallels to those from the Dvaravati sites in Central Thailand and is associated with a calibrated radiocarbon date of AD 570–760 (1390 $\pm$ 70 BP OAEP–1299). The second phase of occupation revealed evidence for cultural contacts with Myanmar in the tenth and eleventh centuries. With the third phase we encounter the influence of Khmer occupation of parts of Thailand during the Bayon period, with imported ceramics of Chinese Song Dynasty origin, dating to the thirteenth century (730 $\pm$ 60 BP, OAEP–1295).[49]

The southern region

Between the fifth and eighth centuries, the influences of Indian civilization were well absorbed by the people of Peninsular Thailand. Various Hindu sects, such as Saivism and Vaishnavism, flourished side by side with Buddhist sects such as Hinayana and Mahayana. On account of their artistic remains, the sites of Chaiya, Nakhon Si Thammarat and Yarang were the most important Buddhist centers in the Peninsula during this period. Sculpture produced here resembles that of the Dvaravati culture of Central Thailand, reflecting the close cultural and commercial exchanges between the Peninsula and Dvaravati communities.[50]

A number of stone *Dharmacakras* dating to the sixth and the seventh centuries have been found at Peninsular sites. Among them, a complete *Dharmacakra* comes from Yarang District of Pattani Province and a fragment of a terracotta *Dharmacakra* has been discovered from Muang District of Nakhon Si Thammarat Province. There is also a fragment of a decorated stone *Dharmacakra* from Chaiya District of Surat Thani Province.

Groups of Buddha images stylistically related to those of the Central Dvaravati region, dated to the eighth century, come from Muang District of Nakhon Si Thammarat Province and from Kanchanadit District of Surat Thani Province. The finest is the bronze Buddha from Yarang District in Pattani Province, in which the double *vitarka mudra* is executed below the level of the waist.[51]

Many types of fired clay votive tablets circulated throughout the Peninsula, most frequently depicting the Buddha giving a discourse on the True Doctrine (The Lotus Sutra) according to Mahayana Buddhism. These have been found at Khao Khanab Nam Cave in Krabi Province, at Khao Ok Thalu Cave in Phattalung Province and at Khuha Phimuk Cave in Yala Province. Similar types of votive tablet have been reported from various Dvaravati sites in Central Thailand, and from further to the south in Kelantan in Malaysia.[52]

A number of Buddhist monuments of this period have been reported from the moated town in Yarang District, Pattani Province. Monument No.3 at Ban Ja Lae, of which only the brick base survives, was excavated by the Fine Arts Department in 1992. It consisted of a central massif of square plan with small indentations, standing on a square base with facings ornamented with mouldings. Votive stupas and votive tablets were found in a small chamber within.[53]

Summary

Literary and archaeological evidence confirm that Central Thailand between the seventh and eleventh centuries was the homeland of a Buddhist kingdom (or kingdoms) referred to as Dvaravati. We may conclude with a fair degree of certainty that the Dvaravati did not form part of the Mon Confederacy centred at Thaton in lower Burma, as previously suggested by some scholars, but developed out of the earlier Austroasiatic-speaking chiefdoms of prehistoric Central Thailand. During that time, local rulers accepted the superiority of Indian concepts in order to give divine legitimacy to their secular rule. They therefore brought to their courts the priests and literati who introduced many elements of Indian culture to the Dvaravati people, such as the system of coinage, seals and sealings, the Pali and Sanskrit languages, religious beliefs, town plans, art and architecture, ceramics, concepts of state and kingship and a variety of musical instruments and dances.

Dvaravati Culture was not restricted to the Central Plains but extended to the Khorat Plateau of Northeastern Thailand and to Lamphun Province in the north. There is also reliable evidence that Dvaravati Culture was well absorbed by the people of Peninsular Thailand and adjacent parts of Malaysia.

Notes

1 Beal 1969; Takakusu 1982.
2 Boeles 1964.
3 Coedès 1925.
4 It is far from certain that Dvaravati was a single state and some authorities believe that the name refers to a number of related but mainly independent small polities.
5 The term "Hoabinhian" is derived from the name of Hoa Binh Province in northern Vietnam where the distinctive stone tools of the late Pleistocene – early Recent foraging peoples of Mainland Southeast Asia were first described. Use of this term in Thailand does not imply close cultural relationships between communities at this time throughout the whole region.
6 You-di 1976; Glover 1990a; Rajpitak and Seeley 1979.
7 Basak 1959.
8 Glover 1990b and Ray 1990, 1994, 1996.

9 Warmington 1928; Margabhandhu 1985; Wheeler *et al.* 1946.
10 Coedès 1928; Picard 1955; Brown and Macdonnel 1989.
11 Boisselier 1965.
12 Bronson 1976; Margabhandhu 1985.
13 Fine Arts Department 1989; Bhattacharyya 1975.
14 Fine Arts Department 1984; Veeraprasert 1986.
15 See Amatayakul 1970; Le and Vu 1996; Boisselier 1968.
16 Dupont 1959.
17 Boeles 1964.
18 Coedès 1964.
19 On the above finds, see Coedès 1956; Dupont 1959, 1968; Yupho 1967; Indrawooth 1985.
20 Lyons 1965; Khambhirayanon 1984.
21 Bronson 1976; Jiachanphong 1996.
22 Maleipan 1979; Varasarin and Imsombat 1981.
23 Boeles 1967; Coedès 1929; Boisselier 1961; Bhumadhon 1983.
24 See Tankittikorn 1991, 1995; Wales 1937; Diskul 1981; Kaewglai 1983; Sukhasvasti 1989; Khan 1963 (Mainamati).
25 Sulaksananont 1987.
26 Pisnupong 1991.
27 Boonprakhong and Thongkhamvarn 1970.
28 On these expansions, see Wales 1937, 1969; Indrawooth 1991; Amatayakul 1970.
29 Gutman 1978.
30 For ceramics generally, see Singh 1969; Indrawooth 1985; Despande 1969; Peacock 1982; Greene 1992.
31 On Mon inscriptions, see Veeraprajak 1986; Wimonkasem 1988; Prapatthong 1979.
32 Temple 1893; Diffloth 1984.
33 Viriyabus 1973.
34 Yamamoto 1979.
35 Boeles 1964; Bhumadhon 1987a.
36 Rhys Davids 1903.
37 Rowland 1953; Drekmeier 1962.
38 Indrawooth 1994; Veeraprasert 1988; Krairiksh 1980.
39 On this material, see Coedès 1958; Lajonquière 1909; Fine Arts Department 1992a.
40 Boisselier 1965, 1968.
41 Ratanakan 1962, 1992; Wales 1969.
42 Takakusu 1982.
43 Mitra 1966, 1971; Owen 1975.
44 Yupho 1967; Coedès 1929; Kern 1884; Nariman 1973; Sirisrap 1981; Chongkol and Woodward 1966.
45 Diskul 1981; Chongkol 1967; Thongjuer 1978.
46 Wales 1969; Indrawooth 1991.
47 Diskul 1956.
48 Indrawooth 1991; Fine Arts Department 1968.
49 On Haripunjaya and Lamphun, see Coedès 1964; Prapatthong 1979; Rungrugee 1985; Indrawooth 1994.
50 Krairiksh 1980; Pantukovit 1987.
51 Chamornman 1985; Pantukovit 1987.
52 On these tablets, see O'Connor 1974; Sooksawasdi 1985; Sirisrap 1981; Adi Taha 1993.
53 Lertrit 1988; Fine Arts Department 1992b; Jacq-Hergoulach 1992.

Select Bibliography

Editors' note on the sources. Most of the recent research on Dvaravati Civilization has been undertaken by Thai scholars and is published only in the Thai language, and often in outlets difficult to access even for Thai readers not resident in the kingdom. However, we have listed a high proportion of these publications below in the hope that they will be of value to scholars wishing to research in this area.

Archaeology other than Thailand

Adi Taha (1993) "Recent *archaeo*logical discoveries in Peninsular Malaysia (1991–1993)", *Journal of the Malaysian Branch of the Royal Asiatic Society* LXVI, Part 1: 67–83.

Coedès, G. (1964) *Les Ètats Hindouises d'Indochine et Indonesie*, Paris: New Edition.

Despande, M. N. (1969) "Roman pottery in India", in B. P. Singh (ed.) *Potteries in Ancient India*, Patna: Patna University, Department of Ancient Indian History and *Archaeo*logy, pp. 275–84.

Glover, I. C. (1990b) *Early Trade Between India and Southeast Asia – a Link in the Development of a World Trading System*, Hull: Centre for Southeast Asian Studies, University of Hull.

Greene, K. (1992) *Roman Pottery*, London: British Museum Press.

Gutman, P. (1978) "The ancient coinage of Southeast Asia", *Journal of the Siam Society* 66: 8–21.

Jacq-Hergoulach, M. (1992) *La Civilisation de Port-Entrepôts du sud Kedah (Malaysia) Ve-XIVe siècle*, Paris: l'Harmattan.

Khan, F. A. (1963) *Mainamati: a Preliminary Report on the Recent Archaeological Excavations in East Pakistan*, Department of Archaeology Pakistan.

Le Xuan Diem and Vu Kim Loc (1996) *Artefacts of Champa*, Hanoi: National Culture Publishing House, pp. 6–9, 114–28.

Malleret, L. (1959–63) *L'Archéologie du Delta du Mekongi*, 4 vols. Paris: École Française d'Extrême-Orient.

Margabhandhu, C. (1985) *Archaeology of the Satavahana Kshatrapa Times*, Delhi: Sundeep Prakashan, p. 261.

Marshall, J. (1975) *Taxila* Vol II. Delhi: Motilal Banasidass, pp. 655–6.

Mitra, D. (1966) *Ajanta*, Archaeological Calcutta: Archaeological Survey of India Government of India.

Mitra, D. (1971) *Buddhist Monuments*, Calcutta: Sahitya Sumsad Press.

Murthy, K. K. (1977) *Nagarjunakonda, a Culltural Study*, Delhi: Concept Publishing, pp. 1–10.

Owen, C. K. (1975) *Buddhist Cave Temples in India*, Bombay: D. B. Taraporevala Sons and Co.

Peacock, D. P. S. (1982) *Pottery in the Roman World. An Ethno-archaeological Approach*, London and New York: Longman.

Ray, H. P. (1990) "Seafaring in the Bay of Bengal in the early centuries AD", *Studies in History* 1(5): 1–14.

Ray, H. P. (1994) *The Winds of Change – Buddhism and the Maritime Links of Early South Asia*, Delhi: Oxford University Press.

Ray, H. P. (1996) "Early trans-oceanic contacts between South and Southeast Asia", in A. Srisuchat (ed.) *Ancient Trade and Cultural Contacts in Southeast Asia*, Bangkok: Office of the National Cultural Commission, pp. 43–56.

Rhys Davids, T. W. (1999) *Buddhist India*, New Delhi, Munisham Manoharlal Publishers.

Rowland, B. (1953) *The Art and Architecture of India* (Buddhidst–Hindu–Jain), London: Penguin Books.

Roy, T. N. (1983) "The Ganges civilization", *The Heritage of Ancient India*, No. II, New Delhi: Ramanand Vidya Bhawan.

Singh, R. C. Prasad (1969) "Spouted vessels in India", in B. P. Singha (ed.) *Potteries in Ancient India*, Department of Ancient Indian History and *Archaeo*logy, Patna University, pp. 118–32.

Takakusu (1982) *A record of the Buddhist Religion as practised in India and the Malay Archiphelogo [AD 671–695] by I-Tsign*, New Delhi: Musharan Manoharlal.

Temple, R. C. (1893) "Notes on the antiquities of Ramannadesa (the Talaing country of Burma)", *Indian Archaeology* 22: 327–66.

Thaw, Aung (1968) *Report on the Excavations at Beikthano*, Rangoon: Ministry of Union Culture, fig. 84.

Wheeler, R. E. M., Ghosh, A. and Krishna Deva (1946) "Arikamedu: an Indo-Roman trading station on the east Coast of India", *Ancient India* 2: 17–124.

Thai archaeology

Amatayakul, T. (1970) *Changwat Suphan Buri* (in Thai), Bangkok: Charoenrat Press, pp. 34–7.
Bhumadhon, B. (1983) *The History of Lopburi during Dvaravati Period* (in Thai), Bangkok: Krung Siam Press, pp.1–16.
Bhumadhon, B. (1984) "Dvaravati uninscribed coins found at Lopburi" (in Thai), *Silpakorn Journal* 28(5): 55–63.
Bhumadhon, B. (1987a) *The Archaeology of Muang Dong Khon* (in Thai), Bangkok: Amarin Printing Group.
Bhumadhon, B. (1987b) *Muang Sab Champa* (in Thai), *Pakpreawkarnchang* 2, Saraburi.
Boeles, J. J. (1964) "The King of Sri Dvaravati and his regalia", *Journal of the Siam Society* 52(1): 99–110.
Boeles, J. J. (1967) "A note on the ancient city called Lavapura", *Journal of the Siam Society* 55(1).
Boisselier, J. (1961) "Un fragment inscrit de Roue de la Loi de Lopburi", *Artibus Asiae* XXIV(3/4): 225–31.
Boisselier, J. (1965) "U-T'ong et son importance pour l'histoire de Thaïlande", *Silpakorn Journal* 9(1): 27–30.
Boisselier, J. (1968) *Nouvelles Connaissances Archéologiques de la ville d'U-T'ong*, Bangkok.
Boisselier, J. (1972) "Travaux de la mission archéologique française en Thaïlande (Juillet–Novembre) 1966", *Arts Asiatiques* XXV: 29, fig. 3.
Boonprakhong and Thongkhamvarn, Ch. (1970) "Khmer inscription on the bronze mirror frame found at Sri Mahosot", *The Collection of Siam Inscriptions* Part IV (in Thai), Bangkok: Office of the Prime Minister, Royal Thai Government, pp. 141–2.
Bronson, B. (1976) *Excavation at Chansen and the Cultural Chronology of Protohistoric Central Thailand*, Ann Arbor, Michigan: University Microfilms International.
Brown, R. L. and Macdonnel, A. M. (1989) "The Pong Tuk lamp: a reconsideration", *Journal of the Siam Society* 77(2): 9–20.
Chamornman, Ch. (1985) *Research on Arts and Archaeology of Muang Yarang, Pattani Province* (in Thai), Nakhon Pathom: Silpakorn University Press.
Chongkol, J. (1967) *The Bangkok. National Museum*, Bangkok: Siwaporn Printing.
Chongkol, J. and Woodward, H. W. Jr. (1966) *Guide to the U-Thong National Museum*, Bangkok: Siwaorn Printing, Fig. 30.
Coedès, G. (1925) "Documents sur l'histoire politique et religieuse de Laos", *Bulletin de l'École Française d'Extrême-Orient* 25 :1–200.
Coedès, G. (1928) "Excavations at Pong Tuk", *Journal of the Siam Society* 21(3): 195–209.
Coedès, G. (1929) "Recueil des Inscriptions du Siam. Pt II", *Inscriptions de Dvaravati, de Crivijaya et de Lavo* (2nd edn), Bangkok: The Siam Society.
Coedès, G. (1956) "Une Roue de la Loi avec inscription en Pali provennant du site de Pra Pathom", *Artibus Asiae* 19(3/4): 221–6.
Coedès, G. (1958) "Nouvelles données epigraphiques sur l'histoire de l'Indochine Centrale", *Journal Asiatique* CCXLVI: 125–42.
Department of Archaeology (1981) *Report and a Study of Ancient Culture at Ban Khu Muang, Amphoe Inburi, Changwat Singburi* (in Thai), Nakhon Pathom: Silpakorn University Press.
Diskul, M. C. Subhadradis. (1956) "Muang Fa Daed. An ancient town in north-east Thailand", *Artibus Asiae* 19(3/4): 362–7.
Diskul, M. C. Subhadradis. (1981) *Art in Thailand* (in Thai) (7th edn), Bangkok: Krung Siam Press.
Dupont, P. (1959) *L'Archéologie Mone de Dvaravati*, Paris: École Française d'Extrême-Orient.
Fine Arts Department (1968) *The Survey and Excavation at Muang Fa Daed Song Yang, Ban Sema, Tambon Nong Pan, Amphoe Kamalasai, Changwat Kalasin*, 1967–8. Bangkok: F.A.D.
Fine Arts Department (1984) *Archaeological Site at Tha Khae* (in Thai), Bangkok: Amarin Press.
Fine Arts Department (1989) *Nern Makok*, a preliminary report of the stratigraphical and archaeological evidence (in Thai), Bangkok: Agricultural Co-operative Federation of Thailand.
Fine Arts Department (1992a) *History and Archaeology of Sri Mahosot* (in Thai), Bangkok: Samaphan Press.

Fine Arts Department (1992b) *Archaeological Survey on Monuments at Muang Yarang* (in Thai), Bangkok: Siam Silpa Press.

Glover, I. C. (1990a) "Ban Don Ta Phet: the 1984–5 excavation", in I. C. Glover and E. Glover (eds) *Southeast Asian Archaeology 1986*, Oxford: British Archaeological Reports, (International Series), 561. pp. 139–83.

Higham, C. F. W. and R. Thosarat (1998) *Prehistoric Thailand. From Early Settlement to Sukhothai*, Bangkok: River Books.

Indrawooth, P. (1983) *The Excavation at the Ancient Town of Nakhon Pathom, Tambon Phra Praton, Amphoe Muang, Changwat Nakhon Pathom* (in Thai), Nakhon Pathom: Silpakorn University Press.

Indrawooth, P. (1985) *Index Pottery of Dvaravati Period*, Bangkok: Thai I. E Printing Group.

Indrawooth, P., Krabuansang, S and Narkwake, P. (1991) "Muang Fa Daed Song Yang: new archaeological discoveries", in Université Silpakorn (ed.) Recentes *Recherches en Archéologie en Thaïlande: Deuxième Symposium Franco-Thai*, Bangkok: Silpakorn University, pp. 98–111.

Indrawooth, P., Krabuansang, S and Narkwake, P. (1994) "The study of ancient civilization from archaeological evidence in Lumphun prior to the 19th century B.E" (in Thai).

Jiachanphong, P. (1996) "Terracotta seals from Khok Chansen", in *Chansen: a Social and Cultural History* (in Thai), Bangkok: Ruen Kaew Printing House.

Kaewglai, C. (1983) "Sanskrit inscription found at Sri Thep" (in Thai), *Silpakorn Journal* 27(2): 55–9.

Khambhirayanon, M. (1984) "Chinese ceramics from Ratchaburi province" (in Thai), *Muang Boran* 10(2): 31–48.

Krairiksh, P. (1980) *Art in Peninsula Thailand Prior to The Fourteenth Century AD*, Bangkok: Amarin Press, Pl. 26.

Lajonquière, M. L. de (1909) "Le domaine archéologique du Siam", *Bulletin de la Commission Archeologique de l'Indochine (Paris) I*, pp. 188–262.

Lertrit, S. (1988) *The Moated Town, Environment and Associated Sites of the Yarang Complex*, Bangkok: Amarin Printing Group.

Lyons, E. (1965) "The traders of Ku Bua", *Archives of the Chinese Art Society of America* XIX: 52–56.

Maleipan, V. (1979) "The excavation at Sap Champa", in R. Smith and W. Watsin (eds) *Early South East Asia: Essays in Archaeology, History and Historical Geography*, Oxford: Oxford University Press, pp. 337–41.

Moore, E. (1988) *Moated Sites in Early North East Thailand*, Oxford: BAR, International Series S-400.

Natapintu, S. (1991) "*Archae*ometallurgical studies in the Khao Wong Prachan Valley, Central Thailand", *Bulletin of the Indo-Pacific Prehistory Association* 11: 153–9.

Noksakul, D. (1983) *A Study of the Culture and the Environment of an Ancient Community at Khok Phanom Di, Changwat Chonburi* (in Thai), Master's Thesis. Bangkok: Silpakorn University.

O'Connor, S. J. (1974) "Buddhist votive tablets and caves in Peninsular Thailand", *Art and Archaeology in Thailand I*, Prachuab Kirikhan: Infantry Center Printing Press, pp. 67–84.

Pantukovit, P. (1987) *A Study of Ancient Sculpture existing in Dvaravati Period at Yarang District, Pattani Province* (in Thai), Master's Thesis, Bangkok: Silpakorn University.

Phaiboonsuwan, P. (1972) *Ancient Objects and Monuments in Changwat Khonkhaen and its vicinities* (in Thai), Bangkok: Religious Affairs Printing Press.

Picard, Ch. (1955) "La Lampe alexandrine de P'ong tuk", *Artibus Asiae* XVIII: 137–48.

Pisnupong, P. (ed.) (1991) *Report on the Excavation of the Sra Morakot Monuments* (in Thai), Bangkok: Samaphan.

Prapatthong, K. (1979) *A Critical Study on the Inscriptions in the Haripunjaya National Museum* (in Thai), Bangkok: Krung Siam Press.

Phaiboonsuwan, P. (1972) *Ancient Objects and Monuments in Changwat Khonkhaen and its vicinities* (in Thai), Bangkok: Religious Affairs Printing Press.

Rajpitak, W. and Seeley, N. (1979) "The bronze bowls from Ban Don Ta Phet: an enigma of prehistoric metallurgy", *World Archaeology* 11(1): 26–31.

Ratanakan, S. (1962) *Archaeological Survey and Excavation at U-Thong* (In Thai), Bangkok: F.A.D.

Ratanakan, S. (1992) *Excavations at Ku Bua* (In Thai), Bangkok: F.A.D.

Rungrugee, B. (1985) *Archaeological Survey and Excavation at Muang Haripunjaya, Lumphun* (in Thai), Bangkok: F.A.D.
Sirisrap, N. (1981) *Dvaravati votive tablets found at Nakhon Pathom* (in Thai), Master's Thesis, Bangkok: Silpakorn University.
Sooksawasdi, M. L. Surasawasdi (1985) *A Study of Southern Thai Votive Tablets* (in Thai), Master's Thesis, Bangkok: Silpakorn University.
Sørensen, P. and Hatting, T. (1967) *Archaeological Investigations in Thailand Vol. II, Ban Kao, Part I: The Archaeological Materials from the Burials*, Copenhagen: Munksgaard.
Sukhasvasti, M. R. Suriyavudh (1989) "Klang Nai: decorative stucco figures of the religious monument", *Muang Boran* Journal 15(1): 41–8.
Sukhasvasti, M. R. Suriyavudh (1984) "Man with monkey in Mon culture (Dvaravati)", *Journal of Silpakorn University (2529)*, Bangkok: Silpakorn University.
Sukpramoon, P. (1991) *Historical Archaeology in Ratchaburi*, Bangkok: Amarin Printing.
Sulaksananont, U. (1987) *A Study of the Ancient Town at Muang Phra Ratha, Amphoe Phanat Nikhom, Chonburi, from Stratigraphy and Archaeology* (in Thai), Master's Thesis, Bangkok: Silpakorn University.
Tankittikorn, W. (1991) *The Settlement Before Muang Sri Thep* (in Thai), Bangkok: Future Press.
Tankittikorn, W. (1995) *Sri Thep* (in Thai), Bangkok: F.A.D.
Thongjuer, Ph. (1978) *The Buddha Images Standing on Vanaspati, found in Thailand*, Master's Thesis, Bangkok: Silpakorn University.
Vanasin, Ph. and Supajanya, Th. (1981) *Ancient Cities on the Former Coastline in the Central Plain of Thailand* (in Thai), Bangkok: Chulalongkorn University Press.
Varasarin, U. and Imsombat, A. (1981) "New inscription from Changwat Lopburi (Sab Champa Inscription I)", in *Ancient Inscription Found at Lopburi and Its Vicinities* (in Thai), Bangkok: Borpit Printing Co., pp. 74–81.
Veeraprajak, K. (1986) "Mon inscriptions found in Thailand", in *Inscriptions in Thailand Vol. II* (in Thai), Bangkok: National Library, F.A.D.
Veeraprasert, M. (1986) "Indian bronze coin from Klong Thom", *Encyclopaedia of Southern Thai Culture* (in Thai), vol. 3, pp. 1206–7.
Veeraprasert, M. (1988) "Tablettes votives bouddhiques de la periode de Dvaravati découvertes à Nadun, Mahasarakham", in Université de Silpakorn (ed.) *La Thaïlande des debut de son Histoire au XVeme siècle: Premier Symposium Franco-Thai*, Bangkok: Silpakorn University, pp. 124–9.
Veeraprasert, M. (1992) "Klong Thom: an ancient bead manufacturing location and its Ancient entrepôt", in I. Glover, P. Suchitta and J. Villiers. (eds) *Early Metallurgy, Trade and Urban Centers in Thailand and Southeast Asia*, Bangkok: White Lotus, pp. 149–61.
Viriyabus, Ch. (1973) *Coins in Thailand* (in Thai), Bangkok: National Museum.
Wales, H. G. Quaritch (1937) "The exploration of Sri Deva, an ancient Indian city in Indochina", *Indian Art and Letters* X: 61–99.
Wales, H. G. Quaritch (1965) "Muang Bon, a town of northern Dvaravati", *Journal of the Siam Society* 53(1): 1–7.
Wales, H. G. Quaritch (1969) *Dvaravati; the Earliest Kingdom of Siam (6th–11th Century)*, London: Bernard Quaritch Ltd.
Wilaikaew, J. (1991) *The Archaeology of Muang U-Taphao* (in Thai), Bangkok: P. Samphan Phanit Co.
Wimonkasem, K. (1988) "Étude paléographique des inscription mones découvertes dans le Nord-Est de la Thailande", in Université de Silpakorn (ed.) *La Thailande des debuts de son histoire au XVeme siècle: Premier Symposium Franco-Thai*, Bangkok: Silpakorn University, pp. 154–65.
You-di, C. (1976) *Ban Don Ta Phet: Preliminary Excavation Report, 1975–6* (in Thai), Bangkok: National Museum.
You-di, C. (1986) *Prehistoric Thailand* (in Thai), Bangkok: Roongsilp Printing.
Yupho, Dh. (1967) *Quartzite Buddha Images of the Dvaravati Period*, Bangkok: Siwaporn Printing.

Art history and history

Bhattacharyya. N. N. (1975) *Ancient Indian Rituals and their Social Content*, London: Curzon Press.
Coomaraswamy, A. K. (1927) *History of Indian and Indonesian Art*, New York: Dover.

Drekmeier, C. (1962) *Kingship and Community in Early India*, Stanford: Stanford Univerity Press.
Pelliot, P. (1904) "Deux itineraires de Chine en Inde à la find du VIIIe siècle", *Bulletin de l'École Française d'Extrême-Orient* 4: 142–3.
Warmington, E. H. (1928) *The Commerce between the Roman Empire and India*, Cambridge: Cambridge University Press.
Wheatley, P. (1961) *The Golden Khersonese*, Kuala Lumpur: University of Malaya Press.
Yamamoto T. (1979) "East Asian historical sources for Dvaravati studies", *Proceedings Seventh Conference, International Association of Historians of Asia, Bangkok, 22–26 August, 1977*, Bangkok: Chulalongkorn University Press, pp. 1137–50.

Buddhism

Basak, R. (1959) *Asokan Inscriptions*, Calcutta: Oriental Press, pp. 63–76.
Beal, S. (1969) *Buddhist Records of the Western World*, London: Oriental Books Reprints.
Bhattacharyya, B.(1968) *Sadhanamala*, Vol.II, Baroda: Oriental Institute.
Cowell, E. B. and Neil, R. A. (eds) (1886) *The Divyavadana*, Cambridge: Cambridge University Press.
Kern, H. (trans.) (1884) *The Saddharma-Pundarika or Lotus of the True Law*, The Sacred Books of The East, Vol. XXI, Delhi: Motilal Banarsidass.
Nariman, J. K. (1973) *Literary History of Sanskrit Buddhism*, Delhi: Motilal Banarsidass.
Rhys Davids, T. W. (1903) *Buddhist India*. London: Publisher unknown.
Rhys Davids. T. W. (trans.) (1956) *Dialogues of the Buddha*, Vol. II, London: Luzac & Co., pp. 92–3.
Takakusu, J. (trans.) (1982) *A Record of the Buddhist Religion as practiced in India and the Malay Archipelago (AD 671–695) by I. Tsing*, second Indian edition, New Delhi: Munshiram Manoharlal, p. 150.

Language and linguistics

Diffloth, G. (1984) *The Dvaravati Old-Mon Languages and Nyah Kur*, Bangkok: Chulalongkorn University Printing House.
Pou, S. and Jenner, P. N. (1974) "Proto-Indonesian and Mon-Khmer", *Asian Perspectives* XVII(2): 112–24.

7

THE ARCHAEOLOGY OF BURMA (MYANMAR) FROM THE NEOLITHIC TO PAGAN

Pamela Gutman and Bob Hudson

In comparison to the rest of Southeast Asia, the archaeology of Burma (Myanmar) has received only sporadic attention, although since the 1880s its various governments have sponsored surveys and excavations, albeit mainly of protohistorical and historical sites. Since 1988 the Myanmar Government Department of Archaeology has concentrated its efforts on restoration of historical monuments and the establishment of local museums, but in recent years a Department of Archaeology has been created at Rangoon (Yangon) University of Arts and Sciences and interest in prehistory has been rekindled.

Burma's geographical position has shaped patterns of human settlement and cultural development. Significantly, it is the only part of Southeast Asia with direct links through mountain passes and river valleys to China and Tibet in the northeast and north and to the Indian subcontinent in the northwest and west. Its situation on the Bay of Bengal gives it relatively easy access by sea to India, and both sea and riverine routes connect it with Thailand to its east. Chains of hills extend north to south. The main river systems – the Kaladan, which flows into the Bay of Bengal, the dominant Irrawaddy (Ayeyarwady) which runs from north to south through the centre of the country, the Sittaung, which empties into the Gulf of Martaban, and the Salween, part of which forms a border with Thailand – are geographically isolated from each other and form individual agricultural areas. Each, with the exception of the unnavigable upper Salween, has its own riverine transport system and access to the sea (Figure 7.1).

Burma is thus quite sharply divided into different climatic zones, which require different water management strategies. The climatic zones correspond to the regions where evidence for urbanization is found: the narrow alluvial valleys in Rakhine (Arakan) state, the "Pyu" region of the central zone, and the Gulf of Martaban between the Sittaung and the Salween rivers. The mountainous coastal strips of Arakan in the west and Tenasserim in the south receive more than 2,000 millimetres of annual rainfall, as do the hill regions along the borders with China and Thailand. The Gulf of Martaban receives the annual monsoon. However, the central plains lie in the shadow of the coastal hills and receive only a little rain. In fact, they may be regarded as semi-arid. Survival here, especially if based on wet-rice (paddy) cultivation, needed techniques for storing and distributing the water available from the perennial rivers, the most important being the Irrawaddy which runs straight through the central dry zone. Those prehistoric sites

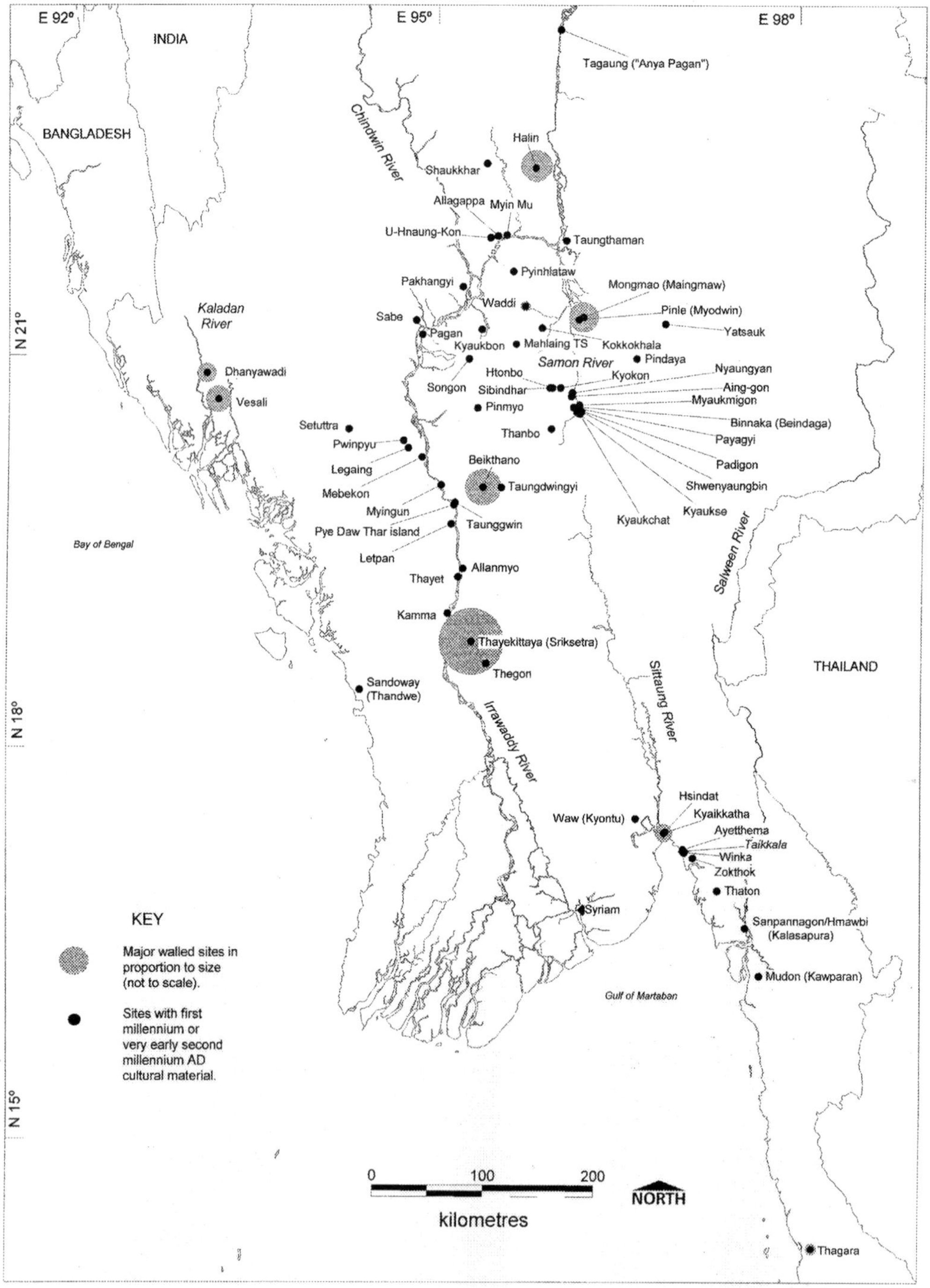

Figure 7.1 The main river systems of Burma, showing walled settlements, Pyu sites and Iron Age archaeological finds.

known to us are for the most part in the upper Irrawaddy valley in the central zone, perhaps reflecting the interests of the Archaeology Department over the years.

The archaeological history of Burma, despite substantial gaps in the evidence, appeared until quite recently to be fairly straightforward. Palaeolithic tools had been found by geologists or collected by colonial administrators, largely in the Upper Irrawaddy Valley. Neolithic polished stone axes and bracelets, and also bronze axes, bracelets and rings, had been making their way into museum collections since the late nineteenth century. However, scholars tended to be more interested in urban sites, notably the Pyu city of Sriksetra (Thayekittaya) and its successor city, the Burman capital of Pagan (sometimes also spelt Bagan).

Prehistory, protohistory and history

G. H. Luce's posthumous work, *Phases of Pre-Pagan Burma: Languages and History* (1985), attempted an account of the Pre-Pagan period using all the sources then available: linguistic analyses, Chinese and other foreign accounts, archaeological investigations of the Pyu sites and reports of other sites and epigraphic evidence. He identified the existence of a number of groups, many of whom had languages influenced by cultures with which they had come into contact. The Austroasiatic Mon-Khmer speakers stretched along the length of the Salween and around the Gulf of Martaban – pioneers, he ventured, of wet rice cultivation. Within the Sino-Tibetan family, the Karen, who had moved south down the ranges between the Salween and the Irrawaddy, were later to be displaced by the Mranma (Burmans) to the southwest across the head of the Delta and down to Tenasserim.

Within the Tibeto-Burman subgroup of the Sino-Tibetan language family, the Sak-Kantu (Thet Kadu) languages once spread from Manipur to north Yunnan. One group, the Loi of Manipur, were recorded in 1859 as being silk manufacturers, smelters of iron, makers of earthenware vessels and polished stone bowls. In the Pagan period the Sak were spread over central Burma, above and below Pagan, while the Kadu were to the east and northeast, their capital being at Tagaung. The Pyu were also Tibeto-Burman speakers whose walled settlements are spread from Halin to Thayekittaya (Sri Ksetra) in central Burma. The Kyan, or Chin, followed the Sak from the northwest, occupying part of the Chindwin valley. The Mru and the Kumi of northern Arakan and the Chittagong Hill Tracts also spoke Tibeto-Burman languages. The Burma-Lolos, Tibeto-Burman speakers who had been forced south from Yunnan, spread as far as Keng Tung in the east. This spread of languages and cultures perhaps reflected the movement of relatively small groups after the beginnings of political centralization on the alluvium, with its high potential for rice irrigation, in the first millennium BC.[1] During the early first millennium AD the languages and cultures of the more powerful and politically organized groups came to dominate.

The Pagan kingdom came to prominence following the decline of an earlier group of settlements in the central zone, enclosed by brick walls and populated by iron-using agriculturalists known today as the Pyu, who called themselves Tircul. According to Chinese sources the Pyu declined after they were attacked by Nanchao, in what is now the Chinese province of Yunnan, in the middle of the ninth century AD. Their fellow Tibeto-Burman speakers, the Burmans, then migrated westward from their agricultural base in the Kyaukse area to establish Pagan.[2] King Anawratha of Pagan is traditionally regarded as having conquered a rival Mon-Khmer speaking kingdom based at Thaton, southeast of the modern capital Yangon (Rangoon), in the eleventh century, bringing captives, Buddhist scriptures and a generally more advanced culture to Pagan. The earliest existing stone inscriptions at Pagan date to around this time. After two centuries of military domination and economic expansion, the kingdom was put under pressure by the Mongols in the thirteenth century. The centre of government then moved north to the area around Mandalay, which sits at the head of the rice-producing Kyaukse valley, and remained there for most of the time until colonization. The geopolitical contraction of Pagan was followed by an expansion of Mon polities in the south, and the rise of Mrauk-U on the west coast.

New research issues

Recent research and new historical models have both changed and complicated the picture of Burma's archaeological past. There is now extensive evidence of Neolithic and Bronze Age cultures in Upper Burma (Figure 7.2). From the evidence of surveys and artefacts collected, many places which yield Neolithic or bronze materials frequently form a continuum of place with later Iron Age sites. This suggests that renewed attention should be paid to the notion of local cultural development, rather than assuming that large-scale internal migration was the key factor involved in intra-regional change. There is radiocarbon evidence of settlement activity at Pagan well before the eleventh century, and new indications of a long-term presence there of the Pyu. This prompts a re-examination of the conventional notion of a rapid Burman migration to establish a settlement at the strategically valuable site of Pagan. As well, the "Mon paradigm", the idea that the Burmans at Pagan emulated the ancient Roman adaptation of Greek culture by absorbing "sophisticated" Mon ways, has come under serious challenge. Paul Strachan[3] has demonstrated that the early architecture of Pagan followed Pyu, not Mon, prototypes. Michael Aung-Thwin[4] has recently suggested, on the basis of inscriptional evidence, that the Pagan conquest of Thaton, and in fact the very existence of a significant Mon polity at Thaton or anywhere else in Lower Burma around or before the turn of the first millennium AD, is based on a later tradition which was wrongly interpreted as factual by European and Burmese historians in the twentieth century.

The Burma Neolithic

Over the past few years, Neolithic materials such as polished stone tools and bracelets (Figure 7.3) have been turning up in increasing numbers in Burma, in museums, private collections and antique shops, as farmers who find them in their fields realize their value. The locations of the known finds are shown in Figure 7.2. So far, the finds have not been put into any formal sequence, none of the sites has been radiocarbon dated, and few have even been professionally excavated. However, in 2001, a preliminary excavation by the Pagan Archaeology department at Letpanchibaw, an apparent early habitation site on the bank of the Irrawaddy north of Pagan, turned up at least four distinct levels of materials. Animal bones and Neolithic tools occurred lower down, and a later layer containing evidence of bronze working. Work on this site is expected to take several more years,[5] but it may be the first excavation in Burma where layers of purely Neolithic material can be

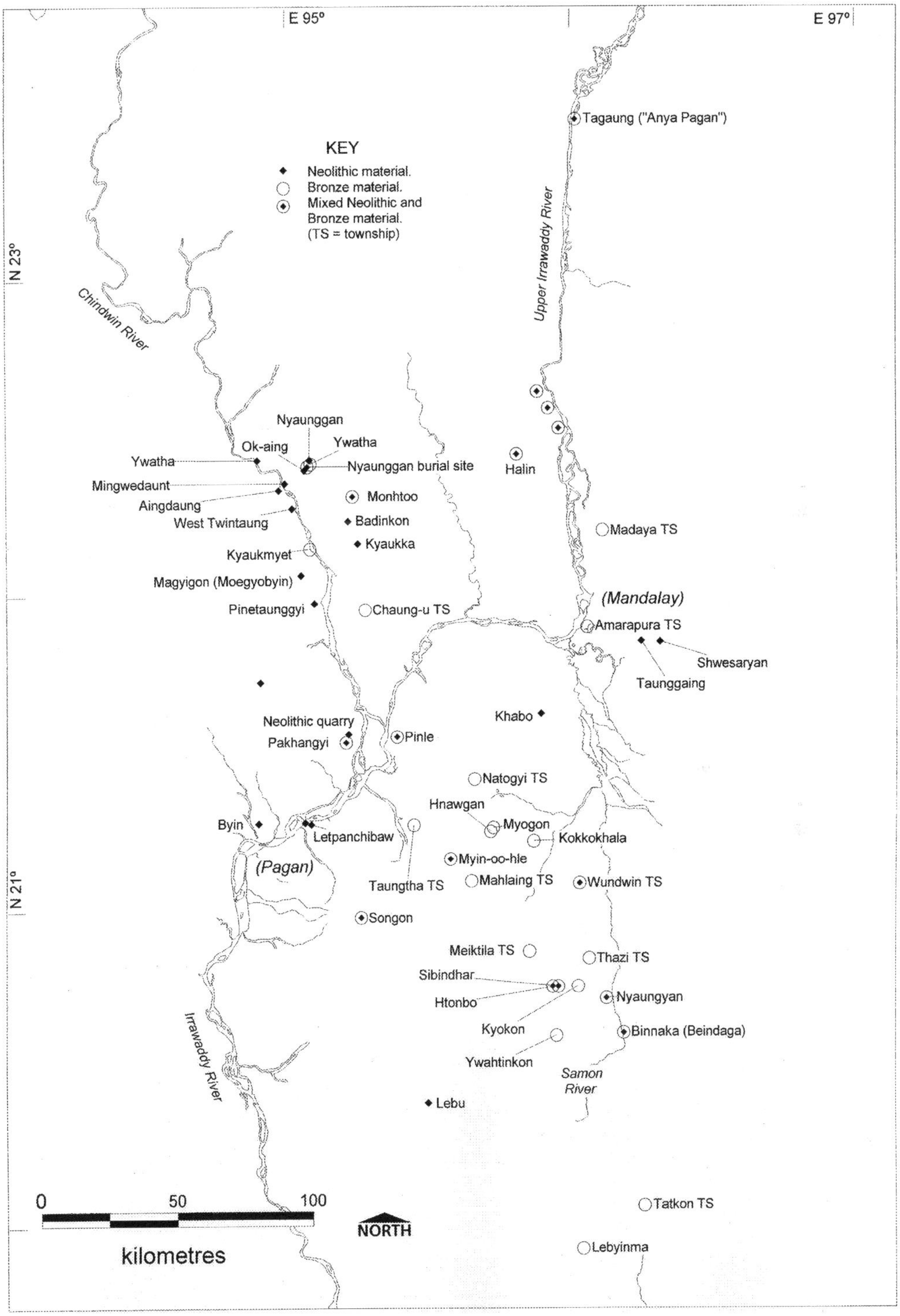

Figure 7.2 Neolithic and Bronze Age archaeological finds in Upper Burma.

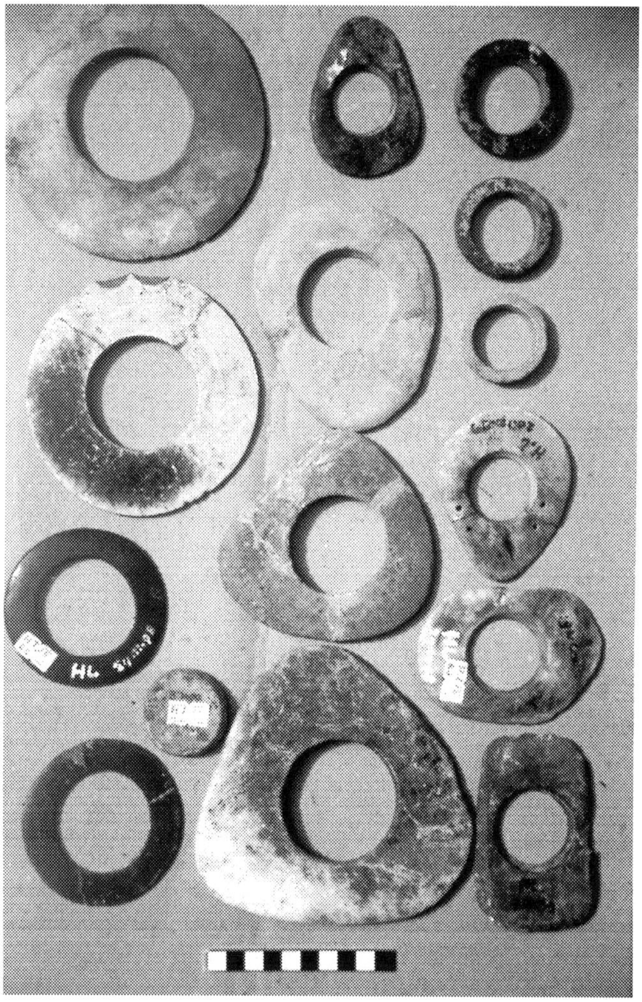

Figure 7.3 Stone bracelets of the Neolithic or early metal age from Halin. (Photograph by Bob Hudson.)

distinguished archaeologically from later layers containing bronze artefacts. As the Letpanchibaw site has evidence of fireplaces, there is potential for radiocarbon dating. Neolithic cultures in the rest of Mainland Southeast Asia date to between perhaps 3000 and 1500 BC.

The Bronze Age: stone and bronze

The excavation in 1998 of a burial site at Nyaunggan spurred new interest in the pre-urban human occupation of Burma. Nyaunggan lies east of the Chindwin River in upper Burma's Monywa district. Socketed bronze spearheads, adzes and arrowheads, and an object described as a socketed flared axe similar to one from Halin, east of Nyaunggan

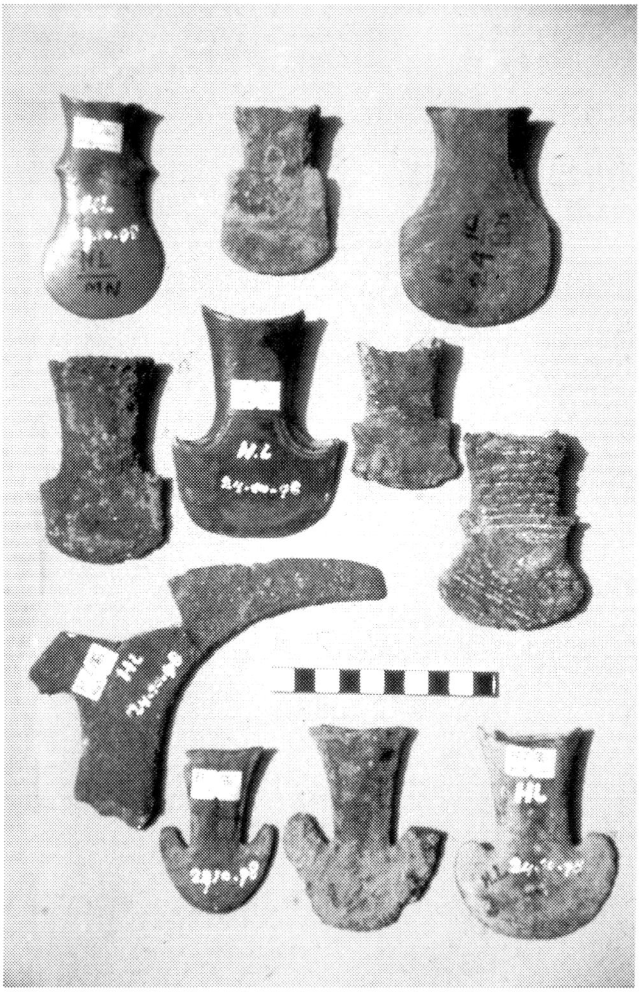

Figure 7.4 Bronze implements from Halin. (Photograph by Bob Hudson.)

(Figure 7.4 lower left) were among the grave goods. Other finds included polished stone bracelets, between 6 and 15 mm thick in the centre, and usually tapering to a sharp edge resemble those from Halin (Figure 7.3). These were mostly found around the wrists of some of the 37 skeletons buried in the cemetery. Some bracelets had been broken and then repaired with bronze wire threaded through carefully drilled holes, suggesting that they were objects of considerable significance to their owners. Similar bracelets have been found in China and Thailand.[6] Pottery vessels buried with the skeletons were thought to have contained food offerings. Stone, earthenware and shell beads were found, suggesting that the deceased were buried wearing jewellery or decorated clothing. The site could date to around 1000 BC, estimated from the chronology of similar sites and assemblages in Thailand, but no viable carbon was found that could provide an absolute date.[7]

New bronze finds in the Samon Valley

The Samon (Figure 7.2) is the only river in Burma that flows north rather than south. It feeds into the Kyaukse Valley, a major irrigated rice-producing area since at least the Pagan period. Eventually it joins the Irrawaddy near Mandalay. The archaeology of the Samon region is so far only known from surveys and casual finds, rather than from excavations. The scientist is presented with a challenging assortment of stone, bronze and iron weapons and tools, carnelian beads, some carved in the form of tigers (Plate 5), etched black and white beads, hoards of Pyu coins (Figure 7.5) and finger-marked bricks.

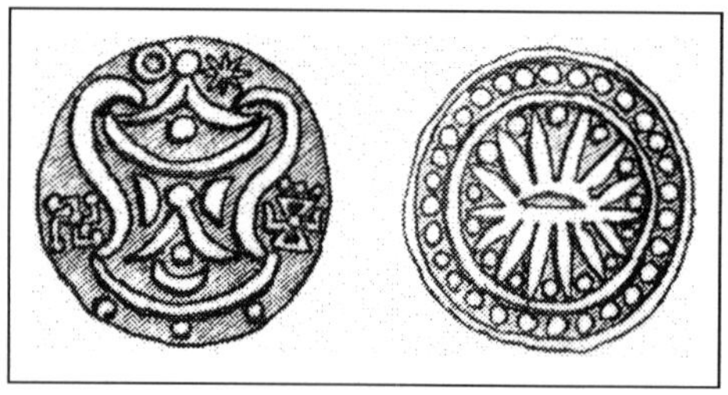

Figure 7.5 Pyu coin from Halin. (Drawing by Tanpawady Win Maung.)

Some of the bronze finds, in terms of their complexity, suggest that they may be younger than the bronzes from Nyaunggan and the other Chindwin sites. These include the beaten-bronze sheets excavated from burials near the villages of Min-oo-hle and Nyaungyan.[8] Some of these (Figure 7.6) appear to represent a human torso and legs, with raised circular sections resembling breasts, along with a larger, lower circle that could represent pregnancy. This has led to the popular interpretation in Burma of the artefacts as fertility figures or "mother goddesses". However, more complex versions have six "breasts" and three "bellies" and it might be more appropriate to view them as funerary decorations of indeterminate symbolism. Other symbolic items found in graves in the Samon valley include flat, leaf-like arrow or spear heads made from beaten bronze and up to 30 centimetres long.

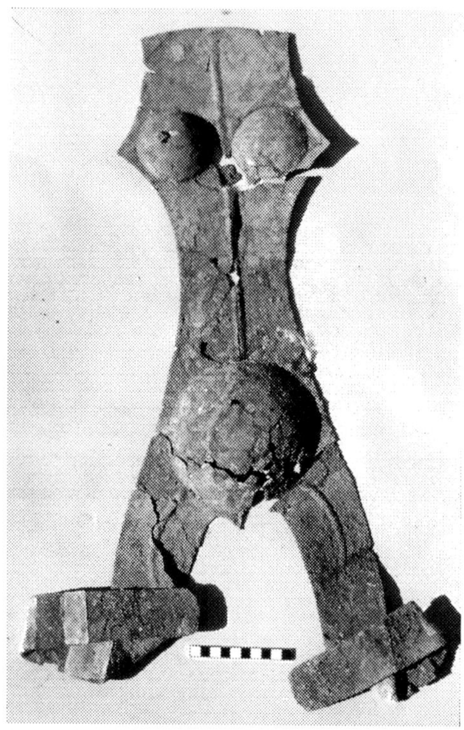

Figure 7.6 Bronze coffin decoration, Samon Valley. (Photograph by Bob Hudson.)

The Iron Age

Iron is a substance linked worldwide with agricultural expansion, as iron tools are more efficient than polished stone or bronze. Iron weapons and tools give an advantage not just because of their strength, but because they can be produced in much greater numbers than bronze, once the extractive and blacksmithing technology has reached the appropriate level. The earliest dated Iron Age site in Burma is Taungthaman, just outside the city of Amarapura, one of Burma's capitals in the eighteenth century and located in the Dry Zone. The site is about 3 metres above the Irrawaddy flood plain. In the late 1960s natural erosion revealed burials and excavations began in the early 1970s under the direction of U Aung Thaw and U Sein Maung Oo of the Archaeological Survey of Burma. Thermoluminescence dates on sherds found in the graves suggest an age in the second half of the first millennium BC.

The iron items recovered with the burials at Taungthaman include a fishhook, knife blades, short swords and several iron lumps. Metallurgical analysis reveals that the iron was smelted at 1,000 degrees centigrade, but the temperature required to burn out impurities (approximately 1,500 degrees centigrade) was not reached. According to Stargardt, Taungthaman represented at about 500 BC the "very last and most sophisticated stage of stone technology co-existing with the beginnings of an initially crude, iron-working metallurgy".[9] This date coincides with the first securely-dated iron artefacts known for China.[10] There are bolder claims for India, where radiocarbon dates associated with iron production appear to go back to the twelfth century BC.[11]

Beikthano Myo, younger than Taungthaman and carbon-dated to the second century BC, had well-established iron-working, with discoveries of caltrops (spikes apparently designed to be strewn on the ground to discomfort horses or elephants in battle), nails, sockets, plates and other construction hardware.[12] Other early urban "Pyu" sites have similar materials.

The early urban period

The early urban sites are situated in the central zone, the Arakan alluvium and around the Gulf of Martaban. They are generally dated from end of the first millennium BC and are characterized by walls of burnt brick, often moated, rhomboid in the case of Beikthano and in other cases varying from round to oval, taking advantage of the local geography for defence and usually situated in the neighbourhood of a river. From this period, if not earlier, irrigation appears to have been based on two principles: either through rivers being redirected through weirs and sluices, or through water distributed by canals fed from artificial tanks.

Similar enclosed settlements appear in other parts of Southeast Asia in the early first millennium AD. A network of moated settlements appears to have formed a regional economic system in the central plain of Thailand by the ninth century.[13] Similar sites, seen as having both water-harvesting and territorial functions, existed in the Mun River basin of Northeast Thailand.[14] In the case of the Myanmar settlements, those of Beikthano, Halin, Mongmao, Thayekittaya (also known as Sriksetra, Hmawza or Old Prome), Dhanyawadi and Vesali all had what appear to be elite enclosures within their outer walls.[15] Indeed, before the eighth century AD the urban sites of central Burma appear to have shared many cultural elements with their counterparts on the west coast, as well as in Thailand, Cambodia and Vietnam. Contact with these is evidenced not only by stylistic comparisons of their palaeography, art and architecture, but also by 'Pyu' coins found in southern Thailand and Vietnam[16] and by identical agate seals found at Halin, Vesali and Oc Eo, inscribed in fourth/fifth-century South Indian script.[17] Chinese sources from as early as the second century BC refer to a Sichuan-Yunnan-Burma-India overland route, while a maritime route from Guangdong province to India was recorded in the first century AD.[18]

Beikthano Myo ("Vishnu City")

The best known of the Pyu sites in the central zone are Beikthano, Halin and Thayekittaya/Sriksetra (Figure 7.1). The radiocarbon dates for the earliest of these, Beikthano, are 1950 ± 90 BP (cal. 180 BC–AD 260), 1890 ± 95 BP (cal. 100 BC–AD 390), 1725 ± 95 BP (cal. AD 80–540) and 1650 ± 85 BP (cal. AD 210–610).[19] The dates indicate activity between outer limits of 180 BC and AD 610. Beikthano shows no evidence of Indian religions in its earliest levels, although certain links with Indian technology have been identified in brick sizes. The excavator of Beikthano, U Aung Thaw, uncovered gateways to the city walls curving gradually inward at the entrance, leading to an inner citadel, monastic buildings and religious structures associated with burial urns. He suggested that these, with the exception of one later eleventh-century structure, belonged to a period of occupation between about the first to the fifth centuries. Pyu elements included masonry structures with massive walls constructed of large bricks, often incised with numerals or deep gouges of between one and three straight, curved or diagonal lines; silver coins bearing auspicious symbols; burial urns of both plain and ornate design; and iron nails and bosses.[20]

The monastery and *stupa* plans at Beikthano bear a considerable resemblance to those found at Nagarjunakonda and the Krishna valley in southeast India, although Buddhist statuary is conspicuous by its absence. This may indicate that the sects at Beikthano did not practice image worship. The most significant features linking Beikthano with other sites are burial urns and coins. It appears that the urns contained secondary burials and were placed in groups in or around sepulchral structures. Stargardt has remarked that the drum-shaped form of these urns recalls the "Dongson" bronze drums of Vietnam and Yunnan.[21] Most early coins in Burma have a symbol on the obverse which may denote the issuing polity. At Beikthano, the majority of coins have a *bhadrapitha* or throne symbol. The reverse has a *srivatsa*, the symbolic home of Sri, the goddess of prosperity. Together with symbols of the sun and moon, representing the heavens, while below is a water symbol, at Beikthano often wavy lines. These symbolize the issuing ruler's role as guarantor of prosperity. Similar symbols are found on terracotta sherds.[22]

Halin

Halin (Hanlin) was explored as early as 1905 and systematically excavated from 1962 to 1967, with further excavations in the 1990s.[23] New data came from a field survey in 2001 by Bob Hudson, Nyein Lwin and Tanpawady Win Maung (Figure 7.7). The four gateways so far excavated (sites 10, 11, 18, 21) turn inward to the citadel, like the gates at Beikthano. Earthenware funerary urns were found buried both within and outside the exposed structures, square or rectangular buildings with a quadrangular projection on one side in some instances, but the earlier *stupa* type has not been found. Sites 5, 8, 12, 13 and 15 appear to be ritual structures. Site 8 contained charred bones, burial pottery and gold ornaments. There are both skeletal and cremation burials within the walls of Halin. Site 17 contained around 50 skeletons and site 20, excavated by Myint Aung in 1995 as a project for his archaeology students, contained up to 5. Site 22 was a brick building with a series of large stones, or megaliths, arranged in front of it. At one location, numerous stretched skeletons were discovered together with funerary urns.[24]

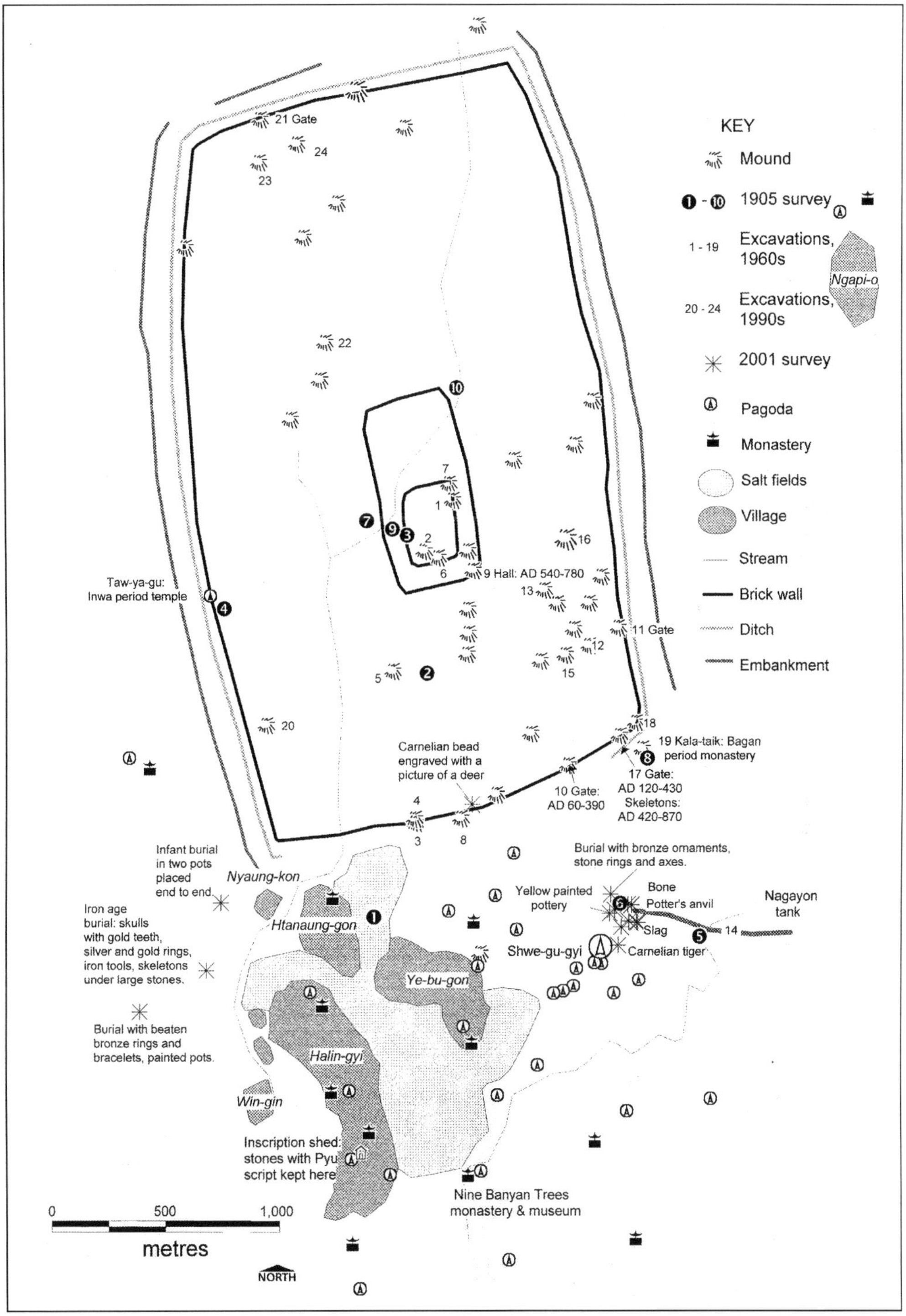

Figure 7.7 Archaeological research at Halin, 1905–2001.

A stone slab inscribed in Pyu[25] possibly mentions the names of kings and events connecting it with the Vikrama and Varma kings of Sriksetra. While occasional words, numbers and proper names have been translated from Pyu, the inscriptions have only been partly deciphered. The script used for the Pyu language is known as "Pyu Tircul" and is derived from eastern Indian scripts from between the fourth and seventh centuries AD. Some, like the Halin slab, have interlinear inscriptions in another, older Indian script described as Brahmi, and may denote musical notations. The coins found at Halin generally have a rising (or perhaps setting) sun on the obverse, and a *srivatsa* on the reverse (Figure 7.5).

The radiocarbon dates from charcoal samples at Halin have been recalculated[26] since they were published by Myint Aung.[27] The new dates are 1369 ± 64 (cal. AD 540–780), 1818 ± 65 (cal. AD 60–390) and 1750 ± 65 (cal. AD 120–430). The Rafter laboratory has also supplied a fourth date for human bone collagen from site 17, which is 1403 ± 98 (cal. AD 420–870).[28] The dates indicate activity at Halin between outside limits of AD 60 and 870.

However, an unusually heavy rainy season at Halin in 2001 uncovered numerous artefacts which provide new evidence for continuity of occupation of the site since well before the period indicated by the radiocarbon dates.[29] These recent finds include polished stone adzes and rings (Figure 7.3), skeletons with rings and bracelets made from beaten (as distinct from cast) bronze strips, and cast bronze axes (Figure 7.4). Some of the skeletons wore both stone and bronze bracelets and some were found under or surrounded by clusters of large stones up to 2 metres long. Local farmers have recovered bronze and iron spearheads, swords with bronze handles and iron blades, skulls with their teeth repeatedly drilled and filled with rolled gold leaf, and a 10-centimetre carnelian pendant in the shape of a tiger carrying a cub in its mouth, similar, but not identical, to "tiger" beads found further south around Binnaka (Plate 5). Glover has reported the finding of a similar feline figure at Ban Don Ta Phet in Thailand (see Plate 3).[30] Some of the new material at Halin was found within the walls, but most came from a cluster of villages on the southern side. These villages sit among fields that are used for salt extraction, an industry that has operated at least since the colonial period.[31] The salt percolates into the soil from underground springs, and would presumably have been present in ancient times.

Mongmao

Mongmao, or Maingmaw, deserves on the basis of size deserves to be considered one of the four major Pyu sites and has been dated comparatively to between the second and sixth centuries AD.[32] The walled settlement today is part of an area under intense irrigation for rice. "Pyu" coins and carnelian beads are still regularly discovered by farmers.

Sriksetra/Thayekittaya ("Noble Field")

The later city of Sriksetra is thought to have attained its height of prosperity between the fifth and ninth centuries. Large stone burial urns have been discovered in association with religious structures. Inscriptions on some of these record the deaths of members of the city's ruling elite in AD 688, 695 and 718. A stone urn unearthed near the Payataung pagoda in March 1993, with a yet largely undeciphered inscription, repeats the names of these three people and adds a further two kings to the list.[33] This evidence suggests a period of dynastic continuity during the late seventh and early eighth centuries.

Roughly circular in shape, Sriksetra's high wall of large bricks encloses an area of more than 12 square kilometres. As with the preceding sites, each gateway has rounded corners turning inwards. The northern half of the city is a low plain dominated by rice fields. Most structures are in the southern sector and outside the city wall. Three tall *stupas*, the Bawbawgyi (Figure 7.8), Payagyi and Payama, are situated respectively to the south, northeast and north of the city wall. Aung Thaw related the Bawbawgyi, with its high cylindrical shape over five round terraces, to the hemispherical *stupas* of Sanchi and Amaravati, first and second century AD sites in central and southeast India respectively.[34] Hollow pagodas, the Bebe, Lemnyethna and the East Zegu, introduce the use of an Indian type of vaulting with bricks laid parallel to the arch face. It has been suggested that this type of vaulting was a local innovation, although slightly later shrines in Orissa use a similar technology.

Figure 7.8 The Bawbawgyi pagoda at Sriksetra (Thayekittaya). (Photograph by Bob Hudson.)

Sculptures in the post-Gupta style indicate that Theravada and Mahayana Buddhism as well as Vaisnavism were followed, and links with the art of Dvaravati and Nanchao can be discerned. Other religious inscriptions such as the Maunggun gold plates use a form of a script known from the fifth century elsewhere in Burma, at Vesali in Arakan and Southeast Asia, notably at Dvaravati sites in Thailand, probably indicating intercourse between the Buddhist *sangha* at the time. It would appear, given the overlap in dates of the major Pyu sites, that each controlled its own sphere of influence and usually cooperated with but at times came into conflict with the others.[35]

The west coast: Dhanyawadi and Vesali

There are enclosed settlements, similar to the Pyu sites of the central plain dating to the early part of the first millennium until at least the tenth century, at Dhanyawadi (Figure 7.9) and Vesali in Arakan (Rakhine) on the west coast of Myanmar. This is an area where the influence of east Bengal is apparent in inscriptions and sculpture.[36] King Anandacandra's *prasasti*, or royal inscription, of *c.* AD 729 gives the names and reign periods of 18 of his predecessors, the earlier of whom may have ruled at Dhanyawadi from the end of the fourth century. Other Buddhist Hybrid Sanskrit *prasasti* and votive inscriptions appear in Arakan from the sixth to the eleventh centuries, their paleography

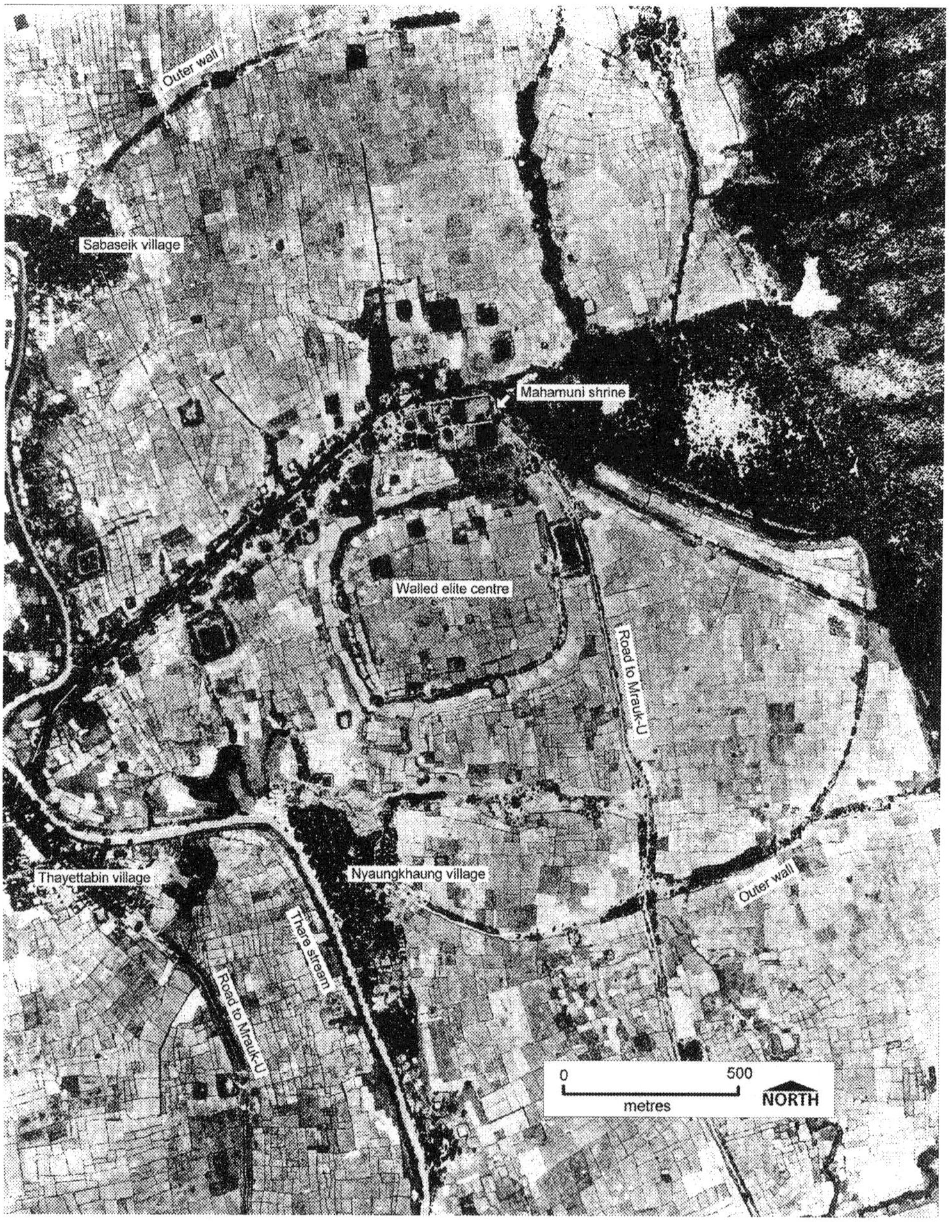

Figure 7.9 A walled elite site at Dhanyawadi surrounded by an irregular, curving outer city wall. The Thare stream forms part of the defensive boundary.

indicating close links with east Bengal but also contact with southeast Indian trading centres. The earlier coins are uninscribed and closely related to the conch/*srivatsa* coins of lower Burma. From the time of Devacandra (c. AD 454–476) until the ninth century the coins have a seated bull on the obverse and are inscribed with the name of the king.

While excavations have not yet been undertaken at Dhanyawadi, the Mahayanist sculpture of the Mahamuni shrine dates from at least the 6th century. At Vesali, excavations in the 1980s uncovered a Buddhist ordination hall, a monastery, and a building which may have been connected with the royal cult since a damaged stone image of a bull on a pedestal was recovered there. Vesali shared with Sriksetra a Visnu cult[37] and there are some remarkable similarities between its sculpture (Plate 6) and architecture and that of Dvaravati and the pre-Angkorian art of Isanapura. A Pyu Tircul inscription found near Sandoway suggests Pyu control of southern Arakan around the seventh century.

Other significant sites

While more than 40 walled sites from various time periods have been located in Myanmar,[38] at least one area in the central plains, a cluster of villages around Binnaka (Figures 7.1, 7.2 and Plate 5), has produced substantial quantities of carnelian beads, cremation urns and finger-marked bricks material identified locally as "Pyu", but with no evidence of enclosure.[39] In the north, the triple-walled city of Tagaung, capital of the Kadu on the east bank of the Irrawaddy (Figure 7.2), has revealed Buddhist votive tablets with Sanskrit inscriptions, some of which pre-date the eleventh century. Tagaung has a cultural assemblage going back to the Neolithic and today is the main market for the salt produced at Halin, which is used to preserve fish.[40]

There are also urban sites, with less secure dates, to the south near the Gulf of Martaban (Figure 7.1). In the south, Kyaikkatha, on the mouth of the Sittaung, has an enclosed area of 3.75 square kilometres and an elite structure surrounded by a series of walls. It has revealed artefacts with Pyu characteristics: beads and glass, earthenware with beaten designs, a cache of hundreds of conch and *srivatsa* coins, as well as laterite stupas, terracotta plaques with an affinity to the art of Dvaravati and, in the upper levels, green glazed wares.[41] Chinese sources and a Sanskrit inscription from Sriksetra refer to Kalasapura, city of jars, which may have been a walled site on the lower Salween river in the vicinity of Martaban (Figure 7.1).[42] Coins with a jar on the obverse and a *srivatsa* on the reverse have been discovered in the vicinity. A relic chamber at Botahtaung pagoda on the Rangoon river bank exposed by a bomb in the Second World War revealed a Pali inscription of the seventh century, with votive tablets and images.[43] Laterite sculptures and architectural fragments usually regarded as Mon have been found near Syriam, Twante and Zokthok (see Figure 7.1 and 7.10), where Sri Lankan-type offering stands are found.[44]

Other sites have revealed traces of south Indian influence. Kyontu, a site about 35 kilometres northeast of Pegu (Bago), with a brick-faced laterite city wall, has at the base of a pagoda platform a series of beaded laterite medallions with low-relief human and animal figures similar to those of the first third of the eighth century at Kanchipuram in India.[45] The walled site of Taikkala is believed to be the city of Suvannabhumi.[46] Conch/*srivatsa* coins have been found at a number of southern sites.[47] Specimens of this type have also been found at a number of Dvaravati sites in Thailand, Vietnam and Bengal. *Bhadrapitha/srivatsa* coins have been reported from Tavoy and southern Thailand, while rising sun/*srivatsa* coins have been discovered at Nakorn Si Thammarat in southern Thailand.

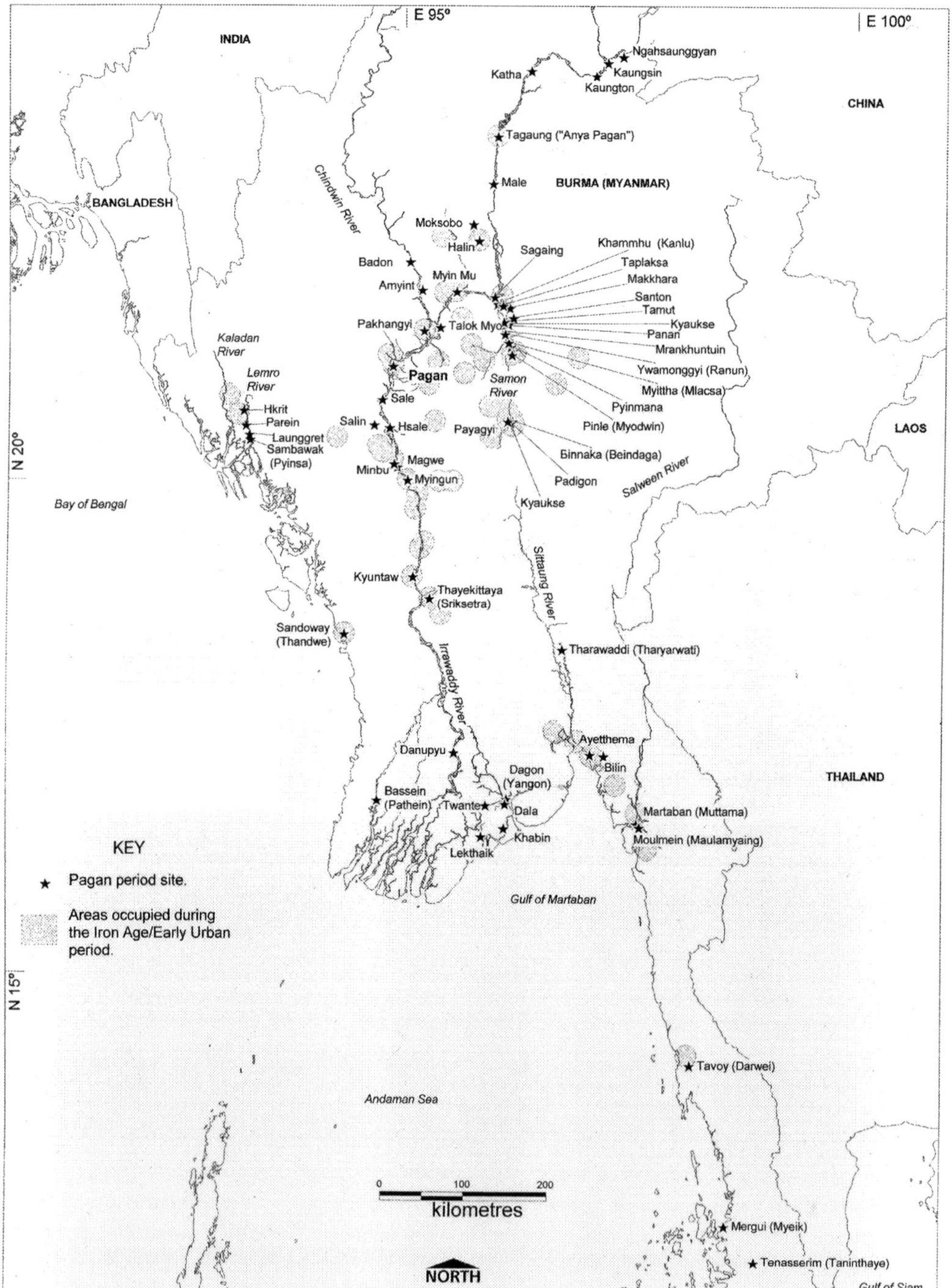

Figure 7.10 Archaeological and epigraphically recorded sites of the Pagan period.

The Mon

There is little or no evidence of the Mon in Lower Burma much before the eleventh century, despite the fact that chronicles and inscriptions written several centuries later give them a much greater antiquity. The founding date for the "Mon capital" of Thaton is in doubt. The city is moated and rectangular in plan, with a palace site at the centre.[48] Archaeological excavation has revealed habitation material under Thaton's stone and laterite wall[49] and a future programme of radiocarbon dating might be able to provide some concrete evidence of the age of the site.

It would appear that Mons were migrating into the Lower Burma region after the decline of Dvaravati in the tenth and eleventh centuries, perhaps partly as a result of Tai and Khmer pressure from the north and east.[50] A large number of people migrated southwestward into what was then sparsely populated Lower Burma during the eleventh century as a result of a cholera epidemic in the Mon city of Haripunjaya (Lamphun). Angkor had been growing since at least the ninth century and continued to do so through the eleventh century, which may have put sustained pressure on the Mons of Dvaravati to move northwestward into the Three Pagodas Pass area. At the same time, the Pagan Empire had also begun to expand southward, into the very area where the Mons had been migrating, squeezing them between the Khmers and the Burmans. There are, nonetheless, indications that Mon culture had a major impact in early Pagan, in the early inscriptions and the adoption of Mon script, in architectural details and in sculpture, as well as through numerous references in the inscriptions to the role of the Mon in Pagan society.

Pagan (Bagan)

Research into this important site has been in progress for a century.[51] Pagan is a historic urban centre on the Irrawaddy River (Figures 7.1 and 7.10), with monuments (Plate 7) dated stylistically to between the eleventh and thirteenth centuries AD. *The Inventory of Monuments at Pagan*,[52] a survey that followed a devastating earthquake in 1975, lists 2,237 Buddhist temples, stupas and monasteries in the eight volumes published or available at the time of writing. Several hundred more structures, mainly small mounds, are shown in the *Inventory's* end-paper maps, and still await publication. Traces of previously unrecorded buildings are still being discovered.

From its beginnings, the architecture of Pagan exhibits an originality and variety which defies categorization. Pierre Pichard in his magnificent *Inventory of Monuments* takes an architectural approach, classifying the buildings according to their constructional elements. Luce, however, approached the subject as an historian. He suggested that the early architecture of Pagan developed from unknown Mon prototypes. This was disputed by Strachan, who has described a logical evolution from Pyu models. It would appear that the earliest *stupas* were based on the bulbous Pyu type, while the large *gu* (cave) temples evolved from the vaulted temples at Sri Ksetra. Although there are no known Mon temples in Burma, certain decorative motifs at Pagan show an affiliation with the art of Thaton and late Dvaravati. Broadly, the early temples were designed to be dark and mystical, with light filtering through to a hall and ambulatory and central image. Around the mid-twelfth century there began a tendency for temples to be raised above subsidiary constructions on a plinth. In the late period, there is a reconciliation in the balance of vertical and horizontal forms. The ground plans become cosmically oriented and the lighter environments illustrate the establishment of Theravada Buddhism as the preferred form of the religion. The influence of northern Buddhism in this period is seen in the adaptation of the Bodhgaya *sikhara* type, and Sri Lankan influence is seen in the square *harmikas* of the *stupas*.

Integral to the architecture were sculpture and painting, which also exhibit a wide range of influences, from Pyu and Mon to the Pala school of north India and related styles in Tibet and Nepal. Massive Buddha images were constructed of stucco over a brick base, while stone (comparatively rare at Pagan), bronze, wood and lacquer were also used. A transition from the sharply defined features of the Pala style to a more stolid, squat conception can be discerned.

Pagan and the Chronicles

The history and dating of Pagan before the period of inscribing temple foundation stones is problematic. A founding date of AD 107 for a confederation of "nineteen villages" based in the eastern hinterland of the present city, a story told in the *Glass Palace Chronicle*,[53] is probably mythological. However, recent investigations in the eastern area have revealed possible Pagan-period buildings, several early pottery production sites, one radiocarbon dated to just after the Pagan period, and hundreds of iron-making furnaces,[54] so the mythology does appear to carry within it information that is worth investigating. The various Burmese Chronicles give a founding date for the existing walled elite centre at Pagan of AD 849, when King Pyinbya, whose origin was supposedly from Pyinbya village to the east of the Pyu city of Beikthano, is said to have built the city walls, the Sarabha gateway and the moat.[55] An eighteenth-century *parabaik* or folding book in the library of the Archaeology Department at Pagan, which described the dimensions and location of a palace, recently led archaeologists to discover previously unrecorded building foundations at the spot indicated by the document.[56] This is another instance where future archaeological excavation could be used to test the claims of the traditional histories.

Pagan inscriptions

Traditional accounts from folklore or from *thamaing*, the histories of towns or individual temples, claim that many of Pagan's buildings were constructed in the eleventh century or before. The *Inventory of Monuments at Pagan* tentatively attributes a number of buildings to the eleventh century (Figure 7.11). However, the *Inventory's* earliest secure date from an inscription is AD 1113, from the Kubyauk-gyi temple near Myinkaba village.[57] Some early Burmese inscriptions exist only as copies, with consequent problems of authenticity. Many have been moved to museums or to other cities, notably by King Bodawpaya (1781–1819), who collected inscription stones to keep in his domain at Amarapura. One of the earliest of these relating to Pagan appears to have had a date of AD 1058, recording a dedication of lands to an unidentifiable *Letthe-she* pagoda.[58] Inscriptions are still being found at Pagan during repairs to buildings and a study of these, along with a reinterpretation of the later copies, could push the chronology further back. The available epigraphic evidence, however, suggests an initial construction cycle in the first half of the twelfth century, with major building then taking place between 1150 and 1200

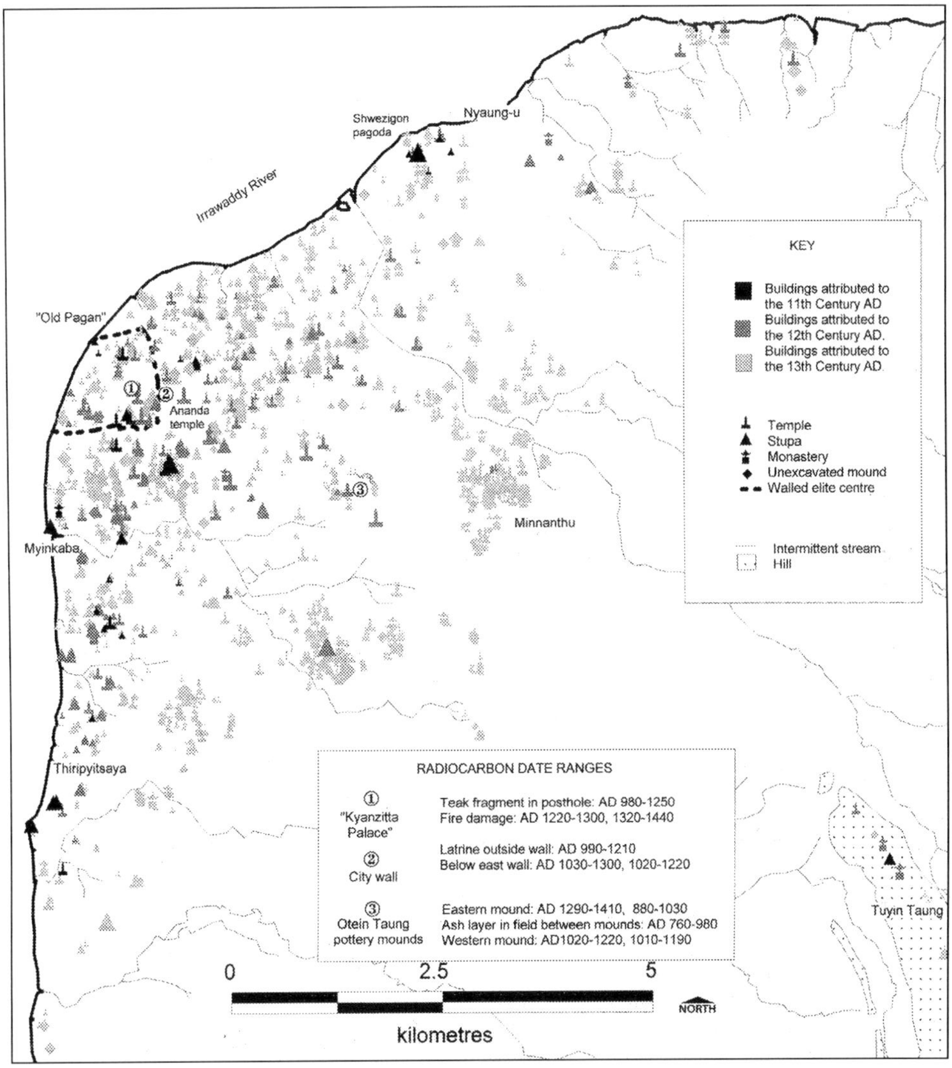

Figure 7.11 Pagan at the end of the thirteenth century AD.

(Figure 7.12). This is much later than the reign of King Anawratha (1044–77), who is credited with imposing Burman hegemony over much of the Irrawaddy valley.

Radiocarbon dates for Pagan

Pagan had not, until the 1990s, been the focus of any programmes of absolute dating. Samples for radiocarbon dating collected by Grave and Barbetti[59] under and near the city wall, and from a large building complex inside the walls which was excavated in the early 1990s, have provided the first scientific evidence with which to test the historical and epigraphic data. The building complex has been interpreted, on the basis of an undated

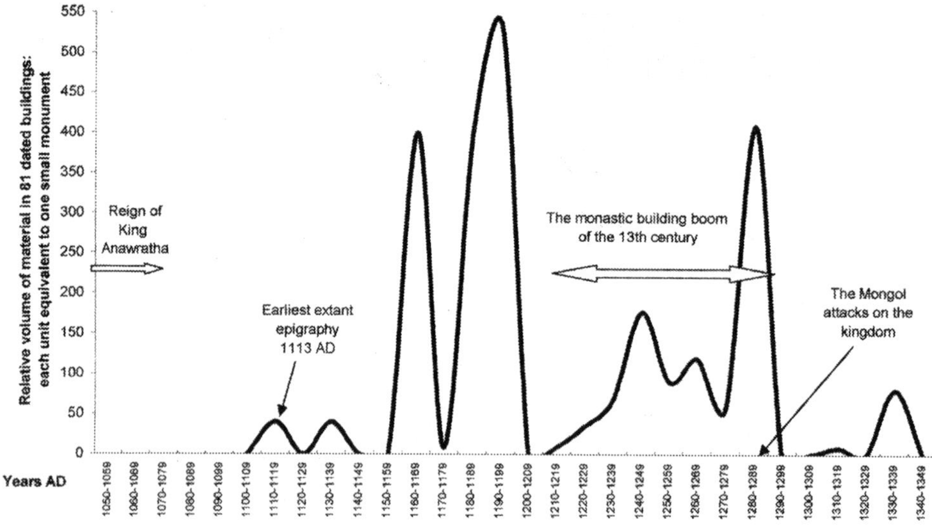

Figure 7.12 The building cycle at Pagan. Epigraphically dated buildings AD 1113–1342.

inscription found nearby describing a dedication ceremony,[60] as being the "great palace" of King Kyanzittha (1084–1111). The dates range between AD 980 and 1440 and thus suggest a later date for the building, although the samples tested may well represent later additions rather than original construction. Other C14 samples taken from under the city's eastern wall when it was being renovated suggest that that section of the wall, at least, was built during or after the eleventh century.

The other radiocarbon dates for Pagan come from Otein Taung, a pottery production site excavated in 1999–2000. A date range of AD 760–1410[61] suggests craft activity at Pagan possibly as early as the eighth century. Otein Taung seems to have supplied stamped pottery to the "Kyanzittha palace" site, and also produced earthenware latrine tubes similar to those found outside the city wall and dated by the above-described C14 samples of Grave and Barbetti (see Figure 7.11).

Burman, Mon and Pyu: the people of Pagan

The ethnonyms Mon, Mranma (Burmese) and Pyu are regularly distinguished from each other at Pagan in early documents or inscriptions. The four-language Myazedi inscription of the early twelfth century[62] distinguishes the Pyu linguistically from the Mon and the Burmese (the fourth language is Pali, the language of Buddhist ritual and scholarship). Kyanzittha's palace inscription of 1102,[63] the first to mention the Burmese (*mirma*) and the first time the word Mon (*rmen*) appears, gives the Mon and the Pyu (*tircul*) particular importance in the dedication ceremonial.

There is increasing evidence of Pyu occupation of the Pagan area before the coming of the Burmans. Strachan's argument that the earliest buildings exhibit an evolution from types developed by the Pyu at Sriksetra is supported by evidence obtained from restoration and conservation efforts since 1994 around Monument 996, southeast of the Lokananda pagoda and an ancient wharf on the Irrawaddy. The work on the structure, which is so far unpublished, has revealed a Pyu stupa encased within a later shrine, with terracotta and stucco decoration identical to fragments found at Sriksetra and remarkably similar to the art of Dvaravati in Thailand in the same period. Importantly, the later structure incorporated earlier architectural elements such as the Gupta-style *caitya* niche.

Other archaeological evidence of a "Pyu" cultural assemblage at Pagan includes the presence of fingermarked bricks, found in large numbers during the past few years as hundreds of buildings have been renovated or rebuilt. Many of these were reconstructed completely from their rubble foundations in an officially sponsored restoration drive.[64] Bricks found at early urban sites across Myanmar are often deeply indented with several strokes, described as fingermarks. Aung Myint had earlier noted the presence of Pyu bricks at Pagan, as distinct from bricks scored or stamped in Old Burmese script with the names of donors or donor villages.[65] Field survey by Win Maung of buildings under renovation since 1998 has now revealed at least 55 structures with bricks that appear to carry Pyu fingermarked designs. These bricks are found in buildings dated from the eleventh through to the fourteenth centuries,[66] though the possibility that some may have been recycled from earlier buildings cannot be discounted.

Pyu-style earthenware vessels were found early last century in an area then known as Myinpagan, outside Pagan's walled core, during the digging of a well.[67] Of "elongated shape and antique pattern", they were identified as Pyu by government archaeologists who, while not of a mindset at the time to seek Pyu material at Pagan, would have been familiar with it from their excavations at Thayekittaya. Bronze Buddha images, reliefs and votive tablets of Maitreya, the Buddha of the future, inscribed in some instances in Pyu script, have been found in relic chambers at Pagan. Gutman suggests that these characteristically Pyu artefacts may represent a Messianic-type cult that emerged in Thayekittaya and was continued possibly by Pyu residents or artisans at Pagan at a time of political uncertainty.[68] All this suggests a long-term presence of members of a group with "Pyu" skills and cultural products, coexisting at Pagan with Mons and Burmans.

Pagan: growth and decline

The epigraphic and other evidence of the *Inventory of Monuments* indicates that the earliest buildings at Pagan marked a substantial stretch of riverside territory, from Nyaung-u to Thiripyitsaya. Mountain-top monuments across the river to the west, and to the east on Tuyin Taung, may have served as boundary markers, defining a sacred space as well as a geographical one. Many of the city's larger monuments, generally sponsored by kings or other members of the elite according to the surviving inscriptions, had been completed by the end of the twelfth century. By the early thirteenth century the area around the walled elite compound now known as "Old Pagan" had become so densely packed with monuments that major new clusters of buildings developed several kilometres to the east (Figure 7.11). These nodes included the monastic area of Minnanthu. The *Inventory of Monuments* indicates that there was a significant upsurge in the building of monasteries and associated small structures during the thirteenth century. This cycle has been linked to dwindling economic resources, hence the smaller buildings, and to a broadening of monastic influence, hence the clustering of the buildings around monastic complexes and often within walled monastic compounds.[69]

By the end of the thirteenth century, as indicated by inscriptions, many translated and kindly supplied by Michael Aung-Thwin, the Pagan presence was strongly felt up the

Ayeyarwady to Kyaukse and downriver to Minbu, the two main rice-producing areas for the city. These granaries, often the subject of religious dedications and donations, were easily accessible due to Pagan's control of the transport infrastructure, this being the river. Inscriptions indicate Burman influence north to the modern Chinese border, downriver to the Irrawaddy delta, south as far as Tenasserim, and west across the Arakan Yoma to the small quasi-autonomous kingdoms of the Lemro valley. Nevertheless, by the middle of the fourteenth century, the locus of power had moved upriver to the area around modern Mandalay.

The conventional explanation for this, the direct invasion and sacking of the city of Pagan itself in the 1280s by Kublai Khan's Mongol forces, is today considered to be poorly supported by historical evidence.[70] A long-term process rather than a single event was the more likely cause. By the time of the Mongol incursions, the city had been through two major resource-depleting construction cycles lasting almost 150 years. These may well have left its economy and administration vulnerable to new stresses. Aung-Thwin has suggested that the provincial administrators charged with defending Pagan's northern frontiers against Mongol incursions actually did so with such success that they became the new power elite. Their domains near modern Mandalay became the locus of Burman administration. This left Pagan a backwater in terms of central control, although records of intermittent construction of buildings indicate that the city remained a monastic and pilgrimage centre, despite regular earthquakes and pillaging, until colonial times and into the modern era.[71]

Conclusion

Burma's archaeology, as Glover and Higham have both recently pointed out,[72] is set for a broad reassessment and in need of expanded programmes of research. Key areas in need of attention include the relationships between Neolithic, Bronze and Iron sites, which on current evidence appears likely to vary in different parts of the country. Another important question concerns the process of transition from Iron Age chiefdoms to Indianized cities such as Beikthano. Cultural elements hitherto identified as Pyu, but also found in Arakan and the Gulf of Martaban, need to be reassessed. Archaeologists and historians also need to pay renewed attention to the possibility of relations with southern China, increasingly apparent from pre-Neolithic times through to the Pagan period.

Some issues have a more definite focus. There is currently strong research interest in glazed ceramics following widespread discoveries of kiln sites.[73] These include a new kiln with glazed potsherds found in 2001 in front of the Abeyadana pagoda at Pagan, a discovery which brings the total of kilns known at Pagan to seven. The local, regional and international contexts of Burmese ceramic production and trade will be valuable in establishing historical links.

Access to remote archaeological sites, often cut off in the past for security reasons, is gradually improving, and there are likely to be many new discoveries in states such as Karen, Shan and Chin. English translation and dissemination of the more recent excavation and field reports held by the Archaeology Department would be of great value. Archaeological studies in Burma should also benefit from an expansion of already-existing areas of international cooperation, the introduction of scientific methods such as Geographical Information Systems (with a commensurate expansion in computer literacy), expanded programmes of radiocarbon dating, and from improved education and training for young archaeologists.

Acknowledgements

The authors wish to thank U Nyunt Han, Director General of Archaeology in Myanmar, and his staff for their continuing cooperation in all aspects of research. Thanks go to Daw Ni Ni Myint and the members of the Universities Historical Research Centre in Yangon, who always provide a friendly forum for academic discourse. Our thanks also to "Tanpawady" Win Maung for access to his collection of artifacts (Figures 7.1–4, Plate 5) and for his collaboration in field trips and data collection, and to all the scholars, monks, village elders, amateur antiquarians and farmers who have enthusiastically shared their ideas and information.

Illustrations by Bob Hudson, except Figure 7.15, drawn by "Tanpawady" Win Maung, Figure 7.9, from the Daw Thin Kyi Archive, and Figure 7.9 and Plate 6, Zaw Min Yu.

Notes

1 Bayard 1979: 280.
2 Luce 1959a, 1959b, 1985.
3 Strachan 1989.
4 Aung-Thwin 2002.
5 U Nyein Lwin, personal communication.
6 Rawson 1996: 84; Higham and Thosarat 1998: 117, 121–23.
7 For more details of the Nyaunggan excavation, see *Proceedings of the Workshop on Bronze Age Culture in Myanmar* 1999; San Nyein 1999; Sein Myint 1999; Tayles, Domett and Pauk Pauk 2001; Moore and Pauk Pauk 2001.
8 Hudson 2001b.
9 Stargardt 1990: 13–14, 28.
10 Wagner 1993: 95–6.
11 Agrawal 2000: 203.
12 Aung Thaw 1968.
13 Vallibhotama 1992; Mudar 1999.
14 Moore 1988, Higham 1989: 217–28.
15 See Aung Thaw 1968: 71; Myint Aung 1970; Sein Maung 1981; ASI 1910, Plate 11; Gutman 1999, 2001a.
16 Gutman 1978, Wicks 1992: 111–21, 157–63.
17 Aung Thaw 1972: 14; Gutman 2001a: 7.
18 Sun 1997: 9–12.
19 *Radiocarbon* 1963 5: 76 Burma date; Stargardt 1990: 408.
20 For further examples of "Pyu" architecture and cultural assemblages, see Aung Thaw 1968; Kan Hla 1979; Stargardt 1990; Aung Myint 1998.
21 Stargardt 1990: 188.
22 For Pyu coins see Gutman 1977, 1978; Mitchiner 1982; Wicks 1992; Mahlo 1998; Miksic 2001: 99.
23 Myint Aung 1970; Pauk Pauk 1999.
24 Aung Thaw 1972: 15.
25 Luce 1985, I: 149, II: Plate 51.
26 Recalibrations by Rafter Radiocarbon Laboratory, New Zealand, in a communication with the authors.
27 Myint Aung 1970: 62.

28 Corresponding lab. numbers are HL 9/NZ 894; HL 10/ NZ 895; HL 17/ NZ 896; and NZ 898.
29 Pauk Pauk 2001a; Nyo Win 2001a.
30 Glover 1991: Figure 5.
31 Nyo Win 2001b.
32 Sein Maung 1981.
33 Blagden 1917: 43; Luce 1969 Vol. 1:5; *Working People's Daily*, 2 April 1993; discussions with U San Win of the Historical Research Commission, August 2001.
34 Aung Thaw 1972: 19.
35 For one such instance, see Luce 1985 I: 51, II: Plates 28–9.
36 Gutman 1977; 2001a.
37 Gutman 1999.
38 Luce 1969; Aung Myint 1999 and personal communication; Win Maung 2000; Hudson 2001a.
39 Win Maung 1981.
40 Luce 1985 I: 40; Win Maung 1997; Sein Myint 2000.
41 Ko Ko 1987; Aung Myint 1999.
42 Luce 1985: 50; Aung Myint 1999: 255–61; Gutman 2001b.
43 Luce 1985 I: 162–3; II Plates 72–3.
44 Luce 1985 I: 159–60, II: Plates 64–71.
45 Luce 1985 I: 166–8, II Plates 76–81; Huntington 1985: Plates 14.36.
46 Myint Aung 1977, 1999.
47 Wicks 1992: 111–14.
48 Aung Thaw 1972: 35–40.
49 Baby 2000.
50 Aung-Thwin 2001.
51 Regular reports on Pagan were published in the *Annual Report of the Archaeological Survey of India* between 1902 and 1934, the *Report of the Superintendent, Archaeological Survey of Burma* between 1901 and 1965, and *Journal of the Burma Research Society* between 1910 and 1980. Key reference works include Luce 1969; Aung-Thwin 1985; Strachan 1989 and Pichard 1992–9.
52 Pichard 1992–9.
53 Pe Maung Tin and Luce 1923.
54 The Taungba pottery site is dated to 530 ± 35 BP (cal. AD 1310–1450, OZE 765). See also Hudson 1999, in press; Hudson *et al.* 2001, 2002.
55 Ministry of Culture 1963: Kan Hla 1977: 15; Khin Maung Nyunt 1989.
56 Hudson in press.
57 Pichard 1995: 250.
58 ASB 1917: 16; Duroiselle 1921: 5.
59 Grave and Barbetti 2001.
60 Blagden 1923.
61 For original radiocarbon results see Hudson *et al.* 2001.
62 Taw Sein Ko and Duroiselle 1919.
63 Blagden 1923; Luce 1969 I: 67–71.
64 Hudson 2000.
65 For examples, see Aung Myint and Moore 1991; Moore and Aung Myint 1993: 63; Aung Myint 1999.
66 Hudson *et al.* 2001.
67 ASB 1917: 42.
68 On these vessels, see Luce 1969, Plates 443–444; Gutman 1996.
69 Aung-Thwin 1985.
70 Aung-Thwin 1998: 63–92.
71 Than Tun 1996.
72 Glover 2001; Higham 2001.
73 Aung Kyaing 1999; Myo Thant Tin 1999; Rooney 1999.

Select Bibliography

Editors' note on the sources. Most of the recent research on Burmese archaeology and history has been undertaken by local scholars and is published only in the Burmese language, and often in outlets difficult to access even for non-resident Burmese readers. However, we have listed a high proportion of these publications below in the hope that they will be of value to scholars wishing to research in this area.

Burma history

Aung-Thwin, M. (1985) *Pagan: the Origins of Modern Burma*, University of Hawaii Press.
Aung-Thwin, M. (1994) "Principles and patterns of the precolonial Burmese State", in U. Gartner and J. Lorenz (eds) *Tradition and Modernity in Myanmar*, Berliner Asien-Afrika-Studien, pp. 14–41.
Aung-Thwin, M. (1998) *Myth and History in the Historiography of Early Burma*, Athens: Ohio University Center of International Studies.
Aung-Thwin, M. (2002) "Lower Burma and Bago in the history of Burma", in J. Gommans and J. Leider (eds) *The Maritime Frontiers of Burma*, Amsterdam: Koninklijke Nederlandse Akademie van Wetenschappen.
Aung-Thwin, M. (forthcoming) *The Mists of Ramanna: The Legend that was Lower Burma.*
Frasch, T. (2002) "Coastal peripheries during the pagan period", in J. Gommans and J. Leider (eds) *The Maritime Frontiers of Burma*, Amsterdam: Koninklijke Nederlandse Akademie van Wetenschappen.
Sun, L. (1997) "Chinese historical sources on Burma: a bibliography of primary and secondary works", *The Journal of Burma Studies*, vol. 2.

Burma archaeology

ASB (Archaeological Survey of Burma) (1901–1965) *Report of the Superintendent, Archaeological Survey of Burma*, Rangoon: Office of the Superintendent, Government Printing. (Volumes from 1901–1905 titled Report on Archaeological Work in Burma).
ASI (Archaeological Survey of India) (1902–1934) *Annual Report of the Archaeological Survey of India*, Manager of Publications, Delhi.
Aung Kyaing (1999) *Ancient Ceramic and Glazed Kilns at Pagan*, Conference on Glazed ceramics of South East Asia, Pagan, Myanmar September 20–22.
Aung Myint (1998) "Site Characteristics of Pyu and Pagan ruins", a comparative study of the dry areas in Southeast Asia: International Seminar, Kyoto, Japan, October 14–16. Conference paper.
Aung Myint (1999) *Ancient Myanmar Cities in Aerial Photos*, (in Burmese) Yangon: Ministry of Culture.
Aung Myint and Moore, E. (1991) "Finger-marked designs on ancient bricks in Myanmar", *Journal of the Siam Society* 72(2): 81–102
Aung Thaw (1968) *Report on the excavations at Beikthano*, Revolutionary Government of the Union of Burma, Rangoon: Ministry of Union Culture.
Aung Thaw (1972) *Historical Sites in Burma*, Rangoon: Ministry of Union Culture.
Aung-Thwin, M. (2001) "Origins and development of the field of prehistory in Burma", *Asian Perspectives* 40(1): 6–34.
Baby, Daw (2000) "Thaton Myohaung, First Excavation Report", (in Burmese) Yangon: Field Report, Department of Archaeology.
Bellwood, P. (1992) "Early Burmese urbanisation: inspired independence or external stimulus?", *The Review of Archaeology*, Fall.
Blagden, C. O. (1917) "The 'Pyu' inscriptions", *Journal of the Burma Research Society* 7(1): 37–44.
Blagden, C. O. (1923) "Mon inscriptions", *Epigraphia Birmanica*, Superintendent of Government Printing, Union of Burma 3(1): 1–68.

Dello Strogolo, S. and Kyaw Nyein (1963) "Report on Pagan trip for analysis of old glazing kiln", privately circulated mimeograph.

Donovan, D. G., Fukui, Hayao and Itoh, Toshikatsu (1998) "Perspective on the Pyu landscape", *Southeast Asian Studies* 36(1): 19–126.

Duroiselle, Chas. (1921) *A list of inscriptions in Burma*, Rangoon: Superintendent of Government Printing.

Fraser-Lu, S. (1994) *Burmese Crafts. Past and Present*, Oxford University Press.

Glover, I. C. 1991. "Beads and bronzes: archaeological indications of trade between Thailand and the early Buddhist civilizations of Northern India", in K. Reinhold Haellquist (ed.) *Asian Trade Routes*, pp. 117–41, London: Curzon Press.

Glover, I. C. (2001) "The past, present, and future of prehistoric archaeology in Burma", *Asian Perspectives* 40(1): 120–26.

Grave, P. and Barbetti, M. (2001) "Dating the city wall, fortification and the palace site at Pagan", *Asian Perspectives* 40(1): 75–87.

Gutman, P. (1977) "Ancient Arakan, with special reference to its cultural history between the fifth and eleventh centuries", unpublished Ph.D. thesis, ANU.

Gutman, P. (1978) "The ancient coinage of Southeast Asia," *Journal of the Siam Society* 66(1).

Gutman, P. (1996) "The Pyu Maitreyas", *Traditions in Current Perspective*, Yangon: Universities Historical Research Centre, pp. 165–78.

Gutman, P. (1999) "Vishnu in Burma", in Stadtner (ed.) *The Art of Burma. New studies*, Mumbai: Marg Publications.

Gutman, P. (2001a) *Burma's Lost Kingdoms: Splendours of Arakan*, Bangkok: Orchid Press.

Gutman, P. (2001b) "The Martaban trade: an examination of the literature from the seventh through eighteenth centuries", *Asian Perspectives* 40(1): 108–18.

Hein, D. (1996) "Ceramic production in Myanmar – further evidence on old traditions", in *Traditions in Current Perspective*, Yangon: Universities Historical Research Centre, pp. 175–205.

Higham, C. F. W. (2001) "Archaeology in Myanmar: past, present and future", *Asian Perspectives* 40(1): 127–138.

Hudson, B. (1997) "Pagan and its monasteries: time, space and structure in Burma's medieval Buddhist city", unpublished B.A Hons thesis, manuscript on file, Archaeology Department, University of Sydney.

Hudson, B. (1999) "The King of 'Free Rabbit' Island: a GIS-based archaeological approach to Myanmar's medieval capital, Pagan", *Proceedings of the Myanmar Two Millennium Conference* 3: 10–20, Yangon: Universities Historical Research Centre.

Hudson, B. (2000) *The Merits of Rebuilding Pagan*, Orientations 31(5): 85–6.

Hudson, B. (2001a) "An archaeological settlement database for Burma/Myanmar", Conference presentation: *Towards an Electronic Cultural Atlas: e-Publishing and Knowledge Management in the Humanities*, Sydney, June 12–13. http://www.archaeology.usyd.edu.au/~hudson/Burma_Myanmar_ database.pdf

Hudson, B. (2001b) "The Nyaungyan 'goddesses': some unusual bronze grave goods from upper Burma", *TAASA Review: The Journal of the Asian Arts Society of Australia* 10(2): 4–7.

Hudson, B. (2003) "The founding villages and early palaces of Bagan – an exploration of some chronicle and parabaik sources via computer mapping, field survey and archaeological excavation", *Proceedings of the "Texts and Contexts" Conference*, Yangon: Universities Historical Research Centre. Vol. 1, pp. 111–33.

Hudson, B., Nyein Lwin and Win Maung (Tanpawady) (2001) "The origins of Pagan: new dates and old inhabitants", *Asian Perspectives* 40(1): 48–74.

Hudson, B., Nyein Lwin and Win Maung (Tanpawady) (2002) "Digging for myths – archaelogical excavations and surveys during the legendary nineteenth founding villages of Pagan", in A. Green and T. R. Blurton (eds) *Burma: Art and Archaeology*, London: British Museum.

Ishizawa, Y. (1989) "Considerations regarding the basic framework of Pagan", *Study on Pagan*, Cultural Heritage in Asia 4, Institute of Asian Cultures, Sophia University, Tokyo, pp. 131–7.

Kan Hla (1977) "Pagan: development and town planning", *Journal of the Society of Architectural Historians* 36(1): 15–29.

Kan Hla (1979) "Ancient cities in Burma", *Journal of the Society of Architectural Historians* 38(2): 95–102.

Khin Maung Nyunt (1989) "The role of Pagan in the history of Southeast Asia", *Study on Pagan Cultural Heritage in Asia 4*, Tokyo: Institute of Asian Cultures, Sophia University, pp. 29–35.

Khin Maung Nyunt (1997) *Hagiography of Maha Thera Shin Arahan and an account of the reconstruction of Shin Arahan's brick monastery*, Myanmar: Ministry of Culture.

Ko Ko, U. (1987) "A preliminary study of Kaikkatha Ancient City", Archaeological Research Cultural Committee, departmental report, in Burmese.

Luce, G. H. (1940) "Economic life of the early Burman", *Journal of the Burma Research Society* 30(1): 284–335.

Luce, G. H. (1948) "A century of progress in Burmese history and archaeology", *Journal of the Burma Research Society* 32(1): 79–94.

Luce, G. H. (1959a) "Old Kyaukse and the coming of the Burmans", *Journal of the Burma Research Society* 42(1): 75–110.

Luce, G. H. (1959b) "Geography of Burma under the Pagan dynasty", *Journal of the Burma Research Society* 42(1): 32–51.

Luce, G. H. (1969) *Old Burma – Early Pagan*, Artibus Asiae and the Institute of Fine Arts, New York: New York University (in three volumes).

Luce, G. H. (1985) *Phases of Pre-Pagan Burma*, Oxford: Oxford University Press (in two volumes).

Mahlo, D. (1998) "Frühe munzen aus Birma: thesen (early coins from Burma – some propositions)", *Indo-Asiatische Zeitschrift* 2: 88–94 (in German).

Maung Hla (1923) "The chronological dates of the kings of Burma who reigned at Thayekhittaya (ancient Prome) and at Pagan", *Journal of the Burma Research Society* 13(2): 82–94.

Miksic, J. (2001) "Early Burmese urbanization: research and conservation", *Asian Perspectives* 41(1): 89–107.

Ministry of Culture, Burma (1963) *Pictorial Guide to Pagan*, Rangoon: Ministry of Culture, Archaeology Department, Socialist Republic of the Union of Burma.

Mitchiner, M. (1982) "The date of the early Funanese, Mon, Pyu and Arakanese Coinages ('symbolic coins')", *Journal of the Siam Society* 70(1 and 2): 5–14.

Moore, E. (1988) "Notes on two types of moated settlement in Northeast Thailand". *Journal of the Siam Society* 76: 275–83.

Moore, E. and Aung Myint (1993) "Beads of Myanmar (Burma)", *Journal of the Siam Society* 81(1): 55–81.

Moore, E. and Pauk Pauk (2001) "The excavations at Halin", *Journal of the Burma Research Society* 53(2): 55–62.

Myint Aung (1970) "The excavations at Halin". *Journal of the Burma Research Society* 53(2): 55–62.

Myint Aung (1977) "The capital of Suvannabhumi unearthed?", *Shiroku* 10: 41–53.

Myint Aung (1999) *The Excavations of Ayethama and Winka (Suvannabhumi)*, studies in Myanma history Volume 1. U Kyi Win, Yangon, Than Tun Diamond Jubilee Publication Committee.

Myo Thant Tin (1999) "The ancient glaze kiln-sites in Myanmar", conference on glazed ceramics of South East Asia, Bagan, Myanmar, September 20–22.

Nyo Win (2001a) "New Discoveries at the Ancient Pyu City of Halin", November 13, *Mandalay Daily*, p. 7 (in Burmese).

Nyo Win (2001b) "Modern-day salt production at the ancient Pyu city of Halin", privately circulated monograph (in Burmese).

Pauk Pauk (1999) "Excavation report on Halin, Mounds 21–24", departmental report (in Burmese), Department of Archaeology, Mandalay.

Pauk Pauk (2001a) "Survey report on Halin, Wetlet Township, Shwebo District", Departmental report (in Burmese), Department of Archaeology.

Pauk Pauk (2001b) "Bronze Age Excavations", unpublished manuscript, Mandalay: Archaeology Department, Mandalay.

Pe Maung Tin and Luce, G. H. (1923) (trans.) *The Glass Palace Chronicle of the Kings of Burma*, Rangoon University Press (reprinted 1960).

Pichard, P. (1992–99) *Inventory of Monuments at Pagan* Vols 1–8 Kiscadale, EFEO, UNESCO (Vol. 1 1992, Vol. 2 1993, Vol. 3 1994, Vol. 4 1994, Vol. 5 1995, Vol. 6 1996, Vol. 7 1999, Vol. 8 2002). KISCADALE EFEO UNESCO.

Proceedings of the Workshop on Bronze Age Culture in Myanmar (1999) Universities Historical Research Centre, Yangon, Myanmar.

Rooney, D. (1999) "New kiln finds in Cambodia and Myanmar (Burma)", *Lotus Leaves* 3(1): 4–6.
San Nyein (1999) *Nyaunggan Bronze Age*, Myanmar 2000 Conference, Yangon, December 1999.
Sein Maung (1981) "Mongmao, a forgotten city", *The Working People's Daily*, 21 and 23 January, 3 February.
Sein Myint (1999) "The archaeological evidence of Nyaunggan excavation site and the neighbouring area", *Myanmar Historical Research Journal* (4): 27–31.
Sein Myint (2000) "Tagaung", *Myanmar Historical Research Journal* 6: 17–19.
Stargardt, J. (1990) *The Ancient Pyu of Burma: early Pyu cities in a man-made landscape*, Cambridge: PACSEA.
Stargardt, J. (2001) "Creation of enduring patterns in the Pyu period", *Newsletter 25: International Institute for Asian Studies (Leiden)*.
Strachan, P. (1989) *Pagan. Art and Architecture of Old Burma*, Arran: Kiscadale.
Taw Sein Ko and Duroiselle, Chas. (eds) (1919) *Epigraphia Birmanica, being Lithic and other inscriptions of Burma*, Superintendent of Government Printing, Burma 1(1).
Tayles, N., Domett, K. and Pauk Pauk, U. (2001) "Bronze Age Myanmar (Burma): a report on the people from the cemetery of Nyaunggan, Upper Myanmar", *Antiquity* 75: 273–8.
Than Tun (1996) "Defacing Old Pagan", *Pagan Lak Thit ("new hand") and other essays*, pp. 182–204, Mandalay: Tun Yin Bookshop.
Thin Kyi, Daw (1964) *The Old City of Pagan*, essays offered to G. H. Luce, Vol. 2, Artibus Asiae.
Universities Historical Research Centre (1996) *Glimpses of Glorious Pagan*, Yangon: The Universities Press.
Win Maung (Tanpawady) (1997) *Exploration of the Tagaung Area*, privately circulated manuscript (in Burmese).
Win Maung (Tanpawady) (1981) *Binnaka Myohaung ("Binnaka Ancient City")*, in Burmese, privately circulated manuscript.
Win Maung (Tanpawady) (2000) "Myittha eleven villages exploration record" (in Burmese), paper read and privately circulated to commemorate the 84th birthday of U Maung Maung Tin, English translation by U. Thaung Lwin.

Archaeology, adjacent regions

Agrawal, D. P. (2000) *Ancient Metal Technology and Archaeology of South Asia: A pan-Asian perspective*, New Delhi: Aryan Books International.
Backus, C. (1981) *The Nan-chao kingdom and T'ang China's Southwestern Frontier*, Cambridge: Cambridge University Press.
Bayard, D. T. (1979) commenting on Shorto, H. L., "The linguistic protohistory of Mainland Southeast Asia", in Smith and Watson (eds) *Early Southeast Asia*, Oxford: Oxford University Press.
Glover, I. C., Pornchai Suchitta and Villiers, J. (eds) (1992) *Early Metallurgy, Trade and Urban Centres in Thailand and Southeast Asia*, Bangkok: White Lotus.
Gutman, P. (1978) "The ancient coinage of Southeast Asia", *Journal of the Siam Society* 66(1): 8–21.
Higham, C. and Thosarat, R. (1998) *Prehistoric Thailand*, Thames and Hudson.
Huntington, S. L. (1985) *The Art of Ancient India*, New York: Weatherhill.
Luce, G. H. (trans.) (1961) *The Man Shu – Book of the Southern Barbarians*, Data Paper 44, Southeast Asia Program, Ithaca: Cornell University.
Mudar, K. M (1999) "How many Dvaravati Kingdoms? Locational analysis of first millennium AD moated settlements in Central Thailand", *Journal of Anthropological Archaeology* 18: 1–28.
Rawson, J. (ed.) (1996) *Mysteries of Ancient China: New Discoveries from the Early Dynasties*, New York: British Museum Press and George Braziller.
Vallibhotama, S. (1992) "Early urban centres in the Chao Phraya valley of Central Thailand", in Glover, Pornchai and Villiers (eds) Early Metallurgy, Trade and Urban Centres in Thailand and Southeast Asia, pp. 123–29, Bangkok: White Lotus.
Wagner, D. B. (1993) *Iron and Steel in Ancient China*, Leiden: E. J. Brill.
Wicks, R. S (1992) *Money, Markets and Trade in Early Southeast Asia*, New York: SEAP, Cornell University.

8

NORTHERN VIETNAM FROM THE NEOLITHIC TO THE HAN PERIOD

Nguyen Khac Su, Pham Minh Huyen and Tong Trung Tin

In this chapter, three Vietnamese archaeologists outline the main stages of cultural development from the mid-Holocene to the Han invasions of the early centuries of the Christian Era. Rather than trying to integrate the different sections, each of which were written separately, the editors felt that it was better to let the three specialists present their independent summaries of an exceptionally rich and complex archaeological record. Only the bibliographic references of the three sections are integrated at the end of the chapter.

PART I: THE NEOLITHIC CULTURES OF VIETNAM

Nguyen Khac Su

Introduction

In contemporary archaeological practice in Vietnam, the term "Neolithic" indicates an evolutionary stage of humankind when stone-grinding techniques and pottery made their appearances. It also is referred to as "the primitive agricultural stage", although there is little or no evidence for actual food production until a late stage of the Neolithic as here defined. The term "Mesolithic", as a phase between the Neolithic and Palaeolithic, is not used in Vietnam.

Conventionally, the Neolithic (Figure 8.1) is divided into three phases by Vietnamese archaeologists – Early, Middle and Late – and each might encompass one or more archaeological cultures. By this term we mean a group of sites in adjoining areas, lasting over some time and expressing characteristics of a durable community in terms of sites and artefacts, distinctive from other synchronic archaeological cultures. In this paper, we will use the concepts and dating recently set out by Ha Van Tan.[1]

The early Neolithic cultures

The Hoa Binh cultural tradition (normally termed "the Hoabinhian" in English)

The French archaeologist Madeleine Colani discovered and excavated many sites in Hoa Binh province, before naming this cultural tradition at the First Conference of the Far

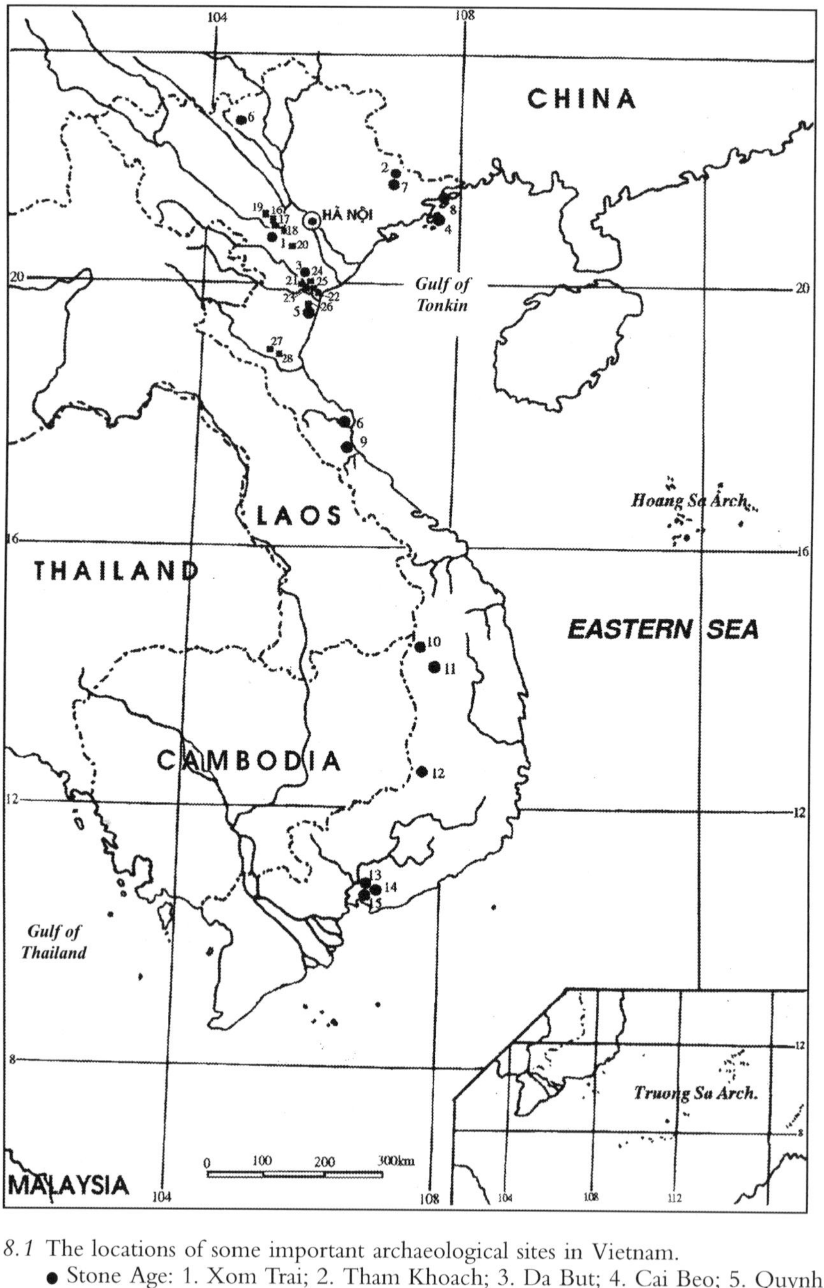

Figure 8.1 The locations of some important archaeological sites in Vietnam.
● Stone Age: 1. Xom Trai; 2. Tham Khoach; 3. Da But; 4. Cai Beo; 5. Quynh Van; 6. Lo Gach; 7. Mai Pha; 8. Ha Long; 9. Bau Tro; 10. Lung Leng; 11. Bien Ho; 12. Buon Triet; 13. Cau Sat; 14. Ben Do; 15. Cu Lao Rua.
■ Metal Age: 16. Phung Nguyen; 17. Go Con Lon; 18. Dong Dau; 19. Go Mun; 20. Duong Co; 21. Con Chan Tien; 22. Hoa Loc; 23. Dong Khoi; 24. Qui Chu; 25. Dong Son; 26. Den Doi; 27. Rú Tran; 28. Lang Vac.

Eastern Prehistory Congress in Hanoi in 1932.[2] It is understood today that the Hoabinhian developed out of the earlier Son Vi Culture, which is not discussed here. So far, over 120 Hoabinhian caves and shelters have been discovered in Vietnam, mostly in Thanh Hoa and Hoa Binh provinces. They have yielded many thousands of stone, bone and shell implements, along with animal bones, shells, hearths and human burials. It is thought by Vietnamese archaeologists that different groups of people each occupied a group of nearby caves and controlled the adjoining limestone valleys. Each cave might be seen as a "house" containing an extended family.

Figure 8.2 Unifacially flaked Hoabinhian pebble tools from Xom Trai Cave. (Photograph courtesy of the Institute of Archaeology, Hanoi.)

Figure 8.3 Hoabinhian flaked axes from Xom Trai Cave. (Photograph courtesy of the Institute of Archaeology, Hanoi.)

Most inhabited caves are located 10–12 metres above the present valley floors and are about 50–150 square metres in floor area. The Hoabinhian economy is presumed to have been based upon hunting and gathering of terrestrial resources, together with the collection of riverine gastropods that occur in large numbers in some sites. Hoabinhians buried the dead within their dwelling places in flexed or extended postures, with small stones, gastropod shells or ash spread under the corpse. Over the burial they often spread ochre. Hoabinhian tools are mostly flaked from river pebbles (Figure 8.2) and there are rare examples of edge-grinding on some of them. The most typical pebble tools may be described as almond-shaped axes (Figure 8.3), discoid scrapers, short "hand axes" and edge-ground axes. Bone and shell implements are rare. Pottery has been found in the later levels of Hoabinhian sites, but no trace of its production has been discovered and Vietnamese archaeologists still dispute whether pottery was an integral part of the Hoabinhian.[3]

The Hoabinhian cultural tradition lasted from the late Pleistocene into the middle Holocene (many of the radiocarbon dates are on freshwater shell and calibrations for this material are unknown), presumably lasting down to the appearance of the pottery traditions described as Middle Neolithic, especially those coastal Neolithic cultures termed "Da But", "Quynh Van" and "Cai Beo" (see pp. 181–3).

The Bac Son Culture (normally termed "the Bacsonian" in English)

The Bacsonian is named after Bac Son district in Lang Son Province, where initial excavations were undertaken early in the twentieth century by the French geologist, Henri Mansuy, in Tham Khoach Cave near Binh Gia town. There he unearthed several edge-ground pebble axes and other finds.[4] By 1925, Mansuy and Colani had together discovered and excavated a dozen sites and established the existence of a distinct Bacsonian Early Neolithic culture, characterized by numerous edge-ground axes (and thus distinguishable from the otherwise-similar Hoabinhian), together with small flat stones with parallel incised grooves on their sides – the enigmatic "Bacsonian marks" or *marques Bacsoniennes*.[5] (Figure 8.4).

Figure 8.4 "Bacsonian marks" on river pebbles from Hang Doi Cave. (Photograph courtesy of Institute of Archaeology, Hanoi.)

Since Vietnamese independence, 53 new Bacsonian sites have been discovered, located mainly in the Bac Son limestone massif north of the Hong (Red) River. This culture lasted from *c.*11000–7000 BP, although again the dates are mostly on freshwater shell and thus cannot be calibrated.[6] On present evidence it seems that the Bacsonian is simply a late facies of the Hoabinhian, since it ended roughly at the same time.[7] Food remains include freshwater molluscs and some forest floor snails (*Cyclophorus* sp.), together with mammal bones. Pottery, although small in quantity, is rich in variety. It is believed that the black, thick, coarse pottery decorated by beating with a cord-wrapped paddle (cord-marked pottery) was made by the Bacsonians, in which case this pottery is the oldest in northern Vietnam and contemporary with similar paddle-impressed traditions in southern China. It is also possible that the Bacsonians practised simple plant cultivation, but there is no certain evidence. Surviving evidence for their artistic sense includes some figures, possibly human, carved in stone and groups of figures incised in clay slabs.

Bacsonians buried the dead in their dwelling places, as both single and collective burials. Nearly a hundred individuals were found in Lang Cuom Cave. Corpses were sprinkled with ochre and sometimes stone tools and marine shell ornaments are found close to the burials, believed by Vietnamese archaeologists to be grave goods.[8] Skeletal remains of the Bac Son people show both "Australoid" and "Mongoloid" phenotypic characteristics and Vietnamese anthropologists believe that they contributed to the gene pool of later Neolithic and Metal Age populations in Vietnam.[9]

The Soi Nhu group of sites

The Soi Nhu sites are named after Soi Nhu Cave in Van Don district, Quang Ninh Province, excavated in 1967.[10] Soi Nhu sites are located mainly on the limestone islands in Ha Long and Bai Tu Long Bays. The excavation of Hang Giua (Middle Cave) at Soi Nhu unearthed edge-ground axes and riverine molluscs, mainly *Cyclophorus* and *Melania*,[11] along with some mammal bones and rare marine fauna. The caves now lie in shallow water in Ha Long Bay. C14 dates[12] indicate that the occupation was contemporary with the Hoabinhian, dating to the terminal Pleistocene. The pebble tools were not of defined shapes – some were made from limestone – and no pottery was present.

The middle Neolithic cultures

The Da But Culture

The Da But shell mound in Thanh Hoa was first excavated by Etienne Patte, but the characterization of the Da But Culture is due to the more recent intensive efforts of Vietnamese archaeologists.[13] Five sites of this culture have been so far discovered in the lower delta of the Ma River.

Da But pottery was made in basketry moulds and has a coarse sand temper (Figure 8.5). Vessels have round bases, no feet, a high straight or slightly flaring rim, and were paddle-beaten. In the earlier phase of the culture, flaked pebble tools and edge-ground axes were predominant; in the middle phase, axes were fully ground on both faces. Small trapezoidal-sectioned axes were popular, together with mortars, pounders, awls, "ringstones", and especially ovoid-shaped net-sinkers made from schist and baked clay with incised grooves to fasten cordage. As sea levels fell following the mid-Holocene high the Da But people cultivated vegetables and tubers in the growing Ma River Delta, and fished in rivers and the sea. Radiocarbon dates range from 6500–6000 BP at Da But to 4700 BP at Go Trung.[14]

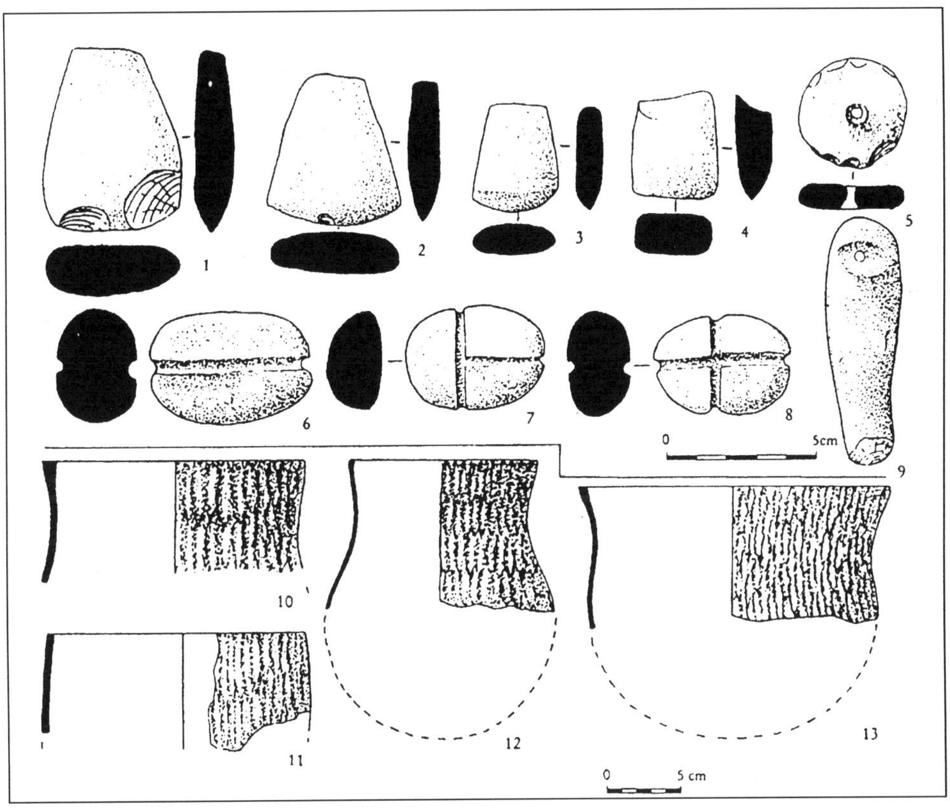

Figure 8.5 Artefacts of the Da But Culture. 1–4 axes; 5 perforated stone disc; 6–9 netsinkers; 10–13 pottery. (Drawing courtesy of A. Reinecke.)

The Quynh Van Culture

The site of Quynh Van, near Cau Giat, was excavated by Colani in 1930 and defined later by Vietnamese archaeologists.[15] Twenty-one sites of this culture have been so far discovered on the coastal plains of Nghe An and Ha Tinh provinces, concentrated around the ancient Quynh Luu Bay. Typical sites are mounds containing marine shells along with remains of crabs, fish, turtles and terrestrial mammals. A dominant feature of the stone implements is the presence of rather crude flaked tools of indefinite form along with many stone pestles and pounders. Some flakes and thin blades are present, but there are very few ground axes. Pottery is common, thick and with coarse fabrics and conical bases (Figure 8.6). Fewer stone tools and more pottery are found in the upper levels of the sites.

Burials were placed in roughly circular graves in the living sites, tightly crouched or flexed on their sides. Skeletons are usually incomplete. Radiocarbon dates run from nearly 5,000 years ago[16] at Quynh Van to only 2000 BP at Con Dat. It is believed that the Quynh Van Culture was derived from a group of Hoabinhian sites in western Thanh Hoa Province, despite the time gap.[17] The later Quynh Van Culture is linked to the late Neolithic Bau Tro Culture.

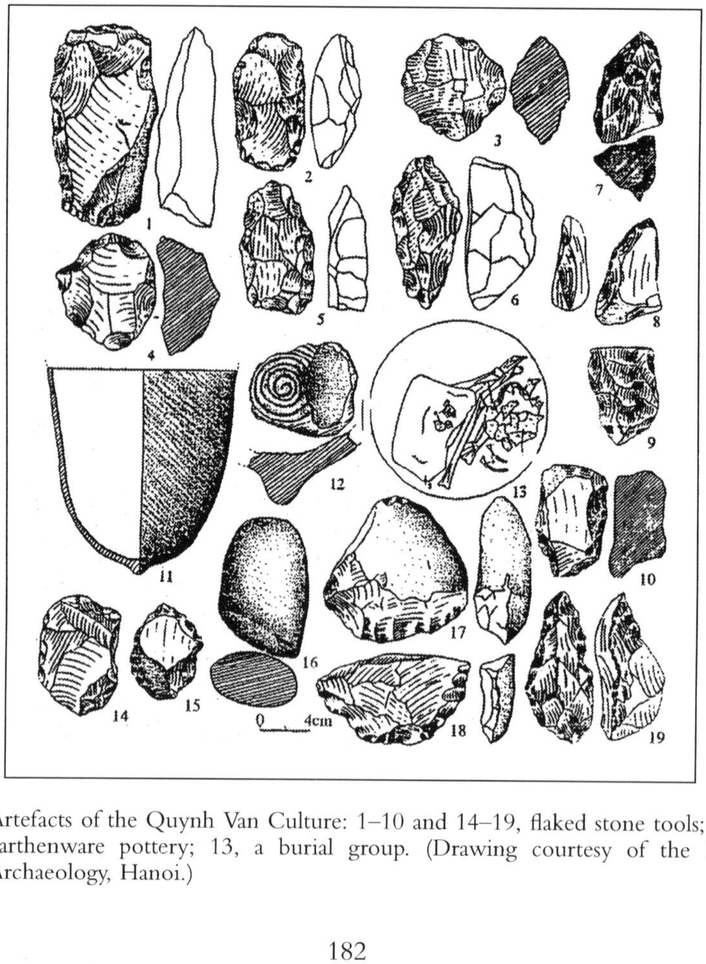

Figure 8.6 Artefacts of the Quynh Van Culture: 1–10 and 14–19, flaked stone tools; 11 and 12, earthenware pottery; 13, a burial group. (Drawing courtesy of the Institute of Archaeology, Hanoi.)

The Cai Beo Culture

This culture is named after Cai Beo Bay in Hai Phong Province.[18] Excavation of the eponymous Cai Beo site was undertaken between 1973 and 1986. Sites containing material similar to that in the lowest layer at Cai Beo have been found on Cat Ba island, in Ha Long Bay and at Bai Tu Long, and provide the basis for identifying a Cai Beo Culture, which is overlain by the Ha Long Culture (see below). Cai Beo stone implements include quadrangular-sectioned untanged axes and adzes (which dominate the assemblages), shouldered axes and chisels. Low-fired, handmade pottery was made from organic-tempered sandy clay. Forms include vessels with straight or everted rims and round or flat bases, decorated on their outer surfaces with basket, comb and cord impressions, short curved incised lines, and punctation. The Cai Beo inhabitants were coastal dwellers using nets and perhaps seacraft for fishing inshore and offshore, and their culture formed the basis for the Late Neolithic Ha Long Culture (Figure 8.7) in northeastern coastal Vietnam.[19]

The late Neolithic cultures

The late Neolithic phase in Vietnam incorporates the Ha Giang, Mai Pha and Ha Long cultures in the north; the Bau Tro, Bien Ho, Buon Triet and Lung Leng cultures in the central zone and western plateaux; and some locations in southeastern Vietnam.

The Ha Giang Culture

This is named after the Lo Gach site in Ha Giang town. Most Ha Giang sites are distributed along the upper courses of the Chay, Gam and Lo rivers and have produced a ground-stone industry of shouldered axes and adzes, bracelets with D and T-shaped cross-sections, and bark-cloth beaters incised with squares. Pottery is rare in the Ha Giang Culture and is mainly coarse and thick-walled, tempered with quartz and mica. Nevertheless, vessel forms are varied. Some vessels have pedestals or ring feet and decoration includes cord-marking, comb-incision, S-shaped patterns of dot impressions and incised leaf-vein patterns. Much of the decoration is concentrated around the outsides of vessel rims.

The Ha Giang Culture is believed to date to *c.*5,000–4,000 years ago and relates to the Ha Long and Phung Nguyen cultures, as well as to various Late Neolithic sites in South China. The people are believed by Vietnamese archaeologists to have been ethnic Tai.

The Mai Pha Culture

This culture is named after a site in Lang Son Province, first excavated by a French plantation owner and published by Mansuy. It was defined after further excavation in 1996.[20] Since then, over twenty Mai Pha sites have been discovered, mainly in Lang Son province to the southwest of the Bac Son limestone massif.[21] Mai Pha stone implements include small quadrangular-sectioned axes and adzes, with a few shouldered but no stepped forms. Also found are stone knives, awls, chisels, polishing slabs, a bark-cloth beater, bracelets and earrings; bone gouges, chisels and bracelets; and shouldered shell axes. Cowrie shells were pierced to be strung as beads.

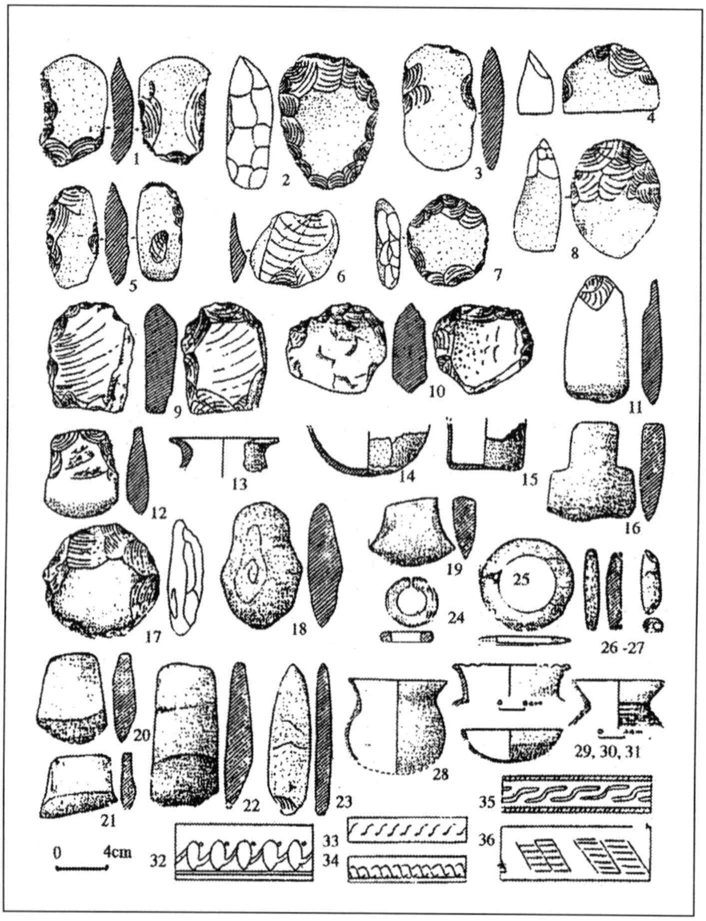

Figure 8.7 Artefacts of the Ha Long Culture: 1–10, 17 and 18, flaked stone tools; 11, 12, 16 and 19–23, polished stone axes and adzes; 13–15 and 28–31 earthenware pottery; 24 and 25, stone bangles; 26 and 27, stone punches; 32–36 decorative designs on pottery. (Drawing courtesy of the Institute of Archaeology, Hanoi.)

The abundant thin-walled Mai Pha pottery was made of fine clay, sometimes coated with a red slip. Most typical are narrow-necked, bell-mouthed vessels with concave bases; ring-footed vases with handles or suspension holes; tall pedestalled trays; and bowls decorated with rosettes and punctation. Baked clay spindle whorls and bow pellets are also found. The Mai Pha people practised hunting and gathering and kept cattle and buffalo, as well as pigs and dogs. A single radiocarbon date places the Mai Pha Culture in the early second millennium BC, and this is supported by its connections with the Ha Long and Phung Nguyen cultures.

The Ha Long Culture

The Dandola Culture was the original name given to this culture by J. G. Andersson,[22] but it was later renamed after Ha Long Bay in northeastern Vietnam. Twenty-seven sites have been so far discovered and studied, distributed along coasts and behind sand dunes.[23] The Ha Long people had mastered techniques of stone grinding, sawing, drilling and polishing, and made high-quality pottery. Dominant Ha Long stone implements are polished untanged, shouldered and small stepped adzes, pestles, and grinding stones with U-shaped grooves known as "Halong marks" (Figure 8.8). The pottery is decorated by punctation, appliqué and incision.

Figure 8.8 Grooved sandstone grinding stones of the Ha Long Culture from Dong Mo site. (J. G. Andersson Collection, courtesy of the MEFA, Stockholm.)

The Ha Long Culture developed during the third millennium BC out of the earlier Cai Beo Culture, and maintained many connections with the Phung Nguyen, Ha Giang and Mai Pha cultures in northern Vietnam, and also with coastal Neolithic cultures in Guangdong and Fujian Provinces in southern China. The population was of Mongoloid skeletal phenotype. There is some evidence to suggest that they were skilful seafarers, probably engaged in coastal trade. They also grew fibre plants for manufacturing fishing nets.

The Bau Tro Culture

This was named after the eponymous site excavated by Etienne Patte in 1923, although the culture has since been defined by Vietnamese archaeologists.[24] Over 20 sites have been discovered, including coastal shell middens, layers in riverside sand dunes and mounds on low hills, distributed along the coastal plains of Nghe An, Ha Tinh and Quang Binh provinces. The most typical Bau Tro implements are shouldered axes and adzes with re-flaked edges. The pottery is highly standardized in terms of fabric, shape, decoration and manufacturing techniques. Vessels may have conical bases with comb-impressed decoration on both inner and outer faces; or round cord-impressed bases. There are also ring-footed vessels with incised decoration; and cord-marked red-painted patterns (Figure 8.9). Based on a single date, the Bau Tro Culture is placed in the mid-second millennium BC[25] and may have been ancestral in some way to the Iron Age Sa Huynh Culture in Central Vietnam.[26]

The Bien Ho Culture

This lies mainly on the Pleiku Plateau. Apart from the two excavated sites of Bien Ho and Tra Dom, over thirty sites of the same character and date have been discovered. Basic artefacts are adzes made from phtanite and shaped like buffalo teeth, shouldered axes, and adzes of chert with reflaked cutting edges patterns (Figure 8.10). The sand-tempered pottery was made on a turntable and fired at a high temperature. Vessels were decorated with incised and impressed patterns. The people practised agriculture close to lakes and had links with the Bau Tro and Lung Leng cultures, as well as with Laos and Cambodia.[27]

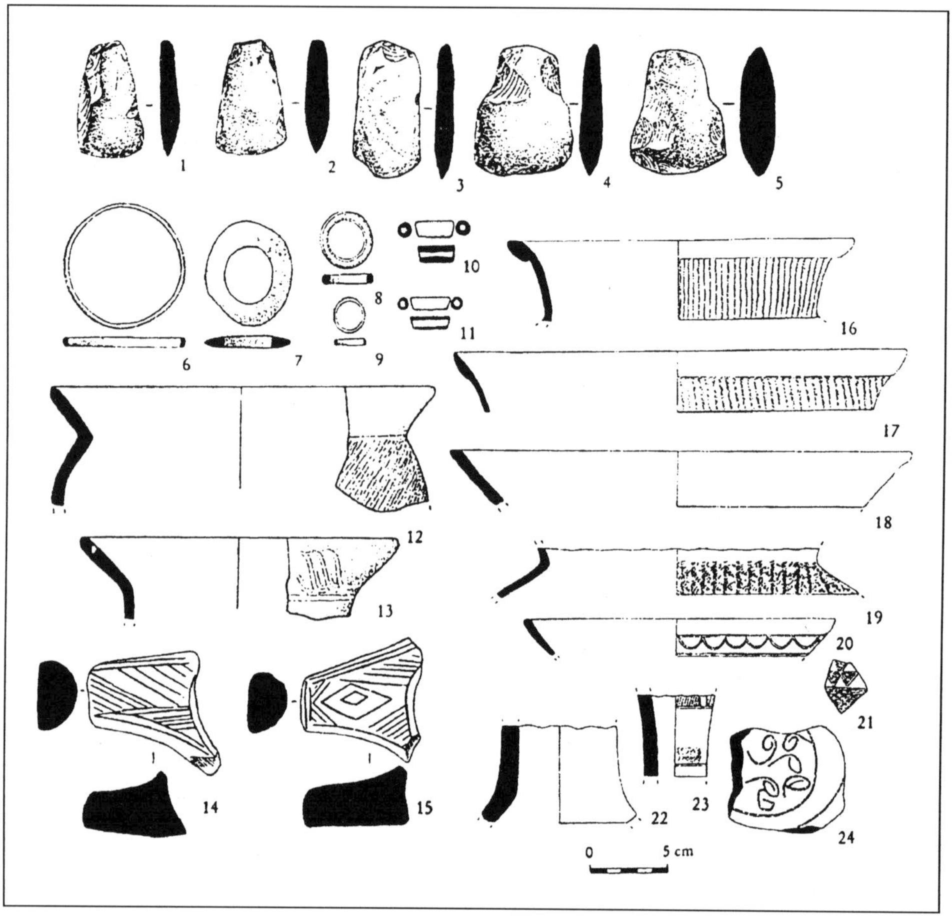

Figure 8.9 Artefacts of the Bau Tro Culture. 1–5, polished stone axes and adzes; 6–9, stone bangles; 10–11 tubular stone beads; 12–34, earthenware pottery and decorative designs on pottery. (Drawing courtesy of the Institute of Archaeology, Hanoi.)

The Lung Leng Culture

This is located in the Kon Tum Basin in the northern part of the Western Plateaux region. Apart from the excavated Lung Leng site itself, nine similar sites have been found. The people made frequent use of square-shouldered hoes made from chert, "buffalo-tooth" hoes and adzes made from phtanite, and much-resharpened shouldered adzes. Also recovered are grindstones, large sandstone saddle-querns, pierced pebbles, and urn burials in which one vessel was placed upside down over another. There are also small, thin and fine wares for domestic use, decorated with beautiful patterns. The Lung Leng people were sedentary river-dwellers, practising agriculture, who had links with the Bien Ho Culture on the Pleiku Plateau, as well as with Bau Tro and other pre-Sa Huynh peoples on the central coast.[28]

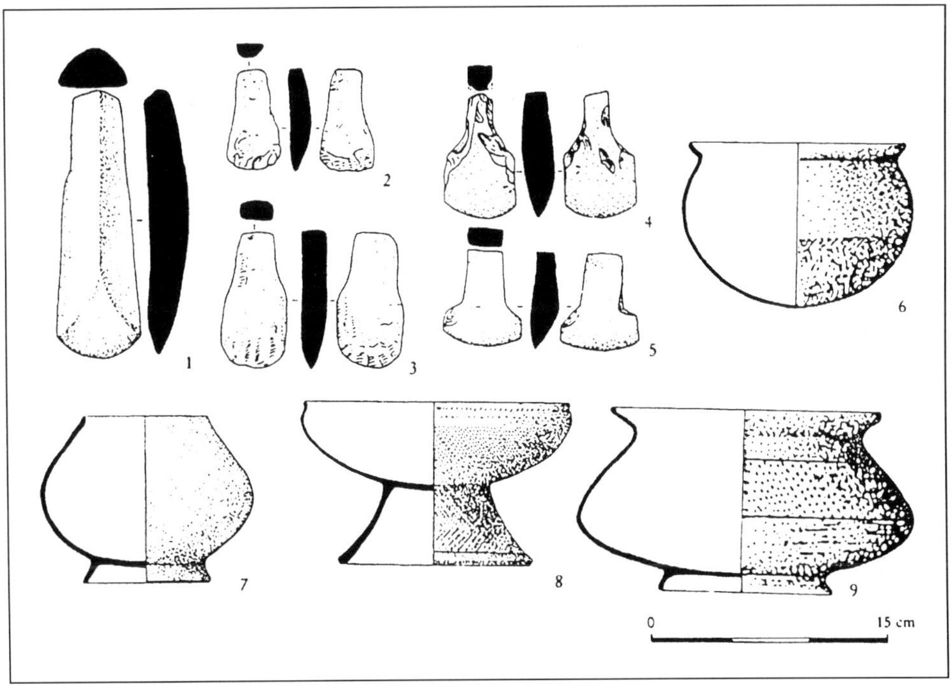

Figure 8.10 Artefacts of the Bien Ho Culture. 1, keeled adze; 2–3, 'buffalo tooth' adzes; 4–5, shouldered adzes; 6–9, pottery. (Drawing courtesy of A. Reinecke.)

The Buon Triet Culture

This is distributed mainly in the southwestern part of the Western Plateaux, in Lac, Dak Nong, Dak Min and Dak R'lap districts of Dak Lak province. Only two sites have been excavated – Buon Triet and Nghia Trang – but nearly 20 other similar ones have been discovered. The main artefacts are trapezoidal-sectioned hoes and adzes made from basalt, pierced hammer stones, and wheel-made sand-tempered pottery with cord impressions, combed and incised motifs. These people were also sedentary agriculturalists around lakes or along rivers, and had extended relations with the Dong Nai Basin to the south and Cambodia to the west.[29]

Since 1975, a wide range of Late Neolithic archaeological sites have been discovered and excavated by Vietnamese archaeologists in southern Vietnam. They divide them into three phases; Cau Sat, Cu Lao Rua and Ben Do. None contain bronze artefacts, yet some researchers classify them as Late Neolithic – Early Bronze Age. We rank them here within the Late Neolithic.[30] The Cau Sat phase includes the Cau Sat and Suoi Linh sites in the Dong Nai Basin. Most common are trapezoidal-sectioned axes and axes with smooth shoulders, sickle-shaped knives, trapezoidal-sectioned bracelets, and coarse, thin, wheel-turned and well-fired pottery. Some sherds have been trimmed into discs.

The Ben Do phase includes many sites, such as Ben Do itself, Phuoc Tan, Hoi Son and Ngai Thang. It is widely distributed in the Dong Nai Basin. Stone hoes, axes and adzes are found; also sickle-shaped knives and chisels and disc-shaped bracelets with triangular cross-sections. Ben Do pottery is more advanced than that of Cau Sat in terms of material and firing techniques. Two radiocarbon dates from Ben Do are 3040 ± 40 and 3000 ± 110 BP.

The Cu Lao Rua phase includes Cu Lao Rua itself, Go Da and the lower layer of the Doc Chua site. The number of hoes decreases and sickles and chisels disappear from the stone tool repertoire. In contrast, shouldered axes and adzes are common and sometimes very large. Bracelets become more oval in cross-section and the pottery is more advanced than in the previous stages. Spindle-whorls and clay bow pellets occur. Two radiocarbon samples from the lower layer at Doc Chua have been dated to 3145 ± 105 and 2990 ± 105 BP.

A common characteristic of these southern sites is a predominance of wholly polished stone implements, which gradually become smaller over time. Shouldered axes are more common in the earlier stages, but untanged trapezoidal-sectioned axes later increase in proportion. Hoes, chisels and sickles become less frequent, while pottery techniques improve and types become more diversified over time. The origins of these late Neolithic cultures are still unclear and at present they represent the earliest well-identified cultural complexes in southeastern Vietnam.

Summary and conclusions: Neolithic cultures in Vietnam

Vietnamese archaeologists draw the following conclusions about the Neolithic in Vietnam:

1 It evolved continuously from the Early Holocene until about 3000 BP, beginning with the Hoabinhian, a cultural complex widely distributed across continental Southeast Asia but best represented in Vietnam.[31]
2 The Early Neolithic of Vietnam also included the Bacsonian and the Soi Nhu sites, the former yielding many edge-ground axes that might have served as a prelude, at least in lithic technology, to the "Neolithic Revolution" in Vietnam.
3 The Middle Neolithic cultures demonstrate multi-faceted cultural evolution, as expressed in the different pottery traditions. This phase probably represents the real "Neolithic Revolution" for Vietnam.
4 The varied Late Neolithic cultures also have distinctive identities. A little later, these identities converged (to a degree) into two Metal Age cultures: the Dong Son Culture in the north and the Sa Huynh Culture in the south.
5 The evolutionary path from Early to Late Neolithic in Vietnam followed a clearly defined pattern. Over time, there was a gradual reduction in the extents of specific cultures – they became more localized and spanned shorter phases of time. There was a development from broad spectrum hunting and gathering to forms of agriculture involving the domestication of a wide range of plant species, and a focus more on cultivation than on animal husbandry.

PART II: THE METAL AGE IN THE NORTH OF VIETNAM

Pham Minh Huyen

Introduction

In the 1920s and 1930s, the prehistoric site at Dong Son in Thanh Hoa Province was investigated by French officials and the Swedish archaeologist Olov Janse.[32] These excavations marked the beginning of research into the Metal Age in Vietnam. After 1954, when the archaeology of an independent Vietnam was founded, Vietnamese archaeologists began to discover sites of the pre-Dong Son Bronze Age and also to recover more information from the Dong Son site itself.

In 1959, the discovery and excavation of the Phung Nguyen site (Phu Tho Province) was a milestone in the study of the early Metal Age in Vietnam. In the 1960s, further pre-Dong Son Metal Age sites were discovered, among them Go Mun in Phu Tho Province and Dong Dau in Vinh Phuc Province. Dong Dau has cultural layers showing three successive phases starting from Phung Nguyen and continuing through Dong Dau to Go Mun. Thus, an evolutionary development of pre-Dong Son cultures had been discovered in the middle valley and delta of the Hong (Red) River.

In the 1970s, many excavations were conducted in the Ma and Lam river basins further to the south. In this area, archaeologists recognized some differences with the pre-Dong Son sites of the Hong River. Metal Age sites were also discovered in the northern mountains and as far south as Quang Binh Province. So much is now known that a single chapter cannot address all aspects of the Metal Age in northern Vietnam and only a few major points can be made concerning developments in the basins of the Hong, Ma and Ca rivers.

The Pre-Dong Son cultures along the Hong River

The Phung Nguyen Culture

The Phung Nguyen Culture marks the beginning of the Bronze Age in Vietnam and commenced a chain of development leading eventually to the Dong Son Culture of the late first millennium AD. More than 50 Phung Nguyen sites have been discovered, mainly in Phu Tho, Vinh Phuc, Hanoi, Ha Tay and Bac Ninh provinces – a broad area centred on the junctions of the Hong, Da, Lo and Day rivers. Settlements extending over more than 10,000 square metres have been recognised, and some individual sites extend over more than 2,000 square metres. Phung Nguyen deposits are typically about 0.7 metres thick, some up to 2 metres. Although many sites have been excavated, structural remains are elusive. Radiocarbon dates place the Phung Nguyen Culture between about 3800 and 3400 BP.[33]

Most Phung Nguyen sites have only one cultural layer, although some contain remains from the succeeding Dong Dau Culture. Three sites contain evidence of workshop activity: Go Che in Phu Tho Province produced stone tools; Trang Kenh produced nephrite bracelets, and Bai Tu (Bac Ninh Province) produced stone drills.[34] These workshop sites usually belong to the late Phung Nguyen or early Dong Dau cultures. The most noticeable cemetery site is Lung Hoa, where 12 graves were found to contain more than 100 stone and pottery artefacts.[35] In other sites, we usually discover only one or two burials in the cultural layer (Figure 8.11).

Stone tools and ornaments are found at most Phung Nguyen sites. From three excavations at Phung Nguyen,[36] 531 adzes and 246 axes were recovered and these are typically small, 3 centimetres long, 2 centimetres wide and 0.5 centimetre thick, made from hard, beautifully coloured stone such as spilite and nephrite. The Bai Tu workshop site produced thousands of jasper stone drills;[37] stone knives, sickles and saws were also made. A few unusual tool types such as harpoons, spearheads, *ko* halberds and barbed arrowheads also occur in Phung Nguyen sites.

Stone ornaments are both diverse and numerous; out of more than 4,000 artefacts at Phung Nguyen, about 600 were ornaments. Van Dien produced 535 stone bracelets out of a total of 1,085 stone objects. Phung Nguyen bracelets have square, round, semi-circular or T-shaped cross sections. Crescent-shaped ornaments, beads and rings were skilfully made from nephrite by sawing, drilling and polishing. Five objects called *chuong* (Chinese *zhang*) of a type typical of cultures of the late Neolithic and Bronze Age in central China have also been found at Phung Nguyen and Xom Ren (Phu Tho Province).

Most Phung Nguyen pottery is coarse with sand or sometimes plant temper in various colours, bright red, dark brown and buff, with occasional higher quality fine wares. Firing temperatures were low at around 700 degress centigrade. Decoration is horizontal, symmetrical and bounded by horizontal incised lines. Typical patterns are made up of straight lines, S-curves, dots and triangles. So far, very little bronze has been found, only at six Phung Nguyen sites, and this is mainly bronze waste material. The late Phung Nguyen site at Dong Vong (Hanoi), discovered in 1997, yielded two baked clay casting moulds.

The Ma Dong, Doan Thuong, Go Con Lon and Quang Huc sites

Contemporary with Phung Nguyen and situated between the sites of this culture are four other sites having quite different cultural characteristics. Researchers have not yet classified these and for the moment call them a "group of sites". They lie on low hills close to the junction of the Hong and Da rivers in Phu Tho and Ha Tay Provinces. The sites are small, short-lived settlements with shallow deposits from 0.40 to 0.45 metres deep. Doan Thuong is a workshop with unfinished shouldered adzes, these being more common here than in Phung Nguyen sites. Pottery is limited in quantity, coarse and low-fired, incised or cord-marked. The more abundant pottery from Ma Dong resembles that of the Hoa Loc Culture (see below) located along the Thanh Hoa coast. Traces of bronze were found in Doan Thuong, which is thought to be the oldest site of this group.[38]

The Dong Dau Culture

This is named after the eponymous site in Yen Lac district, Vinh Phuc Province. Generally, Dong Dau sites are located in the same area as those of the Phung Nguyen Culture but extend further towards the Hong delta. The settlements are usually not large, but Dong Dau itself covers 8 hectares and the deposits are about 1 metre deep. Some yellow earth platforms here are thought to be house foundations. Most Dong Dau sites

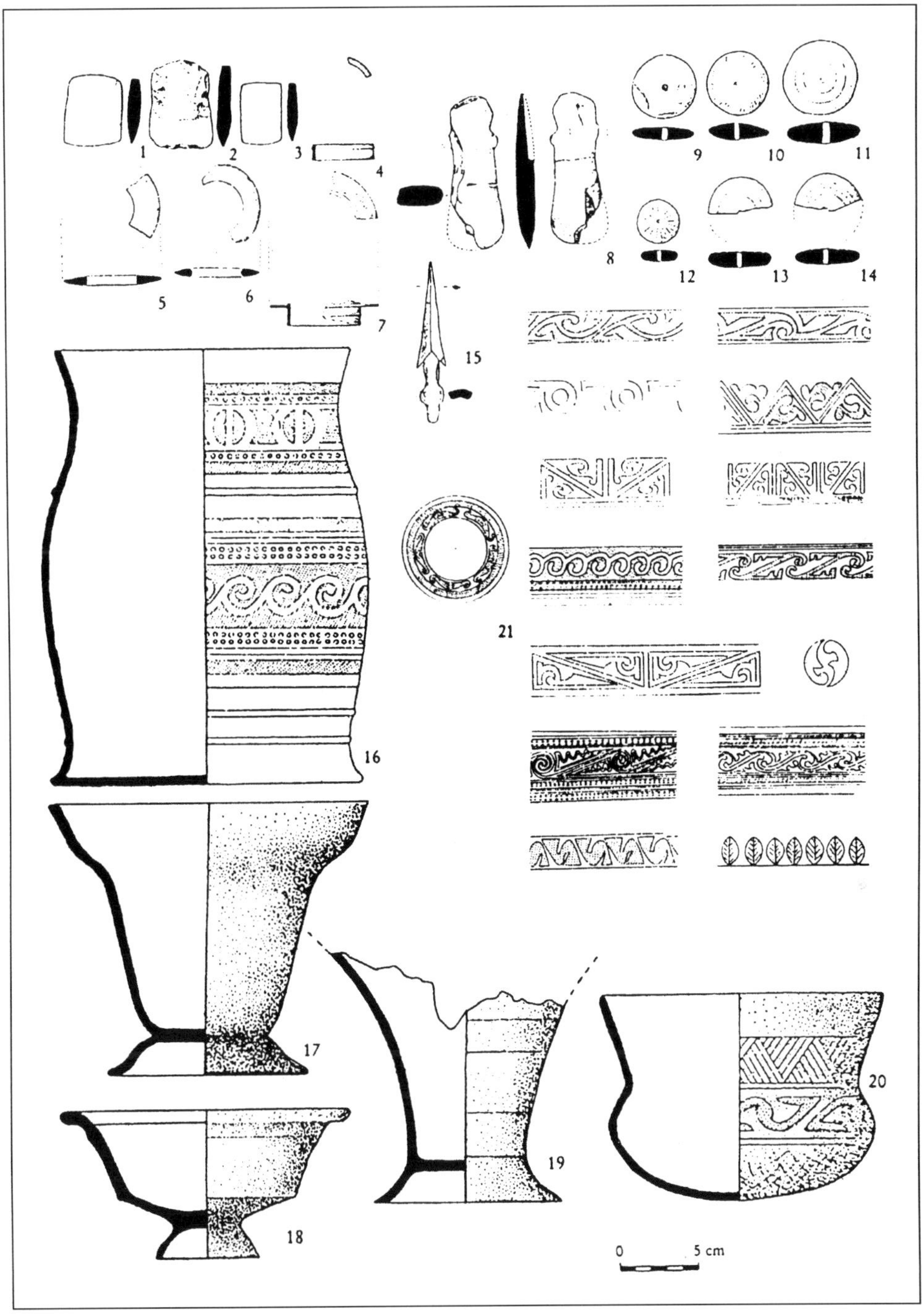

Figure 8.11 Artefacts of the Phung Nguyen Culture. 1–3, polished stone axes and adzes; 4–7, stone bangles; 8 stone *chuong*; 9–14, pottery spindle whorls; 15, bone harpoon; 16–21, earthenware pottery and decorative designs on pottery. (Drawing courtesy of the Institute of Archaeology, Hanoi.)

overlie Phung Nguyen materials and themselves are overlain by Go Mun deposits, thus demonstrating cultural continuity.

Moulds and crucibles for bronze casting have been found in many Dong Dau sites. Thanh Den (Vinh Phuc Province) has yielded 46 stone and ceramic mould fragments and 20 broken casting crucibles, together with the remains of four bronze-casting furnaces and much bronze waste.[39] A true bronze alloy of tin and copper was in use for objects cast in bivalve moulds, such as projectile points, fishhooks, spearheads and axes (Figure 8.12).

Figure 8.12 Double stone mould for casting bronze arrowheads from Dong Dau. (Photograph courtesy of the Institute of Archaeology, Hanoi.)

Dong Dau stone objects are similar to those of the Phung Nguyen Culture, although nephrite ceased to be used for axes and adzes. Projectile points become more common, and the quality of stone used for ornaments diminishes. The blue nephrite bangles with flared ends found in Phung Nguyen contexts no longer occur, but heavy bracelets with D-shaped, trapezoidal and triangular cross sections become more developed.

Ceramics of this phase are harder, larger, thicker walled and fired at higher temperatures. Decoration is dominated by multiple-pronged comb incision with stamped patterns on rims. Radiocarbon dates place the Dong Dau Culture between 3,400 and 3,000 years ago.[40]

The Go Mun Culture

This is named after the Go Mun site in Phu Tho province. Go Mun sites are located in the same area as those of the Dong Dau Culture, but they expand still further towards the delta. Cultural layers are 0.50 to 1 metre thick and generally overlie Dong Dau deposits. The bronze casting technology of the Go Mun Culture is an inheritance from Dong Dau, but the alloys now mix copper and tin in percentages designed to meet the functional requirements for each type of tool.[41]

Stone still remained important for rectangular-sectioned axes and chisels, bracelets with rectangular, trapezoidal and triangular cross sections, and earrings of various forms, many with knobbed projections. Bone artefacts are not common, but they include "charms" of tiger, pig or dog teeth, or of bone carved to the shape of such teeth.

Go Mun pottery technology developed apace; firing temperatures rose to between 800 and to 900 degrees centigrade, giving a very hard thin pottery in dark grey or light red colours. Pottery forms become more complex with higher pedestals and wider bodies. Decoration was done by incision, usually inside the rim, or on the vessel exterior using straight lines, curves, dots, S-shapes and triangles. Radiocarbon dates on charcoal from Go Mun layers show that the Dong Dau-Go Mun transition occurred about 3,000 years ago, and that the transition from Go Mun to Dong Son took place between 2,800 and 2,700 years ago.[42]

Pre-Dong Son in the Ma River area

The deltas of the Ma and Chu rivers in Thanh Hoa Province are in terrain more rocky, mountainous and less fertile than the Hong River delta. Consequently, Metal Age sites are clustered in the Dong Son, Hoang Hoa and Thieu Yen districts, a situation of circumscription that might have led to the rapid emergence of the Dong Son Culture in the second half of the first millennium BC.

Con Chan Tien

The Con Chan Tien stone workshop is located below Mt. Do (Nui Do) and is the only early Metal Age site known in this region, even though it has been excavated twice. Basalt was quarried from Mt. Do to make stone axes of mainly trapezoidal and triangular cross sections. Small nephrite chisels and axes are similar to those of the Phung Nguyen Culture, but clearly were not made at this workshop. Ornaments made of soft colourful nephrite include necklaces, bracelets and earrings, similar to those of Phung Nguyen.

The Con Chan Tien assemblage is distinguished by its rough, hard pottery, some shell-tempered, that includes footed bowls and bowls with rectangular or hexagonal rims in plan. There are also some tripod bowls. The assemblage is unique, and also includes leech-shaped earrings and animal statuettes. Many baked clay anvils were also discovered. The decoration on Con Chan Tien pottery is quite similar to that of Phung Nguyen, with incised linear patterns framing punctations, corded patterns or burnished bands. There are also resemblances with the pottery of the Hoa Loc phase in coastal Thanh Hoa. Although no bronze has been found in Con Chan Tien, the close parallels with Phung Nguyen and Hoa Loc suggest a context at the start of the Metal Age in the Ma and Ca basins.

The Hoa Loc sites

These are named after Hoa Loc in Hau Loc district, northwestern Thanh Hoa Province. Although few sites are known, it is clear that they belong to a different system from Con Chan Tien. The sites are located on sandy hills about 4 metres above sea level and the cultural layers are 0.3 to 0.9 metres thick. Only two metal artefacts were found at Hoa Loc itself: a piece of bronze wire and a bronze awl, confirmed as a tin-copper alloy.[43]

Some 90 per cent of the Hoa Loc stone axes are quadrilateral in section and less than 10 per cent are shouldered, whereas shouldered hoes are more common than untanged ones. There are also stone objects similar to shouldered hoes that have sharp pointed ends and are considered to be ploughshares. Stone bracelets have rectangular, square or oval cross sections (Figure 8.13).

Hoa Loc sites are rich in pottery artefacts with many unusual forms such as bracelets and earrings, ceramic stamps with beautifully incised geometric designs, and pottery boxes with two compartments. Hoa Loc pottery decoration is also distinctive with water drop, "wolf teeth" and wave-like motifs, together with stamped circles, incised curves, cut-out and appliqué decoration. There are also shell impressed and tortoiseshell patterns. However, cord marking is the most common form of surface finish. Some Hoa Loc pottery has been found in Phung Nguyen sites, particularly Ma Dong. Hoa Loc pottery shares some features with Con Chan Tien, and some believe that it has some relationship with the Sa Huynh – Kalanay ceramic tradition of central and southern Vietnam and the Philippines.[44]

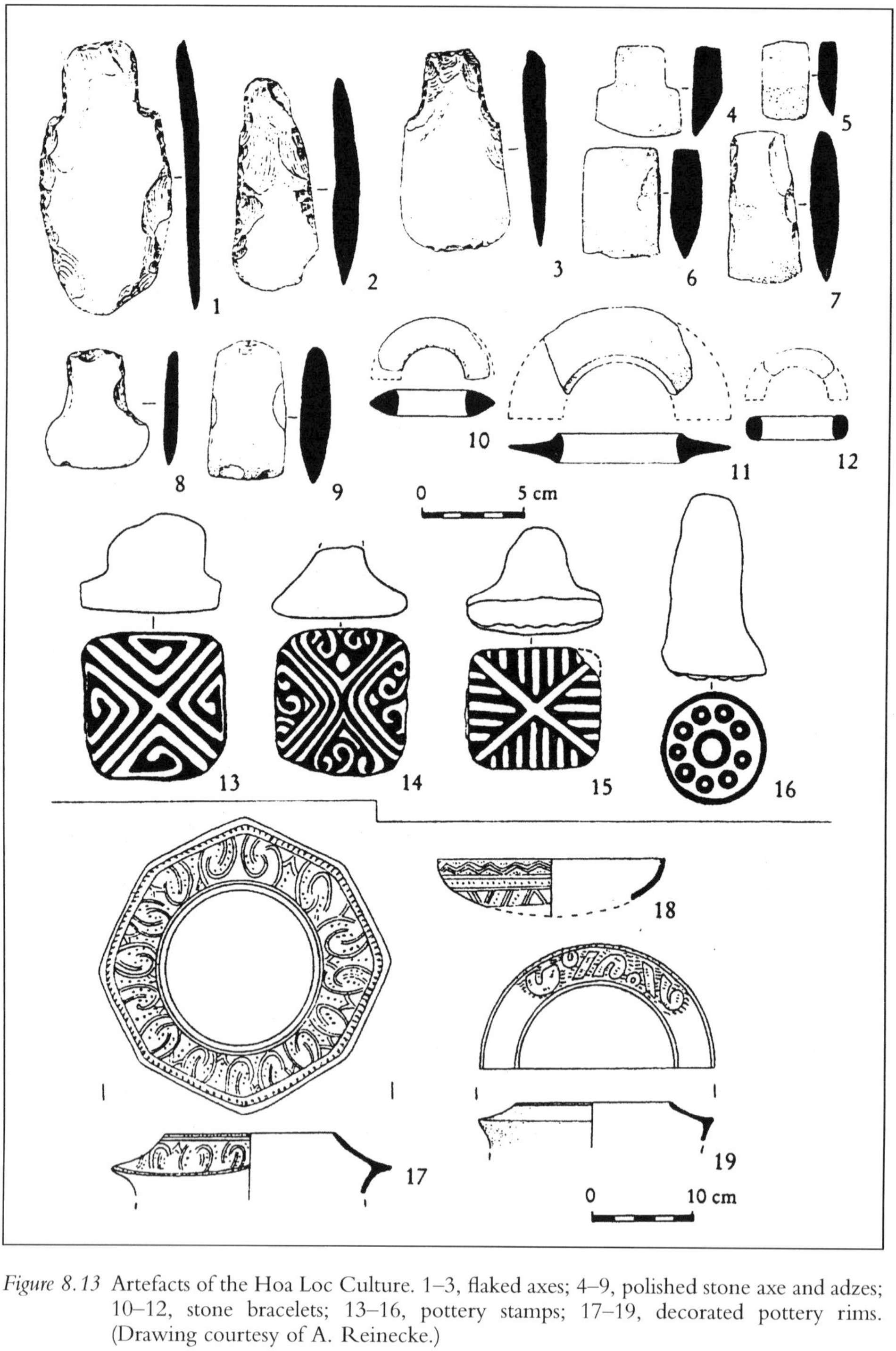

Figure 8.13 Artefacts of the Hoa Loc Culture. 1–3, flaked axes; 4–9, polished stone axe and adzes; 10–12, stone bracelets; 13–16, pottery stamps; 17–19, decorated pottery rims. (Drawing courtesy of A. Reinecke.)

The Dong Khoi and Bai Man sites

Four sites, namely Dong Khoi, Bai Man, Con Cau, the lower layer of Dong Ngam site and probably the lower layer of Thieu Duong are known at the junction of the Ma and Chu rivers in Dong Son and Thieu Yen districts. Although many excavations have been conducted at sites of this phase, no bronze artefacts have yet been found. Nevertheless, the Dong Khoi and Bai Man sites are believed to be contemporary with the Dong Dau Culture in the Hong River area. The stone tools are not so different from those of Con Chan Tien, and materials for the manufacture of stone axes at Dong Khoi were also quarried from Mt. Do. The Dong Khoi and Bai Man pottery resembles that of the previous phase.

The Qui Chu sites

Qui Chu sites occur in Dong Son, Thieu Hoa, Hoang Hoa, Nong Cong and Yen Dinh districts. Many have cultural layers that show continuity into the Dong Son Culture. Burials are found both within and outside the settlements, and the later Dong Son people used the same cemeteries. Bronzes now include socketed axes, spearheads, arrowheads, chisels, hammers, awls, bracelets and necklaces. Much evidence for bronze casting has been found, including many sandstone moulds and casting crucibles.

Qui Chu pottery is hard and fired to a high temperature, and shows relationships with Go Mun pottery to the north and the Ru Tran pottery tradition of the Ca valley to the south (see below). Small pottery replicas made as grave goods appear in this phase, as well as large pots similar in shape to Dong Son drums. Typical pottery decoration includes incised parallel or crossed lines on rims and sharp cord impressions. Mat impressions often occur on flat-based vessels. In the later excavation at Qui Chu we found a different kind of pottery with impressed squares comparable to impressed designs on Shixia pottery from eastern Guangdong.[45] Two samples of charcoal excavated in Qui Chu in 2000 and analysed by the Institute of Archaeology date the phase to between 1000 and 700 BC.[46]

Pre-Dong Son Sites in the Ca Basin

The Ca Basin includes Nghe An, Ha Tinh and Quang Binh Provinces. In comparison to the Hong and Ma river areas, research here is still in an embryonic stage. The site of Den Doi represents the beginning of the Bronze Age of this area and its pottery shows some relationship to the Go Bong phase pottery of the Phung Nguyen Culture and Con Chan Tien in the Ma River area. Sites of the Ru Tran group are found in the Nam Dan area and these contain shouldered and butterfly-shaped bronze hoes similar to the later ploughshares of the Dong Son Culture of the Ma River. The Ru Tran group is considered to be pre-Dong Son, but was probably not in an ancestral relationship to the latter.

The Dong Son Culture

Sites of the Dong Son Culture have been discovered from the northern borders of Vietnam to the Ngang Pass in Quang Binh province, with the densest concentration in the Hong, Ma and Ca valleys. Seventy Dong Son sites have been found to date, in varied

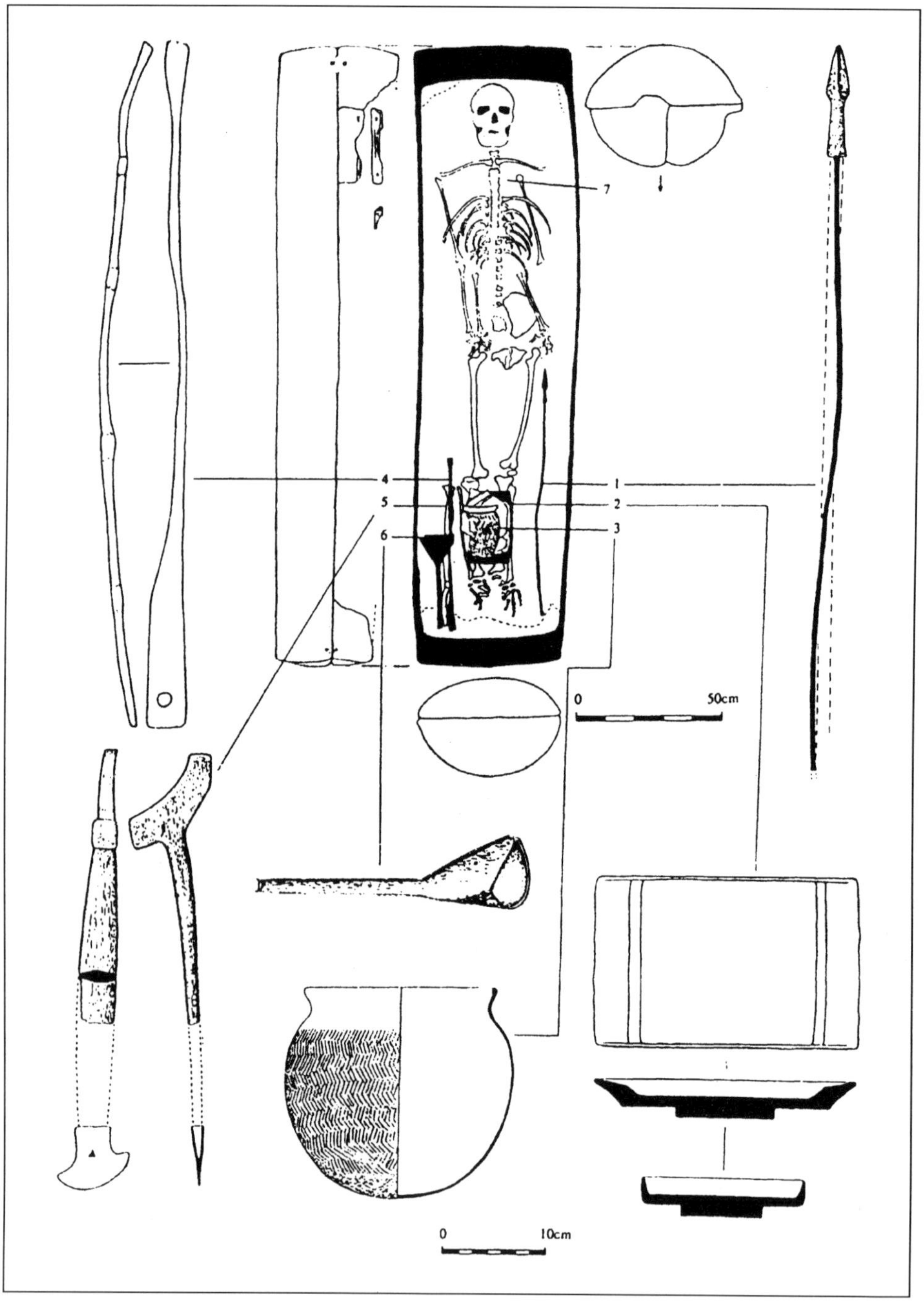

Figure 8.14 Dong Son burial material from Chau Can, Ha Tay Province, 38 km southeast of Hanoi. In the hollow log coffin (upper centre) were, a wooden bow (left), a bronze spear with wooden shaft (right), a bronze shoulder axe with a wooden handle (lower left), a bamboo ladle (centre), a lacquered wooden platter (lower right) and pottery (lower centre). (Drawing courtesy of A. Reinecke.)

environmental circumstances ranging through deltas, coastal areas, and mountains. The large sites often demonstrate a continuous development from pre-Dong Son to Dong Son.

Dong Son sites may be divided into three main types (excluding casual finds) based on their characteristics:

1 Settlement sites are normally close to rivers and areas range from 100 square metres to more than one hectare. Cultural layers are about 0.6 to 1 metre deep and sometimes up to 1.5 metres. Some settlements also contain burials.
2 Cemeteries: many Dong Son burials, including those with dug-out wooden coffins, were located in separate cemeteries away from settlement areas (Figure 8.14).
3 Workshop sites for stone ornaments, only five of which are known, are all located in Dong Son district, Thanh Hoa Province (Figures 8.15 and 8.16).

The greater number of Dong Son bronze artefacts compared to previous phases is a result of progress in casting technology (Figures 8.17–22). In the pre-Dong Son phases, binary

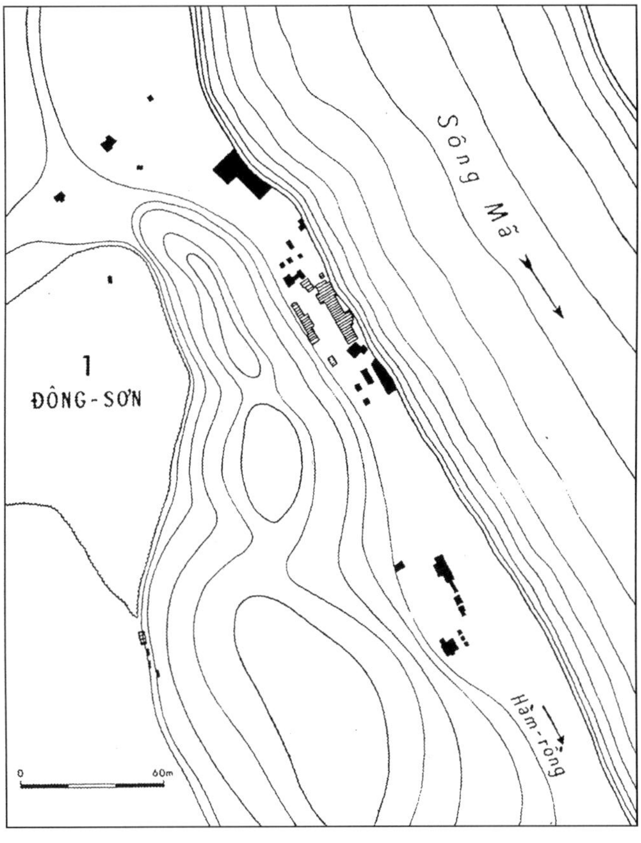

Figure 8.15 Plan of the Dong Son site, Thanh Hoa Province, showing the various excavations between the Ma River and the village of Dong Son. Black areas indicate the French excavations up to 1958; shaded areas locate the excavation in 1958, 1962 and 1970.

Figure 8.16 Excavations at Dong Son in 1960. (Photograph courtesy of A. Reinecke.)

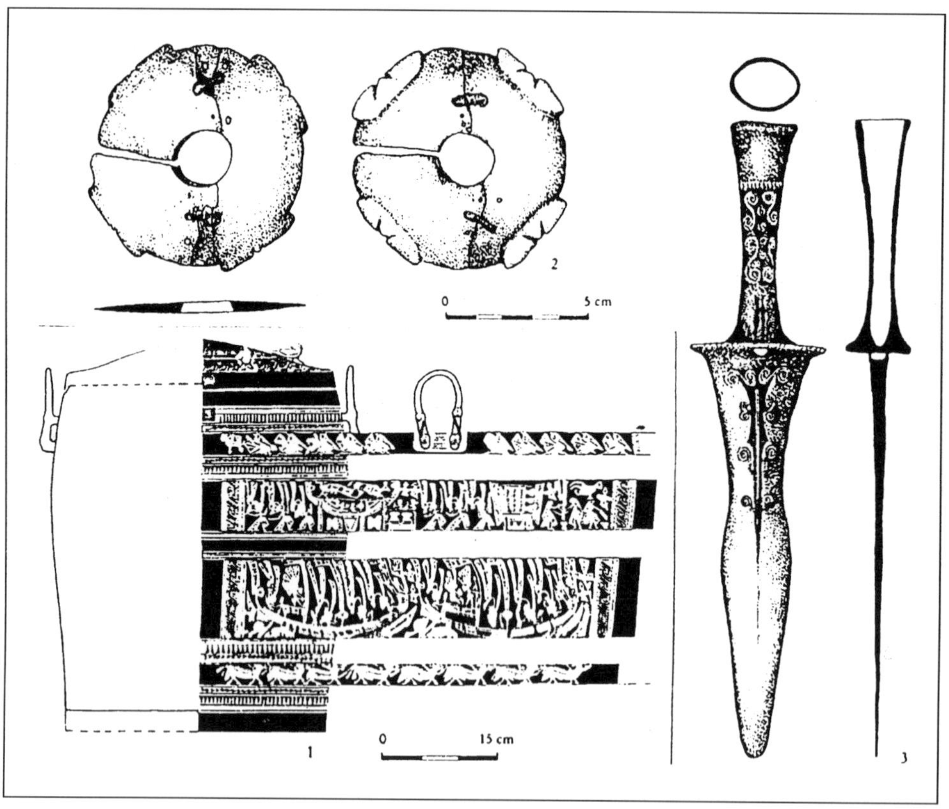

Figure 8.17 Dong Son Culture bronzes from a grave at Hop Minh, Yen Bai Province. 1, decorated bronze situla; 2, stone slit earring; 3, decorated bronze dagger. (Drawing courtesy of A. Reinecke.)

alloys of copper and tin dominate, whereas in the Dong Son Culture the bronze alloys have more elements, among which lead became very important because its addition reduced the melting point of the alloy and made casting easier for large artefacts with delicate patterns,[47] such as the kettle drums and the basket-shaped bronze containers with decorated lids.

Bronze ploughs appear for the first time in Vietnam in Dong Son sites; up to now 200 ploughs of four types, apparently for use in different soils, have been recognized. Other production tools include hoes and shovels; the former are often found in the delta, while shovels are found in the intermediate lands or mountains.

Many bronze axes with various forms and functions have been found and these may be divided into two groups: balanced axes with many blade shapes and pediform socketed axes (Figures 8.18 and 19). The latter are characteristic of the Dong Son Culture and were used as tools as well as weapons. There are two main types: those with a square or round foot are found in the area of the Hong River, while those resembling a shoemaker's last are found in the Ma River area. Other bronze tools include weights, brushes, perhaps for cleaning fibres for textile manufacture (Figure 8.20) and chisels.

Dong Son bronze weapons are numerous and may be divided into projectile weapons such as javelins, socketed spearheads, socketed and tanged arrowheads; close fighting weapons such as swords, fighting axes, daggers, and *ge* (*ko*) halberds; and shields for protection. At Cau Vuc a hoard of about 10,000 tanged projectile points was discovered. Only one complete cross-bow trigger has been found, in a burial at Lang Vac. Daggers were very popular and more than 230 have been discovered in Dong Son burials. They are classified based on the forms of the handle, guard and blade. Those with T-shaped or

Figure 8.18 Dong Son bronze pediform axe from Ha Dong. (J. G. Andersson Collection, courtesy of the MEFA, Stockholm.)

Figure 8.19 Bronze pediform axe and casting mould from Lang Ca site. (Photograph courtesy of Institute of Archaeology, Hanoi.)

Figure 8.20 Bronze toothed implement – possibly a brush used in textile manufacture. (Photograph courtesy of Institute of Archaeology, Hanoi.)

onion-shaped handles were the most popular. The most striking daggers have handles in the forms of human or animal figures that reflect influence from the artistic tradition of the Dien Culture of Yunnan. The short swords are like daggers, but longer.

The *ge* (*ko*) halberd is an ancient Chinese weapon also found in Dong Son Vietnam. In the earlier Phung Nguyen and Dong Dau Cultures, stone *ge* similar to Chinese specimens existed, but these then developed local forms so that those of the Dong Son Culture have their own characteristics. About 30 bronze shields have been found in burials. They are very simple, either square or rectangular with stylized human and animal figures or cross designs. The shields vary in size from about 12.5 centimetres square to 37.5 × 13.7 centimetres.

The most luxurious Dong Son bronze vessels include beautifully-decorated basket-shaped containers with lids (called *thap* in Vietnamese) and bronze vessels thought to be spittoons (*tho*). Some of the larger *tho* carry beautiful and delicate patterns like those on the Ngoc Lu or Co Loa bronze drums. Other household bronze utensils include bowls, plates, spoons and basins. More than 200 bronze kettledrums of Heger type 1 have been found in northern Vietnam (Figure 8.21) and these are the classic "type fossil" for the Dong Son Culture, representing a major technological achievement for the Dong Son people.[48] Some drums show influence from the drums of Shizhaishan and Wanjiaba in Yunnan, and there are also many types of bronze bells.

Figure 8.21 Bronze drum, Heger I type, Dong Son Culture. (J. G. Andersson Collection, courtesy of the MEFA, Stockholm.)

Bracelets are the most common personal ornaments, although necklaces, earrings and belt buckles have also been found. Bronze figurines are rare and most occur as dagger handles (Figure 8.22). These provide naturalistic images of people with their clothing and ornaments, clearer than the very stylized representations on the bronze drums. Animal figurines serving as dagger handles or soldered on to the tympana of drums include frogs, birds, elephants, tigers, snakes, deer, buffaloes, dogs, chicken, fish and snails.

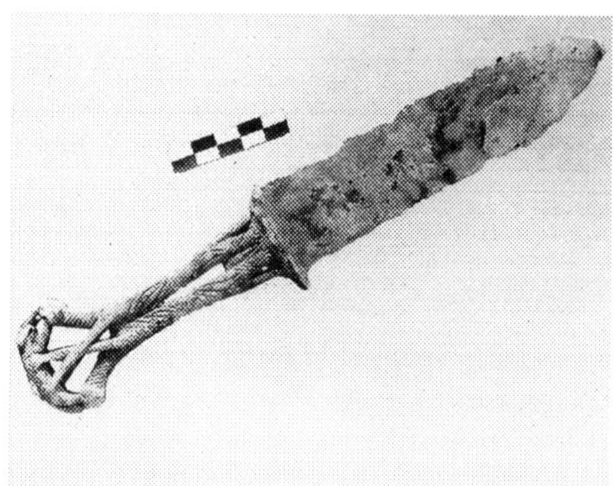

Figure 8.22 Bronze dagger with entwined tigers and elephant from Lang Ca site. (Photograph courtesy of the Institute of Archaeology, Hanoi.)

Iron is far less common than bronze, partly on account of the high humidity and acidity of the soil, but includes weapons, tools and a small number of ornaments. Common forms are axes, hoes, chisels, knives, sickles, spearheads, swords, daggers, vessels, bracelets, necklaces and earrings.

Dong Son pottery continued earlier pottery traditions with dominant cord marking, although it no longer served as a vehicle for artistic expression and so the forms and decoration are quite restricted. That said, pottery kilns had become more advanced and high firing temperatures were achieved. The pottery from Duong Co in the Hong valley was made of carefully selected clay and sand and its light pink colouring marks it as a forerunner of the pottery of the early first millennium AD.

The Dong Son Culture spread over a large area and was relatively uniform in content. In the Hong valley there was a continuous development from the Phung Nguyen Culture through Dong Dau and Go Mun to the Dong Son Culture. In the Ma valley the development was from Con Chan Tien through Dong Khoi-Bai Man to Qui Chu. The Ca valley sequence includes the important burials at Lang Vac in Nghe An Province, although the relationship between Dong Son and pre-Dong Son in this area has not been carefully researched.

The immediate origins of the Dong Son Culture can be found in the Go Mun and Qui Chu sites in the Hong River basin between about 800 and 700 BC. We can say that it ended in AD 43[49] with the failure of the Hai Ba Trung rebellion against the Han, although some elements of Dong Son cultural style lasted into the second and third centuries of the Christian Era.

Conclusion – the Metal Age in Vietnam

The basis of the entire Bronze Age civilization of Vietnam was rice cultivation. In Phung Nguyen times only long-grain rice was known, but by Dong Dau times short and sticky rices were grown as well.[50] Cultivation tools became more varied and also more specialized, even though some were still made of stone. The uses of cattle and buffalo for traction also led to many changes in economy and society.

In Phung Nguyen times, bronze was still rare. During Dong Dau times evidence for bronze casting occurs in many sites. By Dong Son times metalworkers had learned how to use lead to make alloys for more delicate tools and decoration. By this time, metalworking was probably produced in workshops controlled by elites. For example, at Co Loa near Hanoi a hoard of 10,000 bronze arrowheads was found as well as a bronze drum containing about 20 kilograms of broken bronze pieces and about 100 bronze ploughshares. The production of such a large quantity of tools and weapons could hardly be handled by an ordinary village workshop and would have required management by an elite authority of some kind.

Increased production facilitated trade. Weights made of stone and bronze have been found in many sites and the Qui Chu and Dong Son people placed in graves ornaments and semi-precious stones that may have served as exotic valuables. Dong Son bronze artefacts have been found beyond the Dong Son Culture area and such exchanges extended south to the Sa Huynh Culture area and north into southern China.

These economic changes profoundly affected the nature of early society in northern Vietnam and class divisions can now begin to be recognized within the burial system. Incipient distinctions between rich and poor can be seen in Phung Nguyen, Dong Dau and Go Mun burials, but are not as marked as in Dong Son times, when rich tombs with many high-value bronze artefacts occur alongside more numerous poor ones containing no or just a few pots. The development of class divisions led to social conflicts which can be recognized through the increasing numbers of weapons. These conflicts became more serious as an external threat emerged in the form of the Chinese Han Dynasty Empire.

PART III: ARCHAEOLOGICAL ASPECTS OF HAN DYNASTY RULE IN THE EARLY FIRST MILLENNIUM AD

Tong Trung Tin

Introduction – Chinese rule and resistance

In 170 BC, following the defeat of An Duong Vuong, the Au Lac kingdom progressively fell under various Chinese rulers and dynasties. In the old annals, this was referred to as the "Phase of Northern Domination", which lasted for approximately 1,000 years. The Chinese exercized a policy of tribute, taxation and assimilation. Nevertheless, the Viet people resisted absorption by China so that, with the weakening of the Tang Dynasty in the early tenth century, Khuc Hao, a local Viet chief, regained independence for the country.

Chinese rule spanned a long time from the Western Han Dynasty to the Sui-Tang Dynasties. In this section, we examine the results of archaeological research on the period around the turn of the Christian Era, a period that can be divided into three stages: Zhao, Western Han and Eastern Han.

Phase 1 – 179 BC to the beginning of the Christian era

According to the historical annals of both Vietnam and China, the Chinese Zhao dynasty from Guangdong ruled Au Lac via appointed governors from 179 to 111 BC.[51] Archaeological research shows that Dong Son cultural remains occur throughout Au Lac territory at this time, and no material remains distinctive of the Zhao polity itself have yet been discovered, despite the fact that the existence of cultural influence between Dong Son and southeast China is well established archaeologically. Therefore, the Zhao phase can really be considered a cultural continuation of the Dong Son phase in northern Vietnam.

In 111 BC, Han armies invaded northern Vietnam. In the early years, the Western Han administration maintained the same policy over Au Lac as the Zhao rulers. In 106 BC, Han rulers started to reorganize the prefectures and districts. Below the prefectural level, the traditional Dong Son Culture appears to have continued. However, due to stricter administrative control plus increasing immigration of Han people, indications of the Han Chinese presence now become archaeologically visible.

Thieu Duong in Thanh Hoa Province is a major Dong Son site in which 18 graves belonging to the phase of Han domination were discovered. Ten date to the late Western Han (*c.*50 BC to AD 1) and are larger in size than Dong Son graves, with their occupants lying face up or on their sides, with arms and legs extended. Artefacts in these Western Han tombs are typically Han, such as bronze mirrors, furnaces, square-mouthed vessels and Ngu Thu coins.[52] Closer links between Han and Viet cultures become evident during this phase. One of the Western Han tombs in Thieu Duong contained ceramics similar to Dong Son ones. On the other hand, a presumed Viet tomb of this phase had a wooden coffin that contained Han artefacts. The Xuan La coffin grave contained ear-shaped wooden cups (Plate 8) and Dai Tuyen Ngu Thap coins. The Doi Son coffin grave in Ha Nam Province contained Ban Lang (half-ounce) coins. The Minh Duc coffin in Ha Tay province contained square-stamped ceramics.[53]

Phase 2 – Eastern Han first–third centuries AD

Following its victory over Tan Mang, the Han Dynasty further tightened its policy of domination over the Viet people. The oppression even became fiercer after a local uprising led by the Trung sisters that was defeated in AD 43. At this time the Lac Tuong system of the Viet people was revoked, and direct Han rule imposed.

Nevertheless, continuing traces of late Dong Son Culture continued to exist from the first to the third centuries. Interaction between the Viet and Han cultures is shown by Han objects found in the Dong Son graves La Doi, Nghia Vu, Tu Lac, Chau Son and Yen Tu. But archaeological evidence of Eastern Han culture now becomes more common, as at Thieu Duong where eight early Eastern Han tombs of the first century AD have been found. These tombs are similar to those of the late Western Han phase, but the grave goods, such as bronze mirrors, models of barns and furnaces, Ngu Thu coins, vases and vessels, are of Eastern Han forms.

In the second and third centuries, elite Han (and possibly Han-Viet) graves made an appearance. Some were dug deep into the tops of hills, as at Thuy Nguyen in Hai Phong Province. Some, such as the Ngoc Lac tomb in Hai Duong Province, were constructed with wooden sarcophagi. Han-style brick tombs were constructed in many areas, for instance the Nghi Ve 1 tomb in Bac Ninh province (Figure 8.23) which contained 12 rooms. Besides Han graves, ceramic kilns of this phase have also been discovered at Tam Tho in Thanh Hoa Province.[54]

Figure 8.23 Eastern Han Period brick tomb, Mao Khe, Quang Ninh Province. (Photograph courtesy of A. Reinecke.)

The historical annals record that, after having defeated the Trung sisters in AD 43, Ma Yuan was ordered to construct citadels. Remains of one of these can still be seen at Luy Lau in Bac Ninh Province. Many scholars have considered this citadel to have been the prefectural and district capital in the Western Han period. However, recent excavations show that it was constructed in the second century AD.[55]

Sites and artefacts of this phase reflect continuing coexistence between a Viet culture containing remnants of the Dong Son tradition and the Han culture of China. Dong Son objects of this phase, such as a bronze drum from Thuy Nguyen, bronze basins and terracotta trays represent combinations of both Viet and Han style. Within the Eastern Han citadel of Luy Lau the remains of a bronze casting furnace and a casting mould for a Dong Son drum of Heger type I have been found.[56]

Thus, the increase of Han influence and control, combined with closer Viet–Han cultural exchanges despite the political domination, and the prolonged existence of the late Dong Son cultural tradition, are the distinguishing characteristics of Vietnamese culture in this period, before independence was finally regained in AD 905.

Notes

1 Ha Van Tan 1998.
2 Colani 1927, 1932.
3 Hoang Xuan Chinh, 1989.
4 Mansuy 1909.
5 Mansuy 1924; Mansuy and Colani 1925.
6 The earliest dates are 10295 ± 100 BP from Bo Lum Cave and 11000 ± 200 BP from Doi (Bat) Cave. The latest date is 7875 ± 100 BP, also from Bo Nam Cave.
7 Ha Huu Nga 1994.
8 Experience elsewhere suggests that many such items might just be part of the grave fill (eds).
9 Use of terms such as Australoid and Mongoloid is widespread in Southeast Asian palaeoanthropology, the suggestion being that cranial material resembles that from Australia and Melanesia on the one hand, and East Asia on the other. Although many modern anthropologists quibble about the use of such terms since they can imply (in insensitive hands) that human races are absolute and unvariable entities, the editors feel that the author is not using the terms in this fashion and simply wishes to refer to nodes in a field of considerable geographical variation. The terms are thus retained from the original manuscript (eds).
10 Do Van Ninh 1968: 57.
11 This name includes a large number of freshwater species belonging to the Thiaridae.
12 Given in the original manuscript as 14125 ± 180, 15560 ± 180, 12460 ± 60 and 14,300 ± 400 BP.
13 Patte 1932; Bui Vinh 1987: 15–31.
14 6095 ± 60 BP, 6390 ± 60 BP and 6430 ± 60 BP (Bln 3510/IV) at the Da But site. 4700 ± 50 BP at Go Trung.
15 Hoang Xuan Chinh 1966: 73–104.
16 4785 ± 100 BP at Quynh Van and 2010 ± 70 BP at Con Dat. (The latter date seems remarkably recent for an assemblage of such apparently archaic form – eds).
17 Nguyen Gia Doi 2000.
18 Called Baie des Pècheurs by Colani 1938.
19 Nguyen Khac Su 1997: 16–28.
20 Mansuy 1920; Bui Vinh and Nguyen Cuong 1997: 40–54.
21 Nguyen Van Cuong 2001.
22 Andersson 1939: 103.
23 Ha Huu Nga and Nguyen Van Hao 1998: 122.
24 Patte 1924: 521; Ha Van Tan 1983: 142; Le Dinh Phuc 1998; Pham Thi Ninh 2000.
25 3590 ± 80 years BP (Bln 2864) from Con Nen.
26 Although in linguistic terms the Austronesian-speaking southern Vietnamese of Sa Huynh times are likely to have originated in Island Southeast Asia (eds).
27 Nguyen Khac Su 1995: 7.
28 Nguyen Khac Su 2001.
29 Tran Quy Thinh 2001.
30 Ha Van Tan 1999: 384–6.
31 The implication here that all Vietnamese Neolithic cultures descend from the Hoabinhian is widely accepted in Vietnam itself, but to many foreign archaeologists (including one of the editors) such an inbred concept represents a most unlikely possibility (eds).
32 Goloubew 1929; Janse 1958.
33 Pham Ly Huong and Nguyen Quang Mien 2001.
34 Nguyen Th. Kim Dung 1983, 1986.
35 Hoang Xuan Chinh 1968.
36 Hoang Xuan Chinh and Nguyen Ngoc Bich 1978.
37 Nguyen Th. Kim Dung 1983.
38 There is one radiocarbon date from Ma Dong of 4145 ± 60 BP.
39 Ha Van Tan, Nguyen Xuan Manh, Bui Van Loi and Ngoc Toan 1985.
40 Pham Ly Huong and Nguyen Quang Mien 2001.

41 Pham Hong Phi, Nguyen Khac Tung and Hoang Xuan Chinh 1970.
42 Pham Ly Huong and Nguyen Quang Mien 2001.
43 Diep Dinh Hoa 1978.
44 Chu Van Tan 1976.
45 Guangdong Museum 1961; Xu Pin Ji, 1978, Wenwu No. 7: 16–21.
46 Sample HNK-27 from QCHIILII-3 3020 ± 80 BP, Sample HNK-28 from QCHILII-4 2810 ± 80 BP.
47 Trinh Sinh 1989.
48 Heger 1902.
49 AD 43 was a year of great significance at both ends of the Old World, being also the year of the Claudian conquest of Celtic Britain.
50 Dao The Tuan 1988.
51 Zhao Tuo ruled the Nanyue kingdom at Guangdong between 203–137 BC. His son Zhao Mo ruled 137–22 BC; a third king, Zhao Yingqi, 122–13 BC.
52 Le Trung 1966.
53 Bui Van Liem 2000.
54 Janse 1951. Vol. 2, pp. 231–46.
55 Ha Van Tan 2002; Archaeology of Vietnam, Vol. III: 36–41, Hanoi..
56 Nishimura Masarani and associates 2001.

Select Bibliography

Editors' note on the sources for the archaeology of Vietnam. The overwhelming bulk of research on Vietnamese archaeology since independence has been undertaken by local scholars and is published primarily in Vietnamese, and often in outlets difficult to access even for resident Vietnamese readers. However, we have listed a number of these publications below in the hope that they will be of value to scholars wishing to research in this area.

The most useful Vietnamese publication is the journal, *Khao Co Hoc* (Archaeology) which is published four times a year: following Chinese practice only the year and issue numbers are indicated. There is also *Nhung phat hien moi ce Khao Co Hoc Nam* (*New Discoveries in Vietnamese Archaeology*) which presents short reports presented at the annual conference of archaeologists each September in Hanoi. Publication is usually one or two years after each conference. Both these publications are issued from the Institute of Archaeology, 61 Phan Chu Trinh, Hanoi.

The National Museums of History in Hanoi also has a journal, *Thong bao Khoa Hoc cua Vien Bao Tang lich su Vietnam* (Science Publication of the Museum of History in Hanoi) and both this museum and that in Ho Chih Minh City publish occasional reports while the Institute of Archaeology in Hanoi and the Centre for Archaeology of the Institute for Social Sciences, Ho Chih Minh City publishes books and site reports from time to time. Some provincial museums and/or Departments of Culture also publish reports and short booklets from time to time, usually geared to a general audience and almost always in Vietnamese only, on sites and finds in their regions. Thus, as with recent archaeology in China, it is very difficult to keep up to date, and to know what is published where, let alone to acquire the occasional publications without going directly to the museums and offices which issue them.

Some publications in French or English which are not specifically cited by the authors of this chapter are listed at the end of these bibliographic references.

Andersson, J. G. (1939) "Archaeological research in the Fai Tsi Long Archipelago, Tonkin", *The Museum of Far Eastern Antiquities Bulletin*, 11, Stockholm.

Bui Van Liem (2000) "Dong Son graves with boat-coffin in Vietnam", Hanoi: Document of the National Institute of Archaeology (in Vietnamese).
Bui Vinh (1987) "Da But – the archaeological culture and its civilization" (in Vietnamese), *Khao Co Hoc* 3: 15–31.
Bui Vinh (1995) "Initial steps on determining area of distributions and characteristics of stone artifacts of the Ha Giang Culture" (in Vietnamese), *Khao Co Hoc* 3: 33–45.
Bui Vinh and Nguyen Cuong (1999) "Ma Pha Culture after the 1996 excavation in Lang Son" (in Vietnamese), *Khao Co Hoc* 2: 40–54.
Guangdong Musuem (1961) "The artifacts of neolithic in Eastern region of Guangdong province" (in Chinese), *Kaogu*, 12: 650–65.
Colani, M. (1927) "L'Age de la pièrre dans la province do Hoa Binh", *Mémoire de la Societé Géologique de l'Indochine*, XIII (1) Hanoi.
Colani, M. (1938) "Découvertes préhistoriques dans les parages de la Baie d'Along, Bulletin et Travaux", Institut indochinois pour l'ètude de l'Homme, Hanoi.
Chu Van Tan (1976) "Excavation of Tham Khuong" (in Vietnamese), *Khao Co Hoc* 17: 38–40.
Dao The Tuan (1988) "On carbonised grains discovered in Dong Dau (Vinh Phu) in 1984" in Vietnamese, *Khao Co Hoc* 4: 44–6.
Diep Dinh Hoa (1978) "On the metal artifacts from the beginning of the Bronze Age in Vietnam" (in Vietnamese), *Khao Co Hoc* 2: 10–20.
Do Van Ninh (1968) "Excavation at Soi Nhu Cave, Quang Ninh province" (in Vietnamese), *Historical Studies*, 117: 57–59.
Goloubew V. (1929) "L'age du bronze au Tonkin et dans le Nord Annam", *Bulletin de l'École Française d'Extrême-Orient* 29: 1–46.
Ha Huu Nga (1994) "*Bacson Culture and its position in the Neolithic of Vietnam*" (in Vietnamese), unpublished Ph.D. thesis, Institute of Archaeology, Hanoi.
Ha Huu Nga and Nguyen Van Hao (1998) *Prehistory of Ha Long* (in Vietnamese). Hanoi: World Publishing House.
Ha Van Tan (1983) "From Bau Tro site to Sa Huynh Culture" (in Vietnamese), *New Discoveries in Vietnamese Archaeology, 1982*, pp. 142–4.
Ha Van Tan (ed.) (1998) *Vietnamese Archaeology*, Volume I. *The Stone Age* (in Vietnamese), Hanoi: Social Sciences Publishing House.
Ha Van Tan (ed.) (1999) *Vietnamese Archaeology*, Volume II. *The Metal Age* (in Vietnamese), Hanoi: Social Sciences Publishing House.
Ha Van Tan (2002) *Archaeology of Vietnam*, Volume III. Hanoi: Social Sciences Publishing House, pp. 36–41.
Ha Van Tan, Bui Vinh and Vo Quy (1990) "Signs of a new archaeological culture in Ha Tuyen Province" (in Vietnamese), *Khao Co Hoc* 1–2: 34–8.
Ha Van Tan, Nguyen Xuan Manh, Bui Van Loi and Ngoc Toan (1985) "Excavations of Thanh Den site (Hanoi)" (in Vietnamese), *New Discoveries in Vietnamese Archaeology*, 1984: 93–5.
Heger, F. (1902) *Alte Metalltrommeln aus Südostasien*, Leipzig: von Hiersemann.
Hoang Xuan Chinh (1966) "The shell mound sites at Quynh Luu" (in Vietnamese), *Some archaeological materials of Vietnam*, Hanoi: Archaeology Group Publishing House, pp. 37–72.
Hoang Xuan Chinh (1968) *Report on the first excavation of Lung Hoa site* (in Vietnamese), Hanoi: Social Humanities Publishing House.
Hoang Xuan Chinh (ed.) (1989) *The Hoa Binh Cuture in Vietnam* (in Vietnamese), Hanoi: Social Sciences Publishing House.
Hoang Xuan Chinh and Nguyen Ngoc Bich (1978) *The Phung Nguyen archaeological site* (in Vietnamese) Hanoi: Social Humanities Publishing House.
Janse, O. R. T. (1947–51) *Archaeological Research in Indo-China*, (vols 1–2), Cambridge: Harvard-Yenching Institute and Harvard University Press.
Janse O. R. T. (1958) *Archaeological Research in Indo-China – The Ancient Dwelling site of Dong-s'on (Than-hoa, Annam)* vol. III, Institute Belge des Hautes, Bruges: St. Catherine's Press.
Le Dinh Phuc (1998) *Prehistory of Quang Binh* (in Vietnamese), Hanoi: Social Sciences Publishing House.
Le Trung (1966) "Graves of Han domination period in Thieu Duong", in *Some Reports on Vietnamese Archaeology*, (in Vietnamese), Hanoi:

Mansuy, H. (1909) "Gisement préhistorique de la caverne de Pho Binh Gia (Tonkin)", *L'Anthropologie* 20.

Mansuy, H. (1920) "L'industrie de la pierre polie et du bronze dans la région de Luang Prabang (Haut-Laos)". *Bulletin de la Service Géologique de l'Indochine* 7 (2).

Mansuy, H. (1924) "Stations préhistoriques dans les cavernes du massif calcaire de Bac son (Tonkin)", *Mémoire de la Société Géologique de l'Indochine* XI (2) Hanoi.

Mansuy, H. and Colani, M. (1925) "Néolithique inférieur (Bacsonnien) et néolithique supérieur dans le Haut-Tonkin (dermières recherches) avec la description des crânes du gisement de Lang Cuom", *Mémoire de la Société Géologique de l'Indochine* XII (3) Hanoi.

Nguyen Gia Doi (2001) "Mai Da Dieu site and some problems of the Stone Age in western Thanh Hoa province" (in Vietnamese), unpublished Ph.D. thesis, Institute of Archaeology, Hanoi.

Nguyen Khac Su (1984) "Characteristics, origin and transition of the Hoa Binh Culture" (in Vietnamese), *Khao Co Hoc* 1–2: 75–86.

Nguyen Khac Su (1986) "Cai Beo station and prehistory of Northeast seacoast of Vietnam" (in Vietnamese), *Khao Co Hoc* 2: 17–26.

Nguyen Khac Su (1992) "Some features of transitional period from Son Vi to Hoa Binh Culture" (in Vietnamese), *Khao Co Hoc* 2: 13–17.

Nguyen Khac Su (1995) "The Bien Ho culture in the Western Highland" (in Vietnamese), *Khao Co Hoc* 3: 7–16.

Nguyen Khac Su (1997) "Prehistoric maritime culture in Vietnam: a hypothetical model" (in Vietnamese), *Khao Co Hoc* 3: 16–28.

Nguyen Khac Su (2001) "Excavation at Lung Leng site" (in Vietnamese), *New Discoveries in Vietnamese Archaeology, 2001*.

Nguyen Khac Su, Trinh Nang Chung *et al.* (2000) *Prehistory of Ha Giang* (in Vietnamese), Ha Giang: Ha Giang Publishing House.

Nguyen Thi Kim Dung (1983) "Report on the second excavation of Bai Tu workshop site" (Tien Son, Ha Bac) (in Vietnamese), *New Discoveries in Vietnamese Archaeology 1983*: 79–80.

Nguyen Thi Kim Dung (1986) "Report on the second excavation of the Trang Kenh workshop site" Documents at the Institute of Archaeology, Hanoi.

Nguyen Trung Chien (1998) *The Quynh Van Culture* (in Vietnamese), Hanoi: Social Sciences Publishing House.

Nguyen Van Cuong (2001) "The Mai Pha Culture in Lang Son province" (in Vietnamese), unpublished Ph.D. thesis, Institute of Archaeology, Hanoi.

Nguyen Viet (1978) "First researches on pottery from the junction of the Ma and Chu rivers" (in Vietnamese), *Khao Co Hoc* 3: 43–63.

Nishimura Masarani (1998) "A casting mould for a bronze drum found inside the ancient citadel of Luy Lau", *Khao Co Hoc* 4: 99–100.

Pham Hong Phi, Nguyen Khac Tung and Hoang Xuan Chinh (1970) "Spectroscopic analysis of archaeological specimens from Dong Dau" *Khao Co Hoc* 7–8: 130–2.

Pham Ly Huong and Nguyen Quang Mien (2001) "The results of radiocarbon dating methods in Vietnam and some remarks", *Khao Co Hoc* 3: 80–101.

Pham Thi Ninh (1975) "Report on excavation of Bai Man Donh Linh, Dong Son, Thanh Hoa" (in Vietnamese), documents at the Institute of Archaeology, Hanoi.

Pham Thi Ninh (2000) *The Bau Tro Culture* (in Vietnamese), Hanoi: Social Sciences Publishing House.

Patte, E. (1924) "Le kjökkenmödding néolithique du Bau Tro, près de Dong-Hoi (Annam)", *Bulletin de l'École Française d'Extrême-Orient* XXIV 3–4: 521–61.

Patte, E. (1932) "Le Kjökkenmodding néolithique de Da-but et ses sépultures (province de Thanh Hoa, Indochine)", *Bulletin du Service Géologique de l'Indochine* XIX (3), Hanoi.

Praehistorica Asiae Orientalis (1932) "Premier Congrès des Préhistoriens d'Extrême-Orient, 1932", Hanoi: Imprimerie d'Extrême-Orient, pp. 3–15.

Tran Quy Thinh (2001) "The late Neolithic – early Bronze Age in the Western Highland", unpublished Ph.D. thesis, Institute of Archaeology, Hanoi.

Trinh Sinh (1989) "Lead bronze alloys, the Hung Kinh and Dong Son Culture", *Khao Co Hoc* 2: 43–50.

Xu Pin Ji (1978) Xu Pin Xi (1978) "Initial discussion on Shi Xie culture" (in Chinese), *Wen Wu* 7: 16–22.

Publications on Vietnamese archaeology in French, English and German relevant to this chapter but which are not specifically cited by the authors of this chapter are listed below.

Bezacier, L. (1972) *Le Vietnam – de la préhistoire à la fin de l'occupation Chinoise*, Paris: Picard.

Boriskovski, P. (1968–70) *Vietnam in Primeval Times* (trans. from Russian in *Soviet Anthrop. and Arch.* VII–VIII. Very outdated but interesting perspectives on early prehistoric research in northern Vietnam by the newly independent and Marxist-oriented researchers.

Glover, I. C. (1999) "Letting the past serve the present – some contemporary uses of archaeology in Vietnam", *Antiquity* 73 (281): 594–602.

Ha Van Tạn (1980) "Nouvelles recherches préhistoriques et protohistoriques au Vietnam", *Bulletin de l'École Française d'Extrême-Orient* 68: 113–54.

Ha Van Tan (1998) "Different lines of post-Hoabinhian cultural development in the stone age in Vietnam", *Vietnamese Social Sciences* 2: 24–41.

Higham, C. F. W. (1995) "Lingnam and Southeast Asia in prehistory", in C. T. Yeung, and W. L. Li (eds) *Archaeology in Southeast Asia*, Hong Kong: Hong Kong University Museum and Art Gallery, pp. 23–39.

Janse, O. R. T. (1947–58) *Archaeological Research in Indo-China*, 3 vols: Vols 1 and 2 devoted to historical archaeology, vol. 3 to excavations at the Dong Son site in Thanh Hoa Province. Cambridge: Harvard-Yenching Institute.

Le Xuan Diem and Vu Kin Loc (1996) *Artefacts of Champa*, Bilingual and well-illustrated 'catalogue' of a private collection of Sa Huynh Culture and Cham ornaments of gold and silver. Hanoi: Nha Xuat Ban Van Hoa Dan Toc.

Pham, Duc Manh (2000) "Some recent discoveries on the pre- and protohistory of southern Vietnam", in W. Lobo and S. Reimann (eds) *Southeast Asian Archaeology 1998*, Hull: Centre for South-East Asian Studies, University of Hull, pp. 139–48.

Pham Huy Thong, Pham Minh Huyen and Lai Van Toi (eds) (1990) *Dong Song Drums in Vietnam*, A well-illustrated catalogue of all early bronze drums known to that time. Many more have since been discovered, especially in central and southern Vietnam. Hanoi: Social Science Publishing House.

Reinecke. A. (1998) *Einführung in Archäologie Vietnams*, This is more of a Vietnamese-German guide to field methodology for students of Vietnamese archaeology than an overview of archaeological discoveries, but has some useful data, especially on research from the former DDR. Bonn: KAVA and Köln: Linden Soft.

9

THE COASTAL STATES OF CHAMPA

William A. Southworth

Introduction

Champa is a generic name used to describe a series of small coastal kingdoms that developed in central Vietnam during the first millennium AD. Initially based on separate river valley systems flowing from the central Truong Son mountains of Vietnam to the South China Sea in the east – and exploiting the narrow enclaves of cultivable land created by them – these kingdoms gradually became increasingly unified through a complex system of kinship and marital alliances to become a major power in the regional politics of Southeast Asia, particularly during the early second millennium AD (Figure 9.1). Such alliances were often motivated in response to external aggression, either from China or Dai Viet in the north, or from Cambodia in the west, but remained essentially unstable, being based on personal allegiance or kinship ties to a particular ruler or dynasty. Power therefore shifted from one part of the coastline to another in accordance with changes in political and economic advantage.

Although known for periodically disrupting maritime traffic in the South China Sea, the economy of the Champa states, beyond an agricultural and fishing base, was largely centred on the coastal trade with China and northern Vietnam. Champa was the closest source for many of the luxury goods imported by China such as ivory, rhinoceros horn and aromatic woods, while ports such as Hoi An and Nha Trang provided useful shelter and fresh water for ships travelling from Cambodia, the Malay Peninsula, South India, Persia and Oman. During long periods of the first millennium AD, the Champa states are the only recorded trading partners with China from Mainland Southeast Asia, and may well have been instrumental in the redistribution of Chinese goods throughout the mainland. Much of this trade in Chinese silk, iron, and later porcelain, may well have been taken overland, through the mountain passes linking the central coastline of modern Vietnam to the Mekong valley in Cambodia and Laos, and along the Mun and Chi rivers in Northeast Thailand.

The name "Champa" is ultimately derived from India; being the name of an early kingdom in the lower Ganges valley near modern Bhagalpur, and also the common name for the flowering tree *Michelia champaka*. Both plant and kingdom are mentioned in early Indian literature, notably in the epic poem the *Mahabharata*, and the name may well have been transported to Southeast Asia in this way. It was first used in inscriptions at My Son in Quang Nam province from the late sixth century AD. The adoption of Sanskrit and Indian Brahmi scripts; of Indian philosophic, astronomical and calendrical systems of

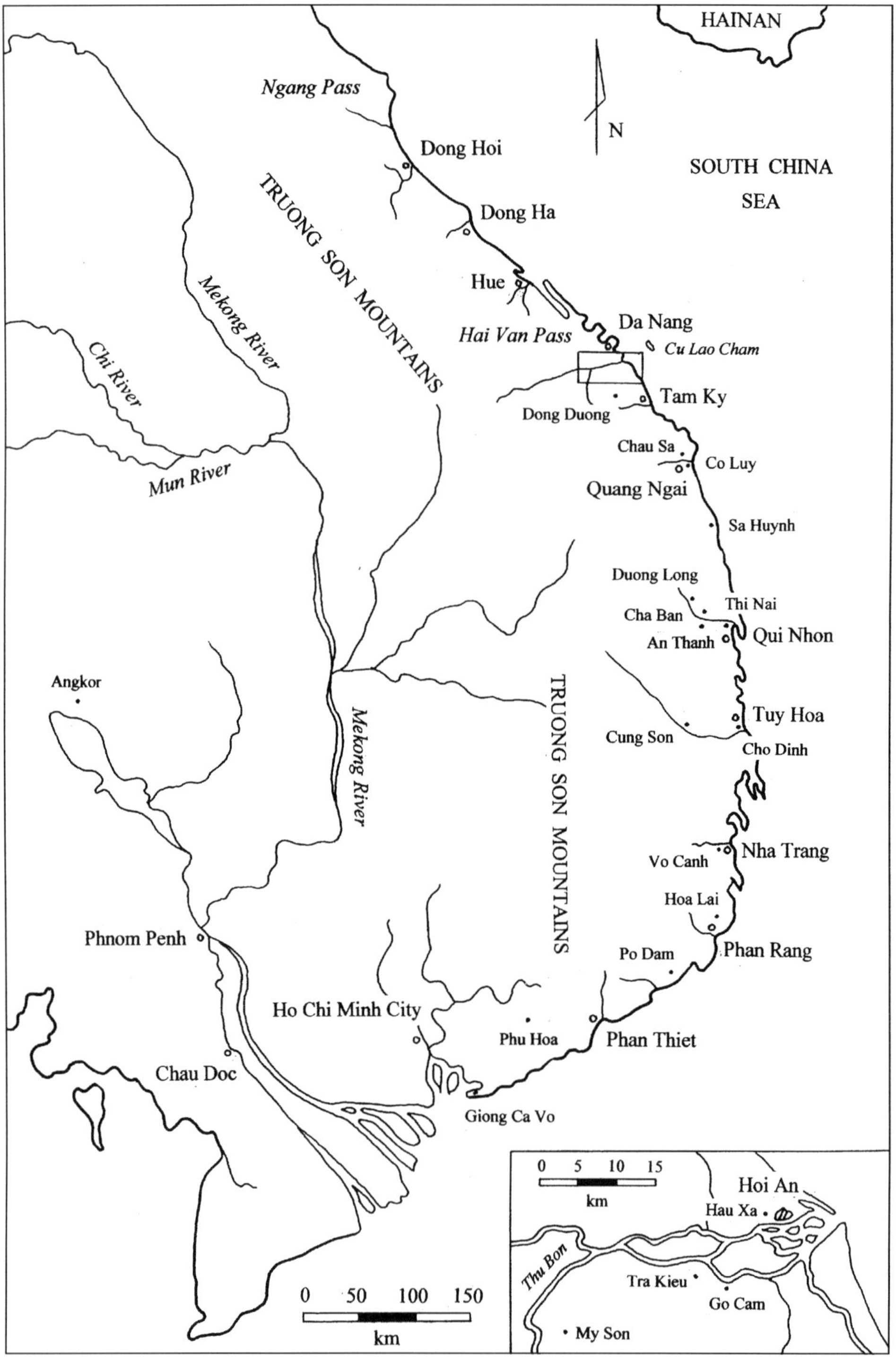

Figure 9.1 Sites of the Champa culture in modern Vietnam. (Map by W. Southworth.)

knowledge; of brick temple construction and of ideas concerning sacred and secular space; and the adoption of Indian religious iconography and concepts, all attest to the intellectual impact of Indian civilization during the first millennium AD.[1] These ideas, however, were absorbed and adapted into a pre-existing social and political environment, with both Hindu and Buddhist temples and monasteries being placed within a largely indigenous ritual landscape of sacred mountains, rivers and springs.

The early Champa culture has historically been associated with the Cham ethnic group, who belong to the Western Malayo-Polynesian branch of the Austronesian language family, a branch which also includes the native peoples of the Philippines, Borneo, Malaysia and most of the Indonesian archipelago, with whom cultural ties were maintained into the modern era. Scattered Cham communities still exist in south-central Vietnam – in particular around the cities of Phan Rang, Chau Doc and Ho Chi Minh City (Saigon). Related communities also survive in Cambodia – notably along the middle Mekong valley, and the Cambodian-Vietnamese border. Although now clustered in the southern part of Vietnam (most probably as the result of ethnic Vietnamese expansion and cultural assimilation from the north), the range of Cham-language inscriptions and the continuation of many Cham placenames suggest that ethnic Cham populations once existed much further north, even beyond the Hai Van Pass or "Pass of the Ocean Clouds".[2] At their fullest extent, however, the Champa states must also have included other Austronesian communities, including perhaps the Jarai and Rhade (E De), and a range of Mon-Khmer peoples who still inhabit the upland plateaux of the Truong Son range.

Much of our current knowledge of the early development of the Champa culture during the first millennium AD has been pieced together from a small number of Sanskrit and Cham-language inscriptions, and from incidental reports in the Chinese dynastic histories of this period. Archaeological research on Champa in general has been extremely limited. During the French colonial era, many of the most important temple sites were cleared and partly excavated: notably by Henri Parmentier and Charles Carpeaux at the Buddhist monastic site of Dong Duong in 1902, at My Son in 1903–4; and by Jean-Yves Claeys at Tra Kieu (Figure 9.2) and at Thap Mam near Cha Ban province in 1934. This research was dominated, however, by the study of brick temple architecture and sandstone sculpture, in common with the academic interests of the time. Only during the last decade have concerted efforts been made to study the ceramic and domestic material from these sites, with archaeological activity since 1990 being concentrated at the "citadel" or urban site of Tra Kieu. Much of the following discussion is based on this research.

Figure 9.2 Jean-Yves Claeys with Henri Parmentier and his daughter at Tra Kieu in 1927. (Photograph courtesy of the EFEO.)

The Sa Huynh Culture and early maritime trade

In recent years, archaeologists have sought to identify the origins of the early Champa states with the prehistoric Sa Huynh Culture, which appears to have occupied the south-central coast of Vietnam between about 500 BC and AD 100.[3] This culture is named after the coastal town of Sa Huynh in Quang Ngai province, where a sequence of jar burials was first reported by a French Customs official in 1909 and later described by Henri Parmentier.[4] Similar jar-burial sites have since been discovered along the whole central coastline, with large, thin-walled, earthenware jars being clustered together in areas of fine sand deposits (Figure 9.3), either on coastal sandbanks or on small tributaries to the major river systems. Grave goods found in association with the burial jars themselves also include low-fired earthenware cooking pots with a variety of impressed and incised decoration, bronze and iron artefacts, and earrings made of nephrite and occasionally glass.

Figure 9.3 Sa Huynh burial jars at Tam My, Quang Nam Province, central Vietnam. (Photograph by I. C. Glover.)

Two types of earrings are commonly found:

1 two-headed animal earrings (Figure 9.4), showing the profile of a deer-like animal with long curved horns, possibly representing *Pseudoryx nghetinhensis*, which was "discovered" in the Central Highlands as recently as 1992.[5]
2 a bulbous form of earring with three external protuberances commonly known as *lingling-o*, a name given to this type in the Philippines where they have occasionally been found and widely copied by local people.

Caches of bicephalous earrings have been found together with an unfinished example at Dai Lanh in Quang Nam province and with a preparatory nephrite block at Giong Ca Vo, southeast of Ho Chi Minh City, suggesting that the earrings were made in more than one locality. Single examples have also been found at quite a number of sites in central Vietnam; at Xuan An, a Dong Son Culture site in Nghe An Province, as well as at Ban Don Ta Phet and U Thong in central Thailand, on Palawan Island in the Philippines and Lan-yu Island, southeast of Taiwan.

Further evidence of overseas trade during the Sa Huynh Culture comes from the discovery of large quantities of glass and semi-precious carnelian and agate beads. Mineralogical analysis of the glass and study of the bead forms has shown that many of these were manufactured in India, or reproduced in Southeast Asia using Indian techniques and raw materials.[6] Evidence of early trade with China has also been revealed by the discovery of a Chinese sword with possible traces of silk at Phu Hoa, east of Ho

Chi Minh City; of Chinese coins from the reign of Wang Mang (AD 9–23) at Hau Xa, west of Hoi An in Quang Nam Province; of Han mirrors of the first century BC in Sa Huynh burial jars; and of Han Chinese sealings (Figures 9.5), roofing tiles and bronze arrowheads and personal ornaments at Go Cam near Tra Kieu.[7] These finds are a physical testimony to the growing importance of trade with China from the end of the second century BC onwards, and form a prelude to the political expansion of China in the first and second centuries AD.

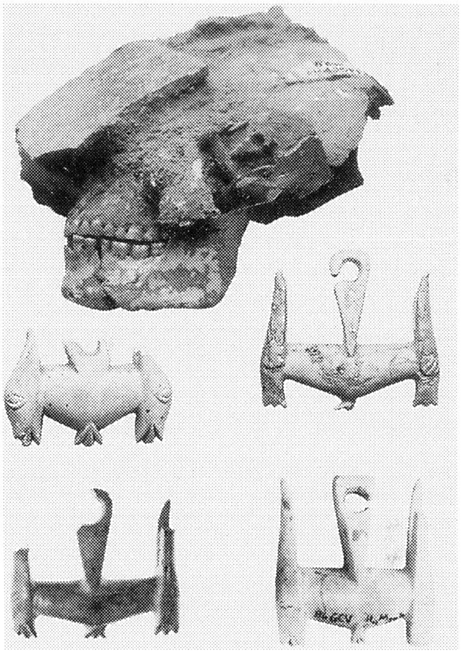

Figure 9.4 Two-headed animal earrings from Giong Ca Vo (Ho Chi Minh City), a site closely related to the Sa Huynh Culture in southern Vietnam. (Photograph courtesy of A. Reinecke.)

Rinan and Han China

The impact of Chinese military, economic and political power in the South China Sea can be dated from the southern campaigns of the first Emperor of China, Qin Shi Huangdi, against the Yue peoples in 221 BC. The Chinese name "Yue" (Viet) was a pejorative term for "outer barbarians" and was applied to many of the non-Chinese populations of the south. This military campaign gave the Qin Empire control of the southern Chinese coastline for the first time, including the strategic port of Nanhai (Canton/Guangzhou) on the Pearl River. Chinese control of this area, however, remained tenuous. Following the collapse of the Qin dynasty in 206 BC the governor of

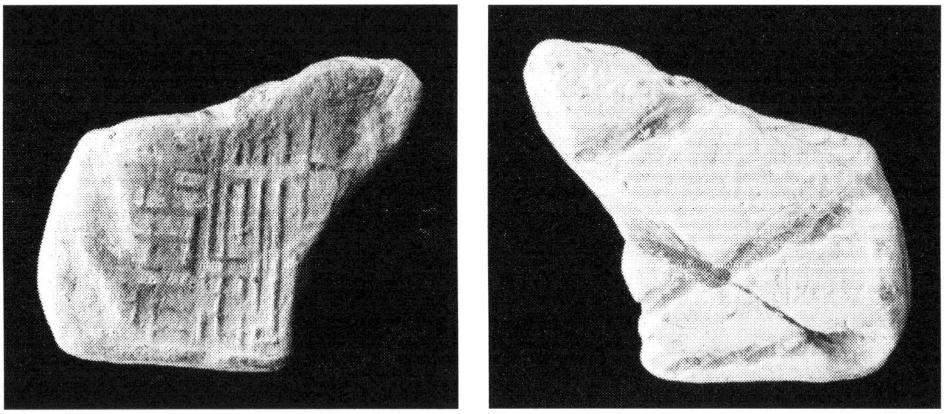

Figure 9.5 Han seal impression from Go Cam, Quang Nam Province. Left: The translation reads, "Seal of the Envoy of the Yellow God". Right: Impression showing marks of binding cords. (Photographs by I. C. Glover.)

Nan Hai blocked the mountain passes giving access to the north and declared himself as an independent sovereign of the new kingdom of Nanyue (Nam Viet). Although culturally close to China, Nanyue successfully resisted the political power of the early Han emperors, and even extended its authority into what is now northern Vietnam. When the kingdom finally fell to the Chinese emperor Han Wudi in 111 BC, this territory was officially incorporated into the Han Empire, and included the southernmost commanderies or "military provinces" of Jiaozhi (the Red River delta), Jiuzhen (the Ma, Chu and Ca rivers) and Rinan (the coastal area to the south of the Ngang pass, formerly known as the *Porte d'Annam*).

The commanderies established in northern and north-central Vietnam were not at first a direct imposition of Chinese dynastic control. Local leaders were given high status within the Han administration and probably ruled much as before, although now under the nominal approval of the Han Emperor and the governor at Nanhai. This was especially true of Rinan, which at this time was probably no more than a small series of coastal chiefdoms with trade agreements with northern Vietnam and southern China. The name Rinan means "south of the sun", denoting only that it lay south of the sun in the summer months.[8] The precise southern boundaries of Rinan are unknown, and almost certainly changed over time. A national census held in AD 2, however, recorded a total population for the commandery of 69,485 people from 15,460 households. Another record, from the same year, of an embassy from the kingdom of Huangzhi – with the gift of a live rhinoceros – is also the first recorded embassy to China of the South China Sea trade. Huangzhi has been located in eastern India, and an itinerary has survived describing the maritime voyage through Southeast Asia. Coastal ports outside Rinan would also have benefited from this maritime commerce, perhaps providing much of the rhinoceros horn, ivory and tortoiseshell associated with the Huangzhi merchandise.

Recent excavations at the site of Go Cam, near Tra Kieu in Quang Nam, have revealed a probable Han stoneware bowl, two fragments of Han seal impressions, Chinese-style crossbow bolts and various Han-style personal ornaments lying among cord-marked earthenware pottery similar to that found in late Sa Huynh burial contexts. Further pottery finds included a spread of over 27 ovoid jars (Plate 9), of a type found in the lowest levels of excavation at the citadel site of Tra Kieu. These thick-walled jars seem to have been used to store vegetable oils.[9] Covering these ceramic layers was a wider spread of broken ceramic tiles of a form typical of tile roof structures in southern China and northern Vietnam (Figure 9.6). These tiles were of two types: a wide, square-shaped tile with a slight curve, originally placed with the concave side upwards across the lateral roofing beams; and a narrower, half-cylindrical tile placed with the concave side downwards to cover the gaps between the square tiles below. Both types of tile had cord-marked impressions on the convex side, and traces of textile impressions on the reverse. These are typical Chinese, rather than Indian, forms. Excavations at Go Cam in 2001 also revealed the remains of a massive timber

Figure 9.6 Roofing tiles of Chinese design excavated at Go Cam in 2000. (Photograph by I. C. Glover.)

Figure 9.7 Remains of a large timber structure from the first or second century AD, excavated at Go Cam, 2001. (Photograph courtesy of Nguyen Kim Dung.)

structure, once raised on low piles with a tiled roof and wall-plastering at one end. This had been burnt allowing many timbers to survive remarkably well (Figure 9.7).

Fragments of later end- or eaves-tiles have also been found at several excavations at Tra Kieu and the Go Cam site.[10] These are circular tablets attached to one end of a half-cylindrical tile to decorate the edge or eaves of the roof. Some show simple stylized flowers, while other examples also display a wide variety of human, animal and demonic *kala* faces (Figure 9.8). Carbon-14 dates from excavations at several locations within the ancient walled city at Tra Kieu suggest that occupation started there in the late centuries BC and continued through the early first millennium AD.

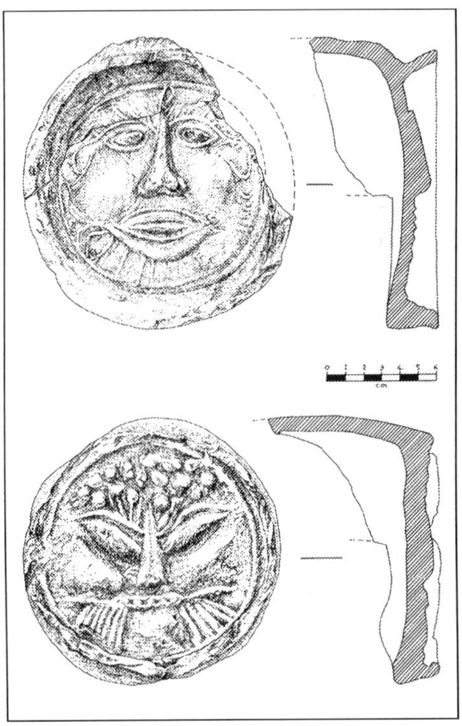

Figure 9.8 Face tiles from the 1993 excavations at Buu Chau Hill, Tra Kieu. (Drawings by William Southworth.)

After the Wang Mang interregnum of AD 9–23 – during which northern Vietnam maintained a largely independent, self-regulating administration – the Han dynasty attempted to reassert its authority. The celebrated revolt of the Trung sisters was largely a reaction to this imposition of direct Chinese rule, and was brutally suppressed by the punitive invasion of the Han general Ma Yuan in AD 43. The southernmost Chinese commandery of Rinan was not involved in these disturbances and was only tentatively under Han control. Chinese prefects appointed to the province were initially tolerant of native customs, and were intended to supervise the trade with China. Attempts to impose a direct system of taxation however led to a major rebellion in AD 100, with further attacks from outside the province occurring in AD 136. Both disturbances were centred on the southernmost district of Xianglin or "elephant forest", possibly located in Quang Nam, or in the region of modern Hue according to others.[11] A second major rebellion occured in AD 144, and in 192 the district magistrate of Xianglin was assassinated by Ou Lian (Au Lien), the son of a district official; an event which led to the establishment of an independent polity known to the Chinese as Linyi (Lam Ap).

The political and cultural transitions of the late second and early third centuries AD can also be recognised in the archaeological assemblages. In excavations conducted at Tra Kieu since 1990, the earliest cultural layer of ovoid jars and cord-stamped earthenware is replaced by a more complex ceramic tradition: comprising flat-based jars with a range of geometric, stamped designs, including lozenge and fishbone patterns – comparable to similar vessels in southern China and northern Vietnam; ring-footed cups of a coarse, highly tempered clay; and dark-coloured, thin-walled, cooking pots – striated at the top and cross-hatched at the base[12] (Figure 9.9). Although partly based on Chinese forms and decorative designs, these ceramics were made from local clay sources and were probably manufactured using traditional techniques of open-fired earthenware production. Changes in roof tile design have also been recorded, with the convex surface of each tile being marked by diagonal striations, and the concave surface left smooth. Tile roofs of this kind would have been extremely heavy and excavations in the Hoan Chau area of Tra Kieu since 1997 have revealed a series of sunken pebble, brick and stone bases used to reinforce the foundations of a series of wooden, columned halls (Figure 9.10).[13]

The Han administration in central Vietnam was therefore strictly limited in duration, in the degree of its control and in its geographic extent. The commandery of Rinan comprised only the most northern section of the present central coastline of Vietnam, and is unlikely to have extended its authority beyond the southern boundary of the Hai Van pass, although some Han involvement in the present-day province of Quang Nam seems probable from recent archaeological evidence. However, the economic and cultural impact of Chinese trade was far-reaching. For the next millennium, this trade provided the main economic basis for political development and expansion in the region. The early states along the central coast of Vietnam were founded on existing social structures, strongly influenced by Indian religious and political ideology, but remained economically dependent on trade with China through the exportation of natural, forest resources and through the establishment of port entrepôts specializing in the transfer of inter-regional trade to the commercial centres of southern China and northern Vietnam.

Linyi: and the early Coastal States

After the final collapse of the Han dynasty in AD 220, China was divided into three kingdoms; northern Vietnam and the south coast of China being ruled by the Wu dynasty, with its capital at Jiangning in the lower Yangzi valley. During the Wu governorship of Lü Dai in northern Vietnam, between AD 220 and 230, an embassy was sent to the south for the encouragement of trade, and three kingdoms sent tribute in return: Linyi, Funan and Tangming. This is the earliest historical reference to individual kingdoms or states in Southeast Asia, with Linyi being located on the north-central coast of Vietnam and Funan

Figure 9.9 The main forms of pottery excavated at Tra Kieu. (Drawings compiled by R. Prior, various scales):
A: Ovoid jar (drawn by M. Yamagata); B: Pedestal cup (drawn by M. Yamagata); C: Flat based stamped jar (drawn by M. Yamagata); D: Kendi from TK90 (after Nguyen Chieu *et al.* 1991: 22); E: Cooking pot from TK90 (after Nguyen Chieu and Lam My Dung 1991).

in southwest Cambodia. Tangming has yet to be identified. The name Linyi means "Forest City" – or alternatively the "City" of "Lin" – and the kingdom was almost certainly based on the former Han prefecture of Xianglin. It is important to remember, however, that the loss of this district was never formally recognized by the dynastic successors of the Han, and the northern parts of Rinan remained at least nominally under Chinese control. In AD 248 an army from Linyi invaded Rinan and attacked the Wu commanderies to the north, setting a pattern of conflict that was to recur over the next 200 years.

During the mid-third century AD, Linyi and Funan appear to have coordinated both their military and diplomatic relations with China. In AD 268, after rebellions in the Wu

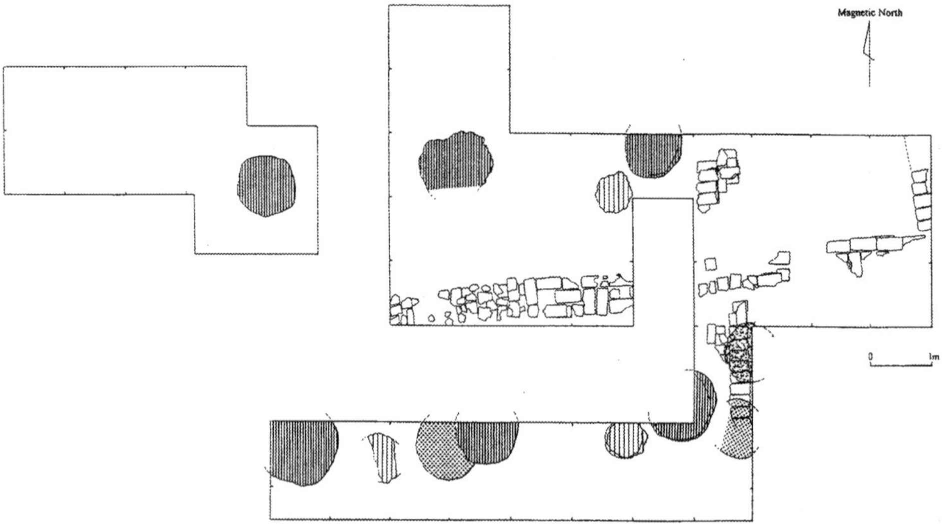

Figure 9.10 Plan of a columned hall at Hoan Chau, Tra Kieu excavated between 1997 and 2000. (Drawing by M. Yamagata.)

provinces of northern Vietnam, both kingdoms sent embassies to the northern Jin dynasty at Luoyang. In the decade that followed the re-establishment of its control in Vietnam in 271, the southern borders of the Wu kingdom were continually harrassed by raids led by Fan Xiong (Pham Hung) the ruler of Linyi, in concert with Fan Xun, the King of Funan. In a report presented to the Jin court after its annexation of Wu in 280, it is stated that: "he [the King of Linyi] is in contact to the south with [the King of] Funan. Their tribes are numerous; their allied troops aid each other. Taking advantage of the ruggedness of their region, they do not submit [to China]".[14]

The acceptance by the Jin emperor of the actual territorial loss of all but the most northern district of the former Han commandery of Rinan led to major changes in the provincial structure of northern Vietnam and heralded a short period of burgeoning international trade. Linyi sent an embassy in late AD 284 or early 285, together with envoys from Daqin, equated with the eastern Roman empire,[15] and in the summer of 285, ten kingdoms including Funan sent envoys to the Jin court from the south. Although only Linyi and Funan are mentioned by name in these reports, it is clear that the political geography of central Vietnam was far more complex than the simple interaction of two major trading powers. Smaller kingdoms and states clearly coexisted alongside them; a further 21 kingdoms from the south, including Funan, sent embassies in 286.

The names of some of these states have survived in later histories and encyclopedias. Foremost among them is the kingdom of Xitu, which was located directly to the south of Xianglin/Linyi, and beyond the former boundaries of Han Rinan. This kingdom was said to have ten smaller kingdoms nearby, all of which were dependencies of Xitu. A second kingdom further south is named Quduqian, and is said to have maintained maritime contact with a gold-bearing island to the east, possibly in the Philippines.[16] These kingdoms are evidence of a series of small trading states that existed separately, and acted largely independently, from the political and military powers of Linyi and Funan, but were nevertheless able to prosper under the liberal trade policy of the early Jin dynasty. The kingdom of Xitu may perhaps be located in modern Quang Nam province, while that of Quduqian may be identified with the port of Nha Trang in Khanh Hoa.

The importance of Nha Trang as an early port and market centre is testified by the discovery in 1885 of the Vo Canh inscription, first reported in fields some five kilometres to the west, upriver from the modern town (Plate 10). This inscription (now in the National Museum of History, Hanoi) has been dated variously from the late first to the early fifth centuries AD, based on palaeographic comparison with scripts found in different parts of the Indian subcontinent. Although no exact identification can be made, the most likely palaeographic source for the inscription is the script of the Ikshvaku dynasty at Nagarjunakonda, dated to the second half of the third century AD.[17] The Ikshvaku dynasty controlled the Krishna and Godavari deltas of modern Andhra Pradesh and appears to have maintained regular trade contact with Southeast Asia. The Vo Canh inscription is written in Sanskrit with several passages of verse and is undoubtedly the oldest Sanskrit text of any length to have been discovered in Southeast Asia. It is inscribed on three sides of an irregular stele standing over 2.5 metres in height, but natural erosion has obscured much of the text. The surviving passages appear to describe a donation of wealth made by "the joy of the family of the daughter of the grandson of the king Shri Mara" to give equality to his sons, brothers and male descendants. This may suggest a matrilineal system, where the king's wealth would normally have been inherited by his daughters and his wife's matrilineage. The theological terms applied in the text are probably Hindu in inspiration, but belong to a pre-Puranic tradition.

Evidence of the cultural impact of trade contacts with China can also be witnessed in the Thu Bon valley of Quang Nam, where excavation has demonstrated the rapid adoption of square-stamped earthenware jars (Figure 9.9), in imitation of similar Chinese wares.[18] These appear together with smooth-walled *kendis* or spouted jars of a form used in the Oc Eo culture of the Mekong Delta, originally derived from India. A group of two *kendis* and four bowls discovered in 1996 within a single domestic or firing context at the Go Du De site at Tra Kieu (Figure 9.11) has been dated from charcoal samples to around the third century AD.[19] A further innovation of this period is the use of end or eaves tiles showing faces with human, animal or demonic features.[20] Many of these were uncovered during excavation at Tra Kieu in 1993, and display a variety of sizes and designs. The earliest tile, found in the lowest level of excavation, featured a composition of three faces combined and may date to the first or second century AD. Two virtually identical tiles were found almost intact, in layers probably dating to the third century AD. These tiles featured a recognizably human face in which the nose and eyebrows had been moulded in the form of a tree with spreading branches (Figure 9.8). The discovery of a third fragment, showing only the nose and eyes, indicated that these pieces had been made using a single wooden or baked clay mould, the only differentiation being caused by the depth

Figure 9.11 Kendis and bowls *in situ* at the Go Du De location, Tra Kieu, 1996. (Photograph by I. C. Glover.)

of impression and the gradual build-up of clay within the mould cavities. Similar, although not identical, tiles have also been found at Co Luy near Chau Sa in Quang Ngai, and demonstrate that this architectural form was not limited to Quang Nam alone. These face tiles are in fact the earliest evidence we have for a figurative artistic tradition in central Vietnam.

In direct contrast to the active trade of the late third century AD, the fourth century appears to have been a disastrous period in the maritime commerce of the South China Sea. High tolls and corruption destroyed trade confidence in the ports of southern China and Linyi became essentially a pirate state, attacking the southern borders of the Jin empire and raiding the coastline of northern Vietnam. Among the main figures of this era was the king Fan Wen (Pham Van). Wen is said to have been born in China, and to have travelled as a merchant adventurer before entering the service of King Fan Yi of Linyi at some time between AD 321 and 326. Wen is accredited with the introduction of many aspects of Chinese civilization to the court of Linyi, including the construction of defensive walls and ditches, the design of palace buildings, the manufacture of weapons and armour and the use of Chinese musical instruments. After succeeding Fan Yi in 336, Fan Wen sent an embassy to the Jin court with a gift of trained elephants and a letter written entirely in "barbarian" characters – a probable reference to the use of an Indian *brahmi* script. His territorial claims were rejected, however, and after a series of military campaigns against China, Fan Wen was defeated and died in 349. Further military incursions by Wen's successors, Fan Fo and Fan Huda, succeeded only in destabilizing the political and economic life of the region and also ended in disaster; Fan Huda being defeated in a major naval battle in AD 420.

The political structure of Linyi at this period was probably based around a loose confederation of coastal states, each maintaining trade and kinship ties with neighbouring centres and the villages and mountain tribes of the interior. While acknowledging the diplomatic and commercial pre-eminence of a particular political centre or lineage, these coastal states were largely self-regulating. It is doubtful whether the Kings of Linyi had any real or lasting control over extensive territory, or over the maritime raids and military incursions conducted by their associates on the southern Chinese border. Continued raids during the reign of Fan Yang Mai (whose name may be a transcription of the Cham title *Yang Mah* or "Golden Prince") prompted a major land invasion of Linyi by the Chinese general Tan Hezhi in AD 446.

A description of Linyi from this period was compiled in a lost book called the *Linyi ji* or "Notes on Linyi", and was later quoted with other sources in chapter 36 of the *Shuijing zhu* or "Commentary on the Water Classic". This account describes two citadels or fortified cities: the citadel of Qusu near the border with China, and the city of Linyi itself. Qusu is described as being situated between two rivers, to the north and south, and having a rectangular system of walls with a perimeter of about two kilometres.[21] These walls consisted of a packed-earth base rising some 7 metres in height, surmounted by a sheer brick wall of 3 metres and by wooden structures or palisades of up to five tiers in height. Thirteen gates gave access to the interior where, according to the text, 2,100 houses were located, with further houses and markets spreading outside the perimeter walls. This fortress was captured by Tan Hezhi at the start of the campaign in AD 446, and all the inhabitants over the age of 15 were put to death.

The capital of Linyi itself is described in similar fashion, with a rectangular surrounding wall measuring up to 4 kilometres in circumference. It was oriented east–west, with a river flowing to the north, and had four gates piercing the walls – the principal gate located on the eastern side. This form of rectangular citadel enclosure, with one lateral side placed on the banks of a river for communication and defence, has been discovered at the site of Thanh Loi, near Hue, on the south bank of the Huong or "Perfume" River, and at Tra Kieu in Quang Nam, on a branch of the Thu Bon. Further examples of this plan can also be seen further south at the "old citadel" of Chau Sa in Quang Ngai, and at the citadels of An Thanh and Thi Nai in Binh Dinh. They may be considered a distinct type of defensive urban enclosure, characteristic of the coastal Champa states during the first and early second millennia AD. The precise location of the capital of Linyi at this period remains unknown, but the literary evidence suggests a settlement somewhere in the region of Hue. Descriptions of the city interior from the *Shuijingzhu* were probably added later,[22] but tell of 50 separate quarters, including eight temples and pagodas, a brick or tiled palace and densely packed housing. The city was captured in 446, and over 100,000 pounds of gold was reputed to have been taken back to China from the looted temples and treasury.

Bhadravarman and the Thu Bon valley

The Chinese punitive expedition of AD 446 seems to have marked a significant change in the political and economic development of the region. The kingdom of Linyi had been created from the former Han commandery of Rinan and appears to have inherited both its export trade and its pattern of border conflict with the Chinese-controlled territories to the north. Its geographical area was probably limited to the narrow stretch of coastline between the Ngang and Hai Van passes. After the destruction of 446, however, this focus changed, with economic and political power shifting further to the south, in particular to the Thu Bon valley of modern Quang Nam. Archaeological excavations at Tra Kieu, Hau Xa and Go Cam have demonstrated that this region was an active participant in the early South China Sea trade from at least the early centuries of the Christian Era and was clearly an important commercial and political area in its own right. In the fifth century, this significance was enhanced by three factors; firstly, a revival of the long-distance maritime trade between the Indian subcontinent (in particular Sri Lanka) and China, in particular from AD 420; second, by China's reversal from a gold-exporting to a gold-importing economy in the mid-fifth century, which gave an added importance to Quang Nam's alluvial gold resources; and above all by the expansion of Guangzhou near modern Hong Kong as China's main commercial port in the south. This expansion highlighted the Thu Bon valley's natural position as a port of call, following the NE–SW trade winds, for ships travelling to and from Guangzhou via eastern Hainan.

The commercial importance of the Thu Bon valley at this time is shown by the inscriptions of King Bhadravarman. A long stele inscription issued by this king was discovered in 1901 at the site of My Son, a religious sanctuary enclosed within a ring of foothills on the edge of the Troung Son mountains, upriver from Tra Kieu and some 25 kilometres from the coast of Quang Nam. It is written in Sanskrit and describes the foundation of a temple to the deity Bhadreshvara, an epithet of Shiva meaning "radiant" or "brilliant". The inscription also honours Shiva as Maheshvara or the "Great Lord" and is clearly *Puranic* in inspiration; the names of Vishnu, Brahma and Uma are also mentioned for the first time. Two rock inscriptions have also been reported from the banks of the Ba Ren River, a branch of the Thu Bon, some 8 kilometres northeast of My Son. These recall the boundaries of land dedicated to the temple of Bhadreshvara, delimited, according to the cardinal directions, by three sacred mountains and the river itself. The immediate landscape and environment, combining the natural features of mountains, rivers and springs, had a primary, sacred significance in Cham religion and thought.[23]

Two further inscriptions have also been attributed to Bhadravarman. The first, a rock-cut inscription discovered in 1885 at Cho Dinh near Tuy Hoa, some 500 kilometres to the south, records a sacrifice or foundation to the god Bhadreshvara, for the benefit of the sons and grandsons of King Bhadravarman. This inscription suggests that Bhadravarman's influence was extensive, but it is unlikely that he retained any direct control over territory so far to the south. These inscriptions have been palaeographically attributed to the fourth or fifth century AD, but attempts to identify Bhadravarman with particular kings of Linyi have proved unsuccessful and his name is not mentioned in later genealogies of the kings of Champa. The script is close to that used by the Vakatakas of the Indian Deccan and it is probable that his reign can in fact be dated to the late fifth or early sixth century. This would make him a contemporary of the king Kaundinya Jayavarman of Funan, who sent an official complaint to China in 484 concerning the actions of a usurper king of Linyi.[24] However, there remains a fundamental disagreement between the Chinese dynastic histories of this period regarding the names and chronology of the kings of Linyi during the fifth century, and it is probable that Bhadravarman was ruling in the Thu Bon valley independently of the traditional royal lineage of Linyi to the north. These two regions were only unified during the campaigns of the King Rudravarman, who sent an embassy to the southern Chinese court in AD 529 or 530, and is the first king to be unequivocally identified from both the Chinese sources and later Sanskrit epigraphy. The second inscription, found in 1936 at Dong Yen Chau, northwest of Tra Kieu, may in fact belong to the early sixth century. It refers to a *nagaraja* or "king of the nagas", perhaps the protective deity of a nearby spring. Although it uses many Sanskrit loan words, this inscription is written in the Cham language and has been considered the earliest text in any Austronesian language.

Figure 9.12 Stone sculpture of a male figure from Phu Ninh, now in the Museum of Cham Sculpture, Da Nang. (W. Southworth.)

Little is known about the sixth century AD in this region, either from historical sources or from archaeology, but it is probable that the earliest sandstone sculpture dates from this period. A series of four sandstone busts were discovered in the 1930s in a river-bank at Phu Ninh near Tam Ky in southern Quang Nam. They are carved in high relief and depict the head and shoulders of a male figure, with heavy curls of hair falling down to the shoulders. Two are now displayed at the Museum of Vietnamese History in Hanoi, and a third at the Museum of Cham Sculpture, Da Nang (Figure 9.12). The subject and purpose of these sculptures is unknown, but the slight downwards angle of each composition suggests that they were originally placed within a raised niche on the outside of a brick temple, or above a doorway. A similar sandstone image was discovered at Hau Xa near Hoi An in 1985, and a further head and bust in terracotta were found at Cung Son in Phu Yen in 1937. In a clear development from these early busts, a full-figure, sandstone relief sculpture was also excavated by Jean-Yves Claeys at Tra Kieu in 1927. It shows a seated male figure with legs crossed at the ankles, and arms spread wide with hands placed on the hips (Figure 9.13). None of these sculptures shows any clear iconographic features, but a second full-figure relief sculpture, formerly housed in the main shrine of the temple of Po Nagar at Nha Trang, and now displayed in the Khanh Hoa Museum, may have had an overarching *naga* hood or multiple-headed cobra, suggesting a *nagaraja* or nature spirit.

Figure 9.13 Stone relief carving of a seated male figure from Tra Kieu, 1927, now in the Museum of Cham Sculpture, Da Nang. (W. Southworth.)

No inscriptions of King Rudravarman have yet been found, but a Sanskrit stele of his son Shambhuvarman has been discovered at My Son. This inscription describes the reconstruction of the temple of Bhadreshvara, which had been destroyed during the reign of his father, under the name of *Shambhubhadreshvara. Shambhu* means "granting welfare" or "well being", and is, like *Bhadra*, an epithet of Shiva. These qualities of the god were almost certainly combined in the worship of a *Shivalinga*, the aniconic, phallic representation of Shiva, housed in a brick shrine on the site of the later remains of My Son A1. The progressive reconstruction and rededication of temples was common practice among the Champa states and makes the dating of surviving temple structures particularly difficult. The inscription of Shambhuvarman also includes the name Champa for the first time, in the form *Champadesha*. The Sanskrit word *desha* has a general meaning of "place" or "country", and is used here in regard to the lands originally prescribed by Bhadravarman for the upkeep of the temple. It is uncertain whether Champa had a wider political meaning and significance at this date, or was being used in a purely local, religious context. The inscription also contains three dates recorded in the *Shaka* era (an Indian solar calendar, calculated from approximately AD 78), but these have become partly effaced. The script is in Pallava Grantha, named after a contemporary Indian dynasty in Tamil Nadu, and the stele can probably be dated to the late sixth century AD. Two trade embassies sent from Linyi to China in 568 and 572 were probably from Shambhuvarman, although the name of the king is not given.

In AD 589 China was reunified under the Sui dynasty, and after suppressing a rebellion in northern Vietnam a Sui army was sent south against Linyi in 605. This expedition seems to have been motivated essentially by plunder, and in the hope of repeating the success of AD 446. An army under the Sui general Liu Fang again captured a citadel called Qusu (probably an urban enclosure northwest of Hue) and after a further eight days' march arrived at the "capital" of Linyi, located almost certainly at Tra Kieu. The

King of Linyi, however, had already escaped by boat; the palace was deserted and the treasury and ritual vessels had all been removed. Only the royal archives and library were found intact, but included 18 gold tablets attributed to the former kings of Linyi and 1,350 Buddhist texts in the Kunlun (Austronesian) language, which were taken back to China.[25] This account suggests that Buddhism may have played an important role in sixth-century and early seventh-century Champa, but was disseminated through Cham-language texts in palm-leaf or other perishable materials rather than by Sanskrit inscriptions in stone. The king of Linyi at the time of the 605 expedition is usually identified with Shambhuvarman, but was more probably his son, Kandarpadharma.

Prakashadharma and the early Tang trade

During the mid-seventh century, a major dynastic crisis occurred. The son and successor of Kandarpadharma – named Prabhasadharma – appears to have died without male heirs and was succeeded by his nephew Bhadreshvaravarman. This king was assassinated, however, by his chief minister in 645, along with all the male members of his family. These events are recounted in both the *Jiu Tang shu* or "History of the Early Tang dynasty" and in inscription C.96 at My Son ordered by King Prakashadharma Vikrantavarman in AD 657. Prakashadharma's father, a nephew of Kandarpadharma, had fled from Champa to Cambodia and had married the daughter of the Khmer king Ishanavarman I. Returning to Champa, their son Prakashadharma was then married to the surviving daughter of Prabhasadharma, thus reuniting the dynasty. This lineage, although ostensibly a list of kings, nevertheless emphasizes the importance of women to the succession – either through the mother or through marriage. Prakashadharma's inscriptions at My Son describe the foundation of two new sanctuaries in honour of Ishaneshvara and Prabhaseshvara. These continue the Shaivite dedication of the site ("Ishana" and "Prabhasa" are both epithets of Shiva), but were also built in honour of Ishanavarman and Prabhasadharma, the fathers of his mother and wife respectively. The inscriptions of Prakashadharma outside My Son are largely Vaishnavite in dedication, and honour Vishnu as Purusha, the primordial "Man" and supreme sentient being. A stele found at Tra Kieu in 1927 also describes the restoration of a temple to Valmiki, the author of the great Indian epic poem, the *Ramayana*. An elaborate sandstone pedestal, showing scenes from the marriage of Rama and Sita[26] may have formed part of this shrine, although its precise date remains uncertain.

The temple constructed by Prakashadharma at My Son for the worship of Shiva as Prabhaseshvara can probably be identified with the ruins of what is now designated My Son E1. This building must originally have consisted of a small, almost square, brick shrine; oriented to the west and raised on a rectangular brick base roughly 2 metres in height. Only the low foundation walls now remain and the original profile of the building is now uncertain. Although two cylindrical sandstone columns found *in situ* on either side of the doorway suggest architectural ties to Cambodia, the overall appearance of the shrine was probably closer to that of the early stone structures of Gedong Songo and the Dieng plateau in Java. When My Son E1 was excavated in 1903, a sculptured pediment and elaborate pedestal base were found. In contrast to the brick temples of pre-Angkorian Cambodia, which use a stone lintel above the doorway as the main surface for relief sculpture, those of Champa have no decorative lintel at all, but use a stone pediment to illustrate mythological or devotional themes. The pediment of My

Son E1 (Figure 9.14) shows the myth of *Vishnu Anantashayin*, in which Vishnu lies asleep on the serpent Ananta or Shesha amid the primordial ocean. As he dreams of the universe, the god Brahma emerges on a lotus flower from his navel to transform it into reality. This story was evidently popular in seventh-century Champa, and is also represented on Khmer lintels from the same period.

Figure 9.14 Sculptured pediment from My Son E1, now in the Museum of Cham Sculpture, Da Nang. (W. Southworth.)

Figure 9.15 Detail of the flautist on the My Son E1 pedestal, now in the Museum of Cham Sculpture, Da Nang. (W. Southworth.)

Also found at My Son E1 was an elaborate, square pedestal measuring 2.7 metres on each side and constructed from 16 individual blocks of sandstone (two of which have not been found). The sides of this pedestal are elaborately carved with scenes showing *rishi* or hermits, depicted in attitudes of teaching, blessing or repose. On the main, west side, are two large figures playing a flute (Figure 9.15) and a harp-like instrument), and on either side of the central stairwell are figures holding a stringed instrument and a book. These last may represent the Shaivite saints Appar and Sambandar, who popularized the worship of Shaivism in southern India during the seventh century AD, in particular through the composition of music and poetry. The pedestal may have been placed in the shrine during the early eighth century, during the subsequent reign of Vikrantavarman II. Although many of the decorative floral designs that appear on the columns, pediment and pedestal from My Son E1 can be compared to similar patterns seen in Cambodia, Thailand and Java, the long sculptural development of the pediment and pedestal in Champa represents a highly distinctive form of cultural and religious expression. In addition to stone-relief carving, freestanding sandstone statues have also been found from this period. The most popular figure is that of Ganesha or Ganapati, the elephant-headed son of Shiva, who was revered as the remover of obstacles and promoter of wealth.

The economy of Champa from *c.* AD 650 to 750 was largely based on trade with early Tang China, for which Quang Nam was ideally situated. At least 20 trade embassies are recorded from Linyi during this period – the most from any Southeast Asian country. Linyi supplied the Tang empire with many of its luxury goods.[27] In exchange, silk and other manufactured goods were sent sent from China, some being traded overland to Cambodia, Laos and Thailand. The Champa of Prakashadharma and Vikrantavarman II was therefore placed at the centre of a highly profitable trade network that helped to finance the religious foundations, sculpture and inscriptions that characterize the cultural life of this era.

Kauthara and Panduranga

The stimulus of trade with early Tang China did not last beyond the mid-eighth century. In AD 755, the great northern cities of Chang'an and Luoyang fell to the An Lushan rebels, cutting the southern ports of China from the major markets of the north. The South China Sea trade to Guangzhou had also been blighted by widespread official corruption, and the port was sacked by Persian traders in 758. After this date, the name Linyi was replaced in the Chinese records by *Huanwang*, possibly a Chinese translation of the Sanskrit title *Dharmaraja*. Only one embassy from Huanwang has been recorded; a gift of live rhinoceros and buffalo made in 793. In the early ninth century, two major raids were made by Huanwang on the southern Tang borders in north-central Vietnam, but the last of these ended in disaster with 59 princes being captured. Two Chinese itineraries describing both a land and a sea journey to Huanwang have also survived and demonstrate that this kingdom was based in Quang Nam and controlled much the same area as the former kingdom of Linyi. Nevertheless, no inscriptions have so far been found in this region that can be identified with Huanwang, and it is possible that the dynasty favoured Buddhism. A large number of bronze Buddhist statuettes have been found throughout central Vietnam from this period, showing in particular the Bodhisattva Avalokiteshvara.[28]

After a decline in the South China Sea trade following the sacking of Guangzhou in 758, commerce was partly resumed in the late eighth century with Long Bien in the Red River Delta as the main focus of trade. This transformation had two major effects. First, the system of recording trade embassies sent from Guangzhou to Luoyang was never applied at Long Bien (which although Chinese administered territory, maintained a partial independence) and so little documentary evidence of this trade has survived. Secondly, the pre-eminence of the Red River Delta encouraged an entirely different network of supply ports, in particular the port of Nha Trang, which provided a natural harbour and fresh water for ships sailing from India, Sumatra and Java to northern Vietnam. A stele inscription from the temple of Po Nagar at Nha Trang describes how the original temple was destroyed by raiders in AD 774 and the linga of Shambhu (Shiva) was lost. However, in 784 the temple was rebuilt by the king Satyavarman of Kauthara, with donations of a linga cover in precious metal embossed with the face of Shiva and statues of the goddess and Ganesha.[29] A second stele inscription from the plain of Phan Rang records how an army from Java destroyed the temple of Bhadradhipatishvara in 787. This temple was reconstructed by King Indravarman of Panduranga in 799, and reconsecrated to the god Indrabhadreshvara.[30]

These inscriptions are the first record of the southern kingdoms of Kauthara and Panduranga. Four additional inscriptions in Sanskrit and Cham from the early ninth century have been found in the Phan Rang area, and an inscription ordered by the *senapati* Par (a military commander) on the northern pillar of the main shrine of Po Nagar at Nha Trang, dated AD 817, suggests that Nha Trang was being ruled from Panduranga at this time. Two important temple sites can also be identified with this kingdom and period. The first is a group of originally three shrines at Hoa Lai, northeast of Phan Rang, each shrine facing east, and aligned in a row from north to south (the central shrine has since collapsed). All three shrines were built entirely of brick; the exterior walls of the central and northern shrines being elaborately carved with vertical floral designs and with figures, including *dvarapalas* or "door guardians", sculpted directly into the brick. The north tower is the most impressive (Figure 9.16), with split pilasters on three sides and a

Figure 9.16 North shrine at Hoa Lai, Ninh Thuan Province. (W. Southworth.)

tiered superstructure in three stages, each stage forming a miniature version of the main walls below. This schema became the standard pattern for brick temples of the Champa culture. A second group of miniature shrines at the site of Po Dam, some 30 kilometres southwest of Phan Rang, also preserves many of the same features of Hoa Lai but on a smaller scale.

The area around Phan Rang is extremely arid, with poor, sandy soil and the lowest rainfall on the central coastline. This region, therefore, and the port of Nha Trang to the north, were extremely sensitive to fluctuations in the maritime trade which necessarily provided the bulk of the region's income. In the ninth century this commerce was supplemented by passing trade carried by Arab merchants from Basrah and Oman. The earliest Arab accounts of Champa are included in the *Kitab al-masalik wa'l-mamalik* of Ibn Khurdadhbih and in the *Akbar al-Sin wa'l-Hind*, both dated to around 850.[31] The first describes a journey of three days from Cambodia (Qmar) to Champa (Sanf), before sailing to Long Bien (Luqin) in the Red River valley. The Cham port used on this journey was probably Nha Trang. The second account describes an itinerary of ten days from Kadrang (possibly Panduranga) to Sanf, where they collected fresh water. They then sailed via Sundur Fulat (the island of Hainan) to the 'Gates of China' at Guangzhou (Canton). This second journey may have stopped in the present-day Quang Nam Province, where large sherds of Islamic pottery from the ninth and tenth centuries have recently been found at Bai Lan on the Cu Lao Cham islands near the Thu Bon River estuary (Plate 11).[32] Both accounts describe the main product of Champa as *Sanfi* aloes wood, which was considered by the Arab author Ya'qubi in the late ninth century to be the finest of the aromatic woods, having the richest and most lasting perfume. This product is sometimes called eaglewood, and denotes the fragrant resinous heart-wood of the species *Aquilaria agallocha*. The heartwood is so dense that it sinks in water, hence its name in Chinese of *Chen mu* or "sink wood".

Dong Duong and Indrapura

The rich trade from the Arab world via the Malay Peninsula and Java to Long Bien in the Red River delta, which had underpinned the late eighth and early ninth century expansion of Kauthara and Panduranga, was destroyed by warfare in the mid-ninth century. From Long Bien, exotic goods had been traded into both southwestern China and northwest into Yunnan, at this time part of the independent kingdom of Nan Zhao. When the Tang dynasty tried to halt this trade to Yunnan, Nan Zhao responded by invading the Red River Delta. The ensuing conflict between these two powers destroyed the stable conditions for overseas trade and the bulk of maritime commerce gradually returned to Guangzhou. The early Tang system of receiving and recording trade embassies was also restored. In 877, a tribute mission was recorded at the Tang court from the kingdom of Zhancheng, which remained the standard transcription of Champa in the Chinese annals from this time.

The return of South China Sea trade to Guangzhou was also complemented by a parallel return to the economic and political prominence of Quang Nam. The extraordinary Buddhist monastic complex at Dong Duong was founded under a new dynasty by the king Indravarman in AD 875, and was probably completed by his maternal nephew Jaya Simhavarman, who has left an inscription at the same site dated 898. The plan of the temple is unique in Champa, being ordered in a succession of three enclosures, with intermediary gateways and columned halls or *mandapas*, and with additional shrines and stupas on either side. This progressional, longitudinal plan corresponds well with the traditional layout of Buddhist monastic buildings in southern China and northern Vietnam, where an official persecution of the Buddhist faith in the mid-ninth century may well have encouraged monks to seek refuge in Champa. Despite the similarity of plan, however, the individual buildings and brick construction techniques are clearly a natural development of the Cham architectural tradition. The temple was dedicated to the Bodhisattva of compassion under the name Lakshmindralokeshvara; a combination of both Hindu and Buddhist elements. A remarkable bronze statue of the female form of Avalokiteshvara (known to the Chinese as Guan Yin and to the Vietnamese as Quan The Am) was discovered at Dong Duong in 1978 (Figure 9.17). This was probably the main image of devotion, while a bronze of the Buddha Gautama, in Amaravati style, was also discovered in 1911.

Figure 9.17 Bronze statue of Tara or a female Avalokiteshvara from Dong Duong, now in the Provincial Museum, Da Nang. (W. Southworth.)

The distribution of inscriptions from the dynasty of Dong Duong suggests that, although based in Quang Nam, their authority extended northwards into the modern provinces of Quang Binh and Quang Tri and southwards into Quang Ngai.[33] Sandstone sculpture in a style derived from or influenced by the royal foundation at Dong Duong, showing in particular the female perception of the Bodhisattva Avalokiteshvara, also mirrors this distribution. However, from AD 939 the influence of Champa to the north was challenged by the newly independent state of Dai Viet in northern Vietnam. The kings of Champa initially followed the Chinese emperors in directly opposing Vietnamese independence, and in 982 were punished for this policy during a major military campaign by the Vietnamese emperor Le Hoan. Although this defeat was clearly a disaster for the northern Champa states (the Vietnamese occupation being recorded by the Arab author, Ibn al-Nadim in 988[34]), the long-term repercussions have been exaggerated. Much of the occupied territory, including the province of Quang Nam, had returned to Cham control by the end of the tenth century. Moreover, the major reconstruction programme that concluded these events was probably responsible for the great series of brick temples that included Claeys' Point A at Tra Kieu, My Son temple A1, and the principal sanctuary of Po Nagar at Nha Trang (Plate 12). Although Claeys' Point A at Tra Kieu has only survived as a range of brick foundations, and My Son A1 was destroyed at the height of the Vietnam War in 1969, this architectural style was nevertheless renowned for the elegance of the pilasters and perpendicular mouldings, which gave an added impression of height to the walls, and for the inclusion of sandstone sculptures into the superstructure of the tower, showing female figures or *devatas* holding a lotus flower to their breasts.

Vijaya and the great powers

The Vietnamese invasion of 982, and further military incursions in the eleventh century, nevertheless had a profound impact on the politics of Champa. A new kingdom, Vijaya, was founded in modern Binh Dinh province and was able to control both the maritime commerce of Quang Nam to the north and that of Nha Trang to the south, as well as promoting its own trade from the Bay of Thi Nai. Although a succession of new temples and shrines were founded in the Binh Dinh region, donations, reconstructions and inscriptions continued to be made to Shiva *Ishanabhadreshvara* at My Son, and to the goddess *Bhagavati* at Nha Trang. It is often assumed that Champa suffered an inexorable decline in the face of Vietnamese pressure from 982 onwards, but in fact the kingdom of Vijaya was undoubtedly more powerful, populous and influential than any of the Champa states that had preceded it. War with Cambodia during the twelfth century led to the sack of Angkor by King Shri Jaya Indravarmadeva of Vijaya in AD 1177, but also to the reciprocal fall of Vijaya to Jayavarman VII in 1191. This kingdom, however, regained its independence in the early thirteenth century and successfully resisted a Mongol invasion in 1283, perhaps with assistance from both Dai Viet and Cambodia. By the late fourteenth century, the Cham king Che Bong Nga was strong enough to lead a series of successful military campaigns against Dai Viet, even occupying Hanoi in 1370.

During this period, fortified citadels were raised in a square or rectangular plan, with earthen ramparts on all four sides and with an additional outer moat. The "new citadel" at Chau Sa in Quang Ngai and the citadel of Cha Ban in Binh Dinh are of this type. The architectural and sculptural work of the period also demonstrates the wealth and physical power of Vijaya. The temple groups of Duong Long and Thap Doi near Qui Nhon originally consisted of three tower-shrines facing East (only two remain at Thap Doi, hence the modern name meaning "twin towers"), and are the largest surviving Cham temples. They are based on a square plan with each side extended outwards in a series of vertical projections from the centre. Like earlier temples they are constructed in brick, but with tiers of the superstructure and external sculpture added in sandstone. The remains of an even larger temple group was excavated by Jean-Yves Claeys at Thap Mam, Binh Dinh, in 1934. Sixty tons of sandstone sculpture were found at the site, including a *Gajasimha* or elephant-lion (Figure 9.18) and the head and torso of a massive *dvarapala* or door guardian with clenched fist, each intricately carved with a variety of decorative fringes and panels sometimes redolent of Chinese monumental sculpture. The temple of Thap Mam may have been destroyed in the immediate aftermath of the Vietnamese invasion of Vijaya in 1471. In contrast to earlier conflicts, Vijaya was subsequently absorbed into the Vietnamese administrative system and its independence was never restored. In the south, a separate kingdom of Kauthara survived at Nha Trang until 1653, while the name of Champa was retained by the kingdom of Panduranga up to its final dissolution in 1832.

Figure 9.18 Gajasimha ('Elephant-lion') from Thap Mam, Binh Dinh, now in the Museum of Cham Sculpture, Da Nang. (W. Southworth.)

Note on sources for the history and archaeology of Champa

Scholarly research on Champa began during the French colonial era in the late nineteenth century and the majority of published material remains in French, with more recent work in English, Vietnamese and Japanese. For this essay, French and English sources have been used and are cited below.

Research on the archaeology and history of Champa was quite intensive between 1900 and 1918, but French scholarship became increasingly focused on the monuments of neighbouring Cambodia, in particular at Angkor. The Second World War and the later struggles for Vietnamese independence and unification meant that little work was undertaken between 1939 and 1975, and indeed many monuments were severely damaged during this period. From 1975, and especially since 1990, a small number of Vietnamese and foreign scholars have again started to take an interest in Cham archaeology and in the earlier prehistory of the region later occupied by the various Champa states. Although still in its infancy, the modern study of Champa is beginning to broaden, and even the entirely neglected field of Sanskrit and Cham epigraphy has begun to be revived.

Notes

1 Recent archaeological work at and around Tra Kieu also shows much more evidence for a Han Chinese role in the emergence of an early, or pre-Champa, polity in the Thu Bon Valley in the late first or early second century BC. In particular the use of heavy terracotta roofing tiles on substantial wooden structures owes more to Chinese practice than to Indian ones, although Indian-inspired decoration was later applied to such tiles (Glover 1995; Glover and Yamagata 1995; Glover *et al.*, in press; Yamagata *et al.* 2001).
2 Chamberlain 1998; Thurgood 1999.
3 Ngo 1991.
4 Parmentier 1924.
5 Reinecke 1996: 30.
6 Theunissen *et al.* 2000; Bellina and D'Errico nd.
7 Yamagata *et al.* 2001; Yamagata in press.
8 Taylor 1983: 30.
9 Glover, Nguyen Kim Dung and Prior in press.
10 Glover 1995.
11 Stein 1947: 318.
12 Prior 1998.
13 Glover, Nguyen Kim Dung and Prior in press.
14 *Jin shu* 57; cf. Pelliot 1903: 255.
15 This embassy corresponds well with the eastern campaigns of the Roman Emperor Carus (AD 282–3), who captured Ctesiphon and Seleucia on the river Tigris gaining short-lived access to the Persian Gulf.
16 *Taiping Yulan* 790; cf. Stein 1947: 116–17.
17 Bhattacharya 1961.
18 Prior 1998.
19 Three samples dated at two laboratories gave closely overlapping results.
20 Glover 1995; Glover *et al.* 1996.
21 Wheatley 1983: 382–418.
22 Wheatley 1983: 391.
23 Mus 1934.
24 Pelliot 1903.
25 Wang Gungwu 1958: 64.

26 Tran Ky Phuong 2000.
27 Wang Gungwu 1958: 90.
28 Boisselier 1963: Figs 28–41.
29 Majumdar 1927 (III): 41–44 (No. 22).
30 Ibid. No. 23.
31 Tibbetts 1979: 25–9.
32 Nguyen Lam My Dzung 1998.
33 Schweyer 2000.
34 Tibbetts 1979: 42.

Select Bibliography

The select bibliography below lists some of the most important publications relevant to the theme of this chapter. Many more, for the period up to 1990, are listed in the *Bibliographie Champa et Cam* compiled by Pierre-Bernard Lafont and Po Dharma (L'Harmattan, Paris 1989).

Archaeology

Claeys, J.-Y. (1931) "Simhapura – grande capitale chame", *Revue des Arts Asiatiques* 7(2): 93–103.

Claeys, J.-Y. (1935) "Thap-mam", *Illustrated London News*, 9 March 1935.

Glover, I. C. (1995) "Decorated roof tiles from ancient Simhapura – an early Cham city in Central Vietnam", in Sri Aroon Khaisri (ed.) *Studies and Reflections on Asian Art History and Archaeology: Essays in Honour of H.S.H. Professor Suphadradis Diskul*, Bangkok: Silpakorn University, pp. 311–22.

Glover, I. C. and M. Yamagata (1995) "The Origins of Cham civilization: indigenous, Chinese and Indian influences in Central Vietnam as revealed by excavations at Tra Kieu, Vietnam 1990 and 1993" in C. T. Yeung and W. L. Li (eds) *Archaeology in Southeast Asia*, Hong Kong: Hong Kong University Museum and Art Gallery, pp. 145–70.

Glover, I. C., Nguyen Kim Dung and Prior R. (in press) "The 2000–01 excavation seasons at the ancient Cham city at Tra Kieu and Go Cam, Quang Nam Province, Central Vietnam", paper presented at the *Conference to Celebrate 100 Years of Archaeology in Vietnam*, Hanoi, December 2001.

Nguyen, Chieu and Lam, My Dzung (1991) "Ceramics from ancient Cham sites at Tra Kieu 1990" *Khao Co Hoc* 1991 (4): 18–30 (in Vietnamese).

Nguyen Lam Thi My Dzung (1998) "Sa Huynh Culture in Hoi An", in M. Klokke and P. Bruyn (eds) *Southeast Asian Archaeology 1996*. Hull: Centre for South-East Asian Studies, pp. 13–25.

Parmentier, H. (1924) "Dépots de jarres à Sa-Huynh (Quang-ngai, Annam)" *Bulletin de l'École Française d'Extrême-Orient* 23: 325–43.

Prior, R. (1998) "The ceramics from early historic sites in Vietnam" in P.-Y. Manguin (ed.) *Southeast Asian Archaeology 1994*, Vol. 1, Hull: Centre for South-East Asian Studies, University of Hull, pp. 94–110.

Southworth, W. A. (2001) "The origins of Champa in central Vietnam: a preliminary review", Ph.D. dissertation, London: School of Oriental and African Studies, London University.

Theunisson, R., Grave, P., Bailey, G. (2000) "Doubts on diffusion: challenging the assumed Indian origin of Iron Age agate and carnelian beads in Southeast Asia", *World Archaeology* 32: 184–105.

Yamagata, M., Pham Duc Manh, and Bui Chi Hoang (2001) "Western Han bronze mirrors recently dicovered in Central Vietnam" *Bulletin of the Indo-Pacific Prehistory Association* 21: 99–106.

Art history

Boisselier, J. (1963) *La statuaire du Champa; recherches sur les cultes et l'iconographie*, Paris: Publications de l'École Française d'Extrême-Orient, vol. LIV.
Parmentier, H. (1909 and 1918) *Inventaire descriptif des monuments cams de l'Annam*, 2 vols, Paris: Ernest Leroux.
Stern, P. (1942) *L'art du Champa (ancien Annam) et son évolution*, Toulouse: Les Frères Douladoure.
Tran Ky Phuong (2000) "The wedding of Sita: a theme from the Ramayana represented on the Tra Kieu pedestal", in M. J. Klokke, (ed.) *Narrative sculpture and literary traditions in South and Southeast Asia*, Leiden: Brill, pp. 51–58.

Inscriptions, epigraphy and linguistics

Bhattacharya, K. (1961) "Précisions sur la paléographie de l'inscription dite de Vo-canh." *Artibus Asiae* XXIV: 219–24.
Chamberlain, J. R. (1998) "The origin of the Sek: implications for Tai and Vietnamese history", *Journal of the Siam Society* 86 (1 and 2): 27–48.
Jacques, C. (ed.) (1995) *Études épigraphiques sur le pays cham*, Paris: Réimpression de l'École Française d'Extrême-Orient No. 7.
Schweyer, A.-V. 2000. La dynastie d'Indrapura (Quang Nam, Vietnam), in W. Lobo and S. Reimann (eds), *Southeast Asian Archaeology 1998*, Hull: Centre for South-East Asian Studies & Ethnologisches Museum, Staatliche Museen zu Berlin, Stiftung Preussischer Kulturbesitz, University of Hull: 205–18.
Thurgood, G. (1999) *From Ancient Cham to Modern Dialects – Two Thousand Years of Language Contact and Change*, Honolulu: University of Hawai'i Press.

History

Majumdar, R. C. (1927) *Ancient Indian colonies in the Far East: Vol. I. Champa*, Lahore: The Punjab Sanskrit Book Depot (Greater India Society publication 1).
Maspero, G. (1928) *Le royaume de Champa*, Les éditions G. Van Oest, Paris and Brussels (reprinted by the École Française d'Extrême-Orient, Paris 1988)
Mus, P. (1934) "Cultes indiens et indigènes au Champa", *Bulletin de l'École Française d'Extrême-Orient* 33: 367–410, (translated by Ian W. Mabbett and David P. Chandler as "India seen from the East: Indian and indigenous cults in Champa", *Monash Papers on Southeast Asia No. 3*, Monash University, 1975)
Pelliot, P. (1903) "Le Fou-nan" *Bulletin de l'École Française d'Extrême-Orient* 3: 248–327.
Southworth, W. (2000) "Notes on the political geography of Champa in central Vietnam during the late eighth and early ninth centuries AD", in W. Lobo and S. Reimann (eds), *Southeast Asian Archaeology 1998*, Centre for Southeast Asian Studies & Ethnologisches Museum, Staatliche Museen zu Berlin, Stiftung Preussischer Kulturbesitz, University of Hull, pp. 237–44.
Stein, R. A. (1947) "Le Lin-yi; sa localisation, sa contribution à la formation du Champa et ses liens avec la Chine", *Han-hiue* 2 (1–3): 1–335.
Taylor, K. W. (1983) *The Birth of Vietnam*, Berkeley and Los Angeles: University of California Press.
Tibbetts, G. R., 1979. *A Study of the Arabic Texts Containing Material on South-East Asia*, Royal Asiatic Society, Oriental Translation Fund, New Series Volume XLIV, Leiden and London: E. J. Brill.
Wang Gungwu (1958) "The Nanhai trade: a study of the early history of Chinese trade in the South China Sea", *Journal of the Malayan Branch of the Royal Asiatic Society* 31(2), (182): 1–135.
Wheatley, P. (1983) *Nagara and Commandery: Origins of the Southeast Asian Urban Traditions*, University of Chicago (Department of Geography Research Papers 207–8).

10

THE CLASSICAL CULTURES OF INDONESIA

John N. Miksic

Introduction

The diversity of ancient Indonesia's cultural development defies efforts to construct a single narrative. For decades, the theme of Indian influence was thought to be sufficient to explain at least most developments from the early centuries of the Christian Era. But in the 1960s a new archaeological paradigm skeptical of diffusion as a general causal factor swept old theories away. No single causal process has since emerged to take its place. Instead, we must now familiarize ourselves with multiple factors if we are to follow this drama as it unfolds.

The division of the drama of Indonesian cultural evolution into "acts" or periods is another difficult enterprise. Indonesian archaeologists reject such terms as Paleolithic, Neolithic, Bronze and Iron Age because technological and social changes do not display the same correlations as in Europe and Western Asia. The introduction of writing into Indonesia did not bring a major change in the trajectory of cultural evolution. When other elements of South Asian culture such as temple architecture or sculpture appeared on the Indonesian scene, they were not accompanied by changes in such basic characteristics as political systems or settlement patterns.[1]

Periodization

This essay will employ the following scheme of periodization. The Protohistoric period begins with the introduction of writing around AD 400. The Early Classic Period begins in the seventh century AD, when enough inscriptions and architectural remains become available to provide coherent accounts of a few areas of Indonesia (Figure 10.1). This phase continues until the early tenth century, when the civilization of Central Java came to an abrupt end. Then begins the Middle Classic period, covering the tenth to the early thirteenth century. The Late Classic period lasted until AD 1500 and was succeeded by the Islamic or Post-Classic era.

The utility of any periodization scheme for ancient Indonesia is further mitigated by the coexistence of cultures with traits diagnostic of different phases. For instance, in the Pakauman district, near Bondowoso in East Java and not far from Late Classic period temples, there are numerous burial sites with stone sarcophagi, a trait associated with the late prehistoric era. One of the sarcophagi contained ninth-century Chinese ceramics, and Chinese coins of the fifteenth century are found in the same fields, demonstrating

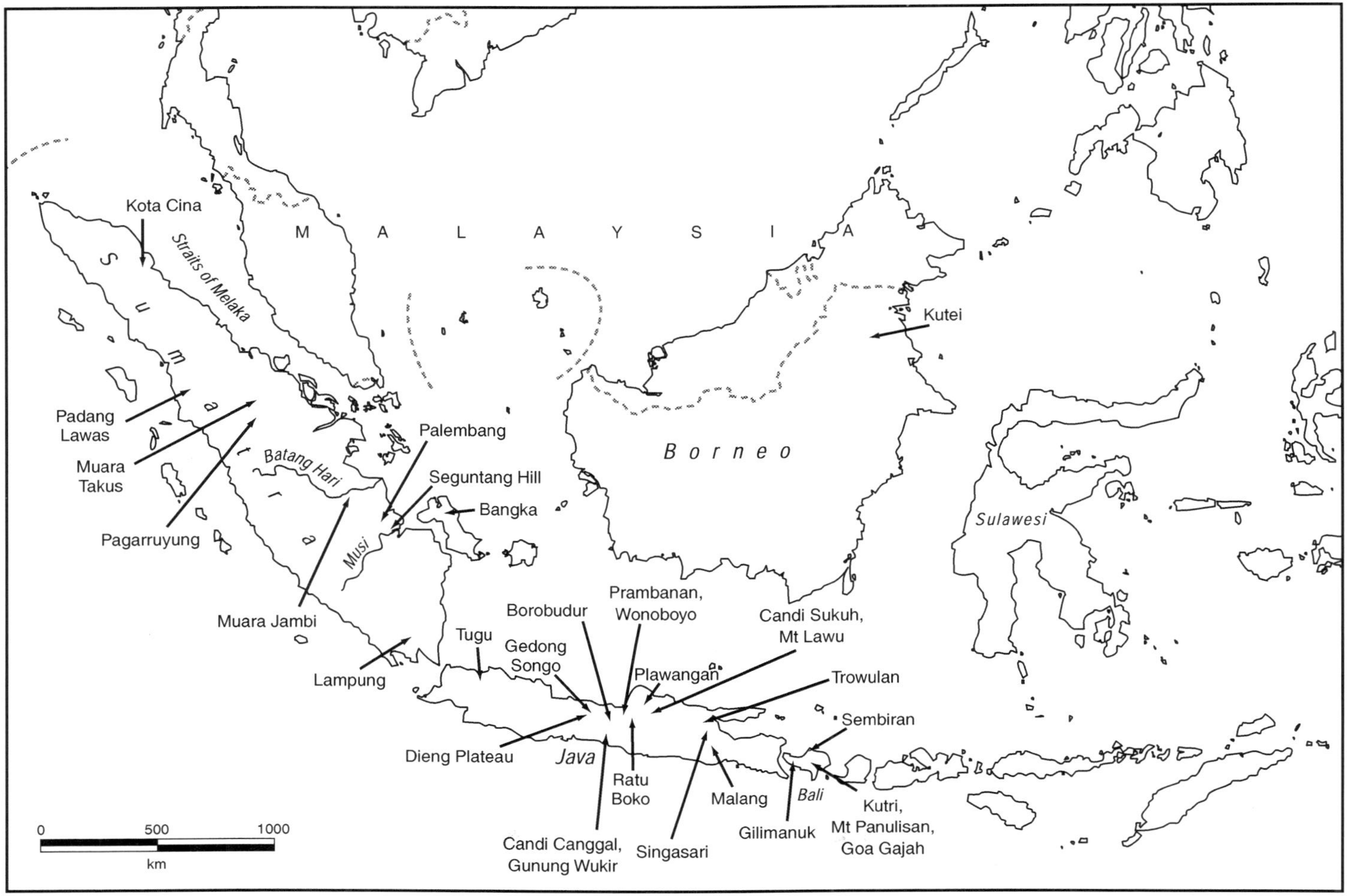

Figure 10.1 Western Indonesia (Sumatra, Java, Kalimantan and Bali) locating places mentioned in the text.

that some groups continued to practice protohistoric or even prehistoric types of burial long after they were abandoned in nearby areas. Ethnographic examples of non-mainstream societies such as the Turunan of Bali, the Tengger of central Java and the Badui of western Java can still be found in many parts of contemporary Indonesia.

Archaism, the revival of practices or motifs characteristic of previous cultural configurations, is another feature of Indonesian cultural development which renders meaningless any attempt to construct a simple unilinear narrative of Indonesian cultural evolution. For instance, protohistoric terraced hillside shrines resembling prehistoric forebears have been found in several parts of West Java. The tradition of constructing such shrines emerged again at the end of the classic period in East Java, and perhaps in Bali as well, although it is uncertain whether the tradition in Bali was ever abandoned.

The lag of three centuries between the appearance of writing in the fifth century and the appearance of masonry architecture in the eighth is evidence that they were adopted at different times, as part of a gradual process of local development. South Asian culture was "Indonesianized", rather than the reverse. The developments of writing and Indic art indicate uneven evolutionary processes, rather than sudden changes in direction. Chronological periods in Indonesian ancient history are arbitrary, inserted by the scholar for heuristic reasons rather than inherent in the data.

Inscriptions and writing

Early Indonesian texts imply that writing had already been practiced for some time before the date of the oldest surviving stone inscriptions. The script used in these is derived from south Indian Pallava writing, but the letters have already diverged from their Indian forebears. A phase during which perishable materials were exclusively used for writing must have preceded the first use of permanent materials.[2]

The first inscriptions in Indonesia come from Kutei in Eastern Borneo (Figure 10.2), at first sight a most unlikely region for such a major discovery owing to its remoteness from the communication routes leading to South Asia. The group of inscribed stones found there dates from approximately AD 400; this date is conjectural since the inscriptions themselves contain no dates, but palaeographic methods have been proven by comparison with other sources to be quite reliable tools in Indonesia. The inscriptions commemorate sacrifices of animals, perhaps horses,[3] in a manner obviously meant to emulate practices

Figure 10.2 The Kutei inscription dated to *c.* AD 400 – perhaps the earliest in Indonesia. (John N. Miksic.)

found in India. Whether such sacrifice was ever conducted at all in Eastern Borneo, where horses have never been useful nor intensively bred, is another question.

The ruler was probably motivated to use imported writing systems and religious ritual in order to enhance his prestige and political status. Erection of inscriptions involving the introduction of new symbols would have facilitated the imposition of a more elaborate status system. The conditions under which these new sets of symbols were introduced no doubt varied significantly from one particular case to the next, rather than being part of a simple process of diffusion.

The next inscriptional evidence comes from a more likely part of the archipelago, this being west Java. A fifth-century kingdom called Taruma is mentioned in texts scattered from the north coast to the southern mountains. These are written in Sanskrit, again undated except through palaeography.

The fact that all the earliest inscriptions from Indonesia are written neither in a local language nor in an Indian vernacular, but in the ritual language Sanskrit, reinforces the inference that the adoption of South Asian cultural elements was a conscious intellectual exercise initiated by Indonesian elites, rather than the result of frequent contact between Indonesians and Indians at the middle level of society.

One of the Taruma inscriptions, at Tugu on the north coast, discusses the construction of a canal, apparently for drainage. Another, from Ciaruton, in the west Java highlands, bears a carved pair of human footprints and the text: "Of the valiant lord of the earth, the illustrious Purnavarman the ruler of Taruma, [is this] the pair of footprints like unto Vishnu's." The nearby Coffee Garden inscription bears carved footprints of an elephant, with the words "these are the footprints of the great elephant belonging to the king of Taruma, which are bigger than those of Airavata." Airavata is the elephant mount of the god Indra, who in ancient Hinduism was the equivalent of Zeus. In later Hinduism he was superseded by other deities, particularly Visnu and Siva, but retained the position of ruler of Mount Meru, at the center of the cosmos, on the slopes of which the gods lived. He was also associated with fertilizing rain; in Mahayana Buddhism he appears to tempt the future Buddha in order to test his resolve to become enlightened.

The Buni Culture

Although no systematic excavations have ever been conducted, a culture known as Buni is known to have existed at approximately the same time as, or slightly earlier than, the kingdom of Taruma. Numerous sites of this culture existed in the coastal plain of northwestern Java. Some of the Buni earthenware resembles that of the Sa Huynh-Kalanay style of the regions around South China Sea; similar material has also been found at Plawangan in north central Java, Gilimanuk in Western Bali, and Sembiran in North Bali. Rouletted pottery (see Figure 2.7) and monochrome glass beads imported from southern India have also been found at Buni and Sembiran.

Most of the Buni sites are only known from looted burials. At two of these sites, Kobak Kendal and Cibutak, several vessels recognized as Indian rouletted ware were found. These probably date back to the first or second century AD.[4] No habitation sites of this culture, or from the Taruma kingdom in general, have yet been identified. Brick foundations east of Jakarta may prove to date from the Taruma period and thus could be the earliest examples of classical architecture constructed in Indonesia.

External contacts

Indonesia's first recorded diplomatic missions may have issued from Taruma. A kingdom called *Holodan* noted in Chinese records sent several diplomatic missions to China between AD 430 and 452. Java was exposed to Buddhism as early as AD 414, when a Chinese monk named Faxian (Fa-hsien) visited western Indonesia on his way to India. An Indian monk named Gunavarman preached in Java shortly before AD 424. A bronze Buddha image found in Sempaga, Sulawesi, has been related to the Amaravati style of the first century AD in South India. Other discoveries suggest that Buddhism enjoyed some influence in early Sulawesi, but firm evidence for this is still lacking.

The early inscriptions in the Strait of Melaka cluster around trading ports. Trade was one important factor favouring increased social complexity, which in turn encouraged elites to compete for imported status symbols. In the fifth century, inscriptions appeared on the Malay Peninsula, precisely at the northern entrance to the Strait of Melaka. Here the religion was Buddhism, and the inscriptions were meant to ensure safe passage across the Bay of Bengal for ship captains. The first Sumatran kingdom found in Chinese records (*Gantoli*) sent envoys to China in AD 454–464. A king of this country named Vijayavarman, perhaps a Hindu, sent another embassy in AD 519. Statues of Visnu, similar to those found in West Java, and like them possibly carved around the fifth century, have been found on the island of Bangka, off the mouth of the Musi River which leads to modern-day Palembang.[5]

More envoys went to China from Sumatra in AD 644–645, from a kingdom called Malayu. In the late seventh century a kingdom named Srivijaya suddenly asserted control over shipping through the Strait of Melaka, the main artery of maritime trade between India and China. In the late 1980s, French and Indonesian archaeologists excavated artifacts from this kingdom in the vicinity of modern Palembang[6] (see Chapter 12). Although recent construction has destroyed much potential information, enough has been learned to enable us to create a relatively detailed depiction of Srivijaya.

In AD 671 the famous Chinese Buddhist monk Yijing sailed from Guangdong to India via Srivijaya in a vessel belonging to the ruler of Srivijaya. His description of the kingdom's capital indicates that Buddhism was flourishing there. Between 682 and 686, several inscriptions were carved in Srivijaya at the order of King Jayanasa. The texts are similar and at least one was intended for an oath of loyalty ceremony. The top of the stele on which the inscription occurs is adorned with heads of seven *naga* or water spirits. Water was poured over the text, and collected from a spout at the bottom. This practice of "drinking oaths" was common in Southeast Asia until recent times (Figure 10.3).

Figure 10.3 The inscription from Telaga Batu recording an "oath drinking" ceremony. (John N. Miksic.)

Other versions of the same oath have been found in the hinterland of modern Jambi Province in eastern Sumatra, on Bangka Island off the mouth of the Musi

River on which Palembang is situated, and at two sites in Lampung Province, near Sumatra's southern tip. This distribution may indicate the extent of the kingdom's sphere of influence.

The inscriptions, in Old Malay larded with many Sanskrit terms, provide useful information on Sumatran society of the time. They indicate the importance of wealth, the employment of armed forces in the kingdom's policies and the prestige of sea captains. The form of Buddhism implied by these texts was quite different from the Theravada form now practiced in Southeast Asia; it combined elements of Mahayanism and esoteric beliefs.

Social and political structures

Early Indonesian societies which adopted either Buddhism or Hinduism shared fundamental assumptions about ideal political structure. Inscriptions refer to kingdoms as *mandalas*, a Sanskrit word with a wide range of meanings. Its simplest connotation is a circle. It can refer to symmetrical arrangements of deities. Beginning around AD 800, Javanese temple complexes were designed as *mandalas*. The ideal kingdom would be a gigantic *mandala*, a replica of the cosmos, with Mount Meru at its center.[7]

Kings thought of themselves as a *Cakravartin*, a Sanskrit term meaning "wheel-turner". According to the ideology there could only be one universal ruler – the *Cakravartin* – who would obtain his position through spiritual rather than military power. Rulers who aspired to be *Cakravartin* sought to attract chiefs of neighboring areas to acknowledge them as supreme rulers through a combination of threats and persuasion. Recognition usually meant no more than providing occasional tribute and participating in state rituals. *Cakravartin* did not usually have the desire or the means to intervene in the internal affairs of their satellites. Such a political structure is reminiscent of the form sometimes known to anthropologists as a segmentary state, which is difficult to distinguish from a highly-developed chiefdom. Such political organization still depended on the personal qualities of rulers.[8]

Social structure in those areas of Indonesia where the earliest historical sources have been found (i.e. South Sumatra, Java, and Bali) was normally based on cognatic kinship – that is, recognizing equally both male and female ancestors. Male primogeniture was not applied to the selection of new rulers. Instead, replacements for kings or queens were usually chosen by a council of nobles from among a range of suitable candidates. Normally some blood relationship to the former ruler was believed to be desirable, but claimants suitably endowed with the qualities of a successful leader often found ways to claim such a relationship through one family connection or another. Such customs made it difficult for dynasties to appear. Female rulers were rare but not unknown. Women had relatively high status in society; they are frequently mentioned in inscriptions as occupying positions of power, and often endowed religious facilities.

Srivijayan inscriptions give us little information regarding economic practices, but recent archaeological research has begun to provide some confirmation of foreign accounts of Srivijaya as a thriving trading centre. Remains of ships dating to the seventh century have now been found, one at the foot of Seguntang Hill in Palembang, mythical center of the ancient kingdom. These ships display Southeast Asian shipbuilding techniques such as lashed-lug construction using no nails or other metal, and rudders mounted at the sides rather than the sterns, reinforcing the conclusion that Indonesians were responsible for carrying a substantial share of maritime trade through Southeast Asia before the coming of the Europeans in the sixteenth century.[9] Research in the late 1990s in waters off south Sumatra yielded much new information, including, from the western Indian Ocean, a wreck of an eighth-century ship which promises to augment knowledge of early Indonesian trade significantly.

Settlements and structures in early Sumatra

Information regarding the settlement pattern of early Palembang is still elusive. Early brick structures may have been built in south Sumatra, but early archaeological expeditions to Palembang report that ancient brick ruins had already been quarried for road building material. Brick ruins from the late first millennium AD have been discovered in the Palembang hinterland, where they have been less disturbed by modern development.

If the early population followed the same custom as many modern residents of Palembang and other parts of Sumatra, they would have built their houses over water rather than on dry land. Palembang, as described by the famous naturalist Alfred Russel Wallace in the mid-nineteenth century, was a populous city several miles long but only one house wide, all dwellings standing on piles over shallow water. Most discarded artifacts would thus fall into the mud, to be deeply buried in river sediments. The search for early Sumatran settlement structures seems to pose problems that are nearly insoluble with our current research tools.

Sumatran sculpture of the seventh and eighth centuries is highly varied and displays international links rather than being distinctively Sumatran. A large granite standing Buddha image from Seguntang Hill belongs to this period.

Srivijaya's last embassy to China arrived in AD 742. Thereafter, neither inscriptions nor foreign sources enlighten us regarding conditions in the kingdom. We can only conclude that, even if Srivijaya remained prosperous, its rulers lacked any desire to leave stone inscriptions. Scraps of data from other parts of the international Buddhist network refer to Srivijaya as an important centre of Buddhist learning throughout the rest of the Early Classic phase. For instance, archaeological research has found large quantities of Chinese green-glazed ceramics in Palembang, indicating flourishing foreign trade during the eighth and ninth centuries, when Chinese pottery first became a significant item of trade.

The Early Classic period in Java

Central Java, which has not yielded any significant sites from the Proto-classic phase, rose to become Indonesia's most highly evolved Early Classic civilization. An undated inscription dated by paleography to the late seventh century is the first indication of this. Next appeared the first dated inscription in Java: the Gunung Wukir text of AD 732, commemorating the foundation of a kingdom by a man calling himself Sanjaya (Figure 10.4).

The oldest permanent structures known in Indonesia are two early complexes of religious buildings on the Dieng Plateau (Figure 10.5) within a volcanic crater 2,000 metres high, and at Gedong Songo much further east. Dieng means "Deified Ancestors". The temples were meant to house symbols of Siva and are clearly inspired by Indian

Figure 10.4 The eighth-century Candi Canggal at Gunung Wukir, Central Java with alterations from around the twelfth century. (John N. Miksic.)

Figure 10.5 The Arjuna group of temples on the Dieng Plateau, Central Java. (John N. Miksic.)

predecessors, but none is modelled directly on any Indian temple. Probably, these structures represent a stage in a process of local development already underway for some time, in which wood had been the main material. Although early Javanese structures are most closely related to early temples of southeast India, Indonesian architects assimilated ideas from several parts of South Asia, recombining various elements in their own fashion.[10]

The temples at Gedong Songo ("Nine Buildings"), situated several hundred kilometers to the east, were probably built between AD 750 and 775. At approximately the same time, other shrines were built near Malang, but these seem to have been an isolated early flowering which did not have any direct descendants. The Malang structures and inscriptions suggest that east Java was not merely an underdeveloped area on the fringe of central Javanese civilization, but was integrated into it.

No concentrated attempts at discovering the precise locations of domestic activities associated with the religious sites have yet been undertaken and we lack any evidence of habitation during this period. Knowledge of Indonesian society during the Early Classic period is almost entirely limited to religion. Information regarding such matters as the economy, settlements and technology can only be inferred from religious structures and texts.

During the eighth and ninth centuries, Java formed an integral part of a far-flung Asian religious and economic network. Archaeological evidence of international trade is difficult to find, due to the perishable nature of many of the commodities concerned, but underwater archaeology has recently begun to show that this situation is not completely irremediable.

Data from the religious sphere, though indirect, is a useful supplement to other indications that communication was flowing smoothly between Java, China and South Asia during the Early Classic. Mahayana Buddhism underwent rapid development during the seventh and eighth centuries. Although no Indonesian texts have survived from this period (the oldest dates from the early tenth century), the originality and sophistication of Javanese Buddhist architecture indicate that Indonesians were making significant contributions to the world's most widespread religion at that time.

Buddhism rose to prominence in central Java after several decades during which Hinduism seems to have been pre-eminent. Major religious complexes were begun and expanded in a relatively short time. The main event of the late eighth century was the start of construction at Borobudur (Plate 13). This, one of the largest Buddhist structures of the ancient world, has a unique design that was never reproduced.

The meaning of Borobudur's name is the subject of conjecture, but a logical guess is that it originally formed part of a longer phrase referring to a mountain where one might accumulate enough merit to become a *bodhisattva* by progressing through ten stages of increasing enlightenment. The genius of the creators of Borobudur is that one monument combines numerous symbolic elements from different sources. It is at once a multi-tiered terraced structure like the prehistoric religious sites of Indonesia; a *mandala* with concentric rows of sculptures representing Buddhist deities; a symbol of royal might composed of over two million large blocks of stone; and a device for inculcating wisdom through its gallery of 1,350 narrative reliefs. Borobudur was built while Mahayana Buddhist ideology was undergoing important evolution, and revisions to the structure were no doubt made to accommodate them; in particular, access to the monument may have been increasingly restricted to elite groups. No texts survive to tell us anything about the purpose of Borobudur, so all we can do is make informed guesses.[11]

A new group of rulers, the Sailendras, displaced the descendants of Sanjaya at the top of the power structure between AD 778 and 832. The Sailendras were interested in esoteric aspects of Buddhism, particularly those which assured them that they were the closest to enlightenment among all members of their society. Their religious structures grew larger, more *mandala*-like and less accessible.

External sources suggest that Indonesians were militarily active along the coasts of Mainland Southeast Asia during this time. Vietnamese annals mention an invasion from Java and "the Southern Islands" in AD 767. In 775 the Maharaja of Srivijaya had an inscription erected in southern Thailand. A Cham inscription records that in 787 an invading army from Java burned a temple. An inscription from Cambodia may refer to a period of Javanese influence there in the late eighth century. The last Sailendra inscription was carved in 824. More Buddhist complexes were built or expanded after this date, but by 842 the ruler of central Java was a Hindu married to a Buddhist queen. For the rest of Classical Javanese history, Buddhism was less influential than Hinduism.

The Ratu Boko *Kraton* (palace) on the Siva Plateau in Central Java overlooks the rich Sorogedug Plain where many of the Early Classic temples were built (Figure 10.6). This tells the story of Buddhism's rise and decline. On a limestone outcrop was erected a complex of stone-faced terraces, reservoirs, walled courtyards and foundations for wooden pavilions. One of these is associated with an inscription stating that a Buddhist monastery was built there in 792. A reference in the text to Abhayagiri Vihara in Sri Lanka, and architectural similarities to a group of ruined monasteries there, prove that the builders had a close relationship with an esoteric Sinhalese sect. The Buddhist remains were later demolished and at least one Shivite temple erected. Inscriptions found around the base of the hill refer to a Javanese ruler in several guises of Siva as destroyer of his enemies.

The most likely conclusion is that a male member of the Sailendra clan, excluded from high position by the pact between the Hindu king and Buddhist queen, sought redress by force. He seems to have failed, and the interfaith pairing prevailed. The story does not

Figure 10.6 The architectural complex at Ratu Boko, Central Java which seems to have combined religious and secular functions. (John N. Miksic.)

end here, though. In about 860 an inscription from Nalanda in Bihar, India, one of the greatest esoteric Buddhist monastic complexes in the world, recorded that a Sailendra with the same name Balaputra as the rebel was ruling in Srivijaya. How he made this transition is a fascinating subject but cannot be answered with the means at our disposal.

Figure 10.7 Carved relief at Candi Loro Jonggrang, with house in the background showing the stressed roof-beam construction. (John N. Miksic.)

In AD 856 the greatest Hindu temple complex ever built in Indonesia, Candi Loro Jonggrang at Prambanan, was consecrated (Figures 10.7 and 10.8). This extensive complex, dedicated to the trinity of Siva, Vishnu, and Brahma, is in many ways a response to Borobudur and Candi Sewu. The latter complex consists of several concentric rows of temples surrounding a principal edifice. Like these two Buddhist structures, the ground plan of Loro Jonggrang resembles a *mandala*; rows of structures are set on successively higher terraces. Two of the main temples contain narrative reliefs from the Ramayana; the third has reliefs depicting the Kresnayana. Thus, whereas the central building houses Siva images, the main reliefs portray texts related to Visnu.

Figure 10.8 Carved relief image of a dancer at Candi Loro Jonggrang. (John N. Miksic.)

Scholars differ on the subject of the relations between Hinduism and Buddhism in ancient Java. Some, noting the use of similar artistic motifs, believe that the two religions cooperated peacefully. The Hindu king who founded Loro Jonggrang also contributed to Buddhist shrines, together with his queen. Others have gone so far as to conclude that Hinduism and Buddhism actually formed a syncretistic union in the succeeding Middle and Late Classic periods. These arguments have been contradicted by the Indonesian philologist Hariani Santiko, who adduces evidence to support the conclusion that, although one thirteenth-century king did indeed have himself commemorated in the same temple as both Siva and Buddha, the two religions remained doctrinally distinct. In fact, later Javanese inscriptions distinguish between three groups: the Buddhists, the Hindus, and the *rishi*, or ascetic hermits. It is likely that the priesthoods retained a firm desire to differentiate themselves from their rivals, although the common people may not have cared much about the finer points of doctrine.

The construction of Loro Jonggrang marked a culmination of Javanese architecture. No more buildings of this scale were erected for almost a thousand years. Inscriptions continued to be carved until the early tenth century, but thereafter the light of Early Classic civilization suddenly died. Numerous explanations have been proposed to account for this sudden extinction of a glorious artistic culture: external attack, perhaps from

Sumatra; destructive volcanic eruptions; droughts; epidemics; all the usual suspects.[12] Later inscriptions only refer to a *pralaya*, or disaster, without specifying its nature. The Wonoboyo site, near Prambanan, central Java, suggests that a volcanic eruption may be at least part of the explanation. Several caches of very impressive gold ornaments and large quantities of gold coins were discovered here in the 1990s. Many other caches of gold objects from the early Classic era have also been found around central Java, whereas such finds are relatively rare in East Java.

Java in the Middle Classic period

The Middle Classic period in Java was marked by the move of the political centre to the Brantas Valley, a few hundred kilometers to the east. There, inscriptions and statues continued to be carved, and some great literary works were composed, but no temples of permanent materials were erected until the mid-thirteenth century, a mysterious hiatus of over 300 years. The patterns of daily life and the standard of living of the common people of Java are better known from temple reliefs and written records than from excavations.

Figure 10.9 Spout of a gold ritual vessel with *makara* face. (John N. Miksic.)

Deposits of metal ores are rare in Java and so much had to be imported, with iron coming from Borneo or Sulawesi, although it is possible that copper was acquired within the island. Nevertheless, Javanese craftsmen were masters of all aspects of their work. Metalsmiths were classified according to the type of metal with which they worked (gold, silver, copper, bronze and iron). Itinerant jewellers had stalls in periodic markets. Many superb examples of gold and bronze jewelry have been discovered (Figure 10.9).

Figure 10.10 Carved relief image of a woman paddling pottery and men carrying clay, second level at Borobudur, Central Java. (John N. Miksic.)

Pottery was a common material, but studies of ancient Javanese ceramics are still scarce. A relief on Borobudur depicts female potters using wooden paddles to shape their pots (Figure 10.10). In the background, men are shown bringing clay to the women. Firing of pottery was probably done in the open rather than in closed kilns.

Other specialized occupations included carpenters, basketmakers, bamboo plaiters, and makers of ceremonial decorations for houses. Inscriptions mention many varieties of textiles and types of clothing, classified by pattern, color and material.

Both common people and royalty dressed in sarongs, without garments on the upper body. Cloth had an important ceremonial meaning in early Java. Visitors attending temple-founding ceremonies were given ritual gifts consisting of gold, silver and pieces of cloth or sets of clothing. Social classes were distinguishable by hairstyle and jewelry.

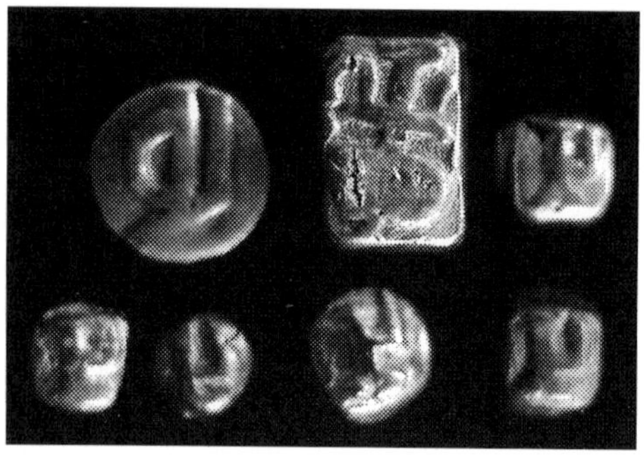

Figure 10.11 Gold coins from Central Java, ninth century. (John N. Miksic.)

The Javanese economy was monetized by the tenth century.[13] The bimetallic coinage system included both gold and silver currency (Figure 10.11). Inscriptions contain terms for "medium of exchange", "market", and various classes of merchants. Goods for sale mentioned in the inscriptions include clothing, rice, sugar, cotton, copper objects, salt, thread, oil, ginger, cardamom and basketry.

An elaborate system of taxation existed in Early Classic Java. The main motivation for erecting stone inscriptions was to record that a certain area had been released from taxation in return for rendering services to a religious complex. Early inscriptions release all people in the specified area from taxation, whereas later inscriptions limit the number of people permitted to reside in the zone. This suggests that many people were dependent on a cash economy and took advantage of the tax-free status of these temple zones. An inscription of AD 929 (the beginning of the Middle Classic period) puts limits on the number of water buffalo and cattle dealers who could live, tax-free, in a temple zone. The inscription also lists such occupations as umbrella makers, drummers and comedians, fire-fighters and pimps. Taxes were levied on agricultural land according to various types. Communities of foreigners, apparently merchants, were also required to pay tax.

Figure 10.12 Carved stone relief from East Java showing an agricultural landscape. (John N. Miksic.)

Archaeology has as yet contributed little to our knowledge of Javanese agriculture. The large numbers of well-made stone tools, including many wood-working tools – some no doubt to make agricultural implements – and the apparent density of population in the island at the beginning of the Classic period, support the inference that intensive rice cultivation had started in prehistoric times. Javanese farmers were no doubt assisted by favorable environmental conditions – rich soils and the mild climate – but we still lack any information concerning the process by which the Javanese evolved the ability to produce the surplus which supported their sophisticated artists.

Inscriptions rarely mention such agriculturally useful activities as the construction of dams and canals, although the Taruma inscription appears to mention flood control. Water control officials belonged to the village level of government, as they still do in many parts of Indonesia. There is no evidence that Javanese kingdoms ever developed state-led bureaucratic institutions for water control.

In the Late Classic period, when narrative reliefs reappear in the Javanese cultural arsenal, agricultural scenes such as villages and their surrounding fields, farmers planting or harvesting rice, become quite common (Figure 10.12). This suggests that the Javanese saw wet rice agriculture as a major constituent of their identity. By the thirteenth century, Java was exporting rice to Sumatra.

Sumatra in the Middle Classic period

At the beginning of the Middle Classic period, when Java was divided and had lost some of its most prominent earlier traditions such as temple construction, Srivijaya enjoyed undiminished political influence in the Strait of Melaka and good relations with its major commercial and diplomatic partners. These included Song Dynasty China and the Chola kingdom of South India. Srivijayan-sponsored temples were built in Guangzhou and at Negapatam on the Coromandel coast of India around AD 1000. This situation abruptly ended when the Chola kingdom invaded the Strait of Melaka in 1025. Chola inscriptions record the defeat and capture of Srivijaya's ruler. The motive for the attack has never been explained.

North Sumatra and the Thai-Malay Peninsula experienced strong south Indian influence during the rest of the eleventh century. South Indian merchant guilds were established in several locations. The Chola kings may even have instituted direct rule over these areas. In addition to Tamil inscriptions, evidence for this comes from typically South Indian temple architecture in Kedah and North Sumatra. After 1100 Tamil power gradually waned as the South Indian political situation became increasingly unstable.

During the Middle Classic phase, when no temples were erected in Java, several extensive complexes were built in Sumatra. One of these is today called Padang Lawas ("Broad Plain"), an environmental anomaly. Here the mountain wall that extends almost the entire length of Sumatra's west coast contains a small gap, though which winds already emptied of their moisture on the west coast can sweep across to the east. These winds have led to the formation of a grassy plain covering several hundred square kilometers.

This barren landscape can never have supported a dense population, but it provided a convenient route between the east and west coasts. This may explain the existence of at least 25 elaborate brick shrines to esoteric Buddhist sects built between the eleventh and thirteenth centuries. Three shrines still bear the folk names Biaro Bahal I, II, and III. Biaro is derived from Sanskrit *vihara*, or monastery. The term *bahal* is still used in Nepal to refer to two-storied temples of the Vajrayana Buddhist sect. Rampant lions on Biaro Bahal I are very similar to contemporary carvings at Polonnaruva in Sri Lanka. Sherds of Chinese porcelain of the Song Dynasty have also been discovered here.

Another important cluster of Middle Classic period brick monuments was constructed in Jambi Province. After Srivijaya's defeat in the early eleventh century, Malayu's capital, which was probably located at the modern site of Muara Jambi on the Batang Hari, seems to have returned to prominence. Jambi's prosperity continued through the twelfth and into the thirteenth centuries. Many Buddhist brick temples at Muara Jambi were built, restored or enlarged during this period. Nine principal structures as well as many smaller edifices were erected along a 5-kilometer left bank stretch of the Batang Hari. Although little archaeological research has been conducted, huge quantities of Chinese ceramic sherds dating from the twelfth through the thirteenth centuries are exposed in the banks of the river at several locations.

Another important Buddhist complex developed around the same time much further inland, at Muara Takus on the upper Kampar River. This site has yielded some Chinese and local ceramics, but its relationship to trading routes and settlement sites remains to be ascertained.

The first archaeological evidence of urban settlements appears during the Middle Classic period in Sumatra, perhaps connected with the arrival of Chinese emigrants. The Song Dynasty, under pressure from the Mongols in the north, ceased to enforce ancient rules against private Chinese commerce with foreigners. By the early twelfth century, Chinese quarters seem to have formed in ports along the Strait of Melaka. Early Chinese settlers built fortified settlements to protect themselves. Marco Polo, who spent five months in north Sumatra in 1292, recorded such a practice:

> This is how we spent our five months. We disembarked from our ships and for fear of these nasty and brutish folk who kill men for food we dug a big trench round our encampment, extending down to the shore of the harbour at either end. On the embankment of the trench we built five wooden towers or forts; and within these fortifications we lived for five months. There was no lack of timber. But the islanders used to trade with us for victuals and the like; for there was a compact between us.[14]

With the decline of the monopolistic trading kingdom of Srivijaya, many new trading centers sprang up where Chinese could settle.[15] The most extensively excavated of these early urban sites is Kota Cina (Chinese Stockade), a site in northeast Sumatra which has yielded a number of radiocarbon dates and a wide range of artifacts dating from 1050 to 1300. Many other areas of Sumatra possess great potential to illuminate this complex and important historical era, but they remain to be explored.

Figure 10.13 Candi Singasari, East Java. (John N. Miksic.)

During the thirteenth century, a newly unified East Javanese kingdom seized the opportunity to assert political ascendency in Sumatra. King Kertanagara of Singasari sent an army to Malayu in 1263 (Figure 10.13). A few years later, esoteric Buddhist statues made in Java began to appear in the upper Batang Hari, evidence of Javanese cultural and political hegemony.

According to a sixteenth-century Javanese text, a Malay princess captured in Sumatra in 1263 married a Javanese prince and had a son named Adityavarman. Adityavarman is one of the few personalities of fourteenth-century Sumatra of whom anything is known (Figure 10.14). He left an early inscription in east Java, and about 30 later inscriptions in Sumatra where he was probably sent as viceroy. His first Sumatran inscriptions were erected in the eastern lowlands, but all subsequent ones are concentrated in the western mountains. We infer from this that Adityavarman threw off allegiance to Java and moved his capital into the hinterland. This move may have been partly dictated by the need to evade Javanese attacks, but an equally strong motive may have been provided by the existence of gold sources in the Minangkabau highlands, particularly in the Buo district and along the Batang Gadis. One of his honorific titles was *Kanakamedinindra*, meaning "Gold Land Lord".

Figure 10.14 Large fourteenth-century stone image of a Bhairawa found in the Rambahan area of Sumatra and considered by some to be a portrait of a ruler, King Adityavarman, as a Tantric initiate. (John N. Miksic.)

West Sumatra is also one of the few regions in equatorial and densely-forested Sumatra where intensive wet-rice cultivation evolved. Such an agricultural system would have been familiar to Adityavarman from his youth in Java, and he would have recognized its potential to support an elaborate court. Legends and archaeological remains indicate that, when Adityavarman entered West Sumatra, society there was characterized by village egalitarianism, religious ceremonies making use of pre-Classic-style stone monuments, and adherence to matrilineal succession and inheritance in important aspects of social organization. Legends depict a struggle between two warriors, one of whom epitomized an egalitarian philosophy, the other striving to impose an aristocratic form of social organization. These legends may preserve a memory of a fourteenth-century attempt to foster a Javanese-style court in an area where the environment resembled that of Java but the culture was very different, sparking a conflict with the indigenous elite.

Adityavarman's experiment aimed at establishing a Javanese-style kingdom in the highlands may have succeeded temporarily, but after his death around 1375 the pre-existing social order reasserted itself. Pagarruyung, the Minangkabau royal centre, retained considerable prestige in the early nineteenth century, but the political structure which early European visitors found bore no resemblance to a Javanese system.

The Middle Classic period in Bali

In the late tenth century a Balinese ruler named Udayana married an East Javanese princess named Gunapriya. In later edicts which they issued jointly, the queen's name appears first. During the decades following this marriage, Javanese cultural influence became quite evident in Bali. Old Javanese language was used for edicts and the court was organized according to the Javanese style, with a council comprising military commanders and Hindu and Buddhist clergy. Gunapriya received a posthumous title meaning "she who is immortalized in Burwan". Burwan may be Buruan, near which is a temple, Pura Kedharman, containing a stone statue of Durga Mahisasuramardini with Javanese Middle Classic traits.

The eldest son of this royal couple, Airlangga, married a Javanese princess. He later defeated the forces which had overthrown his father-in-law and became king of East Java in 1014. Thus, although Airlangga was the eldest son of Balinese rulers, he never ruled there. Instead Bali's next king was Airlangga's younger brother, Dharmawangsa, who ruled between 1022 and 1025. Yet another younger sibling, Anak Wungsu, came to power in 1049. He left a large number of inscriptions which have been found in many parts of the island, evidence that his realm was quite extensive. In 1284 Bali was attacked and subjugated by the Singhasari kingdom of eastern Java. Some inscriptions then refer to an official who may have been appointed by the Javanese as a governor.

Despite strong contacts with Java, Middle Classic period Balinese art developed a distinctive character which evolved continuously into the twentieth century. In the earliest period, around the late tenth and early eleventh centuries, Javanese influence was most marked, as exemplified by the Durga and associated statues of the *Boddhisattva Amoghapasha* and the *Ganesha* at Kutri. The nature of the relationship seems to have changed during the course of the eleventh century, however. At Mount Panulisan, a collection of approximately 50 statues stands in a temple on a peak 1745 meters high. Some bear dates of AD 1011, 1074, 1077, and 1254 (or 1257). Similar statues only appear in Java during the fourteenth and fifteenth centuries, suggesting that Bali may have exerted artistic and religious influence over Java as well as the reverse.

The artificial cave of Goa Gajah can be dated by paleography to the late eleventh century through graffiti on the entrance. A face carved on the cave entrance occupies a position which in Java would be occupied by the *kala* motif, but the style and expression of this image are much more reminiscent of the witch Rangda of modern Balinese dance, or the villain of the Balinese Calon Arang folktale.

Supra-village irrigation organizations called *subak*, found in modern Bali, may already have existed at this time, as indicated by the term *kasuwakan* found in inscriptions. Craftsmen specialized in working gold, silver, iron, copper and bronze, carpentry and boat-building. Merchants and officials in charge of commercial affairs are recorded. The Julah inscription, dated AD 911, mentions a port where foreign ships called. Other inscriptions mention officials who collected many types of taxes, and requests from commoners for tax exemptions.

The Late Classical Period in Java

The Late Classical period was marked by the rise of Indonesia's greatest pre-modern empire, Majapahit, from the ruins of Singasari, which collapsed in 1292 (Figure 10.13).

The period also witnessed the emergence of Islam, a force which ultimately brought that empire down.

The fourteenth century was Majapahit's golden age. Contemporary sources depict a sophisticated court with an urban center at modern-day Trowulan in East Java and a sphere of influence extending from New Guinea to Sumatra. Direct administrative control was limited to East Java and Bali, but Majapahit was able to project military power to other islands when its suzerainty was flouted. A Chinese source reports that Majapahit's commander in chief and his 30,000 soldiers were paid in gold, implying that a standing army existed. Surviving literary sources are largely of religious or poetic genres. They do not enable us to reconstruct the kingdom's bureaucratic structure.[16] One important new development in the kingdom affected the relationship between religion and the government. In 1269 King Kertanagara of Singhasari issued an edict, the "Charter of Sawardharma", which ostensibly freed the priesthood from royal interference. In practice this administrative independence seems to have been purchased at the cost of the loss of royal financial support. No structures on the scale of the enormous Early Classic complexes were built. Religious monuments of the Late Classic period depict local artistic ambitions and religious cults.

Taxes and fines were paid in cash. In about 1300, in the reign of the first king of Majapahit, the system of indigenous coinage which had lasted for 500 years was replaced, for unknown reasons, by imported Chinese copper cash. Certainly the small-denomination copper coins were more convenient for daily transactions than the previous gold and silver currency. One text refers to a court official in charge of markets who received "eight thousand Chinese coins every day". Clay containers for these coins have been found, some in the form of pigs with slits on their backs large enough to admit a coin. Domesticated pigs were probably a source of wealth in fourteenth-century Java.

A text of 1358 mentions 78 ferry crossings in Java, evidence of considerable overland traffic. Other texts refer to many occupational specialties from goldsmiths to drink vendors. Indian, Khmer, Siamese and Chinese were among the foreign merchants in the kingdom, on whom tax was levied.

A poem written in 1365 depicts the palace of Majapahit and its surroundings, but does not describe the non-royal aspects of the capital other than mentioning a marketplace. A book of court etiquette defines the capital as "All where one can go out without passing through paddy fields", implying some sort of urban character. Temple reliefs contain sketches of settlements featuring walled dwelling areas. Texts imply the existence of walled settlement units inhabited by a large number of people under the control of a nobleman. Surrounding the village of Trowulan in East Java is a huge archaeological site covering approximately 100 square kilometers, almost certainly the Majapahit capital. Trowulan possesses monumental remains such as temples, tombs and bathing places. Recent archaeological surveys and excavations show that Trowulan was densely populated during the fourteenth and fifteenth centuries by people engaged in a variety of occupations. Unfortunately, much of the site has been destroyed by people digging for old bricks and artifacts to sell. Much archaeological research is needed before it will be possible to reconstruct even the basic outline of the city; nevertheless, excavations have revealed dwellings with brick floors and foundations of walls, equipped with wells and drains and, in some cases, clay water pipes. Traces of what may have been an urban water system have been discovered, including a large reservoir at the approximate centre of the site, linked by canals to other water storage facilities around the edge of the city. The system was supplemented by wells lined with bricks or clay rings.

Part of the site is still called Kemasan (from *mas* meaning gold). Gold ornaments and tools used for working gold have been found in the vicinity, including small clay cups for melting gold, bronze anvils and stone tripods with flat circular working surfaces. A bronze-working area is marked by a large number of clay crucibles. Bronze statuary from the Majapahit period is rare. Instead the bronze casters applied their considerable skills to the production of such objects as elaborate hanging lamps and rattles which priests jangled as they walked to announce their approach.

The wide range and technical sophistication of pottery products found at Majapahit's capital indicate that specialized craftsmen also engaged in this occupation. The best pottery of Majapahit takes the form of vessels such as water ewers (*kendi*), with thin walled bodies, graceful shapes and glossy red burnished surfaces. Such water containers were probably one of the Majapahit potter's main products. Poetry describes pottery decorations on the roofs of the city. One can gain an idea of their use by observing similar artifacts found in modern Bali. Terracotta figurines were produced in large quantities representing many subjects such as gods, humans, animals, buildings and even landscape scenes. They may have functioned as household decorations.

Sites of the Upper Brantas Valley

Several important religious complexes are found along the course of the Brantas River that winds through much of east Java. The main complex here, Panataran, was developed between about 1345 and 1375. A considerable number of brick and stone structures arose here, but unlike the early Classic complexes Panataran had no overall plan and seems to have grown haphazardly.

By the late fourteenth century, in an interesting example of archaism, the terraced shrines of the preclassic tradition were revived as the main form of religious architecture. The largest concentration of terrace temples is found on Mt. Penanggungan in east Java, where over 80 sites have been identified, with inscriptions stretching over six centuries from 977 to 1511. Penanggungan's popularity may have stemmed from its form: a near-perfect cone flanked by four lesser peaks, distributed in such a uniform pattern as to suggest mythical Mount Sumeru, only 25 kilometers southeast of and clearly visible from the Majapahit capital. Sites on the mountain consist of a series of terraces, usually five, with stone facings and a stairway leading to three altar-like constructions on the uppermost terrace. At a few sites the terraces are faced with carved reliefs illustrating scenes from narratives taken from Hindu epics or Javanese stories based on them such as the Arjunawiwaha.

The most famous monument of this class, Candi Sukuh, stands on the western slope of Mt. Lawu. Inscriptions date this site to the mid-fifteenth century. In the fifteenth century a new form of religious cult devoted to the character Bima, one of the five Pandawa brothers in the Mahabharata epic, seems to have become popular among the Javanese. Bima seems to have been the main figure worshipped at the mountain temples (Figure 10.15). His popularity may have derived from his role in a text called the Sudhamala, wherein he plays the part of a savior who can bring the dead back to life.

Several similar sites lie scattered within a radius of a few kilometers from Candi Sukuh, between elevations of 900 and 1,410 meters above sea level. The largest group of monuments on Mount Lawu, however, is clustered around the summit, over 3,000 meters high. Some are of very large size, with the largest terrace being about 100 meters long and 20 meters wide. All are constructed of unworked boulders. The interesting question remains unresolved as to whether these terraces represent a final stage in the devolution of pre-Islamic Javanese mountain terraces, or a prehistoric complex which survived unaltered.

Figure 10.15 Stone carving of Bima as a blacksmith working a piston bellows, Candi Sukuh, East Java. (John N. Miksic.)

Bali in the Late Classic period

During the fourteenth century a new belief system spread through both Java and Bali which amalgamated with some aspects of pre-Classic religion. This system assimilated a new Hindu sect called Siva-Siddhanta, which de-emphasized the use of statues. In modern Balinese temples, and perhaps in fifteenth-century Java, worship was directed to elevated structures resembling altars but which are actually conceived as stone seats, where the gods can be invoked to manifest themselves invisibly during worship. Old statues were not destroyed, but either stored away or simply abandoned. Terraced temples similar to the fifteenth-century Javanese complexes are found at Sembiran, on the north coast, and at Besakih, still one of the most important Balinese temples.

Bali's economy at the end of the Classic period was apparently not much different from the beginning of the historic era, but more inscriptions are available to give us a detailed picture of it. Regulations governed the division of irrigation water, water taxes, construction of irrigation channels, the protection of certain trees, hunting, and taxes on farmers. The coinage used in markets and for paying taxes remained the same, unlike Java, where it was replaced by Chinese coins.

Javanese sources say that Bali was attacked by Singasari in 1284 and by Majapahit in 1343. Balinese chronicles say that important Javanese moved to Bali after the conquest, but no other sources confirm these stories. In a similar vein, Majapahit's fall in the fifteenth century is said to have caused some loyalists to flee to Bali. There is indirect evidence for this latter account. Balinese literary works of the fifteenth and sixteenth centuries use Middle Javanese language. A stone statue called Kebo Edan, "Crazy Buffalo", has similar attributes to fifteenth-century Javanese images of Bhima.

According to Javanese chronicles, Classical Indonesian culture was fated to meet its armageddon in a great battle between Majapahit and Demak, its Islamic successor, in

1478, which corresponds to Anno Javanensis 1400; (the Javanese calendrical system was based on the Saka era which originated in India). The battle and its date are both apocryphal. In reality, the curtain descended gradually over classic Indonesian culture, rather than falling abruptly. The process began in the late fourteenth century and continued throughout the fifteenth century. Indeed, Majapahit still existed when the Portuguese arrived in the early sixteenth century. Islamic culture, corresponding to the post-Classic phase, infiltrated Indonesia only gradually and in such areas as highland north Sumatra, Sulawesi and Bali it never made a significant impact.

The disappearance of classical Indonesian culture, like its rise, was a complicated drama, enacted over a broad expanse of time and space, with numerous subplots, rather than a single dramatic event. There was no sudden decline, no dramatic disruption in the evolution of Indonesian culture. Even the arrival of the Europeans had no rapid or major discernible effects. New economic and social conditions arising from a variety of factors exerted their influence over developments after 1500. Even Bali, which was the most unaffected by outside forces during the period 1500–1900 of any of the main centers of Indonesian classical culture, did not remain static; culture there was much different at the time of Dutch conquest than it had been in the Majapahit era, despite the fact that Bali remained the only outpost of Hindu culture in Indonesia, indeed in Southeast Asia.

Notes

1 Miksic (ed.) 1996.
2 Casparis 1975.
3 In India such inscriptions refer to the sacrifice of horses, but the Kutei ones are not so specific and as there is no other evidence for horses being known in Kalimantan at this time; other animals such as buffaloes may have been used as substitutes.
4 Walker and Santoso 1977.
5 Dalsheimer and Manguin 1998.
6 Manguin 1987.
7 Dumarçay 1986.
8 Casparis and Mabbett 1992.
9 Manguin 1993.
10 Dumarçay 1986.
11 Miksic 1990.
12 Boechari 1979.
13 Wicks 1992.
14 *The Travels of Marco Polo*, translated and with an introduction by Martin Latham. 1958, p. 254.
15 Wolters 1971.
16 Miksic and Soekatno (eds) 1995.

Select Bibliography

General

Marschall, W. (1988) "On some basic traditions in Nusantara cultures", in D. S. Moyer and H. J. M. Claessen (eds) *Time Past, Time Present, Time Future*, Verhandelingan van het Koninklijk Instituut voor Taal-, Land- en Volkenkunde 131: 69–77.

Miksic, J. N. (ed.) (1996) *Indonesian Heritage. Volume One. Ancient History*, Singapore: Editions Didier Millet.

Miksic, J. N. and Endang Soekatno (eds) (1995) *The Legacy of Majapahit*, Singapore: National Heritage Board.

Archaeology

Ardika, I Wayan and Bellwood, P. (1991) "Sembiran: the beginnings of Indian contact with Bali", *Antiquity* 65: 221–32.
Manguin, P.-Y. (1987) "Etudes Sumatranaises I. Palembang et Srivijaya: anciennes hypotheses, recherches nouvelles" *Bulletin de l'École Française d'Extrême-Orient* 76: 337–402.
Miksic, J. N. (1980) "Classical archaeology in Sumatra", *Indonesia* 30: 43–66.
Walker, M. and S. Santoso (1977) "Romano-Indian rouletted pottery in Indonesia", *Asian Perspectives* 1980: 20 (2): 228–35.

Epigraphy and inscriptions

Casparis, J. G. de (1975) *Indonesian Palaeography: a History of Writing in Indonesia from the Beginnings to c. AD 1500*, Leiden: Brill. Handbuch der Orientalistik: 3. Abt., Indonesien, Malaysia und die Philippinen; 4. Bd. Linguistik, 1. Lieferung.
Coedès, G. and Damais, L-C. (1992) *Sriwijaya: History, Religion and Language of an Early Malay Polity*, Kuala Lumpur: Malaysian Branch of the Royal Asiatic Society Monograph no. 20.

Religion

Casparis, J. G. de and Mabbett, I. (1992) "Religion and popular beliefs of Southeast Asia before *c.*1500", *The Cambridge History of Southeast Asia* I: 276–340.

Architecture and art history

Dalsheimer, N. and Manguin, P.-Y. (1998) "Visnu mitrés et réseaux marchands en Asie du Sud-Est: nouvelles données archéologiques sur le 1er millénaire ap. J. C.", *Bulletin de l'École Française d'Extrême-Orient* 85: 87–123.
Dumarçay, J. (1981) "Candi Sewu et l'architecture bouddhique du centre de Java", *Mémoires Archéologiques XIV*, Paris: École Française d'Extrême-Orient.
Dumarçay, J. (1986) *Temples of Java*, Kuala Lumpur: Oxford University Press.
Edwards McKinnon, E. (1985) "Early polities in southern Sumatra", *Indonesia* 40: 1–36.
Fontein, J. (ed.) (1991) *The Sculpture of Indonesia*, Washington: National Gallery of Art.
Klokke, M. (1992) "Iconographical traditions in late East Javanese narrative reliefs", in I. C. Glover (ed.) *Southeast Asian Archaeology 1990*, Hull: Centre for South-East Asian Studies, pp. 75–84.
Miksic, J. N. (1990) *Borobudur: Golden Tales of the Buddhas*, Singapore: Periplus.
Miksic, J. N. *et al.* (1998) *Indonesian Heritage. Volume Six. Architecture*, Singapore: Editions Didier Millet.
Subhadradis Diskul, M. C. (ed.) (1980) *The Art of Srivijaya*, Kuala Lumpur: Oxford University Press.

History and politics

Boechari. (1979) "Some considerations of the problem of the shift of Mataram's center of government from central to east Java in the tenth century AD", in R. B. Smith and W. Watson (eds) *Early South East Asia – Essays in Archaeology, History and Historical Geography*, London: Oxford University Press, pp. 473–92.
Christie, J. W. (1985) *Theatre States and Oriental Despotisms: Early Southeast Asia in the Eyes of the West*, Hull: Centre for South-East Asian Studies, Occasional Papers No. 10.
Christie, J. W. (1995) "State formation in early maritime Southeast Asia: a consideration of the theories and the data", *Bijdragen tot de Taal-, Land- en Volkenkunde* pp. 235–88.

Kulke, H. (1986) "The early and the imperial kingdom in Southeast Asian history", in D. Marr and A. Milner (eds) *Southeast Asia in the ninth to fourteenth Century*, Singapore: Institute for Southeast Asian Studies, pp. 1–22.
Latham, M. (trans.) (1958) *The Travels of Marco Polo*, Harmondsworth: Penguin.
Wolters, O. W. (1971) *The Fall of Srivijaya in Malay History*, Ithaca: Cornell University.
Wolters, O. W. (1979) "Studying Srivijaya", *Journal of the Malaysian Branch of the Royal Asiatic Society* 52 (2): 1–32.

Trade and exchange

Christie, J. W. (1999) "Asian sea trade between the tenth and thirteenth centuries and its impact on the states of Java and Bali", in H. P. Ray (ed.) *Archaeology of Seafaring: The Indian Ocean in the Ancient Period*, Delhi: Pragati Publications, Indian Council of Historical Research, pp. 221–70.
Manguin, P.-Y. (1993) "Trading ships of the South China Sea", *Journal of the Economic and Social History of the Orient* 36: 253–80.
Wolters, O. W. (1967) *Early Indonesian Commerce*, Ithaca: Cornell University.
Wicks, R. S (1992) *Money, Markets, and Trade in Early Southeast Asia*, Ithaca: Cornell University.

11

THE ARCHAEOLOGY OF THE PHILIPPINE ARCHIPELAGO

Elisabeth A. Bacus

Introduction

The Philippine archipelago, lying between 5 and 20 degrees north latitude, is made up of more than 7,000 islands scattered over a 300,000 square kilometer area. Bounded on the east by the Pacific Ocean and on the west by the South China Sea, the majority of the land mass is composed of eleven islands grouped into three main regions: the northern region with Luzon and Mindoro; the Visayas (or Central Philippines) with Masbate, Palawan, Panay, Negros, Cebu, Bohol, Leyte and Samar; and the southern region with Mindanao along with the smaller islands of Basilan, and the Sulu and Tawi Tawi archipelagos.

The islands are part of a western Pacific arc system that is characterized by active volcanoes. Palawan is the only island in the archipelago that is part of the Sunda continental shelf, the large expanse of land exposed during various times during the Pleistocene when sea level dropped, which may have enabled it to be occupied by humans earlier than the other islands. The latter belong to the biogeographical province of Wallacea and have never been completely joined together as dry land, either with Sundaland or with each other.

The archipelago has a tropical climate, with the southern and eastern parts of the archipelago lying within the equatorial tropics characterized by year-round rainfall, and the northern and western areas lying within the seasonal tropics marked by clearly differentiated wet and dry seasons of varying lengths. These broad divisions in tropical climate tend to be associated with different general types of forest, evergreen rain forest, and more open, deciduous monsoon forest, respectively. Significant differences in altitude, along with those in rainfall, result in marked variation in the types of flora that would have been found in various areas during the prehistoric and protohistoric periods. Tropical plants and trees would have prevailed in the lowland and coastal area, while in the highlands, hardwoods and pines would have covered extensive areas.[1]

The archaeology of the Philippine archipelago encompasses a study of myriad topics: of initial human occupation; of a more than 10,000-year span of hunter-gatherer societies evolving within dynamic environmental and cultural contexts; of Austronesian language expansion; of rice farming communities; of interactions with the larger Asian region; of maritime technology; of elaborate burial practices; of the emergence of trade-oriented polities; and of Spanish conquest, to name a few. While touching on many of these topics, this chapter focuses particularly on the complex lowland polities which arose during the first and second millennia AD in various areas of the archipelago.

Various chronological frameworks exist for understanding prehistoric and protohistoric change and continuity as seen through the archaeological record of the Philippines. While technologically-based periodization is still often used (i.e., Stone Age, Metal Age, and Neolithic), other proposed frameworks emphasize assumed social changes. An example of the latter would be the division of Philippine prehistory into a Formative period, from human occupation of the archipelago until 500 BC, during which a pattern of adaptation to Pleistocene and postglacial Holocene environments developed; an Incipient period, from around 800 BC to AD 1, when the archipelago became less isolated; and a final Emergent period when international contacts greatly expanded and identifiable "Filipino" cultural patterns appeared.[2] The following discussion of the Philippine past does not specifically use terminology associated with any particular periodization, though it does draw on them in identifying periods of significant change. In addition, the establishment of an historical framework in this chapter is based on the use of securely dated sites (see Figure 11.1) for location of all sites discussed); sites that can only be dated by suggested broad similarities in material culture are generally omitted.

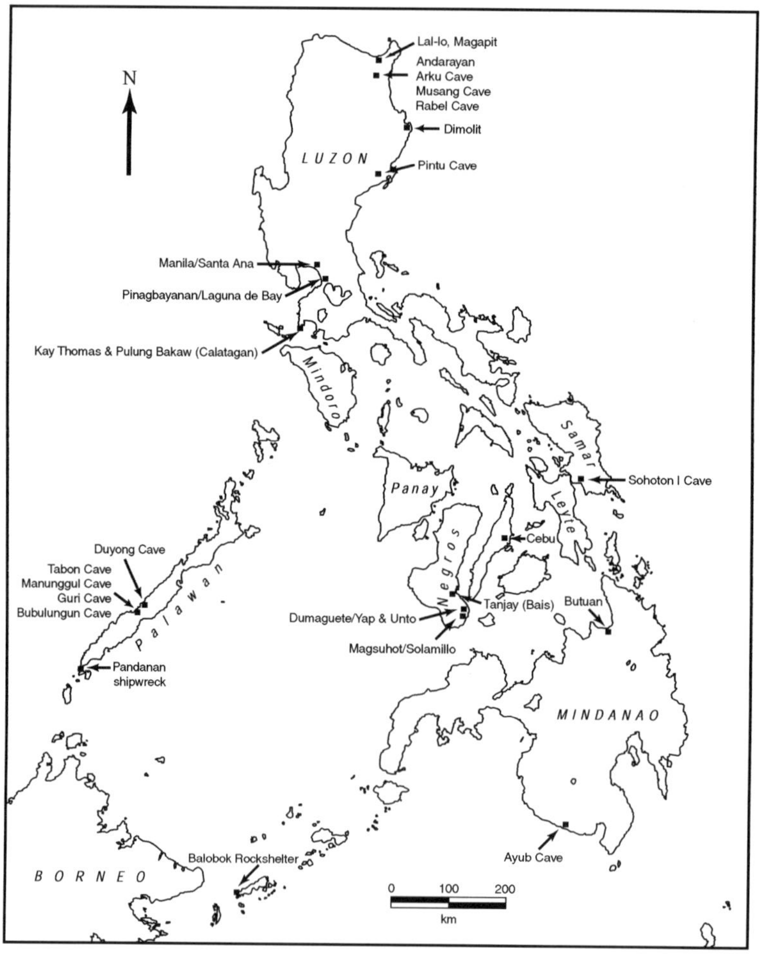

Figure 11.1 Location of archaeological sites in the Philippines mentioned in the text.

Hunter-gatherers to rice farming: the early prehistoric background

Late Pleistocene–Early Holocene hunter-gatherers

Human occupation of the Philippine archipelago occurred by late Pleistocene times and at present the earliest securely dated evidence only dates to around 30,000 years ago. This evidence comes from Tabon Cave located on Palawan, the only main Philippine island that was part of Sundaland, the land mass exposed at various times during the Pleistocene that connected Mainland with parts of Island Southeast Asia. Thus, human expansion into the rest of the archipelago would have necessitated the use of boats. Located on the west coast of Palawan, overlooking the South China Sea, Tabon Cave has yielded evidence of use by hunter-gatherer populations from around 30,000 to 10,000 years ago.[3] This evidence is comprised almost entirely of stone tools, with the earliest remains consisting of flakes, cores and flake tools, together with pieces of charcoal and the bones of small birds, bats and other animals, some of which probably represent hunted prey. Subsequent use of the cave, at around 23,000 years ago, is evidenced again by charcoal and numerous animal bones; hundreds of chert pieces from various stages in the manufacture of flake implements; basalt choppers; and quartz and basalt hammer stones (Figure 11.2). Of particular significance are the cranial fragments of at least three *Homo sapiens* individuals, the earliest such remains in the archipelago.

At around 7–8,000 years ago, hunter-gatherers using nearby Duyong Cave exploited shallow-water marine and brackish water shellfish species as a food source, along with crab and some birds and land animals. The stone tool kits of these populations consisted of small flake tools and blade tools, the latter appearing to have been a new technology.

Hunter-gatherer sites contemporary with the Tabon and Duyong sequences on Palawan are also known from elsewhere in the archipelago, particularly from the northern and central Philippines. The lithic assemblages from such sites include complex and sophisticated industries involving a variety of flake tools, some blades and core tools. In northern Luzon, for example, several cave sites in the Cagayan Valley have yielded pebble tools, with some sites dating to as early as 11,000 years ago. Also around this time, Musang Cave, located in the foothills of the Sierra Madre in northeastern Luzon, was used as a frequentation site by hunter-gatherers who gathered shellfish in the nearby river; hunted wild pig, deer and bird; and used flake tools.[4] On the island of Samar, hunter-gatherers used Sohoton I Cave as a temporary hunting camp as early as around 12–13,000 years ago. They brought marine fish with them to the cave, the sea being approximately 25 kilometers away at that time, and presumably also exploited freshwater fish found in the nearby river. They hunted deer and pig, though the bone remains indicate that they transported most of the meat away from the cave, leaving only butchering refuse and bones from parts bearing little meat behind. Birds, snakes and other small animals were also caught and probably consumed.[5] The southernmost part of the archipelago has also yielded evidence of early Holocene hunter-gatherers. Balobok Rockshelter on Sanga Sanga Island, for example, was occupied around 8–9,000 years ago, and sites dating back to the late Pleistocene are also reported from neighboring Sabah (East Malaysia) on the island of Borneo.

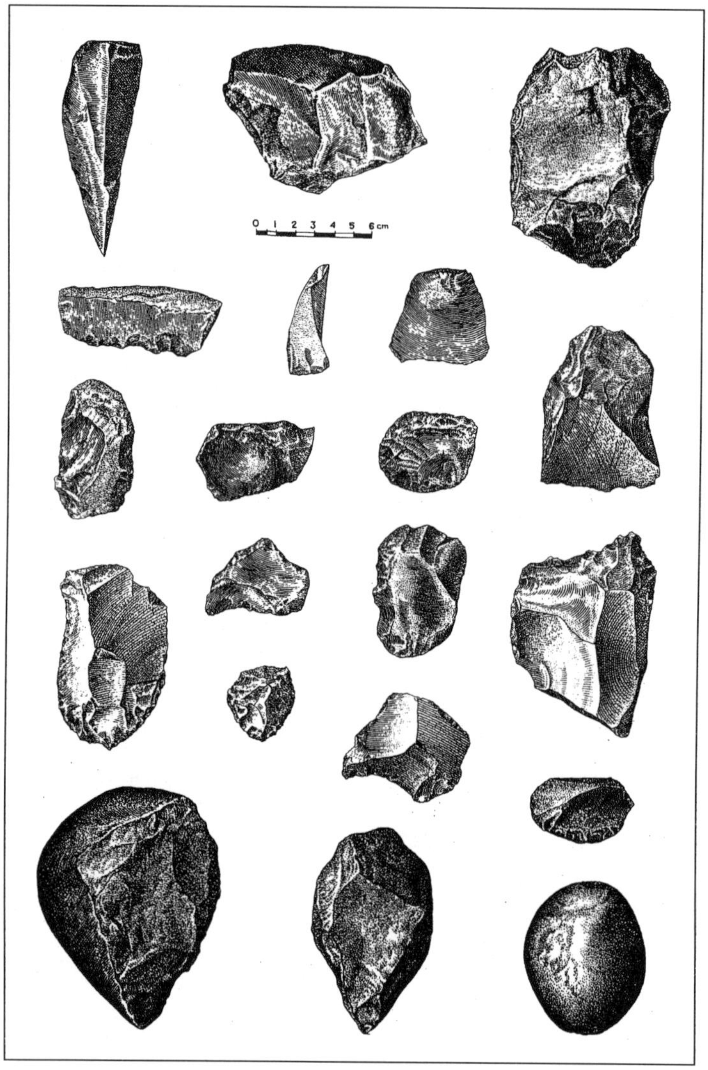

Figure 11.2 Flake tools, basalt chopper (bottom left) and a quartz hammer-stone (bottom right) from Tabon Cave, Palawan. (From Fox 1970: Fig 7.)

Early rice cultivation

In chapter 2, Peter Bellwood discusses models for the spread of rice agriculture and of Austronesian languages through Island Southeast Asia. His chapter is complemented here by a brief consideration of the Neolithic, that is, the period in the Philippines from approximately 5,000 to 2,500 years ago. Traditionally, the term "Neolithic" refers to new categories of material culture and to a change in subsistence economy to one based on the cultivation of domesticated crops and the keeping of animals. In Island Southeast Asia, domestic animals included the pig, dog and chicken. Technological changes entailed the use of pottery, polished stone adzes and stone hoes for forest clearance and gardening activities, implements for cloth making (clay spindle whorls and stone barkcloth beaters), marine shell adzes and fishhooks, and marine shell ornaments.

As in many other areas of Southeast Asia, not all groups incorporated such economic and technological changes. Hunter-gatherer societies thus continued throughout this and subsequent periods, and engaged in various interactions with agricultural communities, through whom they acquired Neolithic material culture (as has been suggested for Musang Cave). Hunter-gatherer groups also interacted with more recent complex societies where they played an important part in the expanding international trade of the late first to mid-second millennia AD. The Neolithic is thus the first period marked by a diversity in cultural practices; that is, in subsistence, settlement, technology, ritual, presumably language and so forth which distinguished communities primarily dependent on cultivated crops – particularly domesticated rice – from those dependent on wild and managed resources. This Neolithic-period diversity is important to consider in reconstructing the fourth to early first millennium BC, in part because the majority of archaeological evidence still comes from caves which were used for various purposes by hunter-gatherers and farmers.

The earliest direct evidence of rice cultivation, dating to around the early to mid-second millennium BC, comes from pottery found at the Andarayan site, an open site located in the Cagayan Valley of northern Luzon.[6] Probably added as temper by local potters to the clay, the carbonized rice inclusions suggest that the makers of the red-slipped pottery concerned (belonging to a widespread style considered a hallmark of the Philippine Neolithic) were part of a settlement cultivating a dryland variety of rice. This community of rice growers also used clay spindle whorls in cloth production, chert flakes and ground stone adzes, and ornamented themselves with ceramic earrings.

Some Neolithic sites, however, suggest even somewhat earlier farming activities in Luzon. Rabel Cave was a frequentation site visited by pottery and flaked-stone using groups beginning around the mid-fourth or late third millennium BC. Pintu Rockshelter was also visited for short periods during the mid-third or mid-second millennium BC by groups with earthenware pottery who produced tool preforms from basalt and other types of stone, and who brought in meat of hunted animals such as pigs and large birds which they had butchered elsewhere.[7]

Rice cultivation though was not necessarily the main form of subsistence engaged in by communities using Neolithic material culture. The Magapit site, located in the limestone hills next to the Cagayan River in northern Luzon, indicates the consumption of freshwater bivalve shellfish by peoples using red-slipped pottery around 1200–800 BC, while a somewhat earlier site (mid-third–late second millennium BC) has a few possible hunted remains of pig and maybe deer, together with pottery.[8] Numerous shell-midden sites are located along this river, some preceramic, some yielding the Neolithic red-slipped pottery, some Iron Age and some containing seventeenth–eighteenth century Asian tradewares, indicating a long period of exploitation of shellfish. Hunter-gatherer shellfish exploitation also continued into the Neolithic at Guri Cave on Palawan Island, a third millennium BC site composed of a marine shell midden, pieces of chert and flake implements with blade tools in the upper levels, and remains of hunted wild pig and deer.

Neolithic-period rice farmers presumably lived in variously-sized residential clusters, though archaeological evidence of domestic structures has rarely been recovered. Only one site, Dimolit, located on the northeast coast of Luzon, provides such remains.[9] Dating to the early third or late second millennium BC, this site has yielded postholes of two seasonally-occupied square houses measuring about three meters on a side (Figure 11.3), each with remains of a hearth, as well as postholes belonging to two other structures. The living floors were littered with plain and red-slipped earthenware sherds from globular pots, shallow dishes on a ring foot (some decorated) and carinated vessels. Flakes (some with silica sheen suggesting their possible use as harvesting knives), mortars, grinders, and two jadeite beads were also found.

Mortuary practices of Neolithic-period groups involved burial in caves, although people presumably also buried their dead near their residences. On Palawan, caves once used for occupation appear to have been selected as a realm for Neolithic burial. Duyong Cave, for example, contained the skeleton of an adult male who was buried in a flexed position and face down with his arms and legs doubled underneath his body. A large polished stone adze or axe and four *Tridacna* (giant clam) shell adz-axes were placed along his sides. He was also buried with two shell ear ornaments – shell disks perforated in their centers – with one lying next to his right ear; a perforated shell pendant (i.e., a shell disk, perforated on the edge) on his chest; and near his feet six *Arca* shells, one of which was filled with lime perhaps chewed with betel nut. This burial may date to within the fourth to mid-third millennium BC and appears to have been contemporary with a cultural layer

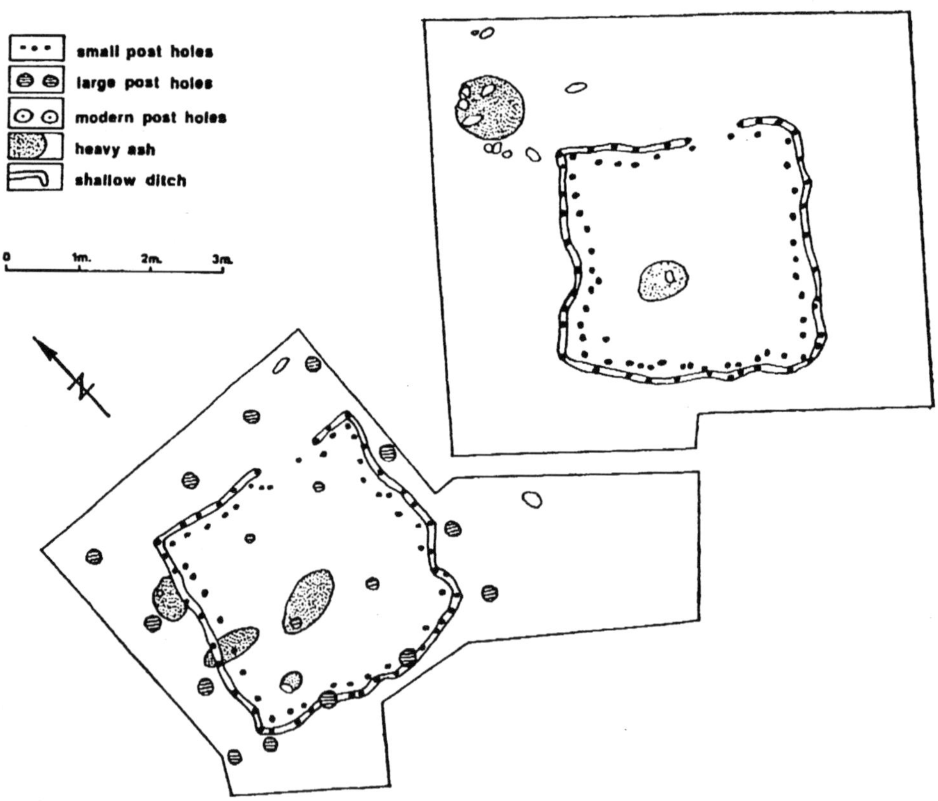

Figure 11.3 House plans from Dimolit, northern Luzon. (From Peterson 1974: Map 2. Reprinted with permission of *Archaeology in Oceania*.)

containing a *Tridacna* shell tool, a piece of a large *Tridacna* shell gouge, a number of shell disk ear pendants, and possible hearth remains.[10]

Towards the end of the Neolithic, the practice of secondary burial, specifically of individuals interred in earthenware jars and placed in caves, may have begun. This form of mortuary ritual becomes more common in subsequent periods, and may be better understood in connection with the emergence of social ranking in the archipelago and related developing links between the Philippines and other areas of Southeast Asia.[11]

Emergent complex society and contacts beyond the archipelago

By around 2,500 years ago, objects crafted of iron, bronze, glass and exotic stone first appeared in Island Southeast Asia and are used as markers for the end of the Neolithic. More significantly, objects such as the knobbed pennanular stone earrings (*lingling-o*) and double animal-headed pendants (Figure 11.4) indicate the participation of Philippine societies in exchange networks that linked them with complex societies on the mainland of Southeast Asia (Thailand, Sa Huynh in Vietnam) and with other parts of Island Southeast Asia (Sarawak). Based on comparative studies of emergent complex societies elsewhere in the world, the appearance of such exotica suggests the emergence of social elites who actively sought these items as markers of their status and links with distant sources of knowledge, as well as for use in the creation of social and economic obligations. The archaeological evidence for this period of emergent complex society (500 BC to AD 500) is far from abundant, deriving primarily from the mortuary use of caves.

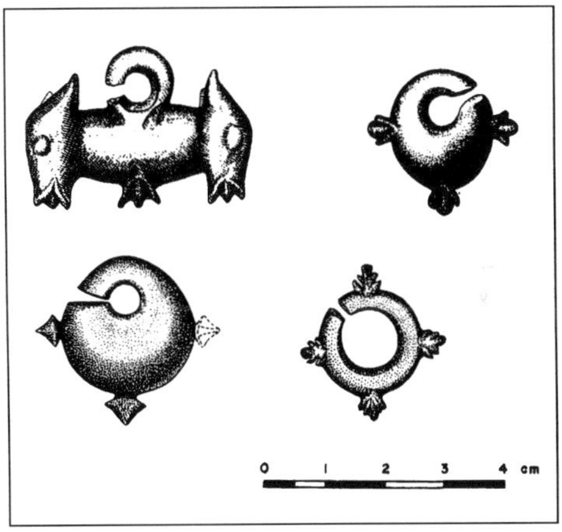

Figure 11.4 Double-headed jade earring/pendant and jade *lingling-o* from Tabon Cave, Palawan. (From Fox 1970: Fig 37.)

Mortuary practices of this period provide some support for developing social complexity. As the sites discussed below suggest, a prevalent practice at this time was secondary burial, often of multiple individuals, in pottery jars or stone urns. Such mortuary practices suggest relatively small, sedentary corporate groups, with some level of internal status differentiation, who controlled stable, localized resources such as land for farming.[12]

The most famous group of jar burials comes from Manunggul Cave Chamber A on Palawan, which may date to slightly before the period under consideration, early first millennium BC (based on dating of "ritual fires"), although this date remains to be securely established. Within this cave, both on the surface and in subsurface layers, lay a total of 78 broken jars, jar covers and smaller earthenware vessels. Amongst these was the "ship-of-the-dead" jar burial (Plate 14), as well as others with sculpted lids including one with three animal or bird heads surrounding the opening. The burial jars and associated earthenwares were often decorated with curvilinear scroll designs on their upper bodies. Body ornaments were an important part of mortuary practice, and included black and white banded agate beads, jade and shell beads and bracelets, agate bracelets, a jasper ear pendant, and a possible red chalcedony or carnelian pendant. Most of these stone materials represent new types not used previously in the manufacture of ornaments in the Philippines.[13]

During possibly the last few centuries BC or early centuries AD, the adjacent Chamber B became a mortuary arena. Sherds of jar burials (now lacking decoration, unlike those in Chamber A) were found together with imported iron objects, glass beads and bracelets, beads of jade, carnelian, etched agate and other stone, and a jade bracelet. Other caves in the area also contain jar burials. Although undated, they are significant in also containing copper/bronze items, including socketed axes and spearheads, a tanged and barbed arrowhead, and a possible barbed harpoon, as well as pottery moulds for casting socketed bronze axes (Figure 11.5). Also present by this time are gold beads, jade *lingling-o* earrings, jade double animal-headed ear-pendants and jade bracelets.

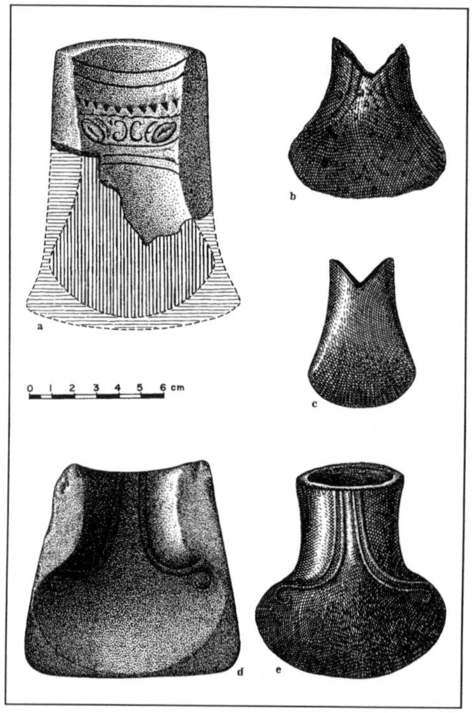

Figure 11.5 Bronze axes, adzes and pottery moulds for casting socketed tools from the Tabon Caves, Palawan: a, from Duyong Cave; b, provenience unspecified; c, possibly from the Tabon Caves area; d, from Batu Puti Cave; e, from Uyaw Cave. (From Fox 1970: Fig 39.)

In Luzon, contemporary groups also practiced secondary burial. At Arku Cave, located in the Cagayan Valley, bones from approximately 60 individuals (mainly adults but also including several children and infants) were interred during the first millennium BC. Various forms of burial were employed, including in jars, one containing the disarticulated bones of two adults, and another containing a skull with the rest of the bones buried outside of the jar; in a small pit which contained bones of two adults; and in groups of four or five adults with a portion of the bones heavily covered in red ocher. Mortuary ritual also involved the placement of red-slipped and polished black earthenware pots, bowls, globular vessels, jars and vessels with ring feet. Ornaments took the form of stone and shell beads, shell bracelets, and earrings of shell, ground stone, jade and fired clay. Four of the stone and all nine of the shell earrings suggest the *lingling-o* style. Other material remains included flake tools, stone adzes, bone points, horn tattooing chisels, a stone barkcloth beater and clay spindle whorls. This is not the only site in Luzon yielding exotica at this time; Pintu Rockshelter in eastern Luzon, while not used for mortuary purposes, also has glass beads dating to about 2,000 years ago.[14]

Portrayal of the deceased individual appears as a theme of secondary burial practice in southern Mindanao.[15] At about 2,000 years ago, mortuary practices in Ayub Cave involved the use of anthropomorphic earthenware jars with features formed as human figures, either moulded, or applied in the cases of the ears, mouths and chins (Figure 11.6). Jar covers took the shape of human heads with faces (49 complete and restorable heads plus around 100 fragments of other heads), some life size, with the bodies of the jars formed as human torsos and sometimes indicating gender. Some also portray jewelry and possibly other forms of body decoration. Some of the heads were plain, some were painted with red hematite and black organic carbon, and others had perforations possibly for the attachment of hair. Not all the jar covers were anthropomorphic; for example, some were of simple rounded shape with four handles while others had appliqué designs. Associated with these burial jars were decorated earthenware vessels, and in some decorated jarlets were teeth and finger bones. A range of ornaments also accompanied the dead, including glass beads and bracelets, earthenware beads and shell ornaments. Suggested differences in quantity and distribution of these with respect to individual burials may indicate variability in the social identities – possibly including status – expressed at death.

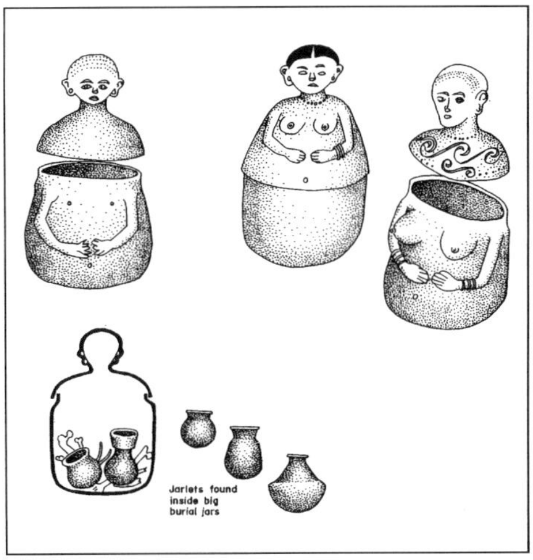

Figure 11.6 Anthropomorphic earthenware burial jars from Ayub Cave. (From Dizon 1996. Reprinted with permission of the author.)

Sometimes, jar burial mortuary ritual also took place outside caves. At Magsuhot in southeastern Negros Island, three groups of secondary burials were interred in an open area and possibly date to the late first millennium BC or early first millennium AD.[16] Burial I included three jars placed within a single grave pit which was lined with earthenware sherds from possibly deliberately broken vessels. This burial also contained 40 earthenware jars and two clay figurines, one of a woman and the other of a calf or young water buffalo. One of the three jars contained the multiple primary burials of an adult female, an infant and a child of 6–7 years of age. With them were placed hundreds of orange glass beads, one orange glass bracelet, two iron implements, and fragmentary chicken and pig bones. Neither skeletal remains nor funerary objects were uncovered in the other two associated burial jars, although hematite was present in one.

Magsuhot Burial II included a large burial jar, presumably once containing skeletal remains that have since disappeared due to soil acidity, as well as glass beads and iron implements. Associated with this burial jar was a pottery coffin containing a single tooth, a glass bead and iron implements, and 70 earthenware vessels, one with two female figures sitting around the opening of the jar (Figure 11.7). More than 20 vessels overlay the burial jar. Magsuhot Burial III consisted of one burial jar which contained neither skeletal remains nor artifacts, though earthenware sherds appear associated with it. As with other jar burial sites, these variations at Magsuhot too are suggestive of status differentiation of the kind found in emergent complex societies.

Unfortunately, despite the detailed information available on mortuary practices, acquisition of exotic goods, involvement in far-reaching exchange networks, body ornamentation and the production of elaborate pottery vessels for ritual purposes, little is known of settlements and details of subsistence during this period. But two open sites, both located in southeastern Negros, were roughly contemporary wth Magsuhot. Solamillo may have been the settlement whose residents interred their dead in the adjacent Magsuhot area. Midden and pit features here have primarily yielded earthenware sherds, some very similar to those found in the Magsuhot burials. There is also a possible hearth and a burial (though no skeletal remains were found). The latter was marked by five partially intact earthenware vessels clustered around a disturbed oval shaped area and surrounded by five postholes, associated with iron fragments, a stone ornament, a glass bead and several pieces of iron slag. The marked difference with the other burials suggests a complexity to mortuary ritual practices, with the jar burials representing only one form and possibly received by only certain social groups.

Figure 11.7 Earthenware vessel with female figures from Burial II, Magsuhot site. (Photograph courtesty of K. Hutterer.)

Apparently contemporary with Solamillo, and possibly with the Magsuhot burials, is the Unto settlement, approximately one hectare in size. This contained at least one residential structure. The pit features and midden deposit contained earthenware sherds with fragments of charcoal and other burnt organic material. Most of the pottery was plain, though some vessels were red-slipped, black burnished/polished, or had incised or other decoration. Vessel types included mainly cooking vessels and at least one bowl, and all appear to have been locally made as there was some evidence for earthenware production. The inhabitants of this settlement appear to have engaged in rice farming as several earthenware sherds contained rice husk impressions.[17]

The patterns of long-distance exchange and emergent social complexity seen in the Philippines during the later centuries BC and early centuries AD, began to intensify and become more evident by the mid–late first millennium AD. The subsequent period, sometimes referred to as the "Porcelain Period", is marked archaeologically by the presence of glazed tradewares from China, and later (during the fourteenth–fifteenth centuries) from Vietnam and Thailand. In this period we witness the development of maritime-trade oriented polities.

The rise of lowland polities and maritime trade

While Philippine communities had clearly engaged in exchange relations involving the larger Southeast Asian sphere since at least the later centuries BC, it was the eventual involvement of China that was to significantly impact the scale of trade from the late first millennium AD onwards. With the closure of the overland silk route, China's maritime trade expanded during the Tang Dynasty (AD 618–907). Beginning in the late Tang or early Song Dynasty (AD 960–1279), Chinese trade with the Philippines and other areas in the South China Sea began to flourish. The most prominent indicators of this early period of trade with China are the presence of Tang and Song glazed tradewares – porcelains and stoneware vessels – which occur in archaeological sites. While the quantities of Tang tradewares are relatively small, particularly in relation to later porcelains and stonewares, they are known from sites in the Babuyan Islands, along the Ilocos and Pangasinan coasts of Luzon, and Mindoro, in the north; from Bohol and Cebu in the Visayas; and in the south along the Mindanao coast, in Cagayan de Sulu and Jolo. By late Song (1127–1279) and Yuan (1280–1368) times, imports of tradewares signficantly and rapidly increased, with sites yielding considerable numbers of southern Song vessels located in the central and northern parts of the archipelago, including Cebu and around Manila Bay and near by Laguna de Bay.

This initial period of early trade, until the end of the protohistoric period (sixteenth century), saw the further development of complex polities in various lowland areas of the archipelago, participating directly and indirectly in international trade. Their involvement was to intensify significantly during the Ming Dynasty, when the Chinese produced ceramics specifically for overseas trade, and lasted until the time of Spanish colonial usurpation of trade in the mid-sixteenth century. The archaeological record of this maritime trade, and of the development of these complex polities, is presented below.

While boats must have been central to human settlement of the archipelago and to later coastal dwelling communities, the earliest boats yet recovered archaeologically in the Philippines date to this period of increasing involvement in long-distance exchange with China. Parts of nine wooden plank boats with internal lashings and the use of dowels to hold the planks together edge-to-edge – a construction method typical of historical Southeast Asian boat-making technology – have been located along the banks of the Libertad River in Butuan, Mindanao.[18] They are associated with evidence of a settlement yielding tradewares (including some Islamic sherds) dating to as early as the nineth–tenth centuries. Three of these boats have been excavated; the timber of the earliest dates to between AD 150 and 650, and belonged to a hull approximately 15 meters in length by 3 meters in width. The other two boats date to somewhat later, to between the late tenth and early thirteenth centuries AD, and the late twelfth and early fifteenth centuries AD. Probably provided with outriggers and propelled either by sail or by paddles, these boats may have carried trade goods brought by the larger Chinese junks to other islands in the archipelago.

The mid-fifteenth century Pandanan shipwreck, located off the southernmost tip of Palawan Island, provides information on the variety of cargo that was brought into the Philippines for trade with later polities.[19] The remains of this wooden boat, perhaps of either Vietnamese construction or southern Chinese construction – though more likely the former, since from 1433 to the 1460s the Ming rulers of China forbade overseas travel and the construction of ocean-going vessels – indicated a vessel approximately 25–30 meters long and 6–8 meters wide. More than 4,700 late Yuan-early Ming period artifacts (fourteenth-mid-fifteenth century) were recovered. The majority were tradewares, with approximately seventy percent deriving from northern and central

Vietnam (Figure 11.8) and the remainder from Thailand and China. Amongst the tradewares were blue and white bowls, cups, saucers, bottles, large plates, jarlets, saucers, covered boxes with inset dishes, kendis, and double-gourd pouring vessels; brown glazed stoneware jars in a range of sizes; and celadon (mainly Chinese) saucers, bowls, plates, cups, bottle, jarlets and kendis. Bowls (from Vietnam) constituted the main vessel form (more than 3,220 out of over 4,700 artifacts).

Figure 11.8 Stoneware jars from Vietnam. (Photograph courtesy of Allison Diem.)

Also recovered (amongst other items) were earthenware globular pots, cooking stones and lids; grinding and sharpening stones; iron cauldrons (probably from China) and tools, a sword/machete and knife; bronze gongs, fish hooks, mirrors, a disk, possible lamp, covered box, and weighing scale; and Chinese coins including one dating to 1403–24. Some of these items were probably for use by the ship's crew and passengers. The cargo also included thousands of glass beads, some of which were stored within stoneware jars for transport. This ship also had two small copper-alloy cannons, though these may have been for social display purposes as they would not have been effective weapons.

Shipwrecks are also known from elsewhere in the archipelago. Near southern Balabac are the remains of two ships containing Song materials, though only porcelain and stoneware sherds, and corroded iron were recovered as the site had been extensively looted. Remains of fourteenth–fifteenth-century Chinese junks have been found off the shores of Zambales and Busuanga near northern Palawan. A shipwreck off the Puerto Galera coast of Mindoro contained Ming period tradewares, and one off of the southwest coast of Marinduque yielded possible Swatow tradewares of the late Ming period (sixteenth century).

While tradewares were clearly the dominant imports, cargo remains together with contemporary accounts indicate the importation of other types of goods including those not archaeologically recoverable (or that could be sourced as foreign), such as silks and other textiles, lacquerware and wine. Iron and glass were probably imported objects that were subject to reworking. In exchange for these foreign goods, Philippine polities offered a range of items, most of which, because of their perishable nature, are primarily known from Chinese and Spanish descriptions. They included forest products such as resins, aromatic woods, rattan and beeswax, textiles of cotton and other plant fibers, unwoven cotton, gold, and marine products such as pearls, bêche-de-mer (sea cucumber), tortoiseshell, and bird's nests.

Complementing the maritime finds are numerous settlements and mortuary remains from various polities located throughout the archipelago. That numerous complex polities (sometimes referred to as "chiefdoms") existed by the early protohistoric period is suggested by intra-site and regional analyses. The archaeological record of several polities located in central Luzon, the Visayas and Mindanao is discussed below. Chinese accounts of Philippine societies commenced possibly as early as the tenth century and continued throughout the protohistoric period. These, with sixteenth-century accounts of Spanish contact, further indicate the pre-Spanish existence of complex lowland societies with a hierarchical sociopolitical structure with hereditary classes. In addition, an apparently authentic tenth-century copper-plate inscription (Figure 11.9) concerning an acquittal of debt, found in the Laguna de Bay area but lacking archaeological context, mentions specific chiefly leaders and nobility.[20]

The Butuan evidence for a polity engaged in large-scale maritime trade, pre- and post-eleventh century, derives not only from the boats, but from settlement and mortuary remains.[21] Butuan may have been the polity recorded in the Chinese *Song Shih* as P'u-tuan, which sent a tributary mission to the imperial court at the beginning of the eleventh century, and was described as having regular connections with Champa. If so, Butuan would have been the first Philippine polity to have sent such a mission. Polities throughout Southeast Asia sent tributary missions to the Chinese court seeking official recognition and the preferred trading status such recognition conferred. Over time, an increasing number of Philippine polities appear to have sent such missions to the Chinese court, suggesting increasing competition for trade goods during the protohistoric period.

The Butuan habitation deposits take the form of a shell midden (located stratigraphically above Boat One) and, extending below it, wooden posts from possibly several small houses. Within the midden were large quantities of ninth–twelfth century Chinese tradewares including Tang, Five and Song Dynasty, Yue, Yue-type and Guangdong wares. Also

Figure 11.9 Copper-plate inscription from Laguna de Bay, Luzon. (Photograph courtesy of A. Postma.)

discovered was a ninth–tenth century Middle Eastern polychrome glass jarlet. Other remains indicate the practice of various crafting activities at Butuan, including weaving (indicated by spindle whorls), wood working (indicated by the presence of wooden tools and animal figures), glass working, and metal working. Glass bead working or reworking is suggested by the presence of incomplete glass beads in various stages of manufacture, and of multicolored drippings in some of the crucibles. The presence of more than 100 clay crucibles, together with wooden tools, iron slag, lead waste and worked and unworked gold fragments indicate the working of various metals. Some of the products may have included iron adzes, blades, knives, points and tangs; bronze basins, bells, cymbals, ear pendants, dishes, gongs and mirror mountings; and gold buckles, ear ornaments and rings. Such items were recovered at Butuan, although some may have been imports.

Whether craft production at Butuan was conducted by full-time specialists or part-time specialists is not yet known. Archaeological and historic evidence from elsewhere in the archipelago (e.g., Cebu, Manila, Dumaguete, Tanjay) suggests that at least some craft production was under elite control and this may have also been the case at Butuan. The location of a gold source in this area may be one reason for the existence of such a large settlement. Butuan's ability to offer gold ore and craft goods would have certainly made it attractive to local and foreign traders alike.

Food remains have also been recovered from the Butuan midden, indicating a range of hunting and fishing techniques. Among the remains were marine and brackish shellfish species, bones of other marine animals such as sharks and sea turtles, and remains of pig, deer and domestic chicken. Bone and shell materials were crafted into implements such as squid lures, shell sinkers and awls, as well as into bracelets, pendants and rings.

Evidence of mortuary activities at Butuan appears in later periods. Four burials, tentatively dated to the fourteenth–fifteenth centuries, were accompanied by numerous grave goods including porcelain bowls, saucers, water droppers and shell bracelets. Wooden coffins appear somewhat later, and are associated with fifteenth–sixteenth century blue and white porcelains, earthenwares, gold jewelery, a bronze gong, and wooden and stone tools.

A large settlement was developing subsequent to Butuan in the Manila area. At Spanish conquest, Manila was one of the most important international trade centers within the archipelago. It may have acted as an entrepôt from which imported goods were then used in exchange relations with smaller polities in the archipelago.[22] The entrance to the port had a wooden palisade, and was defended by warriors and cannons (*lantakas*). This complex polity, probably akin in some aspects to maritime states elsewhere in Island Southeast Asia (e.g., the earlier kingdom of Srivijaya in Sumatra), was ruled by a paramount chief who expressed aspects of Muslim identity, as indicated by his title and name, Rajah Soliman. His residential complex within a fortified settlement in Manila was described by the Spanish as very large and containing valuables such as money, porcelain, copper, iron, and wax; that is, both imported goods and local goods used in exchange. Adjacent to the house was a structure in which were stored iron, copper and cannons, as well as clay and wax molds and unfinished cannons, suggesting that this paramount chief directly controlled their production.

The site of Manila was occupied by at least the eleventh century, as evidenced by a settlement mound underlying Santa Ana church.[23] A thick midden deposit within the mound contained sherds of tradewares and earthenwares, shells, and bones of pig, deer and water buffalo, as well as human burials. Metal crafting was also engaged in at this settlement with one area yielding large quantities of iron slag.

Approximately 300 burials have been excavated from various locations within the Santa Ana area. Of the burials from the churchyard area, 202 were accompanied by more than 1,500 tradewares from the Song to Yuan/early Ming dynasties (i.e., late eleventh–fourteenth centuries). Most of the later period blue and white porcelains were associated with burials located to the north of those with earlier tradewares, indicating expansion of the cemetery over time. Other grave accompaniments, with a smaller number of primarily later period burials, included decorated earthenware vessels, glass and stone beads, metal ornaments, iron and bronze implements, bone artifacts, clay spindle whorls, clay net sinkers, and three eleventh-century Chinese coins. The differential distribution of grave goods suggests that various social identities, probably including statuses, were expressed through mortuary ritual. Within the inner church courtyard were another 78 burials, including some of individuals who had undergone the practice of teeth filing sometime during their life. Accompanying these burials were eleventh–fifteenth century tradewares, spindle whorls, net weights, iron knives, bronze jewelery and animal bones. Some of the ceramic vessels contained grain or seeds. Nails around the edges of the burials suggested placement in coffins. Interestingly, infants and children appear to have been segregated in death; 19 child burials, accompanied by 170 late Song tradewares and one by a dog, were found in an area south of the churchyard. Some were buried with a substantial number of the tradewares, suggesting social differences among children, at least as expressed by the participants in the respective mortuary ceremonies.

Along Laguna de Bay, a settlement and burial site in present-day Pinagbayanan[24] (74 kilometres from Manila, and around 10 kilometres from the location of the copper-plate inscription), contemporary with Santa Ana, shows some of the variability in mortuary practices that existed in different polities during the protohistoric period. While the area may have been used for the burial of a few individuals in the late first millennium AD, in the eleventh–twelfth centuries it was used as a cemetery for inhumation burial. Although with few traces of skeletal remains, 174 excavated burials were accompanied by early Song porcelain vessels, earthenware vessels, spindle whorls, iron blades and other implements, gold ornaments, bronze objects (i.e. bowl, disk, mirror and ornaments), beads, net sinkers, coins, fragments of glass bottles, pottery disks and a glass bracelet. One type of burial practice involved the bundling of the corpse together with grave goods in some type of matting. The non-mortuary context of metal slag in this area suggests that part of the settlement overlapped with the cemetery.

Mortuary practices changed significantly in the following period, around the thirteenth–fourteenth centuries, with cremation appearing as the primary form of treatment of the dead. Of the 55 burials, 50 were cremated, with 38 placed in vessels and 12 in pits. Vessels containing cremated remains ranged from a small, brown four-eared jar to large, brown stoneware jars, the latter being the most common. Other than the vessels in which they were placed, most of the cremations lacked grave goods, though some were accompanied by additional tradeware vessels. A crematory complex was also uncovered at Pinagbayanan. Made of lateric material, this three-chambered structure contained charcoal and other evidence of burning. Smaller basins, possibly for burning only disarticulated skeletal remains, were also found. Above one such basin was a cremation burial in a brown spherical jar.

Settlement evidence is more abundant from this period at Pinagbayanan, though possibly of short duration. Postholes and pit features, along with sherds, net sinkers (some with a phallic shape) and the remains of pig and horse comprised the habitation remains.

Manufacture of textiles and iron goods also took place as indicated by spindle whorls, iron waste and slag.

Around the fourteenth–fifteenth centuries, habitation apparently ceased. Use of the area for burial continued, though apparently to a rather limited extent with only nine burials found. Interestingly, mortuary ritual resumed a pattern similar to that in the eleventh–twelfth centuries, with inhumation burials variously accompanied by grave goods including early Ming blue and white tradewares, celadons, Thai tradewares, glass bracelets, a piece of gold and one spear point.

To the southwest, on the Calatagan Peninsula, there are a number of habitation and cemetery sites contemporary with the Ming period burials at Pinagbayanan. Two of the more extensively excavated cemeteries of the late fourteenth to early sixteenth centuries are Pulung Bakaw and Kay Thomas.[25] A total of 505 graves was excavated, 208 at Pulung Bakaw and 297 at Kay Thomas (including three skeletons without skulls). Accompanying the burials were 521 porcelains and stonewares from China, Vietnam and Thailand – specifically Sawankhalok and Sukothai – along with hundreds of plain and decorated earthenware vessels; some ornaments including hundreds of glass beads, glass bracelets, brass anklets, and gold and copper ornaments; iron tools and weapons such as spear points; a brass spear point; an imported brass plate and brass cover-bowl; iron and brass hardware from two imported chests; and spindle whorls. Food remains, such as shells, fish bones and bones of other animals, were frequently found in the plain earthenware vessels, along with other organic remains, and were often covered with a Chinese porcelain bowl. In some instances, shells were scattered in the graves, particularly giant clam and species of cowries. In a few instances, large bones of pig and deer were found lying beside the skeleton. While children at Santa Ana appear to have been buried in a separate area, at Pulung Bakaw and Kay Thomas infants were included, but received different burial treatment. Each infant, along with smaller porcelain vessels, was placed inside a Ming jar with porcelain bowls or plates used to cover the opening (four at Pulung Bakaw and ten at Kay Thomas).

An interesting find from one of the burials which may date to *c.* AD 1400 (though detailed information is lacking) is a clay medallion of a Buddhist figure, which may be of local manufacture. Such a find is noteworthy not only because of its rarity, but because other possible Hindu-Buddhist items have been found in the archipelago (though again lacking contextual details), such as a late thirteenth to early fourteenth-century figurine (possibly Buddhist) from Mindanao, and a golden Garuda pendant from Palawan (Figure 11.10). While the incorporation of Islamic elements occurred in later polities, leading in one case to the formation of an Islamic state in the Sulu archipelago in the fifteenth century, little is

Figure 11.10 Gold ornament with Garuda image from Palawan. (From Fox 1970: Fig 3.)

known of the extent to which there were other or earlier integrations of foreign religious elements.

Jar burial practice also appears to have continued on Palawan during the protohistoric period, though whether or not it was a common form of burial is difficult to determine given the limited information. At Bubulungun Cave 1-B, a jar burial contained iron and beads and was associated with Song tradewares of the late tenth–eleventh century. Similarly, at Magmisi Shelf, a secondary burial inside an earthenware jar was also associated with late Song tradewares of the eleventh or twelfth centuries.

From the central Philippine islands, several contemporary lowland Visayan polities, such as Cebu, Dumaguete, and Tanjay are archaeologically well known. With a focus on analyses of political centers and their regional contexts, the information on them complements that from the Luzon and Mindanao polities, thus providing further understanding of the dynamic nature of and variability in protohistoric sociopolitical and economic organization. In addition, sixteenth century descriptions (the earliest dating to 1521) of lowland Visayan societies indicate the existence of three largely hereditary classes (although upward/downward mobility apparently was not uncommon).

Among the three polities, Cebu[26] (centered in the area of present-day Cebu City) appears to have been the major political center and international trading port in the Visayas by the time Magellan visited in 1521, and it appears to have been engaged in foreign trade for at least 500 years. Trading vessels came to Cebu from other polities in the archipelago. Cebu's ruling chief appears to have controlled activites at the port, receiving payment from foreign and local vessels before granting them permission to engage in trade.

The earliest known occupation at Cebu dates to around the ninth–tenth century, though this period is less well known than the subsequent fourteenth to mid-sixteenth century settlement. During the protohistoric period, the core settlement area expanded in size from two hectares in the tenth century to 30 hectares in the mid-fifteenth to mid-sixteenth century, with peripheral settlement extending outward along the coast. The growth of the center appears to have correlated with increasing levels of sociopolitical complexity (i.e. from a simple to a more complex chiefdom).

Within the core settlement, porcelain tradewares varied significantly in their density and distribution, suggesting differential access to these tradewares and their use as wealth items or prestige goods. These differences became even more marked over time. Most of the porcelains were dishes/plates and bowls, forms commonly used to serve food, which suggests their use in political activities such as elite-sponsored feasts held as displays of political authority. The earliest historic accounts describe porcelains used for serving, for example, when Cebu's ruling chief feasted Magellan and his crew. Other presumed imported items included carnelian beads, which may have been elite goods.

Residents of Cebu also produced various craft goods, possibly some of which were items destined for trade. From the fourteenth to early sixteenth centuries, iron-smelting and smithing took place, particularly in the south and southwestern parts of the settlement. Iron-working appears to have been under elite control, as suggested by the association of iron slag and possible earthenware crucible fragments with areas of large residential structures and high densities of fine porcelain. Elite control, both over the specialists and the requisite specialized knowledge, appears to have increased over time. Although iron fragments, from possible tools for agricultural and other productive activities, do not appear to have been differentially distributed within the settlement, the elite may have nonetheless controlled the distribution of iron goods. Crafting of decorated hilts for iron knives/daggers, as evidenced by pieces of carved antler (some in the same shape as those found on hilts from burial contexts), also took place. The elite apparently controlled the entire production sequence for crafting iron knives/dagger (Figure 11.11); these items may have been used in intra-archipelago exchange. Given the evidence for the elite control of exchange activities, it is possible that they also controlled the production of goods valued as exchange items. Textile fragments (cotton or abaca) have also been recovered from Cebu burials (of approximately the tenth century and fourteenth–fifteenth century), although evidence of cloth production has not yet been found.

Excavations at Cebu have also yielded locally-made valuables such as gold jewelery, a copper ring, clay and glass beads, and glass and shell bracelets from fourteenth-mid-fifteenth century burial and habitation deposits. Their association with elite residential structures and elite controlled activities suggest they were elite status items or prestige goods.

Archaeological evidence provides little indication of the goods or resources originating from the Cebu polity for export. However, sixteenth century accounts provide some information on items exported or re-exported from Cebu. These included gold, in unspecified form, which was exchanged with Chinese and other foreign traders,

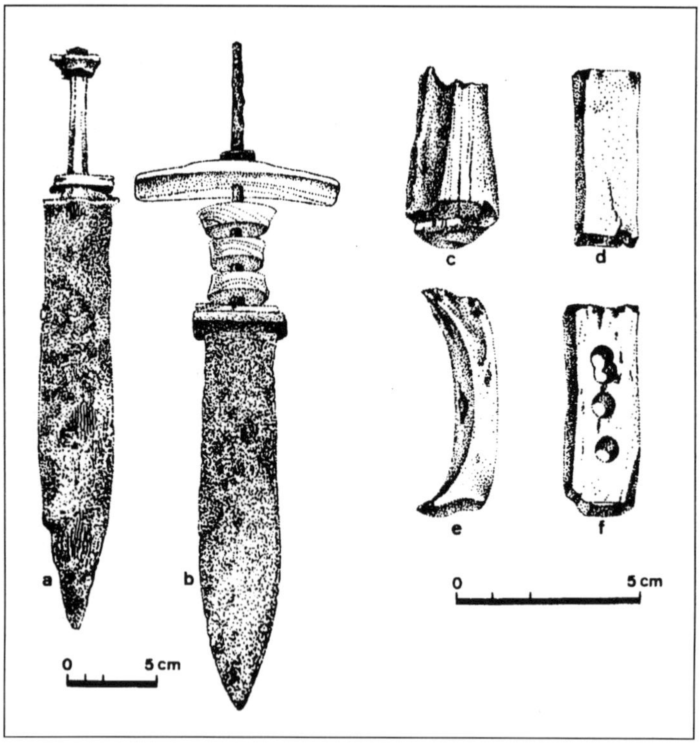

Figure 11.11 Iron daggers: a, from Burial 2 at site LA in Cebu City; b, from Argao, Cebu with shell inlay in the handle; c–f, worked bone and antler for use as inlays in the hilts of iron knives and, daggers. (From Hutterer 1973: Fig. 2. Reprinted with permission of San Carlos University Press.)

though Cebu also imported gold from places such as Thailand; pearls which "Moros" from Luzon and Mindoro received in exchange for their gold and rice; cotton textiles for export to China and elsewhere; and silver. The latter may have been a Spanish-period trade item.

On the nearby of island of Negros, two smaller chiefly polities – Dumaguete and Tanjay – are known to have been contemporary with Cebu. The former was centered at Dumaguete[27] (referred to as the Yap site) and dates from at least the eleventh century to the fifteenth to sixteenth centuries. Elite residential structures are known from the eleventh and fifteenth to sixteenth centuries. The earliest elite residential structures here were ones associated with an extensive midden yielding glass beads, plain and decorated earthenware sherds, iron fragments, and possibly glazed Asian tradewares. The continued presence of elite individuals at Dumaguete in the twelfth to fourteenth centuries is suggested by similar artifact classes including the presence of porcelains, and in the fifteenth to sixteenth centuries by a large residential structure, and possibly others, associated with similar cultural material.

The Yap site, the political center of the Dumaguete polity, appears to have extended along the coast for at least 1 kilometre and inland for at least 0.5 kilometre in the fifteenth to sixteenth centuries, with other settlements of this polity distributed a little further inland. This linear coastal arrangement, similar to Cebu but on a smaller scale, appears to have been the more common of two settlement configurations of political centers described at initial Spanish contact. The other comprised compact nucleated villages found only in a few areas such as Manila. Rice cultivation may have occurred in the area, as suggested by the presence of carbonized rice remains in local earthenware pottery.

Mortuary remains of a single burial (accidentally uncovered during construction activities) from within the Yap settlement lend support to interpreting it as a political center by the fifteenth to sixteenth century. The burial consisted of a log coffin containing glazed ceramic vessels among other items. Though only the log coffin was saved from looting, the type of burial and the nature of the mortuary goods appears similar to those described in early historic accounts of interring high ranking chiefs in "boat coffins".

The Dumaguete polity participated in internationally-connected exchange relations, as indicated by the presence of tradewares from China, Thailand and possibly Vietnam. These ceramics may have been acquired through Dumaguete's direct engagement in long-distance trade relations with China and Mainland Southeast Asian states, either by sending trading vessels, or receiving foreign ships, through exchange and other interactions (e.g. raiding) with polities in the archipelago. However, such Asian tradewares were restricted in their distribution within the polity. Only the chiefly center has evidence of Thai earthenwares and glazed ceramics of the twelfth–thirteenth centuries. During later periods, glazed ceramics continued to be present at the center but also appeared at several other settlements, including ones possibly occupied by lesser elite individuals (Figure 11.12). Such a restricted distribution suggests they were items of wealth used as prestige goods within the polity, at least prior to the sixteenth century, or that they were specific markers of elite status. In the sixteenth century, porcelains begin to appear at smaller, presumably non-elite occupied sites suggesting a change in the value of tradewares or direct elite–commoner relations.

Dumaguete's exchange activities also involved plain and decorated earthenware vessels produced within the archipelago; the decorated vessels may have been locally-made

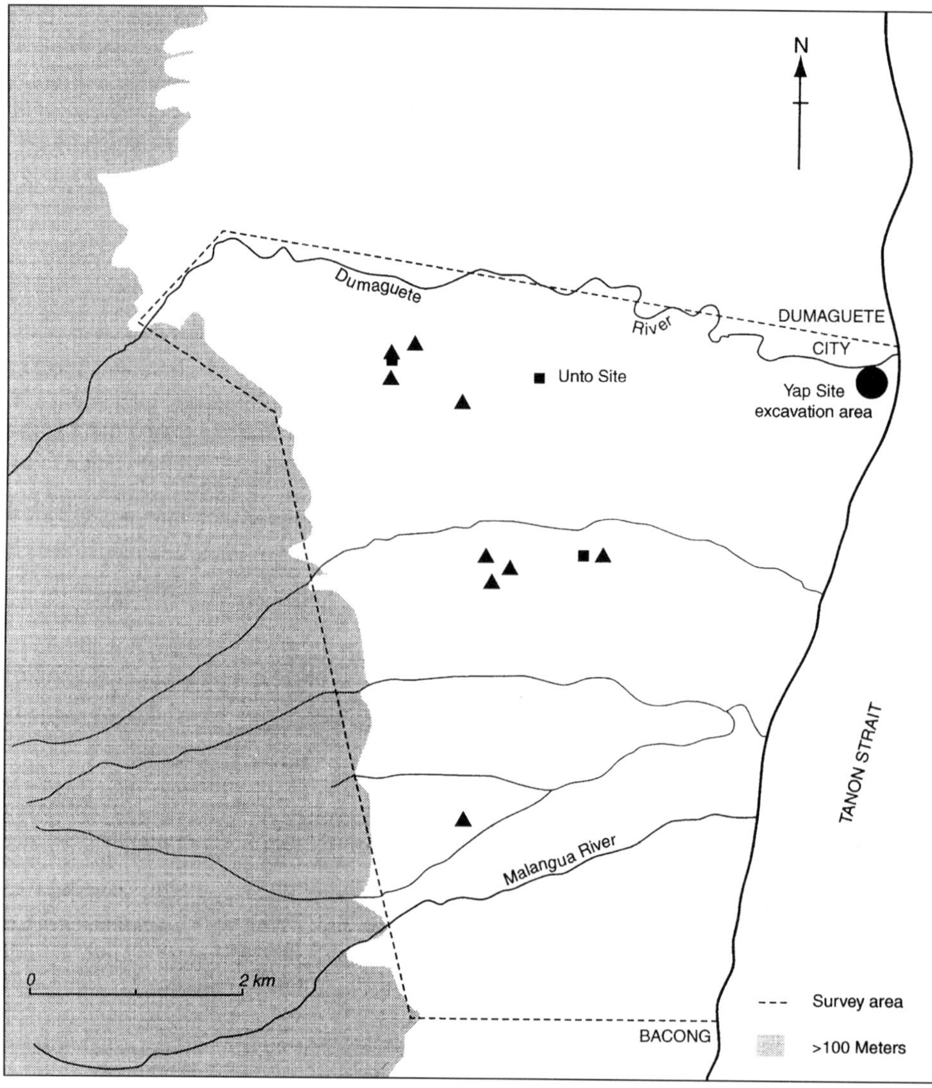

Figure 11.12 Distribution of glazed tradeware ceramics within the Dumaguete polity. The Yap site excavation yielded glazed tradewares from the twelfth and thirteenth to fifteenth and sixteenth centuries. Sites marked with squares yielded fourteenth and fifteenth century tradewares and sites marked with triangles yielded fifteenth to seventeenth centuries tradewares.

prestige items. Exchanges involving earthenware vessels, though only in small numbers, occurred between Dumaguete and Tanjay, Siquijor island, and the Manila area. Beads, also found only at the center, presumably entered through exchange. Whether these are foreign items is not yet known. Both Butuan and Manila have produced evidence for glass bead working, suggesting the possibility that the glass beads from the twelfth to fourteenth centuries occupation at Yap could have been produced within the archipelago.

Political relations among the archipelago's polities, including Dumaguete, may have entailed elite alliances marked by shared decorative styles. Analyses of several protohistoric earthenware styles suggest they were part of elite symbolism, and not items whose similarities and inter-island distributions can be explained by movement of the vessels themselves.

Craft goods were also produced within the Dumaguete polity and such activities probably occurred at the household level. Evidence of pottery production occurred in all periods of occupation at the center, some of which took place within the elite residential areas. Both plain and decorated vessels were produced, and the vessel shapes included globular pots (probably cooking vessels) and various types of bowls. One other site within the polity also yielded evidence of the production of plain and decorated earthenware vessels. Most of these were globular cooking pots or storage vessels, with bowls poorly represented. Interestingly, local decorated earthenwares appear to have been limited in their distribution suggesting restricted access and their use as wealth items. Iron production also occurred at Yap during all periods of occupation. The specialized skills and knowledge required for iron production, and its occurrence within elite residential areas, suggest it was a specialized craft under chiefly elite control, as at Cebu. Around the sixteenth century, one other settlement may have also engaged in iron production within the polity. The types of iron goods produced within the Dumageute polity are not yet known.

The Tanjay polity,[28] with its chiefly center located in what is now the present town of Tanjay, dates also from at least the eleventh century to the fifteenth–sixteenth centuries. During this time the center expanded from 3–5 to 30–50 hectares in size. The patterning of settlements within the region suggests an hierarchical organization, and one that by the later period was regionally-integrated for efficient coastal-interior transport of manufactured goods and possible forest products for use in more intensive participation in external trade. As with other polities of this period, the earliest Tanjay tradewares date from the twelfth to fourteenth centuries, indicating direct or indirect participation in foreign trade. Tanjay's, as well as Cebu's and Dumaguete's, access to or participation in foreign trade increased through the protohistoric period. Such tradewares occurred in higher densities more at elite residences in Tanjay than at non-elite residences, providing further evidence for porcelain vessels as items of prestige. Within the polity, porcelains were also restricted in their distribution, and may have been involved in elite-restricted exchanges. Tanjay also engaged in intra-archipelago exchanges with the center receiving decorated earthenwares produced in or near Kaulungan Island off the west coast of Mindanao.

Tanjay also produced earthenware pottery and iron goods, possibly all for use at the center or within the polity. Pottery making and metal working (of iron and possibly bronze) took place within elite contexts, suggesting it was an elite-sponsored or controlled craft at Tanjay as well. The upland distribution of a standardized earthenware type from Tanjay, and possibly indicative of a presence of full-time pottery specialists, suggests it may have been an item exchanged for those forest products and ores used by chiefs in foreign trade. Within the polity, one fifteenth to sixteenth century settlement also produced evidence of iron extraction and smelting activities. Tanjay's elite may also have sponsored production of high status decorated earthenwares. These wares, along with metal objects and glass beads, appear to have been local prestige goods within the polity.

Figure 11.13 Burials of a fifteenth or sixteenth century mass grave at Tanjay. (E. A. Bacus.)

Tanjay may have been the target of violent raiding or warfare in the fifteenth to sixteenth centuries. Nine (of a total of 17 excavated burials) appear to have been interred in a single-event mass grave (Figure 11.13). These individuals were accompanied by five human crania, possibly heads of enemy individuals captured in raiding or warfare. Visayan societies were noted to have engaged in such activities by Chinese chroniclers, which may have represented alternative strategies for acquiring the foreign and local goods necessary for engaging in maritime trade and hence in the maintenance, politically and economically, of the ruling elite and their polities.

The archaeological record summarized here, together with Chinese and early Spanish accounts, indicates that the protohistoric complex polities of the Philippines shared commonalities, but also varied in their sociopolitical, ideological and economic natures. The long-term processes leading to the formation of these polities, as well as to their individual historical trajectories, are not clearly understood; and more research is needed on all periods of Philippine pre and proto-history. That the initial development of such polities was not a simple result of "trade" alone is clear on both theoretical and archaeological grounds from polities such as Tanjay. At the same time, foreign goods – as prestige goods, elite status items, mortuary necessities, were clearly important for the maintenance and reproduction of lowland polities and their predecessors. They also impacted upon other societies with whom these polities interacted in the archipelago: hunter-gatherer groups and communities based on swidden agriculture, none of which are well-known archaeologically. The contexts in which trade for such goods had long been conducted within the Philippine archipelago, and elsewhere in Southeast Asia, ultimately collided with a system of trade undertaken by an expanding European capitalist system. With this came the establishment of Spanish colonial rule, which consequently led to transformations among the diverse range of societies of the Philippine Islands.

Notes

1 Wernstedt and Spencer 1967.
2 Casal, Jose, Jr., Casino, Ellis and Solheim II 1981.
3 Fox 1970.
4 Thiel 1990.
5 Tuggle. and Hutterer (eds) 1972; Mudar 1997.
6 Snow, Shutler, Nelson, Vogel and Southon 1986.
7 Peterson 1974.
8 Ogawa 1993.
9 Peterson 1974.
10 Fox 1970.
11 New evidence for the Neolithic in the northern Philippines, coming to light as this chapter is published, includes red-slipped, dentate stamped and lime-infilled pottery from beneath the shell mound of Nagsabaran in the Cagayan Valley, and a widespread horizon of stamped and

incised red-slipped pottery with strong southeastern Taiwan affinities on the island of Batan. The Batan sites are buried by deep layers of volcanic ash. These new Cagayan Valley and Batanes sites appear to mark the beginning of a red-slipped pottery tradition which rapidly spread south, about 1500–1000 BC, through the Philippines and into Sabah and eastern Indonesia, emerging in the western Pacific as the Lapita cultural complex. Some of this new material is illustrated in chapter 2.

12 Hutterer 1986.
13 Fox 1970.
14 Thiel 1990; Peterson 1974.
15 Dizon 1993.
16 Tenazas 1974.
17 Bacus 1997.
18 Burton 1977; Clark, Green, Vosmer and Santiago 1993; Ronquillo 1987.
19 Loviny 1996.
20 Postma 1991.
21 Burton 1997; Ronquillo 1987.
22 Peralta and Salazar 1974.
23 Fox and Legaspi 1977.
24 Tenazas 1968.
25 Fox 1959.
26 Nishimuara 1992; Hutterer 1973.
27 Bacus 1999.
28 Junker 1999.

Select Bibliography

Introduction and publications relating to several periods.

Bellwood, P. (1997) *Prehistory of the Indo-Malaysian Archipelago.* Chapter 6. Honolulu: University of Hawai'i Press.

Casal, G., Jose, R., Jr., Casino, E., Ellis, G., and W. Solheim II (1981). *The People and Art of the Philippines.* Los Angeles: Museum of Cultural History, University of California.

Wernstedt F. and Spencer, J. (1967) *The Philippine Island World.* Berkeley: University of California Press.

Early hunter-gatherers

Fox, R. (1970) *The Tabon Caves*, Manila: National Museum of the Philippines.

Hutterer, K. (1985) "The Pleistocene archaeology of Southeast Asia in regional perspective", *Modern Quaternary Research in Southeast Asia* 9: 1–23.

Latinis, K. (1996) "Prehistoric lithic technology, workshops, and chipping stations in the Philippines", *Asian Perspectives* 35: 27–50.

Mudar, K. (1997) "Patterns of animal utilization in the Holocene of the Philippines: a comparison of faunal samples from four archaeological sites", *Asian Perspectives* 36: 67–105.

Thiel, B. (1990) "Excavations at Musang Cave, northeast Luzon, Philippines", *Asian Perspectives* 28: 61–81.

Tuggle, H. and Hutterer, K. (eds) (1972) *Archaeology of the Sohoton Area of Southwestern Samar, Philippines. Leyte-Samar Studies* 6(2).

Neolithic

Bellwood, P., Stevenson, J., Anderson, A. and Dizon, E. (2003) "Archaeological and palaeoenvironmental research in Batanes and Ilocos Norte Provinces, northern Philippines", *Bulletin of the Indo-Pacific Prehistory Association* 23: 141–61.

Ogawa, H. (1993) "Lal-lo shell middens on the lower Cagayan River, Northern Luzon, Philippines", *Japan Society for Southeast Asian Archaeology* 13: 64–66.
Peterson, W. (1974) "Summary report of two archaeological sites from northeastern Luzon", *Archaeology and Physical Anthropology in Oceania* 9: 26–35.
Snow, B., Shutler, R., Nelson, D., Vogel, J. and Southon, J., (1986) "Evidence of early rice in the Philippines", *Philippine Quarterly of Culture and Society* 14: 3–11.
Spriggs, M. (1989) "The dating of the island Southeast Asian Neolithic: an attempt at chronometric hygiene and linguistic correlation", *Antiquity* 63: 587–613.
Spriggs, M. (1999) "Archaeological dates and linguistic subgroups in the settlement of the Island Southeast Asian-Pacific region", *Indo-Pacific Prehistory: The Melaka Papers, Vol 2. Bulletin of the Indo-Pacific Prehistory Association* 18: 17–24.

Emergent complexity

Bacus, E. (1997) "The Unto site: excavations at a late first millennium BC and mid-second millennium AD habitation site in southeast Negros island", *Asian Perspectives* 36: 106–141.
Dizon, E. (1993) "Maguindanao prehistory: Focus on the archaeology of the anthropomorphic potteries at Pinol, Maitum, South Cotabato, Mindanao, Philippines", *National Museum Papers* 4: 1–21.
Fox, R. (1979) "The Philippines during the first millennium BC", in R. Smith and W. Watson (eds) *Early South East Asia*, pp. 227–241, New York: Oxford University Press.
Hutterer, K. (1986) "A balance of trade: the social nature of late pre-Hispanic Philippines", the First Annual Hart Collection Lecture, DeKalb: Northern Illinois University.
Tenazas, R. (1974) "A progress report on the Magsuhot excavations in Bacong, Negros Oriental, summer 1974", *Philippine Quarterly of Culture and Society* 2: 133–55.
Thiel, B. (1989) "Excavations at the Lal-lo shellmiddens, Northeast Luzon, Philippines", *Asian Perspectives* 27: 71–94.
Thiel, B. (1990) "Excavations at Arku cave, northeast Luzon, Philippines", *Asian Perspectives* 27: 229–263.

Lowland complex polities and maritime trade

Bacus, E. (1999) "Prestige and potency: political economies of protohistoric Visayan polities", in E. Bacus and L. Lucero (eds) *Complex Polities in the Ancient Tropical World*, pp. 67–87. Archaeological Papers of the American Anthropological Association No. 9. Arlington: American Anthropological Association.
Blair, E. and Robertson, J., (eds) (1903–07) *The Philippine Islands, 1493–1803, 50 vols*, Cleveland: The Arthur H. Clark Company.
Burton, L. (1977) "Settlement and burial sites in Butuan City: a preliminary report", *Philippine Studies* 25: 95–112.
Clark, P., Green, J., Vosmer, T. and Santiago, R., (1993) "The Butuan Two boat known as a *balangay* in the National Museum, Manila, Philippines", *The International Journal of Nautical Archaeology and Underwater Exploration* 22: 143–59.
Fox, R. (1959) "The Calatagan excavations: two fifteenth century burial sites in Batangas, Philippines", *Philippine Studies* 7: 325–90.
Fox, R. and Legaspi, A. (1977) *Excavations at Santa Ana*, Manila: National Museum Publications.
Hutterer, K. (1973) *An Archaeological Picture of a Pre-Spanish Cebuano Community*, Cebu City: University of San Carlos.
Hutterer, K. (1986) "A balance of trade: the social nature of late pre-Hispanic Philippines", the First Annual Hart Collection Lecture, DeKalb: Northern Illinois University.
Junker, L. (1999) *Raiding, Trading, and Feasting: The Political Economy of Philippine Chiefdoms*, Honolulu: University of Hawai'i Press.
Loviny, C. (1996) *The Pearl Road: Tales of Treasure Ships*, Philippines: Asiatype, Inc. and Christophe Loviny.

Nishimura, M. (1992) "Long distance trade and the development of complex societies in the prehistory of the Central Philippines: The Cebu Central Settlement Case", Ph.D. dissertation, University of Michigan.

Peralta, J. and Salazar, L. (1974) *Pre-Spanish Manila: A Reconstruction of the Pre-History of Manila*, Manila: National Historical Commission.

Postma, A. (1991) "The Laguna-copper plate inscription: a valuable Philippine document", *Bulletin of the Indo-Pacific Prehistory Association* 11: 161–71.

Ronquillo, W. (1987) "The Butuan archaeological finds: profound implications for Philippine and Southeast Asian prehistory", *Man and Culture in Oceania 3* (Special Issue): 71–8.

Scott, W. (1984) "Written Records", in *Prehispanic Source Materials for the Study of Philippine History*, pp. 63–90. Quezon City: New Day Publishers.

Tenazas, R. (1968) "A Report on the archaeology of the Locsin-University of San Carlos Excavations in Pila, Laguna, Manila", unpublished manuscript.

12

THE ARCHAEOLOGY OF EARLY MARITIME POLITIES OF SOUTHEAST ASIA

Pierre-Yves Manguin

Introduction

During the first century of archaeological research in Southeast Asia, orientalist scholars, initially trained in the study of neighbouring Indian or Chinese cultures, chronically disregarded the millennium-long period that led from late prehistory to the emergence, around the fifth century AD, of those civilizations that could be studied with the tools with which they were familiar: philology, epigraphy, art history and monumental archaeology. This disregard for the proto-historical phase of Southeast Asian archaeology, and a focus on little else but monumental archaeology and art history for the historical phase, led to profound misrepresentations of the crucial early developments in state formation and urbanization, best summarized in a blunt statement in George Cœdès' pioneering synthesis on *The Indianised States of Southeast Asia*:

> In most cases, one moves without transition from Late Neolithic to the early Hindu vestiges. . . . One may therefore say, without undue exaggeration, that the peoples of Further India shared a late Neolithic civilisation when the Brahmano-Buddhist culture of India was first brought into contact with them.[1]

For long, the enduring controversies over the processes of "Indianization" (and "Sinicization") of Southeast Asia, while gradually returning responsibility for some of the cultural dynamics to the local people, did not bring about real progress because of lack of solid data to substantiate the various interpretations at hand.

Oliver Wolters' ground-breaking historical study on *Early Indonesian Commerce*,[2] based on textual sources alone, was the first to take into serious consideration the crucial first seven centuries of the first millennium AD in order to understand the economic and political background to the emergence in the seventh century of Srivijaya, the first major state of Insular Southeast Asia. It brought to light the entrepreneurship of the early coastal polities of western Southeast Asia that thrived first on commerce with India, and only later, after the fifth century AD, on direct exchange with China. Another major achievement of the past two decades has been the concentration by archaeologists and historians on sites, many coastal, in both Continental and Insular Southeast Asia with chronological phases bridging the periods between the third century BC and the fifth to seventh centuries AD.

The artefacts brought to light clearly indicate that regular exchange with the Indian subcontinent and, to a lesser degree, with China, had become the rule long before inscriptions, monuments and statuary inspired by India started appearing in Southeast Asian sites, therefore conclusively contradicting earlier assumptions on an abrupt "civilizing" process driven from overseas. These recent finds were reinforced when it was proven that large trading ships built in Southeast Asia using local techniques, distinct from those of the Indian Ocean and China, plied Asian waters during this same period.[3] The passage into Dravidian languages and literature, as early as the first centuries AD, of Austronesian nautical terms (such as *perahu* or *wangkang*, both generic words for "boat") brings further proof of the active participation of Austronesian speakers in Indian Ocean networks in the early centuries of the first millennium AD. One could also argue that the linguistic evidence does not in any way suggest that the Indians taught the Southeast Asian peoples how to trade or sail. Finally, recent progress in the archaeology of early historical sites is now also closing the long-standing gap between prehistory and "classical" Southeast Asia.[4]

As a consequence of the epistemological and methodological leap forward brought about by protohistorical and early historical studies, the emergence of complex polities on the shores of western Southeast Asia during the early first millennium AD can now be firmly associated with regional and long-distance maritime trade networks. Most relevant sites lie along the shores of western Southeast Asia, thus defining a string of favoured coasts astride what was then becoming the enduring trans-Asian maritime route. Due to their exceptional geographical position, the Southeast Asian Mainland peninsulas and the straits that separate them from the neighbouring archipelago soon became an inescapable crossroads between three crucial regions: the two economically and culturally commanding continental masses of China and India, and the multitude of Mainland and Insular Southeast Asian coastal ecosystems, harbouring peoples of various origins, most of them sharing technologically advanced shipping skills and control over valuable and often irreplaceable commodities.[5]

The early coastal polities (*c.* second century BC – third century AD)

Other chapters in this volume take into consideration the archaeological data available from a variety of early Metal Age sites of coastal Southeast Asia that have provided proof of overseas exchange networks. Intra- and inter-regional exchange patterns were solidly established in the late centuries BC (Figure 12.1). Pottery, nephrite ornaments, glass and semiprecious stone beads, bronze bowls and urns, as well as bronze kettledrums, bells and ceremonial weapons from the Dông Son culture in Vietnam help archaeologists to identify these early regional networks. They appear to have carried artefacts a great distance away from their manufacturing sites, probably not in any direct way, but via interconnected local networks. Some artefacts produced beyond Southeast Asia have also been found in a variety of sites strewn along the early Southeast Asian maritime trade routes, clearly indicating regular contacts with Indian Ocean shores. Beads of Indian manufacture made of semi-precious stones and glass became a major trade item in most Southeast Asian sites from the fourth century BC onwards, as best documented at coastal Malay sites and at Ban Don Ta Phet in west-central Thailand.[6] The latter is not a port site but must have been in regular contact with overseas trade, from the west via the Three Pagodas Pass or from the south, via the lower Chao Phraya river basin. Other rare, valuable goods no doubt obtained through trade, especially high-tin bronze knobbed

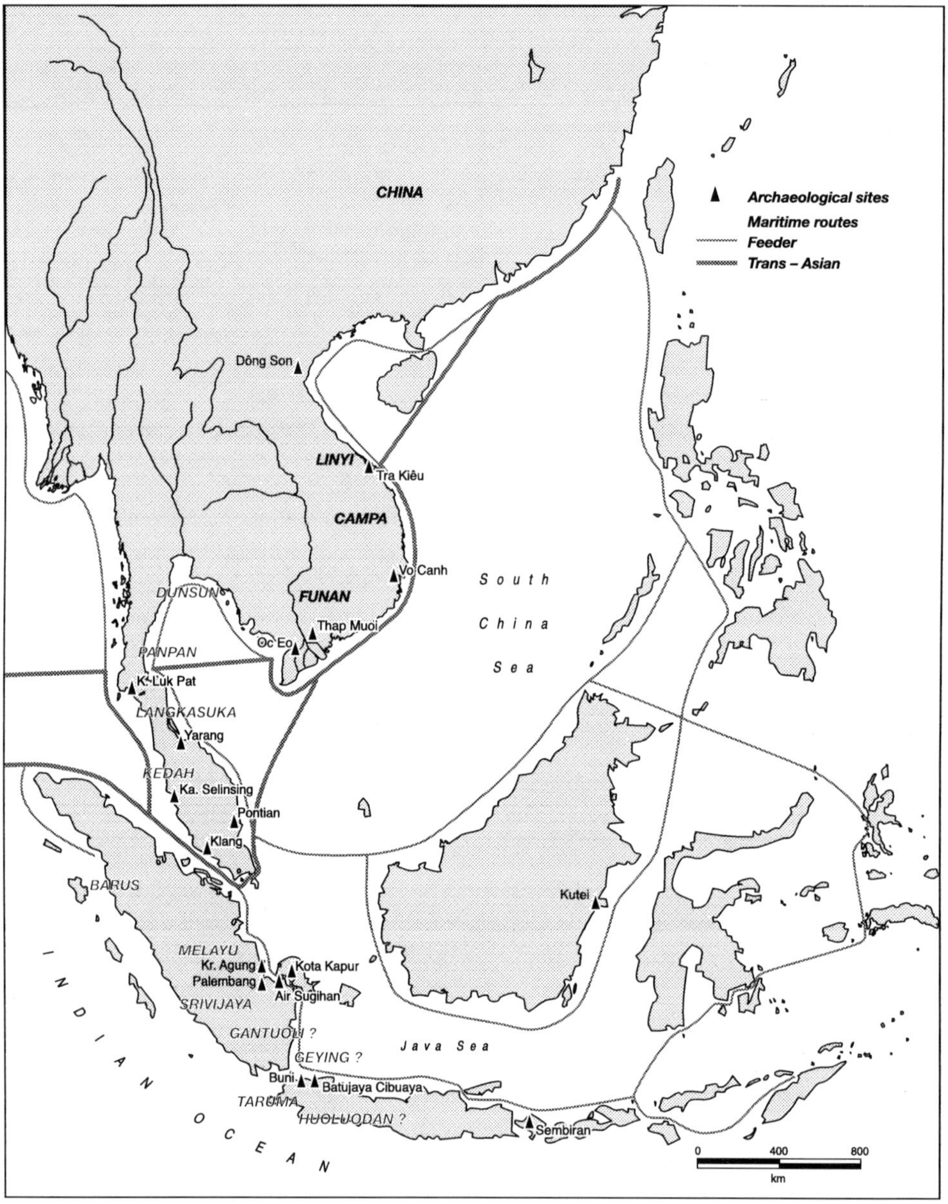

Figure 12.1 Maritime Southeast Asia locating the main known polities (in bold capitals) and major archaeological sites mentioned in the text.

bowls (see chapter 4), also indicate long-distance trade across the Indian Ocean. Such prestige artefacts have been found in burial sites and bear proof of the higher social status of the deceased, therefore also manifesting increasingly ranked societies.

Whatever the original significance of such objects in their foreign place of manufacture, they cannot as yet be used to attest to the adoption of imported religious or political practices in Southeast Asia, although indigenous or foreign merchants as well as indigenous elites could have been aware of such alien thought systems. Much later in the history of Southeast Asia it is well known that it took centuries of contact with foreign Muslim merchant communities before Islam became adopted as a state religion.

The Melaka and Bangka Straits settlements

Some of the first coastal communities of Southeast Asia actively engaged in long-distance maritime trade are located in the Strait of Melaka. Wisseman Christie[7] first brought into clear historical perspective those sites on the west coast of Malaysia, mainly in the Klang and Langat river basins of Selangor, that had attracted only occasional attention in earlier decades.[8] In what appear to have been mound and boat burials dating from the very last centuries BC, she emphasized archaeological assemblages of local and imported artefacts, including an indigenous industry of iron and bronze socketed tools, beads and pottery of Indian origin, cast bronze bells and kettledrums from Dông Son, Vietnam. The sophistication of these burials, their density, and the fact that they provide a richer array of imported goods than the contemporary slab burial sites found further inland in the Malay Peninsula, indicates that they were left by distinctly ranked societies. As these coastal sites are located close to abundant alluvial tin ore deposits, and further had access to upriver sources of alluvial gold, it is surmised that they thrived on the export of these two metals, in high demand in India.

Settlement sites belonging to these early societies have so far never been investigated. However, it is most probable that, to achieve their economic goals, they must already have commanded some sort of symbiotic relationship with the gold-producing inland societies, including those that constructed the slab graves.[9] This in turn implies that these coastal societies belonged to already complex political systems, not far removed from the states that would coalesce in the Straits area later in the first millennium AD, and whose prosperity was also clearly based, among other factors, on the exploitation of a rich hinterland, as will be seen below. This, if confirmed by further archaeological research, would constitute proof of early indigenous entrepreneurship in long distance trade networks.

The earliest coastal settlements with access to overseas trade artefacts date from a slightly later phase of Southeast Asian history (see chapter 3). Some, briefly described below, have long chronological sequences encompassing much of the first millennium AD, but all appear to have been born during the economic boom at the turn of the first millennium, when Roman trade with India was at its peak. The earliest chronological phase is usually dated to the first–third centuries AD – and may date back a century or two earlier depending on the dating of such diagnostic artefacts as the Indian rouletted ware. Much of the information on such coastal sites has been gathered from loosely controlled excavations or chance finds from as early as the 1920s; it has only recently been brought together in order to infuse some meaning into hitherto scattered data.

Systematic excavations of a few of these sites with early phases clearly bridging the late prehistoric and historical periods have been carried out in both Malaysia and Indonesia. Other sites, such as those situated on the South Sumatra coastline, were surveyed and tested in 2001; conclusions reached by these ongoing research programmes must be considered as preliminary.[10] The coherence of the data gathered so far is nevertheless encouraging.

Due to extensive looting, we lack data on the settlement that no doubt would have been found at the site of Khuan Luk Pad ("Bead Mound") in Krabi Province on the south-western coast of Peninsular Thailand. Excavations by Thai archaeologists have nevertheless proved that this large glass and stone bead-producing site was active during the first half of the first millennium AD.[11] The shift of part of the bead production from India to Southeast Asian coastal sites during this period is indicative of the growing dynamics of regional trade. Artefacts other than beads found at Khuan Luk Pad also provide evidence for long-distance trade: Roman intaglios and glass ware, as well as Indian coins from across the Bay of Bengal, and locally smelted tin for export to tin-hungry India (Figure 12.2). Another early bead-making site at Khao Sam Kaeo on the east coast of the Peninsula, about which little is yet known, appears to parallel the activities of the earliest phase at Khlong Thom and further confirms the economic importance of bead-trading activities in Southeast Asian waters during the early first millennium AD.[12]

Figure 12.2 Indian (possibly Satavahana) coin with a ship design found at Khuan Luk Pad, Krabi, Peninsular Thailand. (Photograph courtesy of Wat Khlong Thom collection.)

Pulau Kelumpang, first excavated by Evans in the early 1930s, lies in mangrove forest at the mouth of the Selinsing River on the west coast of the Malay Peninsula.[13] Malaysian archaeologists have intensively investigated it again in recent years.[14] Settlements were built here on wooden piles. Subsistence was clearly marine oriented, with molluscs and fish providing most of the food, but rice also appears to have been part of the diet. The burials, apparently in lashed-plank boats, contained imported beads. Tin rings and ear pendants as well as gold, bronze and iron artefacts are part of the assemblage. People continued to live on this site until the early second millennium AD with access to foreign goods, including pottery and an engraved gemstone matching finds in Funan (in present-day southwestern Vietnam and southern Cambodia), together with Chinese ceramics when these became available after the eighth century. But whereas neighbouring groups in the Sungei Bujang and Sungei Mas sites of Kedah had adopted an Indianised way of life starting around the fourth or fifth century, it is interesting to note that the people of Kuala Selinsing chose not to abandon their indigenous beliefs, practising the same type of burial rituals until the settlement was abandoned some time around the tenth century.

The discovery of comparable coastal sites in Indonesia, spread along the major maritime route passing through the Strait of Bangka and following the northern coasts of Java and Bali, brings the Malaysian sites into a broader perspective. The latter were situated along the Strait of Melaka, on the major thoroughfare between the South China Sea and the Indian Ocean. The Indonesian sites are located not only on the coasts of Sumatra (Karang Agung, Air Sugihan) and West Java (Buni), where much of the economic and political development of the following centuries would take place, but also further east at Sembiran on the northern coast of Bali.[15] Considering the limited economic importance of the Balinese hinterland, one is entitled to interpret the latter as a staging point on the route to Eastern Indonesia, with its renowned spices and precious woods. By then, cloves, which were exclusively cultivated in the Moluccas, were already known as far as Europe and

China and must therefore have transited via such trading sites.

During the 1980s and 1990s extensive areas of freshwater swamp forest along the east coast of South Sumatra, settled only by Kubu hunter-gatherers until the middle of the twentieth century, were cleared to make way for transmigration settlements. The forest was burnt, canals were dug on a geometrical grid and bulldozers created new fields, levelling mounds and filling in old meandering river beds. In the process, many archaeological sites were brought to light. Unfortunately, the first discoverers of these sites, which yielded gold artefacts and beads, were the new settlers who engaged in extensive looting (Figure 12.3).[16]

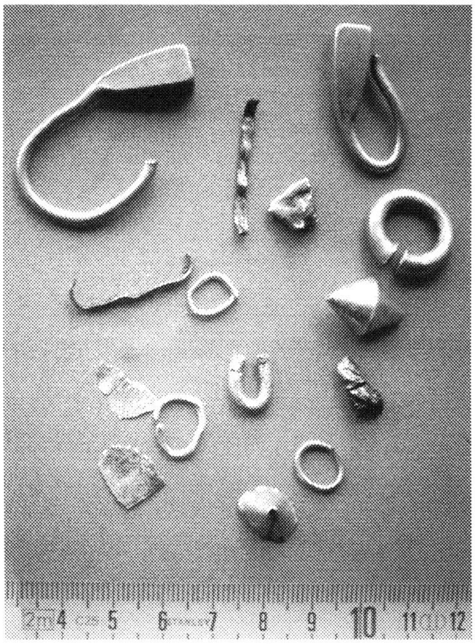

Figure 12.3 Gold ornaments from the site of Air Sugihan (South Sumatra). Identical circular ear rings (top of photograph) and moulds for casting them were found at Oc Eo. (Photograph courtesy of Kanwil Dept. Pendidikan collection, Palembang.)

The area in the vicinity of the Air (river) Sugihan, a few kilometres from the coast, east of the Musi River estuary, was thus brought to the attention of Indonesian archaeologists in the late 1980s. But all that could by then be gathered was an array of artefacts lacking context, roughly dating from late prehistoric to early historic times: coarse pottery, rather crude gold ornaments, large glass and bronze bangles, a quantity of glass and stone beads of various forms and colours, and two whole Chinese ewers dated to the sixth century AD. The area from which settlers excavated these artefacts was vast, and no specific sites were then identified. However, remains found at a new transmigration settlement cleared in the same fashion during the 1990s, northwest of the Musi and Banyu Asin estuaries, have recently been brought to the attention of Indonesian archaeologists. Despite substantial damage to the sites, both by the land-clearing process and by looting, their prompt intervention in 2001 with immediate test excavations allowed for a much better picture of this site complex, known as Karang Agung, to be drawn. Again, as in Air Sugihan, finds of local pottery were scattered over an area some 5 kilometres square, predominantly near old river beds. Much of this area contains large wooden poles, 30 centimetres in diameter, some 2.50 vertical metres of which remained in place under the layers that produced the archaeological finds. One such large house pole has been radiocarbon dated to between AD 220 and 440. Tin net sinkers point to fishing activities and fragments of boat timbers and a rudder, belonging to the ancient "stitched plank and lashed lug" tradition common in Southeast Asia during the whole of the first millennium AD, were also recovered. Gold ornaments with practically no decoration and gold leaf are frequently found and unverified information indicates that a gold leaf eye-cover was found in a burial together with beads, bones and teeth.

At Karang Agung, these indigenous artefacts are accompanied by a broad variety of foreign objects. Again, as in Air Sugihan, bronze and glass bangles are often found. Two small metal pendants are either of Indian manufacture or come from Oc Eo in southern Vietnam, where many comparable ornaments made of bronze or tin have been excavated. Some polished black sherds with a pinkish-grey paste also appear to have been imported from India (though no rouletted ware has so far been identified), as does much of the abundant array of high-quality beads of all sizes and qualities, made of stone or glass. The local pottery assemblage, like that of many other comparable sites of coastal Indonesia, comprised both the coarser cord-impressed type and some finer ware with incised or punctate decoration, including tall-necked *kendis* with a red polished slip.

One other riverine site a dozen kilometres upstream from Karang Agung yielded an archaeological assemblage of large tall-necked carinated pots with geometric punctate decoration, simple socketed iron tools similar to those found in the Klang-Langat sites of Malaysia, and trade beads. All these finds in South Sumatra are clearly indicative of large, well-populated settlements dating back to the first half of the first millennium AD, and possibly starting as early as the last century BC. At Air Sugihan, occupation continued into the historical period. It is too early to ascertain in any detail the part played by such settlements within the trade networks leading further east into Java and Eastern Indonesia. It is manifest, though, that these people were in close contact with foreign traders. Their key location near the estuary of the Musi River, astride the sailing lane passing through the Strait of Bangka, appears to have provided these settlements with the opportunity to act as intermediaries between sea-trading groups and the contemporary societies of the upper valleys of the extensive Musi River basin. Indian beads, Dông Son artefacts and red polished tall-necked *kendis* have been found in the Pasemah megalithic sites (Figure 12.4) and in the Ulu Musi jar burial complexes. These coastal sites, located in an area still rich in natural commodities only a few decades ago (elephant tusks, deer antlers, tortoiseshell, tiger skins, valuable timber and possibly also rhinoceros horns) may have also controlled the flow of alluvial gold and forest products from the upstream valleys.

Figure 12.4 Batu Gaja (Elephant stone) from the Pasemah megalithic site, South Sumatra. It depicts a warrior carrying a Heger I type drum, a sword and leg bands all typical of the Vietnamese Dông Son culture. (Photograph courtesy of Museum Balaputradewe, Palembang.)

Java and Bali

Further east along the maritime route, the complex of sites known collectively as Buni, a few kilometres inland in West Java, gained deserved fame when it yielded the first Indian rouletted wares to be identified in a Southeast Asian context.[17] Judging from a large collection of sherds and whole pots in museum collections, the local pottery assemblage is similar to that of the South Sumatran sites described above. Context-less finds of polished stones, bronze artefacts and rouletted ware suggest a date in the last centuries BC or the early centuries AD. There is also a distinct possibility that this site complex might be identified as the powerful and densely populated polity known from Chinese sources as Geying (Ko-ying), which was still active in the third century AD and was one of the Southeast Asian gates for the India trade.[18] This extended group of sites was not systematically investigated when discovered in the 1960s and most of it is now lost for further research. It was extensively looted for its gold, beads and precious ninth-century Chinese ceramics, and is now situated in a quickly growing urban zone at the eastern edge of Jakarta. It appears, however, to have extended further west along the coast, into the area of Batujaya, where Indonesian archaeologists digging under somewhat later Buddhist structures have identified occupational layers dated to the second–fourth centuries AD and have brought to light Indian rouletted ware.

Figure 12.5 Gold seal of Indian or Hellenistic influence, from Pekalongan, north coast of Central Java. (Photograph courtesy of National Museum, Jakarta.)

So far, no sites of this early phase that show clear links with India have been identified on the central and eastern coasts of Java. The National Museum at Jakarta does hold one gold seal of Indian or Hellenistic influence, acquired in 1917 at the port city of Pekalongan in Central Java (Figure 12.5). It has affinities with pieces found at Oc Eo and Khuan Luk Pad and may have belonged to an assemblage comparable to those of other early first millennium AD sites.[19] The coastal burial sites of Plawangan and Lamongan, in East Java, probably date back to the first centuries AD: they however yielded early metal age assemblages comprising Dông Son bronze artefacts, shell, glass and semi-precious stone beads and local pottery, and do not appear to have been in direct contact with overseas trade networks.[20]

Of all the Indonesian coastal sites that show direct links to long-distance trade networks, only Sembiran, on the north coast of Bali, has so far been systematically excavated, starting in 1987. It is situated near the harbour mentioned in the tenth century AD Julah inscription. A remarkable quantity of Indian pottery (mainly rouletted ware) with striking similarities in shapes and paste composition with those excavated at the South Indian site of Arikamedu was found in the lower archaeological levels. One sherd had characters in Brahmi or Kharoshthi characters inscribed on its surface. This pottery occurred in association with fragments of a volcanic tuff mould for casting a Pejeng-type kettledrum and numerous monochrome glass beads. The appearance of glass beads and semi-precious stones in the well-known burial site of Gilimanuk confirms that they had become a common prestige commodity in Bali by the turn of the Christian era.[21]

The coasts of the Indochinese Peninsula

Sailing northeast from the southern tip of the Malay Peninsula, across the Gulf of Siam, one soon reaches the largest reported group of sites – some 350 so far – many of them coastal and riverine, that have been clearly dated to the first half of the first millennium AD.

Vietnamese archaeologists group the sites in the lower Mekong Basin into what they call the "Oc Eo Culture", after the eponymous site which lies in Vietnamese territory some 20 kilometres east of the present-day coastline of the Gulf of Siam.[22] Oc Eo became famous when Louis Malleret revealed its existence in the early 1940s, suggesting that it had been one major settlement of the polity then known from Chinese sources alone as Funan (first–seventh century AD). Malleret carried out one single but intensive archaeological campaign in 1944.[23] Warfare prevented any further research in the Mekong Delta until 1979. Malleret nevertheless managed to publish, and acquire for what is now the Museum of History of Hô Chi Minh City, an impressive collection of some 10,000 archaeological artefacts (including beads, but excluding pottery), some ninety percent of which came from the Oc Eo area (Figure 12.6). This makes the site one of the richest of Southeast Asia in terms of variety of forms and materials. The largest part of this assemblage is unfortunately

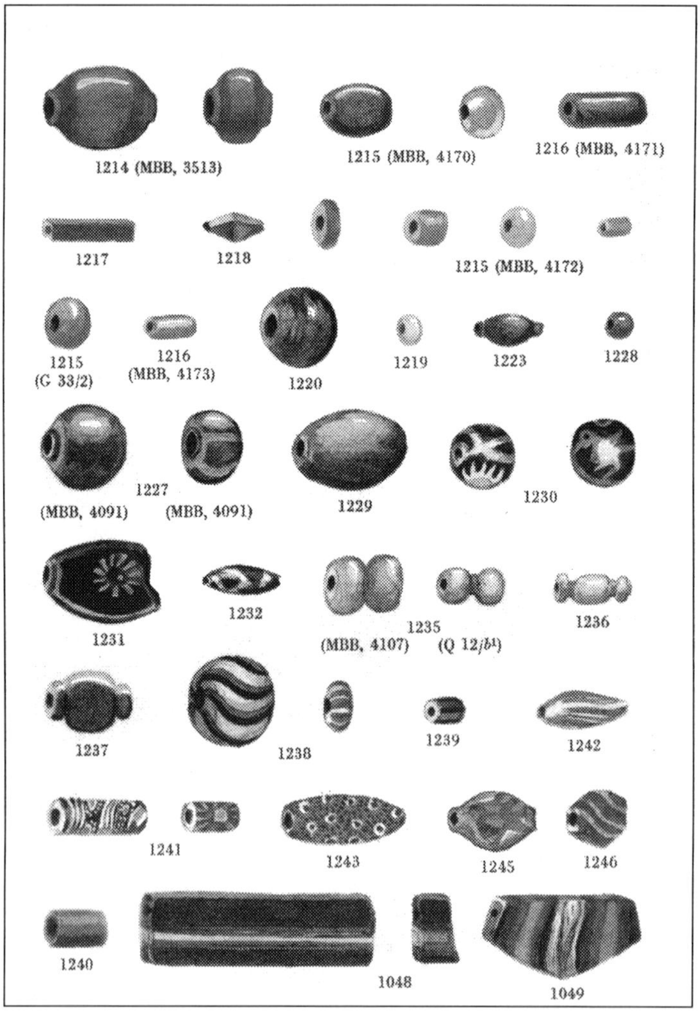

Figure 12.6 Glass and stone beads from Oc Eo. (École Française d'Extrême-Orient photograph from Malleret 1959–63.)

disconnected from its original context and, with few exceptions, it is of little use in dating Funanese sites and determining chronological sequences among them with any precision.

A few years after the reunification of Vietnam, Vietnamese archaeologists resumed investigation of a variety of sites in the Mekong Delta. An ongoing Franco-Vietnamese archaeological programme, started in 1997, concentrates on the sites in the floodplain of Oc Eo and on the slopes of neighbouring Mount Ba Thê.[24] Another archaeological programme is presently investigating the site of Angkor Borei in Khmer territory (see chapter 5). The latter is not technically a coastal site, but it should be remembered that it was linked by a 70 kilometre-long canal to Oc Eo (and therefore to the sea), at least in its later phases.

Preliminary results of recent research at the Oc Eo / Ba Thê complex reveal early Phase I settlements with radiocarbon dates providing a mid-first to mid-third century AD range (Figures 12.7 and 12.8). Remains from the earliest phase are found only on higher ground which floods nowadays only in exceptional circumstances, particularly on the small mounds in the floodplain and at the interface between the floodplain and the lower slopes of Mount Ba Thê. No trace of Phase 1 settlement has been found so far in the annually inundated plain of Oc Eo. Houses in these early settlement sites were built on wooden piles (many of them very large) and some were covered with roofs made of flat terracotta grooved tiles (Figure 12.9) of a type never so far reported for such early sites in Southeast Asia, which may indicate a foreign origin for this technique – possibly Indian.[25]

A jar burial excavated on the slopes of Ba Thê that contained gold foil and carnelian beads probably also dates back to Phase I (Figure 12.10). Apart from beads, the excavations have revealed for Funan Phase I a rich assemblage of locally made pottery, much of it belonging to a category of buff, "fine paste ware". This pottery includes a

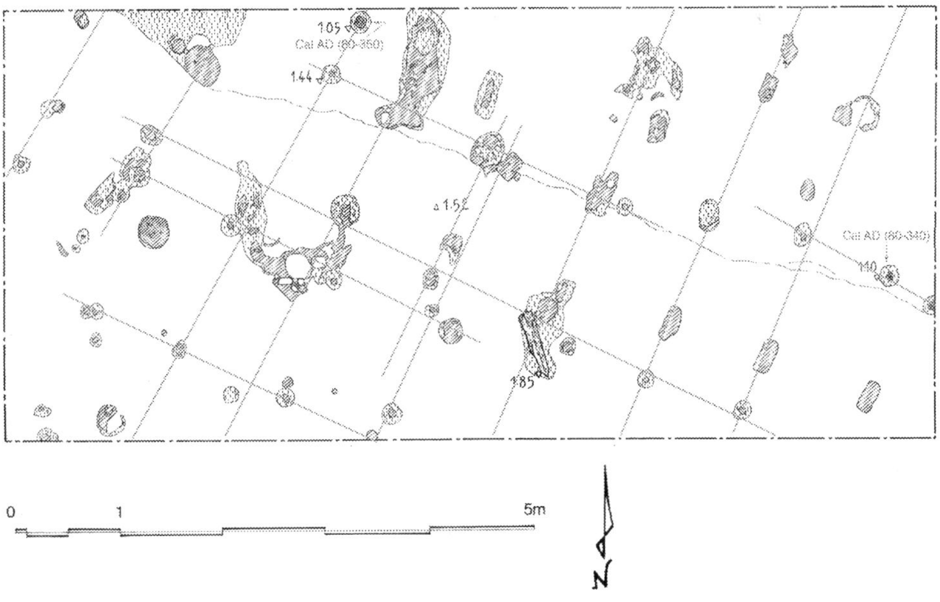

Figure 12.7 Wooden pole pattern from Phase I (first to third century AD) at Go Oc Eo (2001). (Drawing courtesy of EFEO.)

variety of shapes unknown so far in contemporary or later Southeast Asian sites. Many, such as the *kendis*, were clearly influenced by Indian shapes and some sherds of black polished pottery can be counted as direct imports from India. However, no rouletted ware has so far been found, probably because the first settlements at Oc Eo date to the mid-first century AD at the earliest, while the Indian pottery comes from a level dated to AD 50–250. Other ceramic wares, such as Phimai black, attest to exchange with sites further upstream on the Mekong and its tributaries.

Figure 12.8 Wooden pole from Phase I (first to third century AD) at Go Oc Eo (2001). (Photograph courtesy of EFEO.)

So far, no remains of any brick buildings or religious statuary have been found in Phase I levels in any of the excavated sites at Oc Eo, or apparently anywhere else in the Mekong Delta. It appears, therefore, that Phase I, despite significant differences in the pottery assemblage, may be considered as equivalent to contemporary phases of the coastal sites of Insular Southeast Asia described above, again bearing witness to extensive economic and cultural contacts with overseas markets. On-going environmental studies may determine if Oc Eo had access to the sea via now-vanished natural channels, or a manmade canal.

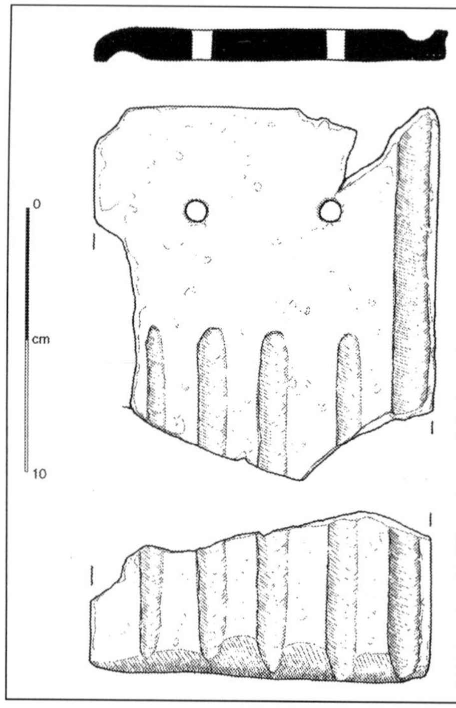

Figure 12.9 Terracotta tile from Phase I (first to third century AD) at Go Oc Eo (2001). (Drawing courtesy of V. Bernard.)

As in contemporary sites in Southeast Asia, artefacts from across the Bay of Bengal that may belong to Phase I of Oc Eo, such as Roman and Middle Eastern medals and intaglios, inscribed Indian gems, beads and ceramics, do not demonstrate any Indianization of Funanese society at this time – just its remarkably cosmopolitan nature. But these remarks are so far valid only for Oc Eo and may not hold true for other parts of the lower Indochinese Peninsula. If the third century AD date for the isolated Vo Canh inscription recovered much further north near modern Nha Trang can be accepted, one has to acknowledge the existence there of a local political power, familiar with Indianized state concepts and contemporary with the end of Phase I at Oc Eo (See chapter 9).

The northern areas of most of present-day Vietnam were under Chinese domination throughout the first millennium AD, but the commandery on their southern borders split off in about AD 192 to become known to the Chinese as Linyi. Here, excavations from 1990 onwards at Buu Câu Hill, Tra Kiêu, also yielded two small rouletted ware sherds in Phase 1 of the Tra Kieu sequence.[26] The early levels there, and the nearby location at Go Cam, provide an "interface between the prehistoric Sa Huynh Culture, early "Indian" contacts, the Han expansion into Central Vietnam, and the early Cham state of Linyi".[27] Together with the riverine sites of the Viêt polities from which the Dông Son bronzes must have been exported, this riverine site most probably constituted the northern limits of those exchange networks that we have seen at work between the third to second centuries BC and the second to third centuries AD in Peninsular and Insular Southeast Asia. Cham polities at Tra Kiêu and nearby areas remained significant powers in international trade during the following centuries and the Cham capitals of Simhapura and Indrapura developed there later in the first millennium AD (see chapter 9 here).

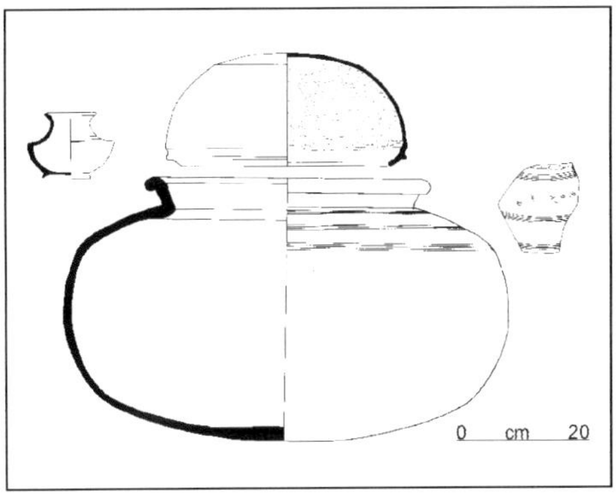

Figure 12.10 Large burial jar with lid and small adjoining jarlet from Linh Son, Oc Eo, Vietnam (1998). (Drawing courtesy of V. Bernard.)

The transition to history

Between the third and fifth centuries AD, the appearance of foreign textual sources with specific information on Southeast Asia brings about a momentous change in our perception of the region. We now progressively enter the historical phase, and historiography will soon be reinforced by the first locally written sources. The earliest of these inscriptions are written in Indian scripts and their language is exclusively Sanskrit. With one debatable exception dated on palaeographic grounds alone to the third century AD – the Vo Canh inscription, possibly engraved for a ruler of Funan – Southeast Asian epigraphs do not appear before the end of the fourth century AD. Starting from then, the corpus of inscriptions grows steadily in size, later switching from Sanskrit to local languages.

The only known Chinese texts describing this early historical period are fragments from lost third to sixth century books, compiled and published centuries later, mainly in official court records, but also in *materia medica*, compendia rich in botanical and pharmacological data. All these texts, despite their limitations, reflect a trading situation outlined above. Early first millennium AD Indian literary or religious sources, albeit less specific than Chinese ones, also reflect the well-established reputation of Southeast Asia as an important source of wealth. The Malay Peninsula and the Indonesian Archipelago were referred to as Swarnadvipa, the "Islands of Gold", and the mainland possibly as Swarnabhumi, "Land of Gold", and the region gained its position in literature as a metaphor for lands where fortunes can be made. Apart from gold, in such great demand in India that its constant flow towards the East alarmed a first century AD Roman emperor, sandalwood, *gharu* wood, cardamoms, camphor and cloves are mentioned among other commodities in early first millennium Indian sources as coming from Island Southeast Asia.[28]

During the first half of the twentieth century, basing themselves largely on this body of foreign and local textual sources, orientalist historians built up, practically from scratch, an impressive reconstruction of Southeast Asian history, culminating in 1944 in Cœdès' first edition of the commanding work subsequently published as *Les États hindouisés d'Indochine et d'Indonésie*.[29] This immediately became and still remains an indispensable reference work for Southeast Asian ancient history. It has to be considered, however, as a product typical of its time. The discourse of Cœdès and his fellow orientalists was twice biased. It was a prisoner as much of the representations conveyed by foreign sources on Southeast Asia as of their own perception of the world in which those scholars lived – colonial and Eurocentric – in which Southeast Asia could only be perceived from the perspective of the "greater civilizations" of Europe and then India or China. It was difficult for European and Indian historians of the time to understand the local factors that provided Southeast Asia with its cultural, economic, and political autonomy and dynamics, and to free its history from the exclusive grip of the two imposing cultural and economic masses of China and India. As noted above, this was never as obvious as in the neglect of the growing body of data that one now ascribes to the early historical period under consideration in this chapter.

The first coastal city-states (*c.* third century–sixth century AD)

Only recently have archaeologists started to consider the early historical period as worthy of attention. The little that remained of monuments of the period, built for the most part in easy-to-reuse bricks, were no match for the temples of later, "classical" ages. The large brick structures brought to light in 1944 by Louis Malleret in the Mekong Delta were seldom discussed until recent archaeological research concentrated again on the Funan sites. And it took until the 1990s to see in print suggestions that the brick monuments of coastal West Java that were being progressively brought to light could have belonged to the fifth–seventh centuries state of Taruma(nagara), long known from inscriptions.[30] Similarly, many an art historian, when confronted with early statues, failed to recognise their antiquity and tended to reject them as either aberrant or degenerate forms, relegating them to an uncharted chronological limbo around the seventh–eighth century (early Buddhist statues somehow managed to escape this curse).[31]

The Malay Peninsula: a stepping-stone

The information gathered from Asian sources and from rare western texts such as the *Periplus of the Erythrean Seas* or Ptolemy's *Geography* all point to the outstanding role played during the early centuries of the Christian era by the isthmian tracts of the Thai-Malay Peninsula, on both sides of the present international border. Their geographical position, facing the Indian coast or the South China Sea, provided convenient harbours for those ships that waited for the monsoon to enter the Strait of Melaka or that wished to connect with the overland portage routes. These harbours were natural havens for merchant communities with close economic ties with India.

Possibly as early as the third century AD, we can recognize on the international scene a group of small coastal polities that are said to have been focused on urban centres enclosed in palisades or walls, with rulers living in palaces. These communities knew writing, practised agriculture and patronized excellent craftsmen. Some of these harbour cities are said to have been host to hundreds of Brahmins and to large merchant communities from India and the Iranian world. Buddhist communities were also active. Some of these polities carried Indian-sounding names such as Takkola, probably on the northwest coast of the peninsula near Takuapa, or Langkasuka, a prosperous and long-lived polity centred on Pattani-Yarang which emerged in the third century AD and survived into the second millennium. Others are only known by the name given them in Chinese records. Panpan (P'an-p'an) was probably on the Bay of Bandon, near modern Chaiya (Figure 12.11), and after its foundation in the third century it seems to have survived for many centuries, well into the "classical" period. Dunsun (Tun-sun), possibly the transcript of a Mon name meaning "five cities", was situated further north on the peninsula and was probably short-lived, around the third century. Jiecha (Chieh-ch'a) appeared in fifth century sources and should be located in South Kedah. Chitu (Ch'ih-t'u, meaning "Red Earth"), possibly south of Langkasuka, was known in Chinese sources only after the seventh century but was probably the same as the Raktamrtikka (with the same meaning) mentioned on a fifth-century Buddhist Sanskrit inscription found in Kedah.[32]

Figure 12.11 Fifth-century mitred Vishnu from Chaiya Peninsular, Thailand, possibly the oldest in Southeast Asia. (Photograph courtesy of EFEO.)

With the exception of Kedah and, possibly, of the ill-studied Takkola/Takuapa sites, larger polities in positions to participate in the various trans-peninsular routes that allowed quick communications between the Indian Ocean and the Gulf of Siam appear to have been primarily located on the eastern shores of the Thai-Malay peninsula, facing contemporary Funan. Most trade commodities, however, particularly the bulkier ones, would have been shipped around the peninsula. The harbours of these east coast polities would therefore appear to have acted as mediators between Funan and the Indian Ocean trade. Funan was by then the dominant economic power in Southeast Asia and, together with the early Cham polities, the gate to the Chinese market. Peninsular sites on both the east and west coasts such as Sathingpra, Pontian (associated with third–fifth-century boat remains) and Kuala Selinsing have yielded sherds of large decorated jars of a type commonly found at Oc Eo. The key position of these peninsular polities in the regional economy is emphasized by the fact that, during the third century, they were "conquered" by Funan as reported by

Chinese sources, or at least integrated into its social space. Nevertheless, they continued to send embassies to China under their own names.[33]

Despite the wealth of archaeological finds gathered during the twentieth century from these isthmian sites, most date to after the fourth century AD. It should be emphasized that no contemporary settlements or religious structures dating to the third–fifth centuries, either Buddhist or Brahmanical, have yet been brought to light in the region. This limits conclusions as to the exact political status of these cosmopolitan settlements. Some seals inscribed with Indian terms may be as old as the third century, but such easily movable objects lack context and tell us nothing about the religious or socio-political circumstances of the sites. We thus have to rely almost solely on Chinese sources for this early period. These texts, compiled in the following period, appear to describe these early polities as city-state-like systems, each centred on a major urban settlement, which acted vis-à-vis the outside world as true states. Whether the Chinese authors who first wrote these accounts (or those who later compiled them) were prejudiced by their own perception of what a state should be, or whether these polities had by then developed from chiefdoms to true city-states, will have to remain a matter of conjecture.

Only when Buddhist and Brahmanical inscriptions become relatively common during the fifth century AD, together with a few contemporary statues, can we infer that the polities in question had significantly moved forward in the process commonly referred to as "Indianization". Indian-inspired political and religious strategies clearly began to be adopted between the third and fourth centuries. By the fifth century, most peninsular polities appear to have become full-fledged city-states, regularly sending and receiving embassies to and from China or India.

The corresponding urban and trading settlements have yet to be identified by excavation. Only in Yarang do we now have evidence, mostly from remote sensing, for the construction of a dense network of (so-far undated) canals linking moated sites to the estuary of the Pattani River, and possibly also to harbour sites. Only religious structures have been brought to light so far. Most of the small brick sanctuaries associated with Visnu statues around Chaiya and Nakhon Si Thammarat that were described in a summary fashion in the early twentieth century – even by then in a sorry state – have now been destroyed. Recent archaeological work by Thai archaeologists at the Khao Sivichai hill site, near Chaiya, has nevertheless revealed a smallish Vaishnava complex dated on stylistic grounds to the sixth century. Further south, larger-scale archaeological research in the vast Yarang complex has brought to light a variety of much larger Buddhist monuments, also said to date back to the sixth–seventh centuries.[34]

The role played by the peninsular city-states in the transformation of Southeast Asia in the very early centuries of the present era is emphasized by recent studies in art history. These confirm that they provided the first impulse for the diffusion of those earliest Indian artistic forms, Vaishnava as well as Buddhist, which rapidly spread to other fast-developing areas such as Funan, Tarumanagara in West Java, and possibly also polities in Eastern and Western Borneo.[35]

The Indochinese Peninsula

Starting in the second century AD, and for the next two to three centuries, Linyi and Funan acted as the gateway to Southeast Asia for those Chinese who grew more and more inquisitive about their southern neighbours and their economic potential. Their interest in the southern maritime routes became particularly acute when overland access to West Asia was made uncertain by instability in Central Asia in the second half of the second century. Access to the overland routes was closed to the Wu government after the partition of China at the fall of the Han, early in the third century. Funan and Linyi are the earliest Southeast Asian polities to enter the system that would provide over the next centuries one general pattern of trade in the South China Sea. Between AD 226 and 231 their ambassadors first presented to the court of China what the Chinese always considered as their "tribute".

Chinese sources provide rather little information on developments during the first half of the first millennium AD in what is now central Vietnam. How Linyi gave place to the Indianized states that are regrouped under the name of Champa remains unclear. The earliest Sanskrit inscriptions by a ruler called Bhadravarman date to the late or mid-fifth century and appear in both Quang Nam and much further south in Phu Yên, indicating that this ruler's political reach was by then already outstanding.[36] The earliest inscription written in an Austronesian language (Dông Yên Châu), in a script of Indian origin, is probably rather later than these early Sanskrit inscriptions: it shows nevertheless that the ancestral Cham language was then used in central Vietnam. This is also when the earlier Saivaite sanctuaries were built in Mi Son, Quang Nam Province. The inscriptions, of which only a few have been translated, together with the temples and statuary – both Saivaite and Buddhist – bear testimony to economic and political developments in Champa during the first millennium AD, and to their already uneasy relation with their powerful Sino-Vietnamese neighbours from the north. Except at Tra Kiêu (see Chapter 9), no systematic archaeological work has been carried out on settlements contemporary with these sites.

Funan soon grew into the privileged partner of the Chinese in Southeast Asia and remained so until the fourth or fifth century. It is from Chinese sources that we learn that the ruler of Funan, during the third century, expanded its power towards the Malay Peninsula, bringing most of the east coast city-states into its sphere of influence. The ports of this enlarged Funanese economic sphere remained for long the terminal of Chinese mercantile activities in Southeast Asian waters. However, it was not the local produce, but trade goods from India and Western Asia, reshipped through the peninsular harbours controlled by Funan, that interested the Chinese government most. In these harbour centres, Chinese merchants also acquired products gathered from the trading polities of Insular Southeast Asia to which they still had no direct access.

In the early centuries of the first millennium AD, the major role of merchants from Central Asia (Sogdania and Bactria) has to be emphasized. Many were stated by Chinese sources to reside in the harbour of Dunsun during the 3rd century. One most probably has to credit these merchant communities with a role in the introduction of the array of precious Indian Ocean and Mediterranean artefacts, such as gems and jewellery, recovered during the past century – the vast majority without archaeological contexts. The numbers of these items is small if compared, say, with indigenous pottery or locally made beads, but their dispersal all over the region is remarkable. The economic importance of Western and Central Asia also finds its reflection in the religious and artistic spheres. Art historians and philologists have for long been aware of marked influence from the Iranian world, as expressed in artistic styles of the fifth to seventh centuries Vaishnava statuary, the associated cult of Surya and the garments worn by Surya statues. Some funerary practices of Funan, attested by both texts and archaeology, may also have been introduced by such contacts.

Whether these influences can be directly attributed to merchants from Western and Central Asia or to indirect contact via northwestern India, remains to be ascertained.

Recent archaeological excavations in the Oc Eo/Ba Thê complex of Funan sites have identified, based on radiocarbon dates, an abandonment phase of marked, if undetermined, length between the late third and the fourth centuries. After this, some two centuries of building activity (Phase II) occurred prior to 650. Many brick temples and burial sites were then built on the lower slopes of Mount Ba Thê and on small, non-floodable mounds in the flood plain of Oc Eo, on which pile dwellings had been constructed during the earlier Phase I (Figures 12.12 and 12.13). At Linh Son, a large religious complex appears to have been inaugurated during this period. However, archaeologists can only excavate its periphery as the centre of the site is occupied by a modern Buddhist sanctuary.[37]

Judging from the statuary from Oc Eo, which is rarely found in context (as elsewhere in the Mekong Delta), and from the few Sanskrit inscriptions available, both Brahmanism and Buddhism were practised during Phase II. The fifth century K5 inscription at Thap Muoi, another important Funan site, bears witness to a Vaishnava cult, which explains the predominance of Vishnu statues in the Mekong Delta. Vishnu statues were recently found close to the large brick temple uncovered at Thap Muoi. A single gold foil Buddhist inscription recently found in a foundation deposit from a temple in the plain of Oc Eo also dates from Phase II.

During Phase II at Oc Eo the archaeological finds are concentrated in two areas separated by approximately two kilometres of low lying floodplain: on the slopes of Mount Ba Thê and, in the plain, on and around a series of higher mounds rising some

Figure 12.12 Brick structure at Go Cây Thi (1999), dating from Oc Eo Phase II (fourth to sixth century AD). (Photograph courtesy of EFEO.)

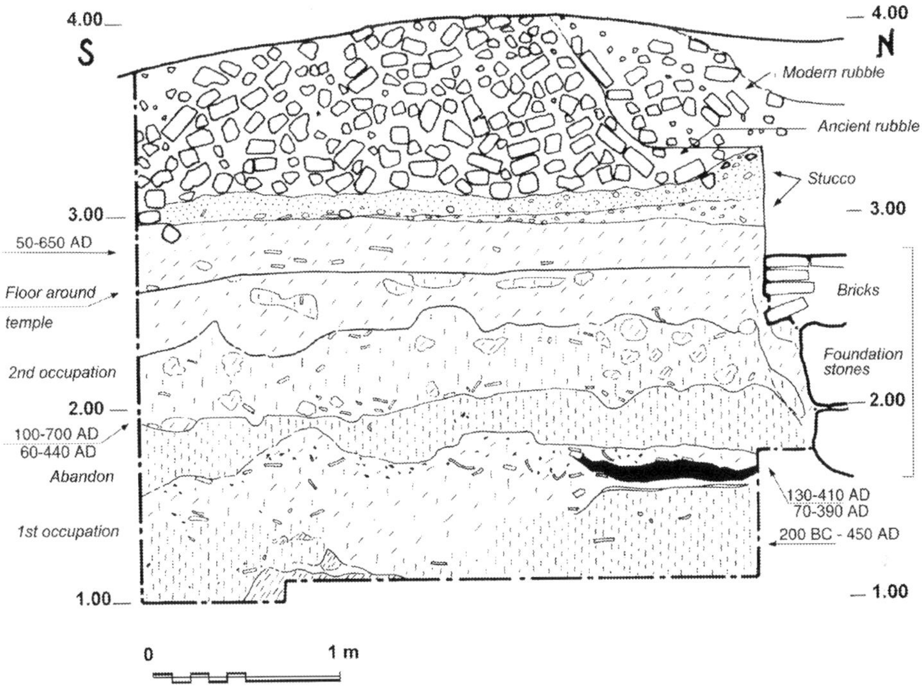

Figure 12.13 Stratigraphical section, Go Cây Thi (1999), showing brick structure and settlement chronology (Oc Eo Phases I and II). (Drawing courtesy of V. Bernard.)

Figure 12.14 Glass effigy of an Iranian-looking man, Oc Eo. (Historical Museum, Ho Chi Minh City.) (Photograph courtesy of EFEO.)

two metres above the mean altitude of the plain. The latter include the eponymous site of Oc Eo (Figure 12.14). As demonstrated by Malleret in his *Archéologie du delta du Mékong*, and verified by recent fieldwork, Oc Eo falls within the limits of a set of parallel moats, visible only on older aerial photographs taken in the 1950s or earlier before intensive paddy cultivation profoundly transformed the local landscape. They mark the rectangular boundaries of a settlement that would have covered the best part of 300–500 hectares of low-lying ground. The northern side of the rectangle is not clearly visible on aerial photographs and the northern limits of the site must therefore remain uncertain. This moated site also appears to have been criss-crossed by a grid of small canals. A larger canal ran precisely across the longest axis of the moated settlement in a north-northeast, south-southwest direction, dividing it into symmetrical halves. In the northeast this main canal joined with another canal that ran in an almost straight line for about 70 kilometres to Angkor Borei in present-day Cambodia (Plate 15). To the southwest, it ran for 16 kilometres towards the former coastline. Towards the southern end of the canal, an important site was found by Malleret, known today as Nên Chua, where remains of a temple and a group of burials have been excavated by Vietnamese archaeologists.

The Phase I settlements at Oc Eo do not appear to have extended into the floodplain since, one may imagine, the flow of flood water had not yet been brought under control. During Phase II, control of the annual floods by the canals would have allowed settlement on the lower ground, leaving the slightly higher mounds for the brick religious monuments. The apparent abandonment of the floodplain sites at the end of Phase II, and the transformation of the sites on the Ba Thê slopes into a largely religious complex during the subsequent pre-Angkorian and Angkorian periods, support the argument that the hydraulic system at Oc Eo and elsewhere in the Mekong Delta had been completed by Phase II.

Due to extensive looting since the early 1940s and intense disturbance for agricultural development since the 1960s, the sites at Oc Eo and Ba Thê may keep forever many of their secrets. Few statues have been found *in situ*, and only a handful of the scores of smaller but precious artefacts thought to have been manufactured locally that were recovered in Malleret's time, or more recently from controlled excavations, have good contexts. However, the information painstakingly gathered by Louis Malleret for the origin and distribution of the extraordinary array of artefacts – most of them coming from the Oc Eo area – does confirm that Oc Eo thrived on maritime trade. Considering the abundant archaeological evidence for local manufacturing of a variety of artefacts (gold, tin and bronze ornaments, beads, pottery, etc), it is quite possible that the urban centre at Oc Eo would have been progressively transformed into a kind of "industrial" site geared towards the production and exportation – inland and overseas – of superbly crafted objects. The commodities obtained must, in their turn, have been fed into the Funanese hinterland via the canal and river network. Ongoing research may also help document other functions of the extensive canal network: it is quite possible that drainage of the floodplain and the newly acquired irrigation control helped open up new tracts of land for rice growing. Rice chaff is commonly found in pottery and bricks at Oc Eo.

The seemingly sudden abandonment, in the mid-seventh century at the latest, of the urban floodplain site of Oc Eo – as opposed to those religious sites on the Ba Thê slopes that survived for five or six more centuries – raises many unanswered questions. What were the shares of environmental, economic or political factors in such radical changes in settlement patterns? Did the digging of the canals put into motion a silting process uncontrollable with the hydraulic technology of the time? The maintenance of the modern hydraulic system, developed after the eighteenth century, often using ancient canal beds, is uncommonly difficult and costly and can only be economically justified by the high yields in rice production of the Mekong Delta. Or, as has been recently suggested,[38] was there an even more radical natural phenomenon, such as a large volcanic explosion inducing a severe change in climate that could have triggered such an irreversible process? We note that the climatic extremes of the late 1990s put considerable pressure on the modern hydraulic system, provoking the longest and highest recorded flood around Oc Eo. Did the growth of agriculture in the interior plains of present-day Cambodia and the progressive shift inland of the political centres of the southern Indochinese peninsula lead to abandonment of the larger coastal centres? It has been argued that, in the face of increasing competition from the Austronesian-speaking states that were fast developing in Insular Southeast Asia in the fifth century, the maritime trade revenues of Funan fell sharply, bringing about the end of its control over trade with China. This, together with internal political strife, could have prompted a shift towards inland agriculture under the pre-Angkorian (Zhenla) and Angkorian Khmer states.

The shift to Insular Southeast Asia

The reorganization of maritime trade networks between the fifth and the seventh centuries appears indeed as a major historical event of Southeast Asian history, as suggested by Oliver Wolters.[39] Until then, the Chinese only had access to the avidly sought Western Asian products and a few pricey Southeast Asian commodities via Funan and Champa and their trade networks. Starting in the third century, indirect information on countries situated further south became available to Chinese writers. These sources suggest that direct and regular contacts with those Malay world polities that had for long entertained trading relations with India and the Indian Ocean were not established before the early fifth century. Overall growth in the South China Sea maritime trade was then encouraged by the disturbances in Northern China and the subsequent movement of Chinese elites towards the southern provinces, fostering a new emerging market that was cut off from its traditional overland access to Western Asia. Those communities in Insular Southeast Asia that had earlier been active in the development of the Indian Ocean trade networks now turned such circumstances to advantage. People of the Malay world were given another chance to show their ability to expand economically and politically, proving their seamanship and commercial acumen, and confirming the fact that commerce played a prominent role in the early formative stages of coastal, harbour-centred political systems.

During the fifth century, written sources, mainly Chinese, bear witness to the political consolidation of a variety of coastal states in Insular Southeast Asia which were sending embassies to China on a regular basis. The most prominent transformation was the progressive introduction and imposition on the Chinese market, between the fifth and the seventh centuries, of Southeast Asian products that acted as substitutes for Western Asian commodities such as frankincense and myrrh which they had helped ship to China in earlier times. Oleoresins from pine trees, benzoin (gum benjamin) and first-grade camphor were common in a variety of Southeast Asian environments, particularly in Sumatra. First traded as by-products of "Persian" aromatics, these new products appeared by the sixth century in Chinese texts as distinct, precious commodities of the Southern Seas.[40]

Not all of the polities that are mentioned in Chinese sources have yet been identified through archaeology. Some of them are only known by the Chinese transcription of their names, and their precise geographical position remains in doubt. For a few others, some of the archaeological proof rests only in the form of Sanskrit inscriptions found on sites that have so far yielded no further reliable data. Such is the case of the polity at Kutei in East Kalimantan that was ruled *c.* AD 400 by a third-generation ruler named Mulavarman. His existence is revealed by a set of pillar inscriptions, dated by palaeography alone, which commemorate a series of lavish cattle donations by the king to Brahmin-like priests.[41] The exploitation of alluvial gold, known to have been abundant in the Mahakam river basin, must have lain at the origin of this coastal state. However, with the single exception of a small Buddha statue in Gupta style, none of the many Indianized remains gathered over the years from Kutei can be dated to such an early period. Buddhist votive rock inscriptions akin to those of the Malay Peninsula were also found in West Kalimantan (Kampung Pahit) and Brunei; they probably also date from the fifth to the seventh centuries and may correspond to an hypothetical polity of Jinlipishi (Chin-li-p'i-shih, Vijayapura?).[42]

So far, only one large site complex, in West Java, can be said to bring together two connected data sets: a corpus of inscriptions dated on palaeographic grounds to the mid-fifth century mentioning a state (*nagara*) named Taruma, and an urban coastal settlement indicated by a growing body of archaeological evidence around the river of Tarum (an Austronesian term for "indigo", sanskritized as Taruma). Fieldwork by Indonesian archaeologists has started to fill in some of the gaps in this early historical period. We have already mentioned the existence, in the same area, of the early first millennium AD Buni complex, and the fact that evidence points to continuity of its occupation until the end of the millennium. It appears that Tarumanagara represents a further progress in local state formation. By the fifth century, Purnavarman, the ruler mentioned in five Sanskrit inscriptions, had clearly adopted Indian stately behaviour (Figure 12.15). He had taken up Brahmanical religious customs and state conceptions: his own footprints were said to represent those of the god Visnu, a divinity closely associated with kingship and political power. According to one inscription found near the coast at Tugu, in what is now East Jakarta, Brahmins were associated with a ritual consecrating a new waterway meant to protect an urban settlement from flooding. Unfortunately this location is today situated in a densely urbanised area of the modern city.[43]

Figure 12.15 Vaishnava inscription of Purnavarman, king of Tarumanagara, at Ci Aruteun, West Java (fifth-century AD). (Photograph courtesy of EFEO.)

At Cibuaya, a coastal site near an ancient bed of the Tarum River, a group of small temples has recently been investigated. The site has been associated with three Visnu statues, probably imported from India, stylistically close to those found in both the Malay Peninsula and the Mekong Delta and believed to date from the fifth century. One small brick platform has been excavated and reveals a building technique that is strikingly similar to that in use in larger brick temples of the fifth–sixth centuries excavated at Oc Eo or at Thap Muoi, in Funan. Another brick temple complex in the same coastal area of West Java, at Batujaya, is tentatively associated with a later phase of Taruma: those structures that have been excavated are in the shape of Buddhist stupas, and small clay votive tablets representing a Bodhisattva indicate that Mahayana Buddhism was practised. Their style could be as late as the seventh or eighth century, but these Buddhist sanctuaries were clearly built on top of earlier settlements: Indian pottery has been excavated and one lower level has been recently radiocarbon dated to the mid-second to fourth centuries.

The coexistence in the Taruma complex of Buddhism and of a Vaishnava form of Brahmanism is worth noting, as this situation appears to be constant in the early phase of Indianization of Southeast Asia, both continental and insular. With the exception of Champa, where early forms of Shaivism appear to have been adopted, data available for this fifth to seventh centuries period overwhelmingly indicate that both Vaisnavism and Buddhism played prominent roles in the early phases of the Indianization process of coastal polities. The corpus of inscriptions and statues found in Funan, in pre-Angkorian Cambodia, along the Malay Peninsula, in Sumatra (as discussed below), in Borneo and in Java is overwhelmingly either Vaishnava or Buddhist. The role of Buddhism in the propagation of Indian civilization in Southeast Asia has long been acknowledged: its universalist doctrines made it a convenient means of proselytizing among foreign people who did not belong to the rigid cast system of India.[44] However, such universalist conceptions were shared with devotional (*bhakti*) sects of Vaisnavism that are also known to have been active in Southeast Asia: one such sect is mentioned in a mid-fifth century inscription of Funan (K5 at Thap Muoi). Shaivaite lingas found in association with such cults appear to have represented a lesser divinity in this period.[45]

Ironically, considering the amount of research that has gone into the later periods of Javanese history, the northern coast of Central and Eastern Java has so far yielded no archaeological remains that can be with any certainty attributed to an Indianized, pre-"classic" chronological phase comparable to that of West Java. One group of statues was reported near Pekalongan in the 1970s, among them a Visnu, which did not appear to fit any "classical" scheme. These reminded one archaeologist of the Cibuaya Visnus, but no further research was carried out and their present location is unknown. The Musée Guimet holds another "un-classical" Surya statue from Java, unfortunately of unknown provenance.[46] Testimonies from Chinese and Indian Buddhist monks sailing into undetermined harbour(s) on the island of Java (Shepo/Shê-p'o), in the first quarter of the fifth century, are conclusive about the progress of their religion among the local people.[47] By 433 and 435, the polity named Shepo was sending embassies to China. Between 430 and 452, however, the rulers of Huoluodan (Ho-lo-tan), a place said to be part of the same island of Java and perhaps located in West Java, were also sending ambassadors to the Middle Kingdom, offering "tribute" comprising Middle Eastern commodities, which probably indicates that their harbour polity was a terminal for Indian Ocean trade. But there is no mention of the name Taruma(nagara) in contemporary Chinese sources, so one cannot be more specific about the social and economic situation on the coasts of central or eastern Java before the trading state named Heling (Ho-ling) appeared in Chinese records in 640 as a steadfast member of the cosmopolitan Buddhist community.[48] Once again, however, the lack of solid contemporary archaeological evidence for the northern coast of Java forbids any reliable assumption regarding the precise situation of the latter coastal state, and one can only surmise that it became incorporated into the growing power of the "classical" inland state of Mataram, some time during the eighth century.[49]

During the fifth and sixth centuries, as mentioned earlier, textual sources bear evidence to the growing control by incipient states of Sumatra over the Chinese market for local forest products such as resins and aromatics. Chinese records mention a variety of polities that engaged in active trade with China, some of them sending embassies bearing "tribute". Unfortunately, with few exceptions, interpretations of these textual sources remain difficult when it comes to precise locations as the Chinese were still unfamiliar with these regions. One prominent such polity was Gantuoli (Kan-to-li), most probably situated on the southeastern coast of Sumatra. This appeared in Chinese records in the mid-fifth century and was still active in 519, by which date a Buddhist king had replaced an earlier Hindu ruler. A Buddhist monk's advice to one ruler of Gantuoli was to "send envoys with tribute [to China]" so that his land would become "rich and happy and travellers would multiply a hundredfold".[50]

Apart from this emphasis on the South China Sea trade, we learn little else from these sources about the internal situation of such polities. By the end of the sixth century, a temporary slump in the Chinese market appears to have provoked their downfall. When the Chinese market recuperated under the Tang dynasty, in the early seventh century, a set of polities quickly rematerialized under different names to take control of local exports and of shipping along the Strait of Melaka. Like Heling in Java, they established themselves as centres of Buddhist scholarship: Chinese pilgrims of the second half of the century spent years in them learning Sanskrit and translating canonical literature into Chinese, before visiting India. Most prominent was the prolific Chinese writer and monk Ijing (I-tsing), whose works provided much of the information on which the history of the region was written until recent archaeological work was carried out. Kedah, Malayu (near Jambi) and Barus (the camphor-exporting centre on the northwest coast of Sumatra) all appear to have shared in the international trade before they were absorbed in the 670s, practically under the eyes of Ijing, into the much broader economic sphere of the political entity known as Srivijaya.[51]

One founding inscription engraved at Palembang by the ruler of Srivijaya in the 680s refers to the outlying polities called *mandala* that he claimed to have brought under his control. It portrays their rulers as powerful local magnates who had to be brought to order as they only uneasily recognized the authority of the new central power.[52] A set of four similar inscriptions, set up by the same expansionist ruler at the periphery of the region under his newly imposed control, draws an almost perfect arc of circle encompassing the south-eastern part of Sumatra, indirectly confirming the fuzzy geographical outline pulled together from Chinese sources. Archaeologists have so far brought to light only one of the four potential sites: a Franco-Indonesian team excavated in 1994 and 1996 the site of Kota Kapur, which appears to have been one of these smaller pre-Srivijaya polities.[53]

The site of Kota Kapur, on the Island of Bangka, facing the straits of the same name and the estuary of the Musi River, was a smallish sixth–seventh centuries coastal settlement with two diminutive Hindu temples complete with their statuary, a 1.5 kilometres-long earthen wall protecting it from outside attacks, and a gathering of riparian settlements. It was built on top of an earlier iron-working site dated to the third–fifth centuries AD. The two temples are simple stone platforms (respectively 5.6 metres and 2.8 metres square) on which, in all probability, wooden structures would have been erected to provide shelter to the images. Statues found in the main sanctuary belong to the Vaishnava cult encountered in most coastal states, starting in the early fifth century AD as described above. These were dated to the late sixth or early seventh century, based on both stylistic considerations and radiocarbon dates (Figure 12.16). The secondary temple contained a coarse *lingga* made of an uncarved natural stone. This coastal settlement was therefore one small link in a long chain of Vaishnava settlements, a merchant network that ran parallel to the similarly widespread Buddhist network.[54] The inscription erected in 686 at Kota Kapur by the Buddhist ruler of Srivijaya, after he gained control of the small polity, also mentions the onset of an attack on neighbouring Java. The state that came under attack from Srivijaya may have been a successor of fifth-century Tarumanagara, in West Java, the ruler of which was Vaishnava, like the people of Kota Kapur more than a century later. There is indeed an isolated mention in Chinese sources of a seventh-century Javanese state named Duoluomo (To-lo-mo), a slightly irregular rendition of Taruma. If confirmed, this could be indicative of severe competition between the Buddhist and Vaishnava trading networks of western Southeast Asia.

Figure 12.16 Vishnu statue from a late sixth- to early seventh-century temple at Kota Kapur, Bangka, South Sumatra (1996). (Photograph courtesy of EFEO.)

The founding of Srivijaya

A momentous event in the 670s was the birth of the state of Srivijaya.[55] We have seen how it came into being by consolidating the activities of smaller polities scattered along the Strait of Melaka. It is the first known large-scale state, clearly of world economic stature, to have prospered in Insular Southeast Asia. In the ninth and tenth centuries, the wealth and prestige of its ruler, the regional eminence of its capital and harbour-cities, and its role as a centre for the diffusion of Buddhism were acknowledged by other world economies, from Baghdad to China. For the first time, a state of Southeast Asia was in a position to concentrate a large measure of control – geographical as well as political – over most of the flow of international trade for several centuries, providing a focal point for the Indian Ocean, South China Sea, and Southeast Asian maritime networks. The fluctuating fortunes of Srivijaya over the next six centuries clearly demonstrate that economic competition was strong. Those regional powers in Sumatra, the Malay Peninsula, and possibly also in West Java and West Kalimantan that came directly into its sphere of political and economic influence were always quick to regain their autonomy when they sensed a weakness at the centre.

For lack of sufficient archaeological data, we are far from understanding all the details of Srivijaya's long history and of its seeming hegemony over part of Insular and Peninsular Southeast Asia. What is clear is that, as an active participant in a growing world economy, Srivijaya always remained dependent on developments taking place in the markets of its two major neighbours, India and China. When these were at peace and domestic demand was on the rise, at foundation times in the late seventh century or during the economic boom of the ninth and tenth centuries, Srivijaya noticeably enjoyed a strong economic and political position. However, during the eleventh to thirteenth centuries, when India and China themselves became major operators in these trade networks – under the Colas in India and the Song in China – Srivijaya progressively lost its commercial importance and foremost stand on the international scene. It was replaced, for a brief period in the fifteenth century, by the Malay city-state of Melaka, its only true successor in the Strait of Melaka.

After decades of controversies following the identification of Srivijaya by George Cœdès in 1918 on textual evidence alone, its physical location in the provinces of South Sumatra, and later in Jambi, where its capital was transferred towards the end of the eleventh century, has now been established beyond doubt. The state of Srivijaya, between the seventh and the thirteenth centuries, produced relatively few inscriptions and practically all of them come from the very first phase, in the 680s. These inscriptions were the first ever to be written in a vernacular language of Insular Southeast Asia, this being Old Malay with a strong Sanskrit lexical input. Because of the paucity of epigraphic evidence, unusual for a "historical" state, only systematic archaeological research in Sumatra can provide some of the answers to the myriad of questions raised by the existence of Srivijaya. A 10-year Franco–Indonesian programme started in the late 1980s has helped to fill some of this gap,[56] and continuing research by Indonesian archaeologists keeps updating the evidence.

The large and still growing body of evidence now proves that the modern city of Palembang in southeastern Sumatra was the political, religious and economic centre of Srivijaya between the seventh and the eleventh centuries. Only the earliest phase of its history (seventh–eighth centuries) is of interest to us here, although no data from controlled excavation has yet been gathered in Palembang city for this early phase. Pre-ninth-century sites without Chinese ceramics produce practically no surface finds, and the little that may have been left to study in the middle of the bustling modern city of Palembang has been heavily looted. The overall picture now gathered at Palembang for the long-lived polity of Srivijaya does, however, help understand the tenuous, context-less archaeological evidence available for foundation times, consisting primarily of late seventh-century inscriptions and statues that are dated on stylistic grounds to the seventh or eighth centuries. Altogether, however, sites in and around the modern city have yielded archaeological evidence for settlement, manufacturing, commercial, religious and political activity at a level that can only be reconciled with it being the capital city of an early Malay state. A riverine pattern, as

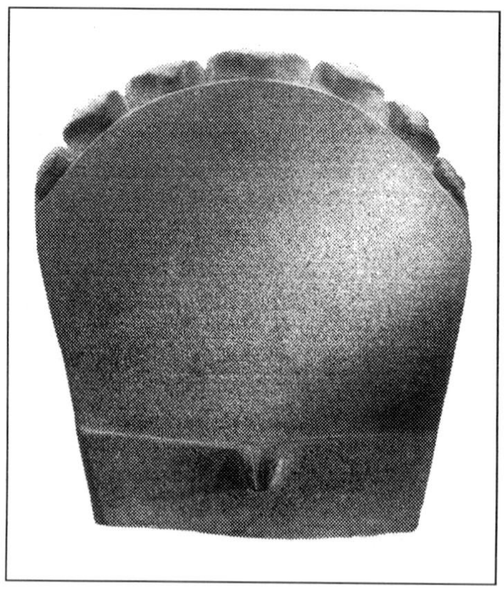

Figure 12.17 Late seventh-century Old Malay 'oath drinking' inscription from Sebokingking, Palembang, South Sumatra. It marked the political centre of the early polity of Srivijaya. (National Museum, Jakarta.) (Photograph courtesy of EFEO.)

expected, is by now clearly discernible. All centres of activity were situated either on the Musi riverbanks or clearly within reach, by water, from the main river and thus from the sea, downstream from Palembang. Many of these finds indicate active, long-distance trade networks and the role of merchants and shipmasters is underscored in local inscriptions. Though no ruler's residence has been located so far, the Sebokingking inscription in East Palembang must have been found close to the political centre of the 680s (Figure 12.17). The politically ominous declaration it contains indicates it was erected at the centre of the polity, at the *kadatuan*, literally the place of the ruler (*datu*), as referred to in the inscription itself.[57]

The picture obtained at Palembang is far removed from the "imperial" state implied by some earlier historians. Careful re-reading of the small corpus of Old Malay inscriptions produced by this polity and of the Chinese sources, in the light of the data produced by recent excavations, allows a scaled-down image to be reconstructed.[58] The structure of the Srivijayan polity was in fact akin to that of later city-states of the Straits area or the Java Sea, these being the Sultanates and harbour-cities of the fifteenth–seventeenth centuries' age of commerce.

Srivijaya, however, was more than just a harbour polity. It was a true city-state in the sense that, immediately after foundation times, it extended its sphere of influence far upstream into one of the largest river basins of Insular Southeast Asia, no doubt allowing it to control the flow of gold and forest products from its hinterland.[59] Brick temple sites situated upstream on the banks of the Musi River or its tributaries have yielded Buddhist statues that can be unmistakably associated with the earliest phase of its history. No

Figure 12.18 A Malay-world sailing vessel depicted on the eighth-century reliefs at Borobudur, Central Java. (Photograph courtesy of EFEO.)

systematic excavations have been carried out yet around these religious sites to investigate the kind of settlement with which they were associated.

After less than a century of intense activity, this first Srivijayan polity appears to have come to a standstill. The last embassy was sent to China in 742. For a while, there are no archaeological or textual data that may be clearly associated with the city-state centred at Palembang. Only on the Malay Peninsula near Chaiya is there a single inscription, dated to the late eighth century, that mentions the name of a ruler of Srivijaya and associates him with the Buddhist Sailendra dynasty known in Java as the builders, among other monuments, of Borobudur (Figure 12.18). Economic activities picked up again in ninth and tenth-century sites at Palembang and upstream in the Musi River Basin, as evidenced by the considerable quantity of Chinese ceramics brought to light. By this time, the Chinese started to give Srivijaya a slightly different name (Sanfoqi/San-fo-ch'i instead of the earlier, more regular transcription Shilifoshih/Shih-li-fo-shih), but they did consider their revived trading partner to be an extension of the earlier polity. By then, however, the ruler was most probably a scion of the Sailendra family, a prince defeated in Java in the 850s, going by the name of Balaputradewa. Srivijaya was by then part of a newly established Southeast Asian "classical" age when powerful states with an agricultural basis, such as Mataram or Angkor, came to dominate much of Southeast Asia. Srivijaya, however, appears to have retained much of its earlier political and economic structure, keeping alive the tradition of the earlier coastal polities.

Notes

1 Coedès 1964.
2 Wolters 1967.
3 Manguin 1980, 1996.
4 Manguin 1992, 1993.
5 Ray 1989; Glover 1990.
6 Glover 1991; Veraprasert 1992.
7 Wisseman Christie 1990.
8 These sites were discovered mainly as a consequence of industrial tin mining.
9 Leong Sau Heng 1990; Wisseman Christie 1990.
10 Tri Manhaeni 2002.
11 Veraprasert 1992.
12 Srisuchat 1996.
13 Evans 1932.
14 Shuhaimi and Arifin 1988; Shuhaimi 1991.
15 Ardika and Bellwood 1991; Ardika 1994; Ardika *et al.* 1997.
16 Lucas, Manguin and Soeroso 1998.
17 Walker and Santoso 1977.
18 Wolters 1967; Wolters 1983.
19 Malleret 1963.
20 Santoso 1990.
21 Ardika and Bellwood 1991; Ardika *et al.* 1997, Ardika 1998.
22 Lê Xuân Diêm *et al.* 1995.
23 Malleret 1959–63.
24 Manguin and Vo Si Khai 2000.
25 Contemporary terracotta tiles, but semi-cylindrical and with decorated end tiles have been excavated at Tra Kieu in Central Vietnam (see chapter 9). These seem to be copied from Chinese roofing materials.
26 Prior 2000; Glover, Nguyen Kim Dung and Prior (in press).
27 Glover and Yamagata 1998.

28 Ray 1989, 1994.
29 Coedès 1964 (last revised French edition in 1964, with an English translation of 1968).
30 McKinnon, Djafar and Soeroso 1998.
31 Dalsheimer and Manguin 1998.
32 Wheatley 1961, Wheatley 1983, Jacq-Hergoulac'h 2002.
33 Wheatley 1961, Wheatley 1983.
34 Jacq-Hergoualc'h 2002.
35 Dalsheimer and Manguin 1998; Dalsheimer 2001.
36 Schweyer 2000.
37 Manguin and Vo Si Khai 2000.
38 Keys 2000.
39 Wolters 1967.
40 Wolters 1967.
41 Casparis 1986.
42 Wolters 1967; Wisseman Christie 1990a; Kartoatmodjo 1994.
43 Vogel 1925; Noordhuyn and Verstappen 1972; McKinnon, Djafar and Soeroso 1998.
44 Ray 1994.
45 Dalsheimer and Manguin 1998.
46 Dalsheimer and Manguin 1998.
47 Damais 1957.
48 Damais 1964.
49 Wisseman Christie 2001.
50 Wolters 1967.
51 Wolters 1967.
52 Kulke 1993.
53 Lucas *et al.* 1998.
54 Dalsheimer and Manguin 1998.
55 Wolters 1967.
56 Manguin 1987; Manguin 1992; Manguin 1993.
57 Kulke 1993; Manguin 2000.
58 Kulke 1991; Kulke 1993.
59 Manguin 2000.

Select Bibliography

General

Bellwood, P. (1997) *Prehistory of the Indo-Malaysian Archipelago*, Honolulu: University of Hawai'i Press, 2nd rev. edn.

Cœdès, G. (1964) *Les États hindouisés d'Indochine et d'Indonésie*, Paris: de Boccard.

Glover, I., Suchita, P. and Villiers, J. (eds) (1992) *Early Metallurgy: Trade and Urban Centres in Thailand and Southeast Asia*, Bangkok: White Lotus.

Higham, C. F. W. (2002) *Early Cultures of Mainland Southeast Asia*, Bangkok: River Books.

Higham, C. F. W. and Thosarat, R. (1998) *Prehistoric Thailand: From Early Settlement to Sukhotai*, Bangkok: River Books.

Jacq-Hergoualc'h, M. (2002) *The Malay Peninsula: Crossroads of the Maritime Silk Road (100 BC–AD 1300)*, Leiden: Brill (Handbuch der Orientalistik).

Kathirithamby-Wells, J. and Villiers, J. (eds) (1990) *The Southeast Asian Port and Polity: Rise and Demise*. Singapore: Singapore University Press.

Keys, D. (2000) *Catastrophe: an Investigation into the Origins of the Modern World*, New York: Ballantine.

Smith, R. B. and Watson, W. (eds) (1979) *Early South East Asia: Essays in Archaeology, History and Historical Geography*, Oxford and Kuala Lumpur: Oxford University Press.

Wheatley, P. (1983) *Nagara and Commandery: Origins of the Southeast Asian Urban Traditions*, Chicago: University of Chicago, Department of Geography (Research Paper no. 207–8).

Wolters, O. W. (1999) *History, Culture, and Region in Southeast Asian Perspectives*. Singapore and Ithaca: Institute of Southeast Asian Studies and Cornell University, Southeast Asia Program Publications (2nd rev. edn).

Archaeology

Ardika, I. W. (1998) "Early evidence of Indian contact with Bali", in P.-Y. Manguin (ed.) *Southeast Asian Archaeology 1994*, Hull: University of Hull, Centre for Southeast Asian Studies, vol. I, pp. 139–46.

Ardika, I. W. and Bellwood, P. (1991) "Sembiran: the beginnings of Indian contact with Bali", *Antiquity*, 65, pp. 221–32.

Ardika, I. W., Bellwood, P., Sutaba, I. M. and Yuliathi, C. (1997) "Sembiran and the first Indian contacts with Bali: an update", *Antiquity*, 71: 193–5.

Evans, I. H. N. (1932) "Excavations at Tanjong Rawa, Kuala Selinsing, Perak", *Journal of the Federated Malay States Museums* 15: 79–134.

Glover, I. and Yamagata, M. (1998) "Excavations at Tra Kiêu, Vietnam 1993: Sa Huynh, Cham and Chinese influences", in P.-Y. Manguin (ed.) *Southeast Asian Archaeology 1994*, Hull: University of Hull, Centre for Southeast Asian Studies, vol. I, pp. 75–93.

Glover, I. C., Dung, N.-K. and Prior, R. (in press) "The 2000–01 excavation seasons at the ancient Cham city at Tra Kieu and Go Cam, Quang Nam Province, Central Vietnam", Paper presented at *the Conference to Celebrate 100 Years of Archaeology in Vietnam, Ha Nôi*, December 2001.

Hoop, A. N. J. Th. A. Th. van der (1932) *Megalithic Remains in South-Sumatra*, Zutphen: W. J. Thieme.

Kempers, A. J. Bernet (1988) "The Kettledrums of Southeast Asia: a Bronze Age world and its aftermath", *Modern Quaternary Research in Southeast Asia*, 10 (special issue).

Lê Xuân Diêm, Dao Linh Côn and Vo Si Khai, (1995) *Van Hoa Oc Eo: nhung kham pha moi*, Ha Nôi: Viên Khoa Hoc Xa Hoi tai Thanh Phô Hô Chi Minh.

Lucas P. K., Manguin, P.-Y. and Soeroso (1998) Kota Kapur (Bangka, Indonesia): "A pre-Sriwijayan site reascertained", in P.-Y. Manguin (ed.) *Southeast Asian Archaeology 1994: Proceedings of the Fifth International Conference of the European Association of Southeast Asian Archaeologists, Paris, October 1994*, Hull: University for Hull, Centre of Southeast Asian Studies, vol. II, pp. 61–81.

McKinnon, E. E., Hasan Djafar and Soeroso, M. P. (1998) "Tarumanagara? A note on discoveries at Batujaya and Cibuaya, West Java", in P.-Y. Manguin (ed.) *Southeast Asian Archaeology 1994*. Hull: University of Hull Centre for Southeast Asian Studies, vol. I, pp. 147–59.

Malleret, L. (1959–63) *L'archéologie du Delta du Mékong*, Paris: École Française d'Extrême-Orient (*EFEO* 43), 4 t. in 7 vols.

Malleret, L. (1963) "Notes archéologiques, II: Pierres gravées et cachets de divers pays du sud-est de l'Asie", *Bulletin de l'École française d'Extrême-Orient*, 51(1): 99–116.

Manguin, P.-Y. (1987) "Palembang et Sriwijaya: anciennes hypothèses, nouvelles recherches (Palembang Ouest)", *Bulletin de l'École française d'Extrême-Orient*, 76: 337–402.

Manguin, P.-Y. (1992) "Excavations in South Sumatra, 1988–1990: new evidence for Sriwijayan sites", in I. C. Glover (ed.) *Southeast Asian Archaeology 1990: Proceedings of the Third Conference of the European Association of Southeast Asian Archaeologists*, Hull: Centre for Southeast Asian Studies, pp. 63–73.

Manguin, P.-Y. (1993) "Palembang and Sriwijaya: An early Malay harbour-city rediscovered", *Journal of the Malayan Branch, Royal Asiatic Society*, 66(1): 23–46.

Manguin, P.-Y. (1993) "Southeast Asian shipping in the Indian Ocean during the first millennium AD", in H. P. Ray and J.-F. Salles (eds) *Tradition and Archaeology: Early Maritime Contacts in the Indian Ocean*, New Delhi: Manohar.

Manguin, P.-Y. and Vo Si Khai (2000) "Excavations at the Ba Thê / Oc Eo complex (Vietnam): a preliminary report on the 1998 campaign", in Wibke Lobo and S. Reimann (eds) *Southeast Asian Archaeology 1998*. Hull and Berlin: Centre for Southeast Aian Studies, University of Hull and Ethnologisches Museum, Staatlich Museen zu Berlin (Veröffentlichungen 70), pp. 107–22.

Noordhuyn, J. and Verstappen, H. Th. (1972) "Purnavarman's River Works near Tugu", *Bijdragen tot de Taal-, Land- en Volkenkunde van de Koninkijk Instituut*, 128: 298–307.
Prior, R. (2000) *Early Historic Ceramics from Tra Kieu, Central Vietnam: typological and petrographic characteristics*, London: Institute of Archaeology.
Santoso S. (1990) "Tinjauan terhadap situs Plawangan", in *Analisis hasil penelitian arkeologi I*, Jakarta: Pusat Penelitian Arkeologi Nasional, vol. II, pp. 6–19.
Shuhaimi, N. H. (1991) "Recent research at Kuala Selinsing, Perak", *Bulletin of the Indo-Pacific Prehistory Association*, 11: 141–52.
Shuhaimi, N. H., (1993) "Pre-Modern cities in the Malay Peninsula and Sumatra", *Jurnal Arkeologi Malaysia* 6: 63–77.
Shuhaimi, N. H. and Arifin, A. L. (1988) "Penyelidikan arkeologi di Pulau Buluh (Pulau Kalumpang), Kuala Selinsing, Perak", *Jurnal Arkeologi Malaysia* 1: 36–41.
Stark, M. T. (1998) "The transition to history in the Mekong Delta a view from Cambodia", *International Journal of Historical Archaeology* 2(3): 175–203.
Sutayasa, I Made (1972) "Notes on the Buni pottery complex, Northwest Java", *Mankind* 8: 182–4.
Tri Marhaeni (2002) "Pemukiman pra-Sriwijaya de Karangagung Tengah: sebuah kajian awal", *Siddhayâtra* 7(2): 65–89.
Veraprasert, Mayuree (1992) "Khlong Thom: An ancient bead manufacturing location and an ancient entrepôt", in I. Glover, Pornchai Succhita and J. Villiers (eds) *Early Metallurgy: Trade and Urban Centres in Thailand and Southeast Asia*. Bangkok: White Lotus, pp. 149–61.
Walker, M. J. and Santoso, S. (1977) "Romano-Indian rouletted pottery in Indonesia", *Mankind* 11: 39–45.

History and Indianization

Casparis, J. G. de (1983) *India and Maritime South East Asia: A Lasting Relationship.*, Kuala Lumpur: University of Malaya.
Chhabra, B. C. (1965) *Expansion of Indo-Aryan Culture during Pallava Rule (as evidenced by inscriptions)*, New Delhi: Munshiran Manohar Lal.
Kulke, H. (1986) "The early and the Imperial Kingdom in Southeast Asian History", in D. G. Marr and A. C. Milner (eds) *Southeast Asia in the Ninth to Fourteenth Centuries*, Singapore and Canberra: Institute of Southeast Asian Studies and ANU, pp. 1–22.
Kulke, H. (1990) "Indian colonies, Indianization or cultural convergence? Reflections on the changing image of India's role in South-East Asia", in H. Schulte Nordholt (ed.) *Onderzoek in Zuidoost-Azie: Agenda's voor de jaren negentig*, Leiden: Rijksuniversiteit te Leiden (Semaian 3), pp. 8–32.
Mabbett, I. W. (1977) "The 'Indianization' of Southeast Asia: reflections on the prehistoric sources and The 'Indianization' of Southeast Asia: reflections on historical sources", *Journal of Southeast Asian Studies*, 8 (1/2): 1–14 and 143–61.
Mabbett, I. W. (1997) "The 'Indianization' of Mainland Southeast Asia: a reappraisal", in N. Eilenberg, M. C. S. Diskul and R. L. Brown (eds) *Living A life in Accord with Dhamma*, Bangkok: Silpakorn University, pp. 352–5.
Manguin, P.-Y. (2000) "Les cités-États de l'Asie du Sud-Est côtière: de l'ancienneté et de la permanence des formes urbaines", *Bulletin de l'École française d'Extrême-Orient*, 87(1): 151–82.
Népote, J. (1999) "Mythes de fondation et fonctionnement de l'ordre social dans la basse vallée du Mékong, accompagnés de considérations sur l'indianisation", *Péninsule*, 38(1), pp. 33–64.
Pelliot, P. (1903) "Le Fou-nan", *Bulletin de l'École française d'Extrême-Orient*, 3: 248–303.
Pelliot, P. (1904) "Deux itinéraires de Chine en Inde à la fin du VIIIe siècle", *Bulletin de l'École française d'Extrême-Orient* 4: 131–413.
Schweyer, A.-V. (2000) "La dynastie d'Indrapura (Quang Nam, Vietnam)", in Wibke Lobo and S. Reimann (eds) *Southeast Asian Archaeology 1998*, Hull/Berlin: Centre for Southeast Aian Studies, University of Hull and Ethnologisches Museum, Staatlich Museen zu Berlin (Veröffentlichungen 70), pp. 205–18.
Vickery, M. (1998) *Society, Economics, and Politics in Pre-Angkor Cambodia: The Seventh–Eighth Centuries*, Tokyo: Toyo Bunko Centre for East Asian Cultural Studies for UNESCO.

Wheatley, P. (1961) *The Golden Khersonese: Studies in the Historical Geography of the Malay Peninsula before AD 1500*, Kuala Lumpur: Oxford University Press.

Wheatley, P. (1982) "India beyond the Ganges – Desultory Reflections on the Origins of Civilization in Southeast Asia", *Journal of Asian Studies*, 42(1): 13–28.

Wisseman Christie, J. (1990) "Trade and state formation in the Malay Peninsula and Sumatra, 300 BC–AD 700", in J. Kathirithamby-Wells and J. Villiers (eds), *The Southeast Asian Port and Polity: Rise and Demise*, Singapore: Singapore University Press, pp. 39–60.

Wisseman Christie, J. (1992) "Trade and settlement in Early Java: integrating the epigraphic and archaeological data", in I. Glover, Pornchai Succhita and J. Villiers (eds) *Early Metallurgy: Trade and Urban Centres in Thailand and Southeast Asia*, Bangkok: White Lotus, pp. 181–97.

Wisseman Christie, J. (1995) "State formation in Early Maritime Southeast Asia: a consideration of the theories and the data", *Bijdragen tot de Taal-, Land- en Volkenkunde*, 151(2): 235–88.

Wisseman Christie, J. (2001), "Revisiting early Mataram", in M. J. Klokke and K. R. van Kooij (eds) *Fruits of Inspiration. Studies in Honour of Prof. J. G. de Casparis*, Groningen: Egbert Forsten, pp. 25–55.

Wolters, O. W. (1967) *Early Indonesian Commerce: A Study of the Origins of Sri Vijaya*, Ithaca: Cornell University Press.

Wolters, O. W. (1979) "Studying Srivijaya", *Journal of the Malaysian Branch of the Royal Asiatic Society* 52: 1–32.

Wolters, O. W. (1983) "A few miscellaneous Pi-chi jottings on early Indonesia", *Indonesia*, 36: 49–64.

Wolters, O. W. (1986) "Restudying some Chinese writings on Srivijaya", *Indonesia* 42: 1–42.

Architecture and art history

Dalsheimer, N. (2001) *Les collections du musée national de Phnom Penh: L'art du Cambodge ancien*, Paris: École Française d'Extrême-Orient, Magellan & Cie.

Le Bonheur, A. (1971) *La sculpture indonésienne au Musée Guimet: Catalogue et étude iconographique*, Paris: Presses Universitaires de France.

O'Connor, S. J. (1972) *Hindu Gods of Peninsular Thailand*. Ascona: Artibus Asiae Publishers.

Inscriptions and epigraphy

Casparis, J. G. de (1956) *Prasasti Indonesia, II: Selected Inscriptions from the Seventh to the Ninth century AD*, Bandung: Masa Baru.

Casparis, J. G. de (1986) "Some notes on the oldest inscriptions of Indonesia", in C. M. S. Hellwig and S. O. Robson (eds), *A Man of Indonesian Letters: Essays in Honour of Professor A. Teeuw.*- Dordrecht, Cinnaminson: *Verhandelingan van het Koninklijk Instituut voor Taal-, Land- en Volkenkunde* 121, pp. 242–56.

Damais, L.-Ch. (1957) "Review of Poerbatjaraka", *Riwajat Indonesia*, vol. I, Jakarta 1952, in *Bulletin de l'École française d'Extrême-Orient* 48 (2): 607–49.

Damais, L.-Ch. (1964) "Etudes sino-indonésiennes. III. La transcription chinoise Ho-Ling comme désignation de Java", *Bulletin de l'École française d'Extrême-Orient* 52: 93–141.

Kartoatmodjo, M. M. Sukarto (1994) "Beberapa temuan prasasti baru di Indonesia", in *Evaluasi data dan interpretatsi baru sejarah Indonesia kuna (Purna Bhakti Drs. M. M. Sukarto Karto Atmodjo, Yogyakarta 1994)*, *Berkala Arkeologi*, 14 (Edisi Khusus): 1–5.

Kulke, H. (1991) "Epigraphical references to the 'City' and the 'State' in early Indonesia", *Indonesia*, 52: 3–22.

Kulke, H. (1993) "Kadatuan Srivijaya – Empire or Kraton of Srivijaya? A reassessment of the epigraphical evidence", *Bulletin de l'École française d'Extrême-Orient*, 80: 159–81.

Vogel, J. Ph. (1925) "The earliest Sanskrit inscriptions of Java", in *Publicaties van de Oudheidkundige Dienst in Nederlandsch-Indie*, 1: 15–35.

Wisseman Christie, J. (1990a) "The Sanskrit inscription recently discovered in Kedah", *Modern Quaternary Research in Southeast Asia*, 11: 39–54.

Trade and exchange

Bellina, B. (1999) "La vaisselle dans les échanges entre le sous-continent indien et l'Asie du Sud-Est à l'époque protohistorique. Note sur quelques marqueurs archéologiques", *Bulletin de l'École française d'Extrême-Orient*, 86: 161–84.

Bronson, B. (1977) "Exchange at the upstream and downstream ends: notes toward a functional model of the coastal state in Southeast Asia", in Karl L. Hutterer (ed.), *Economic Exchange and Social Interaction in Southeast Asia: Perspectives from Prehistory, History and Ethnography*, Ann Arbor: Michigan State University, pp. 39–52.

Dalsheimer, N. and Manguin, P.-Y. (1998) "Visnu mitrés et réseaux marchands en Asie du Sud-Est: nouvelle données archéologiques sur le Ier millénaire apr. J.-C.", *Bulletin de l'École française d'Extrême-Orient* 85: 87–123.

Glover, I. C. (1990) *Early Trade between India and Southeast Asia: A Link in the Development of a World Trading System*, Hull: University of Hull, Centre for Southeast Asian Studies (Occasional paper, no.16, 2nd rev. edn.).

Glover, I. C. (1991) "Beads and bronzes: archaeological indicators of trade between South and Southeast Asia", in K. R. Haellquist (ed.) *Asian Trade Routes*, Copenhagen and London: Scandinavian Institute of Asian Studies (Studies on Asian Topics no.13) and Curzon Press, pp. 117–41.

Leong Sau Heng (1990) "Collecting centres, feeder points and entrepôts in the Malay Peninsula, *c.*1000 BC–AD 1400", in J. Kathirithamby-Wells and J. Villiers (eds), *The Southeast Asian Port and Polity: Rise and Demise*. Singapore: Singapore University Press, pp. 17–38.

Manguin, P.-Y. (1980) "The Southeast Asian ship: an historical approach", *Journal of Southeast Asian Studies*, 11(2): 266–76.

Manguin, P.-Y. (1996) "Southeast Asian shipping in the Indian Ocean during the 1st millennium A.D.", in H. P. Ray and J.-F. Salles (eds) *Tradition and archaeology. Early Maritime Contacts in the Indian Ocean*, Lyon/New Delhi: Manohar (Maison de l'Orient méditeréranéen / NISTADS), pp. 181–98.

Ray, H. P. (1989) "Early maritime contacts between South and Southeast Asia", *Journal of Southeast Asian Studies*, 20(1): 42–54.

Ray, H. P. (1994) *The Winds of Change: Buddhism and the Maritime Links of Early South Asia*, Delhi: Oxford University Press.

Srisuchat, A. (1996) "Merchants, merchandise, markets: archaeological evidence in Thailand concerning maritime trade interaction between Thailand and other countries before the sixteenth century", in Amara Srisuchat (ed.) *Ancient Trades and Cultural Contacts in Southeast Asia*, Bangkok: The Office of the National Culture Commission, pp. 237–74.

Wang Gungwu (1958) "The Nanhai trade: a study of the early history of Chinese trade in the South China Sea", *Journal of the Malayan Branch, Royal Asiatic Society* 31(2): 1–135.

Wicks, R. S. (1992) *Money, Markets, and Trade in Early Southeast Asia: The Development of Indigenous Monetary Systems to AD 1400*, Ithaca: Cornell University, Southeast Asia Program.

13

INDIGENOUS TRADITIONS AND EXOGENOUS INFLUENCES IN THE EARLY HISTORY OF PENINSULAR MALAYSIA

David Bulbeck

Introduction

Tourist guides misunderstand Malaysia in presenting it as a country of rainforests and natural beauty but little historical or cultural interest.[1] To the casual visitor's surprise, Malaya as long as 2,000 years ago was a major node for early maritime trade between the Indian Ocean and the South China Sea. Some of the earliest external references to Southeast Asia describe the Malay Peninsula, which itself contains among the oldest inscriptions in the Indo-Malaysian archipelago.[2] This unusual situation hinges on the repercussions of the major economic activities that generated a surplus in the peninsula, activities like trade in minerals and forest produce, manufacturing, and the provision of strategic port facilities. These neither required nor led to the large populations and associated land shortages that typically befell other places in Southeast Asia with a similarly long history.

Malaya also boasts unequaled cultural diversity in Southeast Asia for a region of equivalent land mass, even if its cultural riches are too subtle to strike a tourist's attention. Speakers of one of the oldest branches of the Austroasiatic language family live cheek by jowl with Austronesian speakers who themselves are apparently represented in several chronological tiers. Indian and Arabic-Persian influences have been felt from ancient times, while early Mons, Khmers and Thais have left behind traces of their visits.[3] Chinese were deeply involved in the fifteenth-century growth of Melaka. To this variety we can add various European colonists and the many Asian groups (Bugis from Sulawesi, Chinese and Indian transmigrants) who found a niche in Malaya during the Modern Era. Malaya's renowned hospitality would appear linked to a sense of complementary opportunities both for newcomers and the locally established residents.

One crux of this diversity is the contrast between the Orang Asli "Aborigines", so variable within Malaya, and whose affinities outside the peninsula tend to be remote, compared to later comers whose wide-ranging networks have each involved a measure of cultural homogeneity across the Peninsula and beyond. This contrast arguably associates the succession of novel cultural phenomena recognizable in the peninsula with the sequential arrival of immigrant groups. The feasibility of this perspective will be explored in this chapter, emphasizing however that it need not make the Orang Asli static relics of the past. Indeed, as we shall see, the "indigenous" groups continually changed over time, in two complementary senses. Already established locals who were not engulfed by the new developments nonetheless absorbed cultural customs and items of material culture from these developments, and sometimes the language that became their mother tongue. Newcomers on the other hand naturalized and blended in over time and, in particular, have come to see their predicament as indigenous in the face of later-arriving newcomers. The term "Aslian" exposes this ambiguity: in a linguistic context it means languages belonging to the Aslian branch of Austroasiatic, even though Austroasiatic languages probably arrived in the peninsula only during the Neolithic; but in other contexts it means any indigenous groups of non-Malay speakers or, following the rise of Melaka and the growth of related Islamic sultanates, people who may speak Malay but have not embraced Islam and the other customs associated with being Malay.[4]

The Melayu or Malays are indeed the exemplar of an externally derived people who have shaped the Peninsula's history, and most scholars would trace their dominance back to Srivijayan times (seventh–thirteenth centuries). However, the *Desawarnana*, written in Java in the fourteenth century, draws a distinction between the lands of the Malays, which are all located in or near Sumatra, and the territory of Pahang which includes places between Singapore (Tumasik) and the Isthmus of Kra. Accordingly, the question of which outsiders most interacted from time to time with people in the peninsula should be approached with an open mind, as we focus on the potential insights from archaeology in this chapter.[5]

Prehistory and human biology

In the author's view, as explained in the Introduction, the Orang Asli cannot be understood except in the context of the peninsula's history (and its historical archaeology) while, reciprocally, an understanding of the peninsula's historical archaeology depends on appreciating the part played by the Orang Asli. Nonetheless the Orang Asli have roots that reach back into prehistory and these are relevant to our discourse. The human biology of the Orang Asli is similarly important here; not to imply that it displays a pattern fossilized in prehistory but, indeed, quite the reverse, to impart a flavor of the dynamism of these various groups' biological characteristics during historical as well as earlier times.[6]

My recent review of the prehistoric archaeology of the Malay Peninsula may be summarized as follows. Several sites reach back to the effective limit of radiocarbon dating (40,000 years ago) though with a hiatus in evidence of habitation between about 25,000 and 15,000 years ago, when sea-levels dropped to their lowest levels in late Quaternary times. Apparently, early hunter-gatherers focused on the lowlands less than 150 meters above prevailing sea-level. After 10,000 years ago, sites with Hoabinhian stone artifacts begin to appear throughout West Malaysia and at all altitudes. Sumatraliths and other pebble tools flaked on only one face tend to be a feature of Hoabinhian assemblages in the western half of the peninsula and in northern Sumatra across the Melaka Strait, whereas pebble tools flaked on both faces tend to characterize assemblages in the eastern half. Pottery is reliably dated to 4–5,000 years ago at several sites in West Malaysia, and tools of polished stone (meeting the formal definition of the "Neolithic") perhaps a millennium later.[7]

It is often presumed that the Semang "Negritos" of Malaya descend from the Hoabinhian hunter-gatherers, while Neolithic immigrants lie at the ancestry of Malaysia's

Senoi swidden farmers, as we see in the following study. Oota and colleagues report extracting and amplifying mitochondrial DNA from human remains in Krabi Province in Thailand's far south, i.e. a Moh Khiew burial supposedly dating to 25,000 years ago, a second Moh Khiew burial which they date to about 12,000 years ago, and four Neolithic Sakai Cave burials which they place in the period between 8,000 and 6,500 years ago (Figure 13.1). The sequences were compared with those from 12 Orang Asli (all Senoi), 6 Malays, 24 Indonesians, 40 Papua New Guineans, and a lone Australian Aborigine. The older Moh Khiew burial fell in a small group with just two of the Papua New Guinea samples; the younger Moh Khiew burial fell in a large group with over half of the Malay and over half of the Papua New Guinea and Indonesian samples, along with a Senoi and the Australian Aborigine; while the four Sakai Cave burials fell in the second

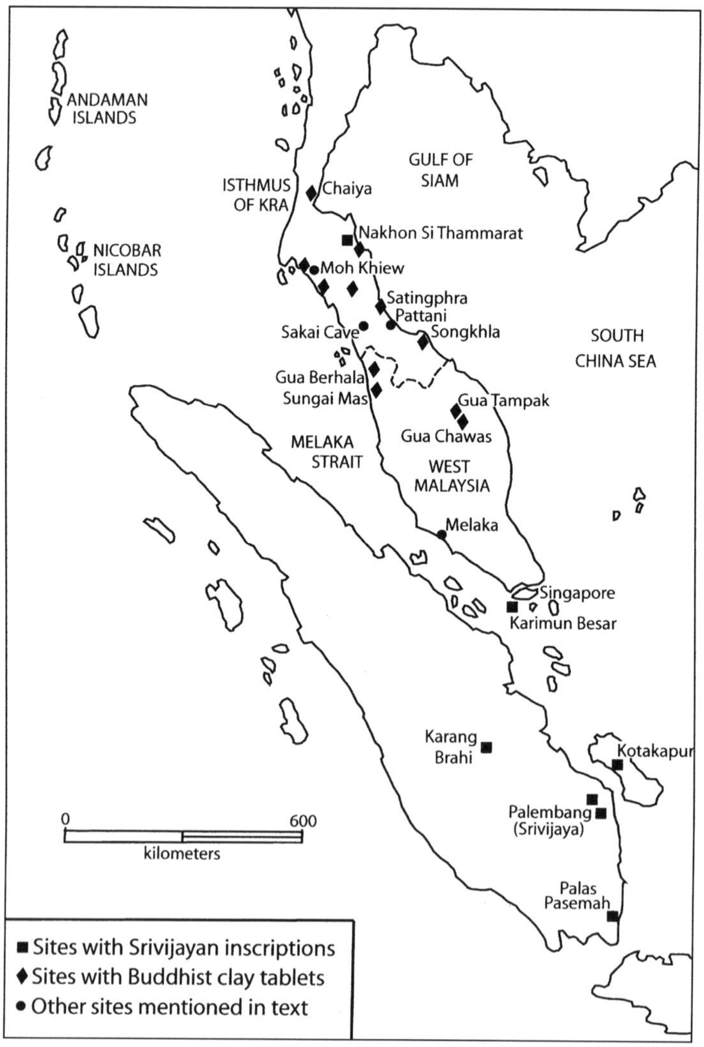

Figure 13.1 West Malaysia and surrounding historical sites. (D. Bulbeck.)

large group that otherwise included eight of the Senoi, three of the Malay, seven of the Indonesian and eight of the Papua New Guinea samples.[8] Although the authors infer a link between the Moh Khiew burials and the Semang, and the Sakai Cave specimens and the Senoi, their results offer no statistically significant associations that might support this presumption.

Similarly, reviews of Malayan prehistory frequently presume an Australoid or Australo-Melanesian affinity for its middle Holocene and earlier inhabitants, but this view enjoys equivocal support at best. The present writer has collected data on all extant archaeological and Orang Asli skulls from West Malaysia, and, whenever at least three of the measurements used in Fordisc analysis are available on a specimen, compared it with the populations measured by W. W. Howells (Table 13.1).[9] This analysis determines the Howells group to which a single specimen is most likely to belong based on the sheer dimensions of its available craniometrics, without making specific allowance for shape

Table 13.1 Fordisc 2.0 analysis of Malay Peninsula craniometric affinities in terms of closest relationship of each specimen to the recent populations measured by Howells.[10]

	Hoabinhian	*Neolithic*	*Iron Age*	*Semang*	*Senoi*	*Aboriginal Malays*
"Mongoloids"						
Easter Island	2	0	1	0	1	0
Eskimos	0	0	1	0	0	0
Arikara	0	0	1	0	0	0
Philippines	0	0	1	1	0	0
Atayal	0	0	0	2	3	0
Santa Cruz	0	0	0	1	0	0
Total	**2**	**0**	**4**	**4**	**4**	**0**
Africans						
Zulu	2	0	0	1	1	0
Teita	0	0	0	1	2	0
Dogon	0	0	0	1	1	0
Bushman	0	0	0	1	0	0
Total	**2**	**0**	**0**	**4**	**4**	**0**
"Australoids"						
Tasmanians	0	3	0	0	0	0
New Britain	0	1	0	0	0	0
Total	0	4	0	0	0	0
Others						
Ainu	0	0	0	2	0	0
Zalavar	0	0	0	1	0	0
Andamanese	0	0	0	3	2	2
Grand Total	**4**	**4**	**4**	**14**	**10**	**2**

comparisons, allometry, or environmental/developmental effects. In-depth exploration of the results lies beyond the scope of this chapter. The purpose of summarizing the results here is to falsify a widely recited myth on Malaya's population history and, further, to indicate that the typological thinking inherent in race-based classifications is wholly inadequate for understanding the dynamism of gene flow and biological adaptation among Malaya's inhabitants.

Fordisc analysis offers no evidence of an original occupation of the peninsula by "Australoid" hunter-gatherers, as the Hoabinhians most resemble Easter Island and Zulu skulls. Apparently, "Australoid" affinities emerge only for the Neolithic specimens, even though this is the period when "Mongoloids" supposedly first entered the Peninsula.[11] The first sign of people with craniometrics similar to those of recent Southeast Asians (Filipinos) dates to the Iron Age when, indeed, all four tested crania are "Mongoloid". Scholars inclined to explain morphological changes in terms of population replacement would be compelled to invoke the immigration of Australoids during the Neolithic and their subsequent replacement during the Iron Age. Despite the small number of tested specimens, many of the differences in Table 13.1 are statistically significant.[12] Further, the Orang Asli crania share their affinities equally with "Mongoloid", African and Negrito (Andaman Islander) groups, without any suggestion that the Semang Negritos resemble Andaman Islanders more than the Senoi and Aboriginal Malays do. The comparisons thus refute any notion of a pristine Negrito occupation of Malaya, because skulls like those of Andaman Islanders appear only among the ethnographic Orang Asli series of crania.

The recent derivation of Negrito craniometrics accords with evidence that the inhabitants of the Peninsula used to be bigger than today's Orang Asli. As shown in Table 13.2, average stature would appear to have dropped by around 10 centimeters between the middle Holocene and the early twentieth century. Stature reduction on the coast would lie in the vicinity of 5–10 centimeters, based on comparing the skeletons in the Guar Kepah middens (dated to about 4–5,000 years ago both on archaeological and geomorphological grounds) with early twentieth-century coastal Malays. It is more marked in the hinterland, amounting to 10–15 centimeters when late Hoabinhian burials are compared to the Orang Asli (Semang, Senoi and Aboriginal Malays). Various lines of evidence suggest that the greater stature decrease in the hinterland is at least in part due to dietary deficiencies as the Orang Asli adapted to restricted territories through body-size reduction.[13] Whether this occurred as a long-term secular process, or as a result of genetic evolution, it offers a critical insight into changes in social organization during the late prehistoric and early historical period.

Table 13.2 Average stature and ranges over time and by location in West Malaysia.[14]

	Males		*Females*	
	Hinterland males	*Coastal males*	*Hinterland females*	*Coastal females*
Middle Holocene	168.3 cm (162,174.5)	168.5cm (168–9)	157.5 cm (155, 160)	153 cm
Late Holocene	157 cm (150–165)	163.5 cm (157–68)	150 cm	153 cm
Early twentieth century	151.6–158.0 cm	159.4–160.0 cm	142.5–147.8 cm	148.0 cm

Stature reduction is in evidence as early as the Neolithic appearance at Gua Cha of burial customs similar to those practiced at Ban Kao and related sites in central Thailand.[15] The similarities – extended burials furnished with stone axes and barkcloth beaters, certain types of decorated pots, and shell jewelery – are so strong that some reviews of the West Malaysian Neolithic assign it to the Ban Kao culture. Certainly, some coastal locations may have been infiltrated by bearers of this culture arriving from central Thailand about 4,000 years ago, as suggested by the dating for the tripod vessels from Jenderam Hilir in the Selangor lowlands, and river mouths would have been prime candidates for settlement by Neolithic immigrants. Unfortunately there are no available descriptions of related skeletal material from coastal sites to test this proposition, but any associated population movement into the hinterland must have been minimal. Neolithic to Bronze Age series in Thailand consistently yield average stature estimates of 164–8 centimeters for males and 154–9 centimeters for females,[16] so the Neolithic decline in stature in the West Malaysian hinterland cannot be attributed to immigrants from Thailand. All three Gua Cha Neolithic crania included in Table 1 resemble Tasmanians, hardly the expected outcome of gene flow from Thailand.[17] Dental morphology also demonstrates that any difference between the Gua Cha Neolithic people and their Hoabinhian antecedents would have involved a more "Australoid" rather than a "Mongoloid" affinity.[18]

The Neolithic in West Malaysia should not be portrayed as the time when farming groups with origins in Thailand began sweeping across the peninsula. Far more relevant is the inauguration of regular trade relationships between coast and hinterland. Gua Cha functioned as a cemetery during the Neolithic, and the grave goods tell us of the prestige goods available to the local people rather than their subsistence economy. Whereas earlier studies attempted to treat the Neolithic Gua Cha people as the direct ancestors of the horticultural Senoi, opinion has switched to Geoffrey Benjamin's view that the Temiar Senoi, who are currently the dominant indigenous group in the area (Figure 13.2), expanded here in more recent times from a homeland west of the main range. Lacking real evidence for farming and/or craft specialization near Gua Cha in Neolithic times, we may more parsimoniously assume the inhabitants had acquired their prestige goods through exchange. To envisage the produce available in sufficient amounts to obtain these goods available from coastal locations, we need look no further than the surrounding equatorial jungle. Honey, resins, bamboo, rattan, fine timber, and hornbill beaks are just some of the rainforest produce traded by the Semang in historical and ethnographic times for rice and manufactured goods.[19]

Gua Harimau, located in the western foothills, points to a different orientation. The site has obtained some notoriety for its claimed bronze dating as far back as 5,000 years ago. This claim is falsified by the unreliable sample (bone and freshwater shell) used to obtain that radiocarbon date, and by all three radiocarbon dates on charcoal from the site which fall between about 3,000 and 2,000 years ago.[20] Contextual analysis suggests a transition from Ban Kao-style Neolithic burials (associated with pots, stone barkcloth beaters, and jewelry of bone and shell) to Early Metal Phase burials (associated with a glass bead and bronze as well as pots and shell jewelry). The state of the teeth is consistent with a farming people, even if they probably lived in a settlement away from the site, and used the Harimau rockshelter only as a stopover camp during forays.[21] Interestingly, four of the seven burials with grave goods include manufacturing tools, either stone barkcloth beaters (Neolithic) or a bivalve mould for bronze axes (Early Metal). Gua Harimau may

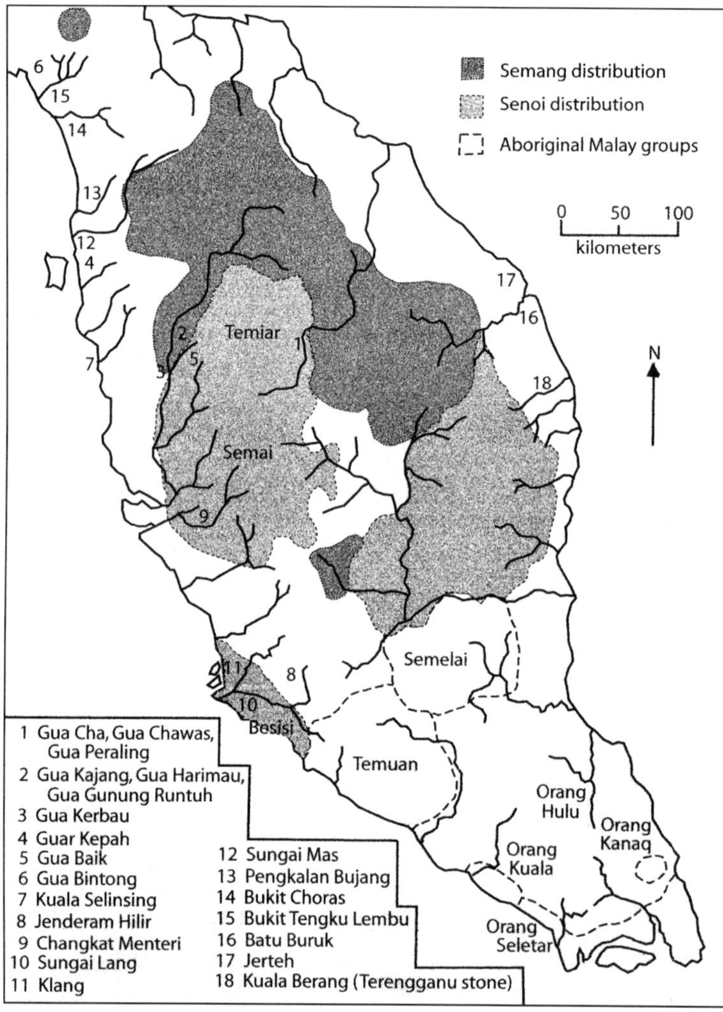

Figure 13.2 Major Malaysian sites compared to Orang Asli groups. (Orang Asli distribution from Rayner and Bulbeck 2002.)

thus represent the more coastally oriented groups who would have produced prestige goods for exchange with forest hunter-gatherers located in the deep hinterland.

Gua Harimau brings us to the verge of Peninsular Malaysia's historical period, a period which can also be treated as the Iron Age, and which includes the Kuala Selinsing burials incorporated into Tables 13.1 and 13.2 above.

Iron, slab graves and early bronzes

West Malaysia is renowned for its idiosyncratic, early iron implements dominated by a range of socketed forms including axes, often shaped like hockey sticks, sickles, knives and spearheads (Figures 13.3 and 13.4). Forms more familiar by standards elsewhere, such as tanged knives, are noted less often. The context of the socketed forms is described as hoards in south Perak, Selangor and Pahang, isolated finds along the Tembeling River, and burial goods in the stone slab graves of the Bernam Valley area of south Perak.[22] The so-called hoards may actually be assemblages of burial goods where all traces of the deceased have dissolved in the acidic soils of the region, by analogy with the slab graves which have never preserved any human bone despite

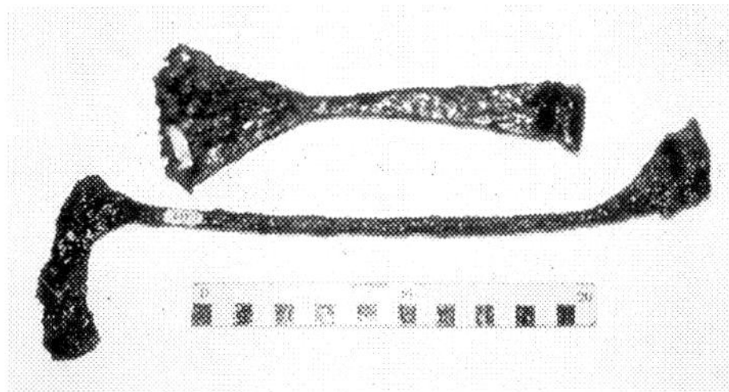

Figure 13.3 Iron tools from Perak slab graves (Perak Museum). Above: a long shafted axe. Below: a *tulang mawas*. Both tools have longitudinal shaft holes, presumably to take wooden hafts. (P. Bellwood.)

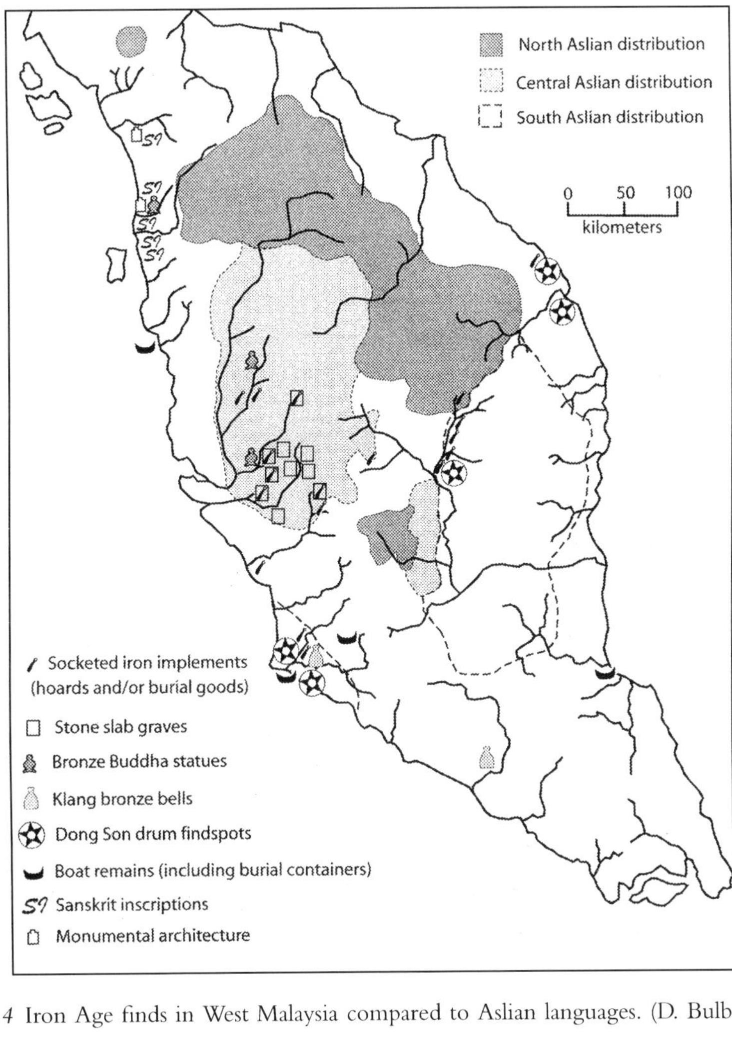

Figure 13.4 Iron Age finds in West Malaysia compared to Aslian languages. (D. Bulbeck.)

the additional protection afforded by their stone casing. Many if not all of the isolated finds might also represent smaller assemblages of grave goods. This consideration is significant as it may suggest these implements be regarded as prestige items, insignia of wealth or authority, even if some also had a utilitarian function.

The slab graves of south Perak and Selangor have conventionally been dated to the first millennium AD. The reported recovery of a Tang Dynasty, Chinese ceramic bowl from one grave at Changkat Menteri suggested either a long period during which the slab graves were constructed or a tendency for them to date late in the millennium. Recently, Leong has obtained radiometric determinations, from four graves, which consistently suggest an age of around 2,000 years ago, along with a decorated bronze from another grave consistent with this age. She also cites a technical report which finds that the supposed Tang ceramic vessel is actually a high-tin bronze.[23] For the moment, the antiquity of these graves should be placed at around the first half of the first millennium AD. Carnelian beads, glass fragments, the stone barkcloth beater and high-tin bronze bowl from Changkat Menteri, and other goods found in the graves would also be consistent with that dating.[24]

The human labor represented by the slab graves and their contents indicates a surplus generated through trade in valuable goods from the Bernam and adjacent valleys. Alluvial tin and gold can be found along these foothills, along with high-quality iron ore,[25] but without complementary evidence from the living sites of the inhabitants, we cannot say whether they merely collected metals (and other produce) for trading, or carried out metallurgy themselves. The slab graves were presumably built for hereditary chiefs or other prominent individuals who supervised the trade (the number of graves could represent no more than a tiny fraction of a viable population). The megalithic status of the slab graves suggests an intrusive Austronesian connection, conceivably but not necessarily speakers of early Malay from Sumatra.[26] However, this intrusive element probably constituted an elite minority attached to Aslian commoners who provided the labor pool.

Leong's model of Iron Age trade identifies the Bernam Valley complex, and Jenderam Hilir where tin ingots were found with Sung ceramics, as upstream collection centers linked to collection centers on the river mouths.[27] No doubt the latter function was exercised at the mouths of the Klang and Langat rivers in Selangor, but in addition this locality may have enjoyed the wider trading relationships of an early entrepôt, to judge from the spectacular nature of its finds (Figures 13.3 and 13.4). In addition to two "hoards" of socketed iron implements from Klang, and a high-tin bowl from Kampung Sungai Lang (Langat), this site complex has produced four of the eight Dong Son bronze drums found in West Malaysia, and three of its four bronze clapperless bells (aptly named Klang bells). A canoe plank recovered from Kampung Sungai Lang, which hints at maritime connections, may date to around 2,000 years ago. A similar antiquity for the Heger I Dong Son drums found in West Malaysia, and a slightly later thermoluminescence date from the core of a Klang bell, confirm the suggestion of a wealthy elite whose members prospered through maritime trade at around 1,500–2,000 years ago.[28] Presumably there was the involvement at some level of the ancestors of the Besisi, a South Aslian-speaking group acknowledged by the *Sejarah Melayu* as the original inhabitants of Melaka, and whose last major outpost today is restricted to the Klang and Langat mouths. This area's continued importance in maritime trade until the rise of Melaka is suggested by the mention of Klang as one of the polities of Pahang in the *Desawarnana*.

Kuala Selinsing, the Andaman Islands and the Bujang Valley

North of Selangor, near the mouth of the Selinsing River (Kuala Selinsing), lie a cluster of offshore islands collectively called Pulau Kelumpang. Early excavations by Evans have been expanded by Nik Hassan Shuhaimi to reveal a thriving maritime community of great importance to understanding the protohistoric period. Radiocarbon dates indicate initial occupation over 2,000 years ago by people with access to imported beads. Imported ceramics demonstrate continued occupation for over a thousand years till the early second millennium AD. The longevity of this offshore community, which must have depended on the mainland for its rice, deer, and other foodstuffs that varied the predominantly marine diet, is remarkable. Industrial production of beads of glass and semi-precious stone after *c.* AD 500 no doubt contributed to the community's success, assuming an efficient maritime exchange network. However, expertise in sailing must have formed the basis for the community's resilience. Occasional burials in canoes (for adults of both sexes) not only underscore the inhabitants' maritime ideology but also their apparent lack of Indic ideology.[29] It would be difficult not to see them as forerunners of the Austronesian-speaking "Sea Gypsies" who still rove along the peninsula's coasts, including the Selung of Thailand, and the "Orang Seletar" based along the strait between Malaysia and Singapore.[30]

The Kuala Selinsing community was undoubtedly involved in the opening of the sea lanes across the Indian Ocean two thousand years ago. In addition to the colonization of Madagascar by Austronesian speakers in the first millennium AD, and Ptolemy's references to the "Golden Peninsula" in the second century AD,[31] the period 2,000–2,500 years ago provides the oldest evidence for habitation of the Andaman Islands, which lie due west of the peninsula. Ming Chinese and earlier sources record three main routes between the Melaka Strait and South Asia, all of which commenced at the Nicobar Islands (due north of Sumatra), and one of which proceeded via the Andamans.[32] The material culture revealed in early Andaman sites and practiced ethnographically by the Andaman Islanders includes canoes with outriggers, earthenware pottery, bone points, flaked pebbles and polished mortars, and bows and arrows (used especially in hunting pigs, of Southeast Asian origin). A material culture of that description would not only have been available in the Malay Peninsula two millennia ago but would also have provided a means to reach the Andamans and successfully exploit the surrounding seas. In particular, Andamanese traditional decorations focus on "Sa-huynh Kalanay" geometric decorations that are remarkably similar to pottery decorations from Kuala Selinsing.[33] Finally, we have the "Negrito" link; from the little known of Andamanese biological anthropology there would be few objections to deriving them from a population closely related to the ancestors of the Orang Asli (e.g. Table 13.1).

The prospect of an Andamanese connection might suggest that crew members on early sailing expeditions were often drawn from coastal peninsula people with Negrito physical features. This suggestion would accord with a sketchy nineteenth-century account of the "Semang Bakow" (mangrove Semang) who formerly frequented the peninsula's shores.[34] The lack of evidence for linguistic connections between the Andamans and elsewhere, including terms for items that must have come from Southeast Asia, could perhaps be explained in part by rapid lexical change among the Andamanese who have avoided using words similar to the names of deceased relatives. Indeed, Aslian resonances in the Nicobar languages might be the relevant evidence pointing to regular links between Aslian-speaking coastal inhabitants of Malaya, and their first stepping stone westwards on any voyage across the Indian Ocean.[35]

An understanding of the languages that used to be spoken along Malaysia's west coast, whether Austroasiatic or Austronesian, would be assisted by ancient inscriptions in a Southeast Asian language, but unfortunately none are known. The earliest inscriptions that have been recorded – all from Kedah – are remarkably homogeneous, involving Buddhist formulae and commendations written in Sanskrit (apart from two later inscriptions, one possibly a Tamil inscription and the other with a single letter in a north Indian script). They include five stone inscriptions dated to the fifth–sixth centuries, and about a dozen later inscriptions, all from the Bujang valley, on a clay plate, bricks, and gold and silver disks.[36] Other early signs of Indian influence in the vicinity include Bukit Choras with its architectural remnants and a ninth-century inscribed stone tablet, 2,000-year-old Indian pottery from Bukit Tengku Lembu in Perlis, and a sixth-century bronze Buddha statue from Ipoh in central Perak.[37] These all support the case for identifying Kedah with the polity recorded (with variations) as Kataha by Chinese, Indian and Arabic-Persian sources between the seventh and fourteenth centuries. The Bujang valley in particular evolved into a center for monumental temples built according to Hindu canons between about 1000 and 1400 (Figure 13.5).[38]

A Mon presence would appear more likely than the usual view that the inhabitants were Malays, as Sanskrit inscriptions are a rarity in the early Malay world, whereas they occur in frequency among the Old Mon alongside Mon and Pali inscriptions.[39] We may never be certain who ruled over the interrelated Sungai Mas and Pengkalan Bujang

Figure 13.5 The Tantric shrine of Candi Bukit Batu Pahat, Bujang Valley, Kedah. (Photograph courtesy of P. Bellwood.)

centers, but, assuming they did not identify themselves as ethnic Indians, they would appear to have depended on Indic specialists for a limited repertoire of literary services. The rich material wealth of the Kedah sites, in terms of foreign crockery, Hindu and Buddhist religious objects, and monumental masonry and brickwork, do not seem to have been accompanied by the establishment of a local literary tradition.

Allen outlines a model placing both the Sungai Mas and Pengkalan Bujang centers on the coastline until the eleventh century. Thereafter, the coastal plain would have rapidly advanced seawards making these centers increasingly reliant on riverine access to the sea. Allen provides geomorphological evidence that dryland farming on the surrounding hills expanded dramatically to cater for the burgeoning population involved in the maritime trade, leading to serious erosion that fed the prograding coastline.[40] Prior to the fifteenth-century rise of Melaka, the longevity of Kataha as a major trading center in coastal Kedah for 500–900 years – depending on precisely whose chronology one follows – indicates impressive stability for this protohistoric entrepôt.[41]

The question of Srivijayan influence in West Malaysia

Nik Hassan Shuhaimi published a map which shows the fleets of the Srivijayan empire supposedly controlling the entire coastline of Peninsular Malaysia and southernmost Thailand.[42] This map is obtained by pushing Srivijaya's limits a little beyond the places where Srivijayan inscriptions in Old Malay have been found in southern Thailand, Bangka and Sumatra (see Figure 13.1). However, whether Srivijaya ever functioned as a monolithic power, rather than as a network connecting particular coastal and riverine centers, should be considered an open question. Archaeological evidence has not to my knowledge been forwarded for any Srivijayan presence at the sites in Kedah or elsewhere along the peninsula's west coast. Now that the archaeology of Srivijaya's capital at Palembang is finally becoming a little known, as discussed in Manguin's chapter, it is possible that future typological comparisons may reveal the Srivijayan influences over Kedah, and other early West Malaysian sites, assumed by most scholars.[43] Till then, it would seem just as likely that Kataha and related early centers operated independently of Srivijaya.

The array of Srivijayan inscriptions to the immediate south of Peninsular Malaysia may suggest that Srivijaya controlled the southeastern gateway to the Melaka Strait. The ubiquity of dialects of Malay in the far south of the peninsula, even among Orang Asli groups, would support this inference. These communities, at least, would be likely examples of the Orang Asli involved in maritime trade whom Nik Hassan Shuhaimi treats as coastal Malays. The fourteenth-century establishment of Tumasik, Melaka's forerunner, at Singapore[44] would have further cemented the Malayic orientation of people on the adjacent mainland. However, these points need not imply any special Srivijayan influence over the communities along the east coast of West Malaysia. Their orientation may have lain towards commercial centers to the immediate north, such as Pattani and Satingphra, and farther afield to mainland centers across the Gulf of Siam, as suggested by sporadic indications of Khmer linguistic influences on Peninsular Malaysia.[45]

Buddhist tablets in Kelantan and the East Coast, prior to the entry of Islam

Trade along the peninsula's east coast may have already been established by the Neolithic, to judge from Gua Cha. As noted above, its "Ban Kao culture" burial goods are best accounted for as prestige items exchanged for forest produce. Subsequent records from eastern Peninsular Malaysia suggest links to Nakhon Si Thammarat and other centers north of the Thailand–Malaysia border. Three Dong Son drums dated to around 2,000 years ago have been recorded at Terengganu along the east coast, two at Batu Buruk and one at Jerteh. The Jerteh drum was excavated as part of a mortuary assemblage that included a bronze vessel, numerous beads, three gold ornaments, and an iron socket resembling the sockets on other early ironwares from the peninsula.[46] The link to the north is suggested by a further Dong Son drum at Nakhon Si Thammarat, and at this age an association with the Mons is likely.[47]

Buddhist clay tablets provide definite evidence of a link between the northern reaches of peninsula Malaysia and Thailand's half of the Peninsula. The open sites with these tablets are a Who's Who of old coastal centers near the isthmus: Chaiya, Nakhon Si Thammarat, Satingphra, Songkhla (identified by some scholars with Langkasuka), and there is even a lone specimen from Sungai Mas. Dates for tablets from open sites (including some farther north) seem to range between the seventh and tenth centuries. However, the deposition of these tablets in cave sites, associated with a tradition of Mahayana Buddhist hermits, may be a slightly later practice. Alastair Lamb dated the tablets from cave sites in Perlis to between the tenth and thirteenth centuries, based on a twelfth-century dating for the script of the Buddhist *ye dharma* text found on some of the stamps. Recently, a cache of 273 tablet specimens was discovered in a small side cavern at Gua Chawas, and several fragments were also found in a hearth in the main cave (Figure 13.6). As the tablets' designs barely differ from those found at open sites, the surprisingly late radiocarbon dates from the hearth (thirteenth–fifteenth centuries) should be treated as the most recent possible dating for the tablets.[48] Lamb's tenth–thirteenth-century dating for the tablets would postdate the time when Nakhon Si Thammarat first fell under Srivijaya's sway, and the small coastal polities in the vicinity probably switched to a Malay identity.[49]

Figure 13.6 A Buddhist votive tablet from the cave of Gua Chawas, Kelantan, showing Buddha Vairocana surrounded by Bodhisattvas. (Photograph courtesy of Adi Haji Taha.)

The potential attractions to traders of the Kelantan region are similar to those already noted for the west coast. Benjamin summarizes a thirteenth-century Chinese description of "Chi-lan-tan" which notes how little land was under cultivation and how the people exported an abundance of forest produce, tin, and manufactured goods. Adi suggests gold may have been of great importance, noting the prevalence of gold panning along the Kelantan River and its feeders in ethnohistorical times.[50] The importance of this region for maritime trade is such that it has yielded a unique record which is the oldest known example of Malay written in the Arabic script, and, equally to the point, the oldest inscription in a non-Indian language in Peninsular Malaysia. This is the fourteenth-century Terengganu stone, its various proclamations couched in the framework of Islamic law,[51] which surely can be seen as a harbinger of the fundamental changes that came to the peninsula with the founding of Melaka.

A dialectic model for indigenous and outsider coexistence over time

A number of thematic arguments have emerged in this chapter's interpretation of the archaeological and historical records. First, the Neolithic is interpreted as the time when newcomers, presumably proto-Aslian speakers, first established a presence along the coast. The importance of river mouths to later historical developments suggests that these communities, at least the successful ones, based themselves on the mouths and lower reaches of Peninsular Malaysia's rivers. Second, Aslian communities may have been partners in all of the historical developments discussed for the west coast, and perhaps the east coast too. Labor is most readily recruited by integrating the local indigenes, and this would explain the lack of evidence from the osteological record for a "Mongoloid immigration" event. Third, the Neolithic involved a dialectic relation between non-Aslian-speaking indigenes, and Aslian-speaking people (at certain locations) of predominantly indigenous descent. During the Iron Age the situation would have progressed to a dialectic relation between these early Aslian speakers, and later comers speaking other languages but who integrated the early Aslians. The gateways for these later comers would have been the same river mouths and lower reaches settled by the early Aslians. South Asians, Mons and Khmers as well as Malays would have been among the exotic elements seeking out opportunities in coastal Malaya for trade and a livelihood.

This sanitized account would not however account for the evidence of conflict in the peninsula, as reflected in the threats to some Orang Asli from slave raiding,[52] or the deterioration in living standards revealed by declining stature over time (Table 13.2). A model based on foraging ranges and the linking trails through the peninsula's forests can accommodate these latter points. I have argued that the Hoabinhians foraged predominantly along well-cleared trails through the jungle; here we can add that these trails probably tended to follow valleys and, given the distinction between unifacial pebble tools west of the main range and bifaces to the east, may have had relatively few connections across the main range.[53] Picture such a network (Figure 13.7a) which connected all the foraging groups' ranges, both along the coast and in the hinterland. This would square with the occasional coastal items found in hinterland Hoabinhian sites[54] and would have accommodated a healthy breeding population with ample opportunity for gene flow between population aggregates. Imagine that, once early Aslian-speaking communities established themselves on the lower reaches of the main rivers, they took over the trails that had linked the residential forager population to its neighbors. Foragers found along these trails may well have been co-opted into the new community to repair the labor shortage. The ranges of independent foragers would have

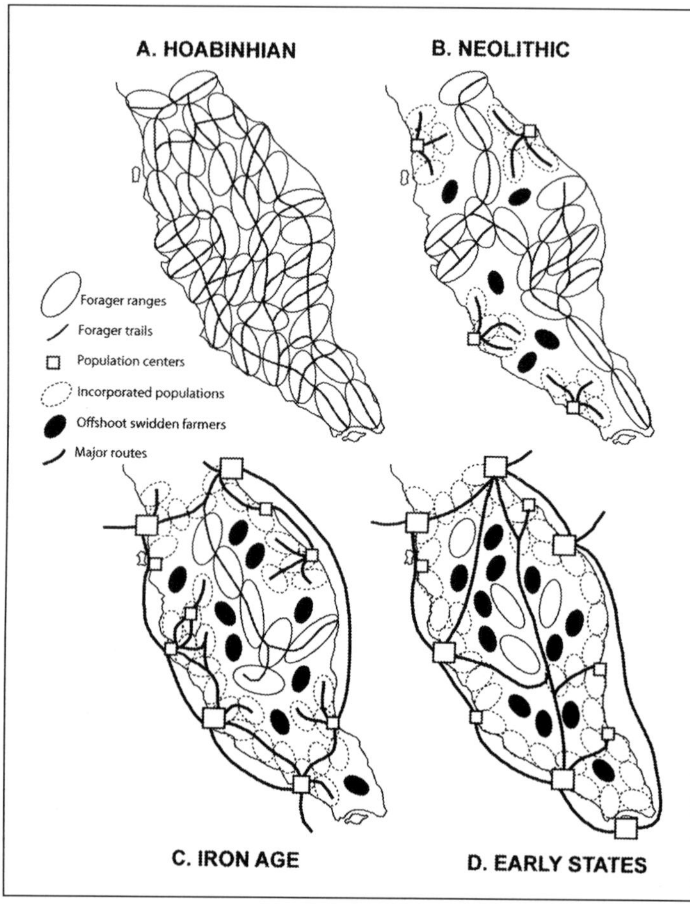

Figure 13.7 A model for changes in group ranges and networks of interconnection in West Malaysia over the last five thousand years. (D. Bulbeck. Drawing D is based on Adi Haji Taha, 2000: 26.)

been distorted to avoid these perilous areas, and the initial set of trails linking all forager communities would have been broken up along the lowland stretches (Figure 13.7b).

Gaps created in the matrix of trails would have provided refuges where Aslian speakers could have established semi-independent communities whose viability depended on swidden agriculture within their restricted territories. In Malaya's dissected terrain, these gaps would have become more common in the later stages of the co-option of Malaya's network of trails into the export-based economy. The second stage would have seen hinterland colonies budding off the main communities based on the rivers' lower reaches, but still connected to them through social and economic relations (Figure 13.7c). Further disruption would have ensued to the foragers' ranges, especially as the last remnants of their connecting trails became the main trans-peninsula routes (Fig. 13.7d). Yet the goods which the external trading network controlled, notably iron, would have acted as an allure to draw foragers into trading relations where they became the specialists in supplying forest produce to the economy.

A model like this would be able to account for the three Orang Asli orientations adumbrated by Benjamin and Rambo.[55] To survive as foragers, a group we now know as Semang (more or less equal to North Aslian speakers) would have had to adapt to drastically reduced ranges in inaccessible regions, navigate the jungle with minimal reliance on the cleared trails that invited penetration by outsiders, and accept a furtive existence. Aslian speakers who sought independence from the main commercial network could have done so by establishing isolated farming communities in the refugia opening up in the hinterland, and here may lie the origins of the Semai and Temiar Senoi. And the Aslian communities who thrived along the rivers and coasts as partners to the growing international commerce provided the basis for Orang Asli who today speak South Aslian languages and dialects of Malay.

Rethinking the evolution of the Orang Asli

The model presented in Figure 13.7 may be critiqued on the grounds that ethnographic observations on the Orang Asli do not tally perfectly with its implications. Actually I would expect this to be the case as a main point of the model is its emphasis on the dynamic circumstances of the Orang Asli up to the founding of Melaka. Therefore, this situation should have changed even more rapidly with the social and political upheavals that have transformed the peninsula over the past 600 years.

Indeed, the ambiguities in the model may provide the key to exploring the Orang Asli past in greater depth.[56] For example, Senoi groups may be split between the Semai and Temiar, speakers of Central Aslian whose growing population and territorial expansion are fuelled by an agricultural economy,[57] and groups to the west and the south whose ranges appear hemmed in, whose numbers are fewer, and whose economic dependence on agriculture is slight. Perhaps, differences in historical origins can explain these distinctions between superficially similar groups; e.g. gene flow from the dominant Malay populations that surround the Besisi combined with these people's "Semang Bakaw" ancestry may have led to their physically intermediate "Senoi" phenotype. Similarly, it is unclear why the ancestors of the Semai (as Figure 13.2 suggests) should be the Orang Asli involved in the social developments producing the Changkat Menteri and related slab graves, and perhaps they were not. Given the expansionist tendencies of the Semai, complementing their concurrent loss of coastal lowlands to Malay immigrants, another Aslian group altogether may have constituted the bulk of the residents of the Bernam and nearby valleys at 1,500–2,000 years ago. As a final example, if we make allowance for the expansion of Malays and a Malayic identity during the Modern Era, then the proximity of Northern Aslian languages to Pangkalan Bujang and Sungai Mas might suggest that the commoners of Kataha had been North Aslian speakers. The prestige and opportunities thus associated with a North Aslian forager-trader network might explain the close correlation between being classified as Semang and speaking a North Aslian language (Figures 13.2 and 13.4).[58]

Juli Edo draws a contrast between inland Orang Asli who tend to see themselves as the original inhabitants, and lowland Orang Asli who claim to be the earliest migrants from overseas before the Malays displaced them from their coastal haunts.[59] The implication of continuous pressure on coastal groups from newcomers with overseas connections provides an apposite perspective for the model proposed in Figure 13.7. Juli stresses that Aslian origin myths provide no basis for accepting the traditional "layer cake" model of successive waves of Semang, Senoi, Aboriginal Malay and Melayu Malay migrations, and the same point applies here. The model's assumption that these groups had arrived fully formed and simply pushed each other inland was a reasonable guess when nothing was known about Malaya's ancient past. Now that scholars are starting to acquire such knowledge, we can see the scope for ethnogenesis within a framework of interaction which would also have included some outside groups, such as the Mons, who are no longer represented in today's ethnic mix.

Juli further points out that the chronicles of Melaka and the other Malay sultanates recognize the services of the "Sakai", who would have included Senoi, as fighters, sailors, rowers, servants and so forth. The dominance of Malay along the coast has presumably therefore resulted from incorporation of these Sakai elements, at least those who were not displaced, into the prevailing Islamic Malay identity. The persistence of coastal Sakai elements until recent centuries followed by their rapid incorporation would argue against the notion of a coastal Malay identity established along West Malaysia's shores as far back as Srivijayan times. Rather, it would serve as an analogy for recognizing that a succession of visitors have interacted with Malaya's indigenes at different places and at different times, resulting in incorporation or displacement in turn, within an overarching framework of ambivalent coexistence.

Acknowledgments

I wish to thank Leonard Andaya for sending me a pre-publication draft of his 2002 paper, which provided numerous pointers for my own investigations, and to thank Stephen Oppenheimer, Wayne Bougas, Niclas Burenhult, and especially Peter Bellwood (as editor) and Geoffrey Benjamin for their valuable comments on this chapter. Any deficiencies or errors that remain are the author's responsibility.

Notes

1 "Malaysia is a country known more for its beautiful scenery than its points of historical or cultural interest" (Turner *et al.* 1994: 431). The passage then mentions how "the people are exceptionally friendly" but, under "Culture", the authors restrict their comments to advice on modest dress and behaviour in this fairly easy-going Muslim nation.

2 See Wisseman-Christie 1990b, and Manguin's chapter in this volume.

3 Benjamin 1997, 2002.

4 The latter sense more or less equates to "tribal" as elaborated by Benjamin (2002) but, to ration the terminology, this chapter retains the term "Aslian". It also departs from Bellwood's use of Aslian in a solely linguistic sense, for several reasons (Aslian in the linguistic sense is a derivative meaning from Aslian in the general sense; Aslian in the general sense serves as a catch-all for indigenous groups in the Peninsula, including as it does those, at various times in the past who may have spoken neither Austroasiatic nor Austronesian languages or alternatively may have spoken both).

5 For a wide-ranging review of Orang Asli–Malay relations during the Modern Era, see Andaya 2002. Andaya notes the problematic *Desawarnana* reference (Robson 1995: 33–4) but still supports the view of Srivijayan dominion over coastal West Malaysia, based on archaeological evidence in Schnitger (1937). However, from my reading of Schnitger this source does not contain the archaeological evidence required to sustain the point.

6 See Rayner and Bulbeck 2002, for a recent demonstration of the dynamic interrelations of the Orang Asli as revealed by their dental morphology.

7 Bulbeck 2003. The term "Hoabinhian" is controversial but seems justified for the West Malaysian industries with their focus on using river pebbles as tools, sometimes with minimal

modification prior to use. We note in passing that claims for the arrival of the Neolithic at Sakai Cave, a short distance north of the Thailand-Malaysia border, as early as 8,000 years ago (e.g. Oota *et al.* 2001) are in conflict with the middle to late Holocene dating of the Neolithic south of the border.

8 Oota *et al.* 2001.

9 Ousley and Jantz 1994; Howells 1973.

10 Hoabinhians: Gua Gunung Runtuh (Matsumara and Zuraina 1999), Gua Peraling 4, treated as female (Bulbeck 2000a), Gua Cha As.33.5.9 & As.33.6.11 (personal data). Neolithic: Gua Cha As.33.5.1, As.33.5.3, As.33.5.10, and Kota Tongkat (personal data). Iron Age: Kuala Selinsing (Bulbeck 1998). Recent: all data from Martin (1905) except the Siong Semang (personal data) and the Jahai, Kensiu and Mendrik Semang measured by Schebesta and Lebzelter (1926). Note that the Arikara and Santa Cruz are North American Indians.

11 e.g. Bellwood 1993, 1997.

12 For instance, according to the Fisher Exact Probability test, the probability of sampling error resulting in four Hoabinhian non-Australoids and four Neolithic Australoids is a paltry 0.014, allowing rejection of the null hypothesis at the conventional 0.05 benchmark. The same result would be obtained when comparing the four Australoid Neolithic skulls with the four Mongoloid Iron Age skulls.

13 Bulbeck 1996, 2003.

14 Hinterland mid-Holocene (Hoabinhian): males, Gua Kerbau, Gua Cha 1 (Bulbeck 1996); females, Gua Kajang (Bulbeck 1996), Gua Peraling 4 (Bulbeck 1997). Coastal mid-Holocene: Guar Kepah (unpublished data). Hinterland late Holocene (Neolithic): males, Gua Baik 94 and six burials from Gua Cha (Bulbeck 1996), and Gua Harimau 1 (unpublished data); females, Gua Cha B8 (Bulbeck 1996). Coastal late Holocene: Gua Bintong 1 (Bulbeck 1996), Kuala Selinsing (Bulbeck 1998). Recent hinterland: Semang, Senoi and Temuan with sample sizes over 30 in Kloss (1915, 1916) and Bulbeck (1996). Recent coastal: coastal Malays with sample sizes over 30 in Annandale and Robinson (1903) and Vickers and Strahan (1937). The Gua Gunung Runtuh skeleton is excluded from Table 2 as it is probably early Holocene and because about 12 cm in body height was lost during life through spinal deformation (Jacob and Soepriyo 1994: 57; Matsumura and Zuraina 1999: 332).

15 See Bellwood (1997: 258–265) for a discussion of Ban Kao parallels in Malayan Neolithic sites.

16 Tayles 1999: 67.

17 Forty sexed, adult skulls from Ban Kao (Sangvichien *et al.* 1969: 37–40) and Khok Phanom Di (Tayles 1999: 88) have three or more published measurements as used in the Fordisc analysis which compares a specimen with the populations measured by Howells. Thirty-one of these – over 75 per cent – would show a "Mongoloid" affinity by the same procedures as used to generate the results shown in Table 13.1.

18 Bulbeck 2000b.

19 Anderson 1824; Noone 1954; Dunn 1975; Endicott 1979.

20 Zuraina 1998: 248.

21 Bulbeck (n.d.) based on personal observations and Zolkurnian (1989, 1998). Habitation refuse reflects the focus on primates and rodents characteristic of late Holocene faunal assemblages in Peninsular rock shelters (Bulbeck 2003).

22 Sieveking 1956.

23 Examination of a fragment of this bowl at the British Museum suggested that the fabric was not ceramic, but a heavily decayed bronze vessel; the whitish cores indicating a high tin content (I. Glover pers. comm. from Dr I. Freestone of the Department of Scientific Research, British Museum).

24 Leong Sau Heng (2000); see also Bellwood (1997: 284). A first millennium dating for the slab graves would also be consistent with a bronze Buddha statue, dated to the ninth century, dredged up in 1936 during tin mining in the vicinity of the slab graves (Jacq-Hergoualc'h 1992: 246–7). There is no evidence assocating it with any slab grave. Thus it may reflect the transition to Buddhism away from home-grown religions in which grave goods were important.

25 Sieveking 1956.

26 Benjamin (1997). Even if early Malay speakers had been involved, there would be no basis to assume a link with Srivijaya, as no evidence has been presented for a Srivijayan association for the early slab graves in Sumatra (Bulbeck 2001: 112).
27 Leong Sau Heng 1990, 1993; Nik Hassan Shuhaimi 1990: 69.
28 Sieveking 1956: 109; Bellwood 1997: 281–4. The Klang bell dated by thermoluminescence is actually the one from Muar in Johor.
29 Evans 1932; Nik Hassan Shuhami 1991, 1997; Bulbeck 2001; Manguin's chapter in this book.
30 Anderson (1824) provides an early historical description of the boat-dwelling inhabitants of coastal Peninsular Malaysia. See Benjamin (2002) for further relevant discussion.
31 Hall 1985; Dewar and Wright 1993.
32 Ptak 1990.
33 For information on the Andaman Islands, see Weber (2002). For points of comparison with West Malaysian prehistoric archaeology, see Bellwood (1997), Adi (2000), Bulbeck (2001, 2003), and Nik Hassan Shuhaimi (1991) for Kuala Selinsing pottery decorations.
34 Anderson 1824: xxxviii.
35 I am grateful to Niclas Burenhult and Geoffrey Benjamin for advice on these points of linguistics, without suggesting that they share my interpretation of the evidence. Even as interpreted here, the evidence need only imply a quantum leap in the population densities on the Andaman Islands at around 2000 years ago, and not necessarily these islands' initial colonization at the time.
36 Wisseman-Christie 1990a; Nik Hassan Shuhaimi and Othman 1990: 60–67; Jacq-Hergoualc'h 1992: 217–36.
37 Jacq-Hergoualc'h 1992; Bellwood 1997: 262. Once again, the Bukit Choras inscription is a Buddhist religious formula in Sanskrit.
38 Nik Hassan Shuhaimi and Othman 1990.
39 Compare Bauer (1992) and Benjamin (1997) with the conventional view of Nik Hassan Shuhaimi and Othman (1990), Jacq-Hergoualc'h (1992: 292), and Allen (2000). Note that all of the Srivijayan inscriptions located in Figure 13.1 are in Old Malay, except the Karimun Besar inscription which, while in Sanskrit, is a mere four words in length. See Indrawoorth's chapter for a review of the inscriptions found at Old Mon sites.
40 Allen (2000).
41 Melaka's ascent would additonally have drawn maritime trade and its personnel away from Kataha, removing the impetus for building new coastal facilities there. Kedah remained sufficiently important into the fourteenth century to have been recorded as one of the polities of Pahang in the *Desawarnana* (Robson 1995: 34).
42 Nik Hassan Shuhaimi (1990: 62), with a very similar map shown by Jacq-Hergoualc'h (1992: 311).
43 For example, Nik Hassan Shuhaimi 1990, Jacq-Hergoualc'h 1992; Andaya 2002.
44 Taylor 1992: 175.
45 Benjamin 1997, 2002.
46 Nik Hassan Shuhaimi and Che Muhamad (1998); see also Nik Hassan Shuhaimi 1997.
47 Mohd. Kamaruzaman 1990; Benjamin 1987: 123–4.
48 Adi (2000) including his assignment of all of the tablets discussed here to Coèdes' Type II. See also Nik Hassan Shuhaimi and Othman (1990: 54) for the Sungai Mas tablet.
49 Bougas 1994: 7–11.
50 Benjamin 1987: 121; Adi 2000.
51 Benjamin 1987: 127; 1997.
52 Endicott 1983, Rambo 1988; Benjamin 2002: 35–6.
53 Bulbeck 2003; see Noone (1954) for a description of hinterland trails' following river valleys. The hypothetical situations depicted in Figure 13.7 obviously cater for reality as reconstructed in this contribution, based on the principle that what may be true exemplifies what is possible, but do not imply any further representations on such matters as the details of former populations' ranges or the particulars of the forager's network.
54 Nik Hassan Shuhaimi 1997.
55 Benjamin 1985; Rambo 1988.
56 See Benjamin 2002 for an example of the depth to which these issues can be explored.
57 Fix 1982; Benjamin (pers. comm.).

58 Allen (2000) assumes that the Kataha commoners were Malays, but without providing any evidence. The Semang/North Aslian correlation is imperfect but much better than the Senoi/Central Aslian or Aboriginal Malay/South Aslian associations.

59 Edo 2000.

Select Bibliography

Anthropology

Annandale, N. and H. C. Robinson (1903) *Fasciculi Malayenses: Anthropological and Zoological Results of an Expedition to Perak and the Siamese Malay States, 1901–2; Anthropology, Part 1*, New York: Longmans, Green & Co.

Benjamin, G. (1985) "In the long term: three themes in Malayan cultural ecology", in K. L. Hutterer, A. T. Rambo and G. Lovelace (eds) *Cultural Values and Human Ecology in Southeast Asia*, pp. 219–71, Ann Arbor: University of Michigan Papers on South and Southeast Asia.

Benjamin, G. (1987) "Ethnohistorical perspectives on Kelantan's prehistory", in Nik Hassan Shuhaimi bin Nik Abd. Rahman (ed.) *Kelantan Zaman Awal: Kajian Arkeologi dan Sejarah di Malaysia*, pp. 108–53, Kota Bahru: Perbadanan Muzium Negara Kelantan Istana Jahar.

Benjamin, G. (1997) "Issues in the ethnohistory of Pahang", in Nik Hassan Shuhaimi bin Nik Abd. Rahman and Ahmad Hakim bin Khairuddin (eds), *Pembangunan Arkeologi Pelancongan Negeri Pahang*, pp. 82–121. Pekan: Muzium Pahang.

Benjamin, G. (2002) "On being tribal in the Malay world", in G. Benjamin and C. Chou (eds) *Tribal Communities in the Malay World: Historical, Cultural and Social Perspectives*, pp. 7–76, Leiden and Singapore: International Institute for Asian Studies and Institute for Southeast Asian Studies.

Dunn, F. L. (1975) *Rain Forest Collectors and Traders*, Kuala Lumpur: Malaysian Branch, Royal Asiatic Society, Monograph 5.

Edo, Juli. (2000) "Stories of migration from native resources: the Semai oral tradition", *Bulletin of the Indo-Pacific Prehistory Association* 19: 42–51.

Endicott, Karen (1979) "Batek Negrito Sex Roles", unpublished MA thesis. Canberra: The Australian National University.

Endicott, Kirk (1983) "The effects of slave raiding on the Aborigines of the Malay Peninsula", in A. Reid (ed.) *Slavery, Bondage and Dependency in Southeast Asia*, pp. 216–44, Brisbane: University of Queensland Press.

Noone, R. O. D. (1954) "Notes on the trade in blowpipes and blowpipe bamboo in north Malaya", *Federations Museum Journal* 1: 1–18.

Rambo, A. T. (1988) "Why are the Semang? Ecology and ethnogenesis of aboriginal groups in Peninsular Malaysia", in A. T. Rambo *et al.* (eds) *Ethnic Diversity and the Control of Natural Resources in Southeast Asia*, pp. 19–36, Ann Arbor: University of Michigan Papers on South and Southeast Asia.

Weber, G. H. J. (2002) *Lonely Islands*, The Andaman Association, Switzerland. <http://www.andaman.org/book/text.htm> (accessed on 17 May 2004).

Archaeology

Adi Haji Taha (2000) "Archaeological Investigations in Ulu Kelantan, Peninsular Malaysia", Unpublished PhD dissertation. Canberra: The Australian National University.

Allen, S. J. (2000) "In support of trade: coastal site location and environmental transformation in early historical-period Malaysia and Thailand", *Bulletin of the Indo-Pacific Prehistory Association* 20: 62–78.

Bellwood, P. (1993) "Cultural and biological differentiation in Peninsular Malaysia: the last 10,000 years", *Asian Perspectives* 32: 37–60.

Bellwood, P. (1997) *Prehistory of the Indo-Malaysian Archipelago*, rev edn, Honolulu: University of Hawai'i Press.

Bulbeck, D. (1998) "Origins of civilization in West Malaysia and the Orang Asli", *Jurnal Arkeologi Malaysia* 11: 95–9.

Bulbeck, D. (2001) "Island Southeast Asia Late Prehistoric: Indo-Malaysian Archipelago Early Metal Phase, Sa Huynh-Kalanay", in P. Peregrine and M. Ember (eds) *Encyclopedia of Prehistory Volume 3: East Asia and Oceania*, chapter 15 (pp. 82–116), New York: Kluwer Academic and Plenum Publishers.

Bulbeck, D. (2003) "Hunter-gatherer occupation of the Malay Peninsula from the Ice Age to the Iron Age", in J. Mercader (ed.) *The Archaeology of Tropical Rain Forests*, pp. 119–60, New Brunswick: Rutgers University Press.

Dewar, R. E. and Wright, H. T. (1993) "The culture history of Madagascar", *Journal of World Prehistory* 7: 417–64.

Evans, I. H. N. (1932) "Excavations at Tanjung Rawa, Kuala Selinsing, Perak", *Journal of the Federated Malay States Museum* 15: 79–133.

Jacq-Hergoualc'h, M. (1992) *La Civilisation de Ports-Entrepots du Sud-Kedah (Malaysia) Ve–XIVe Siècle*, Paris: Editions l'Harmattan.

Leong Sau Heng. (1990) "Collection centres, feeder points and entrepôts in the Malay Peninsula, *c.*1000 BC–AD 1400", in J. Kathirithamby-Wells and J. Villiers (eds) *The Southeast Asian Port and Polity: Rise and Demise*, pp. 17–38, Singapore: Singapore University Press.

Leong Sau Heng (1993) "Ancient trading centres in the Malay Peninsula", *Jurnal Arkeologi Malaysia* 6: 1–9.

Leong Sau Heng (2000) "The chronology of the Bernam cist graves in Peninsular Malaysia", *Bulletin of the Indo-Pacific Prehistory Association* 19: 65–72.

Mohd. Kamaruzaman Abd. Rahman (1990) "Arkeologi di Selatan Thailand", *Jurnal Arkeologi Malaysia* 3: 63–71.

Nik Hassan Shuhaimi bin Nik Abd. Rahman (1991) "Recent research at Kuala Selinsing, Perak", *Bulletin of the Indo-Pacific Prehistory Association* 11: 141–52.

Nik Hassan Shuhaimi bin Nik Abd. Rahman (1997) "Tracing the origins of the Malays and Orang Asli: from archaeological perspective", *Jurnal Arkeologi Malaysia* 10: 95–105.

Nik Hassan Shuhaimi bin Nik Abd. Rahman and Othman Mohd. Yatim (1990) *Antiquities of Bujang Valley*, Kuala Lumpur: Museum Association of Malaysia.

Nik Hassan Shuhaimi bin Nik Abd. Rahman and Che Muhamad Azmi Ngah (1998) "Galicara arkeologi tapak gendang Dong Son di kampong Gaung, Jereh, Terengganu", *Jurnal Arkeologi Malaysia* 11: 61–89.

Schnitger, F. M. (1937) *The Archaeology of Hindoo Sumatra*, Leiden: E. J. Brill.

Sieveking, G. de G. (1956) "The Iron Age collections of Malay" *Journal of the Malayan Branch of the Royal Asiatic Society* 29: 79–138.

Wisseman-Christie, J. (1990a) "Trade and state formation in the Malay Peninsula and Sumatra, 300 BC–AD 700", in J. Kathirithamby-Wells and J. Villiers (eds) *The Southeast Asian Port and Polity: Rise and Demise*, pp. 39–60, Singapore: Singapore University Press.

Zolkurnian Hasan (1989) "Gua Harimau: satu laporan awal", *Jurnal Persatuan Muzium Malaysia* 8: 41–52.

Zolkurnian, Hassan (1998) "Urutan Kebudayaan Prasejarah Lembah Lenggong, Hulu Perak, Perak pada Zaman Holosen", Sarjana dissertation, Penang: Centre for Archaeological Research Malaysia, Universiti Sains Malaysia.

Zuraina Majid (1998) "Radiocarbon dates and culture sequence in the Lenggong Valley and beyond", *Malaysia Museums Journal* 34: 241–9.

Biological Anthropology

Bulbeck, D. (1996) "Holocene biological evolution of the Malay Peninsula Aborigines (*Orang Asli*)", *Perspectives in Human Biology* 2: 37–61.

Bulbeck, D. (1997) "Description and preliminary analysis of the human remains from Gua Peraling, Kelantan, Malaysia", report to the Department of Museums and Antiquity, Kuala Lumpur, Malaysia.

Bulbeck, D. (1998) "Description and preliminary analysis of the human remains from Pulau Kelumpang (Kuala Selinsing), Perak, Malaysia", report to the Department of Museums and Antiquity, Kuala Lumpur, Malaysia.

Bulbeck, D. (2000a) "Multivariate statistical analysis of the Gua Peraling 4 cranium", Appendix 6 in Adi Haji Taha's unpublished PhD dissertation, *Archaeological Investigations in Ulu Kelantan, Peninsular Malaysia*, Canberra: Australian National University.

Bulbeck, D. (2000b) "Dental morphology at Gua Cha, West Malaysia, and the implications for 'Sundadonty'," *Bulletin of the Indo-Pacific Prehistory Association* 19: 17–41.

Bulbeck, D. (n.d.) "Human remains from Gua Harimau, West Malaysia", unpublished manuscript.

Fix, A. (1982) "Genetic structure of the Semai", in M. H. Crawford and J. H. Mielke (eds) *Current Developments in Anthropological Genetics, Volume 2. Ecology and Population Structure*, pp. 179–204, New York: Plenum Press.

Howells, W. W. (1973) *Cranial Variation in Man*, Cambridge: Peabody Museum.

Jacob, T. and A. Soepriyo. (1994) "A preliminary palaeoanthropological study of the Gua Gunung Runtuh human skeleton", in Zuraina Majid (ed.) *The Excavation of Gua Gunung Runtuh and the Discovery of Perak Man in Malaysia*, pp. 48–69, Kuala Lumpur: Department of Museums and Antiquity Malaysia.

Kloss, C. Boden (1915) "Measurements of some Biduanda (Mantra) of Ulu Kenaboi, Jelabu", *Journal of the Federated Malay States Museums* 5: 57–9.

Kloss, C. Boden (1916) "Measurements of some Sakai of Sungkai and Slim, South Perak, with notes on the same", *Journal of the Federated Malay States Museums* 6: 71–84.

Martin, R. (1905) *Die Inlandstämme der Malayischen Halbinsel: Wissenschaftliche Ergebnisse einer Reise durch die Vereinigten Malayischen Staaten*, Stuttgart: Gustav Fischer Verlag.

Matsumura Hirofumi and Zuraina Majid (1999) "Metric analysis of an early Holocene human skeleton from Gua Gunung Runtuh, Malaysia", *American Journal of Physical Anthropology* 109: 327–40.

Oota, H., Kurosaki, Pukajoorn, S., Ishida, T. and Ueda, S. (2001) "Genetic study of the Paleolithic and Neolithic Southeast Asians", *Human Biology* 73: 225–31.

Ousley, S. D. and R. L. Jantz (1994) *Fordisc 2.0 Personal Computer Forensic Discriminant Functions*. Knoxville: University of Tennessee Department of Anthropology.

Rayner, D. and Bulbeck, D. (2002) "Dental morphology of the 'Orang Asli' Aborigines of the Malay Peninsula", in M. Henneberg (ed.) *Causes and Effects of Human Variation*, pp. 19–41, Adelaide: Australasian Society for Human Biology and The University of Adelaide.

Sangvichien, S., Sirigaroon, P. and Jørgenson, J. B. (1969) *Archaeological Excavations in Thailand. Vol. III, Part II: The Prehistoric Thai Skeletons*, Copenhagen: Munksgaard.

Schebesta, P. and Lebzelter, V. (1926) "Schädel und Skelettreste von drei Semang-Individuen", *Anthropos* 21: 959–90.

Tayles, N. G. (1999) *The Excavation of Khok Phanom Di: A Prehistoric Site in Central Thailand. Volume V, The People*, London: The Society of Antiquaries of London.

History

Andaya, L. Y. (2002) "Orang Asli and the Melayu in the history of the Malay Peninsula", *Journal of the Malaysian Branch of the Royal Asiatic Society* 75 (1): 23–48.

Anderson, J. (1824) *Political and Commercial Considerations Relative to the Malayan Peninsula, and the British Settlements in the Straits of Malacca*, facsimile reprint 1965. Kuala Lumpur: Malaysian Branch of the Royal Asiatic Society.

Bauer, C. (1992) "Mon-Aslian contacts", *Bulletin of the School of Oriental and African Studies* 55: 532–7.

Bougas, W. (1994) *The Kingdom of Patani between Thai and Malay Mandalas*, Selangor: Universiti Kebangsaan Malaysia, Institut Alam dan Temadun Malaysia.

Hall, K. R. (1985) *Maritime Trade and State Development in Early Southeast Asia*, Sydney: George Allen & Unwin.

Nik Hassan Shuhaimi bin Nik Abd. Rahman (1990) "The kingdom of Srîvijaya as socio-political and cultural entity", in J. Kathirithamby-Wells and J. Villiers (eds) *The Southeast Asian Port and Polity: Rise and Demise*, pp. 61–82, Singapore: Singapore University Press.

Ptak, R. (1990) "Die Andamanen und Nikobaren nach chinesische Quellen (Ende Sung bis Ming)" *Zeitschrift der Deutschen Morgenländischen Gesellschaft* 140: 343–73.

Robson, S. (trans.) (1995) *Desawarnana (Nāgarakṛtāgama) by Mpu Prapañca*, Verhandelingen van het Koninklijk Instituut voor Taal-, Land- en Volkenkunde 169, Leiden: KITLV Press.
Taylor, K. W. (1992) "The early kingdoms", in N. Tarling (ed.), *The Cambridge History of Southeast Asia. Volume 1: From Early Times to c.1800*, Cambridge: Cambridge University Press.
Wheatley, P. (1983) *Nāgara and Commandery: Origins of the Southeast Asian Urban Traditions*, Chicago: The University of Chicago Department of Geography Research Papers Nos. 207–8.
Wisseman-Christie, J. (1990b) "The Sanskrit inscription recently discovered in Kedah, Malaysia", *Modern Quaternary Research in Southeast Asia* 11: 39–53.

General

Turner, P., Cummings, J., Lyon, J., Peters, J. and Storey, R., (1994) *South-East Asia: A Lonely Planet Shoestring Guide*, 3rd edn, Melbourne: Lonely Planet Publications.
Vickers, N. J. and J. H. Strahan (1937) *A Health Survey of the State of Kedah with Special Reference to Rice Field Malaria, Nutrition and Water Supply*, Kuala Lumpur: Kyle Palmer.

14

RETROSPECT AND PROSPECT

Ian Glover and Peter Bellwood

In the previous 13 chapters of this book the contributors, all of whom are active in Southeast Asian field archaeology, have attempted to trace the various – sometimes quite different – trajectories of cultural development from the establishment of settled village agriculture in the third millennium BC to the emergence of the great civilizations of the historic era. These complex societies, with their Indic religions and philosophies of statecraft, emerged in many parts of the region from about the fifth century of the Christian Era when inscriptions in the Sanskrit language appear in many locations. The chapters mostly follow the framework of the modern nation states of Southeast Asia, meaningless though many of these are for the remote periods of the past we address. Some contributors have also attempted to look beyond these modern boundaries, taking a broader view, to compare and contrast developments across Southeast Asia, as well as with South Asia and China, both areas whose civilizations have impinged on Southeast Asia in many ways and on numerous occasions.

We have also tried to take account of the many significant cultural achievements of Southeast Asian peoples in the past, and of these we must think in the first place of seafaring and the maritime traditions of the region. For we think that it can be shown that the ability to cross major water barriers in order to colonize the island world of the Philippines, Indonesia, Melanesia, Australia, and ultimately the Near Pacific, was first achieved in this region commencing about 50,000 years ago – before, indeed, the time period with which we are mainly concerned in this book. But this precocious familiarity with oceanic travel persisted through subsequent millennia and profoundly influenced many subsequent developments. The dramatic spread of Austronesian languages from a probable homeland in South China and Taiwan, starting some 5,000 years ago, is perhaps the most obvious manifestation of this. From Taiwan to Magadascar to Easter Island, early seafaring peoples extended the Austronesian language family over a greater part of the earth's surface than had any other ethnolinguistic communities before the expansion of some European languages (such as English and Spanish) in the quite recent past.

In the early centuries of the Christian Era, these seafaring traditions enabled isolated polities located along extensive coasts to form trading networks stretching from India to China, and to develop a distinct urban civilized life in regions not always rich in natural resources. In other cultural fields, Southeast Asian peoples enriched culture in many ways. In textiles, basketry, ceramics, metallurgy, architecture, decorative arts and sculpture, many significant and enduring achievements were made, as shown in the chapters by Phasook Indrawooth, John Miksic, and Pierre-Yves Manguin.

Retrospect: the beginnings of archaeology in Southeast Asia

Ian Glover

When we turn to consider the development of the discipline of archaeology in Southeast Asia, it is clear that the early impetus for research and study of the early cultures came, in the most part, from European colonists resident in the region in the nineteenth century. In several articles, Glover[1] has shown that modern archaeology in Western Europe had its roots in antiquarianism and the discovery between the fifteenth and seventeenth centuries of the foundations of European culture in the classical civilizations of Greece and Rome. These publications also examined the distinctions between what Trigger[2] called "colonialist, imperialist and nationalist archaeologies". I will not go over this ground again here, but merely reiterate the proposition that archaeology, and especially prehistoric archaeology, has, almost everywhere, arisen out of an attempt to satisfy nationalist aspirations. The emerging nations of Europe energetically searched for their ethnic and linguistic ancestors through the media of history and archaeology. The European pioneers of archaeology in Southeast Asia were as much concerned with gathering general and comparative data to help them understand the progress from "barbarism to civilization" in Europe, as they were with the specific situations in their colonial territories in Southeast Asia.

I think that it may be taken for granted that all modern nation states attempt to create discourses with the past in order to legitimize and strengthen the position of the state and its dominant political communities. The deliberate invention in various European countries, from the late nineteenth century, of antique rituals and symbols of power with "long-established" credentials has been discussed in a ground-breaking book edited by Hobsbawm and Ranger,[3] and is a practice so widespread that it needs no supporting documentation here. These procedures were also followed in the post-colonial states of Southeast Asia which, in most cases, do not correspond to "natural" nations based on a common language, coherent cultural traditions, shared ethnicity, or long and centralized dynastic rule. The borders, indeed the very existences of the great majority of nation states in the present world, were created as a result of competing spheres of influence of the European and American colonial powers in the nineteenth century. This is true even for Thailand, never a European colony, but whose present borders were forced on to a modernizing monarchy by France and Britain at the beginning of the twentieth century. Thus, the concept of delineated borders within which a single political body claims unique authority is, in Southeast Asia as in many other areas, a product of the nineteenth-century colonial experience. Here archaeology, together with history, is for the most part a state-supported activity and plays a significant role in developing new discourses with the past to the benefit of the ruling elites. Thus writing history, or archaeology, in modern Southeast Asian countries is often problematic since it is yoked to the political demands of the present.

In another seminal book entitled *Imagined Communities*,[4] Anderson comments on the role of archaeology in the chapter, "Census, Map, Museum". Here he notes the way late colonial administrations in India, Burma, the Netherlands Indies and Indochina appropriated the great monuments of decayed Indic civilizations to give some legitimacy to their colonial rule. Substantial resources were put into clearing, excavating and restoring the great temples of Southeast Asia. These reminders of vanished greatness were later appropriated by the first post-colonial regimes, again to give them legitimacy via an often fictitious cultural continuity – and to serve as revenue raisers through tourism.

Prospect: nationalism and archaeology

Ian Glover

In many newly independent countries, forms of nationalist archaeology have developed which are strongest amongst peoples who feel threatened, insecure, or deprived of their political rights by more powerful nations. They also develop in countries where appeals for national unity are being made to counteract serious divisions along class or ethnic lines. Nationalist archaeology tends to emphasize the more recent past, and to draw attention to visible, monumental architecture and centralized political structures. Earlier prehistory, or the archaeology of small-scale preliterate communities, tends to be ignored. The popularity of Classical and Islamic archaeology in Indonesia; the focus on the Late Bronze-Iron Age, Dong Son Culture of northern Vietnam; on the archaeology of Sukhothai and Ayutthaya in Thailand; on the Pagan period in Myanmar, are all cases in point.

Some years ago, when discussing the situation in Indonesia, Glover argued that archaeology, and especially prehistoric archaeology, was an alien European concept and practice introduced into Indonesia in the days of Dutch colonial hegemony and refurbished in a period of European and American intellectual dominance in the mid-twentieth century. He argued then that Indonesian prehistory as reflected, for example, in the books of van Heekeren or in the most recent regional prehistory by Bellwood, was an abstract mental construct, satisfying certain concerns of western academics, but of no significance to more than a handful of Indonesians.[5] Until quite recently, European researchers carried out a very large part of the investigations into Indonesia's prehistoric past, although this situation has changed with the growth of the research programmes of the Indonesian National Research Centre for Archaeology since the 1970s. Quite recently, Bellwood's book has been translated into Indonesian and is used widely in Indonesian and Malaysian universities.[6]

In Thailand, in contrast to the situation in the European-dominated territories of the region, an interest in prehistory was late in developing. Archaeology was, until the early 1960s, largely confined to art-historical studies of sculpture, temples, painting and fine arts, and was mainly the prerogative of aristocratic, western-educated Thais of the royal clan.[7] This delayed start to prehistoric archaeology in Thailand may be explained by the fact that, alone of the Southeast Asian countries, the kingdom was never the colony of a western power. Not having been subjected to alien rule with their political institutions overthrown, Thais could more easily than, say, Vietnamese or Indonesians, take their past for granted. Critical historiography, in Thailand, was not well developed, and the country was an agrarian, quasi-feudal kingdom. Nevertheless, as part of the process of modernization started by King Rama IV (Mongkut) in the mid-nineteenth century, the cyclical timeframe of Buddhist cosmology was slowly replaced by the western concept of linear time. With it developed an interest in the history of the kingdom. Peleggi shows how the antiquarian interests of the princely clan led to the establishment of a museum based on the royal collections which, through a series of transformations, became the National Museums of today. Prince Damrong, younger brother of King Rama V, took it upon himself to search for and document as best he could the ancient cities of the Thai kingdoms. He founded the Fine Arts Department, still the government authority in Thailand responsible for documentation and conservation of the built heritage.

It was not until the early 1960s that systematic investigation of Thai prehistory was initiated by a series of joint field projects. Until about 1980, most sustained work in Thai prehistory was carried out by overseas researchers and was published in English, usually in international journals or monographs published overseas. Today, a new generation of Thais require new explanations of their past. With relatively few historical sources, many Thais have been looking with enthusiasm to archaeology to provide them with this new understanding, but of course the questions they seek to answer from archaeology are not necessarily those favoured by overseas archaeologists.

In particular, only a few Thai archaeologists show an interest in generalized explanations couched in terms of evolutionary processes, and not very much in comparative archaeology outside Thailand.[8] Most resources devoted to archaeology in Thailand go into the reconstruction of the great temples and cities of the Khmer, Sukhothai and Ayutthaya phases of the Thai medieval period. This is archaeology in the service of both nationalism and business, for Thailand is a country where tourism is a major industry.[9] I believe that overseas archaeologists working in Thailand have often been out of step with the concerns of Thai scholars investigating their own past. Yet many Thai archaeologists appear to welcome the presence of foreigners working there – even if they are not too interested in their conclusions – for they see them as a source of new techniques and analytical procedures to stimulate indigenous Thai archaeology.

In Burma, research archaeology is perhaps less well developed than in any other country of the region, not excluding Cambodia and Laos. This has not always been so, for investigation into the history of humankind in Burma started early and there was much pioneering and thoughtful research into the Palaeolithic by geologists. However, it was not until the 1960s that U Aung Thaw, trained at the School of Archaeology of the Archaeological Survey of India at Dehra Dun, brought modern field methods to the study of early Burma. His excavations at Beikthano, and the careful and speedy publication of his discoveries, remain a lonely beacon amid the rather gloomy scene of the archaeology of early Burma. The historian, Michael Aung Thwin, has argued that, given the situation in Burma in the years following independence, "prehistory was a luxury the country could ill afford," and priority had to be given to the great monuments of the medieval period. But this was not inevitable and is in stark contrast with the situation in newly independent, and even more resource-poor North Vietnam after 1954, in which Vietnamese scholars surveyed, recorded, excavated and published more than in all the other newly independent countries of the regions put together. It was not really shortage of funds that held back Burmese archaeology, but a lack of vision on the part of the politicians and the nation's emerging leaders as to how archaeology could serve nation building. A realization of the political (and financial) value of archaeology seems to have come only within the last decade or so, with investment and resources put into the restoration – sometimes even re-invention – of the great monuments at Pagan and elsewhere as a glorification of Myanmar's great and unique past.

In a very recent paper, Miksic (2002) considers the potential value of ancient Burmese cities to the tourist economy. Here he makes a not-too-hidden criticism of both government policies and the implementation of them during the reconstruction projects at Pagan and other historic sites in Burma. Inhabitants were cleared with little warning or compensation from their traditional homes, while ambitious building and reconstruction work was undertaken with too few trained personnel, leading to a substantial lack of the "authenticity" that successful heritage sites require. At Pagan, for example, some ruined temples and stupas have been leased out to wealthy and powerful provincial families to rebuild as they please, as an act of merit with no regard for the original form.

Government acceptance that prehistoric archaeology, rather than the great Buddhist monuments, can contribute to linking the present to an earlier past – and to income from tourists – has appeared only in the last few years, following the discovery of a Bronze Age cemetery at Nyaunggan in central Burma. The finds made there were thought to be significant enough for the Centre for Historical Studies of Yangon University to arrange for an international group of archaeologists to visit the site in early 1999, hold a two-day workshop on the discoveries and comparative perspectives, and to publish a book on this before the end of that year.[10] Perhaps Nyaunggan will be the "Ban Chiang of Burma" and stimulate, among the military elite and intellectuals of Burma, some feeling of national pride in their early indigenous, but non-Buddhist, cultural traditions.

Archaeology in the Philippines presents an instructive contrast. There is no evidence for pre-colonial powerful centralized kingdoms or states leaving behind inscriptions or other written documents, no great standing indigenous monuments as witnesses of a great civilization that can be looked back upon. There are certainly many Spanish colonial forts and churches – fine tourist attractions, but culturally ambiguous and hardly the focus for sustained nationalist pride. Not surprisingly, archaeology in the Philippines is quite strongly focused on the study of prehistory and there is less overt concern with nationalism. Active research groups are based in the National Museum in Manila and in the University of the Philippines. Increasing numbers of Filipino archaeologists are training abroad, especially in the USA, Australia and Britain, and general facility with English allows easier access to the theoeretical literature of archaeology.

In this conclusion I have suggested that archaeology can have, and usually does have, a political function. The uses to which the past is and has been put in Southeast Asia are not so different from those found during the development of archaeology in Europe. Quite recently, a distinguished Japanese prehistorian living and working in Canada commented that archaeology in eastern Asia is not, in general, a generalizing and comparative discipline like anthropology, but is "national history or it is nothing."[11] Archaeology in the service of political nationalism, however, is a two-edged sword. It can be beneficial in so far as it encourages an interest in local origins, and educates a people who may have few sources of information on the remote past to relate to their ancestors and take a pride in their achievements. But nationalist archaeology can also lead to xenophobia, and manipulation by unscrupulous politicians and a media looking for short-term advantage. Archaeologists working in a country with a strong nationalist historical tradition need to be aware of the problem, and to be ready to counter any misrepresentation of their researches by those with other agendas.

I have characterized nationalism in archaeology as a divisive, even malign influence, which I believe it has been in many cases. However, a perceptive article by Filipino archaeologist Victor Paz has made me rethink my position on this. Paz argues that, despite the many excesses of nationalist archaeology, it can be a positive force that helps to strengthen what may be rather recent and artificial national communities. Paz also argues that, when a nation state actively supports archaeology and provides resources and leadership, this can lead to major advances in knowledge of the past that can be used for purposes other than the creation of xenophobic national and ethnic consciousness.[12]

Earlier, I pointed to the fact that the archaeological investigation of Southeast Asia's past was a product of the colonial experience, and until recently most research was carried out by foreign-based archaeologists and published in English, French, Dutch, German and Japanese.[13] This has changed, however, and today, although foreign archaeologists are sometimes made welcome, or at least tolerated and able to work in many countries of the region, the direction of research is firmly in the hands of local academics and government officials. Their agenda is local and for the most part serves to develop a national history for countries that do not have a long written record.

We can only speculate on how the practice of archaeology will develop and change under these new circumstances. Will there be a growing interest in trans-national research and a renewed interest in general and comparative explanations of the trajectory towards civilization in the region? Or will local nationalism and divergent research methodologies and agendas prevail? This we cannot forecast; both trends are present in the region. This book comes at a time of change, almost a watershed in the history of archaeology in Southeast Asia. The two editors and most of the contributors represent the past, and perhaps a passing tradition of research. In the future, we look forward to authoritative books on Southeast Asian archaeology written and edited by local scholars who can make original contributions to our understanding of the past in this rich and varied part of the world.

Prospect: comparison, cooperation and debate

Peter Bellwood

Archaeology is essentially a set of techniques for studying material traces of past human history and behaviour. These traces are mostly inert and fragmentary, but their configurations lie behind many of the manifestations of ethnicity in the modern world. Hence the involvement of archaeology in nationalistic discourse, as described above by my co-editor. The archaeological record also underpins public understanding of remote heritage via education and the management of cultural resources. Today, the leaders of postcolonial nations, bus-loads of tourists, students and intelligentsia, and members of societies facing a dissolution of traditional values, all require periodic injections of heritage, albeit for different purposes.

In order to understand heritage – i.e. "the past" – more fully, whether prehistoric or historic, the results from archaeology must be considered in the light of results from other disciplines: comparative linguistics, genetics, palaeoanthropology, environmental sciences, and so forth. There is also little purpose in being parochial. To explain the prehistory of any small region we must know something of the whole universe, or so I believe. This of course poses a problem, in that most scholars simply do not have full command of the breadth of knowledge that the world of science is continually pouring out every time we take a new breath. Another problem, for those not born in English language communities, is that most of the lexicon of agile theoretical debate in archaeology is based in English and other European languages. English imposes a tyranny on the native speakers of other languages who wish to be quoted trans-nationally. And then there is another deeper problem: the unequal distribution of the world's resources.

Most Southeast Asian countries nowadays have universities and even departments of archaeology, but equality of resources in areas such as libraries, research grants, salaries, and levels of educational training is inadequate for the tasks they face.

Although there are absolutely no indications that the whole world will one day speak English (god forbid!), or that every archaeologist will have access to a radiocarbon laboratory, I do, nevertheless, see signs of hope. For instance, the SEAMEO-SPAFA Regional Center for Archaeology and Fine Arts, currently based in Bangkok, has as its goals across the whole of Southeast Asia (*inter alia*):

1 To promote awareness and appreciation of the cultural heritage of Southeast Asian countries through preservation of archaeological and historical artefacts, and traditional arts;
2 To strengthen professional competence in the fields of archaeology and fine arts through sharing of resources and experiences on a regional basis.

These goals are achieved through regional workshops, training excavations, and the publication of the *SPAFA Journal*.

Likewise, the Indo-Pacific Prehistory Association (IPPA), based in Canberra, has as its major goals:

1 To promote cooperation in the study of the prehistory of eastern Asia (east of 70 longitude) and the Pacific region;
2 To maintain scholarly communication through regular congresses and publications;
3 To uphold ethical standards in prehistorical research.

These goals are achieved through periodic conferences that attract over 200 scholars from Southeast Asia and across the world, the papers from which are published in the IPPA Bulletin series. Since 1985, conferences have been held in the Philippines, Japan, Guam, Indonesia, Thailand, Malaysia and Taiwan.

Both SPAFA and IPPA events and publications give opportunities for archaeologists from all Southeast Asian countries to interact with each other and with foreign scholars. Gone, hopefully, are the days when archaeologists refused to acknowledge the existence of anything remotely relevant beyond the borders of their own country, often because they had no access to any current (i.e. post-colonial) publications that could give them such knowledge. Another trend to be applauded is that whereby graduate students often train in other countries, admittedly mostly western ones (Europe, North America, Australia or New Zealand), but not always. The National University of Singapore, for instance, trains graduates in archaeology from many Southeast Asian countries. One way to improve such circulation would be to provide opportunities for exchange of archaeology teaching staff on short-term contracts between different countries, although large variations in salaries and living standards seem likely to continue far into the future and make this difficult to achieve.

What really drives archaeology, however, and keeps it vibrant and flowing, is debate. Measuring, counting, and putting things in museum stores, even with exemplary publication, will probably produce yawns of increasing magnitude in years to come. Southeast Asian archaeologists need to get to grips with questions that affect all alike. How did agriculture and animal domestication develop in Southeast Asia? How did seafaring skills develop? Do languages and people move together, and, if so, under what circumstances and on what scales? What levels of social complexity developed in Southeast Asia before Indianization? How can the study of DNA assist understanding of population history? Do archaeological patterns reflect interaction or shared ancestry? Do archaeological cultures really reflect history or just random acts of classification? Do ethnic groups exist? Do "peoples" exist? Can archaeologists document demographic changes? And so forth. Archaeology will only survive as a discipline if its practitioners become multidisciplinary in their interests and international in their vision. Otherwise it will simply recombine with the antiquarianism that spawned it. The future looks bright, so we must hope that international and cultural understanding between all the nations of the world will allow archaeology to grow, and not be reduced by increasing political instability to an empty desktop activity. All peoples and cultures deserve to understand their past, using the best of available resources and without prejudice.

Notes

1 Glover 1986, 1993, 1999; Bray & Glover, 1987.
2 Trigger 1984.
3 Hobsbawm and Ranger 1983: 358–60.
4 Anderson 1991: 178–85.
5 Glover 1986; van Heekeren 1958, 1972; Bellwood 1997.
6 Bellwood 2000.
7 Higham, 2002; Peleggi, 2001.
8 Dr Rasmi Shoocondej of Silpakorn Unversity, Bangkok is an exception with her lively interest in world archaeology.
9 Pelaggi 2001.
10 Anon. 1999.
11 Ikawa-Smith 1999: 626.
12 Paz 1998.
13 Vietnam, and to a lesser extent Indonesia, are something of an exception to this statement, with flourishing publication records in their own languages for the past thirty to forty years; likewise Thailand, more recently.

Select Bibliography

[Anon.] (1999) *Proceedings of the Workshop on Bronze age Culture in Myanmar*, Yangon: Universities Historical Centre.

Anderson, B. (1991) *Imagined Communities. Reflections on the Origin and Spread of Nationalism.* London: Verso (rev. edn).

Bellwood, P. (1997) *Prehistory of the Indo-Malaysian Archipelago*, Honolulu: University of Hawai'i Press, (2nd edn).

Bellwood, P. (2000) *Presejarah Kepulauan Indo-Malaysia*, Jakarta: Gramedia.

Bray, W. M. and Glover, I. C. (1987) "Scientific investigation or cultural imperialism; British Archaeology in the Third World" *Bulletin of the Institute of Archaeology* (London) 24: 109–25.

Glover, I. C. (1986) "Some European contributions to the prehistory of Indonesia: a personal view" *Indonesia Circle* 40: 5–16.

Glover, I. C. (1993) "Other peoples' pasts – western archaeologists and Thai prehistory" *Journal of the Siam Society* 81 (1): 45–53.

Glover, I. C. (1999) "Letting the past serve the present – some contemporary uses of archaeology in Vietnam", *Antiquity* 73 (281): 594–602.

Heekeren, H. R. van. (1958) *The Bronze-Iron Age of Indonesia*, The Hague: M. Nijhoff.

Heekeren, H. R. van (1972) *The Stone Age of Indonesia*, (2nd rev. edn) The Hague: M. Nijhoff.

Higham, C. F. W. (2002) *Early Cultures of Mainland Southeast Asia*, Bangkok: River Books.
Hobsbawm, E. and Ranger, T. (eds) (1983) *The Invention of Tradition*, Cambridge: Cambridge University Press.
Ikawa-Smith, F. (1999) "The construction of national identity and origins in East Asia: a comparative perspective" *Antiquity* 73 (381): 626–9.
Miksic, J. (2002) "Early Burmese urbanization; research and conservation", *Asian Perspectives*, 40 (1): 88–107.
Paz, V. (1998) "Is nationalism detrimental to archaeology?", *Hukay*, 1 (1): 17–25.
Peleggi, M. (2001) *The Politics of Ruins and the Business of Nostalgia*, Bangkok: White Lotus.
Trigger, B. (1984) "Alternative archaeologies: colonialist, nationalist, imperialist", *Man* 19: 355–70.

INDEX

Bold numbers denote figures

Abeyadana pagoda 170
Adityavarman 249, **249**
Admiralty Islands 15
adzes shell 15, 261–2; stone 15, 30–1, 42, 44–5, 48, 50, 55–6, 92–3, 261–2, 319 *see also* bronze, iron
agriculture 34; Angkor system 107–8; origins of xix, 12, 21–4, 91–2, 112 *see also* millet, rice
Agta 4
Aï Khanum 77, 83
Air Sugihan 286–7
Airavata 237
Airlangga 250
Ak Yum 93, 101
Akyas 140
Amarapura 157, 166
Amaravati 78, 128, 138, 161, 228
Andaman Islands 318, 323, 332
Andarayan 31, 261
Andhra Pradesh 137, 219
Angkor 60, 64, 89–112, 165, 230
Angkor Borei 60, 97–100
Angkor Thom 104
Angkor Wat 101, 104, 106
ankusa 136
Anuradhapura 74, 77–8
Arabic 4
Arakan 149, 161, 163
Arakan Yoma 170
archaeological training 343
archaeology in Buma 340–1
archaeology in Philippines 341
archaeology in Thailand 340
Arikamedu 74, 76–8, 289
Arku Cave 264
Arretine Ware 71, 122, 135
Arthasastra 68
asbestos 44
Aslian languages 11, 31, 51, 314–5, 321, 327–30
Aung Myint 169
Aung-Thwin, Michael 152, 169–70
Australia 316–7; absence of agriculture 24; first settlement xviii, 5, 7, 12–15
Australian Aborigines *see* Australia
Austric 51
Austroasiatic languages 11, 17–18, 24–5, 28, 31, 34, 51, 151, 314–5, 324
Austronesian language family: Austronesians xviii, xx, 5, 36, 51, 283, 314, 322–4; distribution 1, 11, 24–7; Old Malay 239, 306; subgrouping and migrations 14, 17, 24–36, 257, 337
Ayeyarwady *see* Irrawaddy
Ayub Cave 264–5
Ayutthaya 339

Ba Phnom 100
Babuyan Islands 267
Bactria 122, 297
Badui 236
Bagan *see* Pagan
Bago *see* Pegu
Baiyangcun 48–50
Bakong 105–6
Baksei Chamkrong 93
Balabac 268
Balaputradewa 308
Bali 7, 9, 36–8, 73–4, 78, 239; Late Classical period 253–4; Middle Classical period 250
Balinese 4
Balobok 259
bamboos 18
Ban Chiang 50–3, 74
Ban Don Phlong 60
Ban Don Ta Phet 59, 64, 73–7, 82–4, 122, 128, 160, 283
Ban Ja Lae 142
Ban Kao 51, 122, 319, 326
Ban Khu Muang 80
Ban Krabuang Nok 60
Ban Lum Khao 50, 55
Ban Na Di 53–4, 59, 74
Ban Non Wat 50, 55
Ban Phak Top 50

Ban Takhong 60
Ban Tha Kae 74, 125
Ban U Taphao 73
Ban Wang Hi 59
bananas 9, 30, 36
Bang Pakong Valley 127
Bangka 238, 305, 325
Bangladesh 76, 78
Banteay Mean Chay 96
Banteay Prei Nokor 100–1
Banteay Srei 105
barkcloth 30, 261, 264, 319, 322
Baroda 125 *see also* Bharukaccha
Batan 279
Batanes Islands 30–1, 279
Batang Gadis 249
Batang Hari 249
Batu Gajah 80
Batujaya 289
Bawbawgyi 161
Bay of Bandon 295
Bay of Bengal 238
Bayon 104, 110
beads 36–7, 45, 48–50, 55, 73–5, 79–80, 96, 263–75, 319, 323
Beikthano 80–2, 133, 157–70
Bengal 163
Bernam Valley 321–2, 329
betel 29, 262
bhadrapitha/srivatsa coins 158, 163
Bhadravarman 221
Bhadreshvaravarnman 224
Bharukaccha 122
Bima 252
Binh Dinh 229
Binnaka 160–3
Biora Bahal 247
Bismarck Archipelago 9, 14, 30
Bodhgaya *sikhara* type 166
Bondowoso 234
Borneo 7, 14–16, 28, 31, 34, 37–8, 245, 259
Borobudur 242, 245, **246**, 307–8
bovids 41, 50, 53–8, 92, 265
Brahma 140
Brahma-tin 136
Brahmagiri 78
Brahmi 36, 71, 160
Brahmanical 296
Brantas Valley 245
bronze xix, 36–7, 41, 47, 73, 91, 154, 263–4, 268, 270, 277, 319; bells 285; coins **156**, 157–8, 163; drums 283, 285; early historical bronzes 75–7; geography 149, **150**; inscriptions 166–7; in Mainland Southeast Asia 51–64, 95–6, 112, 320–2; mining in Thailand 52, 54; Neolithic 152–4, **154**; origins of 52; Pagan period **164**, 165–70, **167**; prehistory 152–6, **155**; urbanization 157, **159**, **162**
Bronze Age *see* bronze
Brunei 7
Bubulungan Cave 273
Buddha *see* Buddhism
Buddhism 136, 138; Mahayana 242
Buddhist *sangha* 161
Bugis 314
Bujang Valley 323–5
Bukit Choras 324
Bukit Tengkorak 31–3
Bukit Tengku Lembu 324
Buni 78, 286, 288
Buni Culture 237
burials 42–51, 55–64, 75, 81, 96, 99, 257, 319; cremation 60, 271; jar burial 50, 60, 70, 212, **212**, 263–6, 273; in Philippines 262–6, 270–5; slab graves 320–2; and social organisation 55–8, 265, 271–2, 322
Buriram 109
Burma 6–11, 25, 52, 57, 72–3, 101, 106, 111, 149–71; upper 152 *see also* Myanmar
Burmese *see* Burma
Busuanga 268
Butuan 267–70, 276
Buu Chau 293

Cagayan Valley 31–3, 259–61, 264, 278
Cai Beo 56
Cakravartin 239
Calatagan 272
Cambodia 7, 11, 50, 52, 55, 72; Pre-Angkorian and Angkorian periods 89–112
canals 300
Candi Canggal **241**
Candi Loro Jonggrang 244, **244**
Candi Sukuh 252–3, **253**
canoes *see* watercraft
Carbonel, J.-P. 91–3
cattle *see* bovids
Cebu 257, 267, 270, 273–4, 277
Cemeteries *see* burials
ceramics *see* pottery
Cha Ban 230
Chaiya 137, 141, 295–6, 308, 326
Chakravartin 137
Chamcar-Andong 93
Chams 36–7, 60, 101, 104–6, 111, 269, 297; Arab trade 227–8; history 211; inscriptions 209, 221, 243; tiles 214, **214–15**, 216; language 211, 224; monuments 216; origin of name 209; pottery 214, 216, **210–17**; prehistory 212–13, religion 221–2, 224; sculpture **222–3**, 224–6, **225**, 228; sites **210**; trade with the west 209, 221; trade with China 209, 212, 214, 216, 221, 224–6
Chamic *see* Chams
Champa *see* Chams
Chandraketugarh 78
Changkat Menteri 322, 329
Chansen 71, 80–1, 125, 131, 133, 136
Chao Phraya 59

Chau Sa 220–1, 230
Chau Say Tevoda 95, 104
Chenla 100 *also see* Zhenla
Cheras 68
Chi River 140–1
chickens *see* poultry
Chieng Mai 141
Chin 170
China 4, 11–12, 57, 155; Bronze Age cultures 52; Chinese coins in Indonesia 234; contact and trade with Southeast Asia 36–8, 41, 70, 111, 266–77, 282–3, 314; documentary sources on Southeast Asia 97–101, 278, 326; early agriculture in 23–4, 35; language families in 9–10, 28; Neolithic archaeology in 29–30, 46, 50–1
Chindwin: River 154; Valley 57
Chinese languages 4, 29
Chitu 295
Ciaruton 237
Cibutak 237
Cibuya 302
Chou Ta-kuan 102, 105, 107, 111
Chula Paton Chedi 130, 138
Chumphon 127
Chup-Thmar Pich 93
Claeys, Jean-Yves **211**, 223, 229–30
cloves 286
Co Loa 47, 58
Co Luy 220
coastal states 283
coconuts 29
Coedès, George 9, 120, 129, 282, 294, 306
Con Nen 50
Culao Cham 228
Cung Son 223

Da But 56
Da Nang 223, 225
Dadunzi 48–50
Dai Viet 209, 229–30
Damrong, Prince 339
Demak 253
Desawarnana 315, 322
Devacandra 162
Dhanyawadi 161–3
Dharma 138
Dharmachakra 128
Dharmawangsa 250
Dian 11, 57–8
Dieng Plateau 224, 240, **241**
Dimolit 261–2
DNA *see* genetic data
dogs 24, 29–30, 42, 45, 51, 55–6, 260
domestication *see* agriculture
Dong Dau 55–6
Dong Duong 228–9
Dong Khon 127, 136, 143
Dong Son 37, 56–9, 70, 75, 80, 130, 287, 289, 322, 326
Dongson drums 158
Dubois, Eugene 12
Dumaguete 270, 273–7
Dunsun 297
Duong Long 230
Dupont Pierre 120, 128
Durga 250
Duyong Cave 259, 262
Dvaravati 64, 80–1, 104, 120, 128–9, 142, 161–5; ceramics 135; excavations 128–31; kingdoms 125, 136–40; languages 135–6; material culture 132–4; regional cultures 140–2; religion 138–40; sculpture and terracottas 128, **128–30, 134**; seals, amulets and coins **131**, **133**; sites **126–7**, **129**

École française d'Extrême-Orient 91, 102
East Mebon 105
East Zegu 161
Easter Island 25, 31
Erlitou 49

Fa-hsien *see* Faxian
farming *see* agriculture
faunas 7, 12; translocation 15
Faxian 238
fish hooks 44, 53, 56, 261, 268
Flores 13
founder-focused ideology 34
Fujian 29
Funan 68, 98–9, 216–8, 286, 290–1, 295–7
future of archaeology in Southeast Asia 342–3

Gaja-Laksmi 131, 140
Ganesha 250
Ganga Valley (Ganges) 68, 77, 133
Gansu 52
Ganuoli (Kan-to-li) 303
Garuda 128
ge 49
Gebe 15
Gedong Sogo 224
General Ma Yuan 215
genetic data 22, 51, 316
Geying (Ko-ying) 289
Gilimanuk 73, 289
Giong Ca Vo 73
glass 59–62, 71–6, 79, 96, 263–75, 283, 287, 319, 322–3
Glass Palace Chronicle 166
Go Bong 48
Go Cam 214–15, 293
Go Cay Thi 298–9
Go De De 219
Go Mun 56
gold 270–4, 322, 324, 327; alluvial 301; eye covers 287; gold ornaments 287
Groslier, B.-P. 93, 102, 108, 111
Gua Cha 319, 326

Gua Chawas 326
Gua Harimau 319–20
Gua Sireh 30
Guangdong 29, 46, 51–2, 157, 238, 269
Guangxi 29, 52
Guangzhou 228
Guar Kepah 318
Guimet Museum 303
Guizhou 29
Gujarat 139
Gulf of Martaban 149–70
Gunapriya 250
Gunavarman 238
Gunung Wukir 240
Guptas 68, 81, 131, 135
Guri Cave 261

Ha Giang culture 50
Ha Long 56
Hai Van Pass 216
Halin 81, 133, 153–63, **159**
Halmahera 15
Han China: ceramics 214; emperors 213–15; expansion 213; Rinan commandery 213–6; seal impressions **213**, 214
Hariharalaya 101, 104–5
Haripunjaya 141, 165
harmika 166
Hau Xa 223
Heling 304
Hemudu 30
Hinayana 138, 141
history of archaeology 338; in Southeast Asia 338–9
Hmong-Mien language family 11, 25
Hoa Lai 226, **227**
Hoa Loc 56–7
Hoabinhian 16, 25, 92, 122, 315–19, 327, 330–1
Hoi An 209, 213, 223
Homo erectus 12–13
Hong Kong 52
Hoop, A. N. J. van der 79
Huanghe *see* Yellow River
human biology 315–19
hunting and gathering economy 11–16, 41–6, 91, 257–61, 315, 327–9
Huoluodan (Ho-la-tan) 303

Ijing (I-tsing) 304
India: maritime connections with Southeast Asia xx, 4, 36–8, 59, 68–83, 91, 314, 324
Indian beads 288
Indian gems 292
Indianization 97
Indonesia 7, 11–16, 27–31, 36–7, 70–3, 83, 316–17; external trade 238–9; inscriptions and writing **236**, 236–7; periodization 234; social and political structure 239–40
Indo-Roman 122
Indrapura 228, 293
Indratataka 107
IPPA 343
iron 36–7, 41, 57–64, 70–1, 91, 96, 156, 263–77, 320–2, 328
Iron Age *see* iron
Irrawaddy 149–70
irrigation *see* water control by Khymers
Isanapura 100, 120, 163
Islam 270, 315

jade *see* nephrite
Jaggayyapeta stupa 137
Jambi 238, 248, 306
Janse, Olof 75–7
Japan 15, 42
Java 7, 9, 12, 16, 30–1, 37–8, 78–80, 288–9; coinage **246**, Early Classical period 240–5; economy 246, 251; Gold **245**; 246; Late Classical period (Central) 240–7, 250–3; Middle Classical period 245–7
Javanese 4, 25, 31
Jayavarman II 97, 100–5
Jayavarman VII 104–5, 109–11, 230
Jenderam Hilir 51, 319, 322
Jolo 267
Jomon 42
Jula inscription 250

Kadai languages 11
Kadu 163
Kaladan River 149
Kalaspura 163
Kalimantan *see* Borneo
Kampung Sungai Lang 322
Kanchanaburi 120, 122
Kanchipuram 83, 163
Kantarodai 77
Kao Klang Nai 138
Karaikadu 74, 77–8
Karang Agung, 286–8
Karen 9, 170
Kataha 324–5, 329
Kaulungan 277
Kausambi 80, 133
Kebo Edan 253
Kedah 286, 324–5
Kelantan 326–7
Kelumpang 286
kendi 80, 288, 292
Keng Tung 151
Khao Jamook 82
Khao Kwark 75
Khao Sam Kaeo 73–4, 286
Khao Sivichai 296
Khao Wong Prachan 52–3
Kharoshthi 36, 71, 289
Khmer 4, 11, 25, 97–112, 132, 314, 325–7 *also see* Angkor, Cambodia
Khmers *see* Khmer

Khmer political organisation 108–11
Khok Phanom Di 42–6, 55, 331
Khok Plub 122
Khorat Plateau 89, 140, 142
Khuan Luk Pad 71, 73–5, 125, 285, 289
Ki Muang 136
King Anandacandra 161
King Anawratha 151, 167
King Bodawpaya 166
King Jayasa 238
King Kertnagara 248, 251
King Kyanzittha 135, 168; palace 168
King Pyinbya 166
King Rama IV 339
King Sri Isanavarman 138
Klang 285–6, 322, 332
Kobak Kendal 237
Kok Ra Ka 74
Kolhapur 83
Kompong Cham 93
Kompong Thom 95, 100
Kondapur 81–3
Kota Cina 248
Kota Kapur 304–5
Krabi Province 285
Krek 93–4
Kresnaya 244
Krishna 131
Krishna: River 138; Valley 158
Ku Bua 127, 130–8
Kuala Selinsing 73–4, 320, 323
Kubera 140
Kublai Khan 170
Kubu 287
Kubyauk-gyi temple 166
kundika 80
Kushanas 68, 81
Kutei inscription 236, 301–2
Kwo Lo Wan 52
Kyaikkatha 163
Kyaukse 151, 170
Kyhber Pass 122
Kyontu 163

Laang Spean 92–3
Laguna de Bay 267–71
Lajonquière 120
Lake Mungo 14
Lam Ap *see* Lin Yi
Lamongan 289
Lamphun *see* Haripunjaya
Lampung 239
land bridges 7
language shift 35
Langasuka 295
Laos 6–8, 11, 37, 91, 100–1, 111
Lapita 36, 279
Le Hoan 229
Leang Buidane 73
Leer, W. J. van 72
Lemro Valley 170
Letpanchibaw 152, 154
Leur, J. C. van der 72
Lesser Sundas (Nusa Tenggara) 7, 16, 25, 37
Lévy, Paul 96
Liangzhu 46
Lin Yi 216–18, 220, 223, 226, 293, 296–7
lingling-o 263
Lingnan 49, 52, 57
lithic technologies 14–16, 31, 259–262
Lo River 50
Lokananda pagoda 168
Lolos 151
Long Bien 228
Lopburi 137
Lopburi–Pasak Valley 127, 131
Lotus Sutra 139
Luce G. H. 165
Lung Hoa 49
Luzon 9, 31, 257–61, 267–72, 275

Madagascar 11, 25, 29, 31, 36, 38, 323, 337
Maharakam River 301
Magapit 261
Magellan, Ferdinand 273
Magmisi Cave 273
Magsuhot 265–6
Mahabharata 137, 252
Mahamuni 163
Mahastangarh 76–8
Mahayana 149–71
Maitreya Buddha 169
Majapahit 251–4
Majumdar, R. C. 68
Malacca *see* Melaka
Malang 242
malaria 31, 45
Malay, Malays 4, 25, 31, 36–7, 60, 315–30, 332
Malayo-Polynesian languages *see* Austronesian languages
Malaysia: archaeological record in 51, 314–33; human biology 315–9; Peninsular 7, 11, 14, 16, 29, 31, 34, 37, 70–5, 80, 101, 142
Malayu 238, 248
Malleret, Louis 93, 290, 294, 299–300
mandala 96, 239, 243, 304
Mandalay 156, 170
Mangkalihat Peninsula 16
Mani 4
Manila 267, 270, 275–6
Manipur 151
Mansuy, Henri 96
Mantai 74, 77
Manunggul Cave 263–4
Maori 34
Marco Polo 248
Mariana Islands 30
Marinduque 268

maritime technology *see* watercraft
Maros points 16–17
Marshall, Sir John 125
marsupial translocation 15, 18
Martaban jars 163
Mataram 308
Mathura 81
Maunggun gold plates 161
Mauryas 68, 77, 122
megaliths 71, 79–80, 84, 322
Meklong–Ta Chin Valley 122, 127
Mekong River 50, 52, 57, 59–63, 68, 89, 91, 97 *passim*, 111, 289–92, 300
Melaka 285, 304–6, 314–5, 322, 327–32
Melanesia 35–6
metallurgy *see* bronze, iron
Micronesia 31, 34
millet: broomcorn (common millet) 23–4, 29; foxtail 9, 23–4, 29
Mimot 93
Minangkabu 249
Minbu 170
Mindanao 257, 264–5, 267, 272, 277
Mindoro 267–8, 275
Minnanthu 169
Misool Island 15
Mlu Prei 96
Moh Kiew 316–7
Moluccas (Maluku) 7, 9, 14–16, 25, 28, 31, 38, 70
Mon 25, 110, 120, 165–8, 314, 324–7, 330
Mon-Khmer languages 51, 151; Old Mon 135
Mongmao 157, 160
Mongols 152, 170
Mount Ba The 291
Mount Meru 237–9
Mount Panulisan 250
Mount Penanggungan 252
Mount Lawu 252
Monywa district 154
Mranma (Burmans) 151, 168
Mrauk-U 152
Muang Bon 133
Muang Fa Daed 132, 137, 140
Muang Phra Mahosot 132, 134
Muang Phra Rot 132
Muang Sema 137
Muara Jambi 74
Muara Takus 248
Mukhalinga 138
Mulavarman 301
Mun Valley 50, 55, 60, 64, 209
Mundas, Mundaic 11, 51
Musang Cave 259, 261
Musi River 239, 287–8, 304
mutisalah 74
My Son 209, 221, 224, 230
Myanmar 133, 141
Myinkaba village 166
Myinpagan 169
Na Dune 137
Naga 128, 238
Nagarjunakonda 138, 158, 219
Nagsabaran 278
Nakhon Pathom 127, 133, 134, 138, 139
Nakhon Sawan Province 133
Nakhon Si Thammarat 141, 296, 326
Nakorn Si Thammarat 163
Nalanda 244
Nan-kuan-li 30
Nan Zhao 228
Nanchao 151, 161
Nationalism and archaeology 339, 341–2
Negapatam 247
Negritos 315–9, 323
Negros 257, 265
Nepal 166
nephrite 24, 48–9, 52, 59, 70, 73, 75, 262–4, 292
Nern Hin 128
Nern Makok 125, 136
New Britain 15, 31
New Guinea 7, 9, 12, 14, 16, 34–7; early agriculture in 24, 27, 30–1
New Ireland 15
New Zealand 25, 31
Nha Trang 219, 226–7, 229–30, 292
Niah Caves 13, 16
Nicobar Islands 11, 51, 323
Nil Kham Heng 53
Noen Ma Khok 59
Noen U-Loke 60–3, 73
Non Kao Noi 50
Non Muang 74
Non Nok Tha 50–5
Non Pa Wai 51–3
Non Yang 60
Nong Nor 42–4, 53–5
Nyaunggan 57, 154–7
Nyaung-u 169
Nyein Lwin 158

obsidian 15, 31
Oc Eo 71, 73, 75, 80, 99–100, 128, 135, 157, 219, 289–2, 295–300
oleoresins 301
Ongbah 59
Orang Asli 314 *passim*
Otein Taung 168

P'eng-hu 30
Padang Lawas 247
Paduranga 226, 230
Pagan 104, 111, 149–70, **164**
Pagarruyung 249
Pahang 315, 321
Pala School 166
palaeography 157
Palawan 257 *passim*
Palembang 238–40, 307, 325

Pali 130–1, 135, 139, 142, 168, 324
Pallavas 68, 125, 236; Grantha script 223
palynology 31
Pamittan 31
Panay 257
Pandanan 267
Panpan 295
Papuan languages 25, 34
Parmentier, Henri **211**, 211–2
Pasemah Plateau 80; megaliths 288
Pataliputra 133
Pattani 325
Payagyi 161
Payama 161
Payataung pagoda 160
Pearl Delta 16, 24
Pearl River 52
Pegu 133, 163
Pejeng 38, 289
Pekalongan 303
pellet bow 48
Pelliot, Paul 68, 98, 103, 120
Pengkalan Bujang 324–5, 329
Pengtoushan 46
Perak 321–2, 324
Periplus 294
Perlis 326
Petchabun Province 131
Phan Rang 226
Phanom Wan 64
Philippines 7, 12–14, 27–31, 35–8, 59, 70, 73; archaeological record 257–78
Phimai 60, 64, 104, 109; black ware 292
Phnom Bakheng 105
Phnom Da 98
Phnom Kulen 109
Phnom Loang 92
Pho Dam 227
Pho Nagar 223, 226, 228
Phra Praton 81
Phu Lon 52
Phu Ninh 222
Phum Snay 96
Phung Nguyen 47–50, 55–7
Picard, Ch. 122
pigs 24, 29–30, 41, 50, 53–8, 61, 259–61, 265, 270–2
Pinagbayanan 271
Pintu Shelter 261
Plawangan 289
Pleistocene Epoch 7, 11–16
Pliny 72
Polynesia 30–1, 34–6
Pompeii 72
Pong Tuk 122, 125
post-Gupta 135
pottery 24, 29–33, 36–8, 92–3; early historical ceramics 78–83; Khmer 103, 109; in Malaysia 315, 319; in Philippines 261–78; in Thailand 42–6, 60–3; in Vietnam 48–50
poultry 24, 29–30, 260, 265, 270
Pra Paton Chedi 128–9
Prachinburi Province 132
Prakashadharma 224
Prasat Muang Singh 74, 109
pre-Angkorian 300; art 163
Pre Rup 102, 105
Preah Khan 104
Preah Ko 105
Ptolemy 72, 294, 323
Punan 4
Purnavarman 237
Pyinbya village 166
Pyu 80–2
Pyu Tircul 160, 163

Rabel Cave 261
Rajah Soliman 27
Rajasuya 137
Rakhine *see* Arakan
Rama 137
Ramayana 224, 244
Rangoon 149, 163
Rattanakiri 96
Ratu Boko 243
Red River 47, 50, 55, 58, 228
Rice 9, 11, 57–8, 61–3, 101, 266, 275, 323; Neolithic cultivation of 29–31, 42–6, 50–1, 257, 261; origins of cultivation xix, 24
Roman Empire 59, 70–2; coins 122
Roti 13
Rouletted Ware 36, 73, 78–9, 84, 122, 237, 285, 289
Rudravarman 222–3

Sa Huynh 60, 64, 70, 73, 75, 127, 212–13, 263
Sa Huynh-Kalanay pottery style 38, 237, 323
Sab Champa 131
Sabah 16, 31, 259
sago 29–30
Sahul Shelf 14
Sai Yok 120
Sailendras 242–3, 308
Saivism 138
Sak-Kantu (Thet Kadu) languages 151
Saka era 254
Saka-Kshatrapas 130, 139
Sakai Cave 316–17, 331
Sakya Simha 140
salt 63–4
Salween River 149, 151, 163
Samar 257, 259
Sambor Prei Kuk 95, 100
Samoa 31
Samon Valley 156–7
Samrong Sen 50, 89, 95
Sanchi 161
sandalwood, gharu wood, cardamoms, camphor and cloves: trade in 293

Sandoway 163
Sanga Sanga 259
Sangiran 12
Sanjaya 240–2
sankha 136
Sanskrit 4, 37, 91, 97–102, 135, 142, 161, 163, 219, 223, 237, 298, 301, 324
Santa Ana 270–2
Sanxingdui 49
Sarawak 13, 30–1, 263
Sarnath 129
Satavahanas 68, 72
Satingpra 74, 325–6
Satyavarman 226
Saurin, W. 91
Sawankhalok 272
sea level changes 7, 315
seafaring *see* watercraft
Sebokingking Hill 306
Seguntang Hill 239–40
Selangor 285, 321–2
Selinsing River 286
Semai 329
Semang 4 *also see* Negritos
Sembiran 36–7, 75, 78, 237, 286
Senoi 316–9, 329–30
Shaka era 223
Sham Wan 52
Shambhuvarman 223
Shan 170
Shek Pik 52
Shepo 303
Shiva *see* Siva
Shixia 46
Sichuan-Yunnan 157
Simhapura 293
Singapore 315, 325
Sino-Tibetan language family 9, 24–5, 28, 151–2
Siquijor 276
Sisupalgarh 76, 78
Sittaung River 149–63
Siva: Saivism 105–7, 111, 140, 237, 240, 243–4; Sivalinga 223, 226
Siva-Siddhanta 253
slab graves 285
Sogdiana 297
Sohoton Cave 259
Solamillo 266
Solomon Islands 30–1
Song Dynasty 141, 247
Songkhla 326
Songkhram Valley 50
SPAFA 343
spices 70
spindle whorls *see* weaving
Sras Srang 102, 104
Sravasti 139
Sri Ksetra 81, 120, 165
Sri Lanka 72, 83, 163, 243
Sri Thep 131, 138
Sriksetra *see* Thayekittaya
srivatsa 158, 163
Srivijaya 100, 270, 282, 304, 307–8, 315, 325–6, 330–2
stegodonts 7
Strabo 72
stone beads 283
Strait of Bangka 286–8
stupa 158
Sudhamla 252
Sui Dynasty 223
Sukhothai 111, 272, 339
Sulawesi (Celebes) 7, 14, 16, 28, 31, 37–8, 245, 314
Sulu 257, 272
Sumatra 7, 16, 30–1, 37, 100, 270, 315, 322, 325; Middle Classical period 247–9
Sunda Shelf (Sundaland) 7, 37, 80, 257–9
Sungei Bujang 286
Sungei Mas 286, 324–6, 329
Supajanya Thiwa 125
Surya 131, 297, 303
Suryavarman II 104, 106
Suvannabhumi 163
Swarnabhumi 293
sweet potato 24
Syriam 163

Ta Chin River 128
Ta Prohm 104
Tabon Caves 13, 259–64
Tagaung 163
Tai language family 11, 24–5, 28, 37, 51
Taikkala 163
Taiwan 11, 14, 16, 24–5, 28–31, 71, 279, 337
Takkola 295
Takuapa 295
Talaud Islands 14, 31, 73
Tamil 324
Tamil Nadu 125, 223
Tamluk 78
Tamralapti 68, 122
Tang China 224–5, 228
Tanjay 270, 273–8
taro 9, 29–30, 36
Taruma 237, 238, 247, 294, 302–3
tattooing 29, 264
Taungthaman 156–7
Tavoy 163
Taxila 76–7, 82, 122, 125
Tembeling River 321
Temiar 6, 319, 329
Tenasserim 170
Tengger 236
Ter 82–3
Terengganu 326–7
Tha Muang 75
Thailand 7, 11, 16, 29, 37, 41, 52, 101, 111, 120, 155, 263, 275, 325–7; Bronze Age cultures in

52–7; early contacts with India 70 *passim*, 91, **121**, 122–5; human biology 316–19; hunters and gatherers 42–6; Iron Age cultures in 59–64; Neolithic cultures in 46, 50–1, 319; Thais 4, 314; tradewares in Philippines 266–8, 272, 275
Thanh Den 56
Thap Doi 230
Than Loi 221
Thap Mam 230
Thap Muoi 298, 302–3
Thaton 120, 135–6, 152, 165
Thayekittaya **150**, 151, 158, 161, 169
Theravada Buddhism 166
Thiripyitsaya 169
Three Pagoda Pass 165, 283
Thu Bon Valley 221
Tibet 149, 166
Tibeto-Burman languages *see* Sino-Tibetan language family
Timor 6, 9, 14, 16
tin 55, 69, 112, 286, 322, 327
Tingkayu 16–17
Tircul 151
Toalian industry 16
Toba eruption xix
Tonle Sap 91, 97, 101, 111
Tra Kieu 78, 80, 213–16, 221, 293, 297
Trang Kenh 48
Trapeang Phong 95
Trinil 12
Trowulan 251
Trung Sisters rebellion 215
Truong Son range 209
Tu Yu 136
Tugu 237, 302
Tung-tien 136
Turunan 236
Tuyin Taung 169
Twante 163

U Aung Thaw 157–8
U-Thong 71, 122, 125–8, 133, 136, 128, 140
Udayana 250
Ujjain 81, 122, 125
Ulu Musi 288
Unto 266

Vaishnava 305
vajra 136
Valabhi 139
Valmiki 224
Vanasin 125
Vanaspati 139
Varanasi 76, 133
Varma 160
Vesali 157–63
Victorinus 122
Viet Khe 58
Vietnam 7, 11, 16, 29, 34, 37–8, 41, 52, 89, 98, 101; Bronze Age cultures in 55–7; early contacts with India 70 *passim*, 91; hunters and gatherers 42–6; Iron Age cultures in 58–60; Neolithic cultures in 46–52; tradewares in Philippines 266–8, 272, 275
Vietnamese language *see* Vietnamese people
Vietnamese people 4, 11, 25, 37; annals 243
Vidisa 122
Vijaya 229–30
Vijayavarman 238
Vikrama 160
Vikrantavarman 225
Vishnu 131, 140, 237–8, 298
Vjarayana School 140
Vo Canh inscription 219, 292–3

Wallace, Alfred Russel 7, 240
Wallacea 7, 14, 16, 257
Wat Klong 130, 138
Wat Kukut 141
Wat Mahathat, Lopburi 131
Wat Phu 100
water buffalo *see* bovids
water control by Khmers 107–8, 111
watercraft 13–15, 29, 34–5, 44, 71, 267, 286, 323, 337
weaving 24, 29, 48, 58, 261, 264, 270–4
West Baray 106
Wheeler, Sir R. E. M. 78, 83
Winka 80
Wolters, Oliver 68, 96, 282, 301
Wu 98

Xom Ren 49

yams 9, 29–30
Yangzi River 16, 24, 41, 46, 50–2
Yap 275–7
Yarang 137, 142, 296
Yashodharatataka 107
Yasodharapura 105
yazhang 49
Yellow River 24, 50
Yijing 238
Yudhisthra 137
Yunnan 37–8, 48–50, 57–8, 73, 158

Zambales 268
Zancheng 228
Zhejiang 29
Zhenla 301
Zokthok 163